GREAT ATHLETES

OLYMPIC SPORTS

GREAT ATHLETES

OLYMPIC SPORTS

Volume 2

Dick Fosbury–Jon Lugbill

Edited by
The Editors of Salem Press

Special Consultant
Rafer Johnson

SALEM PRESS

Pasadena, California   Hackensack, New Jersey

Editor in Chief: Dawn P. Dawson

Editorial Director: Christina J. Moose *Photo Editor:* Cynthia Breslin Beres
Managing Editor: R. Kent Rasmussen *Acquisitions Editor:* Mark Rehn
Manuscript Editor: Christopher Rager *Page Design and Layout:* James Hutson
Research Supervisor: Jeffry Jensen *Additional Layout:* Frank Montaño and Mary Overell
Production Editor: Andrea Miller *Editorial Assistant:* Brett Weisberg

Cover photo: © Icefields/Dreamstime.com

Library of Congress Cataloging-in-Publication Data

Great athletes / edited by The Editors of Salem Press ; special consultant Rafer Johnson.
    p. cm.
    Includes bibliographical references and index.
    ISBN 978-1-58765-473-2 (set : alk. paper) — ISBN 978-1-58765-483-1 (vol. 1 olympic sports : alk. paper) — ISBN 978-1-58765-484-8 (vol. 2 olympic sports : alk. paper) — ISBN 978-1-58765-485-5 (vol. 3 olympic sports : alk. paper) — ISBN 978-1-58765-486-2 (vol. 4 olympic sports : alk. paper) — ISBN 978-1-58765-487-9 (set olympic sports : alk. paper)
    1. Athletes—Biography—Dictionaries. I. Johnson, Rafer, 1935-   II. Salem Press.
    GV697.A1G68 2009
    796.0922—dc22
    [B]
                                                                            2009021905

First Printing

Contents

Complete List of Contents

Volume 3

Volume 4

GREAT ATHLETES

OLYMPIC SPORTS

Dick Fosbury

Born: March 6, 1947
    Portland, Oregon
Also known as: Richard Douglas Fosbury (full name)

Early Life

Richard Douglas Fosbury was born on March 6, 1947, in Portland, Oregon. He grew up in Medford, a small southwest Oregon town just north of the California border. His father was a truck sales representative, and his mother was a secretary. Dick was a tall, slender, and awkward young boy. He participated in sports but seldom notably. In the fifth grade, Dick tried out for the school track team, trying every event without much success. His best performance, although not spectacular, was the high jump, so he stuck with it. In high school, he was on the third team in football and sat on the bench on the basketball team. However, track kept his interest. He ran hurdles but kept coming back to the high jump.

The Road to Excellence

When Dick was learning to high jump, he was taught the "straddle" technique. He worked hard to master it but simply could not learn the correct form. He gained more success doing the "scissor" method that had been out of fashion for many years. His best jump with this style was 5 feet 4 inches. At the age of sixteen, he tried to lay his body back and push off his back leg, going over the bar head and back first. Over a short period, this evolved into the jumping style that became popular subsequently. The first time he tried his new style, he increased his personal best to 5 feet 10 inches. His high school coach Dean Benson, thinking Dick had become confident enough, tried to ease Dick back to the straddle style but with no success. The coach saw that Dick's personal style was more effective and wisely allowed him to develop his own form.

Dick won the National Junior Olympics his senior year in high school with a jump of 6 feet 7 inches. Throughout Dick's high school career, no colleges expressed any interest in him and his strange style of jumping. No one thought it would catch on. Berny Wagner, the head track coach at Oregon State University (OSU), took a chance on Dick and offered him a scholarship after he won the Junior Olympics. Wagner tried unsuccessfully to change Dick's style. After his freshman year, Dick weight trained to develop his strength. In 1967, in the first meet of his sophomore year, he cleared 6 feet 10 inches using his jumping style. Soon, his technique became known as the "Fosbury Flop."

The Emerging Champion

As a junior, Dick became more proficient in his unique style. In January, 1968, he jumped 7 feet for the first time and won the National Collegiate Athletic Association (NCAA) Indoor Championship. By the end of the outdoor season, he was the most consistent 7-foot high jumper in the country; he won the high jump title at 7 feet 2¼ inches at the NCAA Championships.

Dick Fosbury executes "the Fosbury flop" in 1968. (AP/Wide World Photos)

Dick was fortunate that his most successful year came in 1968, the year of the Mexico City Olympic Games. At the Olympic team trials, Dick jumped 7 feet 3 inches using the "Fosbury Flop" to make the U.S. team. Still, many people thought that the young high jumper would not be able to handle the pressure of Olympic competition. The high jump competition of the nineteenth Olympic Games was on the afternoon of October 14, 1968. Three hours later, after all but two competitors were eliminated, Americans Fosbury and Edward Carruthers, the bar was raised to 7 feet 4¼ inches. Carruthers was eliminated after missing the height three times. Dick missed on his first two attempts. Only one jump remained between him and the gold medal. On his final attempt, Dick cleared the bar a full 1⅕ inches above his former personal best, setting a new Olympic record.

Continuing the Story

Dick's track and field career had reached its zenith. He returned to his hometown for a ticker-tape parade. He appeared on the "Johnny Carson Show" and met famous celebrities. He never fully regained his top form, however. Dick returned to OSU to continue his studies in engineering. The newfound status took its toll on the twenty-one-year-old. He traveled to many events and eventually defended his high-jump crown at the 1969 NCAA Championships, his final major competition. Realizing that his future was in engineering, Dick took a year off from competition to concentrate on his studies at OSU. He graduated and never again

---

Major High-Jump Championships

Year	Competition	Place	Height
1968	Olympic Games	Gold	7′ 4¼″ OR, AR
	NCAA Outdoor Championships	1st	7′ 2¼″
	NCAA Indoor Championships	1st	7′ 0″
	Pacific-8 Championships	1st	7′ 0″
1969	NCAA Outdoor Championships	1st	7′ 2½″
	National AAU Championships	1st	7′ 0″

Notes: OR = Olympic Record; AR = American Record

---

found the competitive edge he needed for top-level performance.

In 1973, he joined the now-defunct professional track circuit but with small success. He finally retired from his sport. Dick was a philosophical young man who saw, and enjoyed, the inner satisfaction of competition. "As time passed, I realized some of what I did was remarkable," he said in 1989. "That has helped to motivate me in everyday life: take the drive behind those athletic achievements and translate it into other areas."

Summary

Dick Fosbury was an innovator who changed his sport. He was not deterred by criticism or skepticism. His style was considered a fad but instead became the standard utilized by most major high jumpers, including the first man to jump more than 8 feet, Javier Sotomayor of Cuba.

Rusty Wilson

Additional Sources

Dunaway, James. "Five Game-Changers." *Coach and Athletic Director* 75, no. 10 (May/June, 2006): 62-64.

Kemp, Justin, and Damian Farrow. *Why Dick Fosbury Flopped: And the Answers to Other Big Sporting Questions.* Crows Nest, N.S.W.: Allen & Unwin, 2006.

Rubin, Debra K. "Olympic Gold Medalist Now Competes in Different Arena." *Engineering News Record* 253, no. 7 (August 16, 2004): 18-20.

Honors and Awards

1968	*Track and Field News* Number One High Jumper
1981	Inducted into USA Track and Field Hall of Fame

Greg Foster

Born: August 4, 1958
     Maywood, Illinois
Also known as: Gregory Foster (full name)

Early Life

Gregory Foster was born in Maywood, Illinois, a suburb of Chicago, on August 4, 1958. As a young boy he was very athletic, participating in many different sports; however, running appealed to him most. His tall, lanky build and long legs provided him with an amazing stride and gave him the perfect build for running the hurdles. During high school, Greg's accomplishments as a hurdler brought him to the attention of many of the country's best track coaches. In 1977, after graduating from Proviso East High School, Greg went west to attend the University of California at Los Angeles (UCLA) and became a member of one of the nation's best college track programs. During his sophomore year at UCLA, he began to make his mark in the track world.

The Road to Excellence

Track was Greg's all-consuming interest as a young athlete. He did not let any distractions interfere with his quest to become the best hurdler in the country. In his first season with the Bruins, Greg took third place in the National Collegiate Athletic Association (NCAA) Championships and was ranked third in the world.

In 1978, the UCLA sophomore was one of the best high-hurdlers in the world. He won the NCAA championship with a new American record. His time of 13.22 seconds in the 110-meter hurdles was

Greg Foster wins the 55-meter hurdles in 1988. (AP/Wide World Photos)

329

Major Hurdles Championships

Year	Competition	Event	Place
1978	NCAA Championships	100-meter high hurdles	1st AR
1979	NCAA Championships	200-meter high hurdles	1st
1980	NCAA Championships	110-meter high hurdles	1st
1981	World Cup	110-meter high hurdles	1st
1983	World Championships	110-meter high hurdles	1st
1984	Olympic Games	110-meter high hurdles	Silver
1986	Goodwill Games	110-meter high hurdles	2d
1987	World Championships	110-meter high hurdles	1st
1991	World Indoor Championships	60-meter high hurdles	1st
	World Championships	110-meter high hurdles	1st

Notes: AR = American Record

---

the fastest time in the world that year and was just .01 second off the world record. At the time, another young hurdler, Renaldo Nehemiah, was at the University of Maryland. For the next five years, Greg and Renaldo engaged in one of the most famous rivalries in track history. During this period, the two met thirty-four times in competition; Renaldo had a clear advantage with twenty-eight wins to Greg's five, with the pair tying once. Although the record of the rivalry did not reflect it, Greg pushed Renaldo to three world records. As Renaldo said to Greg after one world-record race, "If it hadn't been for you, I wouldn't have run that time." In the same race, Greg finished in 13.03 seconds, the third-fastest 110-meter hurdle time in history. Throughout this phase in his career, Greg never quit, while fighting to perfect his talents, both mentally and physically.

The Emerging Champion

Tenacity was a major component of Greg's personality. In 1982, his persistence finally paid off when he was ranked number one in the world. This determination was best exemplified when he won his event at the first World Track and Field Championships in Helsinki, Finland, in 1983. After getting a characteristically quick start, Greg was going great when he hit the ninth hurdle and fell over the tenth but still staggered over the finish line to capture his first world championship.

Greg was hampered by untimely injuries and miscalculations. The first of many came in 1984 during the Los Angeles Olympic Games. After winning his second straight Mobil Indoor Championship and Mobil Indoor Grand Prix title, Greg was an odds-on favorite to win the Olympic 110-meter

hurdle gold medal. Greg led the field over all ten hurdles when he made the mistake of looking over his shoulder for his opponent. As he turned his head to look, he was passed at the finish line by teammate Roger Kingdom for the gold medal. Once again, Greg took the defeat in stride and returned in 1985 to take his third straight Mobil Indoor Championship and Mobil Grand Prix title. In 1985, Greg suffered his greatest loss when his mother and three family members were killed in a car accident. By 1986, he had refocused his concentration and recaptured his number-one world ranking. In 1987, at the first World Indoor Championships, adversity struck again when Greg collided with Canada's Mark McKay and did not finish the race. He returned months later at the second World Track and Field Championships in Rome and retained his world title. However, in 1988, another Olympic year, Greg suffered more misfortune.

Continuing the Story

The Olympic year began well, with Greg winning his fifth Mobil Indoor Championship and Grand Prix crown. During a training session just two weeks before the Olympic trials, however, he caught his trailing leg on a hurdle, fell, and suffered a compound fracture of his left forearm. Greg still competed in the trials despite a cast on his arm. He won the first heat and advanced to the semifinals, where he hit the seventh hurdle and dropped out of the race, failing to make the Olympic team. Early in 1989, Greg was playing a pick-up basketball game when he fell and broke his left forearm again.

Greg gradually regained his form, and despite a broken foot, he started to move back up the rankings. By 1990, he was ranked fourth in the world, and he ran the year's second-fastest time with a 13.10. Within the year, Greg regained his old form and was reaching for new heights. Early in 1991, Greg won his sixth Mobil Indoor Championship

---

Honors, Awards, and Milestones

1977-92	Held world ranking 15 of 16 years
1987	Set world record in 60-meter hurdles
1998	Inducted into USA Track and Field Hall of Fame

---

and Grand Prix crown. By winning the championship, he placed second, behind Harrison Dillard's all-time record of nine, for most national hurdle titles. In a European meet prior to the World Track and Field Championships in Tokyo, Greg ran a 13.06, his best time in ten years. During the semifinals of the World Track and Field Championships, he suffered a deep cut on his right knee, but he came back in the finals to edge out teammate Jack Pierce in a meet-record 13.06. At the age of thirty-three, Greg became the first athlete to win three straight world track and field championships.

Greg was in the world rankings in fifteen of sixteen years between 1977 and 1992. In 1987, he broke the world record in the 60-meter hurdles, with a time of 7.36. After his retirement, Greg focused on promoting track and field programs for children. In 1998, he was inducted into the USA Track and Field Hall of Fame.

Summary

For sixteen years, Greg Foster was a driving force in track and field. His duels with Renaldo Nehemiah were some of the most dramatic confrontations in track history. His impressive list of accomplishments in the face of numerous injuries, personal obstacles, and tragedies was evidence of his tenacity and commitment. For years to come, aspiring hurdlers will look to Greg's career as an example of what can be accomplished with dedication and hard work.

Rusty Wilson

Additional Sources

Hickok, Ralph. *A Who's Who of Sports Champions.* Boston: Houghton Mifflin, 1995.

Wallechinsky, David, and Jaime Loucky. *The Complete Book of the Olympics: 2008 Edition.* London: Aurum Press, 2008.

Dawn Fraser

Born: September 4, 1937
  Balmain, near Sydney, New South Wales,
  Australia
Also known as: Dawn Lorraine Fraser (full name)

Early Life

Dawn Lorraine Fraser, the youngest of eight children, was born in the living room of a little house on Birch Grove Road, in Balmain—a suburb of Sydney, Australia—on September 4, 1937. In Balmain, a lower-middle-class community, the Frasers often struggled to survive. Dawn was a tough little girl who thought nothing of hurling a stone at a streetlight or stealing fruit from a neighborhood street stall. Dawn idolized her older brother Don. Sadly, he died of leukemia when only twenty-one years old. He was seven years older than Dawn and had introduced her to swimming at the Balmain Baths. He did not live long enough to see her win in world competition. She dedicated her first Olympic medal to him and his memory.

Dawn Fraser at the Rome Olympics in 1960. (Courtesy of International Swimming Hall of Fame)

The Road to Excellence

The same year that Dawn's brother died, her Scottish-born father became ill with bronchial asthma and her mother became an invalid with a heart condition. Suddenly, at thirteen, Dawn's life changed from that of a happy-go-lucky street child to the family provider. All her older brothers and sisters had married and left home. She had to do all the housework—washing, sewing, and cooking for her parents—as well as make her own clothes. At night she hung around the neighborhood gang at the local milk bar, smoking cigarettes and getting into trouble in small ways. She had no time for school.

Dawn finally left school to stay at home and take care of her mother. After two visits, the truant officer gave her special permission to drop out of school before the legal age. When her mother was better, Dawn took a job in a dress factory. By then she had met coach Harry Gallagher, who convinced her she had championship swimming potential. She raced from breakfast, to training, to her job, and then back for more training. After that, she was on to her favorite milk bar, where she worked in the evening.

The Emerging Champion

When Dawn was fourteen, she moved to Adelaide with Gallagher, who obtained a lease on a pool there and found Dawn a job as a floor walker in an Adelaide city store. She was working normal hours and eating regular meals at last. She was able to commit fully to swimming, with regular hours for practice. Her coach helped her find the self-discipline to achieve success in her sport. At seventeen, she won her first big race, the 220-yard freestyle championships of Australia, held at her new home pool in Adelaide. As if to show her coach that she had not competely given in to her training regimen, she warmed up for the race with three hours of jumping and diving into the pool from the 10-meter high diving tower. Gallagher had made a rebellious girl see beyond the corner milk bar and the juke box in Balmain. Dawn began to think about competing in the Olympics and Empire

Records

First woman to break 1 minute for the 100-meter freestyle

First person to win gold medals in 3 consecutive Olympic Games

Broke women's world record for the 100-meter freestyle nine successive times between 1956 and 1964

Her mark of 58.9 seconds set in 1964 was unbroken until 1972 by Shane Gould (58.5 seconds)

Winner of seven Australian National Championships in the 110-yard freestyle

Winner of eight Australian National Championships in the 220-yard freestyle

Winner of five Australian National Championships in the 440-yard freestyle

Honors and Awards

1962   Associated Press Female Athlete of the Year

1965   Inducted into International Swimming Hall of Fame

Games. Her dying brother's last words, "Keep on with the swimming, kid. You'll be a champ one of these days," were about to come true.

On February 25, 1956, in Sydney, Dawn set her first world record in the 200-yard freestyle. On October 25, 1962, she became the first woman to break 1 minute for the 100-meter freestyle; she remained the only woman to do so for two years, until the American Sharon Stouder did it at Tokyo, finishing second to Dawn. Dawn won the 100-meter freestyle gold in three Olympics: Melbourne, in 1956; Rome, in 1960; and Tokyo, in 1964. She was twenty-seven when she took the gold medal at Tokyo in 1964, and her world-record time of 58.9 seconds, set earlier that year, as well as her 1964 Olympic record time, remained unbroken until the 1972 Olympics.

Continuing the Story

Dawn's good times were not all in the water. Her rule-breaking was almost as dramatic as her record breaking. She was finally suspended by the Australian Amateur Swimming Union at the 1964 Games for climbing the wall of Emperor Hirohito's palace to steal a souvenir flag from his garden. She watched from the grandstand at Mexico City because the suspension had not been

lifted to let her swim. The gold went elsewhere, but the glory still belonged to Dawn.

Summary

Dawn Fraser was the first woman to swim under 1 minute for the 100-meter freestyle and the first person to win gold medals in three straight Olympics. She was banned from the 1968 Games, where she was favored to win a fourth gold medal. In 1965, Dawn was enshrined in the International Swimming Hall of Fame in the charter group of honorees. She later entered politics as a representative for her hometown of Balmain. In 2000, she was one of the torch bearers at the Opening Ceremony of the Sydney Olympics. She remains a national icon in Australia.

Buck Dawson

Additional Sources

Fraser, Dawn. *Dawn: One Hell of a Life.* Sydney: Hodder Headline Australia, 2002.

Greenberg, Stan. *Whitaker's Olympic Almanack: An Encyclopaedia of the Olympic Games.* Chicago: Fitzroy Dearborn, 2000.

Wallechinsky, David, and Jaime Loucky. *The Complete Book of the Olympics: 2008 Edition.* London: Aurum Press, 2008.

Major Swimming Championships

Year	Competition	Event	Place	Time
1956	Olympic Games	100-meter freestyle	Gold	1:02.0 WR
		400-meter freestyle	Silver	5:02.5
		4×100-meter freestyle relay	Gold	4:17.1
1957	AAU Outdoor Championships	110-yard freestyle	1st	1:03.9 WR
1958	Commonwealth Games	110-yard freestyle	1st	1:01.4 WR
		4×110-yard freestyle relay	1st	4:17.4
1960	Olympic Games	100-meter freestyle	Gold	1:01.2 OR
		4×100-meter freestyle relay	Silver	4:11.3
		4×100-meter medley relay	Silver	4:45.9
1962	Commonwealth Games	110-yard freestyle	1st	59.5 WR
		440-yard freestyle	1st	4:51.4
		4×110-yard freestyle relay	1st	4:11.1
		4×110-yard medley relay	1st	4:45.9
1964	Olympic Games	100-meter freestyle	Gold	59.5 OR
		4×100-meter freestyle relay	Silver	—
	Commonwealth Games	100-meter freestyle	1st	58.9 WR

Notes: OR = Olympic Record; WR = World Record

Gretchen Fraser

Born: February 11, 1919
Tacoma, Washington
Died: February 17, 1994
Sun Valley, Idaho
Also known as: Gretchen Claudia Kunigk Fraser
(full name); Gretchen Claudia Kunigk (birth
name)

Early Life

Gretchen Fraser was born Gretchen Claudia Kunigk on February 11, 1919, in Tacoma, Washington. Both her parents were born in Europe. Her father, William A. Kunigk, came to the United States from Germany when he was twenty-two. Her mother, Clara Andersen Kunigk, moved to the United States from Norway at the age of twenty. Although Gretchen's mother was an avid skier, Gretchen did not start skiing until she reached her late teens. Her mother eventually taught her a love of skiing, though, and Gretchen began to race soon after she took up the sport.

The Road to Excellence

Gretchen's first skiing experiences were at Mt. Rainier in Washington. She began to win novice races almost immediately. In 1937, at the age of eighteen, at a novice race, she met Donald W. Fraser, who had been a member of the 1936 U.S. Olympic ski team. Gretchen attended the University of Puget Sound in Washington until she married Donald in 1939. The couple moved to Sun Valley, Idaho, where Gretchen began to excel in skiing. Both Gretchen and Donald made the 1940 U.S. Olympic ski team, but with the advent of World War II, the Games were never held. The 1944 Olympics was also canceled.

Nevertheless, Gretchen continued to ski. In the early 1940's, she dominated women's skiing in the United States. In 1941, only about five years after taking up the sport, she won the national downhill championship and the combined championship; the latter included the slalom and downhill races. In 1942, she won the national slalom championship. On an international level, that might not have meant much. American skiers were rarely taken seriously by the Europeans, who dominated the

sport. The highest any American had ever finished in Olympic ski competition was eleventh—in a jumping event. The war kept Gretchen from competing in the international events.

The Emerging Champion

Finally, in 1948, Gretchen got the chance to compete internationally. She qualified for the U.S. Olympic ski team, earning the first spot during the Olympic trials despite skiing with a cracked rib. Most considered Gretchen a long shot to win at the Olympics in St. Mortiz, Switzerland. In her first race, the downhill, she finished eleventh. Then in the slalom, the second half of the combined event, she finished fast enough to clock the second-quickest time in the combined. Her silver medal in the combined was the first Olympic medal ever won in skiing by an American. She had proved that an American skier had the talent to be among the best in the world.

The following day her success continued in the special slalom, which was later known as the giant slalom. In the first of two runs, Gretchen posted the fastest time, only one-tenth of a second ahead of the closest follower. As she stood in the starting gate for the second run, there was suddenly a problem with the telephone line that ran from the finish to the start of the course. Race officials searched for a break in the line so that the start and finish officials could communicate. Gretchen stood in the gate in the cold for seventeen minutes, until the problem was solved. She burst out of the gate and clocked a much faster time than her first run. Antoinette Meyer of Switzerland was the only racer with a faster second run, but she could not make up enough time to beat Gretchen's combined times

Major Skiing Championships

Year	Competition	Event	Place
1941	U.S. National Championships	Downhill	1st
		Slalom	1st
1942	U.S. National Championships	Slalom	1st
1948	Olympic Games	Giant slalom	Gold
		Downhill	11th
		Combined	Silver

from both runs. Gretchen won by a half-second and took the gold medal.

Continuing the Story

During the late 1940's, Gretchen and her husband lived in Vancouver, Washington, where they operated a small oil and gas distribution company. Eventually, they moved back to Sun Valley, Idaho. She continued to support skiing. Gretchen felt it was important to give back to her sport. She worked with ski racing organizations, helping to raise money, and in 1952, she managed the U.S. women's Olympic ski team.

Gretchen and her husband also founded the Flying Outriggers, the first U.S. amputee ski club. She felt it important to work with disabled people, and she also helped with the Special Olympics over the years. Gretchen was an outstanding athlete, and although she was famous for skiing, she was accomplished in horseback riding and swimming, which she also taught to the disabled. Amazingly, Gretchen was hit by cars three times over a fifteen-year period, but her determination helped her recover each time. She also battled cancer and underwent surgery several times. Gretchen died in 1994. She was elected to the National and the Intermountain Ski Halls of Fame.

Summary

Gretchen Fraser was more than a sports champion. Although she was a great athlete in several sports, and remarkably became a champion skier after taking up the sport so late in life, she was also a community leader. She combined her mother's love of skiing and sports with her father's altruism, and became a longtime advocate of physical fitness. She made tremendous contributions to programs for the disabled and in organizations sponsoring skiing and horseback riding.

Robert Passaro

Records and Milestones

Awarded the first Olympic medal ever won by a U.S. ski team member, in 1948
Cofounder of the Flying Outriggers, the first amputee skiing club in the United States
Managed the U.S. women's Olympic ski team in 1952

Honors and Awards

1948	Norwegian Crown Prince Olaf Award for outstanding achievement in winter sports
1949	Perry Medal
1961	Inducted into U.S. National Ski Hall of Fame

Additional Sources

Fry, John. *The Story of Modern Skiing.* Hanover, N.H.: University Press of New England, 2006.

Pfeifer, Luanne. *Gretchen's Gold: The Story of Gretchen Fraser, America's First Gold Medalist in Olympic Skiing.* Missoula, Mont.: Pictorial Histories, 1996.

Smith, Lissa, ed. *Nike Is a Goddess: The History of Women in Sports.* New York: Grove Atlantic, 2001.

Wallechinsky, David, and Jaime Loucky. *The Complete Book of the Olympics: 2008 Edition.* London: Aurum Press, 2008.

Cathy Freeman

Born: February 16, 1973
　　Mackay, Queensland, Australia
Also known as: Catherine Astrid Salome Freeman
　　(full name)

Early Life

Catherine Astrid Salome Freeman was born to Cecilia and Norman Freeman in Mackay, Queensland, Australia, on February 16, 1973. Her mother and grandmother had been separated under the former policy of forced Aboriginal assimilation. Cathy was one of five children. Her parents separated when she was a child. Cathy's mother subsequently converted to the Baha'i religion and Cathy later credited the faith for her strength. She was nine when her mother married Bruce Barber and the family moved from place to place, struggling to make ends meet.

Cathy enjoyed sports in grammar school, and when her athletic ability became apparent, her stepfather encouraged her and played a key role in her development as a runner. He noticed that she had powerful legs and a natural flowing gait when running. Cathy practiced in bare feet because the family could not afford track shoes.

Barber predicted to a shy ten-year-old Cathy that she would one day compete in the Olympics. Her mother also had high expectations for Cathy and had her write an affirmation of her ability, which she hung on the wall as constant reinforcement. However, Cathy's older sister Anne-Marie, born with cerebral palsy, was Cathy's greatest inspiration. She came to realize, through Anne-Marie, that when one is able to do something well, one should not waste the opportunity. Cathy was motivated to chart the limits of her abilities; however, she did not consciously set out to be the first person of Aboriginal descent to perform a certain task.

At the age of twelve, Cathy attended the Australian Institute of Sport at Canberra to get an assessment of her athletic ability. By the time Cathy had won an athletic scholarship to attend boarding school at Fairholme Girls College in Toowoomba at the age of thirteen, she had already made it onto the state teams for touch football, basketball, and baseball.

The Road to Excellence

In 1988, Cathy experienced her first track success at the age of fifteen at the National School Championships in Melbourne. She performed well in the hurdles, jumps, and sprints, winning the 400 meters. Since Australia was in need of sprinting talent, Cathy decided to focus on running. At another boarding school, Kooralbyn International, Cathy received her first professional coaching. She sought selection to the Australian 4×100-meter relay team at the 1990 Commonwealth Games in New Zealand. She succeeded in her quest, winning a surprise gold medal in the event, beating the favored English team. She was sixteen years old.

In the 1990 National Championships, Cathy won the 200-meter title to become the youngest-ever winner. Also that year, she represented Austra-

Cathy Freeman winning the 400-meter final at the 2000 Olympic Games in her native Australia. (Mike Powell/Getty Images)

Major Sprint Championships

Year	Competition	Event	Place
1990	World Junior Championships	100 meters	3d
		200 meters	5th
	Commonwealth Games	4×100-meter relay	1st
1992	Olympic Games	400 meters	5th
	World Junior Championships	200 meters	2d
1993	World Championships	200 meters	5th
1994	World Cup in Athletics	200 meters	3d
	IAAF/Mobil Grand Prix Final	400 meters	2d
	Commonwealth Games	200 meters	1st
		400 meters	1st
1995	IAAF/Mobil Grand Prix Final	200 meters	7th
	World Championships	400 meters	4th
		200 meters	5th
1996	Olympic Games	400 meters	Silver
	IAAF/Mobil Grand Prix Final	400 meters	1st
	Olympic Games	200 meters	6th
1997	World Championships	400 meters	1st
1999	World Championships	400 meters	1st
2000	Olympic Games	400 meters	Gold
2002	Commonwealth Games	4×400-meter relay	1st
2003	Australian Championships	400 meters	1st

lia at the World Junior Games in Bulgaria and ran in the 200-meter- and 4×100-meter relay finals. She was named the 1990 young Australian of the year and the 1991 Aboriginal athlete of the year. Cathy had become a symbol of hope and success in a country whose indigenous people had a legacy of repression. She began to focus on the 200-meter and 400-meter sprint events. She earned a place in the 400 meters at the 1992 Olympic Games but did not progress past the second heat. She ran in the 4×100-meter-relay final, although she did not place.

The Emerging Champion

Cathy persevered, assisted by boyfriend Nick Bideau, a Melbourne journalist who, after their breakup in 1996, continued to serve as Cathy's manager until 1998. Cathy won the silver medal in the 200 meters at the 1992 World Junior Championships. In 1993, she reached the semifinals in the 200 meters at the World Track and Field Championships.

In 1994, Cathy won both the 200-meter and 400-meter events at the Victoria Commonwealth Games. This led to a high world ranking and marked her as a world track star. Though initially reluctant to speak out about racial injustice, at this event she made a statement of pride in her cultural heritage by taking a victory lap draped in both the Aborigine and Australian flags, which sparked controversy. It soon became clear, however, that most Australians, especially schoolchildren, admired and supported Cathy.

In 1995, Cathy finished a disappointing fourth in the 400 meters at the World Track and Field Championships. She was determined, however, and, in 1996, cracked the 50-second barrier for the first time and set four national records for the 400 meters. Her efforts culminated in her silver-medal win behind her fiercest competitor, Marie-Jose Perec, at the 1996 Atlanta Olympic Games. In the event, Cathy finished in a personal best 48.63 seconds, making her the sixth fastest woman ever in the 400 meters.

Cathy had more success at the 1997 World Track and Field Championships in Athens, Greece, where she earned the gold medal in the 400 meters, becoming the first Aboriginal woman to win a world title. This win also earned her a number-one world ranking in the 400 meters. Cathy was named 1998 Australian of the year, one of the country's highest civilian honors. Her winning streak of twenty-two consecutive 400-meter finals continued until a foot injury led to a fourth-place finish at the 1998 Bislett Games in Oslo, Norway, and kept her from competing in the 1998 Commonwealth Games. Cathy bounced back in 1999, winning the 400 meters at the World Track and Field Championships in Seville.

Continuing the Story

Cathy married Nike executive Alexander "Sandy" Bodecker in September, 1999. He took a two-year

Honors and Awards

1990	Young Australian of the Year
1991	Aboriginal Athlete of the Year
1998	Australian of the Year
2000	Selected to light Olympic cauldron at Olympic Opening Ceremony
	Laureus Female Athlete of the Year
2001	Arthur Ashe Courage Award

leave of absence to support her in her quest for the 400-meter gold medal in the 2000 Sydney Olympic Games. On September 25, 2000, Cathy appeared on the track in a full bodysuit in the Australian colors of green and gold. Her shoes were yellow, red, and black, the colors of the Aboriginal flag. She won the event by a wide margin, making Olympic history by becoming the first indigenous Australian to win an individual gold medal. She once again ran her victory lap carrying both the Australian and the Aboriginal flags, while the crowd roared its approval. Her win, and her selection to light the Olympic cauldron at the Opening Ceremony, served as significant symbols of Australian social healing as well as Aboriginal pride. A song inspired by Cathy's "Cos I'm free" tattoo even became a hit for an Aborigine artist.

Following the Olympics, Cathy took a break from running to nurse her husband through throat cancer. The couple lived in relative anonymity in Portland, Oregon. At the 2002 Winter Olympics at Salt Lake City, as a noncompetitor, Cathy carried the Olympic flag in the Opening Ceremony. Returning to competition at the 2002 Commonwealth Games, she helped her team win the 4×400. Cathy subsequently lost interest in racing and retired on July 15, 2003. She worked as a writer for the magazine *Deadly Vibe* and the English newspaper *The Daily Telegraph.*

Summary

Cathy Freeman's indomitable spirit, unaffected charm, enthusiasm for her sport, and quiet dignity made her an endearing Australian icon and an international hero despite her natural reluctance to be in the spotlight. Her perseverance as an athlete made her a role model for women and aspiring athletes everywhere, perhaps especially for the indigenous people of her native Australia.

Barbara C. Beattie, updated by Caryn E. Neumann

Additional Sources

Abrahamson, Alan. "Runner Is a Symbol of Aboriginal Freedom." *Los Angeles Times,* September 25, 2000, p. A1.

Basquali. *Catherine: Intimate Portrait of a Champion.* London: Birdy Num-Num, 2000.

Freeman, Cathy, and Scott Gullan. *Cathy: Her Own Story.* New York: Viking, 2003.

Gordon, Henry. *The Time of Our Lives: Inside the Sydney Olympics, Australia and the Olympic Games, 1994-2002.* London, Ontario, Canada: Centre for Olympic Studies, 2004.

McGregor, Adrian. *Cathy Freeman: A Journey Just Begun.* New York: Random House, 2000.

Phillips, Andrew. "A Race for All Australia." *Maclean's,* October 9, 2000, 51.

Sieg, Lindstrom. "Freeman Captivates a Nation: One for the Home Team." *Track and Field News,* December, 2000, 44-45.

Dave Freeman

Born: September 6, 1920
     Pasadena, California
Died: June 28, 2001
     San Diego, California
Also known as: David Guthrie Freeman (full
  name)

Early Life

David Guthrie Freeman was born September 6, 1920, in Pasadena, California. Dave grew up with two brothers and two sisters. One of his brothers, Robert, became a prominent doctor. His other brother, Fulton, was a foreign ambassador. Both of Dave's parents were well-educated professionals. His father was the minister of the First Presbyterian Church of Pasadena, California. His mother was a professor of religion at Occidental College in Eagle Rock, California. Dave was a well-disciplined student and a good athlete. He was the best ping-pong player in his elementary school and the fastest runner of the 50-yard dash. Living and growing

Dave Freeman. (Herbert Gehr/Time & Life Pictures/ Getty Images)

up in Southern California helped Dave become a good tennis player, too.

The Road to Excellence

Dave began his competitive career by playing in a ping-pong tournament when he was twelve years old. As a sign of things to come, Dave won the thirteen-and-under championship. Dave also won several junior tennis tournaments. He first started playing badminton when he read about a tournament for school children in Pasadena. He and a friend put a badminton net in Dave's backyard and began to play. After only two weeks of practice, he entered the Pasadena City Schools Badminton Tournament and won the fifteen-and-under championship as a fourteen-year-old.

After returning to tennis for most of the following year, Dave again practiced badminton for about two weeks—this time inside a gymnasium—and won the eighteen-and-under Pasadena City Schools Badminton Tournament as a fifteen-year-old. With his success, Dave started to play badminton more seriously the next year. Partly because of his experiences with other racket sports like ping-pong and tennis, Dave was able to improve in badminton quickly. In 1937, Dave's extra practice paid off when he won the California State Badminton Singles Championship as a seventeen-year-old. Although not particularly powerful, Dave was quick and intelligent. He was also competitive; he loved to win and fought extremely hard to do so.

The Emerging Champion

With his success at the 1937 California State Championships, Dave decided to enter the 1938 U.S. National Badminton Championships. Although he lost his first bid to become a national champion in 1938, he came back the following year to win his first U.S. National Badminton Singles Championship without losing a game. Dave dominated U.S. badminton for the next ten years. From 1939 to 1943, he won five straight national singles championships. In fact, Dave did not lose a game, much less a match—two out of three games—from 1939 to 1949.

Dave hit many unique and deceptive shots to confuse his opponents. He did not overpower his opponents; rather, he ran them into the ground. Always in superb condition and extremely quick, Dave could routinely play 50- to 75-shot rallies for a single point. Other players simply could not outlast him. He was too quick and too smart for his opponents.

The late 1930's and early 1940's were the "glory years" for American badminton. Several Hollywood film stars popularized the game with the help of badminton professional Jack Purcell. The impact of World War II changed everything. The U.S. National Championships were not played from 1943 to 1947, and after the war, many of the best athletes who might have played badminton became involved in sports with greater financial rewards, such as tennis or baseball.

Like many Americans, Dave served in the Army during the war. In 1947, when the U.S. National Championships were first played after the war, Dave was stationed in Panama. As in his earlier years, Dave practiced for a couple of weeks and won both the California State and U.S. National Singles Championships. Although Dave did not possess the single best strokes in the country, he had no weaknesses either. He could do everything well. His solid strokes, coupled with his competitive desire and quickness, made him easily the best American player.

In 1949, Dave journeyed to the All England Badminton Championships—the unofficial world championships—to play the best in the world. The combination of Dave's defensive retrieving style and offensive shot-making style was too much for his opponents. Dave easily won the world title, beating Ooi Teck Hoc of Malaysia, then thought to be the best player in the world, 15-4 and 15-5. Dave's performance was the first time an American won the men's singles title. He was the only American ever to be the top player in the world.

Continuing the Story

Like many great athletes, Dave had other things in his life besides his sport, such as his family and medical school. He had proven he was the best in the world at badminton, and it was time to move on. In 1949, Dave prematurely retired from competitive badminton. After finishing medical school, Dave completed his residency in neurosurgery with-

Major Badminton Championships	
1937, 1947	California State Badminton Singles Championship
1939-49, 1953	U.S. National Badminton Championships
1949	All-England Badminton Championships

out playing much badminton. Then, in 1953, he was asked to play a local tournament in San Diego, California, appropriately named the Dave Freeman Open. After practicing enough to return to his winning form, Dave decided to play in the U.S. National Championships as well. In 1953, Dave won both the first Dave Freeman Open and the national title without losing a game. He officially retired in 1953, at thirty-three years old, because he loved to win so much that he could not continue playing while his skills declined with age. Also, Dave decided to retire to establish his medical practice as a brain surgeon.

Dave was a great champion in his professional career too. He was one of the top neurosurgeons in the nation. His wife, Dolly, and daughter, Diana, both worked with him. His two sons also became respected professionals: Rees, his oldest, a neurosurgeon, and David, Jr., a lawyer. Although Dave no longer played competitive badminton, the ability to handle pressure and to perform at his best were competitive qualities he used daily as a surgeon.

Summary

It is difficult to argue about the best player in the history of any sport. Three great champions are recognized in badminton history, Dave Freeman of the United States, Erland Kops of Denmark, and Rudy Hartono of Indonesia. It is impossible to say who was the all-time best in the world, but no one can deny that Dave was the best the United States ever had.

Jon R. Poole

Additional Sources

Hickok, Ralph. *A Who's Who of Sports Champions.* Boston: Houghton Mifflin, 1995.

Levinson, David, and Karen Christensen, eds. *Encyclopedia of World Sport: From Ancient Times to the Present.* Santa Barbara, Calif.: ABC-Clio, 1996.

Litsky, Frank. "Dave Freeman, a Champion in Badminton, Is Dead at Eighty." *The New York Times,* July 28, 2001, p. C15.

Fu Mingxia

Born: August 16, 1978
    Wuhan, China

Early Life

Fu Mingxia was born August 16, 1978, in the small town of Wuhan, Hubei Province, along the Yangtze River in central China. She was the second of two girls in a poor family. Ironically, Fu, the family name, means financial prosperity in Chinese. Mingxia started diving around the age of seven, even before she knew how to swim. In late 1987, Yu Fen, a female diving coach from Beijing, visited Wuhan in search of young divers with potential for success. Yu selected nine-year-old Mingxia and three other aspiring athletes, and officials made arrangements for them to move to Beijing for training and competition with the national diving team.

The Road to Excellence

Sports for young Chinese athletes were tied to success in studies at sports school. Three years after her start in diving, Mingxia had become an athlete with obvious promise.

As a participant in a 1989 competition in Seattle, Washington, Mingxia became the youngest champion in the history of diving. Her performance at the meet gave her wide exposure, and she received attention as a potential medal contender for future Diving World Cup and Olympic competitions.

The Emerging Champion

Twelve days prior to her official twelfth birthday, Mingxia competed in the 1990 Goodwill Games in the United States. The platform diving title at the competition brought the spotlight to Mingxia; she defeated Olympic platform champion Xu Yanmei of China and Olympic bronze medalist Wendy Lian Williams of the United States. Mingxia became an immediate celebrity in China, enjoying a life of travel and parties. On the other hand, she was able to see her family only two times a year. Even at Chinese sports meets that her parents attended, they could not meet.

Mingxia's platform title initiated changes in the rules for Olympic competition. The International Swimming Federation (FINA), the governing body for aquatic events, passed a rule that mandated that a diver must turn fourteen in the year of competition in order to take part in the Olympics, World Diving Championships, or Diving World Cup meets. This ruling was ironic, as, up to this point, Chinese authorities had tried to portray Mingxia as young as possible. As a result, the ruling limited Mingxia to competition within China and forced her to miss the 1991 Diving World Cup.

One month after the 1990 Goodwill Games, Mingxia competed in the Asian Games. The combination of her young age, celebrity status, and reduced training time took its toll, and she fell to a

Fu Mingxia diving in the three-meter springboard event during the 2000 Olympic Games at Sydney. (Sean Garnsworthy/Getty Images)

Major Diving Championships

Year	Competition	Event	Place
1990	Alamo International	10-meter platform	1st
	Goodwill Games	10-meter platform	1st
1991	World Championships	10-meter platform	1st
1992	Olympic Games	10-meter platform	Gold
1993	World Championships	10-meter platform	Gold
1994	World Championships	10-meter platform	Gold
1995	World Championships	3-meter springboard	Gold
		10-meter platform	Gold
1996	Olympic Games	10-meter platform	Gold
		3-meter springboard	Gold
2000	Olympic Games	3-meter springboard synchronized	Silver
		3-meter springboard	Gold

third-place finish with a score of 465.33. After this dose of reality, she returned to the pool for hours of practice and intense training under the watchful eye of Yu. Three months later, Mingxia rebounded to win the world title.

In January, 1991, Mingxia captured the platform-diving world title with an impressive score of 426.51 at the World Aquatics Championships held in Perth, Australia. The competition was significant for all of China: Mingxia and her teammates collected eight gold medals—four for swimming, four for diving—at the championships. China placed second in the medal standings. Mingxia earned an additional honor from her homeland when she was named one of the twenty best swimmers and divers for China in 1991.

Mingxia set her sights on the 1992 Olympic Games in Barcelona. Spain. If she won a gold medal, she would be the second-youngest Olympic diving champion in history. On the day of the platform finals in Barcelona, she was still officially thirteen years old but would turn fourteen, the required age, one week after the closing of the Games. Thus, she met FINA requirements.

At the 1992 Summer Games, Mingxia charmed the world with her grace and flawless performances on the 10-meter platform. Her sweet smile came forth each time she popped out of the water to the thunderous applause of spectators. She selected the toughest optional dives of any woman at Barcelona, and the gamble paid off. She won the gold medal for her performance with a score of 461.43, beating the runner-up by 49.80 points.

Continuing the Story

After the 1992 Olympics, Mingxia remained in Beijing, still residing with Yu. Training schedules and competition limited her opportunities to return to Wuhan to visit her parents and sister. Her incredible success continued after Barcelona. She won the World Diving Championship in the 10-meter platform competition in 1993, 1994, and 1995, as well as the World Diving Championship in the 3-meter springboard in 1995. She exceeded all expectations in the 1996 Olympic Games in Atlanta, Georgia, when she became only the fourth woman in Olympic history to win the gold medal in both the 10-meter platform and the 3-meter springboard competitions.

After the Olympic Games, Mingxia retired from diving to study economics at Qinghua University in Beijing. After two years she returned to the pool, diving for her university's team. With a less strenuous schedule, comparable to that of Western athletes, and with weekends off, she found renewed enjoyment in athletics. Mingxia rejoined the Chinese national team in time for the 2000 Sydney Olympics.

At the 2000 Olympic Games, Mingxia extended her medal streak, adding the gold in the 3-meter springboard and the silver in the synchronized 3-meter springboard. After her triumph at the 2000 Sydney Olympics, Mingxia continued her studies in Beijing. In November, 2001, at the Chinese National Games, she performed her last professional dives and then retired.

The same month, Mingxia met Antony Leung Kam-chung, then the financial secretary of the Hong Kong Special Administrative Region. Born in 1952, divorced but childless, Antony won Mingxia's heart in a whirlwind romance. The couple was married in Honolulu, Hawaii, on July 15, 2002, a date in Chinese tradition that symbolized changing the past and moving to a new era. In February, 2003, Mingxia gave birth to a baby daughter at Hong Kong's Queen Mary Hospital. In December, 2004, she had her first son.

In May, 2005, Mingxia was inducted into the International Swimming Hall of Fame. While supportive of the 2008 Beijing Olympics, Mingxia did not play a major role in part because in April, 2008, she gave birth to her second son.

Summary

For divers and spectators throughout the world, Fu Mingxia was a delightful athlete to watch. Her pleasant attitude, friendliness, and obvious enjoyment of life contributed to her popularity and made her a model representative of a new generation of Chinese athletes. By the age of twenty-two, Mingxia was a veteran of three Olympic Games, the youngest Olympic champion, and the first female diver to win four Olympic gold medals. With her decision to quit diving in 1996 until granted a less rigorous training schedule and by winning at the 2000 Sydney Olympics, Mingxia demonstrated great independence of spirit.

Marcia J. Mackey, updated by R. C. Lutz

Additional Sources

Barnes, Simon. "Fu the Bearer of Eternal Flame." *The Times* (of London), August 9, 2008, p. 75.

Kristof, Nicholas. "At Fourteen, a Diver Reaches New Heights." *The New York Times*, May 4, 1992, p. C8.

Levinson, David, and Karen Christenson, eds. *Encyclopedia of World Sport: From Ancient to Present.* Santa Barbara, Calif.: ABC-Clio, 1996.

Montville, Leigh. "Fu's Gold." *Sports Illustrated*, August 12, 1996, 66.

Pucin, Diane. "Sydney 2000/Summer Olympics Games, Fu Makes a Splash in Record Books, Not Much in Pool." *Los Angeles Times*, September 29, 2000, p. U4.

Jim Fuchs

Born: December 6, 1927
Chicago, Illinois
Also known as: James Emanuel Fuchs (full name)

Early Life

James "Jim" Emanuel Fuchs was born in 1927, in Chicago, Illinois. He was an all-around star athlete in his Chicago high school. At the age of seventeen, he won the Illinois state 100-yard-dash championship with a time of 9.9 seconds. He also won a 220-yard-sprint title and played running back on his high school football team. He entered Yale University in 1946 and became an outstanding collegiate athlete. He excelled on the Yale football team as a halfback. However, the shot put was the sport in which Jim became a world champion.

The Road to Excellence

At 6 feet 1½ inches and 224 pounds, Jim was well-sized for both speed and weight competitions. However, his mastery of shot put owed more to his innovative technique than his strength. Like many of the Olympic weight events, the shot put has its origins in ancient Scotland and Ireland. As a test of strength, competitors threw a heavy stone. The "shot" is a 16-pound ball made of brass or iron. The ball is "put," which means that the athlete must keep the shot above his shoulder at all times and push the shot. The putter is confined to a shot circle in which he or she must build up the momentum for the put, release the shot, and complete the hurl. The circle is 7 feet (2.134 meters) in diameter. A shot putter is entitled to several attempts at each competition. Given the constraints of the circle and the weight of the shot, the successful shot putter must perfect a technique of turns, spins, or glides, creating the torque necessary to propel the shot from the circle. Jim used a quarter-turn throwing technique in which he began his put with his nonthrowing arm nearest the toe board. This technique allowed Jim to use the width of the circle to full effect, generating explosive force. With power derived from his legs and inclined trunk, Jim created a long channel to apply pressure to the ball.

While at Yale, Jim won both the Intercollegiate and National College Athletic Association Championships in shot put twice. Jim's 1950 throw of 17.57 meters (57 feet 6 inches) was a Yale record for fifty-seven years. In 1948, he competed in the Olympic Games in London and shot put 16.42 meters (53 feet 10 inches), good enough for third place and a bronze medal. He also won the Amateur Athletics Union (AAU) national outdoor title in 1949 and 1950 and the indoor titles in 1950, 1951, and 1952.

The Emerging Champion

From 1949 to 1950, Jim had two of the most incredible seasons in the history of the shot put. On July 28, 1949, at Oslo, Norway, he set a new world record of 17.79 meters (58 feet 4 inches). On April 29, 1950, in Los Angeles, California, he set a second world record of 17.82 meters (58 feet 5½ inches). On August 20, 1950, at Visby, Sweden, he set a third world record of 17.90 meters (58 feet 9 inches). Two days later in Eskilstuna, Sweden, he set his fourth and final world record of 17.95 meters (58 feet 11 inches). During this period, Jim won an incredible eighty-eight consecutive meets, one of the longest streaks in the history of track and field. *Track and Field News* ranked Jim first in the world in each of these two seasons. For his achievements,

---

Major Shot Put Championships

Year	Competition	Result
1948	Olympic Games	Bronze
1949	Intercollegiate Association of Amateur Athletes of America Championships	1st
	NCAA Outdoor Championships	1st
	U.S. Outdoor Championships	1st
1950	U.S. Outdoor Championships	1st
	U.S. Indoor Championships	1st
	Intercollegiate Association of Amateur Athletes of America Championships	1st
	NCAA Outdoor Championships	1st
1951	U.S. Indoor Championships	1st
	Pan-American Games	1st
1952	U.S Indoor Championships	1st
	Olympic Games	Bronze

he was inducted into the USA Track and Field Hall of Fame.

Continuing the Story

In 1951, Jim's remarkable winning streak finally came to an end when he was defeated by Parry O'Brien at the AAU Championships. O'Brien had a career that marked him as perhaps the greatest shot putter of all time, and he pioneered a glide technique that replaced Jim's quarter-turn method. In 1951, Jim competed in the Pan-American Games in Buenos Aires, Argentina. He won a gold medal for his shot put of 17.25 meters (56 feet 7 inches) and a gold medal in the discus for a throw of 48.91 meters (160 feet 5½ inches). In 1952, Jim finished third at the Helsinki Olympics, winning a bronze medal with a shot put of 17.06 meters (55 feet 11½ inches).

After graduating from Yale in 1950, Jim became a successful businessman. He worked as chairman and chief executive officer of several companies, including the Cosamar Group and the Grenfox Group. He also served the community as director of the local boys and girls club. Jim was president, chairman, and executive director of the Silver Shield Foundation, which provided financial assistance for the education and support of families of police officers and firefighters who have died in the line of duty. Jim has five daughters and two sons.

Summary

During a fourteen-month span in 1949 and 1950, Jim Fuchs had one of the most remarkable streaks in the history of track and field. He won an amazing eighty-eight consecutive competitions, and set four world records along the way. Although subsequent shot putters employed spin or glide techniques to surpass Jim's marks, Jim's explosive use of the quarter-turn method was an important advance in shot-putting technique.

Howard Bromberg

Additional Sources

Quercetani, Roberto. *A World History of Track and Field Athletics: 1864-1964*. London: Oxford University Press, 1964.

Silvester, Jay, ed. *Complete Book of Throws*. Champaign, Ill.: Human Kinetics, 2003.

Wallechinsky, David, and Jaime Loucky. *The Complete Book of the Olympics: 2008 Edition*. London: Aurum Press, 2008.

Grant Fuhr

Born: September 28, 1962
      Spruce Grove, Alberta, Canada
Also known as: Grant Scott Fuhr (full name)

Early Life

Grant Scott Fuhr was born on September 28, 1962, in Spruce Grove, Alberta, Canada. His birth parents were unwed teenagers of different races. His father was black and sixteen years old; his thirteen-year-old mother was part Caucasian and part American Indian. Too immature and poor to raise a baby, the parents allowed the Canadian government to put the child up for adoption. Grant was adopted and named by a Caucasian couple, Robert and Betty Fuhr, when he was just thirteen days old. The Fuhrs had no biological children, but they later adopted a Caucasian-American Indian girl. Grant and his sister were raised in a stable, small-town, middle-class household.

The Road to Excellence

Like many Canadian youngsters, Grant learned to skate and play hockey before he was old enough to go to school. A natural athlete, Grant excelled in both hockey and baseball as a teenager. Although left-handed, Grant was a catcher on his high school baseball team and was good enough at the position to be drafted by the Pittsburgh Pirates. However, he loved hockey so much that he turned down the opportunity to be a professional baseball player. Meanwhile, he was having an outstanding junior hockey career as a goaltender.

Canada has a complex and comprehensive network of junior league hockey teams in which teenagers hone their skills. Many of the better players are drafted by NHL teams while playing for these junior teams. In the 1979-1980 and 1980-1981 seasons, Grant was a member of a Victoria, British Columbia, team in the Western Hockey League—one of the three highest-rated junior leagues in the country. His combined record for those two seasons was seventy-eight wins, twenty-one losses, and one tie. His statistics were so impressive that the Edmonton Oilers selected Grant in the first round

Grant Fuhr celebrating the Edmonton Oilers' Stanley Cup win in 1987. (Bruce Bennett/Getty Images)

NHL Statistics

Season	GP	W	L	T	GAA	PIM
1981-82	48	28	5	14	3.31	6
1982-83	32	13	12	5	4.29	6
1983-84	45	30	10	4	3.91	6
1984-85	46	26	8	7	3.87	6
1985-86	40	29	8	0	3.93	0
1986-87	44	22	13	3	3.44	6
1987-88	75	40	24	9	3.43	16
1988-89	59	23	26	6	3.83	6
1989-90	21	9	7	3	3.89	2
1990-91	13	6	4	3	3.01	0
1991-92	66	25	33	5	3.66	4
1992-93	58	24	24	6	3.30	10
1993-94	32	13	12	3	3.68	16
1994-95	17	2	9	3	4.03	2
1995-96	79	30	28	16	2.87	8
1996-97	73	33	27	11	2.72	6
1997-98	58	29	21	6	2.53	6
1998-99	39	16	11	8	2.44	12
1999-2000	23	5	13	2	3.83	2
Totals	868	403	295	114	3.38	120

Notes: GP = games played; W = wins; L = losses; T = ties; GAA = goals against average; PIM = penalties in minutes

of the 1981 NHL draft. He played his first game for the Oilers on October 14, 1981, less than a month after his nineteenth birthday.

The Emerging Champion

The Oilers were the best team in the NHL during the middle and late 1980's, and Grant's performance as the squad's goaltender was an important component of the team's success. The Oilers won the Stanley Cup four times during the decade—in 1984, 1985, 1987, and 1988. Grant played in six league all-star games between 1982 and 1989, and he was the most valuable player of the all-star contest in 1986. In 1988, he received the Vezina Trophy as the NHL's best goaltender. That year, Grant won the sixteen games required for a team to earn the Stanley Cup—four wins in each of four rounds of playoffs—while losing only two games. During his decade in Edmonton, Grant was at the pinnacle of his career.

Then, Grant almost lost everything he had achieved as a hockey player. First, in the 1989-1990 season, the Oilers's management replaced him as the team's starting goaltender—relegating him to backup duty. The team won another Stanley Cup in 1990, but Grant, who had played in only twenty-one games during the regular season, did not see any action in the playoffs. Then, in September, 1990, as another season was about to begin, the NHL suspended Grant for six months because of his admission to using illegal drugs. He played in only thirteen regular-season games in 1990-1991. Although he was once again the Oilers starting goaltender during the 1991 playoffs, the team did not win another Stanley Cup. After the season, the Oilers traded Grant to another Canadian team, the Toronto Maple Leafs.

Continuing the Story

Grant was not as productive during the 1990's as he had been during the 1980's. For one thing, he played for five different teams after leaving the Oilers. After two seasons in Toronto, Grant spent two and one-half years with the Buffalo Sabres, part of a season with the Los Angeles Kings, and four years with the St. Louis Blues, before closing out his career in 1999-2000 as a member of the Calgary Flames. Moreover, he was sometimes—but not always—a starter. His greatest success during this time occurred in St. Louis: He won 108 games in four years. In the 1995-1996 season, he appeared in seventy-nine regular-season games—a record for a goaltender. However, none of the teams for which he played during the last half of his career won a Stanley Cup. Thus, after leaving the Oilers, Grant never experienced the extraordinary success that he had achieved in Edmonton.

Grant's last season was especially disappointing. In a backup role, his record was a paltry 5 wins, 13 losses, and 2 ties. However, those five victories allowed him to reach a career milestone rarely achieved in the NHL: He became only the sixth goaltender in league history to record 400 regular-season wins. Grant's nineteen years in the NHL resulted in 403 wins, 295 losses, and 114 ties in the regular season and 92 wins and 50 losses in the playoffs. These statistics led to Grant's election to the Hockey Hall of Fame in 2003. After his retirement, Grant remained active in sports as the goaltending coach for the Phoenix Coyotes and as a profes-

NHL Records

Most points by a goaltender in one season, 14 (1983-84)
Most games played by a goaltender, 75 (1987-88)
Most games played by a goaltender, 79 (1995-96)
Most consecutive starts, 76 (1995-96)

Honors and Awards

1980	Stewart (Butch) Paul Memorial Trophy
1982, 1984-86, 1988-89	NHL All-Star
1988	Vezina Trophy
1994	William M. Jennings Trophy
2003	Inducted into Hockey Hall of Fame

sional golfer, playing in several minor-league and celebrity tournaments.

Summary

Grant Fuhr's hockey career was significant for two reasons. First, he was one of the best goaltenders who ever played in the NHL. Second, in a league that has had few players of African descent, Grant was the first black hockey player to have a career worthy of election to the Hockey Hall of Fame.

Roger D. Hardaway

Additional Sources

Harris, Cecil. *Breaking the Ice: The Black Experience in Professional Hockey.* Toronto: Insomniac Press, 2003.

Murphy, Austin. "Old Faithful." *Sports Illustrated* 84, no. 7 (February 19, 1996).

Wiley, Ralph. "The Puck Stops Here." *Sports Illustrated* 68, no. 1 (January 11, 1988).

Dan Gable

Born: October 25, 1948
Waterloo, Iowa
Also known as: Daniel Mack Gable (full name)

Early Life
Daniel Mack Gable was born on October 25, 1948, in the farming community of Waterloo, Iowa, to Mack Gable, a real-estate salesman, and Katie. Although Dan did not grow up on a farm, he was not unfamiliar with hard work. Whether on a job or training for athletics, he always did much more than was asked or expected.

Surprisingly, swimming, not wrestling, brought Dan his first success in sports. He was the state Young Men's Christian Association (YMCA) backstroke champion at the age of twelve. There was no swimming program in the junior high school he attended, so he participated in football, baseball, and wrestling. A close friend of Dan's father had two sons, Bob and Don Buzzard, who wrestled at East Waterloo High School and went on to become all-Americans at Iowa State University. East Waterloo was Dan's favorite team, so he went to all the meets and watched the Buzzards wrestle—he wanted to be just like them.

The Road to Excellence
By ninth grade, Dan had developed into a wrestling prospect. He suffered his first loss in wrestling during his freshman year at West Junior High. Ron Keister, a ninth-grader from Edison Junior High, not only beat Dan but also pinned him. Dan was so upset that when he got home, he locked himself in his room and later went out and shoveled the driveway. When he came back in from shoveling, he vowed that he would never again lose a match in high school. Dan's promise proved to be prophetic. In his sophomore year, his record was 20-0; he also won the state championship. During the summer following his sophomore year, his family experienced personal tragedy. Diane, the Gables' only other child, was raped and murdered by a younger male acquaintance while Dan and his parents were away on a fishing trip. The Gables were a close family and this was a shattering experience. The senseless end to Diane's life became a motivating force for Dan. Whenever a tough match came up, Dan told his father not to worry, he was going to win for Diane.

Dan's drive and determination produced another flawless record in his junior year, when he finished 21-0 with another state championship to his credit. Bob Siddens, Dan's wrestling coach at West High School, commented that he had seen many young men with more natural ability than Dan, but none with such intensity and sheer dedication. In his senior year, Dan posted a 23-0 record, winning a third state championship. His stellar high school career concluded with a total of 64 wins, no defeats, and three state titles.

The Emerging Champion
Following his senior year, Dan had another experience that spurred him to greatness. Bob Buzzard, one of the wrestlers that he admired, was home for the weekend from Iowa State. Dan invited Buzzard to his house to work out on his wrestling mat. Buzzard beat him so

NCAA Records

Most consecutive victories, 100
Most falls, national tournaments, 13
Most consecutive falls, national championship, 10

Honors, Awards, and Milestones

1964-66	Iowa State High School Champion
1968-70	NCAA champion
1969-71	U.S. freestyle champion
1971	U.S. Pan-American Games gold medalist
	World Championships gold medalist
1972	U.S. Olympic gold medalist
1977-97	Big Ten Championship Team coach
1978-86, 1991-93, 1995-97	NCAA Championship Team coach
1980	Inducted into National Wrestling Hall of Fame
	Amateur Athletic Union Wrestling Coach of the Year
1984	U.S. Olympic Team coach
1985	Inducted into U.S. Olympic Hall of Fame

soundly that Dan cried—he did not believe anyone could beat him that easily. Dan realized that three state championships were not good enough to win in big-time wrestling. He knew that he would have to push much harder to be successful at the national level.

When choosing a college, Dan selected Iowa State University because it was the closest college with a wrestling program that suited his needs. After arriving on campus, wrestling with his more experienced teammates made him realize, once again, that he still had a lot to learn. During his first year, although freshmen were not permitted to compete at the varsity level, he wrestled unofficially in several tournaments and recorded a 17-0 mark.

While in his sophomore year, Dan spent time at an Olympic tryout camp with Rick Sanders of Portland State University, who added perhaps the mightiest weapon to Dan's wrestling arsenal. Sanders taught him to effectively use arm bars to pin opponents. Subsequently, Dan pinned sixty of the last sixty-five opponents he faced in college, not losing a match until he was beaten by Larry Owings of the University of Washington in the National Collegiate Athlete Association (NCAA) finals of his senior year. He compiled an unprecedented 138-1 record, including three NCAA championship titles, during his collegiate career.

Continuing the Story

By the time he finished college, Dan Gable was well known in international wrestling; he won world championships and beat men who became his challengers at the 1972 Olympic Games in Munich, Germany. The Soviets vowed to find someone to beat Dan. Following the Olympic tryouts—where Dan faced Owings again, but soundly defeated him this time, 7-1—he was off to Munich. At the Olympics, he completely dominated the best wrestlers in the world. Incredibly, Dan won six matches without yielding a single point and won the gold medal. In 1974, Dan married Kathy Carpenter and they had four daughters: Jennifer, Annie, Molly, and MacKenzie.

After returning from Munich, Dan accepted an assistant coaching position under Gary Kurdelmeier at the University of Iowa. In 1975 and 1976, the Kurdelmeier-Gable teams produced consecutive national championships. When Kurdelmeier accepted the assistant-athletic-director position, Dan took over as head wrestling coach. After the team finished third in the country in his first year as head coach, he led the University of Iowa to nine consecutive national titles.

Dan coached the Hawkeyes to Big Ten Conference titles in every year of his tenure, from 1977 to 1997, as well as seventeen national titles. He compiled a career record of 355-21-5, and, in that time, he produced forty-five national champions and ten Olympians. In 1997, Dan underwent hip replacement surgery and announced his retirement at the end of that season. He was selected as the head coach of the U.S. freestyle team for the 1999 World Wrestling Championships and cohead coach of the 2000 Olympic Games. In 2006, Dan returned to the University of Iowa as assistant wrestling coach. He also served as assistant athletic director.

Summary

Dan Gable is generally recognized as the greatest amateur wrestler the United States has ever produced; his name is synonymous with excellence. He compiled the unbelievable record of 182-1 while in high school and college and won many national and international awards. He continued to leave his mark in the world of wrestling by coaching his University of Iowa Hawkeyes to nine national titles.

Glenn A. Miller

Additional Sources

Chapman, Mike. *Wrestling Tough*. Champaign, Ill.: Human Kinetics, 2005.

"Dan Gable." *Current Biography* 58, no. 8 (1997).

Hoffer, Richard. "The Pride of Iowa." *Sports Illustrated* 106, no. 11 (March 12, 2007): 56-60.

McCormick, John. "The Babe Ruth of Wrestling." *Newsweek* 134, no. 19 (1999).

Zavoral, Nolan. *A Season on the Mat: Dan Gable and the Pursuit of Perfection*. New York: Simon & Schuster, 2007.

Gao Min

Born: September 7, 1970
Zigong, China

Early Life

Gao Min was born in Zigong, in China's Sichuan Province, on September 7, 1970. Min first became interested in gymnastics, then began diving for fun. At the age of nine, she started platform diving. By eleven, she was attending a sports school in Chengdu, the capital of Sichuan Province.

The Road to Excellence

Moving to Beijing, Min began a daily routine that included five hours of intense training. She also attended academic tutorials, played afternoon soccer and volleyball, and frequently won at a Chinese card game called *gong zhu*. In 1985, she moved away from platform diving to devote her attention to the 3-meter springboard event.

In 1986, sixteen-year-old Min competed in her first international meet, the World Aquatics Championships in Madrid, Spain. She then entered and won the 1987 Diving World Cup, the most prestigious of all diving competitions. After her victory, she continued to be almost unchallenged in world championship competitions.

The Emerging Champion

Min was the first female diver ever to score higher than 600 points in springboard diving in international competition. At the China Open in April, 1988, she scored the unprecedented total of 611.14. By May, 1988, she had broken the 600-point barrier twice more. The 1990 Asian Games was the backdrop for a dynamic performance that earned her an unofficial record 630.66 points. Despite her success, Min sustained years of pain and interrupted training as a result of various injuries.

By 1988, China had become recognized as a diving power, especially in the women's events. Min's performances strengthened this reputation. She won her first Olympic gold medal in the springboard competition with a 50-point victory over teammate Li Qing, the greatest point spread between two Olympic diving medalists since 1956.

In 1991, Perth, Australia, hosted the World Aquatics Championships. The meet marked the first time the Chinese team, or any Asian individual, brought home any gold medals from the world championships. By winning in Perth, Min completed the "triple crown" of diving, earning victories in the Olympics, the Diving World Cup, and the World Aquatics Championships.

Continuing the Story

After the 1988 Olympics, Min added three new 2½-somersault dives in the pike position to her repertoire. She often won through her consistency and the superiority of her entries into the water rather than with exceptionally difficult dives. She was known for her refined movements and for entering the water with precision on each dive.

As Min prepared for the 1992 Barcelona Olympics, a shoulder injury bothered her. She missed the 1991 Diving World Cup because of the injury.

Gao Min diving in the 3-meter springboard competition at the 1992 Olympic Games, where she won the gold medal. (Anja Niedringhaus/AFP/Getty Images)

After she won the World University Games in July, 1991, she did not compete until February, 1992.

Min wanted to win the gold medal in springboard diving at the 1992 Summer Olympic Games in Barcelona, Spain. She entered the competition with an opportunity to be the first woman to win consecutive gold medals in diving since Ingrid Kraemer of East Germany in 1960 and 1964. After the preliminaries, however, Min was only in third place and was plagued with shoulder problems. After the fifth round of dives in the finals, she moved up to second place. She took over the lead in the seventh round. By the tenth round, she had first place secured with nearly a 60-point lead over the runner-up, and she earned the gold medal once again.

Min had become well known for her winning smile. In Barcelona, as she stood on the victory stand, her face held a smile, but her eyes were filled with tears. While some tears were of joy and pride, others were of sadness. She knew that Barcelona would be her last appearance in any diving competition. She planned to retire after the Games.

In November, 1992, Min married Su Dong. This meant her retirement from diving competitions was final because, at that time, Chinese athletes had to be single. In December, 1992, Min auctioned one of her two gold medals from the 1991 World Aquatics Championships to raise money to support mainland China's bid for the 2000 Olympics and to set up a diving foundation.

In 1997, after several years away from competition, Min became head coach for the Edmonton Kinsmen Diving Club in Canada, which was a state-of-the-art training center for national and Olympic diving competitions. In recognition of her unprecedented domination of the springboard competi-

Honors and Awards

1986-92	Women's World Springboard Diver of the Year
1998	International Swimming Hall of Fame
2003	Inducted into International Women's Sports Hall of Fame

tion, Min was inducted into the International Swimming Hall of Fame in 1998 and the International Women's Sports Hall of Fame in 2003.

In 2005, Min left her coaching position and returned to China. There, she wrote her autobiography and became an active supporter of the 2008 Beijing Olympics. On the opening day of the Beijing Olympics, Min was the second of the ten final torch bearers that brought the Olympic flame into Beijing National Stadium. Throughout the event, she was a gracious host to international athletes and guests. She gave strong support to a new generation of Chinese women divers who in turn admired her greatly.

Summary

From 1986 to 1992, Gao Min won gold medals at every international championship in which she competed. She became a champion through long hours of training and persisted through painful injuries. She made immeasurable contributions to women's diving. Min's great commitment to the Olympic spirit made her a welcome presence at the 2008 Beijing Olympics.

Marcia J. Mackey, updated by R. C. Lutz

Additional Sources

Bagchi, Rob. "Beijing 2008: Day Twelve." *The Guardian*, August 20, 2008, p. 31.

Eskenazi, David. "Springboard's New Dawn: China First, U.S. Shut Out." *The New York Times*, August 4, 1992, p. B11.

Feitelberg, Rosemary. "Athletes Offer Some Expert Advice." *WWD*, October 23, 2003, 13.

Levinson, David, and Karen Christenson, eds. *Encyclopedia of World Sport: From Ancient to Present.* Santa Barbara, Calif.: ABC-Clio, 1996.

Spolar, Christine. "Retiring Gao Repeats Title, U.S. Shut Out." *The New York Times*, August 4, 1992, p. C5.

Wallechinsky, David, and Jaime Loucky. *The Complete Book of the Olympics: 2008 Edition.* London: Aurum Press, 2008.

Major Diving Championships

Year	Competition	Event	Place
1986	World Championships	3-meter springboard	1st
1988	Olympic Games	3-meter springboard	Gold
1989	World Cup	3-meter springboard	1st
1990	China Open	3-meter springboard	1st
	Goodwill Games	3-meter springboard	1st
		1-meter springboard	1st
1991	World Championships	3-meter springboard	1st
1992	Olympic Games	3-meter springboard	Gold

Rulon Gardner

Born: August 16, 1971
         Afton, Wyoming

Early Life

The youngest child of Reed and Virginia Gardner, Rulon Gardner was born on August 16, 1971, in Afton, Wyoming. Rulon grew up with his eight siblings on a 250-acre dairy farm. He was a descendant of the area's original Mormon settlers. He developed strength and stamina while performing chores on the family farm. He often carried 100-pound calves, heavy bales of hay, and 5-gallon milk pails. A large child, he weighed 125 pounds by the age of ten years.

Rulon began wrestling in a little league program in kindergarten, sometimes competing against older children because of his bulk. Bullies teased Rulon about his plumpness. He decided to view his size as a strength and became motivated by these taunts, enjoying his nickname, "Tiny." Because Rulon had a learning disability, some teachers discouraged his ambitions, but such dismissive attitudes only encouraged him to persevere. However, when Rulon was eight years old, his brother Ronald, who had aplastic anemia, died. Furthermore, the family lost a milking barn to a fire, which caused financial problems.

The Road to Excellence

Rulon wrestled for Star Valley High School and earned the Wyoming state heavyweight championship in 1989, the year he graduated. During his senior football season, Rulon's weight peaked at 315 pounds, and he lost 40 pounds to meet the state's 275-pound limit for wrestlers. He often qualified at weigh-ins by running several miles in sweats prior to meets. He also excelled at other sports, setting a long-standing school shot-put record of 48 feet 9 inches.

Attending Ricks College in Rexburg, Idaho, Rulon won the 1991 national junior college heavyweight title. After he transferred to the University of Nebraska at Lincoln, he earned fourth place at the 1993 National Collegiate Athletic Association (NCAA) Wrestling Championships. Opponents misjudged Rulon's pudgy appearance and were stunned by his powerful agility.

While he competed for Nebraska, Rulon learned about Greco-Roman wrestling and began training for that event in 1993. He won the 1995 and 1996 U.S. national championships for heavyweight Greco-Roman wrestling, the 1995 Pan-American gold medal, and the 1996 World Cup championship. In December, 1996, he completed a bachelor's degree in secondary education with a major in physical education and health and secured his teaching certificate. He married Stacy, a social studies teacher, that year. Rulon married and divorced three times.

The Emerging Champion

Rulon dreamed of winning an Olympic medal in Greco-Roman wrestling. Determined to compete in the 2000 Olympics, he re-

Rulon Gardner (right) wrestling Aleksandr Karelin during the 2000 Olympic Games at Sydney. (Billy Stickland/Getty Images)

located to Colorado Springs, Colorado, to train at the Olympic wrestling facility there. Wrestling at international meets, including Cuban and East European matches, he demonstrated his strength and skill. In 1997, Rulon was decisively beaten by the powerful Russian wrestler Aleksandr Karelin, who threw Rulon on his head at the Greco-Roman World Championships. Rulon placed fifth at that competition.

Despite that setback, in 1998, Rulon defeated Olympic gold medalists Andrew Wronski and Hector Milan. In 1999, he lost in the finals of the U.S. nationals, and *Sports Illustrated* designated Rulon one of the top fifty Wyoming athletes of the twentieth century. At the June, 2000, Olympic trials in Dallas, Texas, Rulon defeated Matt Ghafarri, an Olympic silver medalist, and spent most of August at the Olympic training camp in Colorado Springs.

Continuing the Story

The 6-foot 3-inch, 286-pound Rulon, with a 54-inch chest circumference, was an unknown underdog when he marched in the Opening Ceremonies at the Sydney Olympics. He was not expected to win a medal. After defeating four wrestlers in preliminary Greco-Roman wrestling rounds, he reached the finals. His opponent, the three-time Olympic gold medalist Karelin, had dominated the international heavyweight class for thirteen years, never losing a match during that time. Rulon did not anticipate defeating Karelin and relied on his work ethic honed from years of dutifully performing farm chores despite grueling conditions. Their legs locked in a regulation stance, the rivals clenched each other. Pressing against Karelin, Rulon, who had planned his strategy, was determined not to quit nor to permit Karelin to execute the notorious "Karelin Lift" to twist him

down to the mat. Neither wrestler scored points during the first round.

In the next round, Rulon implemented his defensive tactic of slightly wriggling his hips, which he compared to a worm's movement. The startled Karelin momentarily relaxed his hold on Rulon, who was awarded one point. Rulon, amazed at Karelin's mistake, wrestled conservatively from his crouch stance and pushed against Karelin the way he shoved cows back on the farm. Karelin, who had already wrestled in two matches that day, was fatigued and let go of Rulon with only seconds re-

Major Wrestling Championships

Year	Competition	Event	Place
1989	Wyoming State High School Championships	Heavyweight wrestling	1st
1991	NJCAA Championships	Heavyweight wrestling	1st
1993	NCAA Championships	Heavyweight wrestling	4th
1994	University National Championships	Freestyle wrestling	1st
	Pan-American Games	Freestyle wrestling	1st
1995	Pan-American Games	Greco-Roman wrestling	1st
	Granma Cup	Greco-Roman wrestling	1st
	U.S. National Championships	Greco-Roman wrestling	1st
	University National Championships	Greco-Roman wrestling	1st
		Freestyle wrestling	1st
1996	World Cup	Greco-Roman wrestling	1st
	Sunkist International Invitational	Greco-Roman wrestling	1st
1997	ASU/Sunkist Invitational	Greco-Roman wrestling	1st
	World Championships	Greco-Roman wrestling	5th
	Poznan Tournament	Greco-Roman wrestling	1st
	World Team Trials	Greco-Roman wrestling	1st
	U.S. Nationals	Greco-Roman wrestling	1st
1998	Vantaa Cup	Greco-Roman wrestling	1st
	Winter Classic International Tournament	Greco-Roman wrestling	1st
	Sunkist Kids International Tournament	Greco-Roman wrestling	1st
	Pan-American Games	Greco-Roman wrestling	1st
	Hungarian Grand Prix Championships	Greco-Roman wrestling	1st
	Cuba Grand Prix Championships	Greco-Roman wrestling	1st
	Colorado Open Championships	Greco-Roman wrestling	1st
1999	U.S. National Championships	Greco-Roman wrestling	2d
2000	Olympic Games	Greco-Roman wrestling	Gold
2001	World Wrestling Championships	Greco-Roman wrestling	1st
	World Team Trials	Greco-Roman wrestling	1st
	U.S. Nationals	Greco-Roman wrestling	1st
2003	New York Athletic Club (NYAC) Christmas Tournament	Greco-Roman wrestling	1st
	Sunkist International Tournament	Greco-Roman wrestling	1st
	Pan-American Games	Greco-Roman wrestling	2d
	Dave Schultz Memorial Tournament	Greco-Roman wrestling	2d
	Kurt Angle Classic	Greco-Roman	1st
2004	Olympic Games	Greco-Roman Wrestling	Bronze
2005	New Year's Eve Pride Fight (versus Hidehiko Yoshida)	Mixed martial arts	winner

maining in an overtime round required when nei-ther wrestler scored a minimum of three points. Rulon reacted to his 1-0 victory, one of the most amazing upsets in sports history, by leaping into a cartwheel and somersault. He humbly told Karelin that he was the better wrestler despite his loss.

Rulon enjoyed immediate accolades at the Games. His Olympic teammates elected him to carry the American flag in the closing ceremonies. His hometown hosted a celebratory parade in his honor; Rulon arrived on a tractor. He earned many honors including the prestigious Sullivan Award, which is given annually to the top amateur athlete.

After returning to Colorado Springs, he began training for the 2004 Olympics. He also contrib-uted to developing future wrestlers' potential by establishing camps to teach advanced wrestling tech-niques. He vowed to return to public school teach-ing and coaching after he retired from wrestling.

Prior to his defense of his gold medal, however, Rulon gained attention for a brush with death. In 2002, he was involved in a snowmobile accident, the vehicle plunging into an icy river. After seven-teen hours of surviving in sub-zero temperatures, Rulon was rescued, but not before suffering frost-bite. All of his toes were damaged, and one had to be amputated. Naturally prone to accidents, as a child, Rulon had accidentally stabbed himself in the stomach with a hunting arrow he had taken to school for show-and-tell. In 2004, while riding his motorcycle, Rulon hit the side of a car that had pulled out in front of him. Though he was not wearing a helmet at the time and was thrown over the hood of the car, he suffered only bruises. In-credibly, in 2007, Rulon and two of his friends sur-vived the crash of a single-engine plane when it lost altitude over Lake Powell, near the Utah-Arizona border. The plane went down in the lake, and Rulon dove into forty-four-degree water. Not a strong swim-mer, he managed to backstroke his way to shore. He and his friends survived the night and were res-cued the next morning by a passing fisherman.

Rulon's participation in the 2004 Athens Olym-pic Games did not seem certain. With the damage to his feet and a dislocated wrist held together with pins, Rulon won the Olympic trials in Indianapolis, Indiana. At the age of thirty-three, Rulon, who did not make his high school wrestling team until his senior year and who pulled off what some people believe was the greatest Olympic upset of all time, was ready to lace up his shoes one last time. At the end of the day, as wrestling tradition dictates, he would leave those shoes on the mat out of respect for the sport. Rulon went to the 2004 Olympics for his final match to prove his amazing 2000 victory in Sydney, Australia, was no accident. As it turned out, Rulon won the bronze medal, which, given the ob-stacles he had to overcome, was still remarkable.

Rulon debuted as a commentator for NBC Sports at the 2008 Beijing Olympics, working as one of the 106 broadcasters covering the Games for the network. Rulon also became a motivational speaker. His main interest was in working with chil-dren with learning disabilities.

Summary

Significant for defeating one of Russia's greatest athletes, Rulon Gardner also became the most out-standing Greco-Roman wrestler in the United States. His determination and perseverance al-lowed him to overcome one of the most decorated wrestlers of all time and to win an Olympic gold medal in the process. His story of success was one of the most amazing of the 2000 Summer Games.

Elizabeth D. Schafer, updated by Randy L. Abbott

Additional Sources

Chapman, Mike. *Wrestling Tough.* Champaign, Ill.: Human Kinetics, 2005.

Fitzgerald, Terence J. "Gardner, Rulon." *Current Bi-ography* 65, no. 11 (November, 2004): 13-18.

Gardner, Rulon. *Never Stop Pushing: My Life from a Wyoming Farm to the Olympic Medals Stand.* New York: Carroll & Graf, 2006.

Tyson Gay

Born: August 9, 1982
Lexington, Kentucky
Also known as: Lightning Bolt

Early Life
Tyson Gay was born on August 9, 1982, in Lexington, Kentucky, to Daisy Lowe. As a child, Tyson raced his older sister Tiffany but could not beat her in a race until he was fourteen years old. Tyson's excuse: "She had a quick start." Nonetheless, Tyson had plenty of speed as a child to be a proficient base stealer in baseball. Tyson attended Lafayette High School in Lexington and became a three-time Kentucky class 3A, 100-meter dash champion and set the state-meet record in the 100-meter dash, running in 10.46 seconds. He set the record in 2001, when he was a senior in high school.

The Road to Excellence
After Tyson placed fifth in the 100-meter dash at the National Scholastic Track and Field Championships, he earned a spot on Barton County, Kansas, Community College's track and field team, which was coached by Lance Brauman. Tyson ran the 100-meter and 200-meter dashes for Barton County Community College. In 2002, he finished first in the 100-meter dash but did not finish the 200-meter dash at the junior college nationals as a freshman. In the same year, he finished sixth at the 2002 USA Outdoor Track and Field Championships by running a 10.28 in the 100 meters. As a sophomore, he finished second in the 200 meters and third in the 100 meters at the junior college nationals.

Tyson's speed earned him a spot on the University of Arkansas's track and field team. He ran the 100- and 200-meter races as well as the 4×100-meter relay. In his first season with Arkansas, he won the Southeastern Conference Track and Field Championships in all three events. He then shocked many people by becoming the first sprinter from the University of Arkansas to win the 100-meter dash at the National Collegiate Athletic Association (NCAA) Men's Outdoor Track and Field Championships while running a then personal best 10.06. He also ran in the 2004 Olympic trials but did not advance past the semifinals of the 100-meter event. His work was enough for *Track and Field News* to rank him ninth in 100-meter dash and eighth in the 200-meter dash in the United States.

The Emerging Champion
Tyson's second year at Arkansas was not as impressive as his first, but it was still great. Tyson finished third in the 200-meter at the NCAA Men's Outdoor Track and Field Championships and then turned professional. He finished second at the USA Outdoor Track and Field Championships and finished fourth at the World Outdoor Track and Field Championships in the 200-meter. He was victorious at the World Athletics Finals and earned a ranking of third best in the world in the 200-meter according to *Track and Field News*.

Tyson Gay winning the 100-meter semifinals at the 2008 Olympic Games in Beijing. (Matthew Stockman/Getty Images)

In 2006, Tyson had a breakout year: He was dominant in both the 100- and the 200-meter races worldwide. In the 100-meter event, he won the USA Outdoor Track and Field Championships, was second at the Adidas Classic, the Reebok Grand Prix, and the Stockholm, Sweden, meets. In the 200-meter event, Tyson won the London Grand Prix and finished second at the Lausanne, Switzerland, meets. In 2006, Tyson was ranked second in the world in the 100 meters and first in the world in the 200 meters. Also, he run both the 100- and the 200-meter events with his best times of 9.84 and 19.68, respectively.

In early 2007, Coach Brauman was sentenced to one year in at a minimum-security prison in Texarkana, Arkansas, for embezzlement and mail fraud. However, Brauman was wise enough to prepare Tyson's training program for the entire 2007 season. Tyson was able to win the 100-meter, 200-meter, and the 4×100-meter relay events at the World Track and Field Championships. By the end of the season, *Track and Field News* ranked Tyson first in the world in both the 100 and the 200 meters.

Continuing the Story

Entering 2008, Tyson was the favorite to win both the 100- and the 200-meter dashes at the Olympic Games in Beijing, China. However, Jamaican Usain Bolt came to the forefront of the track and field world. On May 31, Tyson and Bolt raced in the 100 meters in New York City; Usain ran much faster than Tyson, while setting a world record time of 9.72. This loss stuck with Tyson. He trained with his new coach Jon Drummond and surprised the nation at the Olympic trials. In the second round of the 100-meter event, he set a U.S. record of 9.77. In the finals of the trials, he ran what was initially thought to be a world-record in 9.68. Even though the time was better than Bolt's record in New York City, it was not considered an official record because Tyson was running with the aid of high winds blowing at his back. Despite Tyson's success in

Major Sprint Championships

Year	Competition	Event	Place
2003	Southeastern Conference Championships	100 meters	1st
		200 meters	1st
		4x100-meter relay	1st
2004	NCAA Outdoor Championships	200 meters	3d
	USA Track and Field Outdoor Championships	200 meters	3d
2006	USA Track and Field Outdoor Championships	100 meters	1st
	IAAF World Cup	100 meters	1st
2007	World Championships	100 meters	1st
		200 meters	1st
		4x100-meter relay	1st
	USA Track and Field Outdoor Championships	100 meters	1st
		200 meters	1st

the 100-meters, he had to give up his 200-meter chances because of an injury to his hamstring.

At the Olympics, Tyson ran in the 100-meter dash and the 4×100-meter relay. He had a forgettable Olympic experience. His struggles first began in the 100-meter dash: He not only failed to run a sub-10-second time in the event but also failed to advance past the semifinals. Then in the 4×100-meter relay, he dropped the baton on an exchange in the first round, which resulted in an automatic disqualification for the relay team.

Summary

Tyson Gay, a sprinter respected worldwide, failed in his chance to claim Olympic glory. At the age of twenty-six, he was running against people five years younger than him. However, he set numerous American and Olympic records during his track career and was regarded as one of the finest runners of his era.

Paul C. Alexander II

Additional Sources

Layden, Tim. "Panic Speed." *Sports Illustrated* 109, no. 1 (July 7, 2008).

_____. "Speed to Burn." *Sports Illustrated* 107, no. 1 (July 2, 2007).

Zinser, Lynn. "Gay Takes Philosophical View of Defeat, but It Still Hurts." *The New York Times*, August 18, 2008.

Haile Gebrselassie

Track and field
(long-distance runs)

Born: April 18, 1973
    Asella, Arsi Province, Ethiopia
Also known as: The Emperor; Gabe; Haile
Gebreselassie

Early Life

Haile Gebrselassie was born on April 18, 1973, in Asella, Arsi Province, in central Ethiopia, a region famous for producing great long-distance runners. Haile's family was extremely poor and lived in a one-room house. One of ten children born to parents who were peasant farmers, Haile was running from a young age. He ran barefoot 6 miles a day to and from school and frequently exasperated his father because his running kept him from working on the farm. Haile's father could afford only one pair of running shoes, which Haile shared with a brother and sister.

Haile's running style was affected by his daily trip to school: He had to run with his schoolbooks held against his left side to keep from dropping them. Throughout his career, Haile ran with his left arm pressed against his body, instead of the usual swinging gait favored by other distance runners.

The Road to Excellence

After his mother died, Haile became even more interested in running. Inspired by his countrymen, Ethiopian marathon legend Abebe Bikila and Olympic gold medalist Miruts Yifter, he began to train on his own, pushing himself in his solitary runs over the hilly Ethiopian countryside. Once, he met a group of runners whose trainer invited him to join their club. He began to train with them and soon, against his father's wishes, went to live with his brother and continued training in Addis Ababa. At the age of sixteen, he entered the Addis Ababa marathon and finished ninety-ninth. His father urged him to give up running, believing Haile's efforts were futile, but Haile persisted.

The Emerging Champion

Soon after the Addis Ababa marathon, Haile plunged into an intensive two-year training program that prepared him to represent Ethiopia in international competition. The 5-foot 3-inch, 119-pound runner first gained international fame in 1992, when he won the 5,000-meter and the 10,000-meter races in the World Junior Track and Field Championships. At the World Track and Field Championships in 1993, he won the 10,000 meters and placed second in the 5,000 meters. In 1994, in Hengelo, Netherlands, Haile

Haile Gebrselassie (1658) leading his 10,000-meter heat at the 2000 Olympic Games in Sydney. (Jeff Haynes/AFP/Getty Images)

World Record and Championship Times

10,000 Meters

1993	World Championships: Stuttgart, Germany	27:31.62 (WR)
1995	World Championships: Hengelo, Netherlands	26:43.53 (WR)
1996	Olympic Games: Atlanta, Georgia	27:07.34 (Gold, OR)
1997	World Championships: Oslo, Norway	26:32.31 (WR)
1998	World Championships: Hengelo, Netherlands	26:22.75 (WR)
2000	Olympic Games: Sydney, Australia	27:18.20 (Gold)

5,000 Meters

1994	World Championships: Hengelo, Netherlands	12:56.96 (WR)
1995	Weltklasse Meet: Zurich, Switzerland	12:44.39 (WR)
	Indoor World Championships: Paris, France	13:10.98 (WR)
1997	Weltklasse Meet: Zurich, Switzerland	12:41.86 (WR)
	Indoor World Championships: Stockholm, Sweden	12:59.04 (WR)
1998	World Championships: Helsinki, Finland	12:39.36 (WR)

2 Miles

1995	World Championships: Hengelo, Netherlands	8:07.46 (WR)
1997	World Championships: Hengelo, Netherlands	8:01.08 (WR)

3,000 Meters

1996	Memorial Van Damme: Brussels, Belgium	7:30.72 (WR)
1997	World Indoor Championships	7:40.97
2003	World Indoor Championships	7:53.57

2,000 Meters

1998	Indoor World Championships: Birmingham, England	4:52.86 (WR)

1,500 Meters

1997	Indoor World Championships: Stuttgart, Germany	3:32.39 (WR)
1999	World Indoor Championships	3:33.77

Marathon

2007	Berlin Marathon	2:04:26 (WR)

Half-Marathon

2001	World Half-Marathon Championships	1:00:03

Notes: WR = World Record; OR = Olympic Record

lap, he passed Tergat for the gold medal in an Olympic record time of 27 minutes 7.34 seconds. However, the hard Olympic track blistered Haile's feet, preventing him from competing in the 5,000-meter race.

At the awards ceremony, Haile's eyes filled with tears as the Ethiopian flag was raised and the sounds of Ethiopia's national anthem flooded Centennial Olympic Stadium. Nearly one million people greeted him upon his return home and proclaimed him Ethiopia's ambassador to the world. A short time later, Haile married Alem Tellahun and settled in Addis Ababa.

Continuing the Story

Having claimed victory at the Olympics, Haile, perceived by many as the greatest distance runner of all time, continued to set records. In February, 1997, he set a world record in the 1,500 meters, an event in which he did not normally compete. Later that month, he set a world record at an indoor 5,000-meter race in Stockholm, Sweden. In Oslo, Norway, in July, 1997, he set another 10,000-meter world record followed by yet another world championship in the 10,000 meters in September of that year.

In 1998, Haile reclaimed the 5,000- and 10,000-meter world records set by Kenya's Daniel Komen and Paul Tergat, respectively. In that same year, he was elected the international amateur athlete of the year. In 1999, in Seville, Spain, he won another 10,000-meter world championship.

After 2000, Haile entered a long competition with Kenenisa Bikele, also Ethiopian. The two traded top honors in the 5,000 meters. From 1998 to 2003, Haile held the world indoor record until Bekele broke the mark by almost two minutes. The following year, Bekele also took Haile's 10,000-meter record. At this point, Haile began to concentrate full time on the marathon.

Hampered by a sore Achilles tendon, Haile entered the 2000 Olympics in Sydney, Australia, at the last moment. In the closest finish in that event in Olympics history, he barely edged past his old rival, Tergat, to win his second Olympic gold medal in

broke the six-year-old world record in the 5,000-meter competition.

At a meet in England in 1995, Haile got off to a bad start and finished a disappointing fourth. However, that same year, he came back and set a new world record in the 2-mile race. Later that summer, he set a second world record and won a gold medal in the 10,000-meter category. By August, he had brought his number of world records to four. By the end of the year, he had set two more world records—an indoor 5,000-meter race clocked at 13 minutes 10.98 seconds and a 3,000-meter run in 7 minutes 30.72 seconds.

In 1996, Haile represented Ethiopia at the Olympic Games in Atlanta, Georgia. Throughout most of the 10,000 meters, he ran behind the leaders but remained within striking distance. By the twenty-fourth lap, he had moved into second position behind Kenyan Paul Tergat, and in the final

the 10,000 meters. Next, he decided to train for the 2004 Olympic Marathon.

In 2002, Haile placed first in the London Marathon, and he followed that with first-place finishes in Amsterdam, Netherlands; Berlin, Germany; Fukuoka, Japan; and London, England. In 2007, he won in London again and set a world record in Berlin with a time of 2 hours 4 minutes 26 seconds (2:04:26). In 2008, he won the Dubai Marathon with the second-fastest time in history (2:04:53).

Haile decided to bypass the marathon at the 2008 Beijing Olympics, fearing that the air quality would aggravate his asthma. Instead, he ran the 10,000 meters but finished sixth. He indicated that he would continue to run the marathon. However, after retiring, he planned to enter politics in his home country.

Haile seemed well suited to distances of 3,000 meters and above and possessed amazing speed for a long-distance runner. However, such racing requires tough preparation. In addition to long training sessions twice a day, Haile's regimen consisted of a series of 2,000 meters, 1,000 meters at a fast pace, and then fifteen 400 meters at 56 seconds each, with a 1-minute break in between. Regularly, he ended training sessions with 100-meter sprints, which may partly account for his incredibly fast finishes.

The speed at which Haile was able to run makes distance running seem more like sprinting. He was one of a small, elite group of runners whose running speed elicits a level of pain former runners were unwilling to endure. As he kept running faster and breaking his own records, Haile had to train harder, pushing himself toward the edge of endurance.

Summary

Because Haile Gebrselassie hailed from a relatively poor country, he constantly prepared for the future. In a country where athletes were not allowed to earn money prior to 1991, Haile was fortunate to be able to command handsome fees for appearances and product endorsements. For a time, he made more than $1 million per year for appearances and endorsements, and he was the one-million-dollar winner of the AF Golden League in 1998. Haile also received several luxury cars, although he never learned to drive. He extended his fortune beyond his family, however, using his Adidas Global Club to train and manage young athletes in his country. He believed strongly that his success should provide opportunities for Ethiopian athletes and ensure Ethiopia's future in distance running.

Mary Hurd, updated by Norbert Brockman

Additional Sources

Brant, John. "Hope and Glory: Ethiopia's Haile Gebrselassie, World Record Holder at 5,000 and 10,000 Meters, Carries the Hope of His Country into the Olympic Games." *Runner's World* 31, no. 7 (July, 1996): 94-104.

Burfoot, Amby. "Summer Spectacular." *Runner's World* 32, no. 11 (November, 1997): 74-88.

Denison, Jim. *The Greatest: The Haile Gebrselassie Story.* Halcottsville, N.Y.: Breakaway Books, 2004.

Eyestone, Ed. "Be Like Haile." *Runner's World* 43 (August, 1999): 42.

Layden, Tom. "Distance Thunder." *Sports Illustrated* 89, no. 3 (July 20, 1998): 34-38.

_____. "Inside Olympic Sports." *Sports Illustrated* 93, no. 17 (August 21, 2000): 78.

Bernie Geoffrion

Born: February 16, 1931
　　Montreal, Quebec, Canada
Died: March 11, 2006
　　Atlanta, Georgia
Also known as: Bernard Joseph André Geoffrion
　(full name); Boom Boom

Early Life

Bernie "Boom Boom" Geoffrion was born on February 16, 1931, in the city of Montreal, Quebec, Canada. On the outdoor rinks of inner-city Montreal, Bernie got his first experience with hockey. On most winter Saturdays, after spending the day playing and practicing, Bernie would head downtown to the Forum, home of the Montreal Canadiens, to watch the team play and root for his hero, Maurice "The Rocket" Richard. As soon as he was able, Bernie joined a local team and started making a name for himself on the ice.

The Road to Excellence

At the age of fourteen, while playing for the Immaculate Conception parish team, Bernie had an argument with his coach, who suggested that Bernie should pursue another sport. In fact, this coach threw all of Bernie's equipment on the floor, told him he would never amount to anything in the sport, and sent him home. This was one of the turning points in Bernie's career. He was so mad and so sure that his coach was wrong that he was determined to try harder. He was soon on another team and proving to the world that he did belong on the ice. In fact, as he progressed toward the National Hockey League (NHL), Bernie impressed so many people that he never played hockey in the minor leagues. He jumped straight from junior hockey right into the big leagues.

During his junior hockey days, Bernie picked up a nickname that stayed with him for the rest of his career. While Bernie was practicing his slap shot, a Montreal sportswriter noticed the sound that the puck created when it hit the boards. In an indoor arena, the booming noise was unavoidable. The name "Boom Boom" stuck. The hard slap shot would be a trademark of this great right wing.

Bernie was brought up to the big club, the Canadiens, during the 1950-1951 season. In eighteen games, he averaged just under a point a game. The next year, in his first full season, Bernie won the NHL rookie of the year award (Calder Memorial Trophy).

The Emerging Champion

Bernie's slap shot was earning him the respect of all goalies. The shot was not only powerful but also controlled and accurate. Bernie was a natural goal scorer. At the time he was playing, he was only the second player, other than Maurice Richard, to score 50 goals in a season. He accomplished that feat in the third to last game of the 1961 season. He tried to break that record but scored no points in the final two games. Through sixteen years as a player, fourteen with Montreal and two with the

Bernie Geoffrion during his years with the Montreal Canadiens. (Courtesy of Amateur Athletic Foundation of Los Angeles)

NHL Statistics

Season	GP	G	Ast.	Pts.	PIM
1950-51	18	8	6	14	9
1951-52	67	30	24	54	66
1952-53	65	22	17	39	37
1953-54	54	29	25	54	87
1954-55	70	38	37	75	57
1955-56	59	29	33	62	66
1956-57	41	19	21	40	18
1957-58	42	27	23	50	51
1958-59	59	22	44	66	30
1959-60	59	30	41	71	36
1960-61	64	50	45	95	29
1961-62	62	23	36	59	36
1962-63	51	23	18	41	73
1963-64	55	21	18	39	41
1966-67	58	17	25	42	42
1967-68	59	5	16	21	11
Totals	**883**	**393**	**429**	**822**	**689**

Notes: GP = games played; G = goals; Ast. = assists; Pts. = points; PIM = penalties in minutes

New York Rangers, Bernie proved that he was one of the greatest scorers ever. He won the scoring title (Art Ross Trophy) in 1955 and again in 1961. He claimed that winning the scoring title the second time was much more satisfying because it proved that the first time was not just luck. In 1968, when Bernie retired as a player, he was fifth in goals scored and eighth in all-time point production. He had been on six Stanley Cup teams and won the Hart Memorial Trophy as the league's most valuable player in 1961.

Continuing the Story

Throughout his career, Bernie dealt with a temper and a rash of injuries that would have ended the career of a less determined man. In 1958, he ruptured a bowel during a practice session. He almost died from that injury and most people, including his doctors, thought that he was finished as a hockey player. At best, they thought he might attempt a comeback the following season. Bernie proved them all wrong, returning to the ice less than six weeks later, just in time to participate in the playoffs against archrival Boston. In the sixth and final game of that series, Bernie scored the first goal, assisted on the second, and then scored the game winner as Montreal won the Stanley Cup.

In 1964, Bernie retired from the Montreal Canadiens to take a coaching job with the Quebec Aces

of the American League. He stayed there until he was lured out of retirement. In 1966, when the New York Rangers needed a team boost, they called on Bernie. The Rangers made the playoffs in each of Bernie's two seasons with the team. Finally, in 1968, he retired for good as a player but continued with the Rangers as the team's coach. Once again, one of his many ailments and injuries derailed him. An ulcer got so bad that doctors ordered Bernie to quit the game or his life would be in jeopardy. This time, he had no choice but to say good-bye to hockey.

Summary

A man of intense pride and great determination, Bernie Geoffrion played the game with the best. By his own admission, he was not one of the better skaters in the league, but hard work helped him to achieve greatness. His ability to propel the puck accurately and at great speed was only one of many talents he possessed on the ice. He played the game when only six teams made up the league. The level and standards of hockey were high and Bernie was able to excel at a game he loved. Bernie died of stomach cancer on March 11, 2006—the day the Montreal team was set to retire Bernie's number.

Carmi Brandis

Additional Sources

Goldstein, Richard. "Bernie Geoffrion, Seventy-five; Popularized the Slap Shot." *The New York Times*, March 13, 2006, p. A19.

McDonell, Chris. *For the Love of Hockey: Hockey Stars' Personal Stories*. Richmond Hill, Ont.: Firefly Books, 2004.

_____. *Hockey's Greatest Stars: Legends and Young Lions*. Richmond Hill, Ont.: Firefly Books, 2005.

O'Donnell, Chuck. "For the Man They Called 'Boom Boom,' Life Goes On." *Hockey Digest* 25, no. 6 (1997).

Honors and Awards

1952	Calder Memorial Trophy
1955, 1960	NHL Second Team All-Star
1955, 1961	Art Ross Trophy
1961	Hart Memorial Trophy
	NHL First Team All-Star
1972	Inducted into Hockey Hall of Fame

Jean-Sébastien Giguère

Born: May 16, 1977
Montreal, Quebec, Canada
Also known as: J. S.; Jiggy; Jigs; Jigger

Early Life

Jean-Sébastien Giguère was born on May 16, 1977, in Montreal, Quebec, Canada, to Claude, a prison warden, and Gisele, a school bus driver. The youngest of five, Jean-Sébastien was recruited by his siblings to play goalie in their practice games. The oldest brother Stephane, later drafted by the Toronto Maple Leafs; sister Isabelle, who became a hockey referee and officiated an Olympic women's finals; and another brother and sister put Jean-Sébastien at the goal net, where he took their practice shots aimed for his head. He showed he could take the challenge. When he was twelve years old, his parents mortgaged their house to buy him the necessary goalie gear and to pay for him to attend summer hockey school. There Jean-Sébastien was trained by the legendary François Allaire, a hockey great best known as the godfather of the goaltending technique called the modern butterfly. This methodology had been honed to perfection by Patrick Roy, the esteemed goaltender of the Montreal Canadiens. Although the young Jean-Sébastien was not a Canadiens fan, Roy was his favorite player, and so Jean-Sébastien practiced hard to emulate the famous goalie. Added to his motivation was the day at pee-wee team practice when he found himself in possession of Roy's old goal stick: Jean-Sébastien cherished the item, taping it repeatedly whenever it took a cracking blow.

The Road to Excellence

After the pee-wee period, Jean-Sébastien joined the junior hockey team the Halifax Mooseheads of Quebec. By 1995, the eighteen-year-old was hired by the Hartford Whalers. When the Whalers' goalie Sean Burke got injured in December, 1996, Jean-Sébastien was called up. His debut performance with the new team was against the Philadelphia Flyers. He saved an impressive twenty-seven of thirty shots and sports aficionados said he proved he could compete with the best of the top shooters.

After seven more games with the Whalers in the 1996-1997 season, Jean-Sébastien was traded to the Calgary Flames, where he performed unremarkably for the next two years. A goalie with the gift for simple and sure technique, Jean-Sébastien began to add complexity to his game, reacting instead of acting at the moment he was facing the puck. Calgary became disappointed in him, and he was sent to the St. John Flames, the New Brunswick, Canada, American Hockey League (AHL) farm team. While there, he played well enough to earn, with Tyler Moss, the Harry Holmes Award for the lowest goals against average. However, in 1999-2000, he played only seven games and, in the off-season, was traded to Anaheim to play with the Mighty Ducks (now Ducks) starting in 2000.

The Emerging Champion

Jean-Sébastien's confidence had slowly eroded, and his demotion to the minor leagues further affected his self-esteem. Allaire, the goaltending consultant for the Ducks, helped Jean-Sébastien regain his confidence. He and Jean-Sébastien retrained and rebuilt Jean-Sébastien's style. By the middle of his first season with the Ducks, Jean-Sébastien was in top form, again rising in the ranks. In 2003, he became the first goaltender in fifty-eight years to post three shutout games in the West-

NHL Statistics

Season	GP	W	L	T	GAA	PIM
1996-97	8	1	4	0	3.65	0
1998-99	15	6	7	1	3.21	4
1999-00	7	1	3	1	2.72	2
2000-01	34	11	17	5	2.57	8
2001-02	53	20	25	6	2.13	28
2002-03	65	34	22	6	2.30	8
2003-04	55	17	31	6	2.62	4
2005-06	60	30	15	0	2.66	20
2006-07	56	36	10	0	2.26	0
2007-08	58	35	17	0	2.12	4
Career	411	191	151	25	2.43	78

Notes: GP = games played; W = wins; L = losses; T = ties; GAA = goals against average; PIM = penalties in minutes. 2004-05 NHL season canceled because of lockout.

ern Conference Finals. Furthermore, Jean-Sébastien had secured Anaheim's place in the Stanley Cup Finals against the New Jersey Devils. He and his team forced the Devils to seven games. Though the Ducks lost, Jean-Sébastien was awarded the coveted Conn Smythe Trophy and named the finals' most valuable player.

Continuing the Story

Jean-Sébastien was re-signed by the Ducks and awarded a $20-million, five-year contract. He had a varied 2003-2004 season, playing inconsistently despite his best efforts to retain what he had learned with Allaire. After the lockout canceled the 2004-2005 season, however, Jean-Sébastien began to regain his form in the 2005-2006 season. In April, 2006, he and his team again made the playoffs. Jean-Sébastien played only four games; he was replaced by rookie Ilya Bryzgalov, who matched Jean-Sébastien's three-shutout-game record, and the Ducks ultimately lost in the playoffs. However, Jean-Sébastien recouped once more: In October, 2006, the first month of the season, he did not lose a single game. In 2007, Jean-Sébastien guided his team to the Stanley Cup Finals and to a 6-2 win in the fifth game to clinch Anaheim's first championship. Despite the team's first-round defeat by the Dallas Stars in the 2008 playoffs, Anaheim gave Jean-Sébastien another multiyear contract.

Summary

Spending the largest portion of his time in the minors, Jean-Sébastien Giguère nevertheless made a significant impact on hockey throughout his career. He showed potential early, when he played with the Halifax Mooseheads of Quebec Major Junior Hockey League, and at seventeen, was considered a world-class goalie on the junior level. When

---

Anaheim Ducks Records

Lowest single-season goals against average, 2.12 (2007-08)
Lowest single-season save percentage, .9224 (2007-08)
Most wins in season, 36 (2007)
Most career wins, 174
Most career shutouts, 28

---

he was recruited by the Hartford Whalers in 1996, he was drafted thirteenth overall. After his NHL debut in 1998, Jean-Sébastien proved a goalie with which to be reckoned. He won a share of the Harry Holmes Award for the lowest goals against average in the AHL. After he was traded to the Anaheim Ducks, a team with a last-place reputation and little esteem, Jean-Sébastien took his team to the 2003 Stanley Cup playoffs. Leading the Mighty Ducks by dominating some of the best teams in the NHL, he finished the playoffs with a remarkable 1.62 GAA. Furthermore, he had a scoreless streak of 168 minutes and 27 seconds, the longest in playoff history. Ultimately, he took home the Conn Smythe Trophy, becoming only the fourth player from a losing team to win the award. In 2007, he led his team to a championship and had a 36-10-7 record with a 2.12 goals against average, the best numbers of his hockey career.

Roxanne McDonald

Additional Sources

Gilchrist, Alex, and Lauren O'Gorman. *Anaheim Ducks Stanley Cup Champions NHL 2007-08 Media Guide*. Anaheim, Calif.: Anaheim Ducks, 2007.

"Jean-Sébastien Giguère." *Newsmakers*. Detroit: Gale, 2008.

"Jean-Sébastien Giguère: NHL Goaltender." In *Contemporary Canadian Biographies*. Detroit: Gale, 2003.

Diana Golden

Born: March 20, 1963
Lincoln, Massachusetts
Died: August 25, 2001
Providence, Rhode Island
Also known as: Diana Golden Brosnihan (full name)

Early Life

Diana Golden was born on March 20, 1963, in Lincoln, Massachusetts, near Boston. She lived in a big colonial-style house with her parents and a brother and sister. Her family also owned a home in Franconia, New Hampshire, and Diana spent many happy days there as a child. Snow skiing was a popular sport in the Franconia area, and Diana had learned to ski by the time she was five. In fact, she learned to ski before she could ride a bike. Although she was not considered a great athlete, Diana loved to ski.

One day in 1975, when she was twelve, she was in Franconia in the woods with some friends when suddenly her right leg gave out and she collapsed. Her parents took her to a doctor, who told her that

Diana Golden skiing with only one leg.

she had bone cancer in her leg. The cancer was spreading and the only way to save Diana's life was to amputate her leg above her right knee. Diana asked her doctors if she would still be able to ski and was assured that she would. Although the prospect of life with only one leg was frightening, Diana was determined to live a normal life and to continue skiing. Diana was soon fitted with an artificial limb, or prosthesis. She underwent chemotherapy to eliminate the cancer. Because of the treatment, her hair fell out and she had to wear a wig. Despite the change in her life, Diana returned to her school and friends and continued to do well in her classes. She did not have to take physical education classes anymore, which made her glad, but she was determined to ski again. She entered a ski program for the physically challenged, and, seven months after her surgery, Diana was skiing.

The Road to Excellence

Diana learned to ski fairly well on one ski. She did not wear her prosthesis when she skied. She used outriggers, which are ski poles with short skis on the bottom. The high school ski-team coach, Dave Livermore, thought Diana showed considerable natural ability and determination, and he asked her to join the ski team. Diana had never ski raced before, but she accepted the challenge and made the team. She eventually became one of the better skiers on the team. When she was seventeen, she placed first in both the downhill and the slalom in the United States Disabled National Championships. In 1982, she again took first in the slalom and the giant slalom.

After high school graduation, Diana entered Dartmouth College. She continued to race and won her first World Disabled Championship in 1982. She stopped racing shortly after the World Championships, however. She tired of people thinking she was something special because she was skiing so successfully on only one leg. She did not want people to focus on her disability; she wanted to be known as a great athlete. In 1984, she graduated from college with a degree in English. She realized soon after, though, that she missed

Major Skiing Championships

Year	Competition	Event	Place
1981	U.S. Disabled National Championships	Downhill	1st
		Slalom	1st
1982	U.S. Disabled National Championships	Giant slalom	1st
		Slalom	1st
	World Disabled Championships	Downhill	1st
		Giant slalom	2d
1985	Canadian Disabled National Championships	Giant slalom	1st
	U.S. Disabled National Championships	Downhill	1st
1986	World Disabled Championships	Downhill	1st
		Giant slalom	1st
		Slalom	1st
		Combined	1st
1987	U.S. Disabled National Championships	Downhill	1st
		Giant slalom	1st
		Slalom	1st
		Combined	1st
1988	Olympic Games	Giant slalom	Gold
	U.S. Disabled National Championships	Giant slalom	1st
		Slalom	1st
		Super-G	1st
		Combined	1st
	World Disabled Championships	Downhill	1st
		Giant slalom	1st
	Canadian Disabled National Championships	Downhill	2d
		Giant slalom	1st
		Slalom	1st
1989	Canadian Disabled National Championships	Giant slalom	1st
	U.S. Disabled National Championships	Downhill	1st
		Slalom	1st
		Super-G	1st
1990	U.S. Disabled National Championships	Giant slalom #1	1st
		Giant slalom #2	1st
		Slalom	1st
	World Disabled Championships	Giant slalom	1st
		Slalom	1st
		Super-G	1st

other physically challenged athletes. A rule named for Diana, called the Golden rule, gives physically challenged skiers favorable positions in races against able-bodied skiers. Diana was also one of the first physically challenged skiers to use regular ski poles instead of the outrigger type. With her drive for perfection and constant upbeat personality, Diana continued to win friends and races.

In 1986, Diana won four gold medals at the World Disabled Championships in Sweden. The United States Ski Association (USSA) presented Diana with the Beckwith International Award given to the best American skier in international skiing. She was given this award because the USSA felt she was the best overall skier that year, not because she was a disabled skier. This was important to Diana. In 1987, she placed first four more times in national competition. In 1988, Diana participated in the 1988 Winter Olympic Games in Calgary, Alberta, Canada. Disabled skiing was an exhibition sport for which no Olympic medal was awarded. Diana demonstrated her outstanding abilities by placing first in the giant slalom competition. Later that year, the United States Olympic Committee named her the female skier of the year.

Continuing the Story

Diana continued to perform well in the years after the 1988 Winter Olympic Games. In 1990, she placed first two times in the United States Disabled National Championships and three times in the World Disabled Championships. At one point in competition, Diana was timed at sixty-five miles per hour. Diana announced her retirement shortly after the 1990 ski-race season. Over the course of her career, Diana won ten world

racing. She learned to accept that people looked at her as an example. She decided to do some things to help herself and other physically challenged skiers.

The Emerging Champion

Diana knew that in order to be a champion, she had to work at it almost full time. She made good use of her popularity and asked companies to financially sponsor her training. She became the first physically challenged ski racer ever to be financially supported by a ski company. Because of this, companies began to sponsor other physically challenged athletes. Diana had not only helped her own career but also helped the careers of

Honors and Awards

1986	U.S. Skiing Association Beckwith International Award
1988	U.S. Olympic Committee Female Skier of the Year
1991	Women's Sports Foundation Flo Hyman Award
1997	Inducted into U.S. National Ski Hall of Fame
	Inducted into International Women's Sports Hall of Fame
2006	Inducted into U.S. Olympic Hall of Fame

championship event gold medals, nineteen United States National Championship events, and a Winter Olympic Games first place. In 1991, Diana was awarded the Women's Sports Foundation Flo Hyman Award, which is given to women athletes who exemplify dignity, spirit, and commitment to excellence.

Diana continued to be a spokesperson for the physically challenged in sports. Her fantastic record as an athlete and her tireless promotion of sports for the physically challenged were instrumental in changing the way people perceive the physically challenged athlete. In 2001, Diana died at the age of thirty-eight after losing her last fight with cancer. She was inducted into the U.S. Olympic Hall of Fame in 2006.

Summary

Diana Golden's drive for excellence and her refusal to accept the limitations of a physical disability made her an inspiration to many athletes and physically challenged people. Despite her physical shortcomings she is still considered one of the finest American skiers ever.

Michael Salmon

Additional Sources

Wallechinsky, David, and Jaime Loucky. *The Complete Book of the Winter Olympics.* Wilmington, Del.: Sport Media, 2005.

Woolum, Janet. *Outstanding Women Athletes: Who They Are and How They Influenced Sports in America.* Phoenix, Ariz.: Oryx Press, 1998.

Gong Zhichao

Born: December 15, 1977
Anhua City, Hunan Province, China

Early Life
Gong Zhichao was born December 15, 1977, in Anhua, Hunan Province, China. She grew up in a poor family. When she was about eight years old, she observed her physical education teacher at Ziang Hua Zi Di Primary School playing badminton with his daughter. Zhichao was so impressed with the game that she asked the teacher to show her how to play. He immediately taught her the basics of the game, and she practiced diligently thereafter.

When Zhichao first began playing badminton, her family was supportive of her efforts. Although the family was poor, her mother sacrificed to make sure that she had the proper food to maintain athletic stamina. After Zhichao's older brother noticed that Zhichao's grip on the badminton racket had caused blood blisters to form on her hands, her family urged her to give up the game. However, Zhichao was steadfast in her desire to play. Eventually the family accepted her wishes.

The Road to Excellence
After learning to play badminton, Zhichao became a member of her school team, where her coach Wen Juguang helped her to develop her skills. She put a great deal of effort into developing her natural talents. After jogging every morning, Zhichao attended class during the day and then practiced badminton in the afternoon. Her school team won the Hunan provincial championship, and, in 1989, Zhichao was selected for the Hunan provincial team. Li Fang, coach of the provincial team, recognized her potential and took great interest in helping her develop it.

In 1996, Zhichao was selected for the Chinese national team, which was one of the two goals her father had set for her from his deathbed. The other was to win a gold medal. The coach of the national team, Yong Bo Li, developed rigorous training activities for Zhichao. In order to increase her stamina, she was required to run up a mountain wearing clothing in which had been sewn sandbags weighing 13 pounds. Another part of her practice routine included throwing a metal ball against a wall and then catching it.

The Emerging Champion
Zhichao's rigorous training paid off. In 1997, she won the Swedish Open and was the runner-up in the Korean Open. In 1998, she won the Japan Open. After winning the event, she experienced a twenty-six-month dry spell in which she achieved no championships. However, in March, 2000, her luck changed when she won the All England Badminton Championship, beating world champion and silver medalist Dai Yun. Later in the year, Zhichao won the Malaysia Open and the Japan Open.

Gong Zhichao competing at the 2000 Olympic Games in Sydney. (Michael Steele/Getty Images)

Major Badminton Championships

Year	Competition	Place
1997	Ericsson Swedish Badminton Open	1st
	Ra Kyung Min Badminton Open	Runner-up
1998	Japan Badminton Open	1st
2000	All England Badminton Open	1st
	Malaysia Badminton Open	1st
	Japan Badminton Open	1st
	Olympic Games women's singles badminton	Gold

Continuing the Story

In 2000, in Sydney, Australia, Zhichao became an Olympic gold medalist, winning the women's singles badminton title. Going into the competition, Zhichao was the second seed behind Danish player and female world champion Camilla Martin. However, Zhichao overcame Martin fairly easily: The game was finished within eleven minutes.

The match provoked controversy because some felt that the head coach of the Chinese badminton team had ordered fellow Chinese badminton Olympian Ye Zhaoying to lose deliberately to Zhichao in the semifinals because Zhichao had a better chance to defeat Martin. Ye lost against Zhichao as ordered, but won the bronze medal and retired after the Olympics. In November, 2007, coach Li admitted to making the controversial order.

In March, 2001, Zhichao competed in the All England Badminton Championship. In the final, she beat fellow Chinese player Mi Zhou. In November, 2001, she won the singles competition in the Chinese National Badminton Tournament. Exhausted and tired, Zhichao requested to be allowed to retire from the Chinese national badminton team. Soon after, officials granted her request.

In December, 2004, Zhichao returned briefly. In October, 2005, at the Chinese National Badminton Games in Kunshang, Zhichao contributed to her Hunan Province team's victory over favored Guangdong Province. On January 6, 2008, Zhichao carried the Olympic flame through the city of Changsha in her home province of Hunan on its way to Beijing for the 2008 Olympics.

Summary

Gong Zhichao spent many years working for the goal that she finally achieved: an Olympic gold medal. An intense player, Zhichao was highly regarded by fans, coaches, and other players for her great mental strength and her quick ability to cover the court. She was spurred onward by her love for her dead father, whose nationalistic pride led him to urge her to make the Chinese national team and to win a gold medal for her country. She was part of a Chinese national team that made an impressive showing in the 2000 Olympic Games in Sydney, where it won five of the eight gold medals awarded for badminton competition.

Annita Marie Ward, updated by R. C. Lutz

Additional Sources

Mallozzi, Vincent. "Champions 2000." *The New York Times*, December 31, 2000.

N. N. "Badminton: Chinese Claim Honours in Birmingham." *The Guardian*, March 13, 2000, p. 10.

Wallechinsky, David, and Jaime Loucky. *The Complete Book of the Olympics: 2008 Edition.* London: Aurum Press, 2008.

Brian Goodell

Born: April 2, 1959
        Stockton, California
Also known as: Brian S. Goodell (full name)

Early Life
Brian S. Goodell was born in Stockton, California, on April 2, 1959. Brian is a small man with the arms and shoulders of a wrestler. At six, he was afraid to go to a pool without his life jacket. At eight, his family moved to Mission Viejo, California, and lived behind the swimming pool where young Mark Schubert was molding a no-nonsense program based on hours of practice with the Mission Viejo Nadadores Swim Club. The carefree Brian was an easygoing backstroker who cared more about his junior high

Brian Goodell. (U.S. Swimming)

school football team than swimming. In high school, the football coach admitted that Brian was tough enough but said he was just too small to have much of a future in football. At 5 feet 9 inches and less than 150 pounds, he also did not have an ideal swimmer's build.

The Road to Excellence
The ambitious Schubert finally convinced Brian that his dreams of greatness could be fulfilled in the pool right next to his house. Although Brian had been slow to convince, once sold, he was committed to his sport. "Old Salt Mine," as Brian's mother called him, began swimming twenty thousand yards a day in tough two-a-day workouts. His immediate goal was to see how many miles he could swim every day. He became the "swimming machine" in the "animal lane," the side of the pool Schubert reserved for the grueling workouts of his best-disciplined, hardest-working swimmers. As Schubert said, "He possessed uncanny determination and talent."

The Emerging Champion
Within two years, the Nadadores, coached by Schubert and led by Brian, was on its way to becoming the United States' top swim team. Brian set five world records and eight American records and won ten national championships with the Nadadores. His college coach at the University of California at Los Angeles (UCLA), Ron Ballatore, said, "He has a will to win that I have seen in few other athletes. . . . He won't let himself be beaten. He can summon up those hidden reserves and turn it on when someone's after him like few others."

How he accomplished this is best illustrated by one of Brian's favorite stories, frequently told on the banquet circuit, where he was in much demand after winning gold medals in the two longest swimming events at the 1976 Montreal Olympics. He related that,

in the early morning mist and pre-dawn fog . . . We pretended that swimmers such as Michael Gross of Germany and Vladimir Salnikov, the great Russian, were in the next lanes. We also squinted when

370

we turned to breathe and we could see the huge Olympic crowd cheering us on. The noise was building up length by length as the cheering got louder and louder. Our adrenaline was really pumping. There were Olympic flags out there in the mist around the top of the pool stadium and pretty women were walking around the deck yelling "faster."

Brian's record, both in practice at Mission Viejo and at UCLA, attest for how well these dreams worked. Brian's rise to swimming heights occurred the summer after his first year of high school, when he made it to the U.S. nationals. The summer following his second year at Mission Viejo High School, Brian won the silver medal in the 1,500-meter freestyle at the World Aquatics Championships, finishing just behind the world record holder Tim Shaw, his Long Beach rival and friend.

Continuing the Story

In 1976, Brian shone the international spotlight on Mission Viego when he won a pair of gold medals at the Montreal Olympics and broke world records in the 400-meter freestyle (3 minutes 51.93 seconds) and 1,500-meter freestyle (15 minutes 2.40 seconds). In 1977, at a dual meet in East Berlin, he lowered his 400-meter world mark to 3 minutes 51.56 seconds. That same year, he recorded the world's fastest times in the 800-meter and 1,500-meter freestyle events. In 1978, Goodell's

quiet self-confidence was tested when he did not make the fifteen-member U.S. team at the World Aquatics Championships trials because of strep throat. He took a short two-month layoff and came back in the fall, stronger than ever. In the 1979 National Collegiate Athletic Association (NCAA) Championships, Brian won three individual events. Later that year, he brought home two individual gold medals from the Pan-American Games in Puerto Rico. While swimming for UCLA, Brian was almost invincible, winning three NCAA titles, in 1978, 1979, and 1980. During the 1978-1979 collegiate season, he did not lose a single race all year, even in dual meets.

Brian's big chance to beat Vladimir Salnikov, his Soviet long-distance rival, was to be in the Moscow Olympics. He was preparing for the showdown when President Jimmy Carter decided that the United States would boycott the Moscow Olympics. Brian's disappointment must have been great, but he made a simple announcement, "I've accomplished all that I've really wanted to," and he retired. In 1986, Brian was inducted into the International Swimming Hall of Fame. He kept busy with public appearances, his own business, and playing all the sports he so enjoyed growing up—especially tag football.

Records

Five world records (400- and 1,500-meter freestyle)

Eight national records (400- and 1,500-meter freestyle, 500- and 1,650-yard freestyle, and 400-yard individual medley)

Won nine NCAA Championships

Won ten National AAU Championships (500-, 1,000-, and 1,500-yard freestyle, and 400-, 800-, and 1,500-meter freestyle)

Honors and Awards

1977	World Swimmer of the Year
	Robert J. H. Kiphuth Award, Long Course
1977, 1979	World's Top Male Swimmer
1979	Robert J. H. Kiphuth Award, Short Course
1986	Inducted into International Swimming Hall of Fame

Major Swimming Championships

Year	Competition	Event	Place	Time
1975	World Championships	1,500-meter freestyle	2d	15:39.00
1976	Olympic Games	400-meter freestyle	Gold	3:51.93 WR, OR
		1,500-meter freestyle	Gold	15:02.40 WR, OR
1978	NCAA Championships	500-yard freestyle	1st	4:18.05
		1,650-yard freestyle	1st	14:55.53
		400-yard individual medley	1st	3:53.61
1979	Pan-American Games	400-meter freestyle	1st	3:53.01 PAR
		1,500-meter freestyle	1st	15:24.36 PAR
		4×200-meter freestyle relay	1st	7:31.28
	NCAA Championships	500-yard freestyle	1st	4:16.43
		1,650-yard freestyle	1st	14:54.13
		400-yard individual medley	1st	3:50.80
1980	NCAA Championships	500-yard freestyle	1st	4:17.81
		1,650-yard freestyle	1st	14:54.07
		400-yard individual medley	1st	3:51.38

Notes: OR = Olympic Record; WR = World Record; PAR = Pan-American Record

Summary

Brian Goodell was twice named world swimmer of the year, in 1977, after winning two gold medals at the 1976 Montreal Olympics, and again in 1979. He held five world records and eight American records during his reign as king of the 400- and 1,500-meter freestyle events.

Buck Dawson

Additional Sources

Gonsalves, Kelly, and Susan LaMondia. *First to the Wall: One Hundred Years of Olympic Swimming.* East Longmeadow, Mass.: FreeStyle, 1999.

Greenberg, Stan. *Whitaker's Olympic Almanack: An Encyclopaedia of the Olympic Games.* Chicago: Fitzroy Dearborn, 2000.

Wallechinsky, David, and Jaime Loucky. *The Complete Book of the Olympics: 2008 Edition.* London: Aurum Press, 2008.

Ekaterina Gordeeva and Sergei Grinkov

Ekaterina Gordeeva

Born: May 28, 1971
Moscow, Soviet Union (now in Russia)
Also known as: Ekaterina Alexandrovna
Gordeeva (full name); Katia

Sergei Grinkov

Born: February 4, 1967
Moscow, Soviet Union (now in Russia)
Died: November 20, 1995
Lake Placid, New York
Also known as: Sergei Mikhailovich Grinkov (full
name)

Early Lives

Ekaterina Alexandrovna Gordeeva's father was a Russian folk dancer who wanted his daughter to become a ballet dancer. Her mother was a teletype operator for a Soviet news agency. Sergei Mikhailovich Grinkov's parents were employed in the Moscow police department. Ekaterina started skating at the age of four, and both she and Sergei became child beneficiaries of the Soviet Union's emphasis on excellence in sports. When Ekaterina was eleven years old she was teamed for pairs skating with Sergei, and both had to undergo considerable retraining to perform together as a team.

The Road to Excellence

Traveling to numerous competitions around the world, the working relationship between Ekaterina and Sergei matured into a close personal friendship. Having placed fifth at the Junior World Figure Skating Championships in Sapporo, Japan, in 1983, they trained with greater determination and won this Junior World Figure Skating Championships the following year in Colorado Springs, Colorado. In 1986, they ranked second in both the Soviet National Championships and at the European championships in Copenhagen, Denmark.

Ekaterina and Sergei—known as "G and G" within the international skating community—won their first gold medal at the 1986 World Figure Skating Championships in Geneva, Switzerland. They repeated this feat the following year in Cincinnati, Ohio, and also secured victory in the Soviet National Championships, held in Vilnius, Lithuania. International recognition of their considerable skill and talent followed their first American skating tour that year.

The Emerging Champions

In 1988, the duo won the European championships at Prague, Czechoslovakia, and won gold at the Olympics, in Calgary, Canada. In 1989, as their homeland was undergoing massive political change, Ekaterina and Sergei continued their stunning victories in the World Figure Skating Championships in Paris, France, followed by the European championships at St. Petersburg in 1990. That year they also won the World Figure Skating Championships held in Halifax, Canada.

In 1990, the pair decided to turn professional. Their close personal friendship had blossomed into mutual love, and when Sergei at last acquired the title to a small apartment in Moscow, he proposed to Ekaterina. They were married on April 28, 1991. That year they joined the touring show "Stars on Ice" and secured victories in two important competitive events, the World Professional Figure Skating Championships, held in Landover, Maryland, and the Challenge of Champions in Oslo, Norway. The following year, their daughter, Daria, was born. Because it became possible for professional skaters to request amateur status in order to compete in the Olympics, Ekaterina and Sergei decided to go for the gold once again. In 1994, their victory in the Russian National Championships landed them a spot on the Russian Olympic team. They won the coveted gold medal at the Olympic Games held in Lillehammer, Norway, as well as the European championships in Copenhagen, Denmark. Having resumed professional status after the Olympics, they went on to win the World Professional Championships in 1994 and the Challenge of Champions the following year.

Major Figure-Skating Championships

Year	Competition	Place	Year	Competition	Place
1984	Junior World Championships	5th	1990	European Championships	1st
1985	Junior World Championships	1st		World Championships	1st
	Soviet National Championships	6th		Goodwill Games	1st
	Skate Canada	1st		World Professional Championships	2d
	Prize of *Moscow News*	4th		Challenge of Champions	2d
1986	Soviet National Championships	2d	1991	World Professional Championships	1st
	European Championships	2d		Challenge of Champions	1st
	World Championships	1st	1992	World Professional Championships	1st
	Skate Canada	2d	1993	Skate Canada	1st
1987	Soviet National Championships	1st	1994	Russian National Championships	1st
	European Championships	Disqualified		European Championships	1st
	World Championships	1st		Olympic Games	Gold
	Prize of *Moscow News*	1st		North American Open	1st
1988	European Championships	1st		Canadian Professional Championships	1st
	Olympic Games	Gold		World Team Championships	1st
	World Championships	2d		World Professional Championships	1st
1989	World Championships	1st	1995	Challenge of Champions	1st
	NHK Trophy	1st			

Continuing the Story

In 1995, at the height of Ekaterina and Sergei's skating careers and international fame, Sergei had a massive heart attack while practicing on a rink in Lake Placid, New York. He died on November 20, 1995, at the age of twenty-eight. Although Sergei had suffered from back trouble and foot problems, there was no prior indication of heart disease. His sudden death was a shock that reverberated around the world. Sergei and Ekaterina were widely admired both for their skating and for the joy their performances brought to so many millions of people. Sergei was popular in the international skating community, and his kindness to his colleagues, his love for his wife and daughter, and his independent spirit endeared him to all. Ekaterina's grief was shared across the world as friends mourned in the United States and again at a large funeral in Russia, which drew thousands.

Struggling through immense personal grief, Ekaterina found solace in her daughter. She eventually returned to the ice rink, which had been the focal point of her life. She had to learn to skate alone, no small feat for an athlete who had always been part of a pair. The skating community honored Sergei in a special celebration of the duo's art and skill, but Ekaterina performed alone. She recounted the story of their life and love in a tribute to her husband, *My Sergei: A Love Story* (1996), cowritten by E. M. Swift. The book became a best-seller and was followed by *A Letter for Daria,* coauthored by Antonina Bouis and published in 1998. Having always relied so much on her husband, Ekaterina struggled to find her own path through life and raise her daughter as well. She decided to settle in the United States, where Daria had been born.

In 1996, Ekaterina and Sergei were inducted into the World Figure Skating Hall of Fame. Besides a successful writing career, Ekaterina has worked on television shows, done product endorsements, and commentated for CBS at the Olympics. In 2002, Ekaterina married Russian figure-skating champion Ilia Kulik. The couple had a daughter the previous year. In 2003, Ekaterina returned to the ice, this time with Daria.

Summary

Ekaterina Gordeeva and Sergei Grinkov entranced the world with their grace and skill as skaters. However, their personal love story made them media celebrities. In 1994, *People* magazine named Ekaterina one of the fifty most beautiful people in the world. The tragedy that struck at the height of their glory resonated with the skating community, and Ekaterina's personal journey to overcome her grief and emerge triumphant was an inspiration. The pair was significant because their care for each other transcended the world of skating and made their art inspiring, exemplifying beauty and grace to many around the world.

R. K. L. Panjabi

Additional Sources

Gordeeva, Ekaterina, and Antonina W. Bouis. *A Letter for Daria.* Boston: Little, Brown, 1998.

Gordeeva, Ekaterina, and E. M. Swift. *My Sergei: A Love Story.* New York: Warner Books, 1996.

Hines, James R. *Figure Skating: A History.* Urbana: University of Illinois Press, 2006.

Wallechinsky, David, and Jaime Loucky. *The Complete Book of the Winter Olympics.* Wilmington, Del.: Sport Media, 2005.

Shane Gould

Born: November 23, 1956
       Sydney, New South Wales, Australia

Early Life

Shane Gould was born on November 23, 1956, in Sydney, Australia, just seven days before the Olympic Games began in Melbourne. In her early childhood, her family lived in the Fiji Islands for seven years, and she used to spend entire days in the water because of the heat—and because she loved to swim. According to her mother, Shane's love affair with the water began before she could walk. As a baby, she cried when bath time ended; she crawled down the beach straight into the waves of Sydney Harbour; she bobbed about in a rubber tire smiling with satisfaction before she was a year old. Before she was three, she could swim underwater with her eyes open and soon after she turned three she managed a respectable dog paddle.

The Road to Excellence

At six, Shane had her first lessons from a professional swimming coach. By eight, she was reasonably proficient in all swimming strokes except for the butterfly. At fourteen, she said, "Breaking world records is more thrilling than going to parties and out with boys." Said Selwyn Parker, "Out of the pool, she has a Gidget-like personality. Inside the pool or before a key race, she switches off and becomes a dedicated (if youthful) athlete." She showed such concentration that Australian hall-of-famer Murray Rose called her "more focused on what she's doing than any athlete I've ever seen!" In 1972, at sixteen, Shane Gould was destined to be one of Australia's greatest Olympic swimmers and, at the 1972 Olympic Games in Munich, a female counterpart of Mark Spitz. No girl has achieved so much Olympic success so soon and then retired before reaching the normal age of an athlete's achievement, even in women's swimming, where girls start and finish early.

The Emerging Champion

Shane's greatest triumphs came before the age of sixteen. During her short career, Shane held every freestyle world record—the 100, 200, 400, 800, and 1,500 meters—and the four-stroke 200-meter individual medley record. She broke the longest-standing record in the books when she beat Dawn Fraser's freestyle 100-meter world record at Sydney on January 8, 1972, in 58.5 seconds. Fraser had held the record almost sixteen years, since December 1, 1956. From April 13, 1971, until January 8, 1972, Shane set seven world records. In gold medals won, she was second only to Spitz at the 1972 Olympics in Munich, winning five individual medals in swimming.

Each time she won a gold medal at the 1972 Olympics, Shane waved her toy kangaroo in triumph. She won three events, two in world-record

Shane Gould during the 1972 Olympics in Munich. (Courtesy of International Swimming Hall of Fame)

Major Swimming Championships

Year	Competition	Event	Place	Time
1972	Olympic Games	200-meter freestyle	Gold	2:03.56
		400-meter freestyle	Gold	4:19.04 WR, OR
		200-meter individual medley	Gold	2:23.07 WR, OR
		800-meter freestyle	Silver	8:56.39
		100-meter freestyle	Bronze	59.06
1973	AAU Indoor Championships	1,650-yard freestyle	1st	16:46.659
		200-yard butterfly	1st	2:02.720
		400-yard individual medley	1st	4:27.115

Notes: OR = Olympic Record; WR = World Record

time. She also won a silver medal in the 800-meter freestyle and a bronze in the 100-meter freestyle. Her 100-meter time was 59.06 seconds. She had previously set a world-record time of 58.50, which stood after the Olympic event was over, even though the winner, Sandra Neilson of the United States, had set an Olympic record with her time of 58.59 seconds. It is no wonder that at the Munich Games, the U.S. team, in an attempt to boost its own morale, wore T-shirts that read, "All that glitters is not Gould." In fact, two Americans beat her in the 100-meters, Neilson and Shirley Babashoff.

Continuing the Story

After Shane's gold-medal performance in the Olympics, she came to the United States to "combine [her] education with swimming." She trained under one of the United States' top coaches, Nort Thornton. After all of the hard work and discipline in preparation for the Olympics, Shane took it easier while in the United States. "I swim for pleasure more than before the Olympic Games." Despite her ability, Gould retired a year after the 1972 Olympics, at sixteen. She wanted more in life than the all-consuming discipline of competitive swimming. Immediately following her Olympic win, Shane's mother wrote a book *Swimming the Shane Gould Way* (1972), in which she traced Shane's swimming career, using a factual approach sprinkled with motherly pride, and revealing the diet, determination, and training regimen that worked so well for Shane. Shane went on to operate a sheep ranch with her husband in Western Australia. In 2000, she was a torch bearer for the Sydney Olympics.

Summary

Shane Gould broke Dawn Fraser's 100-meter freestyle world record and every other freestyle mark there was. She retired at sixteen after winning five medals in the 1972 Olympics. For her achievements, Shane was inducted into the International Swimming Hall of Fame in 1977 and the International Women's Sports Hall of Fame in 2006.

Buck Dawson

Additional Sources

Gonsalves, Kelly, and Susan LaMondia. *First to the Wall: One Hundred Years of Olympic Swimming.* East Longmeadow, Mass.: FreeStyle, 1999.

Gould, Shane. *Tumble Turns.* New York: HarperCollins, 2003.

Wallechinsky, David, and Jaime Loucky. *The Complete Book of the Olympics: 2008 Edition.* London: Aurum Press, 2008.

Record

Set eleven world records in the freestyle, from 100 to 1,500 meters

Honors and Awards

1970-71	World Swimmer of the Year
1973	Robert J. H. Kiphuth Award, Short Course
1977	Inducted into International Swimming Hall of Fame

Cammi Granato

Born: March 25, 1971
    Downers Grove, Illinois
Also known as: Catherine Michelle Granato (full name)

Early Life

Catherine Michelle Granato was born into a hockey family: "All hockey, all the time," in her words. She and her brothers and sister played on a nearby pond, flooded their backyard when the pond ice was too thin, and even practiced in their basement in the summer. When Cammi was four years old, her mother bought her a figure-skating outfit and lessons, but from the first lesson, Cammi walked out of the rink to watch the action in the hockey rink instead.

A natural athlete, Cammi played Little League baseball, batting cleanup for her team. However, hockey was her passion. She played on the Downers Grove Huskies from early childhood until her junior year in high school. She did not notice that she was unique until she was about ten years old, when she had to move out of the locker room to change in the women's room. Although she hated feeling weird and different, she wanted to play. Her mother tried to persuade Cammi to change sports, and she did play on her high school soccer, volleyball, basketball, and tennis teams. She even won team-handball medals at the 1989 and 1990 U.S. Olympic Festivals. Cammi finally stopped playing for the Huskies, though, because opposing players were trying to injure her.

The Road to Excellence

Although the University of Wisconsin recruited her for soccer,

Cammi accepted a hockey scholarship to Providence College in Rhode Island. Playing center, Cammi was Eastern College Athletic Conference player of the year in 1991, 1992, and 1993, and a conference all-star all four of her years. Her records still stood in 2008: all-time leading goal scorer, 139; points scored, 256; single-season points, 84; single-season goals, 48; and single-season assists, 43. Cammi graduated with a degree in social science in 1993.

The Emerging Champion

In 1990, Cammi made the U.S. national team and was elected its first captain—a position she held throughout her tenure with the team. The squad maintained a hot rivalry with the number-one Canadian women for its first six years. Cammi was rec-

Cammi Granato (center) and teammates celebrating the U.S. victory over Canada in the IIHF Women's World Championship in Sweden in 2005. (Sven Nackstrand/AFP/Getty Images)

College Hockey Statistics

Season	GP	G	Ast.	Pts.
1989-90	24	24	22	46
1990-91	22	26	20	46
1991-92	25	48	32	80
1992-93	28	41	43	84
Totals	99	139	117	256

Notes: GP = games played; G = goals; Ast. = assists; Pts. = points

National Team Hockey Statistics

Season	GP	G	Ast.	Pts.
1990	5	9	5	14
1992	5	8	2	10
1994	5	5	7	12
1995	5	4	7	11
1996	5	6	3	9
1997	5	5	3	8
1998	6	4	4	8
2002	5	6	4	10
Totals	41	47	35	82

Notes: GP = games played; G = goals; Ast. = assists; Pts. = points

ognized as 1996 U.S. women's player of the year. In 1997, she led her team to the International Ice Hockey Federation Championship and was voted all-tournament player. That year, the New York Islanders of the NHL invited Cammi to its training camp for a tryout, but she decided that, at 5 feet 7 inches tall and 140 pounds, she was too small and vulnerable to injury. No one doubted her toughness, however: At the 1995 Pacific Rim tournament, a Chinese player broke a bone in Cammi's leg. Since the bone was not weight-bearing, Cammi played four more games with the injury.

Women's hockey became an Olympic sport in the Nagano, Japan, Olympics in 1998. Cammi, playing forward, was team captain. Propelled by Cammi's 4 goals and 4 assists in six games, the U.S. women won the first-ever gold medal, with Canada and Finland placing second and third, respectively. Cammi had the honor of carrying the flag on behalf of the entire U.S. team during the closing ceremonies at Nagano. She even appeared on Wheaties cereal boxes after the Olympics.

Continuing the Story

During the 1998-1999 NHL season, Cammi worked as a radio commentator for the Los Angeles Kings, only the second woman to be invited to do so. She also founded her Golden Dreams for Children Foundation, supporting children with special needs. However, hockey remained her focus, as she continued to lead the U.S. team in international competition. She was the only American women's hockey player to participate in all championship games between 1990 and 2005, and scored 44 goals and 34 assists in total. She was voted best forward and elected to the all-star team in 1992 and 1997. She captained the Olympic team again in 2002,

when it took the silver medal beside the mighty Canadian team.

In 2006, Cammi was abruptly cut from the national team by the U.S. coach. Her elimination shocked everyone and was widely perceived as unjustified. Most observers thought she remained one of the best forwards on ice; Cammi was puzzled also. No explanation was ever offered, although fans protested, and the coach was strongly criticized by sports commentators.

Later, Cammi started a hockey camp for girls and women; thus, she continued to influence the success of the U.S. women's hockey teams. She married Ray Ferraro, a former NHL player, and the couple had a son, Riley, in 2006. Cammi's brother Tony, who had a long career as both player and coach in the NHL, admitted that he was only the second-best player in the Granato family—an opinion shared by hockey experts and fans.

In 2007, Cammi was one of four recipients of the Lester Patrick Trophy, honoring her contributions to U.S. hockey. She had previously won the trophy

Honors and Awards

1991-93	Eastern College Athletic Conference player of the year
1996	USA women's hockey player of the year
1997	International Ice Hockey Federation all-tournament player (World Championships)
1998	Gold medal, Olympic ice hockey
2002	Silver medal, Olympic ice hockey
2007	Lester Patrick Trophy
2008	Inducted into International Ice Hockey Federation Hall of Fame

in 1999, as a member of the women's Olympic team. Providence College inducted Cammi into its athletic hall of fame in 2008.

Summary

Although Cammi Granato was never the fastest skater or the most powerful shooter, she possessed an innate passing sense and an accurate wrist shot. Because of her enthusiasm and dazzling play, she encouraged hundreds of girls and young women to take up hockey seriously and showed men that the women's game could be fast and exciting, too. Her influence on ice hockey surpasses that of all but a few male players.

Jan Hall

Additional Sources

Loverro, Thom. *Cammi Granato: Hockey Pioneer.* Minneapolis: Lerner, 2000.

Paré, Michael A. *Sports Stars, Series 5.* New York: UXL, 1999.

Turco, Mary. *Crashing the Net: The U.S. Women's Olympic Ice Hockey Team and the Road to Gold.* New York: Harper Collins, 1999.

Debbie Green

Born: June 25, 1958
     Seoul, South Korea

Early Life

Debbie Green was born on June 25, 1958, in the city that was the site of the 1988 Summer Olympic Games: Seoul, South Korea. Her mother, a native of South Korea, and her father, a native of the United States, met in South Korea just after the Korean War. They moved their family to Orange County, California, shortly after Debbie was born. Coming from a middle-class suburban family, Debbie had the opportunity to engage in a variety of activities while she was in grade school. Debbie played soccer and basketball and participated in gymnastics and tennis.

At the age of fourteen, Debbie became a member of the Orange County Volleyball Club. Although her volleyball skills were, at the time, mediocre, she was determined to improve. With the encouragement of her father, Don, who founded the American National Volleyball Association, Debbie was the starting setter of a newly formed junior national team by the next year. Debbie devoted as much energy as she could to volleyball. The team practiced for as many as forty hours a week, the equivalent of a full-time job. Debbie still managed to do well in school. At the age of seventeen, she was selected as the youngest United States

Volleyball Association All-American in the history of volleyball.

The Road to Excellence

While attending the University of Southern California (USC), Debbie led her team to two Association of Intercollegiate Athletics for Women (AIAW) National Championships, and was a two-time AIAW All-American. Debbie knew that she could fulfill the challenging role of setter at the international level. In 1978, with the encouragement of her junior national team, USC coach Chuck Erbe, and her father, Debbie made the U.S. national team. Arie Selinger, the newly selected coach of the U.S. women's team, trained the team in the new Olympic Training Center in Colorado Springs. Despite little money, little tradition, and no continuity, they soon took the world by surprise.

The Emerging Champion

During the 1978 world championships held in the Soviet Union, Debbie contributed greatly, helping the U.S. women's team earn a top-five world ranking. By 1979, they were ranked second, beating Japan, the Soviet Union, and South Korea; the team qualified for the Olympic Games in 1980. The Olympic boycott by the United States, however, prevented the team from competing at the Moscow Games. Since 1973, Debbie and the team had trained for the opportunity to play in the Olympic Games. Disappointed, Debbie continued to train for the 1984 Games.

Continuing the Story

By this time, Debbie was ranked as the best setter in the United States and among the top three in the world. She had mastered the jump set, adding a new dimension to the U.S. game. She was capable of attacking the second touch by dumping or spiking the ball. By jumping with almost every set, she was able to confuse opponents about her eligibility to attack the ball. Because she could jump with a "one" hitter on the way, action was also created in front of the opponents' middle blocker. The middle

---

Honors, Awards, and Milestones

1974-77	Women's U.S. Junior National Team
1975	USVBA Nationals Championship Team
1975-77	USVBA All-American
1976-77	AIAW All-American
1977	AIAW All-Conference Team
	AIAW National Championship Team
1978	Women's U.S. National Team
1979	Women's U.S. Pan-American Games volleyball team
1980, 1984	Women's U.S. Olympic volleyball team
1982	U.S. World Championships bronze medalist
1983	U.S. Pan-American Games silver medalist
1984	U.S. Olympic silver medalist
1986	Volleyball Hall of Fame All-Time Great Volleyball Player
1988	Inducted into Volleyball Hall of Fame Court of Honor

---

blocker was more likely to stay in the middle, leaving outside hitters with only one blocker. This provided great versatility for the team's offense.

In 1984, The U.S. women's team used a blend of transition-attack systems. This meant that the system was dependent upon the opponent and the situation, using Debbie as the primary setter. Debbie's talent, determination, and intelligence, combined with that of her teammate, 6-foot 5-inch Flo Hyman, made the U.S. attack almost unbeatable. At one point, Debbie and Hyman were selected cocaptains of the team. This was a reward for past performance and an opportunity for Debbie to develop leadership in the position. She recognized that the job carried the three "R's" of leadership: role definition, responsibility, and relationship development between her teammates. Frequently, she set the standard for self-discipline and a positive attitude, thereby defining her role as setter and leader. She assisted the coaches as one of the on-the-floor leaders and enforced standards of performance and behavior, which served as a measure of success for the team. Debbie's sensitivity and warmth as a person helped her to develop relationships with her teammates and coaches in order to meet team and individual goals.

In 1984, the U.S. women's volleyball team was awarded a silver medal in the Olympic Games in Los Angeles. This was the best finish ever recorded by a U.S. women's volleyball team. Debbie accomplished her goal: to participate on a medal-winning volleyball team that represented the United States in the Olympic Games.

After the 1984 Games, Debbie toured the United States, hosting her own volleyball clinics. In 1986, she was asked by Long Beach State's head volleyball coach, Brian Gimmillaro—who had worked with the 1984 Olympic team—if she would like to coach at the university level. She accepted a position as assistant volleyball coach at Long Beach State and helped lead the team to a national championship in 1998. Debbie was inducted into the Volleyball Hall of Fame in 1995 and the American Volleyball Coaches Association (AVCA) Hall of Fame in 2004.

Summary

Although Debbie Green is only 5 feet 4 inches tall, she was one of the best setters in the world. Her impact on the international game made her one of the world's most outstanding champions to play the game. As a player, she was a leader on and off the court. She led the USC team to the collegiate championship and the U.S. women's team to a silver medal in the Olympic Games. She was an excellent coach and role model for her players. Her international and national playing experience, coupled with her constant search for excellence, makes Debbie one of the most respected professionals in volleyball.

Darlene A. Kluka

Additional Sources

Greenberg, Stan. *Whitaker's Olympic Almanack: An Encyclopaedia of the Olympic Games.* Chicago: Fitzroy Dearborn, 2000.

Levinson, David, and Karen Christensen, eds. *Encyclopedia of World Sport: From Ancient Times to the Present.* Santa Barbara, Calif.: ABC-Clio, 1996.

Wallechinsky, David, and Jaime Loucky. *The Complete Book of the Olympics: 2008 Edition.* London: Aurum Press, 2008.

Maurice Greene

Born: July 23, 1974
Kansas City, Kansas

Early Life

Maurice Greene was born on July 23, 1974, in Kansas City, Kansas, the youngest of Ernest and Jackie Greene's four children. Maurice followed the lead of his older siblings, all of whom participated in track and field. Elder brother Ernest—who reached the semifinals at the 1972 Olympics—introduced eight-year-old Maurice to coach Al Hobson. Recognizing the young boy's talent, Hobson mentored Maurice. Even at an early age, Maurice had the confidence that was to become a trademark: At the age of ten, he remarked that someday he would be the world's fastest man. As a teenager, Maurice attended F. L. Schlagle High School. He vowed he would someday beat his idol, Carl Lewis.

The Road to Excellence

Under Hobson's coaching, Maurice began winning track meets. He captured numerous Amateur Athletic Union titles as well as Kansas state titles in the 100-, 200-, and 400-meter events for three consecutive years while he was in high school. He also played football and was offered a scholarship to junior college. Maurice attended community college for two years and was awarded a scholarship provided by the Kansas City Royals baseball team and Project Choice, while continuing to train privately with Hobson. Maurice was not interested in competing on the collegiate level, however; he was still obsessed with achieving his childhood goals.

In 1995, Maurice achieved the first of his goals when he defeated Lewis at the Texas Relays with a 100-meter time of 9.88 seconds. Later that year, Maurice finished second in the men's 100 meters at the USA Outdoor Track and Field Championships. With a time of 10.23 seconds, Maurice earned a place on the American team competing in the 1995 World Track and Field Championships. However, an unfortunate mistake eliminated him from competition in the quarterfinals. After the World Track and Field Championships, Maurice's focus shifted to the 1996 Summer Olympics. All his training ended in disappointment, however, when he injured a hamstring during the Olympic trials and could not qualify for the team.

The Emerging Champion

The pre-Olympic letdown forced Maurice to make the most difficult decision of his life. Although it meant leaving the security of his home and family and a coach who was like a father to him, in September, 1996, Maurice moved to Los Angeles to train with John Smith, an Olympian in 1972.

Maurice joined Smith and his other runners at the University of California at Los Angeles

Maurice Greene running a 100-meter heat at the 2004 Olympic Games in Athens. (Gary Hershorn/Reuters/Landov)

383

Major Sprint Championships

Year	Competition	Event	Place
1997	World Championships	100 meters	1st
1999	World Championships	100 meters	1st
		200 meters	1st
		4×100-meter relay	1st
2000	Olympic Games	100 meters	Gold
		4×100-meter relay	Gold
2001	World Championships	100 meters	1st
2004	Olympic Games	4×100-meter relay	Silver
		100 meters	Bronze

(UCLA), where he met Ato Boldon, a Trinidadian who had won a bronze medal in the 1996 Olympics. Smith's training was demanding. He pushed Maurice until the runner felt he had no more to give and then pushed him a little harder. Smith reworked Maurice's stride, improved an already fast start, and added weight training to his regimen to provide strength.

Under Smith, Maurice began improving. At the 1997 U.S. Outdoor Track and Field Championships, he won the men's 100-meter sprint with a time of 9.90 seconds. Only six men had ever run faster. Later that year, Maurice came closer to achieving his dream of becoming the fastest man in the world when he won the men's 100-meter competition at the 1997 World Track and Field Championships. In a field that included Boldon and 1996 Olympic champion Donovan Bailey, Maurice pulled out to an early lead and was never challenged. He won in 9.86 seconds, tying the World Track and Field Championships record.

Maurice returned to Los Angeles with increased confidence and continued training. When he finished second in the voting for the Jesse Owens Award in 1997, he knew that, despite his confidence and recent wins, there was more training to do and more meets to win before the ultimate test at the 2000 Olympics. Every day, he and Bolden raced each other. In the march toward the Olympics, Maurice continued winning important meets, including the 1999 World Track and Field Championships, in which he became the first athlete to win both the 100- and 200-meter sprints. During that same year, he set world records in 100 meters and 60 meters to become the only sprinter ever to hold world records at both distances simultaneously.

Continuing the Story

In September, 2000, all the training and hard work came down to one race: the men's 100 meters at the Sydney Olympics. Although Maurice had been boasting, he looked nervous as he approached the line. However, he took off to an early and fast lead and maintained it. The race was over in 9.96 seconds, and Maurice had earned the right to call himself the fastest man in the world. After hugging Boldon, who finished second, Maurice wowed the appreciative crowd when he threw his red, white, and blue Nike shoes into the stands. Several days later, Maurice won his second Olympic gold medal as a part of the men's 4×100-meter relay team.

In 2001, Maurice again defended his 100-meter title at the World Track and Field Championships. The following year, injured, he could only watch as fellow American Tim Montgomery broke his 100-meter world record, running the race in 9.78 seconds. Though Montgomery's record was later disallowed because Montgomery had used performance-enhancing substances, in 2005, Asafa Powell broke the record without dispute.

In 2004, Maurice returned to prominence at the Summer Olympics in Athens, Greece. He won a bronze medal in the 100-meter dash and a silver medal in the 4×100-meter relay, missing gold by just .01 second. Though he continued to compete at a high level for several more years, other activities took precedence. In 2006, Maurice, appeared on the television game show *Identity* and the television show *Blind Date*. In 2008, he was a contestant on *Dancing with the Stars*. In the same year, Maurice announced his retirement from competition. Months afterward, he became another of the many track and field athletes to be accused of using performance-enhancing substances.

Summary

Maurice Greene's career was defined by a confidence he maintained in the face of victories and defeats. From an early age, he single-mindedly pursued his goal of becoming the fastest man in the world. An injury that denied him a place on the 1996 U.S. Olympic team only fueled his desire to try harder. His incredible determination paid off at the 2000 Olympics when he claimed the title of fastest man in the world. Holder of numerous records and championships at distances from 50 meters to 400 meters, Maurice had his performances cast into doubt by charges that he cheated with the use of illegal doping.

Deborah Service, updated by Jack Ewing

Additional Sources

Jendrick, Nathan. *Dunks, Doubles, Doping: How Steroids Are Killing American Athletes.* Guilford, Conn.: Lyons Press, 2006.

Layden, Tim. "Gold Standard: Once Going Nowhere Fast, Sprinter Maurice Greene Has Found His Stride." *Sports Illustrated* 90, no. 26 (June 28, 1999): 58.

Posnanski, Joe. "Greene's Long Journey Ends in 9.87 Seconds." *The Sporting News*, October 2, 2000, p. 10.

Ramsak, Bob. *The Track Profile Reader 2004: Interviews, Profiles and Reports Chronicling International Track and Field in 2003.* Cleveland: Track Profile Press, 2004.

_____. "The World's Fastest Man (and Mouth)." *Newsweek* 136 (September 11, 2000): 40.

Wallechinsky, David, and Jaime Loucky. *The Complete Book of the Olympics: 2008 Edition.* London: Aurum Press, 2008.

Nancy Greene

Born: May 11, 1943
   Ottawa, Ontario, Canada
Also known as: Nancy Catherine Greene (full
   name); Tiger

Early Life

Nancy Catherine Greene was born May 11, 1943, in Ottawa, Ontario, Canada. During World War II her family had moved to Ottawa for her father's work. About the time Nancy was two years old, she and her family moved to Rossland, British Columbia. As Rossland was in snow country, everyone skied, and Nancy was no exception. She started skiing on homemade skis when she was three years old. She and her brothers and sisters learned to ski at nearby Red Mountain, which was so steep that Nancy skied with a rope around her waist, so that

Nancy Greene celebrating her victory in the giant slalom at the 1968 Winter Olympic Games in France. (AFP/ Getty Images)

when she fell, her father could reel her in. Although she participated on the Rossland High School ski team, she was not particularly attracted to competitive skiing.

The Road to Excellence

In 1958, her attitude toward competitive skiing changed when the Canadian Junior National Championships were held at nearby Red Mountain. Nancy's sister, Elizabeth, was a member of the British Columbia team, but Nancy was not. The night before the meet, though, the coach of the British Columbia team asked Nancy if she would substitute for some injured skiers. Much to everyone's surprise, Nancy did well, finishing third in the slalom race and second in the downhill race behind her sister. At the age of fourteen, Nancy had become a serious competitor. Over the next two years she and her sister would be fierce rivals. Nancy made the Canadian team for the 1960 Olympic Games and competed at Squaw Valley, California, finishing twenty-sixth in the giant slalom. At that point in her career, Nancy still lacked the experience and technical skills to be a world-class champion, but she received inspiration to continue working at the medal ceremonies. While watching Ann Heggtveit receive her gold medal for her slalom victory, Nancy resolved to win one for herself and for her country.

To fulfill her quest, Nancy trained hard to become the champion of her dreams. The sport of alpine skiing is physically demanding. The racers must have the strength and stamina to negotiate courses set on the sides of steep and often icy mountainsides. During Nancy's racing era, alpine skiing consisted of three types of races: slalom, giant slalom, and downhill. Slalom races have two runs on similar courses with forty to fifty gates that each racer must pass through. In slalom, the racer going through all the gates and having the lowest combined time for the two runs is the winner. A giant slalom race has fewer gates, set farther apart, allowing the racers to ski faster. In the downhill race, because control gates are set only for safety, the skiers take the straightest line possible, achieving very high speeds and often flying through the air during the course of the race. Most racers finish the courses in from two to four minutes; there is not much room or time for errors.

The Emerging Champion

From 1960 to 1967, Nancy worked hard perfecting her craft. She had her first international tour in 1961, skiing with the Canadian team at many European meets. At home she experienced success. She was Canadian National Champion six times. In the 1964 Olympics at Innsbruck, Austria, she showed improvement, finishing seventh in the downhill. However, she still lacked the technical skills and experience to be an Olympic champion.

Nancy's persistence and aggressive style earned her the nickname "tiger." Her style also led to some of her rather spectacular falls. One such fall took place at Portillo, Chile, in 1966, when Nancy fell while skiing at about 40 miles per hour. Turning cartwheels, losing her helmet, poles, and skis, she tore ligaments and broke her coccyx. During her career she also suffered a broken leg, a dislocated shoulder, and a sprained ankle. However, the "tiger" always battled back.

In 1967, the skiing world started the World Cup competition, leading to the crowning of a World Cup champion at the end of the season. Nancy was ready. After the first three European meets, she had collected five wins and was in the lead, but the Canadian team had to return home, forcing her to miss three meets. When the Canadians returned to the competition in Jackson Hole, Wyoming, Nancy was in third place. She would need eighteen points to win the World Cup title. She got them, winning the final race by .07 second.

By 1968, Nancy had become the skier to beat. That year, the Olympics were held at Grenoble,

Major Skiing Championships

Year	Competition	Event	Place
1960	Olympic Games	Giant slalom	26th
		Downhill	22d
1962	World Championships	Downhill	5th
1964	Olympic Games	Downhill	7th
1966	World Championships	Giant slalom	4th
		Slalom	7th
1967	World Cup	Overall	1st
1968	Olympic Games	Giant slalom	Gold
		Slalom	Silver
		Downhill	10th
	World Cup	Overall	1st

France. Nancy was leading the World Cup by 30 points—having won the first two events—when disaster struck at Badgastein, Austria. She slipped during a training run and ended up hanging from a tree by her skis. There were no fractures, but Nancy had severely injured the ligaments of her right ankle. She could not practice, let alone race, until the injury healed.

By the time Nancy arrived at Grenoble, she could ski and do light exercise—but it was unknown whether she would be able to race. The first race was the downhill and proved to be a big disappointment. Her coach had predicted great things, proclaiming it the "perfect" course for her, but her ski wax picked up some dirt, slowing her down, and she finished a disappointing tenth. Nancy handled this situation by avoiding the crowds and concentrating on the next race—the slalom. The course was difficult, with fifty-six gates. By concentrating hard, Nancy won her first Olympic medal—a silver—after putting together two good runs. The final race, the giant slalom, was a very technical course, dropping 450 meters over a 1,610-meter course with sixty-eight gates. Nancy drew a good start number after her archrival Marielle Goitschell. Nancy pushed the entire course and won the gold medal by 2.64 seconds, an almost unheard-of margin in world-class skiing.

Continuing the Story

The Canadian "tiger" finished the 1968 ski season at a torrid pace, posting nine straight victories, including one at Red Mountain, British Columbia, her home area. She captured the World Cup title for the second straight year. Just as important,

Milestones

Member of the order of Canada
Member of British Columbia's Order of Dogwood

Honors and Awards

1967	Inducted into Canada's Sports Hall of Fame
1967-68	Canada Athlete of the Year
1969	Inducted into British Columbia Sports Hall of Fame
1999	Canadian Female Athlete of the Century

Nancy also passed her final exams at the University of Notre Dame at Nelson, British Columbia, and earned her bachelor's degree. Nancy retired from competitive skiing after the 1968 season, but she stayed involved in skiing. She helped to found The Nancy Greene League, a developmental ski program for Canadian children. Nancy also had success as a ski resort developer. In 1996, she published a guide for beginning skiers. In 1999, she was named the Canadian Female Athlete of the Century.

Summary

Nancy Greene battled to be world champion two years in a row. Once she retired, she took steps to help others to follow in her footsteps. She is considered one of the greatest skiers of all time.

Suzanne M. Beaudet

Additional Sources

Barber, Terry. *Nancy Greene*. Edmonton, Alta.: Grass Roots Press, 2007.

Fry, John. *The Story of Modern Skiing*. Hanover, N.H.: University Press of New England, 2006.

Levinson, David, and Karen Christensen, eds. *Encyclopedia of World Sport: From Ancient to Present*. Santa Barbara, Calif.: ABC-Clio, 1996.

Wallechinsky, David, and Jaime Loucky. *The Complete Book of the Winter Olympics*. Wilmington, Del.: Sport Media, 2005.

Wayne Gretzky

Born: January 26, 1961
      Brantford, Ontario, Canada
Also known as: Wayne Douglas Gretzky (full
    name); the Great One

Early Life

Wayne Douglas Gretzky was born in Brantford, Ontario, Canada, on January 26, 1961. He was the first of five children born to Walter and Phyllis Gretzky. Wayne's father worked for the telephone company, but hockey had been his hobby since childhood, when he played in the Junior B league in Canada.

Wayne's father taught Wayne to skate when he was only two years old and, soon after, was instructing his son on how to use a miniature hockey stick.

Wayne Gretzky after winning an NHL game in late 1984.
(AP/Wide World Photos)

He even built a backyard hockey rink, complete with lights for night practice sessions, and personally coached his son with special drills, many of which he invented.

The Road to Excellence

Wayne entered his first hockey youth league as soon as the rules allowed; he was six years old. Despite his small size, he excelled at the technical aspects of hockey: skating, shooting, and passing. He scored only 1 goal that season but made the all-star team because of his superior skills against the older and larger boys.

Even after he began league play, Wayne continued to practice at home. When there was ice, he held after school tournaments with neighborhood friends. He also studied televised hockey games and often practiced for a little while longer before bedtime. In his second year in league play, seven-year-old Wayne scored 27 goals. The following year, newspapers were interviewing the boy who had made 104 goals that season.

By the time Wayne was ten years old, his fame had spread. Television and newspapers across Canada were running stories about the 4-foot 4-inch, 70-pound wonder. He scored 378 goals in sixty-eight games that season. Wayne was even invited to speak at a banquet with Gordie Howe, one of the greatest NHL players in history.

In order to improve, Wayne needed more competition than his local team could provide. At the age of fourteen, he left home for the first time to live with some friends in Toronto, where he could play Junior B hockey. In his second year, he impressed everyone with his 70 goals and 112 assists.

At the age of sixteen, Wayne was selected for the Junior A league, the final stepping-stone to professional hockey. He had to move again, living with different family friends to be near his team, the Sault Sainte Marie Greyhounds in Ontario, Canada. Still an amateur, Wayne received $75 a week for expenses.

Two things happened to help Wayne to fame in Sault Sainte Marie: Fans began calling him "The Great Gretzky," and he was given the uniform number 99. The number 9 had been worn by some of the greatest players in hockey history. His career as a hockey prodigy mirrored that of Boston Bruins legend Bobby Orr. Like Orr, Wayne transformed the nature of the offensive attack in hockey.

The Emerging Champion

Wayne turned professional at the age of seventeen, joining the Indianapolis Racers of the World Hockey Association (WHA) for the 1978-1979 season. He signed a contract for seven years and $1.75 million.

The Racers sold Wayne's rights to the Edmonton Oilers, who gave him a $5 million, twenty-year contract. He finished his second professional season with 46 goals and 64 assists in eighty games. At eighteen years old, Wayne showed so much promise that record-keepers were holding a place for him in the Hockey Hall of Fame.

In 1980, Wayne became the youngest hockey player to score 50 goals in one season. Sportswriters awarded the young superstar two major hockey honors: the league's most gentlemanly player award and the first of nine most valuable player awards he received over ten years.

NHL Statistics

Season	GP	G	Ast.	Pts.	PIM
1978-79	80	46	64	110	19
1979-80	79	51	86	137	21
1980-81	80	55	109	164	28
1981-82	80	92	120	212	26
1982-83	80	71	125	196	59
1983-84	74	87	118	205	39
1984-85	80	73	135	208	52
1985-86	80	52	163	215	46
1986-87	79	62	121	183	28
1987-88	64	40	109	149	24
1988-89	78	54	114	168	26
1989-90	73	40	102	142	42
1990-91	78	41	122	163	16
1991-92	74	31	90	121	34
1992-93	45	16	49	65	6
1993-94	81	38	92	130	20
1994-95	48	11	37	48	6
1995-96	80	23	79	102	34
1996-97	82	25	72	97	28
1997-98	82	23	67	90	28
1998-99	70	9	53	62	14
Totals	1,567	940	2,027	2,967	596

Notes: GP = games played; G = goals; Ast. = assists; Pts. = points; PIM = penalties in minutes

At 5 feet 11 inches tall and 165 pounds, Wayne was much smaller and physically weaker than most professional hockey players, but his skating speed was far faster than that of his larger teammates. Besides his quickness, Wayne always studied what was happening on the ice and used his speed to react instantaneously.

Hockey has a reputation as a violent sport. Wayne, however, hardly ever received a penalty. He was never one to argue with his coach. He was a tough player but stayed out of brawls on the ice. For his twenty-first birthday, the Oilers gave Wayne a pay raise—to about $1 million a year. He was also in demand to endorse products. Thirteen songs were written about "The Great Gretzky." _The Sporting News_ named him athlete of the year for 1981. Wayne led his team to four Stanley Cups between 1984 and 1988, along the way becoming a national hero in Canada.

Continuing the Story

On August 9, 1988, the citizens of Canada mourned as twenty-seven-year-old Wayne traded in his orange, white, and blue uniform for a black and silver Los Angeles Kings jersey. The Oilers had traded its star player for $18 million, and Wayne signed a new eight-year contract for $24 million.

The previous month, Wayne had married American actress Janet Jones in what the Canadian press called the "Royal Wedding." She lived in Los Angeles and was blamed by angry Oiler fans, who felt betrayed by Wayne's decision to leave Edmonton.

Fans in Los Angeles, on the other hand, were thrilled to call "The Great One" their own. Attendance at Kings games increased as season ticket sales more than doubled, and hockey was suddenly in the sporting forefront in a city known for championship basketball, football, and baseball.

Wayne had an immediate effect on the performance of his new team. The Kings, long an NHL doormat, vaulted from eighteenth to fourth place in the overall standings in Wayne's first season with the club. Even with Wayne's help, though, the Kings were swept by the eventual Stanley Cup winners, the Calgary Flames, in the second round of the playoffs. Nevertheless, Wayne won the Hart Memorial Trophy as the NHL's most valuable player for a record ninth time, and Kings fans looked forward to further improvement the following season.

Shortly after the start of the 1989-1990 season, Wayne made more headlines when he broke Howe's NHL career scoring record. Howe had taken twenty-six seasons to establish his mark, and Wayne had surpassed the record in a little more than ten seasons. Though Wayne went on to claim his eighth NHL scoring title, the Kings slipped by eight games. The team salvaged something from its season by upsetting the defending champion Calgary Flames in the first round of the playoffs, but Wayne's former teammates from Edmonton eliminated the Kings in the next round. Wayne was merely a spectator when the Oilers went on to take the Stanley Cup, the team's first ever without him.

The Kings rebounded the next season to post the best record in franchise history and claim their first Smythe Division title. The team was considered among the favorites for the Stanley Cup. Again, though, Edmonton defeated the Kings in the playoffs, and Los Angeles hockey fans began to learn that even a player of Wayne's ability could not guarantee a championship.

During his eight seasons with the Kings, Wayne continued to set records, scoring his two thousandth career point in 1990, passing Howe's all-time goal-scoring record in 1994, and leading the Kings to the playoffs five times.

With the Kings enmeshed in controversy surrounding then-owner Bill McNall, and with free agency coming up in the next year, Wayne pushed to be traded during the 1995-1996 season. He signed with the St. Louis Blues in 1996 and came close to winning a fifth Stanley Cup. Following his first season with the Blues, Wayne became a free agent and joined his former teammate Mark Messier with the New York Rangers. Together, they led the Rangers into postseason play, where Wayne

NHL Records

Most goals, 894
Most points, 2,857
Most assists, 1,963
Most points in a season, 215 (1985-86)
Most goals in a season, 92 (1981-82)
Most assists in a season, 163 (1985-86)
Most assists in a game, 7 (three times: 1980, 1985, 1986) (record shared)
Most goals in a period, 4 (1981; record shared)
Most consecutive games scoring points, 51 (1983-84)
Most Stanley Cup Playoff points, 382
Most Stanley Cup Playoff goals, 122
Most Stanley Cup Playoff assists, 260
Most points in one Stanley Cup Playoffs, 47 (1985)
Most assists in one Stanley Cup Playoffs, 31 (1988)
Most assists in a Stanley Cup Playoff game, 6 (1988; record shared)

Honors and Awards

Year	Award
1979	WHA Rookie of the Year
	WHA Second Team All-Star
1980-88, 1990	Hart Memorial Trophy
1980, 1988-90, 1994, 1997-98	NHL Second Team All-Star
1980, 1991-92, 1994, 1999	Lady Byng Memorial Trophy
1981	*Sporting News* Athlete of the Year
1981-87, 1989, 1991, 1994	Art Ross Trophy
1981-87, 1991	NHL First Team All-Star
1982	*Sports Illustrated* Sportsman of the Year
	Associated Press Athlete of the Year
1982-85, 1987	Lester B. Pearson Award
1982-88	Seagram's Seven Crowns of Sports Award
1983-85, 1987	Emery Edge Award
1983, 1989, 1999	NHL All-Star Game most valuable player
1985-87	Chrysler/Dodge NHL Performer of the Year
1985, 1988	Conn Smythe Trophy
1987	Canada Cup most valuable player
1998	Made Officer of the Order of Canada
1999	Inducted into Hockey Hall of Fame
2000	Inducted into International Ice Hockey Federation Hall of Fame
	Uniform number 99 retired by National Hockey League

scored a hat trick against the Florida Panthers in the first round. The Rangers fell to the Flyers in the conference championship.

Wayne played two more seasons with the Rangers and announced his retirement in April, 1999. At a ceremony during his final game in New York, NHL Commissioner Gary Bettman permanently retired Wayne's number 99 jersey. Wayne left the game holding or sharing sixty-one records, many of which were thought to be unbreakable. The Hockey Hall of Fame waived its traditional waiting period and inducted Wayne in November, 1999. In November, 2000, Wayne was named the executive director for the Canadian Olympic men's hockey team. He also received numerous honors from his countrymen. Highways and roads were named for him throughout Canada.

Wayne entered a successful career as a hockey businessman and executive. In 2002, he became part owner of the Phoenix Coyotes, and in 2005, he became the Coyotes' coach. He also was part owner of a Toronto restaurant and sports equipment manufacturer. Wayne coached the Canadian national hockey team at the 2002 and 2006 Winter Olympics.

Wayne and Janet had five children. In 2006, rumors circled that Janet and Coyotes' assistant coach Rich Tocchet had bet on NHL games. Although Tocchet pleaded guilty to gambling charges in 2007, there was no allegation that Janet was involved in wrongdoing.

Summary

Wayne Gretzky's polite and serious nature and his superb grace and speed on the ice separated him from the other players in the NHL. Training from the time he was a toddler, Wayne broke records steadily throughout his professional career.

A popular figure, Wayne has used his influence to condemn hockey violence and to promote the positive aspects of his sport. He was called the most valuable player in the history of hockey and proved his worth to every NHL team for which he played. His name appears frequently on lists of the twentieth century's greatest athletes. Many believe that Wayne's impact on hockey exceeded that of all other athletes on their chosen sports.

Leslie A. Pearl, updated by Howard Bromberg

Additional Sources

Benson, Michael. *Wayne Gretzky: Hockey Player.* New York: Ferguson, 2004.

Fortunato, Frank. *Wayne Gretzky, Star Center.* Springfield, N.J.: Enslow, 1998.

Gretzky, Wayne. *Gretzky: An Autobiography.* New York: HarperCollins, 1990.

Kramer, Sydelle. *The Great Gretzky.* New York: Grossett & Dunlap, 2000.

Messier, Mark, et al. *Wayne Gretzky: The Making of the Great One.* Kansas City, Mo.: Beckett, 1998.

Podnieks, Andrew. *The Great One: The Life and Times of Wayne Gretzky.* Chicago: Triumph Books, 1999.

Santella, Andrew. *Wayne Gretzky: The Great One.* New York: F. Watts, 1998.

Florence Griffith-Joyner

Born: December 21, 1959
     Los Angeles, California
Died: September 21, 1998
     Mission Viejo, California
Also known as: Florence Delorez Griffith (birth
     name); FloJo

Early Life

Florence Delorez Griffith was born on December 21, 1959, in Los Angeles, California, the seventh of eleven children born to Robert and Florence Griffith. Her father was an electronics technician, and her mother was a seamstress. When Florence was four, her mother moved her and the other children to the Watts area of Los Angeles. The family was poor, but Florence recalled her childhood as happy.

When Florence was seven, she began attending the Sugar Ray Robinson Youth Foundation sports days, running in the 50- and 70-meter dashes and always beating the boys. When she was fourteen, she won the annual Jesse Owens National Youth Games; the following year she won it again. At Jordan High School in Los Angeles, she set school records in the sprint and long jump. After graduating in 1978, she attended California State University, Northridge (CSUN), planning to major in business.

The Road to Excellence

Florence dropped out of college after her freshman year because of a shortage of funds, and for a while she worked as a bank teller. Bob Kersee, the assistant track coach at CSUN, persuaded her to apply for financial aid and return to school. In 1980, when Kersee moved to the University of California at Los Angeles (UCLA), Florence followed him there, switching her major from business to psychology. She got serious about running and thought that Kersee was the best coach for her. Kersee decided that she should specialize in the 200 meters because she was not quick enough off the starting blocks for the 100 meters. Kersee was an expert on the technical aspects of coaching, and at first Florence found it difficult to take in all his

advice and instructions. She had relied solely on her natural abilities and her flair and determination to put her ahead of the field, but she realized that if she were to succeed, she needed to learn from a professional coach. At UCLA, Florence had the opportunity to compete against some of the finest American athletes, and her partnership with Kersee was soon paid dividends. She only narrowly missed selection for the U.S. Olympic team in 1980.

The Emerging Champion

In 1982, Florence became National Collegiate Athletic Association (NCAA) champion in the 200 meters; the following year she won the 400 meters in

Florence Griffith-Joyner after winning the 100-meter dash at the 1988 Olympic Games in Seoul. (Tony Duffy/Getty Images)

Major Sprint Championships

Year	Competition	Event	Place	Time
1981	U.S. Nationals	200 meters	2d	23.09
1982	U.S. Nationals	100 meters	3d	11.15
		200 meters	2d	22.58
1983	World Championships	200 meters	4th	22.46
	U.S. Nationals	200 meters	3d	22.23
1984	Olympic Games	200 meters	Silver	22.04
		400 meters	3d	51.56
1987	World Championships	200 meters	2d	21.96
		4×100-meter relay	1st	41.58
	U.S. Nationals	200 meters	2d	21.7
1988	Olympic Games	100 meters	Gold	10.54 OR
		200 meters	Gold	21.34 WR
		4×100-meter relay	Gold	41.98
		4×400-meter relay	Silver	3:15.51

Notes: OR = Olympic Record; WR = World Record

the same championship. In 1984, she won the silver medal in the 200 meters at the 1984 Los Angeles Olympic Games, coming in second to her great rival, Valerie Brisco. In this race, Florence first attracted widespread attention to her spectacular appearance on the track: her 6½-inch fingernails were painted red, white, and blue.

Florence was disappointed by her failure to win the Olympic gold medal, and for a while she lost her enthusiasm, taking a job with a bank and neglecting her training. In 1987, Bob Kersee got her back on the right track, and at the World Track and Field Championships In Rome she won the silver medal in the 200 meters and a gold medal as a member of the U.S. 4×100-meter relay team. Florence was not yet satisfied with her performance and set out to be the best in 1988. Guided by Kersee, she embarked on a rigorous weight-training program to improve her technique and increase her strength. She was still working a full-time job, and her schedule became extremely demanding: She worked out during lunch hours and sometimes trained until after midnight. In addition to weight training, she ran 3.7 miles a day and also studied a video recording of Ben Johnson's record-breaking run in the 100 meters in Rome, convinced that Johnson's lightning start was the key to his success.

Just before the U.S. Olympic trials in July, 1988, Florence told her coach that she felt ready to break the world 200-meter record. She was at a peak of strength, endurance,

technique, and self-confidence. These qualities produced some of the most astonishing results in the history of women's athletics.

Continuing the Story

In the Olympic trials, Florence broke the world record in the 100 meters with a time of 10.49 seconds. This was more than a quarter of a second faster than the previous record, an amazing feat. In the space of four days, she ran the four fastest 100 meters in women's track history. Florence also added to her reputation for glamour, wearing a one-legged blue leotard and a white bikini in the final. After her spectacular performances in the Olympic trials, Florence became a media darling, not only in the United States but also around the world. *Paris Match* called her "la tigresse noir," or "the black tigress," and she was sought after by film producers and fashion magazines.

Before the 1988 Olympic Games in Seoul, South Korea, in September, Florence parted company with her coach, Bob Kersee, putting her husband, Al Joyner, the 1984 Olympic triple jump champion and the great heptathlete Jackie Joyner-Kersee's older brother, in charge of her preparations. In the Olympics, Florence—nicknamed FloJo—lived up to expectations. She set two Olympic records in the 100 meters and won the gold medal. She then smashed the world 200-meter record twice, in the semifinals and then again in the final, which she ran in 21.34. Then she won her third gold medal in the 4×100-meter relay, as well as a silver medal in the 4×400-meter relay. Only one female athlete in Olympic history, Fanny Blankers-Koen, in 1948, had had greater success.

In February, 1989, Florence announced her retirement. She founded the FloJo International Track Club and became president and coach. She

Honors, Awards, and Records

1988	Jesse Owens Award
	Associated Press Female Athlete of the Year
	James E. Sullivan Award
	Set World and American outdoor records at 100 meters (10.49)
	Set World and American outdoor records at 200 meters (21.34)
1989	U.S. Olympic Committee Award
	Harvard Foundational Award for Outstanding Contribution to Society
	Golden Camera Award
1995	Inducted into International Track and Field Hall of Fame

still felt the need to compete, however, and in 1991, she announced that she was starting to train for a marathon. Problems with her Achilles tendon forced her to abandon the effort. Following her retirement, Florence was named cochair of the President's Council on Physical Fitness and Sports and pursued a career in acting and writing, publishing several books on running and general fitness.

In 1996, Florence suffered a seizure and was hospitalized briefly. For the next two years, she continued to promote fitness and focus on her acting career, appearing in an episode of the CBS series *The Brian Benben Show* in 1998. On September 21, 1998, at the age of thirty-eight, and in presumably superb physical condition, Florence Griffith-Joyner died in her home of an apparent heart seizure. Speculation on the cause of her death focused on rumors throughout her career that she used performance-enhancing drugs. However, Florence never failed a drug test, and her autopsy revealed that her death was not as a result of drug use.

Summary

Beautiful, swift, and powerful, with a flair for fashion, Florence Griffith-Joyner captured the world's attention with her stunning performances on the track. Her untimely death was a shock to her fellow athletes and to the nation as a whole, which had been captivated as much by Florence's remarkable athletic abilities as by her charm and grace.

Bryan Aubrey

Additional Sources

Posey, John R., and Margo J. Posey. *Portraits in Excellence.* Dallas, Tex.: BSPIN, 2004.

"Ten Greatest Women Athletes." *Ebony* 57, no. 5 (March, 2002): 74-77.

Wallechinsky, David, and Jaime Loucky. *The Complete Book of the Olympics: 2008 Edition.* London: Aurum Press, 2008.

Woolum, Janet. *Outstanding Women Athletes: Who They Are and How They Influenced Sports in America.* Phoenix, Ariz.: Oryx Press, 1998.

Guo Jingjing

Born: October 15, 1981
  Baoding, Hebei Province, China

Early Life

Guo Jingjing was born on October 15, 1981, in Baoding, ninety miles south of Beijing, China. In 1987, Jingjing was six years old and rather frail. Therefore, her parents let a talent scout take her to Baoding Diving Training Base to gain strength through sports. When Jingjing started training in competitive diving one year later, her scout objected to her protruding kneecap. Jingjing's father corrected the problem in two years by sitting on Jingjing's kneecap while she stretched out her leg in the evening. Jingjing's mother took care of her when she was in the hospital with a sports injury. At the age of ten, in 1992, Jingjing was selected to dive for the Chinese national team. She moved into a dormitory. For the next thirteen years, Jingjing rarely saw her parents.

The Road to Excellence

After three years of hard training, in September, 1995, at the Diving World Cup in Atlanta, Georgia, Jingjing won her first gold medal, for 10-meter-platform synchronized diving with partner Rui Wang. At the 1996 Atlanta Olympics, Jingjing took fifth place in 10-meter platform diving. She was too nervous at this height.

In 1998, Jingjing's coach Zhong Shaozen, a former diving champion, switched Jingjing to the 3-meter springboard. This became Jingjing's event. In single 3-meter springboard diving, Jingjing won silver at the World Aquatics Championships in Perth, Australia, and gold at the Asian Games in Bangkok, Thailand.

Jingjing trained hard for the next Olympics. Her weekday started early in the morning and included 9 to 10 hours of training. At 10 P.M., the lights went out in the athletes' dormitories. In 1999, Jingjing won the synchronized springboard event and was third in the single 3-meter diving event at the World Cup. Early in 2000, she won World Cup gold in singles and silver in synchronized diving.

At the 2000 Sydney Olympics, Jingjing and her synchronized diving partner, Fu Mingxia, lost the gold to the Russian team. In the single 3-meter diving, Fu won the gold and Jingjing earned the silver. For Jingjing, this meant defeat. It took Coach Zhong's solace, and perhaps the retirement of Mingxia, for Jingjing to dive again.

Major Diving Championships

Year	Competition	Event	Place
1995	World Cup	3-meter synchronized springboard	1st
		Synchronized platform	1st
1996	Olympic Games	Platform	5th
1998	World Championships	3-meter springboard	2d
1999	World Cup	3-meter springboard	3d
		3-meter synchronized springboard	1st
2000	World Cup	3-meter springboard	1st
		3-meter synchronized springboard	2d
	Olympic Games	3-meter springboard	2d
		3-meter synchronized springboard	Silver
2001	World Championships	3-meter springboard	1st
		3-meter synchronized springboard	1st
2002	Asian Games	3-meter springboard	1st
		3-meter synchronized springboard	1st
	World Cup	3-meter springboard	1st
		1-meter springboard	1st
		3-meter synchronized springboard	2d
2003	World Championships	3-meter synchronized springboard	1st
		3-meter springboard	1st
	Australia/China Grand Prix	3-meter springboard	1st
		3-meter synchronized springboard	1st
2004	Olympic Games	3-meter synchronized springboard	Gold
		3-meter springboard	Gold
	World Cup	3-meter springboard	2d
		3-meter synchronized springboard	1st
2005	World Championships	3-meter synchronized springboard	1st
		3-meter springboard	1st
2006	Asian Games	3-meter synchronized springboard	1st
2007	World Championships	3-meter springboard	1st
		3-meter synchronized springboard	1st
2008	Olympic Games	3-meter synchronized springboard	Gold
		3-meter springboard	Gold

The Emerging Champion

At the 2001 World Aquatics Championships in Fukuoka, Japan, Jingjing won the 3-meter synchronized springboard event with her new partner, Wu Minxia, and took gold in the single 3-meter springboard event. In the next year, at the World Cup in Seville, Spain, Jingjing earned three gold medals: She won the 3- and 1-meter springboard events and 3-meter springboard synchronized event. At the Asian Games in Pusan, South Korea, Jingjing and Wu won gold medals for synchronized diving. Jingjing beat Wu for gold in the 3-meter singles two days later. In the Chinese national diving team, athletes who were partners in team events had to compete fiercely against each other in single events.

In October, 2002, Jingjing entered Renmin University in Beijing for a six-year program for student athletes in the school of humanities. In 2003, Jingjing won a gold medals in both the single and synchronized 3-meter diving events at both the Grand Prix and the World Aquatics Championships. Jingjing's preparations for the next Olympics took a temporary setback when she fell off the springboard at the Grand Prix in Atlanta in May, 2004. Jingjing called it a stupid mistake.

Jingjing's sixteen-year dream of winning an Olympic gold medal came true at the 2004 Athens Olympics. On August 15, she and Wu won the synchronized springboard dive, beating the Russian team of Yulia Pakhalina and Vera Ilyina, the same divers who beat Jingjing and her former partner in 2000. On August 26, Jingjing won the Olympic gold medal for the single 3-meter springboard dive, beating her synchronized-diving partner.

Continuing the Story

After the Olympics, Jingjing celebrated her success and signed lucrative advertisement deals. She was romantically linked to Kenneth Fok, son of International Olympic Committee member Timothy Fok and grandson of Hong Kong tycoon Henry Fok. In November, 2004, Zhou Jihong, head coach of the Chinese national diving team, dropped Jingjing from the national roster for excessive commer-

cial activities. Jingjing apologized to Coach Zhou. In February, 2005, Jingjing spent Lunar New Year with her parents for the first time since 1992.

Jingjing won gold in synchronized springboard diving with Li Ting at both the 2005 World Aquatics Championships in Montreal, Quebec, Canada, and the 2006 Asian Games in Doha, Qatar. In 2007, Jingjing teamed up with Wu again. They won the synchronized springboard diving at the World Aquatics Championships in Melbourne, Australia. Jingjing also won the singles event. This gave her an unmatched four consecutive gold medals at the world championships.

Diving in front of an enthusiastic home crowd at "the Water Cube" at the 2008 Beijing Olympics, Jingjing and Wu won gold in synchronized springboard diving. Their score of 343.50 included three perfect tens in the second round, and they defeated the Russian team again. In the single springboard diving, Jingjing won gold with 415.35 points.

Summary

Guo Jingjing's total of four gold and two silver Olympic medals made her the most decorated female Olympic diver. She proved a worthy successor to Chinese women divers Gao Min and Fu Mingxia. Beginning with Gao's gold in 1988, six consecutive Olympic gold medals went to Chinese divers in 3-meter springboard diving. Jingjing became extremely popular in her home country: Her endorsement deals made her one of the richest athletes in China.

R. C. Lutz

Additional Sources

Anderson, Kelli. "Two Good: In Synchronized Diving the Chinese Still Rule the Pool." *Sports Illustrated* 101, no. 7 (August 23, 2004): 60.

Beech, Hannah. "She Always Makes a Splash." *Time,* August 4, 2008, 60.

Lloyd, Janice. "Getting to Know Guo Jingjing." *USA Today,* August 14, 2008, p. 2D.

Weir, Tom. "Diving in and out of Controversy, Guo Still a Splashing Star." *USA Today,* August 18, 2008, p. 8D.

Tatiana Gutsu

Born: September 5, 1976
   Odessa, Soviet Union (now in Ukraine)
Also known as: Tatiana Konstantinovna Gutsu
   (full name)

Early Life

Tatiana Konstantinovna Gutsu was born to Constantin and Elena Gutsu on September 5, 1976, in the Black Sea port of Odessa, Ukraine (then part of the Soviet Union). She was the second of four daughters. At the age of six, Tatiana was one of many little girls selected from her kindergarten to practice gymnastics. "She was at once a little bit different," recalled her coach, Victor Dikii. "She was a little bit faster, quicker and stronger than the other kids." Dikii and his wife, Tamilla Evdokimova, trained Tatiana with solid physical preparation—stretching and strength exercises—and firm attention to the basics of the sport. Tatiana steadily progressed, eventually gaining a spot on the Soviet Union's junior national team.

The Road to Excellence

At the 1990 Goodwill Games in Seattle, Tatiana, at thirteen, was an alternate to the competitive team. Instead of warming the bench, however, she was allowed to perform in exhibition in place of an injured gymnast from another country. While audience interest centered on the spirited battle between the United States and the Soviet Union, those who watched carefully saw a star in the making. Tatiana performed some of the most difficult skills yet shown by a female gymnast. Any male gymnast would have been proud of her ambitious tumbling on floor exercise, while her balance beam work, packed full of tricks, resembled a high-wire act. Moreover, she competed with the confidence of a veteran.

However, beyond the awesome stunts, Tatiana's routines lacked polish and style. She returned to the Soviets' training center outside Moscow to work toward the next stage.

Tatiana showcased her improvement at the 1991 European Cup in Belgium. Though the big names in the sport stayed away, Tatiana outshone a talented young field to win the all-around competition. By that autumn's World Gymnastics Championships, Tatiana was among the Soviet Union's best, but because of her youth and the depth of her team, Tatiana did not secure the all-important top spot in the lineup. She paid her dues, contributed to the team gold, and ended up fifth in the all-around despite a fine performance. In the event finals, Tatiana earned silver medals for her bars and beam work. To the Soviet coaches, Tatiana had shown that she could complete her intricate exercises without fault in a major competition. In short, she was ready for the big time.

Tatiana Gutsu performing on the balance beam to win the gold at the Barcelona Summer Olympics in 1992. (AP/Wide World Photos)

The Emerging Champion

By 1992, Tatiana was a leader. She won Moscow's Stars of the World competition, usually an accurate Olympic predictor, en route to the European championships in Nantes, France. The European championships were a preview of the Barcelona Olympics. Defending two-time champion Svetlana Boginskaya of Belarus, Tatiana's Soviet teammate, was heavily favored, but she faltered on her final exercise. Tatiana stepped into the spotlight with more new skills and won her first major title. Her success at the European championships gained Tatiana the envied cleanup slot at the Olympics, along with the attendant pressures. Because scores in gymnastics tend to rise as team members compete, the cleanup slot is worth precious tenths that can make the difference between champion and runner-up.

At the Olympics, when every tenth of a point counts, performing the "big trick" is not always worth the risk. A difficult routine may be rewarded, or it may not, but an error always produces a deduction. One flinch and all is lost. Tatiana, as always, competed without hesitation. In the team competition, she mounted the beam with a daunting layout somersault and fell. Thinking her Olympics were over, she completed her routine, then began crying. Only a few minutes later, she clinched the gold for the Unified Team with a spectacular tumbling display during the floor exercise.

Tatiana's overall score was the fourth best on her team. Thanks to a three-per-country limit, she had not qualified to compete for the women's all-around gold, the prize trophy of Olympic gymnastics. However, she would once again benefit from a substitution. This time, teammate Roza Galieva was pulled out because of an unspecified injury. While the experts debated the authenticity of the injury claim, Tatiana prepared for the biggest day of her life.

After three of four events in the all-around, Tatiana held a small lead, tied with Romania's Lavinia Milosovici. Like Mary Lou Retton in 1984 and Soviet Olympic champ Elena Shushunova in 1988, she would have to vault for gold. American

Major Gymnastics Championships

Year	Competition	Event	Place	Event	Place
1990	U.S.S.R. Championships	All-around	2d		
1991	European Cup	All-around	1st		
	World Championships	All-around	5th		
		Balance beam	2d	Team	1st
		Uneven bars	2d		
1992	European Championships	All-around	1st	Balance beam	2d
		Floor exercise	3d	Uneven bars	1st
		Vault	1st		
	Olympic Games	All-around	Gold	Floor exercise	Bronze
		Team	Gold	Uneven bars	Silver

Shannon Miller made a grandstand play with a near-perfect effort, leaving it up to Tatiana, who needed 9.95 for the gold. Her first vault was good, but a quiver on the landing left her with 9.925. The second had to be better. She ran, took flight, and landed without a quiver. A 9.95 flashed on the scoreboard, and a relieved Tatiana was the Olympic champion.

Continuing the Story

In the individual event finals, Tatiana added two more medals, then went home to a changed life. The Ukrainian government rewarded her with a car, a larger apartment for her family, and 340,000 rubles, about four years' earnings for an average citizen. She spent a month touring the United States, giving exhibitions and earning more money. When the new year approached, gymnasts began to prepare for the next Olympic cycle. Tatiana, burned out from the stress of the previous year, took a break. She decided to retire late in 1992, apparently washed up at the age of sixteen. She performed in a show in the United States, then disappeared.

After a period of rest, she was persuaded to return by world and Olympic champion turned entrepreneur Dimitri Bilozerchev, who had gathered the remnants of the disbanded Soviet team to establish a professional competitive and exhibition team. In the spring of 1993, Tatiana went to Moscow to begin pursuing the new style of gymnastics in the old Soviet Union. She then moved to the United States. After a brief, failed marriage, a few coaching jobs, and exhibitions, she left the sport.

Later, as Tatiana became more comfortable with her English and life in the United States, she returned to the gym and to coaching in Detroit, Michigan. She attempted to make the U.S. Olympic team in 2004, but failed.

Summary

Tatiana Gutsu will be remembered as the shy blond who risked the big tricks at the biggest meet of them all, the Olympic Games. For her daring, she won gymnastics' ultimate prize: The Olympic all-around gold medal. She was also the last Olympic champion produced by the Soviet dynasty.

Nancy Raymond

Additional Sources

Greenberg, Stan. *Whitaker's Olympic Almanack: An Encyclopaedia of the Olympic Games.* Chicago: Fitzroy Dearborn, 2000.

Wallechinsky, David, and Jaime Loucky. *The Complete Book of the Olympics: 2008 Edition.* London: Aurum Press, 2008.

Glenn Hall

Born: October 3, 1931
      Humboldt, Saskatchewan, Canada
Also known as: Glenn Henry Hall (full name);
  Mr. Goalie

Early Life

Glenn Henry Hall was born on October 3, 1931, in Humboldt, Saskatchewan, Canada. Located in the center of the province, Humboldt served as a railway center for western Canada. Glenn's father worked for the Canadian National Railroad as an engineer. Growing up on a farm, Glenn learned to appreciate the quiet of country life and the vast open spaces around him. He was first introduced to hockey on the outdoor rinks of his hometown. Hockey was very popular with the boys of the town,

and they played on the outdoor rinks whenever they had the time. At times, the temperature dropped to forty degrees below zero, but that would not stop Glenn from joining the other boys of the town in a game of hockey.

The Road to Excellence

By the time Glenn was a teenager, he was playing goalie for the junior team of the Humboldt Indians. In 1949, while playing for the junior team, he was spotted by Fred Pinkney, a scout for the Detroit Red Wings. Because of Pinkney's positive report, Detroit wanted to sign young Glenn to a contract. Glenn accepted the offer, and he was sent to join Detroit's junior farm team, the Windsor Spitfires of the Junior A Ontario Hockey Association. Glenn played well for his new team, and for the 1950-1951 season he was awarded the Red Tillson Trophy as the most valuable player of the Ontario Junior A League. For the next season, he was moved up to the Indianapolis Caps of the American League.

Glenn stayed with the Caps only for the 1951-1952 season. He was then sent to the Edmonton Flyers of the Western League. He spent three seasons with the Flyers. During his years with the Flyers, Glenn proved that he was a fine prospect for the National Hockey League (NHL). At the time, the Detroit Red Wings had an outstanding young goalie by the name of Terry Sawchuk, so it did not look like Glenn would be moving up to the Detroit team in the near future. He did get a chance to play with the Red Wings when Sawchuk was injured, though. Glenn played in eight NHL games during his tenure with Edmonton, and Detroit management was so impressed

Glenn Hall during his years with the Chicago Blackhawks. (Courtesy of Chicago Blackhawk Hockey Team)

NHL Statistics

Season	GP	W	L	T	GAA	PIM
1952-53	6	4	1	1	1.67	0
1954-55	2	2	0	0	1.00	0
1955-56	70	30	24	16	2.11	14
1956-57	70	38	20	12	2.24	2
1957-58	70	24	39	7	2.89	10
1958-59	70	28	29	13	2.97	0
1959-60	70	28	29	13	2.57	0
1960-61	70	29	24	17	2.57	0
1961-62	70	31	26	13	2.66	12
1962-63	66	30	20	16	2.55	0
1963-64	65	34	19	12	2.31	2
1964-65	41	18	18	5	2.43	2
1965-66	64	34	21	7	2.63	14
1966-67	32	19	5	5	2.38	10
1967-68	49	19	21	9	2.48	0
1968-69	41	19	12	8	2.17	20
1969-70	18	7	8	3	2.91	0
1970-71	32	13	11	8	2.42	0
Totals	**906**	**407**	**327**	**165**	**2.51**	**86**

Notes: GP = games played; W = wins; L = losses; T = ties; GAA = goals against average; PIM = penalties in minutes

with Glenn's play that they traded Sawchuk to the Boston Bruins to make room for Glenn as the team's full-time goaltender.

The Emerging Champion

During Glenn's first complete season with the Red Wings, he proved his excellence. He was the NHL's leading goalie, with twelve shutouts, and he allowed only 2.11 goals per game. For the outstanding season he had in 1955-1956, Glenn won the Calder Trophy as the NHL's rookie of the year. His second year with the Red Wings turned out to be his last, however. Glenn had a respectable regular season and was named to his first NHL all-star team, but Detroit was eliminated in the first round of the playoffs by the Boston Bruins. Glenn was tagged by Detroit management as a goalie who could not come through with great performances when it counted most. During the off-season, the Red Wings reacquired Terry Sawchuk, and Glenn was traded to the Chicago Blackhawks. The trade was traumatic for Glenn, and he became a loner after the move to Chicago. Glenn was determined to prove that Detroit had made a mistake by trading him.

The Blackhawks were in the process of rebuilding. Glenn played a major role in turning the team around. He became a favorite of the Chicago fans, who gave him the nickname "Mr. Goalie." Glenn played in every game during his first five years with Chicago, and the Blackhawks became a powerhouse team with the addition of such quality young players as Bobby Hull and Stan Mikita. Chicago won its first Stanley Cup in twenty-three years at the end of the 1960-1961 season, and Glenn's goaltending was one of the key ingredients in Chicago's triumph.

The Blackhawks were one of the NHL's most exciting teams. Most of the players on the team were extroverts, but Glenn was quiet. He did not like going out in public and looked irritated when forced into public situations. He played for the Blackhawks for ten seasons, and even though the team did not win another Stanley Cup, Glenn had earned the name Mr. Goalie.

Continuing the Story

During his tenure with the Blackhawks, Glenn was named five times to the NHL all-star first team and three times to the second team. He was not sidelined in his NHL career until the 1962-1963 season. Glenn played in 502 consecutive games, a tremendous accomplishment. In those days, NHL teams did not use substitute goalies to give the first-string goaltenders a rest, so Glenn played all of those 502 games in their entirety. By the late 1960's, a two-goalie system was initiated by the NHL teams, since the number of teams in the league had been increased and the schedule had been expanded to seventy-eight games. In 1967, Glenn and the second goaltender for Chicago, Denis DeJordy, combined to win the Vezina Trophy for having the lowest goals against average in the league.

Despite Glenn's success, the Blackhawks did not protect the thirty-six-year-old Glenn in the 1967 expansion draft. He thought about retiring, but a high salary offer convinced him to sign with the expansion St. Louis Blues, and the new team reached the Stanley Cup finals against the Montreal Canadiens. The Blues lost to Montreal, but Glenn had

Honors and Awards

1956	Calder Trophy
1957-58, 1960, 1963-64, 1966, 1969	NHL First Team All-Star
1963, 1967, 1969	Vezina Trophy
1968	Conn Smythe Trophy
1975	Inducted into Hockey Hall of Fame

been instrumental in getting St. Louis to the finals. He was awarded the Conn Smythe Trophy as the most valuable player in the playoffs. Another aging goalie was added by the Blues the next season, the great Jacques Plante. The two goaltenders combined to win the Vezina Trophy and lead St. Louis back to the Stanley Cup finals, where they lost again to Montreal.

Glenn played two more seasons for the Blues and, in 1971, retired after sixteen seasons. The strain of playing goalie in the NHL was finally over for Glenn. Throughout his career, he was often sick to his stomach before games. Glenn returned to his farm in Alberta, which he had seen only during the off-season. In 1972, he came out of retirement to be an assistant coach for the World Hockey Association's Alberta Oilers, but after a few months Glenn returned to his farm for good. In 1975, Glenn was inducted into the Hockey Hall of Fame.

Summary

Glenn Hall was one of hockey's most durable and outstanding goaltenders. He had a unique style of play that relied on wonderful eyesight and quick reflexes. Glenn worked hard and brought out the best in himself and his teammates. Glenn won the Vezina Trophy as the league's top goalie three times and ranks near the top in career shutouts, with 84.

Jeffry Jensen

Additional Sources

Adrahtas, Tom. *Glenn Hall: The Man They Call Mr. Goalie.* Tampa, Fla.: Albion Press, 2003.

Conner, Floyd. *Hockey's Most Wanted: The Top Ten Book of Wicked Slapshots, Bruising Goons, and Ice Oddities.* Washington, D.C.: Brassey's, 2002.

Weekes, Don. *The Big Book of Hockey Trivia.* Berkeley, Calif.: Greystone Books, 2005.

Dorothy Hamill

Born: July 26, 1956
    Chicago, Illinois
Also known as: Dorothy Stuart Hamill (full
    name)

Early Life

On July 26, 1956, Dorothy Stuart Hamill was born
to Carol and Chalmers Hamill in Chicago, Illinois.
The family soon moved to Riverside, Connecticut.
Dorothy grew up there with her older brother,
Sandy, and sister, Marcia. Her father was an executive at Pitney Bowes Company.

Dorothy and her siblings often visited their
grandparents, Esther and Willis Clough, in Wellesley, Massachusetts. In the wintertime, the children
skated on Morse's Pond behind the Clough home.
When Dorothy was about eight years old, she skated
there for the first time, wearing a borrowed pair
of old skates that were much too big for her. When
she got back to Riverside, Dorothy begged for
skates of her own. She received her first pair that
winter.

Dorothy Hamill holds her Olympic Gold medal in 1976. (AP/Wide World
Photos)

The Road to Excellence

Dorothy joined a local skating class and loved her
lessons. When summer came, skating lessons began
to conflict with swimming, and Dorothy decided
that she wanted to quit swimming. Her mother refused to let her, saying that Dorothy had made a
commitment, and commitments must be honored.

As her skill improved, Dorothy's enthusiasm returned and expanded. In the fall of 1965, she began weekly private lessons with a local teacher,
Barbara Taplan. Dorothy was impatient, but Taplan made her learn slowly and carefully, building a
strong basis for the many years of championship
skating to come. That same year, Dorothy entered
her first competition, the Wollman Open, held annually in New York City's Central Park. Despite inexperience and fear, Dorothy took second place.

The following spring, she started lessons with
Otto Gold, a Czechoslovakian who was a former
European skating champion. Gold was a strict
disciplinarian, and Dorothy's skating improved
quickly under his instruction. At Gold's urging,
Dorothy began to take—and pass—
the United States Figure Skating
Association tests, which are used to
establish levels of competence in
figure skating.

By the time she was only nine, Dorothy's whole life revolved around
skating. In the summer of 1966, she
left her family and friends to study
with Gold at Lake Placid, New York,
an important summer training center for skaters. At the end of the
summer, Gold concluded that Dorothy was an extremely skilled technical skater for her age, but he said
she needed more experience and
training.

Dorothy came home extremely
disappointed. Rather than give up,
however, she became more determined to improve. Referring to this
as a turning point in her life, Dorothy said, "I made a commitment to

myself, and from that moment on there was no turning back."

The Emerging Champion

Dorothy's coach assured the Hamills that their daughter had the talent to be a champion. Dorothy began a rigorous schedule of lessons and practice, getting up early to skate before school. In the spring of 1967, Dorothy entered the Wollman Open for the second time and won a gold medal. When summer came, she again went to Lake Placid to train, this time with the great Swiss coach Gustav Lussi.

During the next year, Dorothy set high standards for herself and made steady progress in her skating. Her new teacher was Sonya Klopfer Dunfield, the 1951 national ladies' champion. In order to study with Dunfield, Dorothy had to commute three hours a day from Riverside, Connecticut, to New York City.

Under Dunfield's guidance, Dorothy won the national novice ladies' championship in 1969. By this time, because of her intense skating schedule, Dorothy had missed a lot of school and had fallen seriously behind in her work. Rather than reduce her skating, however, Dorothy decided to move to New York City, stay with friends, and work with private tutors there.

Dorothy devoted all her time to skating lessons, practice, and competition. In 1970, she won the eastern U.S. junior ladies' title and came in second in the national junior ladies' competition. At the Pre-Olympics in Japan, she won the silver medal. There she also met Carlo Fassi, one of the best coaches in the world, who invited her to study with him in Colorado. While studying with Fassi, Dorothy enrolled in Colorado Academy, the school from which she received her high school diploma.

In 1973, at the age of sixteen, Dorothy took second place in the national senior ladies' competition. In 1974, she won that championship. She was also national senior ladies' champion in 1975 and 1976.

To achieve such success, Dorothy and her family

Major Figure-Skating Championships

Year	Competition	Place
1969	U.S. National Novice Ladies Championships	1st
1970	U.S. National Junior Ladies Championships	2d
1971	U.S. National Senior Ladies Championships	5th
1972	U.S. National Senior Ladies Championships	4th
1973	U.S. National Senior Ladies Championships	2d
	World Championships	4th
1974	U.S. National Senior Ladies Championships	1st
	World Championships	2d
1975	U.S. National Senior Ladies Championships	1st
	World Championships	2d
1976	U.S. National Senior Ladies Championships	1st
	Olympic Games	Gold
	World Championships	1st

made sacrifices. Dorothy trained seven hours a day, six days a week, eleven months a year while preparing for major competitions. Much of the time, she lived away from her family. She had their strong support, however. When Dorothy moved to Colorado to train with Fassi, her mother went with her. The Hamills reportedly spent as much as $20,000 a year on lessons, travel, costumes, and living expenses.

The highlight of Dorothy's career was her almost perfect performance in the 1976 Olympic Games. Millions of television viewers watched her skate brilliantly to win the gold medal. Her trademark haircut also became well known to her fans. Shortly after the Olympics, Dorothy won the 1976 ladies' world figure skating title as well.

Continuing the Story

Throughout her career, Dorothy set new standards. She considered figure skating to be a sport, not an art, and performed in a unique, bold manner. Dorothy combined athletic skill with a fluid style, developing and perfecting daring spins and jumps. One of them, a spiral spin, became well known as the Hamill Camel.

As a performer, Dorothy was outgoing but sensitive. Before important competitions, she was nervous and sometimes doubted her ability. At those times, coach Lussi's advice echoed in her ears. He had told her, "You have to have guts to be a great skater. . . . Go out there and give every move you do everything you've got."

After winning her 1976 Olympic gold medal,

Honors and Awards

1991	Inducted into U.S. Olympic Hall of Fame
	Inducted into U.S. Figure Skating Association Hall of Fame

Dorothy signed a lucrative contract to skate professionally with the Ice Capades. In addition to hundreds of performances a year, she made personal appearances, endorsed products, and appeared in television specials. After three years, Dorothy decided to change her difficult schedule. She began to skate only part time with the Ice Capades and became more selective about her personal appearances and skating exhibitions. During the 1980's and 1990's, she also successfully competed in professional competitions, winning five world professional championship titles.

One of Dorothy's continuing interests was children. Dorothy gave ice-skating clinics for children with disabilities. She served as the American Cancer Society's national youth chairperson, and her skating exhibitions often benefited organizations such as Big Brothers and Big Sisters of America and the American Cancer Society. She also became involved in the President's Council on Physical Fitness and Sports, and she raised millions of dollars for AIDS causes and for Ronald McDonald House.

Dorothy's first marriage, to Dean Martin, Jr., son of the entertainer, ended in divorce. In 1987, she married sports medicine doctor Kenneth Forsythe, a former member of the Canadian Olympic ski team. Their daughter, Alexandra, was born in 1988. However, this marriage also ended in divorce. In 1993, Dorothy bought the financially ailing Ice Capades. Despite her name recognition, innovations in the treatment of performers, and the critically acclaimed redesign of the shows, she was unable to save the touring show and sold her interest in it in 1994. Dorothy continued to be a favorite performer at professional competitions, in exhibitions, and in special shows.

Summary

Dorothy Hamill was known for introducing a daring, athletic style into her sport, quite different from the traditional, graceful form of previous women figure skaters. She had natural talent, but self-discipline and dedication to excellence made her a champion.

Dorothy radiated a genuine graciousness to those around her. As a child, she was crushed when a famous movie actor refused to give her an autograph. Dorothy vowed then that if she ever became famous, she would never unreasonably refuse an autograph. Like the commitment to herself and her skating that Dorothy made and kept over the years, she continued to keep this commitment to her fans.

Jean C. Fulton

Additional Sources

Hamill, Dorothy. *Skating Life*. New York: Hyperion, 2007.

O'Neil, Dana Pennett, and Pat Williams. *How to Be Like Women Athletes of Influence: Thirty-one Women at the Top of Their Game and How You Can Get There Too*. Deerfield Beach, Fla.: Health Communications, 2007.

Platt, Jim, and James Buckley. *Sports Immortals: Stories of Inspiration and Achievement*. Chicago: Triumph Books, 2002.

Scott Hamilton

Born: August 28, 1958
    Toledo, Ohio
Also known as: Scott Scovell Hamilton (full name)

Early Life

Scott Scovell Hamilton was born in Toledo, Ohio, on August 28, 1958. When he was six weeks old, he was adopted by Ernest and Dorothy Hamilton, both of whom were college professors at Bowling Green State University, in Ohio. He has an older sister, Susan, and a younger brother, Steven, who is also adopted.

Scott was in and out of hospitals throughout most of his childhood. Stricken by a mysterious illness at the age of two, Scott's body stopped growing, and he was bedridden for the next few years. When Scott was eight years old, the doctors mistakenly pronounced his condition cystic fibrosis. Shocked by the news that Scott had only a few months to live, his parents took him to Boston Children's Hospital. This time, Scott was correctly diagnosed as having Schwachmann's syndrome, which is paralysis of the intestinal tract. After Scott was fortified with a vitamin-enriched, high-protein diet, the disease was arrested.

The Road to Excellence

Scott first became interested in ice skating shortly after his return to Bowling Green from the hospital. Even though he had a feeding tube running from his nose to his stomach, he began skating with his sister. His natural ability captured the attention of the rink's skating professionals, who suggested that he sign up for lessons. Six months after Scott started skating, his life changed dramatically. He became a member of his elementary school's hockey team. He also began competing in local and regional skating contests. Most important, his body began to grow again as a result of the exercise that he was getting on the skating rink. Still, he was told he would always be shorter than other boys his age.

Scott's formal training began at the age of thirteen, when he left home to work with a former Olympic gold medalist named Pierre Brunet in

Rockton, Illinois. Over the next few years, Scott's education was interrupted many times as his training and competitions took him to all parts of the country. After graduating from high school, Scott decided to quit skating competitively and to enroll at Bowling Green State University because his parents could no longer afford to support him. However, a wealthy couple agreed to sponsor him, and Scott resumed his training under Carlo Fassi and Don Laws in Denver, Colorado.

Despite having some of the best trainers in the world, Scott did not work as hard as he should have. In 1977, for example, he finished a disappointing ninth at the U.S. National Figure Skating Champi-

Scott Hamilton performing at the World Figure Skating Championships in Helsinki, Finland, in 1983. (Juha Jormanainen/AFP/Getty Images)

onships. When his mother died a few months later, Scott remembered how much she had sacrificed for his career. Ashamed for having taken his talent for granted, Scott began to train in earnest.

The Emerging Champion

Scott's renewed enthusiasm and dedication transformed him into an entirely different skater over the next few years. Undaunted by a skating judge's observation that he was too short to ever be a serious contender, Scott simply altered his style so that he would appear to be taller. By 1980, Scott had improved so much that he took third place in the nationals and was chosen for the U.S. Olympic figure skating squad. His teammates were so impressed by Scott's perseverance that they asked him to lead the troupe into the arena on the opening day ceremonies at the 1980 Winter Games at Lake Placid, New York. He eventually placed a respectable fifth in competition.

Scott's goal for the next year was to win the national and world skating championships. In 1981, he easily won first place in the national championships in San Diego, California; the 1981 world competition, on the other hand, was much more difficult. His program got off to a bad start with a spill while he was running on the ice. Refusing to give in to frustration, Scott regained his composure and did so well that the judges awarded him first place anyway. Scott's primary goal for the next three years was to hold on to his national and world championships. In order to make his dream a reality, he practiced eight hours a day, six days a week. He also supplemented his technical training with dance lessons. As a result, he kept his national and world titles in 1982 and 1983. Experts hailed him as the United States' greatest hope for winning a gold medal in the 1984 Winter Olympics.

As he began preparing for the 1984 Olympics, Scott wanted to add an increased aura of masculinity to the sport. He rejected the two-piece uniform

Major Figure-Skating Championships

Year	Competition	Place
1976	U.S. National Junior Men's Championships	1st
1978	U.S. National Senior Men's Championships	3d
	World Championships	11th
1979	U.S. National Senior Men's Championships	4th
1980	U.S. National Senior Men's Championships	3d
	Olympic Games	5th
	World Championships	5th
1981	U.S. National Senior Men's Championships	1st
	World Championships	1st
1982	U.S. National Senior Men's Championships	1st
	World Championships	1st
1983	U.S. National Senior Men's Championships	1st
	World Championships	1st
1984	U.S. National Senior Men's Championships	1st
	Olympic Games	Gold
	World Championships	1st

worn by most figure skaters in favor of the one-piece uniform worn by speed skaters, because he was convinced that figure skating should be a sporting event instead of ballet. Nevertheless, the aesthetic element of his skating was so pronounced that he became the sport's only all-around performer, equally good at athleticism and artistry.

Even though Scott was heavily favored to win the gold medal in men's figure skating, he was totally unprepared for the tremendous pressure of Olympic competition. He placed first in the compulsory school figures but came in second to Brian Orser in the two-minute short program that includes seven required elements. His performance in the free-skating segment was even more disappointing: he scored only six 5.9's, compared to Orser's eleven. Nevertheless, Scott had accumulated enough points in the other two events to win the gold medal.

Continuing the Story

Scott did some serious self-examination after his victory at the 1984 Olympics. Because he had been taking antibiotics before the competitions, he seemed to have an excuse for his poor performance. Nevertheless, Scott placed the blame entirely on his own shoulders. Filled with the desire to prove to the world and to himself that he was indeed a true champion, Scott went on to win the world championship in Ottawa, Canada, a month later.

Scott retired from active competition soon after his victory at Ottawa because he realized that he was no longer willing to make the commitment

Honors and Awards

1987	Olympic Spirit Award
1990	Inducted into U.S. Olympic Hall of Fame
	Inducted into World Figure Skating Association Hall of Fame

that a contender has to make. In 1984, he signed on with the Ice Capades so that he could remain in the sport that he loved so much. Throughout the remainder of the decade, Scott delighted sold-out crowds with his enthusiastic performances. Then, in 1991, he became coproducer of "Discover Card Stars on Ice," which toured both the United States and Canada. Scott's likable personality also made him a popular television commentator for CBS from 1985 to 1998.

Scott also made solo appearances on various television specials. In December, 1990, Scott hosted a Home Box Office (HBO) special entitled *A Gold Medal Tradition: Lake Placid Figure Skating.* His easygoing personality and sense of humor have made him one of the most popular figure skating champions. Scott's childhood bout with disease was the primary impetus behind his involvement in tournaments that benefit children's charities. He became a strong supporter of drug prevention and rehabilitation.

In 1997, Scott faced another great struggle when he was diagnosed with testicular cancer. He was open with the news, and—with a positive attitude and the support of many friends, family, and fans—he decided to aggressively fight the cancer. After submitting to chemotherapy and surgery in June, 1998, he was given a clean bill of health and was back on the ice, performing, by October. He officially retired in 2001 but continued to skate.

At this point, Scott started dedicating even more of his time to charity causes and fund raising. He started the Scott Hamilton C.A.R.E.S. Initiative for cancer research and education; he sponsored the Scott Hamilton Circle of Friends Invitational Golf Tournament in benefit of Target House at St. Jude's Hospitals in Memphis, Tennessee; and he was in-volved in the March on Washington conducted by the National Coalition of Cancer Survivors. Other causes he supported are pediatric AIDS research, the Make-A-Wish Foundation, and animal rights. Scott married in 2002, and he and his wife have two children.

Scott's short stature was ideally suited to figure skating. Because he has a lower center of balance, Scott did not have as much body to adjust when he made a mistake. Thus, his ability to give seemingly flawless performances helped him to become the first American man to win three consecutive world titles since David Jenkins in 1957-1959. In 1984, he also became the first American man to win the men's single Olympic gold medal since David Jenkins in 1960.

Summary

Scott Hamilton's life is the story of one man's struggle to overcome his bodily weaknesses. With the support of his parents and coaches, Scott transformed himself from a sickly child into a strong athlete. By making the most of what he had, Scott triumphed over his physical shortcomings and over his opponents on the ice as well.

Alan Brown

Additional Sources

Hamilton, Scott, and Lorenzo Benet. *Landing It: My Life on and off the Ice.* New York: Kensington, 1999.

Hines, James R. *Figure Skating: A History.* Urbana: University of Illinois Press, 2006.

Shaughnessy, Linda. *Scott Hamilton: Fireworks on Ice.* Parsippany, N.J.: Crestwood House, 1998.

Shulman, Carole. *The Complete Book of Figure Skating.* Champaign, Ill.: Human Kinetics, 2002.

Paul Hamm

Born: September 24, 1982
     Washburn, Wisconsin
Also known as: Paul Elbert Hamm (full name)

Early Life

Paul Elbert Hamm grew up with his twin brother Morgan on a farm in Waukesha, Wisconsin. His father, Sandy, and his mother, Cecily, operated the farm. Both Paul and Morgan began learning gymnastics when they were both seven years old because their older sister Betsy was a gymnast. Sandy noticed their interest in gymnastics and built the twins gymnastics equipment using items found on the farm. He used an old maple tree, foam, and leather from a car to build a pommel horse; he hung rings in the attic of the farmhouse; he used a stairway railing for parallel bars; and he placed a trampoline in the barn. As Sandy realized Paul and Morgan were maintaining interest in gymnastics, he had the boys join the Swiss Turners gymnasium, where Stacy Maloney started coaching Paul.

The Road to Excellence

Paul enjoyed his childhood and maintained his love for gymnastics. In 1999, he competed in the United States Gymnastics Championships and finished eleventh in the all-around event. In 2000, he finished third in the all-around at the United States Gymnastics Championships and then qualified for the Olympic team by finishing second in the all-around and winning the pommel-horse events at the 2000 Olympic trials. He skipped the beginning of his senior year at Waukesha South High School to compete in the 2000 Olympic Games in Sydney, Australia, with his brother Morgan and finished fourteenth in the all-around event. Paul and Morgan were the first pair of twins to compete together for the U.S. Olympic team.

In 2001, at the World Gymnastics Championships, Paul continued to improve. He finished seventh in the all-around events, helping the U.S. team earn a silver medal, its second-ever medal at the World Gymnastics Championships. In 2002, Paul rose to elite status in the gymnastics world. He dominated the 2002 United States Gymnastics Championships by winning the all-around, pommel horse, and vault. His all-around victory also ended Blaine Wilson's streak of five consecutive national titles. At the 2002 World Gymnastics Championships, Paul finished third in the floor exercise.

The Emerging Champion

In 2003, Paul advanced in the gymnastics hierarchy by winning not only the all-around at the United States Gymnastics Championships but also both the all-around and the floor exercise at the World Gymnastics Championships in Anaheim, California. Paul won the all-around title by defeating China's Yang Wei. Entering the final rotation, Paul trailed Yang by .05 and performed a difficult high-bar routine to earn the title. Paul's victory was the first time an American male had won the all-around title and was the first medal performance since Kurt Thomas in 1979.

In 2004, Paul competed at the Olympic Games in Athens, Greece, and did not disappoint his con-

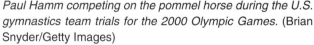

Paul Hamm competing on the pommel horse during the U.S. gymnastics team trials for the 2000 Olympic Games. (Brian Snyder/Getty Images)

Major Gymnastics Championships

Year	Competition	Event	Place
1999	United States Gymnastics Championships	All-around	11th
2000	United States Gymnastics Championships	All-around	3d
	U.S. Olympic trial	All-around	2d
		Pommel horse	2d
	Olympic Games	All-around	14th
2001	World Championships	All-around	7th
		Team	2d
2002	United States Gymnastics Championships	All-around	1st
		Pommel horse	1st
	United States Gymnastics Championships	Vault	1st
	World Championships	Floor exercise	3d
2003	World Championships	All-around	1st
		Floor exercise	1st
		Team	3d
2004	Olympic Games	All-around	Gold
		Team	Silver
		Horizontal bar	Silver
2007	United States Gymnastics Championships	Floor exercise	1st

stituency. Once again competing with his brother, Paul led the U.S. team to a silver medal in the team competition. Two day later, he competed in the all-around as the favorite. However, during the team competition, Paul had anchored the team by competing in eleven of the twelve events. His contribution to the team tired his body and his mind.

Paul started the all-around event solidly by winning the floor competition, finishing fourth in the pommel horse, and finishing eighth in the rings. However, in the fourth event, he fell while attempting his vault routine. The misstep dropped Paul to twelfth in the standings. However, after multiple errors by other gymnasts, Paul was able to win the last two events and capture the gold medal by a margin of .012, which was the closest finish in Olympic gymnastics history.

Continuing the Story

Just days after Paul won the all-around competition, the International Gymnastics Federation (IGF) determined that South Korean bronze medalist Yang Tae-young was unfairly docked .10 of a point on the parallel bars, while Paul scored a meet-high 9.837 in the final event. Yang's complaint was that the one-tenth taken off his start value was the difference between gold and bronze. The IGF agreed with Yang but could not change the results

of the event. Then IGF president Bruno Grandi sent a letter to Paul via the United States Olympic Committee (USOC) asking Paul to return his gold medal to portray the "ultimate demonstration of fair play by the whole world." The USOC did not grant IGF's request, stating that fault lay with the international organization. International Olympic Committee president Jacques Rogge also condemned IGF's request. After failing in his appeal, Yang appealed the decision to the Court of Arbitration for Sport (CAS) in Lausanne, Switzerland. On September 27, 2004, Paul appeared before the CAS in a hearing to decide Yang's appeal. The CAS ruled that Paul could keep his gold medal and the results were irreversible.

After the Olympic Games, both Paul and Morgan enrolled at Ohio State University but were ineligible to compete at the collegiate level. Paul did not stop practicing his gymnastics and won the floor competition at the 2007 United States Gymnastics Championships. He was set to compete in the 2008 Olympic Games in Beijing, China, when disaster struck for the champion gymnast. At the 2008 United States Gymnastics Championships in Houston, Texas, Paul had a big lead after the first day. However, during the competition, he broke his hand and was forced to miss not only the Olympic trials but also the Olympic Games.

Summary

Paul Hamm's journey to gymnastics stardom started humbly at his family's farm in Wisconsin. Despite the controversy surrounding his 2004 Olympic gold medal in the all-around, Paul ascended into the realm of U.S. gymnastics greats. He rejuvenated the U.S. gymnastics team to the level of international respectability. His impact was evident at the 2008 Olympics when the U.S. team shocked the world with a silver-medal winning performance.

Paul C. Alexander II

Additional Sources

Cazeneuve, Brian. "Break Point." *Sports Illustrated* 108, no. 22 (June 2, 2008).

Macur, Juliet. "Setback Forces Paul Hamm to Withdraw from U.S. Team." *The New York Times*, July 29, 2008.

Swift, E. M. "How the Fallen Was Mighty." *Sports Illustrated* 101, no. 8 (August 30, 2004).

Lis Hartel

Born: March 14, 1921
    Hellerup, Denmark
Also known as: Lis Hartel-Holst (full name); Lis
    Holst (birth name)

Early Life

Lis Holst was born on March 14, 1921, in Hellerup, Denmark. In a sense, she was born in the saddle, because her mother, Else Schmidt Holst, was an instructor in the Copenhagen Riding Club. Early in life, Lis became interested in dressage, the most exacting and difficult part of horse showmanship. Dressage is a kind of horse ballet requiring the highest degree of coordination and understanding between horse and rider. The rider must take the

Lis Hartel with her horse after winning a silver medal in dressage during the 1956 Olympics, whose equestrian events were held in Sweden. (Hulton Archive/Getty Images)

horse through all the tests without obvious effort and make it seem to the observer that the horse is in control of all movements and completely self-disciplined.

Before Lis's time, the field of dressage was completely dominated by men, often professional cavalry officers—this was a barrier she had to overcome. Despite this obstacle, Lis made remarkable progress. In 1943, at the age of twenty-two, and in 1944, she won the Danish National Prize in Dressage with her horse Gigolo. She repeated her triumph in 1952, 1954, and 1959.

The Road to Excellence

In 1944, Lis's future in dressage seemed assured. She and her husband, Poul Finn Hartel, whom she had married in 1941, were expecting their first child. Then tragedy struck: In September of that year Lis awoke with a headache and a strange stiffness in her neck. Then paralysis began to spread throughout her body. She was a victim of polio, a terrible and incurable disease that usually leaves its victim crippled.

Lis, however, was determined to overcome her great handicap and continue her career. She gave birth to a healthy daughter and, through constant exercise, gradually regained the use of her arms and the upper part of her body. She had to learn to do without the muscles below the knees, as they remained paralyzed. Trying to bring back the muscles necessary to keep her from falling was at first so hard that she had to rest for two weeks before she could try a second time. However, her efforts paid off. She regained her skill as a horsewoman.

The Emerging Champion

Just three years after the onset of the disease, Lis was able to compete in the Scandinavian Riding Contest, finishing second in women's dressage. She felt confident enough for the ultimate prize—individual dressage at the Olympic Games. She underwent strenuous training with the noted Scandinavian horseman, Gunnar Andersen. Luck was with Lis. The rules for Olympic dressage changed between 1948 and 1952, and, for the first time, women were allowed to compete. Lis was thrilled when, in 1952, she was chosen to represent Denmark in the Helsinki Olympics.

Even though Lis had to be helped on and off her horse, she won the silver medal in dressage, losing to the Swedish rider Henri Saint Cyr. When Saint Cyr helped Lis onto the victory platform for the medal presentation, it was a momentous and emotional occasion in Olympic history. Lis was the first woman to medal in the Olympic equestrian contest.

Continuing the Story

Only a small margin prevented Lis from winning the gold medal, and this disturbed many professionals in the field of dressage. Her graceful carriage, her firm mount, and, above all, her wonderful understanding of her horse convinced them that she should have been first. In 1954, in Aachen, Germany, she was named World Dressage Champion. In 1956, at the Stockholm Olympics, Lis again competed against Saint Cyr and again failed to win the gold medal by a slender margin: 860 to 850. Many felt the judges had been unfair. The German judge, for example, ranked the German riders first, second, and third; the Swedish judge did the same for the Swedish riders. As a compromise, the Swedish rider was given the gold medal, Lis was given the silver medal, and the German rider Liselott Linsenhoff was given the bronze medal.

Major Equestrian Championships

Year	Competition	Event	Place
1943-44, 1952, 1954, 1959	Danish National Prize	Dressage	1st
1947	Scandinavian Riding Contest	Women's dressage	2d
1952, 1956	Olympic Games	Individual dressage	Silver
1954	World Championship	Dressage	1st

Good sport that she was, Lis accepted the decision without complaint.

Stockholm was the last Olympics in which Lis participated. She became an instructor in a leading Danish riding school. More important, she traveled extensively through Europe, giving lectures to the physically challenged, assuring them through her example that, with will and effort, the greatest of handicaps could be overcome.

Summary

Lis Hartel was the first woman to break the male barrier in the Olympic equestrian events. Her feat was even more remarkable because of her battle with polio. Lis became an inspiration to many around the world.

Nis Petersen

Additional Sources

Slaughter, Jane R. *The Woman Equestrian*. Terre Haute, Ind.: Wish, 2003.

Smith, Lissa, ed. *Nike Is a Goddess: The History of Women in Sports*. New York: Grove Atlantic, 2001.

Wallechinsky, David, and Jaime Loucky. *The Complete Book of the Olympics: 2008 Edition*. London: Aurum Press, 2008.

413

Rudy Hartono

Badminton

Born: August 18, 1949
Surabaja, Indonesia
Also known as: Rudy Hartono Kurniawan (birth name)

Early Life

Rudy Hartono Kurniawan, known as Rudy Hartono, was born on August 18, 1949, in Surabaja, an eastern seaport city on the island of Java, the major island of Indonesia. Rudy grew up with seven brothers and sisters. One of his sisters, Utami Dewi, was a badminton champion, winning the national Singles Badminton Championship of Indonesia four times and playing on several Uber Cup teams (the women's international badminton team championship). Rudy's father worked hard in the dairy business to provide for his family. A good athlete himself, he made time to help all his children learn and play various sports, especially the national sport of Indonesia, badminton.

The Road to Excellence

Rudy began playing badminton when he was just seven years old under his father's tutelage. Rudy learned early the basics of good badminton: solid footwork and smooth movement around the court. As he grew older and stronger, he began to train every day after school at a local badminton club in Surabaja. Under the watchful eye of local coaches, Rudy trained extremely hard. He was disciplined as a young boy, as he already knew he wanted to be the best badminton player in the world. To accomplish that, Rudy knew, he would have to push himself both on the badminton court and off the court during his workouts.

Rudy sometimes played older, more powerful players for five hours at a time. He won easily when he played junior tournaments against opponents his own age because he was accustomed to playing boys much older and stronger. By the time Rudy was a teenager, he was one of the top players in the country. Rudy was more powerful, faster, stronger, and more agile than any other player in the country. Known as the "boy wonder," Rudy burst upon the international badminton scene as a seventeen-year-old player training year-round at the Indonesian National Badminton Center.

The Emerging Champion

When Indonesia and Malaysia squared off for the 1967 Thomas Cup—the men's international badminton team championships, played every three years—Rudy shocked the best players in the world by winning all of his matches. Although Malaysia would go on to win the 1967 Thomas Cup, in 1970, Rudy led Indonesia back to the Thomas Cup title. In 1968, Rudy began a domination of international badminton that would last for close to a decade. In 1968, at the age of eighteen, Rudy won his first All

Rudy Hartono. (Preben Soborg, Denmark)

414

Major Badminton Championships

1968-74, 1976, 1980	All England Badminton Championships
1970, 1973, 1976, 1979	Thomas Cup Championship team
1972	World Invitation Men's Singles Championship
1980	World Championship
1981	Japan Open Men's Championship

England Badminton Singles Championship—the unofficial world championship. He went on to win an incredible seven in a row from 1968 to 1974.

Rudy was a tireless worker. His love for badminton pushed him through incredibly demanding workouts. He believed that if he were in the best possible shape, the odds of losing were reduced. He was right. Rudy's hard work off the court made his play on the court look easy. Graceful, yet powerful, Rudy was once described as the world's most fit and perfect athlete. Because of his superior conditioning, Rudy was never completely out of a match. He felt he could wear down any player in the world.

Continuing the Story

Rudy achieved legendary status in his native Indonesia. He was a national hero and a role model for Indonesian youth. He appeared on television, starred in films, and even had his face on a postage stamp. His seven straight All England Singles Championships are still, and might always be, a record.

Rudy's gracious and classy style of play on the court endeared him to players and fans alike. In one of his last tournaments, the 1980 World Badminton Championships held in Jakarta, Indonesia, Rudy faced America's top player, Chris Kinard. In a match watched by fifteen thousand fans and a television audience, Rudy continued his dominance of the world by beating Kinard and later capturing the world championship.

In 1982, Rudy retired at thirty-three years old, quite old by badminton standards. The physical de-

mands of training, and a desire to spend more time with his wife and two children, Christopher and Christina, persuaded Rudy to give up full-time badminton. Although Rudy was no longer involved with badminton competitively, he continued to contribute to the sport. Players eager to follow in his footsteps copied his strenuous workouts and style of play. Rudy had a wonderful impact on the sport. His records, his physically demanding practices and workouts, and his gracious style of play are the standards by which all future champions would be compared. These standards would be difficult for some players to live up to. Liem Swie-King, the Indonesian world champion following Rudy, was always compared to and measured against Rudy, which was like a comparison with the great Babe Ruth in baseball.

Summary

For many people in the United States, badminton is something one plays on weekends in the backyard. However, in many parts of the world, especially Asian countries, badminton is the national sport. The simple mention of the name Rudy Hartono in those countries is equivalent to mentioning the great Pelé to soccer fans. Although it is difficult to say who was the greatest player in badminton history, Rudy, based on his record and achievements, is often considered the best ever to play.

Jon R. Poole

Additional Sources

Bloss, Margaret Varner, and R. Stanton Hales. *Badminton.* Boston: McGraw-Hill, 2001.

Fortin, François. *Sports: The Complete Visual Reference.* Buffalo, N.Y.: Firefly Books, 2000.

International Badminton Federation. *Sixty Years, 1936-1996: Sixtieth Jubilee Factbook.* Colorado Springs, Colo.: United States Badminton Association, 1996.

Levinson, David, and Karen Christensen, eds. *Encyclopedia of World Sport: From Ancient Times to the Present.* Santa Barbara, Calif.: ABC-Clio, 1996.

Doug Harvey

Born: December 19, 1924
   Montreal, Quebec, Canada
Died: December 26, 1989
   Montreal, Quebec, Canada
Also known as: Douglas Norman Harvey (full
   name)

Early Life

Douglas Norman Harvey was born in 1924, to Alfred and Martha Harvey in the Notre-Dame-de-Grâce neighborhood of Montreal, Quebec. Doug had a sister, Mary, and two brothers, Alfred, Jr., and Howard. All three Harvey boys were superb athletes, playing lacrosse, soccer, baseball, and ice hockey. Doug was a star in baseball and football, and at sixteen, he began to excel in hockey. In his senior year at West Hill High School, he helped lead the hockey team to an undefeated season and the league championship. In 1942, the Junior Royals, the Quebec Senior Hockey League farm team of the Montreal Canadiens, signed Doug. Doug also enlisted in the Royal Canadian Navy and

NHL Statistics

Season	GP	G	Ast.	Pts.	PIM
1947-48	35	4	4	8	32
1948-49	55	3	13	16	87
1949-50	70	4	20	24	76
1950-51	70	5	24	29	93
1951-52	68	6	23	29	82
1952-53	69	4	30	34	67
1953-54	68	8	29	37	110
1954-55	70	6	43	49	58
1955-56	62	5	39	44	60
1956-57	70	6	44	50	92
1957-58	68	9	32	41	131
1958-59	61	4	16	20	61
1959-60	66	6	21	27	45
1960-61	58	6	33	39	48
1961-62	69	6	24	30	42
1962-63	68	4	35	39	92
1963-64	14	0	2	2	10
1966-67	2	0	0	0	0
1968-69	70	2	20	22	30
Totals	1,113	88	452	540	1,216

Notes: GP = games played; G = goals; Ast. = assists; Pts. = points; PIM = penalties in minutes

was promptly assigned to the naval hockey team. Although occasionally stationed as a gunner on merchant ships, Doug spent much of the World War II years playing hockey. He also earned a most valuable player award for his contribution to the navy football team.

The Road to Excellence

After the war, Doug returned to the Royals, playing exclusively as a defenseman. In May, 1947, he helped the Royals win the Allan Cup. In 1947-1948, he played his first season in the NHL, with the Canadiens. With his exceptional skating skills and ability to control the puck, the left-handed-shooting Doug was a top prospect. However, his methodical style of play and ability to pace himself was taken for laziness. He seemed unfocused, playing semi-professional baseball in the off-season. He showed enough promise in that sport, however, to be drafted by the Boston Braves and offered a contract by the St. Louis Cardinals. In May, 1949, Doug married Ursula Hardie. Doug, Jr., the first of the couple's six children, was born in February, 1950.

The Emerging Champion

In the 1951-1952 season, Doug began to emerge as a champion. He was named to the NHL's all-star team for the first of eleven consecutive times. Over the following years, he became the leading defenseman in the league. In the 1954-1955 season, he won the James Norris Trophy for best defenseman. That same year, he became the first defenseman ever to have more than 40 assists, with 43. He became a leader for the Canadiens' exciting "firewagon," up-tempo, style of hockey. Starting in 1955-1956, the Canadiens won five consecutive Stanley Cups, dominating the league in every respect. Winning seven Norris Trophies in eight seasons, Doug showed a new way to play his position. He combined superb, combative defense in his own zone with a transition-oriented outlook and was always alert to make plays. On defense, he was strong, could block shots, and was hard to get around. When he got the puck, he took it up the ice, looking for a streaking forward to whom a pinpoint pass could mean a breakaway or a quick shot on the net. With his skating speed, he could insert himself into the offense; occasionally, he got past the opposing defense for a goal. He directed Montreal's power play so efficiently that the league changed the rules to allow only one score per penalty. In his ability to control the puck and the tempo of the game, Doug influenced the great Bobby Orr.

In his fourteen years with the Canadiens, Doug was selected to the first-team all-stars ten times. He won the Norris Trophy six times. He played in ten Stanley Cup finals; the Canadiens won six times. In his final year with the Canadiens, he became team captain.

Continuing the Story

Doug also tried to improve the lot of hockey players, who were essentially a poorly educated group controlled and manipulated by the team owners. In 1957, Doug, Detroit Red Wings player Ted Lindsay, and other player representatives announced the creation of a players association. Doug was vice president. The team owners reacted harshly, trading many of the players association leaders from their teams. Within a year, the association was defunct. Doug also lobbied for an improvement in player pensions.

In the spring of 1961, Doug was traded to the New York Rangers, becoming, by some accounts, the highest paid player in the league and also the player-coach of his new team. Doug brought a touch of the "firewagon" style to the Rangers. In the 1962-1963 season, the Rangers made a rare playoff appearance; Doug was again named an all-star and won his seventh Norris Trophy. The following year, he gave up coaching to concentrate on playing. However, with a decline in his skills, he was sent down to the minor leagues. He spent five years as a minor-league journeyman, playing a few games with the Red Wings during that time. In 1968-1969, at the age of forty-four, Doug spent his final hockey season as a player and assistant coach with the St. Louis Blues.

Retirement was not easy for Doug. His personality was always feisty and independent. Doctors eventually diagnosed Doug with bipolar disorder; his behavior was increasingly erratic. He drank heavily. He remained bitter toward the league's owners and officials and did not show up for his in-

Honors and Awards

1952-62, 1969	NHL All-Star
1955-58, 1960-62	Norris Trophy
1973	Inducted into Hockey Hall of Fame
1985	Uniform retired by the Montreal Canadiens

duction into the Hockey Hall of Fame in August, 1973. In 1980, Doug and his wife separated, and he began living with his girlfriend. He worked briefly for the World Hockey Association. In 1985, the Canadiens retired his jersey and hired him as a part-time scout. In 1988, Doug was diagnosed with cirrhosis of the liver. After eleven months in Montreal General Hospital, he died in December, 1989.

Summary

Doug Harvey is considered the greatest defenseman in the history of hockey before the arrival of Bobby Orr. In pure defensive ability, Doug had few rivals. He was an incredible natural athlete, becoming a star football and baseball prospect with his thoughtful, methodical approach to sport. He may well have been a successful Major League Baseball player. However, he chose ice hockey for his career and became one of the few players in its history to revolutionize his position. He initiated a transition offense, in which he carefully brought the puck up the ice, looking to direct an accurate pass on the fly to a streaking forward. Canadien forward Bernard "Boom Boom" Geoffrion said that Doug "changed the whole game." Doug also foreshadowed the modern world of professional sports in his fight to create a players association to get better wages and pensions for Canadian hockey players, who were often treated as commodities.

Howard Bromberg

Additional Sources

Brown, William. *Doug: The Doug Harvey Story.* Montreal: Véhicule Press, 2003.

McDonnell, Chris. *Hockey's Greatest Stars: Legends and Young Lions.* Buffalo, N.Y.: Firefly, 2007.

McFarlane, Brian. *Best of the Original Six.* Bolton, Ont.: Fern, 2004.

Robinson, Chris. *Stole This from a Hockey Card: A Philosophy of Hockey, Doug Harvey, Identity, and Booze.* Roberts Creek, B.C.: Nightwood Editors, 2005.

Dominik Hasek

Born: January 29, 1965
    Pardubice, Czechoslovakia (now in Czech
    Republic)
Also known as: The Dominator

Early Life

Dominik Hasek was born on January 29, 1965, in Pardubice, Czechoslovakia (now in Czech Republic). When he was six years old, his father took him to a hockey tryout. He did not have real skates; he had only blades that screwed onto the bottoms of his shoes. The team for which he was trying out was so impressed by his physical flexibility and agility that it made him its regular goaltender. By the time he was sixteen, Dominik was playing on the professional team in his hometown, Pardubice Tesla. He played on that team for eight years and was named Czech goalie of the year each season he played.

The Road to Excellence

Dominik was selected by the Chicago Blackhawks in the tenth round in the 1983 NHL draft. He played in Czechoslovakia for the next several years and did not make his NHL debut until November 6, 1990. Dominik played for Chicago for two seasons, and in 1992, he was traded to the Buffalo Sabres. After he was traded to the Sabres, his rise to stardom began. He played nine seasons with Buffalo, and in 1994-1995, he won the Jennings Trophy, awarded to the goaltender with the lowest goals against average. Furthermore, he won the Vezina Trophy, awarded to the goaltender voted most valuable to his team, five times in six years. During the 1995-1996 season, Dominik helped the Sabres to an Eastern Conference Championship and played in his first all-star game.

In the 1996-1997 season, Dominik became the Sabres' all-time leader in shutouts. That season, he won the Hart Trophy, given to the player voted most valuable to his team during the regular season. Dominik was the first goalie to win the Hart

Dominik Hasek celebrating the Detroit Red Wings' winning of the Stanley Cup in 2008. (Bruce Bennett/Getty Images)

NHL Statistics

Season	GP	W	L	T	GAA	PIM
1990-91	5	3	0	1	2.46	0
1991-92	20	10	4	1	2.60	8
1992-93	28	11	10	4	3.15	0
1993-94	58	30	20	6	1.95	6
1994-95	41	19	14	7	2.11	2
1995-96	59	22	30	6	2.83	6
1996-97	67	37	20	10	2.27	30
1997-98	72	33	23	13	2.09	12
1998-99	64	30	18	14	1.87	14
1999-00	35	15	11	6	2.21	12
2000-01	67	37	24	4	2.11	22
2001-02	65	41	15	8	2.17	22
2003-04	14	8	3	2	2.20	8
2005-06	43	28	10	0	2.09	2
2006-07	56	38	11	0	2.05	16
2007-08	41	27	10	0	2.14	20
Totals	735	389	223	82	2.20	170

Notes: GP = games played; W = wins; L = losses; T = ties; GAA = goals against average; PIM = penalties in minutes. 2004-05 NHL season canceled because of lockout.

Trophy since Jacques Plante in 1962. Furthermore, he won the Lester B. Pearson trophy awarded to the NHL's outstanding player during the regular season. In 1997-1998, he won the Hart and Pearson awards again.

The Emerging Champion

In the 1998 Winter Olympics in Nagano, Japan, Dominik distinguished himself as one of the world's best goalies while playing for the Czech Republic. In his team's semifinal win over Canada, he stopped all 5 of the Canadians' penalty shots in the overtime shootout. In the final game against the Soviet Union, he recorded 20 saves and helped the Czech team win the Olympic gold medal.

In 1998-1999, Dominik led Buffalo to the Eastern Conference Finals. The following season, Dominik helped the Sabres to the franchise's first Stanley Cup appearance in twenty years.

In July, 1999, Dominik announced his retirement from hockey. At the time of his announcement, he was known as "The Dominator" and for six consecutive seasons had been voted the most valuable player on the Sabres. Dominik retired at the

top of his game because he and his wife preferred to raise their children in the Czech Republic, where the children could learn about their heritage and know their family members. Moreover, Dominik did not enjoy the media attention in the United States.

At the time of his retirement, Dominik held every major goaltending record in the history of the Sabres. He had played the most games, 491; compiled the most wins, 234; and tallied the most shutouts, 41. He also had the best career goals against average.

Dominik returned to play for the Sabres during the 1999-2000 season. However, because of injury he missed most of the regular season. He was chosen for the all-star game, but the injury prevented him from playing. During the 2000-2001 season, Dominik won thirty-seven games. He had an excellent 2.11 goals against average, but the Sabres missed the playoffs. During the off-season he was traded to the Detroit Red Wings. He had his best season with Detroit in 2001-2002. He appeared in sixty-five games and won a league-leading forty-one of them. He played all of Detroit's twenty-three playoff games and recorded and NHL record of 6 shutouts. He led Detroit to a Stanley Cup, Dominik's first.

Dominik did not play in the 2002-2003 season, stating he wanted to spend more time with his family. He came back in 2003-2004 but played just fourteen games with Detroit because of injury. He did not play in the NHL in the 2004-2005 season because of the lockout. Then, he was traded to the Ottawa Senators, playing in forty-three games. That

Records and Milestones

1994   Set Buffalo Sabres record for shutouts in one season (7)

     Set Buffalo Sabres record (with Grant Fuhr) for team shutouts in one season

     Set Buffalo Sabres record for goals against average

     Set Buffalo Sabres record for save percentage

     First European-trained goaltender to lead the NHL in goals against average (1.95)

1998   Set Buffalo Sabres record for shutouts in one season (13)

2001   Set Buffalo Sabres records for career games played by a goaltender (491), career wins (234), career shutouts (55), and lowest goals against average (GAA; 2.22)

2002   Set Detroit Red Wings single-season playoff records for most games played by a goaltender (23), most minutes played by a goaltender (1,455), most shutouts (6), and most wins (16; record shared)

2008   Most career games (European-born goaltender; 735)

year, 2006, he represented the Czech Republic at the 2006 Olympics. In 2006-2007, he was traded back to Detroit, splitting the goaltending duties with Chris Osgood. In 2008, he won his second Stanley Cup, when Detroit beat the Pittsburgh Penguins.

Summary

Dominik Hasek is considered one of the greatest goaltenders ever to play professional hockey and was known for his unorthodox style of goaltending. He played in sixteen NHL seasons and in 735 games, winning 389 and recording 82 shutouts. His career goals against average was an outstanding 2.20. During his career, he played in the all-star game five times. Dominik won the Vezina Trophy an incredible six times and the Hart Trophy twice. He won the Pearson Trophy twice and the Jennings Trophy three times. At forty-three years of age, Dominik retired on June 9, 2008. He will be remembered as one of the greatest goalies in the NHL and will undoubtedly be inducted into the Hockey Hall of Fame.

Annita Marie Ward, updated by Timothy M. Sawicki

Honors and Awards

Year	Award
1981-89	Czechoslovakian Goaltender of the Year
1986-89	Czechoslovakian Player of the Year
1987-89, 1990-91	Czechoslovakian First-Team All-Star
1992	Upper Deck/NHL All Rookie Team
1993	*Hockey News* Goaltender of the Year
	Upper Deck Goaltender of the Year
	Sporting News Second Team All-Star
	All-Beckett Hockey Team
	All-Beckett Hockey Player of the Year
	Reeds Jewelers Most Popular Player award winner
	Memorial Trophy (team most valuable player, voted by teammates)
1993, 1995, 1997	Star of the Stars Trophy
1994-95, 1997-99, 2001	Vezina Trophy
1994, 2001	Jennings Trophy
1995	Official NHL First Team All-Star
	Sporting News All-Star First Team
	Frank Eddolls Memorial Trophy
1997	*Hockey News* All-Star Team, most valuable player
	Hockey News Player of the Year
	Hockey News Goalie of the Year
1997-98	Hart Memorial Trophy
	Lester B. Pearson Award
	NHL All-Star Team
1998	Voted starting goalie for World Team
	Gold medal with Czech Olympic team
1998-99	Official First Team All-Star
2000	NHL All-Star Team

Additional Sources

Burgan, Mike. *Dominik Hasek.* Broomall, Pa.: Chelsea House, 1999.

Caroll, Michael R. *The Concise Encyclopedia of Hockey.* Vancouver, B.C.: Greystone Books, 2001.

Dowbiggen, Bruce. *Of Ice and Men: Dominik Hasek, Chris Chelios, Steve Yzerman.* Toronto: Macfarlane, Walter, and Ross, 1999.

Hornsby, Lance. *Hockey's Greatest Moments.* Toronto: Key Porter Books, 2004.

Morrison, Scott. *By the Numbers.* Toronto: Key Porter Books, 2007.

Rossiter, Sean. *Dominik Hasek.* Vancouver, B.C.: Greystone Books, 1999.

Dale Hawerchuk

Born: April 4, 1963
> Toronto, Ontario, Canada

Also known as: Dale Martin Hawerchuk (full name); Ducky

Early Life

Dale Martin Hawerchuk was born to parents of Ukrainian ancestry on April 4, 1963, in Rexdale-Thistledown, a community within the city limits of Toronto, Ontario, Canada. When Dale was still an infant, his parents, Ed and Eleanor Hawerchuk, moved the family east to Oshawa. Like many youngsters in Canada, where ice hockey has been a national obsession for more than one hundred years, Dale received his first pair of ice skates when he was just a toddler and learned to skate before he could walk.

By the age of four, Dale had begun to play hockey competitively and showed excellent skating and stickhandling skills. He improved as he advanced through the various juvenile divisions: Mite, ages 3-4; Tyke, ages 4-6; Novice, ages 7-8; Atom, ages 9-10; Peewee, ages 11-12; Bantam, ages 13-14; and Midget, ages 15-17. At a Peewee tournament, he scored 8 goals in a game to set a national record.

The Road to Excellence

In 1978, Dale tried out for the Oshawa Generals, a junior team in the Ontario Hockey League, but did not make the club. The following year, however, the Cornwall Royals of the Quebec Major Junior Hockey League (QMJHL) selected him. Dale made an immediate impact, scoring 103 points during the 1979-1980 season to earn rookie of the year honors. During the QMJHL playoffs, he scored 45 points in eighteen games and was named most valuable player (MVP) while leading the Royals to the Memorial Cup championship. For his performance, Dale won the most sportsmanlike player award and made the QMJHL all-star team at left wing. The Royals represented Canada at the 1981 World Junior Hockey Tournament, where Dale tallied 9 points to tie for the scoring lead.

During the 1980-1981 season, Dale again dominated the QMJHL with 81 goals and 183 points. The Royals swept to another Memorial Cup championship behind Dale's tournament record 8 goals. He was selected for the QMJHL all-star team, named Canadian major junior player of the year, and was Memorial Cup MVP and the tournament's all-star center. After his outstanding performance in major junior hockey, Dale was destined for better things. He was ready for the big leagues.

Dale Hawerchuk skating in an NHL game in late 1991. (Rick Stewart/Getty Images)

NHL Statistics

Season	GP	G	Ast.	Pts.	PIM
1981-82	80	45	58	103	47
1982-83	79	40	51	91	31
1983-84	80	37	65	102	73
1984-85	80	53	77	130	74
1985-86	80	46	59	105	44
1986-87	80	47	53	100	54
1987-88	80	44	77	121	59
1988-89	75	41	55	96	28
1989-90	79	26	55	81	70
1990-91	80	31	58	89	32
1991-92	77	23	75	98	27
1992-93	81	16	80	96	52
1993-94	81	35	51	86	91
1994-95	23	5	11	16	2
1995-96	82	17	44	61	26
1996-97	51	12	22	32	32
Totals	1,188	518	891	1,409	742

Notes: GP = games played; G = goals; Ast. = assists; Pts. = points; PIM = penalties in minutes

The Emerging Champion

During the 1981-1982 season, the NHL Winnipeg Jets (later the Phoenix Coyotes), possessor of the first overall pick in the draft because of a last-place finish in the previous season, selected Dale. He quickly paid dividends, leading the team to one of the most startling turnarounds in NHL history: a 48-point improvement. Dale scored 45 goals and handed out 58 assists for 103 points to become the youngest player in league history to break the 100-point barrier, a feat unequaled until 2006, when Sidney Crosby of the Pittsburgh Penguins broke the mark. Dale was named rookie of the year and an all-star.

During nine seasons with Winnipeg, from 1981 to 1990, Dale gained a reputation as one of the NHL's best forwards. He topped 100 points six times, including four consecutive seasons, 1983-1988, and led the Jets in scoring. His best season was 1984-1985, when he scored 53 goals and 77 assists for 130 points. In 1982, 1986, and 1989, he was a member of Team Canada at the Ice Hockey World Championships, helping the team to two bronze medals and one silver medal. In 1987, he was a key member of Team Canada at the 1987 Canada Cup tournament and was named the MVP of the deciding championship game.

Despite his skills as a playmaker and goal scorer,

he was never able to inspire the team to the Stanley Cup because of powerful division rivals the Edmonton Oilers and the Calgary Flames. Before the 1990-1991 hockey season, he was traded to the Buffalo Sabres.

Continuing the Story

In his first season in Buffalo, Dale scored 31 goals and dished out 58 assists, for a respectable 89 points, while recording his 1000th career NHL point. He was also a significant contributor to the Team Canada championship effort at the 1991 Canada Cup.

In five seasons with the Sabres, 1990-1995, Dale amassed 375 points in 323 games. However, injuries had diminished his skills, and in 1995, the St. Louis Blues signed him as a free agent. Toward the end of that season, he was traded to the Philadelphia Flyers. Injuries again took their toll, and Dale retired in 1997, after playing in 1,188 NHL games and compiling 518 goals, 891 assists, and 1,409 points. When his playing career ended, Dale ranked twenty-first all-time in the NHL in goals scored and tenth in assists and total points. He was inducted into the Hockey Hall of Fame in 2001.

Though Dale had left competition, he did not vanish from the consciousness of Canada's faithful hockey fans: In 2005, a Quebec rock band, Les Dales Hawerchuk, released an album in his honor. Nor did Dale stray far from hockey. He became associated with the Orangeville Crushers of the Ontario Provincial Junior A Hockey League, first as president and primary owner, then as director of hockey operations. In 2007, his name was installed in the Phoenix Coyotes' Ring of Honor. In 2008, he was elected as a second vice chairman of the Ontario Provincial Junior A Hockey League.

Honors and Awards

1981	Memorial Cup most valuable player
	Canadian Major-Junior Player of the Year
1982	Calder Memorial Trophy Winner
	Bronze medal, World Championships
1986	Bronze medal, World Championships
1987	Canada Cup Championships
1989	Silver medal, World Championships
1991	Canada Cup Championships
2001	Inducted into Hockey Hall of Fame

Summary

One of the premier scoring and playmaking centers in the NHL from the early 1980's to the early 1990's, Dale Hawerchuk was the youngest player to score 100 points until 2006. He had the misfortune of playing for mediocre teams throughout his professional career. As a consequence, he appeared in only one Stanley Cup final, in his last season of competition. Though injuries cut short his career, he finished with more than 1,400 points and was elected to the Hockey Hall of Fame.

Jack Ewing

Additional Sources

Anderson, H. J. *The Canada Cup of Hockey Fact and Stat Book.* Victoria, B.C.: Trafford, 2005.

Conner, Floyd. *Hockey's Most Wanted: The Top Ten Book of Wicked Slapshots, Bruising Goons, and Ice Oddities.* Dulles, Va.: Potomac Books, 2002.

Pelletier, Joe, and Patrick Houda. *World Cup of Hockey: A History of Hockey's Greatest Tournament.* Toronto, Ont.: Warwick, 2004.

Taylor, Scott. *The Winnipeg Jets: A Celebration of Hockey in Winnipeg.* Winnipeg, Man.: Studio Books, 2007.

Bob Hayes

Born: December 20, 1942
      Jacksonville, Florida
Died: September 18, 2002
      Jacksonville, Florida
Also known as: Robert Lee Hayes (full name);
   Bullet Bob
Other major sport: Football

Early Life

Robert "Bob" Lee Hayes was born in Jacksonville, Florida, on December 20, 1942. Bob said that his mother, Mary Hayes, considered him a lazy boy. He took a long time to learn to walk as a baby. Bob got along well with his elder brother Ernest, who dreamed of becoming a professional boxer. Bob's first exposure to athletics was accompanying Ernest on road runs to build up leg strength and stamina. At Matthew W. Gilbert High School in Jacksonville, Bob found his athletic outlet. He joined the football team and found that his powerful physique and blazing speed made him an exceptional performer.

The Road to Excellence

Soon, the speed Bob demonstrated on the football field attracted the attention of the high school track team. Bob recalls a challenge race—the winner was to receive a nickel—in which he beat the track team's top sprinter by five yards. Head track coach Bill Cannon knew he had a remarkable talent when he first watched Bob in action. Cannon was convinced that, on a good track and in ideal conditions, Bob could run a 9.5-second 100-yard dash. Bob performed nearly as well in the 220 yards and was a fearsome anchor runner in the 440-yard relay team. His best high school time was 9.6 seconds for the 100 yards. Jake Gaither, the head football coach at Florida Agricultural and Mechanical University (Florida A&M), in Tallahassee, Florida, vigorously recruited Bob. After graduating from high school in the summer of 1960, Bob enrolled at Florida A&M.

The Emerging Champion

Bob was the star halfback for the Rattlers and eventually led the team in rushing yards, pass receptions, and touchdowns. Despite the fact that football was Bob's favorite athletic pursuit, it was in sprinting that he displayed his championship ability. In June, 1961, in Sioux Falls, South Dakota, Bob equaled the world record for the 100 yards with a time of 9.3 seconds.

In 1963, Bob enjoyed an even more successful year with two world records. Indoors he ran the 70 yards in 6.9 seconds, and outdoors he clocked an amazing 9.1 seconds for the 100 yards. In some circles, he was dubbed "The World's Fastest Human." A year later, in 1964, Bob set another world record with a time of 5.9 seconds for the 60-yard indoor dash. *Sports Illustrated* writer John Underwood, in a May 18, 1964, profile of Bob, captured

Bob Hayes. (Courtesy of Amateur Athletic Foundation of Los Angeles)

the unique running style of an athlete who, though well built, could fly over the ground: "Hayes does not run a race so much as he appears to beat it to death . . . the wonder then is not the completion of the trip so much as the speed of it."

At the 1964 Olympics in Tokyo, Japan, Bob was the favorite. Still, favorites, especially in the dash, had been upset before. Four years previously at the Rome Olympics, Ray Norton of the United States was expected to take the gold and instead finished last in the 100 meters. With Bob, however, his triumph was spectacular. He ran in 10.00 seconds to equal the world and Olympic record. His winning margin of two meters was the greatest in the Olympic history of the event. Bob's greatest moment may have been six days later, when he ran a magical anchor leg for the U.S. 4×100-meter relay team. He received the baton in fifth place, three meters behind the leader, and at the finish line was the winner by three meters. In that one performance, Bob may have run faster than any human being before or since. One watch had him clocked at 8.9 seconds for his 100-meter leg.

Continuing the Story

On December 8, 1964, Dallas Cowboys general manager Tex Schramm signed Bob to a two-year contract. There were those who felt that Bob would not make it in the National Football League (NFL). Other great track runners—for example, Ray Norton and Frank Budd—had tried and failed. What was ignored was the fact that Bob's first love was football and that he had been a star football player in high school.

Early in 1965, Bob played poorly. He repeatedly fumbled the ball. Nevertheless, he worked and practiced for hours at a time until he was the major offensive weapon for the Dallas Cowboys. His statistics for his rookie season silenced the critics who had talked of Bob's blazing feet and buttery hands. Bob, in fourteen games, caught 46 passes for more than

Major Sprint Championships

Year	Competition	Event	Place	Time
1963	National AAU Outdoor Championships	100 meters	1st	9.1
1964	Olympic Games	100 meters	Gold	10.0 WR, OR
		4×100-meter relay	Gold	39.0 WR, OR
	NCAA Outdoor Championships	200 meters	1st	20.4
	National AAU Indoor Championships	60 yards	1st	5.9 WR
	National AAU Outdoor Championships	100 meters	1st	10.3

Notes: OR = Olympic Record; WR = World Record

National Football League Statistics

Season	GP	Rec.	Yds.	Avg.	TD
1965	13	46	1,003	21.8	12
1966	14	64	1,232	19.3	13
1967	13	49	998	20.4	10
1968	14	53	909	17.2	10
1969	10	40	746	18.7	4
1970	13	34	889	26.1	10
1971	14	35	840	24.0	8
1972	12	15	200	13.3	0
1973	13	22	360	16.4	3
1974	12	7	118	16.9	1
Totals	128	365	7,295	19.9	71

Notes: GP = games played; Rec. = receptions; Yds. = yards; Avg. = average yards per reception; TD = touchdowns

Records

Equaled the world record for 100 yards in 1961 (9.3 seconds)

Set a world indoor record at 70 yards in 1963 (6.9 seconds)

Set a world outdoor record at 100 yards in 1963 (9.1 seconds)

Set a world indoor record at 60 yards in 1964 (5.9 seconds)

Holds the NFL record for the highest average in yards per punt return in a postseason game, 47.0 (1967)

Honors and Awards

1962	Inducted into Florida Sports Hall of Fame
1963	Dieges Award
1965	Inducted into Helms Athletic Foundation Track and Field Hall of Fame
1965-68	*Sporting News* NFL Eastern Conference All-Star Team
1966-68	NFL Pro Bowl Team
1966, 1968	NFL All-Pro Team
1976	Inducted into USA Track and Field Hall of Fame

1,000 yards and 12 touchdowns. After more than a decade of success as a Cowboy, Bob retired from football. His subsequent career hit rock bottom, however, when he pleaded guilty to selling cocaine. He died of kidney failure in 2002. Two years later, he narrowly missed election to the Pro Football Hall of Fame.

Summary

At the 1964 Olympics, Bob Hayes rocketed to two gold medals and subsequently achieved star status as a receiver for the Dallas Cowboys. Despite the tragedy of his conviction for drug trafficking and a jail sentence, his athletic feats were remarkable. Many friends from his athletic past rallied around him, hoping to assist Bob in reestablishing his life.

Arthur Ashe, the former Wimbledon champion, noted in his *A Hard Road to Glory* (1988) that Bob was "filled with remorse for his deed."

Scott A. G. M. Crawford

Additional Sources

Carroll, Bob. *Total Football: The Official Encyclopedia of the National Football League.* New York: Harper-Collins, 1999.

Hayes, Bob, and Robert Pack. *Run, Bullet, Run: The Rise, Fall, and Recovery of Bob Hayes.* New York: Harper & Row, 1990.

Wallechinsky, David, and Jaime Loucky. *The Complete Book of the Olympics: 2008 Edition.* London: Aurum Press, 2008.

Chad Hedrick

Born: April 17, 1977
      Spring, Texas
Also known as: The Exception
Other major sport: In-line skating

Early Life

Chad Hedrick was born in Spring, Texas, on April 17, 1977. His parents owned a roller rink, where Chad started skating at seventeen months old. Chad's talent on traditional four-wheel roller skates was recognized at an early age, and he was outskating children three times his age by the time he was two.

Chad's father was the coach of the local roller-skate speed-racing team. As soon as Chad was old enough, he joined the team and began his lifelong career of speed racing. By the age of eight, Chad won his first national championship. At ten years old, he was devoted to the sport and, with the support of his parents, practiced 6 to 7 hours every day.

In the late 1980's and early 1990's, in-line skates were introduced into the marketplace, forever changing the roller rink and roller-skating culture. Rather than the traditional roller skates that placed two sets of wheels side by side, in-line skates consisted of four thin wheels in a row, which allowed for greater speed and agility. In-line skates were also more conducive to skating long distances and skating outdoors, resulting in the birth of a new outdoor-racing scene of long courses and high prize money. As with speed skating, because of his competitive nature Chad immediately embraced and excelled in the new sport.

The Road to Excellence

Adapting to the new equipment and necessary changes in techniques, Chad was able to master in-line skating quickly. In 1993, at fifteen, he easily qualified for the U.S. junior national team; at the age of sixteen, Chad became the youngest skater to join the senior national team. That same year, 1994, he won his first world championship.

Chad is credited with developing a skating technique to increase speed that initially was dubbed "The Scissors" or "The Chad." Coaches and officials dismissed the technique as unconventional, but the technique quickly became a standard in the sport and was renamed the "Double Push" or the "DP." Suddenly every serious in-line speed skater began copying the technique in order to remain competitive.

Chad, an intense competitor, continued to dominate the sport, winning every world championship title available while racing on the top in-line teams, Rollerblade and Hyper. In 2000, Chad won his fiftieth world championship title in Oostende, Belgium, setting a world record.

The Emerging Champion

While at the height of his in-line racing career, Chad needed further incentive and inspiration to remain competitive. He began seeking new challenges and trials. Chad discovered his new passion when he watched fellow in-line skater Derek Parra win a gold medal in the 1,500-meter speed-skating heat at the 2002 Salt Lake City, Utah, Olympic Games. Chad became obsessed with conquering this new challenge and worked hard to master this new sport.

Chad Hedrick competing in Germany in early 2008. (John Mac-Dougall/AFP/Getty Images)

World In-Line Skating Championships

Year	Event	Place
1994	20,000 meters (track)	2d
1994-95, 1997-98	1,500 meters (track)	1st
1995	Marathon	1st
1995-96	20,000 meters (road)	1st
1995-97, 1999-2001	10,000 meters (road)	1st
1995-2001	10,000 meters (track)	1st
1996	1,500 meters (track)	2d
	5,000 meters (track)	1st
1996-98	1,500 meters (road)	1st
1996, 1998-99	500 meters (track)	2d
1996-2000, 2002	20,000 meters (track)	1st
1997	Marathon	3d
	300-meter time trial	2d
	5,000 meters (road)	2d
	5,000 meters (track)	2d
1997, 1999, 2001	20,000 meters (road)	1st
1998	Marathon	2d
	300-meter time trial	3d
	10,000 meters (road)	3d
1998-99, 2001	15,000 meters (track)	1st
1998, 2000	15,000 meters (road)	1st
1999	1,000 meters (road)	1st
1999, 2001-02	1,000 meters (track)	1st
	500 meters (road)	2d
2000	1,000 meters (track)	2d
	20,000 meters (road)	3d
2000-01	1,000 meters (road)	2d

The transition was not an easy one, but with his determination, Chad qualified for the U.S. national team after only three months on the ice. A little more than one year after making the team, Chad became the third American to win the World Allround Speed Skating Championships in Hamar, Norway, as well as winning World Cup races. In 2004, he won the World Single Distance Championships in Seoul, South Korea. In 2005, Inzell, Germany, Chad retained his 5,000-meter world title but lost the all-around speed-skating title to fellow American Shani Davis.

Continuing the Story

As the 2006 Torino, Italy, Winter Olympics approached, Chad found himself in the best condition of his career. Before the Games, he had set world records in the 1,500-, 5,000-, and 10,000-meter sprints. At the 2006 Olympics, he won a gold medal in the 5,000 meters, a silver medal in the 10,000 meters, and a bronze medal in the 1,500 meters, becoming only the third American, after Eric Heiden and Sheila Young, to win medals in all three events in one Olympic Games.

After the 2006 Olympics, Chad won a 1,500-meter race in the Netherlands and earned the World Cup title in that event. Chad attempted to win the all-around championships in Calgary, Alberta, Canada, but made a crucial mistake, turning into the inner lane of the track instead of his scheduled outer lane, and was motioned off the track.

Summary

Chad Hedrick excelled in in-line skating and speed skating throughout his career. Not only did he enhance the sports with his enthusiasm and passion, but also he helped to popularize the sports across the United States. In his career, he won ninety-three national championships and fifty world championships. He pioneered the Double Push technique, which enables in-line skaters to increase their speed, and had a brand of in-line skates named after him. In 2005, Chad's contributions and talents in speed skating were recognized when he was awarded the Oscar Mathisen Memorial Trophy, becoming the third American, behind Bonnie Blair and Eric Heiden, to receive the honor.

Sara Vidar

Additional Sources

Marsico, Katie. *Speed Skating.* Lafayette, La.: Cherry Lake, 2008.

Powell, Mark. *In-Line Skating.* Champaign, Ill.: Human Kinetics, 1997.

Publow, Barry. *Speed on Skates: A Complete Technique, Training, and Racing Guide for In-Line and Ice Skaters.* Champaign, Ill.: Human Kinetics, 1999.

Speed-Skating Championships

Year	Competition	Event	Place
2004	World Championships	Allround	1st
		5,000 meters	1st
		10,000 meters	3d
2005	World Championships	Allround	2d
		5,000 meters	1st
		10,000 meters	3d
2006	Olympic Games	5,000 meters	Gold
		10,000 meters	Silver
		1,500 meters	Bronze

Eric Heiden

Born: June 14, 1958
    Madison, Wisconsin
Also known as: Eric Arthur Heiden (full name)

Early Life

Eric Arthur Heiden was born on June 14, 1958, in Madison, Wisconsin. He grew up in a family of skaters. Encouraged by his parents and supported by the well-organized local skating clubs, Eric and his younger sister, Beth, began skating almost as soon as they could walk. By the time Eric was fourteen he was totally committed to ice skating and devoted all of his time to the sport. Beth also would develop into a world-class competitive speed skater.

In 1972, Eric's training took a dramatic turn when Dianne Holum, an Olympic speed skating champion (1968 and 1972), moved to Madison, took notice of Eric, and started him on a training program that prepared him for greatness. Coach Holum's training stressed "dry-land exercises," particularly bicycling, weightlifting, and duckwalking, all exercises designed to increase Eric's already enormous upper-leg strength and endurance.

Eric Heiden in 1980. (AP/Wide World Photos)

The Road to Excellence

By the time Eric reached his full height of 6 feet 1 inch in his late teens, he had a 32-inch waist and 27-inch thighs, making him a strong competitor. However, speed skating also requires flawless technique, for the skater must be able to build speed and then maintain it through the straightaways and grueling turns of the rink. Eric's winning technique was based on his ability to accelerate through the turns, a technique he learned under Holum's guidance. During training, Holum simulated the rink turns on a track. First she would tie a length of surgical tubing around Eric's waist. Then, while she held onto the other end of the tubing and leaned back, Eric would duckwalk in a skater's stance as if he were negotiating turns on the ice.

This early training was exhausting, but Eric always trained harder and longer than any of his teammates. Teammates and coaches respected him not only for his tremendous strength but also for his total commitment to becoming the fastest skater in the world. He was, as one of his coaches remarked, "very mind-strong." Eric trained always with his eyes focused toward the Olympics, but he decided early that winning the World Speed Skating Championships was "the true meaning of success." His first entry into international competition was in the 1975 Junior World Speed Skating Championship in Sweden, where he placed tenth. At the 1976 Winter Olympics in Innsbruck, Austria, he placed a respectable seventh in the 1,500-meter and nineteenth in the 5,000-meter events.

The Emerging Champion

In the 1977 World Speed Skating Championships, in Heerenveen, the Netherlands, Eric won the overall title at the age of nineteen, the first American to do so in the seventy-six-year history of the event. That same year, he won the World Sprint Championship and the World Junior Speed Skating Championship. Suddenly, the skating world took notice.

Between 1977 and the 1980 Winter Olympic Games at Lake Placid, New York, Eric won nine world titles: two Junior World Speed Skating Championships, three World Speed Skating Championships, and four World Sprint Skating Championships. He won his races by unprecedented margins, leading one writer to call him the "Secretariat of speed skating," after the racehorse renowned for his record-setting performances. By the time he won his third straight world overall title in Oslo, Norway, in February, 1979, Eric had achieved international superstar status. In a scoring system where a winning margin of one point is considered

significant, Eric finished 4.8 points ahead of the second-place finisher, Jan-Egil Storholt of Norway; only 4.2 points separated Storholt from the fifteenth-place finisher. Eric had clearly become the greatest skater of his day. After his overwhelming victory in Oslo, the U.S. ambassador to Norway honored Eric's achievement by appointing him honorary sports ambassador to Norway.

Continuing the Story

When Eric arrived for the Winter Olympic Games at Lake Placid in February, 1980, he knew the rink well, having won the World Sprint Championships there only the week before. When the Games were over, Eric had five gold medals, in the 500, 1,000, 1,500, 5,000, and 10,000 meters. Eric's domination of his sport was without precedent. Never before had one athlete been consistently able to sweep all the world titles in both speed and sprint skating, where different skills and techniques are required. Often winners and losers are separated by mere hundredths of a second—it is a supreme test of speed and nerves.

Soft-spoken, unfazed by pressure, completely confident in his preparation, Eric possessed the winning combination of strong body and mind required to propel him to victory at all levels of competition. The 1980 Winter Olympics marked the end of Eric's competitive skating career. Immediately after the Winter Games, he turned his attention to cycling and qualified as an alternate for the 1980 U.S. Olympic cycling team. From 1981 to 1986, he raced as a professional cyclist and competed in the 1986 Tour de France.

While at the University of Wisconsin, Eric had majored in pre-medicine, and in 1986, he entered Stanford University Medical School, specializing in sports and orthopedic medicine. He was the team physician for the 2002 and 2006 U.S. Olympic speed skating team. He also served as team doctor for the National Basketball Association's (NBA's) Sacramento Kings. He has been inducted into both the National Speedskating Hall of Fame and the U.S. Bicycling Hall of Fame.

Summary

Those who witnessed Eric Heiden's success in the 1980 Olympics will long remember his powerful grace and his sincere humility in victory. His greatest contribution to his sport, in addition to his

Major Speed-Skating Championships

Year	Competition	Event	Place
1976	Olympic Games	1,500 meters	7th
		5,000 meters	19th
1977	World Championships	Overall	1st
		500 meters	1st
		1,500 meters	3d
		5,000 meters	9th
		10,000 meters	3d
	World Sprint Championships	Overall	1st
		500 meters #1	2d
		500 meters #2	6th
		1,000 meters #1	1st
		1,000 meters #2	1st
1978	World All-Around Championships	Overall	1st
		500 meters	1st
		1,500 meters	1st
		5,000 meters	1st
		10,000 meters	5th
	World Sprint Championships	Overall	1st
		500 meters #1	1st
		500 meters #2	2d
		1,000 meters #1	1st
		1,000 meters #2	1st
1979	World All-Around Championships	Overall	1st
		500 meters	1st
		1,500 meters	1st
		5,000 meters	1st
		10,000 meters	1st
	World Sprint Championships	Overall	1st
		500 meters #1	1st
		500 meters #2	1st
		1,000 meters #1	1st
		1,000 meters #2	1st
1980	Olympic Games	500 meters	Gold
		1,000 meters	Gold
		1,500 meters	Gold
		5,000 meters	Gold
		10,000 meters	Gold

world records, may be that he almost single-handedly rekindled the American public's interest in speed skating. After retiring from speed skating, he continued to personify in his private life and career the values of hard work and dedication that any athlete must possess to be a true champion.

William C. Griffin

Record

Set world records in the 500, 1,000, 1,500, 3,000, and 10,000 meters

Honors and Awards

1980   James E. Sullivan Award
1983   Inducted into U.S. Olympic Hall of Fame
1990   Inducted into Wisconsin Sports Hall of Fame

Additional Sources

Cazeneuve, Brian. "Eric Heiden." *Sports Illustrated* 101, no. 2 (July 12, 2004): 134.

Cook, Stephanie. "Speed Skater Eric Heiden." *Christian Science Monitor* 92, no. 249 (2000).

Publow, Barry. *Speed on Skates.* Champaign, Ill.: Human Kinetics, 1999.

Uschan, Michael V. *Male Olympic Champions.* San Diego, Calif.: Lucent Books, 2000.

Wallechinsky, David, and Jaime Loucky. *The Complete Book of the Winter Olympics.* Wilmington, Del.: Sport Media, 2005.

Carol Heiss

Born: January 20, 1940
New York, New York
Also known as: Carol Elizabeth Heiss (birth name); Carol Elizabeth Heiss Jenkins (full name)

Early Life

Carol Elizabeth Heiss, the first child of Edward Heiss, a baker, and Marie Gademann Heiss, a textile designer, was born on January 20, 1940, in New York City. Her parents both emigrated from Germany to the United States, where they met and married. Carol had a younger sister and brother who also became excellent competitive skaters. The Heiss family lived in Ozone Park, close to New York City, in a seven-room, white stucco house.

Carol tried on her first pair of roller skates in the family's basement when she was only three and one-half years old. She found her balance and skated on her own almost immediately. Realizing that Carol had a special gift, her parents soon enrolled their daughter in ice skating classes, and she appeared in her first ice show before she was old enough for school.

The Road to Excellence

Carol's parents took her to the Junior Figure Skating Club in New York City to skate for coaches Andree and Pierre Brunet, former Olympic pairs champions. The Brunets immediately spotted Carol's potential. She possessed enormous natural talent, but even more important, they felt she had the nerve and heart of a true champion. Andree coached Carol until she was seven, when her husband, Pierre, took over. He predicted that, with hard work, Carol could be "on top" in ten years, and from that time on Carol worked toward that goal. The road to the top was grueling and not without detours. Carol practiced five to eight hours every day, studied piano to get a better feel for music, took dance lessons to improve her grace and rhythm, and attended school.

At the age of ten, Carol entered her first important figure skating competition, the Middle Atlantic Ladies Pairs Championship, with her sister Nancy. They placed first, and the next day Carol won the Junior Ladies Singles title as well. These victories marked the beginning of years of winning titles and trophies. At eleven, Carol won the National Novice Ladies title, and at twelve, the National Junior Ladies Championship. She was also the youngest member of the U.S. team at the World Figure Skating Championships at Davos, Switzerland, placing fourth.

Carol's career took a detour on January 1, 1954, when she collided with her sister Nancy during practice and Nancy's skate cut a deep gash into the muscle of Carol's left leg, severing a tendon below the calf. The doctors said she might never skate again, but, like a true champion, she came back to place second to fellow teammate and chief rival Tenley Albright in the 1955 World Figure Skating Championships. Carol's success in the 1955 competition, however, was overshadowed by the discovery that her mother, her greatest inspiration and biggest fan, was suffering from cancer.

Carol Heiss in 1960. (Hulton Archive/Getty Images)

Major Figure-Skating Championships

Year	Competition	Place
1951	U.S. National Novice Ladies Championships	1st
1952	U.S. National Junior Ladies Championships	1st
1953	U.S. National Senior Ladies Championships	2d
	World Championships	4th
1954	U.S. National Senior Ladies Championships	2d
1955	U.S. National Senior Ladies Championships	2d
	World Championships	2d
1956	U.S. National Senior Ladies Championships	2d
	Olympic Games	Silver
	World Championships	1st
1957	U.S. National Senior Ladies Championships	1st
	North American Championships	1st
	World Championships	1st
1958	U.S. National Senior Ladies Championships	1st
	World Championships	1st
1959	U.S. National Senior Ladies Championships	1st
	North American Championships	1st
	World Championships	1st
1960	U.S. National Senior Ladies Championships	1st
	Olympic Games	Gold
	World Championships	1st

The Emerging Champion

The 1956 Winter Olympics in Cortina d'Ampezzo, Italy, began a period of great trial as well as great success for Carol. The youngest woman ever to skate for the U.S. team in the Olympics, she hoped to win her first gold medal for her ailing mother. She almost succeeded, finishing just 1.5 points behind Tenley Albright to place a close second. Carol had another chance to take first place two weeks later at the World Figure Skating Championships in Germany, and this time she succeeded. The years of work and sacrifice had finally paid off, and Carol earned the gold medal she so desperately wanted for her mother.

Marie Heiss died on October 30, 1956, and Carol, although grieving, carried on. Carol practiced five hours every morning, attended classes at New York University in the afternoon, then hurried home to finish homework and housework before her 9:00 P.M. bedtime. Carol's chief competition, Albright, retired from skating in 1957, and Carol went on to win four straight world titles, four straight national titles, and two North American titles. Her primary goal was a gold medal at the 1960 Winter Olympics at Squaw Valley, California.

Carol prepared the most difficult program she could devise for the Olympics, including twenty of the twenty-six possible difficult jumps. In a brilliant red costume and with a tiara in her honey-blond hair, she dazzled the world with a spectacular display of skating. When she was finished, the crowd of 8,500 stood and cheered. Carol won the first gold medal awarded to an American in the 1960 Winter Olympic Games.

Continuing the Story

Carol returned to New York to a ticker-tape parade attended by 250,000 people and received a medal from the mayor, inscribed "To Carol Heiss, figure skater extraordinaire, inspiration to our youth, admired daughter of New York." Her skating dreams had all come true.

Four weeks after her Olympic victory, she announced her retirement from amateur skating, and on April 30, 1960, she married figure skater Hayes Alan Jenkins, the 1956 Olympic men's champion. Carol went to Hollywood to make a movie, *Snow White and the Three Stooges*, and then settled with her husband in Akron, Ohio. The couple had three children, and Carol went on to teach and coach.

Summary

Carol Heiss earned a special place in the hearts of Americans, not only because of her spectacular natural talent as a figure skater but also because of the determination, strength of character, and heart she showed under adversity. Through injury, illness, and the death of her mother, she continued working hard to achieve the goals she had set as a child.

Mary Virginia Davis

Additional Sources

Hines, James R. *Figure Skating: A History*. Urbana: University of Illinois Press, 2006.

Wallechinsky, David, and Jaime Loucky. *The Complete Book of the Winter Olympics*. Wilmington, Del.: Sport Media, 2005.

Woolum, Janet. *Outstanding Women Athletes: Who They Are and How They Influenced Sports in America*. Phoenix, Ariz.: Oryx Press, 1998.

Honors and Awards

1973	Inducted into Ice Skating Hall of Fame
1976	Inducted into U.S. Figure Skating Association Hall of Fame

Bud Held

Born: October 25, 1927
      Los Angeles, California
Also known as: Franklin Held (full name)

Early Life

Franklin "Bud" Held was born in Los Angeles, California, in 1927. As boys, Bud and his brother Dick played baseball constantly; their father spent hours training them in proper throwing technique. Bud attended Grossman High School in San Diego. At Grossman, he participated in pole-vaulting, a track and field event requiring superb technique. Although Bud was rated one of the best high school pole-vaulters in the nation, he was frustrated by the toll the sport took on his body. In 1948, he enrolled at Stanford University in Palo Alto, California, where he took up the sport of javelin throwing. He was a quick learner and, as a freshman, made a remarkable throw of 213 feet (64.92 meters).

The Road to Excellence

At 6 feet 1 inch and 165 pounds, Bud had a lean, muscular build well-suited for the javelin event, which requires both a fast run-up and a strong throw. Javelin throwing is one of the oldest known sports, related to hurling a spear, an essential skill for hunters and warriors in ancient civilizations. Modern-day specifications for javelin throwing are highly regulated, both to standardize the sport and to prevent injuries to judges and spectators. Male competitors use a javelin that weighs 800 grams (1 pound 12 ounces) and is 2.6 meters long (8 feet 6 inches). The javelin consists of three parts: a shaft, a cord for gripping, and a metal pointed head. For a throw to count, the metal head must pierce the ground. Unlike other throwing sports, like the shot put and hammer throw, javelin throwers use a runway to gain momentum. Bud skillfully concentrated his technique on transferring his forward momentum from his body to the javelin.

Bud won the National Collegiate Athletic Association javelin championship three years in a row while at Stanford, in 1948, 1949, and 1950. In 1951, he set an American record with a throw of 249 feet, 8 inches (76.1 meters). He set five additional American records for the javelin throw in the following years. He also won the American Athletic Union Championship six times, in 1949, 1951, 1953, 1954, 1955, and 1958. Javelin throwing was a sport long dominated by Scandinavians. Some doubted whether or not Bud could beat the Scandinavian champions in international competitions. In 1952, Bud competed on the U.S. Olympic team, but because of a shoulder injury, he only managed to place ninth.

The Emerging Champion

On August 8, 1953, in a meet in Pasadena, California, Bud threw the javelin 80.42 meters (263 feet, 10 inches). This incredible throw broke Yrjö Nikkanen's fifteen-year-old world record. The throw was the first to exceed 80 meters and the first world record throw by an American. Two years later on May 21, 1955, Bud set a new world record at the Modesto Relays with a throw of 81.74 meters (268 feet, 2 inches). His throw of 69.77 meters (228 feet 11 inches) won him a gold medal in the 1955 Pan-American Games in Mexico City. The following year, Bud threw his personal best, hurling the javelin 82.30 meters (270 feet). As recognition of these achievements, Bud was inducted into the USA Track and Field Hall of Fame in 1987.

Bud also participated in important technological breakthroughs in modern javelin throwing. In 1953, with the help of his brother Dick, he invented a hollow javelin, greatly increasing the flight and landing capacity of the javelin. Bud's hollow javelin was too effective; the International Association of Athleticss Federation banned it in part because the increased distances made injuries to spectators possible.

Milestones and Awards

1948-50	National Collegiate Athletic Association champion (javelin)
1949-55, 1958	Amateur Athletic Union champion (javelin)
1952	Olympic Games, 9th place
1955	Pan-American Games, gold medal
	Inducted into Stanford University Athletic Hall of Fame
1987	Inducted into USA Track and Field Hall of Fame

In 1954, Bud developed a metal javelin, without the weighted steel tip but with a thick middle section in the shaft. By altering the javelin's center of gravity, he was able to throw it.

Continuing the Story

Bud's athletic career after his days as champion was equally remarkable. He became one of the great senior athletes of track and field. While pursuing a career as a businessman selling sports equipment, Bud occasionally competed as a senior athlete. At the age of sixty, he became active in Master Championships, competitions for athletes older than thirty-five, divided by age levels. In 1970, Bud set a U.S. national Masters record with a javelin throw of 69.88 meters (229 feet, 3 inches). On May 15, 1993, Bud set a world record in the M65 javelin throw with a throw of 55.02 meters (180 feet 6 inches). In 2004, when he was seventy-seven, Bud set a record for the M75 pole vault, at the Decatur Masters Nationals, clearing 2.76 meters (9 feet). In 2007, at the age of seventy-nine, Bud bested his own mark with a 3.04-meter (10-foot) pole vault at the Striders Meet of Champions in Long Beach, California. He set a world record in the M70 high jump at 1.52 meters (5 feet). He also ranked number six in the M75 discus with a throw of 34.63 meters (113 feet 7 inches). All in all, he became the holder of three world records in the M70 and M75 categories.

Summary

In a sport that had been dominated by Scandinavians, in 1953, Bud Held became the first American world record holder when he hurled the javelin more than 80 meters 262 feet 5½ inches. He set a second world mark two years later. His engineering expertise rendered several improvements in the design of the javelin. As a senior Master athlete, he set three world records and was the first person older than seventy to pole-vault more than 10 feet.

Howard Bromberg

Additional Sources

Quercetani, Roberto. *A World History of Track and Field Athletics: 1864-1964.* London: Oxford University Press, 1964.

Silvester, Jay, ed. *Complete Book of Throws.* Champaign, Ill.: Human Kinetics, 2003.

Watman, Mel, ed. *Encyclopedia of Track and Field Athletics.* New York: St. Martin's Press, 1981.

Sonja Henie

Born: April 8, 1912
      Kristiania (now Oslo), Norway
Died: October 12, 1969
      Ambulance plane between Paris and Oslo

Early Life

Born in Kristiania (now Olso), Norway, on April 8, 1912, Sonja Henie was the younger of two children of Hans Wilhelm Henie, a wealthy fur merchant and former bicycle champion, and Selma Henie. In her autobiography, *Wings on My Feet* (1940), Sonja recalls a girlhood in which outdoor activities were encouraged. Oslo itself was covered with snow half the year, and the family had a hunting lodge at Geilo, a mountain village where they skied instead of walked. On skis, Sonja could follow her brother Leif wherever he went. The climate and the activities that her father's wealth made possible gave direction to her life.

The Road to Excellence

Before trying to skate, Sonja had already become a strong and agile skier. This ability gave her a feeling for rhythm and balance in motion. She had also shown an interest in dance. At four or five, she took clothing from her mother's closet and dressed up for what she called family dancing recitals. She arranged the living room into box seats, made out tickets, ushered in her audience, and performed to a record player. Her parents decided she should be given formal instruction and sent her to Love Krohn, an Oslo ballet master who had once taught famous Russian ballerina Anna Pavlova.

At the age of six, Sonja convinced her father to give her ice skates, although he believed she was too young. Rejecting skates with double blades as toys for babies, she started with a pair of skate blades attached to her shoes and took her first falls following and imitating her older brother. Although she often fell, she quickly learned that skating was all she wanted to do. In 1940, in her autobiography, she claimed that, since she was nine years old, she had never been off the ice for more than three weeks at a time. She practiced three hours in the morning and two in the afternoon. For her academic education, she was privately tutored. At seven, she entered an Oslo children's competition, and at eight, she won the Junior Class Competition and was ready to move

Sonja Henie practicing for the Winter Olympic Games in Switzerland in 1928. (Getty Images)

directly to the Senior A competition, the national championship of Norway.

The Emerging Champion

In 1923, at the age of ten, Sonja was national figure skating champion of Norway. In 1924, she entered the Winter Olympic Games at Chamonix in the French Alps. She claimed to have placed last in that competition; actually, she was fifth of seven. Sonja's unsurpassed rise to fame then began. She was the silver medalist in the World Figure Skating Championships at Stockholm in 1926, and took her first world championship at Oslo in 1927.

Then, in a superlative show of courage for a young woman still in her early teens, she changed the nature of figure skating. At the 1928 Olympic Games in Switzerland, she introduced dance routines into the free-skating part of the competition. Only eight years before, U.S. skater Theresa Weld supposedly was scolded for "unfeminine" behavior when she performed the first jump by a woman in major competition. Sonja, profoundly influenced by Anna Pavlova, introduced ballet patterns, giving form and flow to what had been a routine series of spins and jumps. She developed nineteen types of spins, in some of them whirling around as many as eighty times. By introducing shorter skirts, she gave herself freedom while adding a theatrical element to her performance.

Sonja won the World Figure Skating Championship each year from 1927 to 1936 and was gold medal winner in the Olympics of 1928, 1932, and 1936. Her record of ten world titles was not surpassed for many years, and only Irina Rodnina, in the pairs skating events of 1972, 1976, and 1980, tied her record of three Olympic gold medals.

Continuing the Story

By 1937, Sonja's competitive career was ending. A woman of lesser strength might have rested on her victories or become embittered as age limited her athletic power. Instead, Sonja changed careers and became the first skater to popularize figure skating with the general public.

In 1927, Sonja had made a Norwegian film, *Syv Dager for Elisabeth* (seven days for Elisabeth). For some years, she had given exhibition performances in Europe, and, thus, she contracted for a U.S. series. In Los Angeles, she rented a rink and performed to a Hollywood audience that included many of the great stars of the period. As a result, she signed a movie contract with Twentieth Century-Fox. *One in a Million* (1936) was the first of twelve films that were to make her the number three box-office attraction—behind Shirley Temple and Clark Gable—by 1939. Her film career spanned two decades.

As her film career came to an end, she began a new project, this time producing her own ice shows, which she continued until 1951, when a block of seats in a Baltimore armory collapsed, injuring 250 persons. Although she was cleared of any responsibility, she gave up production. She continued to appear personally and had her own television special. She was the first woman athlete to earn one million dollars and, in fact, by her death her earnings were estimated at $47 million.

Sonja and her third husband, Niels Onstad, retired to Norway. They established the Sonja Henje-Niels Onstad Art Centre. It opened in Oslo fourteen months before her death. Within a few months of returning to Norway, she found that she was ill with leukemia. She was in Paris when her condition worsened, and the decision was made to fly

---

Major Figure-Skating Championships

Year	Competition	Place	Year	Competition	Place
1924	Olympic Games	5th	1932	European Championships	1st
1926	World Championships	2d		Olympic Games	Gold
1927	World Championships	1st		World Championships	1st
1928	Olympic Games	Gold	1933	European Championships	1st
	World Championships	1st		World Championships	1st
1929	European Championships	1st	1934	European Championships	1st
	World Championships	1st		World Championships	1st
1930	European Championships	1st	1935	European Championships	1st
	World Championships	1st		World Championships	1st
1931	European Championships	1st	1936	European Championships	1st
	World Championships	1st		Olympic Games	Gold
				World Championships	1st

Honors and Awards

1936	World Trophy
1963	Inducted into Ice Skating Hall of Fame
1976	Inducted into U.S. Figure Skating Association Hall of Fame

her home to Oslo. She died in the plane during the flight on October 12, 1969.

Summary

In the 1920's, 1930's, and 1940's, girls interested in athletics could find few role models. Sonja Henie was such a model, not only for her accomplishments but also for her courage. Her success in her sport—she changed the nature of her sport and brought it to the general public—would be inspiring at any time but was especially so during the years of her most spectacular achievements.

Betty Richardson

Additional Sources

Kirby, Michael. *Figure Skating to Fancy Skating: Memoirs of the Life of Sonja Henie.* Raleigh, N.C.: Pentland Press, 2000.

Kuhlman, Erika A. *A to Z of Women in World History.* New York: Facts On File, 2002.

Wallechinsky, David, and Jaime Loucky. *The Complete Book of the Winter Olympics.* Wilmington, Del.: Sport Media, 2005.

Woolum, Janet. *Outstanding Women Athletes: Who They Are and How They Influenced Sports in America.* Phoenix, Ariz.: Oryx Press, 1998.

Jimmie Heuga

Born: September 22, 1943
     San Francisco, California
Also known as: James Frederic Heuga (full name)

Early Life

James "Jimmie" Frederic Heuga was born on September 22, 1943, in San Francisco, Calfornia, and grew up in Lake Tahoe, California. Lake Tahoe is located in Northern California near Squaw Valley, the site of the 1960 Winter Olympic Games. Jimmie began skiing when he was two. Jimmie's competitive career began at the age of five. Jimmie's father had immigrated to the United States from France. He was a close friend of Émile Allais, an excellent ski racer who later became the U.S. Olympic ski coach. Allais was the most influential ski instructor early in Jimmie's career.

Jimmie Heuga skiing in a slalom event. (Courtesy of Amateur Athletic Foundation of Los Angeles)

The Road to Excellence

Jimmie seemed to possess natural skill as a skier and was successful right from the start. At the age of fifteen, he became the youngest male ever to ski on the U.S. ski team. When Jimmie competed, there were three events in alpine skiing, the slalom, giant slalom, and downhill. In the slalom event, competitors must ski through combinations of poles, called gates. Jimmie skied in all three events, but his best event was the slalom. He was about 5 feet 6 inches tall and had great quickness, which proved to be an advantage when making the tight turns on a slalom course.

In 1962, in St. Moritz, Switzerland, at the age of eighteen, Jimmie won his first international race. As a member of the 1964 U.S. Olympic team, Jimmie was part of a close-knit group of American skiers. Included on the men's team were Billy Kidd, Buddy Werner, Chuck Ferries, Bill Marolt, and Ni Orsi. All these skiers had the potential to beat the best skiers from Europe. Beginning with the 1948 Winter Olympic Games at St. Moritz, where Gretchen Fraser won gold and silver medals, American women had taken several Olympic medals in skiing. The men's team, however, had not done so well.

The Emerging Champion

No American man had ever won an Olympic medal in alpine skiing prior to 1964. The American men's team, under the leadership of coach Bob Beattie, was determined to win a medal at the Winter Olympic Games at Innsbruck, Austria. During the first days of competition, the Americans were disappointed by their performance. The men did not win any medals in either the downhill or the giant slalom. Their only remaining hope was a medal in the slalom.

The slalom event consists of two runs down the course. Jimmie's first run was one of the fastest of the day. Sometimes, slalom skiers who have a good first run ski too carefully on their second run. Jimmie did not wilt under the pressure. Before thirty thousand spectators on a very icy course, Jimmy turned in another fast

Major Skiing Championships

Year	Competition	Event	Place
1964	Olympic Games	Slalom	Bronze
1967	World Cup	Giant slalom	Bronze
		Overall	6th
1968	Olympic Games	Slalom	7th
		Giant slalom	10th

run. He finished in third place, less than .40 of a second behind the winner, and won the bronze medal. His teammate Billy Kidd joined him as the first American men to win a skiing medal by winning the silver medal.

At the end of the 1964 season, Jimmie finished third in the World Cup giant slalom standings. The World Cup standings were determined by his performance over the entire year. In 1967, three years after winning his Olympic medal, Jimmie became the first American to win the prestigious Arlberg-Kandahar event in Germany. Jimmie competed in the 1968 Winter Olympic Games in Grenoble, France. He skied well but did not win a medal. As usual, his best event was the slalom. Jimmie finished seventh. In the giant slalom, he placed tenth in a field of one hundred skiers. Later that year, he retired from the national team and became a professional skier.

Continuing the Story

As early as 1967, Jimmie began to have problems with his vision. On one occasion, his feet became numb. At first he did not pay much attention to these problems, but they persisted. Finally, in 1970, a doctor informed Jimmie that he had multiple sclerosis (MS), a mysterious nerve disorder. Doctors are not sure what causes it. About half a million people in the United States have MS. Many MS patients eventually lose control of their muscles, and about a third of all MS patients eventually must use a wheelchair.

Doctors advised Jimmie to avoid physical activity. For the next several years he followed their advice. The lack of activity made him feel less healthy and energetic, so, in 1976, he began an exercise program that he hoped would give him a sense of control over his life. Jimmie's training program included swimming, bicycling, and stretching and strength exercises. By 1977, he was able to resume skiing. Jimmie was

not cured; there is no known cure for MS. However, Jimmie felt that he had taken charge of his own life.

Jimmie worked for three years with the Multiple Sclerosis Society, helping other MS patients to develop programs to meet their individual needs. In 1984, he opened the Jimmie Heuga Center in Colorado. The center conducts scientific research in MS and provides assistance to those affected by MS and other physical challenges. Many of the world's most famous skiers have helped the Jimmie Heuga Center raise money. In 1986, Jimmie organized a series of ski events, called the Jimmie Heuga Express, designed to raise money for the center. Every year the Jimmie Huega Center stages events in the United States and Canada.

Summary

Jimmie Heuga's bronze medal at Innsbruck, in 1964, ensured his place in skiing history. He may be even better remembered for his courage and determination in dealing with MS. He was elected to the U.S. National Ski Hall of Fame in 1976, and he has received numerous awards for his work in helping people to understand MS.

Wayne Wilson

Additional Sources
Fry, John. *The Story of Modern Skiing.* Hanover, N.H.: University Press of New England, 2006.

LaFontaine, Pat. *Companions in Courage: Triumphant Tales of Heroic Athletes.* New York: Warner Books, 2001.

Lombardi, Chris. "Jimmie Heuga: Changing the Face of MS." *Inside MS* 19, no. 4 (Fall, 2001): 32-36.

Russell, Margot. *When the Road Turns: Inspirational Stories About People with MS.* Deerfield Beach, Fla.: Health Communications, 2001.

Records and Milestones

Youngest male ever to make the U.S. Ski Team

First American man, with Billy Kidd, to win an Olympic medal in skiing (bronze medal in slalom, 1964)

Honors and Awards

1976	Inducted into U.S. National Ski Hall of Fame
1989	National Academy for the Advancement of the Handicapped DACI (Determination, Achievement, Courage, and Inspiration) Award

Charlie Hickcox

Born: February 6, 1947
Phoenix, Arizona
Also known as: Charles Hickcox (full name)

Early Life

Charles Hickcox was born on February 6, 1947, in Phoenix, Arizona. There were five brothers and sisters in the Hickcox family. For a long time, his sister Mary Sue, a national ten-and-under age group champion, was the swimmer in the family. Charlie took up basketball and eventually made his high school basketball team. When Mary Sue began training for the Olympics, Charlie became excited about swimming even though he did not start until he was thirteen. He had a great coach, hall-of-famer Walt Schlueter, who stressed fundamental stroke workouts.

The Road to Excellence

Charlie learned to swim all four strokes, which prepared him well for the four-stroke individual medley, the "decathlon of swimming." Charlie was not at his best with the breaststroke, but he set records in the butterfly, the backstroke, and the crawl. In spite of his success on the basketball team, his parents kept him out of football, fearing injury, and kept urging him into swimming. Charlie's swimming earned him a full scholarship to Indiana University, where he blossomed into a multi-world-record holder. The active, articulate, and fun-loving Charlie was perhaps the best captain Coach "Doc" Counsilman ever had at Indiana, and the leader of a multitalented team that had such great stars as world record holders Gary Hall, Mark Spitz, and John Kinsella.

Charlie showed early signs of greatness as a butterfuly swimmer but later broke the world record as a backstroker—although his specialty was always the four-stroke individual medley, reflecting his early training with Schlueter. The flamboyant Charlie also demonstrated early on that he responded well to pressure. He decided that he would do his best and would not worry if that was not good enough.

Charlie also had a way of adjusting to adversity. As an age-group swimmer in local meets and as a regional and state champion, he was always expected to win and he nearly always did. At Indiana, he set

Charlie Hickcox. (Courtesy of International Swimming Hall of Fame)

441

freshman class records in four events—the 100- and 200-meter backstroke and the 100- and 200-meter butterfly. He also swam a leg on the 4×100-meter freestyle relay team that tied a national record.

The Emerging Champion

Charlie was gaining confidence with each year at Indiana. He lifted weights to build up his shoulders. He won for himself and his team. Although many thought he was a bit of a show-off, Charlie said he would just as soon not be noticed. At 6 feet 3 inches and 165 pounds, and wearing his Indiana University letter jacket, he was often mistaken for one of Bobby Knight's Hoosier basketball players, which pleased him.

Charlie led the Indiana team to three straight National Collegiate Athletic Association (NCAA) championships, but, he said, "If I got last place, and we won as a team that would be good enough for me." His big meets leading into the 1968 Mexico City Olympics included the little Olympics, also at Mexico City—his first high-altitude meet, where he was voted the outstanding men's swimmer after winning gold medals in six events; the 1967 Pan-American Games, where he won the 100-meter and 200-meter backstroke and swam on the winning 4×200-meter freestyle relay team; and the World Student Games in Tokyo, where he won four gold medals and set two world records.

Continuing the Story

At the Mexico City Olympics, Charlie handled the altitude better than most swimmers. Although all of his eight world records were set prior to the Olympics, he still dominated the competition. His three gold medals and one silver medal tied Sharon Stouder (1964) for the second highest medal total for a swimmer in a single Olympic Games up to that time. Don Schollander led with four in 1964, and Mark Spitz, Charlie's Indiana teammate, was still four years away from his seven golds at Munich. While at Indiana, Charlie won sixteen titles—seven NCAA championships and nine national Amateur Athletic Union (AAU) championships—causing his Hall of Fame coach Doc Counsilman to comment, "Coaching is a pleasure, and it sure is easier when Charlie is your captain." Charlie was named world swimmer of the year in 1968.

After his retirement from swimming, Charlie be-

Major Swimming Championships

Year	Competition	Event	Place	Time
1966	AAU Indoor Championships	200-yard backstroke	1st	1:59.9
	AAU Outdoor Championships	100-meter backstroke	1st	1:01.0
		200-meter backstroke	1st	2:12.4
1967	World University Games	100-meter backstroke	1st	59.3 WR
		200-meter backstroke	1st	2:09.4 WR
	Pan-American Games	100-meter backstroke	Gold	1:01.2
		200-meter backstroke	Gold	2:13.05
		4×00-meter freestyle relay	Gold	8:00.41
	NCAA Championships	100-yard backstroke	1st	53.17
		200-yard backstroke	1st	1:55.30
	AAU Outdoor Championships	100-meter backstroke	1st	59.7
		200-meter backstroke	1st	2:12.3
1968	Olympic Games	100-meter backstroke	Silver	1:00.2
		200-meter individual medley	Gold	2:10.0 OR
		400-meter individual medley	Gold	4:48.4
		4×100-meter medley relay	Gold	3:54.9 WR, OR
	NCAA Championships	100-yard backstroke	1st	52.18
		200-yard backstroke	1st	1:54.66
		200-yard individual medley	1st	1:52.56
	AAU Indoor Championships	100-yard backstroke	1st	52.51
		200-yard backstroke	1st	1.54.93
		200-yard individual medley	1st	1:53.30
	NCAA Championships	200-yard backstroke	1st	1:53.67
		200-yard individual medley	1st	1:54.43
		400-yard medley relay	1st	3:25.89

Notes: OR = Olympic Record; WR = World Record

Records

Set eight world records

Won nine national AAU championships

Won seven NCAA Championships

Honors and Awards

1968	World Swimmer of the Year	
	Robert J. H. Kiphuth Award, Short Course	
1976	Inducted into International Swimming Hall of Fame	

came a coach of the Cincinnati Marlins and a television color commentator on swimming with Jim McKay and the ABC program *Wide World of Sports.* He also became a successful businessman with emphasis on sales. His younger brother Tom, following Charlie's lead, became U.S. national champion in the 200-meter freestyle, missing the world record by .37 second.

Summary

Charlie Hickcox was one of the greatest team captains in U.S. college history. He was elected to the International Swimming Hall of Fame in 1976. His success in the pool mirrored the success of his Indiana University teammates in the late 1960's.

Buck Dawson

Additional Sources

Gonsalves, Kelly, and Susan LaMondia. *First to the Wall: One Hundred Years of Olympic Swimming.* East Longmeadow, Mass.: FreeStyle, 1999.

Hammel, Bob, and Kit Klingelhoffer. *The Glory of Old IU.* Champaign, Ill.: Sagamore, 2000.

Wallechinsky, David, and Jaime Loucky. *The Complete Book of the Olympics: 2008 Edition.* London: Aurum Press, 2008.

Taufik Hidayat

Born: August 10, 1981
      Bandung, Jawa Barat, Indonesia
Also known as: Opik; Ucil

Early Life

Taufik Hidayat was born August 10, 1981, in Bandung, the capital of Jawa Barat (West Java), an island and the most populous province in the archipelago of Indonesia. Taufik and his siblings, Dewi and Desti Siswanti, are the children of a former Indonesian badminton player, Abu Harmee, and Enak Dartilah.

Taufik began playing badminton as a child. Originally, European colonists introduced the sport to Indonesians, and it became a national obsession, particularly because Indonesia won gold medals in badminton at every Olympics beginning when the sport debuted in Barcelona, Spain, in 1992. By the time Taufik was nine years old, he had committed to the sport and joined a badminton organization. Each day, he traveled for two hours from his home in Pengalengan, in Bandung's suburbs, to a downtown training compound, where he practiced for six hours. A talent scout eventually noticed Taufik's dedication, and at the age of sixteen, Taufik earned a place in the national badminton association, the Badminton Association of Indonesia, which governs the Indonesian national team.

The Road to Excellence

Taufik made an immediate impact as a member of the badminton team, winning the men's badminton singles at the 1997 Brunei Open. In 1998, he reached the All England Badminton Championship finals. In 1999, he played for the Sudirman Cup and won the men's singles at the Indonesia Open for the first time.

In 2000, Taufik helped lead Indonesia to the Badminton World Federation (BWF) World Men's Badminton Championships, capturing the Thomas Cup. That year, Taufik repeated as Indonesia singles champion, won the Asian Badminton Championships (later known as the Badminton Asia Championships), took the Malaysia Open, and was again runner-up at the All England finals.

By the 2000 Sydney Olympic Games, Taufik, just nineteen, was the number-one ranked men's badminton player in the world, thanks to a dazzling array of shots, a smooth playing style, and excellent footwork. His backhand smash had been clocked at more than 120 miles per hour, and his forehand jump smash came over the net at more than 180 miles per hour. More than just a power player, Taufik also beat opponents with clever forehand drop shots, uncanny reverse slices, and deceptive fakes. Though he was the top seed at the Sydney Olympics, Taufik lost in straight sets to gold-medal-winner Ji Xinpeng of China in the quarterfinals. Only a victory in men's badminton doubles kept Indonesia's Olympic gold-medal streak alive.

The Emerging Champion

After personal disappointment at the 2000 Olympics, Taufik rededicated himself to his sport, play-

Taufik Hidayat competing in the badminton singles event in the Beijing Olympic Games in 2008. (Michael Steele/Getty Images)

ing with more determination than ever. He added the 2001 Singapore Open singles title to his list of accomplishments and inspired his team to a runner-up position at the 2001 Sudirman Cup. The following year, he led Indonesia to its second consecutive championship at the Thomas Cup. He also won men's singles at the Indonesia Open—his third such title and the first of three consecutive singles crowns at the event—and at the Asian Games.

Tuning up for the 2004 Olympics in Athens, Greece, Taufik took men's singles at the Asia Championships again and participated at the Thomas Cup competition. At the Olympics, Taufik kept his volatile emotions in check to defeat Japan's Hidetaka Yamada and Malaysia's Wong Choong Hann in the first rounds. He edged Denmark's Peter Gade in the quarterfinals and crushed Thailand's Boonsak Ponsana in the semifinals. In the finals, Taufik dominated South Korea's Shon Seung-mo to claim the men's badminton singles gold medal.

Following his Olympic triumph, Taufik continued to play well, though the luster of his many achievements was tarnished by his sometimes ill-mannered on-court behavior. In one match, he disputed a line call and stalked off, forfeiting to his opponent. In another contest, after loudly exchanging taunts, he charged into the stands to pummel a heckler.

Continuing the Story

Despite such fits of rage and lapses in judgment, Taufik remained one of the world's best badminton players. In 2005, he captured men's singles at the World Badminton Championships, won again at the Singapore Open, and assisted the Indonesian team to a runner-up position at the Sudirman Cup. In 2006, he took his sixth singles title at the Indonesia Open, won singles at the Asian Games, and performed well at the Thomas Cup. That same year, Taufik married Ami Gumelar, daughter of Agum Gumelar, former president of the Indonesian national sports committee and of the national football association and once a minister in the Indonesian government.

The following year—when Taufik's wife gave birth to their daughter, Natarina Alika—Taufik was again a key player in Indonesia's runner-up placement at the Sudirman Cup. He also won singles at

---

Major Badminton Championships

1997	Brunei Open
1999-2000	All England Open (runner-up)
1999-2000, 2002-04, 2006	Indonesia Open
2000	Malaysia Open
2000, 2002	Thomas Cup (team)
2000, 2004, 2007	Badminton Asia Championships
2001, 2005	Singapore Open
2002, 2006	Asian Games
2004	Olympic Games (gold medal)
2005	World Championships
2007	Southeast Asian Games (individual and team)
2008	Macau Open

---

the Badminton Asia Championships and captured the gold in men's singles at the Southeastern Asian Games. Hoping to repeat as gold medalist at the Summer Olympics in Beijing, China, Taufik continued his outstanding play, performing well at the 2008 Thomas Cup and adding a new men's singles title to his collection: the 2008 Macau Open Badminton Championships.

At the Beijing Olympics, Taufik was seeded seventh. Though he played well, he lost in straight sets to Wong of Malaysia and did not qualify for the medal round. Taufik achieved much in a short period of time and hoped to compete at the 2012 London Olympics.

Summary

Taufik Hidayat, one of the world's top men's badminton stars, won championships at every level of international competition during a decade of play. He was the gold medalist in men's singles at the 2004 Olympics and became the first badminton player to capture titles in successive Olympics and World Badminton Championships. Taufik was a six-time champion at the Indonesian Open and the possessor of the game's fastest backhand and forehand smashes.

Jack Ewing

Additional Sources

Grice, Tony. *Badminton: Steps to Success.* Champaign, Ill.: Human Kinetics, 2007.

Hong, Fan. *Sport, Nationalism and Orientalism: The Asian Games.* New York: Routledge, 2006.

Mangan, J. A. *Sport in Asian Society: Past and Present.* Portland, Oreg.: Frank Cass, 2002.

Jim Hines

Born: September 10, 1946
    Dumas, Arkansas
Other major sport: Football

Early Life
James Ray Hines was born on September 10, 1946, in Dumas, Arkansas, to Charles and Minnie Hines. Jim spent most of his youth in Oakland, California, where his father was a construction worker. Jim attended McClymonds High School and starred on

Jim Hines running in the 4x100-meter relay final during the 1968 Olympic Games in Mexico City. (Popperfoto/Getty Images)

the track team for three years. He was captain of the football team in 1963, and as a running back in his senior year he rushed for 869 yards, caught passes for 500 yards, and scored 13 touchdowns.

The Road to Excellence
After graduation from high school in 1964, Jim entered Texas Southern University, where he became a member of the track team. He continued to perform well in track and field. His specialties were the sprint races. These distances of 100 and 220 yards were the distances in which Jesse Owens had excelled. Athletes who held the world record in the 100-yard event were considered the fastest humans on earth. Jim was determined to be one of those athletes.

Jim's track coach, Stan Wright, considered Jim one of the best sprinters he had ever coached. Under Wright's guidance, Jim's performances gradually improved. In 1965, he was second at the Amateur Athletic Union (AAU) Championships 220-yard event. At the 1966 AAU Championships he came in second in the 100- and 220-yard events. Then, at the 1967 AAU Championships, he won the 100-yard dash in 9.3 seconds and was second in the 220-yard event. Although Jim was beginning to make his mark in the track world, his greatest achievements were ahead of him. He knew he was capable of even better times, and his drive for excellence made him work even harder. He did not have to wait long for results.

The Emerging Champion
In June of 1968, at the AAU Championships in Sacramento, California, Jim turned in the performance of a lifetime. Jim was scheduled to race in the 100-meter event. One hundred meters is a little longer than 100 yards because a meter is about 3 inches longer than a yard. No one had ever run 100 meters in under 10 seconds. The athletes had to run several heats, or races, in the 100 meters in order to qualify for the final race.

Major Sprint Championships

Year	Competition	Event	Place	Time
1965	National AAU Championships	220 yards	2d	—
1966	National AAU Championships	100 yards	2d	—
		220 yards	2d	—
1967	National AAU Outdoor Championships	100 yards	1st	9.3
		220 yards	2d	—
	NAIA Indoor Championships	60 yards	1st	5.9
1968	Olympic Games	100 meters	Gold	9.95 WR, OR
		4×100-meter relay	Gold	38.2 WR, OR
	National AAU Championships	100 meters	2d	—

Notes: OR = Olympic Record; WR = World Record

National Football League Statistics

Season	GP	Rec.	Yds.	Avg.	TD
1969	10	2	23	11.5	0

Notes: GP = games played; Rec. = receptions; Yds. = yards; Avg. = average yards per reception; TD = touchdowns

In his first heat, Jim was timed at 9.8 seconds, and he thought he had set a new world record. The track and field judges, however, determined that the wind was too strong to consider his time legal. A wind that is too strong is thought to give athletes an unfair advantage. Although Jim won the heat, his world record was not allowed. In the semifinal heat, Jim ran the 100 meters in 9.95 seconds. This time the judges determined that the wind had not helped him, and the world record belonged to Jim. He had become the world's fastest human. In the final race of the 100-meter event, Jim had a bad start and came in second. Although disappointed at finishing second in the final, Jim was thrilled with his new world record.

Jim was also affiliated with a track club called the Houston Striders. Coached by former Olympian Bobby Moore, Jim trained hard and was chosen as a member of the 1968 U.S. Olympic track and field team. The Olympic Games were to be held in Mexico City, and Jim felt that he was as good as anybody in the world in the 100-meter event.

Continuing the Story

The competition in Mexico City was fierce. A runner from East Germany ran a very fast 10.2 seconds and still did not make the finals. Jim ran his first two heats in 10.0 seconds, only one-tenth of a second slower than his world-record time of 9.9 seconds, and qualified for the finals. The final race was the first time in Olympic history that all the finalists were of African heritage. Jim took his place on the track, and his-tory was about to be made. When the gun sounded to start the race, Jim exploded out of his starting blocks. After 70 meters Jim was well ahead, and he blasted past the finish line in 9.95 seconds to win the gold medal. His time of 9.95 seconds was considered the real world record because it had been timed electronically. His 9.9 seconds in Sacramento the year before had been timed with a less accurate, handheld timer. Jim had broken the world record in the 100 meters again. He was still the world's fastest human. There was no official change to Jim's record after the race, and his time of 9.95 seconds in the 100-meter event remained a world record for fifteen years.

Jim's Olympic triumphs continued. He ran the last lap in the 4×100-meter relay race, and the United States won the gold medal in a world-record time of 38.2 seconds. Jim's accomplishments as a member of one of the most successful U.S. Olympic track and field teams ever were incredible. Four days after competing in the Olympic Games, Jim signed a contract to play professional football with the Miami Dolphins. He played briefly for Miami in 1969. Jim kept active in track and field back home in Oakland, California. He represented the Northern California Seniors Track Club in the age thirty-and-over category competitions. He was elected to the USA Track and Field Hall of Fame in 1979. In April of 1984, when Jim was thirty-seven years old, he ran the 100 meters in 10.9 seconds in

Records

Co-held the 100-meter and 100-yard world records
Set a 100-meter world record of 9.9 seconds at the National AAU Championships in 1968

Honor

1979   Inducted into USA Track and Field Hall of Fame

the first annual Olympics Meet at the University of California at Los Angeles (UCLA).

Summary

Among Jim Hines's greatest accomplishments in track and field are his 100-yard and 100-meter records and his participation on the 4×100-meter world record relay team. In 1967, Jim equaled the indoor 60-yard dash world record of 5.9 seconds. As a world-record holder in the 100-meter event, Jim was temporarily the world's fastest human, an achievement few can claim. He is truly a track and field legend.

Michael Salmon

Additional Sources

Ashe, Arthur. *A Hard Road to Glory, Track and Field: The African American Athlete in Track and Field.* New York: Amistad, 1993.

Wallechinsky, David, and Jaime Loucky. *The Complete Book of the Olympics: 2008 Edition.* London: Aurum Press, 2008.

Nancy Hogshead

Born: April 17, 1962
    Iowa City, Iowa
Also known as: Nancy Lynn Hogshead (full
    name)

Early Life
Nancy Lynn Hogshead was born April 17, 1962, in the university town of Iowa City, Iowa. She is the daughter of Dr. Howard Paul Hogshead, an orthopedic surgeon, and Janet Bartel Hogshead, who was a fund-raiser for schools and clubs. By the time Nancy started swimming at the age of seven, her family had moved to Gainesville, Florida. Because her parents purchased a boat, they had her take swimming lessons to be safe around the water. She has an older brother, Andy, who rowed on the Harvard varsity eight crew, and a younger sister, Sally.

The Road to Excellence
Nancy's first swim instructor was Eddie Reese, assistant swim coach at the University of Florida, who later became a highly successful coach at the University of Texas. When Nancy first started swimming, Reese predicted that she could become a world-class swimmer. Later, Reese was Nancy's first coach at the Gainesville Golf and Country Club. At the age of twelve, while in junior high school, Nancy entered the 1975 Amateur Athletic Union (AAU) Indoor Championships.

In high school, Nancy swam on the Jacksonville, Florida, Episcopal High School swim team. Her senior year, she transferred to Gainesville High School, where, coached by Terry Schlichenmaier, she began to concentrate on training for the 1980 Olympics. While in high school, she earned all-state honors in nine events and all-American honors in three events. In 1978, Nancy was awarded the Nathan Mallison Award as Florida's most outstanding amateur athlete. In 1977, she es-

tablished national high school records in the 100-yard butterfly and the 200-yard butterfly. At the 1978 World Aquatics Championships, she was silver medalist in the 200-meter butterfly. She did not compete for her high school team in 1979 and 1980 because she was training for the 1980 Olympics. She earned a spot on the 1980 Olympic team in the 200-meter butterfly and the 400-meter individual medley, and she was terribly disappointed that the United States boycotted the 1980 Moscow Olympic Games.

The Emerging Champion
Nancy went to Duke University, in North Carolina, and swam under Coach Bob Thompson. She selected Duke because she did not want to put swimming ahead of academic achievement. The frustra-

Major Swimming Championships

Year	Competition	Event	Place	Time
1977	AAU Long Course	100-meter butterfly	2d	—
		200-meter butterfly	1st	—
		200-meter individual medley	2d	—
		400-meter individual medley	2d	—
	AAU Short Course	100-yard butterfly	1st	—
		200-yard butterfly	2d	—
		200-yard individual medley	3d	—
1978	World Championships	200-meter butterfly	2d	2:11.30
	AAU Long Course	200-meter butterfly	2d	—
		400-meter individual medley	2d	—
	AAU Short Course	100-yard butterfly	2d	—
		200-yard butterfly	1st	—
		200-yard individual medley	3d	—
		400-yard individual medley	3d	—
1979	AAU Short Course	400-yard individual medley	3d	—
1983	U.S. Nationals	200-meter butterfly	3d	2:12.45
1984	Olympic Games	100-meter freestyle	Gold (tie)	55.92
		200-meter individual medley	Silver	—
		200-meter butterfly	4th	—
		4×100-meter freestyle relay	Gold	3:43.43 AR
		4×100-meter medley relay	Gold	4:08.34

Note: AR = American Record

tion of the Olympic boycott caused her to drop completely out of collegiate and AAU swimming for two years. With the 1984 Olympics approaching, however, she decided to leave school for a year and concentrate only on swimming. She moved to California, where she joined the Concord-Pleasant Hill Swim Club. She was coached by Mitch Ivey, who put her on an extremely heavy training schedule; she practiced seven hours a day, six days a week. On Sundays her workouts were lighter, averaging only an hour or two. She spent five to six hours each day in the pool; the other hour was devoted to running or lifting weights. Ivey not only encouraged Nancy to increase her workload but also convinced her to switch her specialties from individual medley and butterfly to sprint freestyle. In 1983, she returned to swim for the Florida aquatic swim team, where she swam on the world record-setting U.S. 4×100-meter freestyle relay team. For that accomplishment as a sprinter, Nancy won the United States Swimming (USS) 1983 comeback swimmer of the year award.

Nancy returned to the Concord-Pleasant Hill Swim Club and began seeing an internationally recognized sport psychologist, Dr. Thomas Tutko of San Jose State University, California. Tutko helped Nancy use a form of self-hypnosis to relax, and he was a constant source of support for her both at the Olympic trials, when she was having trouble sleeping, and at the Olympic swimmers'

camp at Mission Viejo, California, before the 1984 Olympic Games.

In 1984, Nancy swam extremely well at the USS international invitational and the national outdoor championships. She qualified for the 1984 Summer Olympic Games in four events: the 100-meter freestyle, the 100-meter and the 200-meter butterfly, and the 200-meter individual medley. At the 1984 Los Angeles Summer Olympic Games, Nancy was at the top of her career. She earned the silver medal in the 200-meter individual medley and gold medals in both the 4×100-meter freestyle relay and the 4×100-meter medley relay. The highlight of her career, however, occurred when she placed in a dead heat with American teammate Carrie Steinseifer for a gold medal in the 100-meter freestyle.

Continuing the Story

After the 1984 Summer Olympic Games, Nancy retired permanently from competitive swimming. In 1986, she graduated with honors from Duke, earning her bachelor's degree in political science and women's studies. She considered entering law school. While at Duke, she received recognition for counseling work with disadvantaged youth and for serving as a caseworker in the Women's Health Clinic. Since graduation, she has taken a leadership role helping women, children, and athletes deal with health problems. She has testified before the 1984 United States Senate Subcommittee on Drug Abuse and the 1985 Children's Health in America Subcommittee. Because Nancy has had problems with asthma all her life, she is particularly interested in bettering the sport life of the asthmatic. She has been spokesperson for a pharmaceutical firm that produces medication for asthmatics, has produced an exercise video appropriate for asthmatics, and, in 1990, coauthored a text on the effects of exercise on the chronic asthmatic. In 1997, she received her law degree from Georgetown University Law School. In 2001, she became a professor at Florida Coastal School of Law.

Records and Milestones

Won four national titles

Ranked first in the world (1977)

Swam second fastest 100-meter freestyle in U.S. history in 1984 (55.99)

World record in 4×100-meter freestyle relay (1983)

American record in 200-yard butterfly (1977)

Best times: 100-meter butterfly (1:00.47), 100-meter freestyle (55.99), 200-meter freestyle (2:01.42), 200-meter butterfly (2:11.25), 200-meter individual medley (2:15.24), 400-meter individual medley (4:52.29)

Spokesperson, Olympic Athlete at the Republican National Convention (1984)

Spokesperson, Women on the Run (1985)

Honors and Awards

1978	Nathan Mallison Award
1983	U.S. Swimming Comeback Swimmer of the Year

Summary

Nancy Hogshead was a dedicated competitive swimmer who earned international recognition while still in high school. After the pride of qualifying for the 1980 Summer Olympic Games, she suffered great frustration when the United States boycotted those games. Her frustration led her to retire from competitive swimming during her freshman year at Duke University. Her competitive nature, however, caused her to take a year off from college and train hard for the 1984 Summer Olympic Games. Her dedication and hard work paid off when she earned three gold medals. In retirement from competitive swimming, Nancy has been an author, spokesperson for the asthmatic athlete, lawyer, and professor.

Carol Cooper

Additional Sources

Cole, C. L. "Playing the Quota Card." *Journal of Sport and Social Issues* 27, no. 2 (May, 2003): 87-99.

Hogshead-Makar, Nancy, and Andrew S. Zimbalist. *Equal Play: Title IX and Social Change.* Philadelphia: Temple University Press, 2007.

Gordie Howe

Born: March 31, 1928
Floral, Saskatchewan, Canada
Also known as: Gordon Howe (full name); Mr. Hockey

Early Life

Gordon "Gordie" Howe was born March 31, 1928, in Floral, Saskatchewan, Canada, a small town on the outskirts of Saskatoon. When Gordie was three months old, the Howe family moved to Saskatoon, a hockey town of about fifty thousand people. Gordie was one of nine children of Albert and Katherine Howe. Gordie was big, awkward, and shy while growing up and had few friends. Because school was difficult for him, he quit after his first year of high school. Gordie got his first pair of used skates when he was about six years old and his first hockey stick when he was nine. From that time on, hockey became his way of life. Even when the temperatures dropped to 40 degrees below zero, Gordie skated on an outside rink, and he had a hockey stick in his hands everywhere he went all year round.

The Road to Excellence

When Gordie was nine, Ab Welsh, a forward for the Saskatoon Quakers, gave him his first hockey stick. Always Gordie's favorite, Welsh was strictly a position player whose techniques the young boy watched and studied. In the beginning, Gordie played goalie, wearing shin pads composed of magazines and mail-order catalogs stuck in his socks. At the age of eleven, he was shifted to right wing. Meanwhile, Gordie was still growing. Summers he worked for a construction company and on farms. By the age of fifteen, Gordie was heavily muscled and weighed 200 pounds. No longer awkward, he was perfectly balanced, quick, and confident on the ice.

The summer that Gordie was fifteen, he was selected for the New York Rangers training camp in Winnipeg, Manitoba, but he returned home before camp was over. The fol-

lowing summer was more successful. He attended the Detroit Red Wings camp in Windsor, Ontario, and was signed to a contract for the 1944-1945 season and assigned to their team in Galt, Ontario. However, because his transfer from a western to an eastern province was ruled illegal, he was allowed on the ice only for practice sessions and exhibition games. For the 1945-1946 season, Gordie was assigned to Omaha, Nebraska. That season, he made it big; he scored 22 goals and had 26 assists. Within a few weeks of his Omaha debut, fans began lining up for his autograph.

Gordie Howe during his years with the Detroit Red Wings.
(Courtesy of Amateur Athletic Foundation of Los Angeles)

NHL Statistics

Season	GP	G	Ast.	Pts.	PIM
1946-47	58	7	15	22	52
1947-48	60	16	28	44	63
1948-49	40	12	25	37	57
1949-50	70	35	33	68	69
1950-51	70	43	43	86	74
1951-52	70	47	39	86	78
1952-53	70	49	46	95	57
1953-54	70	33	48	81	109
1954-55	64	29	33	62	68
1955-56	70	38	41	79	100
1956-57	70	44	45	89	72
1957-58	64	33	44	77	40
1958-59	70	32	46	78	57
1959-60	70	28	45	73	46
1960-61	64	23	49	72	30
1961-62	70	33	44	77	54
1962-63	70	38	48	86	100
1963-64	69	26	47	73	70
1964-65	70	29	47	76	104
1965-66	70	29	46	75	83
1966-67	69	25	40	65	53
1967-68	74	39	43	82	53
1968-69	76	44	59	103	58
1969-70	76	31	40	71	58
1970-71	63	23	29	52	38
1973-74	70	31	69	100	46
1974-75	75	34	65	99	84
1975-76	78	32	70	102	76
1976-77	62	24	44	68	57
1977-78	76	34	62	96	85
1978-79	58	19	24	43	51
1979-80	80	15	26	41	42
NHL totals	1,767	801	1,049	1,850	1,685
WHA totals	419	174	334	508	339

Notes: GP = games played; G = goals; Ast. = assists; Pts. = points; PIM = penalties in minutes

The Emerging Champion

When eighteen-year-old right wing Gordie joined the Red Wings for the 1946-1947 season, the dominant teams in the National Hockey League (NHL) were the Montreal Canadiens and the Toronto Maple Leafs. The best player was Montreal's right wing Maurice "Rocket" Richard, who had dominated hockey throughout the 1940's. However, Gordie would dominate the 1950's. Following World War II, at a time when interest in hockey was at a low, Gordie's style and ability sparked new enthusiasm in the sport.

Gordie's first two seasons with the Red Wings were not impressive, but during the 1949 Stanley Cup playoffs in his third season, Gordie emerged

as a star. Although the Red Wings came in second in the playoffs, Gordie had the most points. In eleven games, he had 8 goals and 3 assists. In the 1949-1950 season, Gordie was the league's third-highest scorer. During the 1950-1951 season, he reached a major milestone in his career, not only scoring his 100th goal but also displacing Richard at right wing position on the first team all-stars. He was becoming the most celebrated player in professional hockey.

Continuing the Story

Gordie was a superb stick handler, equally capable with either hand. He was able to send a puck flying at 120 miles per hour with a flick of his wrists and scored repeatedly with his quick, forceful shot. Gordie used a 21-ounce stick—the heaviest used by any NHL player—because ordinary sticks broke in his powerful hands.

The enormously strong, 6-foot-tall, 205-pound Gordie played aggressive, tough hockey that opponents feared and respected. As a result, he had many injuries, the most serious occurring during the opening game of the 1950 Stanley Cup playoffs. When an opponent sidestepped his check, Gordie, skating full speed, crashed headfirst into the boards, fracturing his skull, cheekbones, and nose. Near death, he was rushed to a hospital, where brain surgery saved his life. Released from the hospital in time to watch his team win the championship game, the big right wing carried the Stanley Cup off the ice.

Gordie's most important goal—the 545th of his career, scored on November 10, 1963, in his home arena—was followed by a ten-minute standing ovation. He had broken Richard's all-time record. Not counting playoff goals, Gordie scored 801 goals in his NHL career, a record that held for many years.

Gordie married Colleen Joffa in 1953. They had three boys and one girl. Two of their sons, Marty and Mark, played hockey. After the 1970-1971 season, Gordie retired from the Red Wings, having played more seasons in the NHL than any other player. In 1973, Gordie's dream of playing hockey with his sons, Marty and Mark, was realized when the three Howes signed with the Houston Aeros of the rival World Hockey Association. In 1977, Gordie signed with the Hartford Whalers, playing with them until his retirement at the age of fifty-two, following the 1979-1980 season.

Gordie's jersey, number 9, was retired by the Red Wings (1971), the Houston Aeros (1977), and also the Hartford Whalers (1981). His career point total of 1,850 points stood as the NHL record until broken by Wayne Gretsky on October 15, 1989. In 2007, the Red Wings erected a statue of Gordie outside Joe Louis Arena.

Summary

Gordie Howe is the standard by which many hockey players measure their achievements. He set records that will be broken, but he endured as an outstanding professional hockey player for thirty-two seasons, a record that will not be easily broken. Known as "Mister Hockey," Gordie is regarded by many as the best hockey player of all time.

Louise Crain

Additional Sources

Allen, Kevin. *Mr. and Mrs. Hockey: A Tribute to the Sport's Greatest Couple.* Wayne, Mich.: Immortal Investments, 2004.

Duff, Bob. *History of Hockeytown: Detroit Red Wings, Seventy-five Years.* Detroit: Olympia Entertainment, 2002.

Howe, Gordie. *Gordie Howe: My Hockey Memories.* Buffalo, N.Y.: Firefly Books, 1999.

McDonell, Chris. *For the Love of Hockey: Hockey Stars' Personal Stories.* Richmond Hill, Ont.: Firefly Books, 2004.

_____. *Hockey's Greatest Stars: Legends and Young Lions.* Richmond Hill, Ont.: Firefly Books, 2005.

Platt, Jim, and James Buckley. *Sports Immortals: Stories of Inspiration and Achievement.* Chicago: Triumph Books, 2002.

NHL Records

Most goals, 801
Most games, 1,767
Most years in Stanley Cup playoffs, 20
Most years played, 26

NHL-WHA Record

Most points, 2,358

Honors and Awards

Year	Award
1949-50, 1956, 1959, 1961-62, 1964-65, 1967	NHL Second Team All-Star
1951-54, 1957-58, 1960, 1963, 1966, 1968-70	NHL First Team All-Star
1951-54, 1957, 1963	Art Ross Trophy
1952-53, 1957-58, 1960, 1963	Hart Memorial Trophy
1965	NHL All-Star Game MVP
1967	Lester Patrick Trophy
1972	Inducted into Hockey Hall of Fame
1974	Howe Trophy
	Gary L. Davidson Trophy
	Team Canada Member
1974-75	WHA First Team All-Star
1975	Inducted into Canada's Sports Hall of Fame
	Uniform number 9 retired by Detroit Red Wings, Houston Aeros, and Hartford Whalers

William DeHart Hubbard

Born: November 25, 1903
   Cincinnati, Ohio
Died: June 23, 1976
   Cleveland, Ohio

Early Life

William DeHart Hubbard was born November 25, 1903, in Cincinnati, Ohio. As a child, he liked to run and was always the fastest among his schoolmates. William attended Douglass School and Stowe School before entering Walnut Hills High School. There, he starred in football, baseball, gymnastics, and track. In practicing for jumping events, William pioneered the "hitch kick," in which the athlete continues to run in the air after takeoff. The style, which later became a standard technique, added distance to a jump. In conjunction with his dedication to sports, William was also an excellent student. He maintained an A-minus average during four years of school.

The Road to Excellence

After graduating from Walnut Hills High School in 1921, William received a scholarship to the University of Michigan. In college, William focused on track and field. He competed in 60- and 100-yard dashes and in the long jump and the triple jump. In his first year of competition, he won Amateur Athletic Union (AAU) championships in both the long and the triple jumps. He captured both titles again in 1923, the same year he won the National Collegiate Athletic Association (NCAA) long-jump championship.

In 1924, William again took first in the long jump at the AAU championships and was selected for the U.S. Olympic team. At the Paris Olympics, he represented the United States in both the long jump and the triple jump. Before sailing to Europe, William promised his mother to do his best to achieve the ultimate goal of amateur athletics: to compete against the world's best and to be crowned champion.

William kept his promise. At Paris, he leapt 24 feet 5 inches to win the long jump and became the first African American to win an individual Olympic gold medal. In 1908, in London, John Taylor, had been the first African American to win a gold medal of any kind, as a member of the U.S. medley-relay team. However, William's feat was only second best in distance at the Olympics. Teammate John LeGendre, competing in the pentathlon, soared 25 feet 5¾ inches to break the world long-jump record.

The Emerging Champion

Despite intensive training to compete at Big Ten Conference and international levels, William maintained good grades. In 1925, he graduated with honors, one of only 8 African Americans in a class of more than 1,450 students. William continued to run and jump throughout his collegiate career and beyond.

William's senior year in college was particularly memorable. He won his fourth consecutive AAU long-jump title. He also won the NCAA 100-yard dash, tying the world record of 9.6 seconds. His fantastic season culminated with the NCAA long-jump title after a prodigious leap of 25 feet 10¾ inches, which shattered LeGendre's world record.

Following graduation from the University of Michigan, William worked in Cincinnati as a recreation supervisor of the Department of Colored Works, part of the Public Recreation Commission. Meanwhile, he continued to train and compete, winning his final three AAU titles as an unaffiliated, or independent, athlete. In 1928, he was a member of the U.S. Olympic team again but did not win any medals. Though his own track and field career was over, William remained close to sports for many years.

Records and Milestones

1924	First African American to win Olympic gold medal (individual)
1925	Set world record in the long jump (25 feet 10¾ inches)
	Tied world record in the 100-yard dash (9.6 seconds)
1979	Inducted into USA Track and Field Hall of Fame
	Inducted into University of Michigan Hall of Honor

Continuing the Story

In 1934, William took on a new sporting venture. He founded the Cincinnati Tigers, a professional baseball team that played briefly in the Negro Leagues. Wearing second-hand Cincinnati Reds uniforms, the Tigers played three seasons as an independent team. In 1937, the Negro American League began. The Cincinnati Tigers, a charter member of the league, battled such teams as the Kansas City Monarchs, Chicago American Giants, Memphis Red Sox, and Birmingham Black Barons. At home, the Tigers played games at the Reds' park, Crosley Field, where the team often drew more than 15,000 fans. Though the Tigers finished in third place that inaugural season, the team beat the Chicago American Giants in the playoffs to win the Negro League Championship. Then, the team folded.

William continued to work with the Public Recreation Commission in Cincinnati until 1941. He managed Valley Homes, a public housing project, for a year, before moving to Cleveland, Ohio. There, he was employed with the Federal Housing Authority. A race-relations adviser, he worked to improve housing for minorities.

During the 1950's, William had one last major encounter with sports. An avid bowler, he served as president of the National Bowling Association (formerly the National Negro Bowling Association). As president, William helped promote professional African American bowlers, who at the time were not allowed to compete with the segregated American Bowling Congress.

Finally recognized for his athletic achievements, William was elected to the USA Track and Field Hall of Fame in 1957. He was also inducted into the Black Athletes Hall of Fame. He retired from the Federal Housing Authority in 1969. He died in Cleveland in 1976. A Cincinnati playground was named for him in 2001. In 2006, the refurbished Walnut Hills High School track was dedicated in his honor.

Summary

An early African American superstar, William DeHart Hubbard dominated track and field jumping and short-sprint events during the 1920's. Competing both on national and on international levels, he was the first African American to win an individual Olympic gold medal. His feats as an athlete served as a model for such later outstanding multi-event performers as Carl Lewis. William's work to improve the status of African American professional athletes helped set the stage for full integration in American sports.

Jack Ewing

Additional Sources

Barber, Gary. *Getting Started in Track and Field Athletics: Advice and Ideas for Children, Parents, and Teachers.* Victoria, B.C.: Trafford, 2006.

Dabney, Wendell Phillips. *Cincinnati's Colored Citizens.* Reprint. Cincinnati: Ohio Book Store, 1988.

Entine, Jon. *Taboo: Why Black Athletes Dominate Sports and Why We're Afraid to Talk About It.* New York: PublicAffairs Books, 1999.

Findling, John E., and Kimberly D. Pelle, eds. *Encyclopedia of the Modern Olympic Movement.* Westport, Conn.: Greenwood Press, 2004.

Bobby Hull

Born: January 3, 1939
     Point Anne, Ontario, Canada
Also known as: Robert "Bobby" Marvin Hull, Jr.
  (full name); the Golden Jet

Early Life
Robert "Bobby" Marvin Hull, Jr., was born in Point Anne, Ontario, Canada, on January 3, 1939, the fifth of eleven children. His parents had a farm, but his father was also a cement company foreman. His father's own dreams of a professional hockey career were fulfilled by two sons, Bobby and Dennis, the latter playing for the Chicago Blackhawks from 1964 to 1977.

Bobby was skating on his first pair of skates at Christmas 1942, before he was four years old. Bobby recalls rising at 5:00 A.M. as a child and skating alone for hours. At the age of twelve, he played on the Belleville, Ontario, team with his father. He was already powerfully built, on his way to his full size of 5 feet 10 inches and 195 pounds. Bobby attributes his strength to farm work, especially chopping wood. He returned to farming and cattle raising after his retirement.

The Road to Excellence
The Chicago Blackhawks acquired Bobby almost accidentally. In 1951, scout Bob Wilson spotted him in a Bantam game at Belleville while waiting to observe a Blackhawk farm team's prospects. One look at Bobby in action was enough. Wilson immediately telephoned National Hockey League (NHL) offices in Montreal to place Bobby's name on the Blackhawk "negotiation list." This action prevented other teams from approaching him. Wilson became Bobby's lifelong friend.

Bobby was only thirteen when he left his family for the Hawks' Hespeler, Ontario, juvenile team. The next season, 1953-1954, he led Woodstock to a Junior B championship. At sixteen, he moved to St. Catharines in the Junior A Ontario Hockey Association, the toughest amateur league in Canada and the last step before the NHL. In his second year with St. Catharines, Bobby led the team in scoring. Still, it was a troubled year for him. Rather than accept coach Rudy Pilous's decision that he must shift from center to left wing, Bobby left the team for four games. Also, his first marriage, at seventeen, failed. Bobby's second marriage, in 1960, produced five children, and his son Brett eventually became a star with the St. Louis Blues.

The Emerging Champion
In 1957, Bobby signed his first NHL contract with the Blackhawks. That fall, he worked out with the

Bobby Hull during his years with the Chicago Blackhawks. (Courtesy of Chicago Blackhawk Hockey Team, Inc.)

NHL Statistics

Season	GP	G	Ast.	Pts.	PIM
1957-58	70	13	34	47	62
1958-59	70	18	32	50	50
1959-60	70	39	42	81	68
1960-61	67	31	25	56	43
1961-62	70	50	34	84	35
1962-63	65	31	31	62	27
1963-64	70	43	44	87	50
1964-65	61	39	32	71	32
1965-66	65	54	43	97	70
1966-67	66	52	28	80	52
1967-68	71	44	31	75	39
1968-69	74	58	49	107	48
1969-70	61	38	29	67	8
1970-71	78	44	52	96	32
1971-72	78	50	43	93	24
1972-73	63	51	52	103	37
1973-74	75	53	42	95	38
1974-75	78	77	65	142	41
1975-76	80	53	70	123	30
1976-77	34	21	32	53	14
1977-78	77	46	71	117	23
1978-79	4	2	3	5	0
1979-80	27	6	11	17	0
NHL totals	1,063	610	560	1,170	640
WHA totals	411	303	335	638	183

Notes: GP = games played; G = goals; Ast. = assists; Pts. = points; PIM = penalties in minutes

Hawks at the team's St. Catharines training camp. His two goals in an exhibition game against the New York Rangers convinced Coach Tommy Ivan that he was ready to move to Chicago. Completion of high school would have to wait.

Bobby's first two seasons under new Hawk coach Rudy Pilous were not spectacular, but Pilous finally moved Bobby to left wing and the Hawks began to improve in the standings. In the spring of 1959, as a guest player with the Rangers on a European tour, Bobby scored 15 goals in twenty-one games. He felt this experience was a turning point for him: He learned to pace himself. In the following season, 1959-1960, Bobby, twenty-one, won his first scoring title. In 1960-1961, the Blackhawks ended the Montreal Canadiens' five-year dynasty, capturing Chicago's first Stanley Cup since 1938.

One explanation for Bobby's rapid rise in scoring was the improved accuracy of his explosive slap shot. His style—soon to become famous—was an end-to-end rush at nearly thirty miles an hour to just inside the opponents'

blue line. From there, he would let go the hardest shot ever clocked: 120 miles per hour. Goalies claim that all they saw was a blur as the puck rose or dropped unpredictably as it passed them. Hockey fans had never before seen anything like it. Another feature of Bobby's game was his development of the curved blade, which added a slingshot effect to his wrist shots. In fact, Bobby says, he scored more goals with this shot than with his vaunted slap shot.

In 1961-1962, Bobby scored fifty goals. That feat had been accomplished only twice before, by Maurice "Rocket" Richard in 1944-1945 and by Bernie "Boom Boom" Geoffrion in the previous season. During Bobby's run at the record, one goal was wrongly credited to Ab McDonald. Bobby characteristically never complained, although he was thus deprived of a record 51st goal.

Bobby rarely lost his temper or retaliated, even when provoked. Opposing teams began to assign their best checker to "shadow" Bobby—the purpose was to draw him into penalties. Bobby did not succumb to the tactic; he reasoned that one cannot score from the penalty box.

In 1964-1965, Bobby had a great start: 35 goals in thirty-eight games. The "Golden Jet" was on a pace to equal Richard's 50 goals in fifty games. A knee injury intervened, however, and Bobby slumped, finishing with a disappointing 39 goals.

Honors and Awards

1960, 1962, 1964-70, 1972	NHL First Team All-Star
1960, 1962, 1966	Art Ross Trophy
1962	NHL All-Star Game MVP
1963, 1971	NHL Second Team All-Star
1965	Lady Byng Memorial Trophy
	Canadian Press Athlete of the Year
1965-66	Hart Memorial Trophy
1969	Lester Patrick Trophy
1970-71	Sport magazine Hockey Player of the Year
1973, 1975	Howe Trophy
1974	Team Canada Member
1974-75	WHA First Team All-Star
1976, 1978	WHA Second Team All-Star
1983	Inducted into Hockey Hall of Fame
	Uniform number 9 retired by Chicago Blackhawks and Winnipeg Jets

Not until the 1965-1966 season did Bobby begin to take some retaliatory penalties against his "shadows." Still, his 54 goals and 97 total points were then NHL records.

Continuing the Story

Bobby scored 50 or more goals nine times in all, reaching a high of 58 in the NHL in 1968-1969 and 77 in the World Hockey Association (WHA) in 1974-1975. His Blackhawks finished out of the playoffs only once from 1958 to 1972. In each of Bobby's last four years, the Hawks finished first in the division. In 1972, Bobby astonished the hockey world, and Chicago fans in particular, by accepting nearly three million dollars to play for the Winnipeg Jets of the newly formed WHA. He was "possessed of a pioneer spirit and the notion that he was improving the lot of all players." The NHL saw it differently, however, initiating lawsuits that delayed Bobby's entry into the new league. Others followed him, and Gordie Howe even came out of retirement to play in the WHA.

The WHA lasted only seven years, but Bobby's Winnipeg Jets survived to become one of the expansion teams of the NHL. The Jets' financial success was the result of the crowd appeal of Bobby Hull. Bobby's son Brett followed in his father's footsteps, becoming a star in his own right with the St. Louis Blues. Together, they are the only father-son duo to score 600 goals and 1,000 points in the history of the league. After his retirement in 1980, Bobby became a commentator for the Canadian television broadcast *Hockey Night in Canada*.

Summary

Bobby Hull's conduct both off and on the ice was an example of sportsmanship, gentlemanly graciousness, and excellence. He seldom refused an autograph or interview. He retired in 1980 and was inducted into the Hockey Hall of Fame three years later. In the days of the original six-team NHL, when every roster was filled with the premier players in North America, Bobby was the best. One can only guess how many points he might have scored had he played at his prime in the expanded NHL of today.

Daniel C. Scavone

Additional Sources

McDonell, Chris. *For the Love of Hockey: Hockey Stars' Personal Stories.* Richmond Hill, Ont.: Firefly Books, 2004.

_____. *Hockey's Greatest Stars: Legends and Young Lions.* Richmond Hill, Ont.: Firefly Books, 2005.

MacInnis, Craig. *Remembering the Golden Jet: A Celebration of Bobby Hull.* Vancouver, B.C.: Raincoast, 2003.

Brett Hull

Born: August 9, 1964
Belleville, Ontario, Canada
Also known as: Brett Andrew Hull (full name);
the Golden Brett; Hully; the Yankee

Early Life

Brett Andrew Hull was born at his family's Canadian summer home in Belleville, Ontario, one of five children and four boys. Because his father was National Hockey League (NHL) all-star Bobby Hull and his mother Joanne was a professional figure skater, Brett had the pedigree to become a skater. His father, a hall of famer whose nickname was the Golden Jet, and mother separated in 1979. By then, Brett was beginning to draw attention as one of the premier junior players in North America. In 1984, he was drafted by the NHL's Calgary Flames with the 117th overall pick. After two years of college hockey at the University of Minnesota-Duluth and after leading Team USA in scoring during the 1986 Ice Hockey World Championships, Brett made his professional debut for the Flames during the 1986

NHL Statistics

Season	GP	G	Ast.	Pts.	PIM
1986-87	5	1	0	1	0
1987-88	65	32	32	64	16
1988-89	78	41	43	84	33
1989-90	80	72	41	113	24
1990-91	78	86	45	131	22
1991-92	73	70	39	109	48
1992-93	80	54	47	101	41
1993-94	81	57	40	97	38
1994-95	48	29	21	50	10
1995-96	70	43	40	83	30
1996-97	77	42	40	82	10
1997-98	66	27	45	72	26
1998-99	60	32	26	58	30
1999-00	79	24	35	59	43
2000-01	79	39	40	79	18
2001-02	82	30	33	63	35
2002-03	82	37	39	76	22
2003-04	81	25	43	68	12
2005-06	5	0	1	1	0
Totals	1,269	741	650	1,391	458

Notes: GP = games played; G = goals; Ast. = assists; Pts. = points; PIM = penalties in minutes. 2004-05 NHL season canceled because of lockout.

Stanley Cup Finals. He spent the next season in the minors, where he was an American Hockey League all-star for the Moncton Golden Flames.

The Road to Excellence

By the 1987-1988 season, Brett was in the NHL to stay. On March 7, 1988, the Flames traded him to the St. Louis Blues. Prior to joining St. Louis, Brett was best known as the son of the Golden Jet. During his eleven seasons with the Blues, he became one of the best right wingers in NHL history and earned a nickname of his own, a play on his father's nickname and Brett's gold-blond hair: "the Golden Brett."

In 1990-1991, playing on a scoring line with fellow all-star Adam Oates, Brett set an NHL record for goals by a right winger, with 86; the third-highest total for a single season in NHL history at the time. The record earned the Hart Memorial Trophy as the league's most valuable player. He and Bobby Hull became the first father-son duo to win Hart Trophies. After Oates was traded during the 1991-1992 season, Brett never approached the historic levels of production he had achieved early in his career. With Oates as a linemate, Brett scored 72 goals in 1989-1990, 86 in 1990-1991, and 70 in 1991-1992. Without Oates, he still managed to score 54 and 57 goals in 1992-1993 and 1993-1994, respectively. On December 22, 1996, against the Los Angeles Kings, Brett completed a hat trick on his 500th career goal. At the age of thirty-two, Brett had, with that scoring milestone, secured his place beside his father in the Hockey Hall of Fame. However, Brett's career seemed incomplete: He had not won a Stanley Cup Championship.

The Emerging Champion

Brett made the playoffs every season he played for the Blues, but St. Louis never won the championship during his eleven-year tenure. In 1998, the seven-time all-star signed a free-agent contract with the Dallas Stars. The prime of his career was behind him; however, Brett still managed to score 32 goals, including the 600th of his career, and played an integral role in securing a playoff berth for Dallas.

During the playoffs, Brett's experience was a critical ingredient to the Stars' success. Dallas advanced to the Stanley Cup Finals against the Eastern Conference champion Buffalo Sabres. In twenty-two postseason games that season, Brett scored 8 goals and contributed 7 assists for 15 total points. His eighth goal of that postseason was one of the most controversial in NHL playoff history. It came in the third overtime of game six of the best-of-seven series and gave the Stars and the state of Texas their first Stanley Cup title. For years afterward, Sabres fans insisted that the goal never should have counted.

The goal was controversial because overhead replays showed that Brett's skate was in the crease in front of the goal mouth when he scored, a violation of a rule in place at the time that was later eliminated from the NHL rule book. As Buffalo goalie Dominik Hasek flailed in front of the net in an attempt to prevent the game-winning goal, Brett took three quick shots in succession as the puck rebounded toward him. Video replay officials declared that Brett had control of the puck when he shot, which created an exception to the in-the-crease rule. Brett and his Stars' teammates already were well into their postgame celebration when the goal was ruled legal.

Continuing the Story

Brett and the Stars returned to the Stanley Cup Finals in 1999-2000. Brett, thirty-five years old at the time, led the NHL in playoff goals, 11; assists, 13; and points, 24. However, the Stars' quest to repeat as champions was derailed by all-star goalie Martin Brodeur and the New Jersey Devils. Brett's third and final season with Dallas was his finest. He scored 39 goals and finished with 79 points, but the Pacific Division champion Stars were swept out of the playoffs in the second round by Brett's former team, the Blues.

At the age of thirty-seven, Brett continued to play at a high level. Prior to the 2001-2002 season, he signed a free agent contract with the Detroit Red Wings. He played all eighty-two regular-season games and was instrumental, along with former Sabres goalie Hasek, in helping the Red Wings win the 2002 Stanley Cup. Brett again led the NHL in postseason goals with 10. Brett also played for the

Honors and Awards

1987	Dudley "Red" Garrett Memorial Award
1990	Lady Byng Memorial Trophy
1990, 1992-94, 1996-97, 2001	NHL All-Star
1991	Hart Memorial Trophy
	Lester B. Pearson Award
2002	Silver medal, Olympic games
2003	USA Hockey distinguished achievement award
2006	Uniform number 16 retired by the St. Louis Blues
	Uniform number 29 retired by the University of Minnesota-Duluth
2009	Inducted into Hockey Hall of Fame

silver-medal-winning American team in the 2002 Winter Olympics.

Brett's playing career was coming to an end after his second Stanley Cup victory, but his production remained impressive. In 2002-2003, he scored 37 goals, including the 700th of his career. In 2003-2004, his final full season in the NHL, he scored 25 goals and had 43 assists. Brett then signed a free agent contract with the Phoenix Coyotes, but a labor dispute between the NHL owners and the players association canceled the entire 2004-2005 season. In 2005, Brett played five games before announcing his retirement at the age of forty-one and after twenty seasons. In 2007, having joined the Dallas Stars' front office in a support capacity, Brett was named co-general manager of the team with Les Jackson.

Summary

Brett Hull finished his NHL career with 741 goals, the third-most in NHL history. His jersey number, 16, was retired by the Blues in 2006. Having begun his career in the shadow of his famous father, Brett carved a substantial place for himself as one of hockey's all-time greatest scorers. In 2009, he joined his father as a member of the Hockey Hall of Fame.

Carter Gaddis

Additional Sources

Davidson, John, and Chris McDonell. *For the Love of Hockey: Hockey Stars' Personal Stories.* Rev. ed. Richmond Hill, Ont.: Firefly Books, 2007.

Diamond, Dan. *Total Hockey.* 2d ed. Toronto: Sport-Classic Books, 2003.

Hull, Brett, and Kevin Allen. *Brett: His Own Story.* Chicago: Triumph Books, 1999.

Flo Hyman

Born: July 29, 1954
Inglewood, California
Died: January 24, 1986
Matsue, Japan
Also known as: Flora Jean Hyman (full name)

Early Life

Flora Jean Hyman was born on July 29, 1954, in Inglewood, California. Inglewood is near the volleyball-playing beach communities of the South Bay. When she was young, Flo towered over the other children her age. When her schoolmates were 4 feet tall, she was 5 feet tall. Because of her unusual height, she had the nickname "Jolly Green Giant."

Flo's parents were also tall, but they were not athletes. Her father was a janitor with the Southern Pacific Railroad. Her mother, who died in 1978, cleaned houses until she later opened her own

Flo Hyman in 1979. (AP/Wide World Photos)

café, the Pink Kitty. Flo's parents gave her an important model: to set a goal and be willing to work for it. Flo also had two older sisters, who played volleyball with her at Inglewood's Morningside High School.

The Road to Excellence

The Morningside High School varsity team was the first volleyball team on which Flo played. As a freshman, she was allowed to try out for the varsity team, but she walked in the gym the first day of practice, saw the team playing, and walked out. Flo felt lanky and uncoordinated. The next year, however, she played on the varsity team. She did not learn to hit well until her senior year, when she was voted the team's most valuable player.

From the day Flo heard that volleyball was an Olympic sport, she knew she was going to be on the national women's team and play in the Olympics. Her coach in high school, Beth Di Stefano, took Flo and her teammates to United States Volleyball Association tournaments on Saturdays. They were searching for a club team where they could gain some playing experience. Flo first chose the Long Beach Hangers, based on the club's teamwork and stylish uniforms. She then moved up to play for the South Bay Spikers, who became the U.S. champions in 1977.

In 1974, the citizens of Pasadena, Texas, began providing homes, jobs, and scholarships at the University of Houston for women volleyball champions to train for the 1980 Olympics. Flo was asked to join the national team. She studied mathematics on her volleyball scholarship at the University of Houston. In 1974, she led her team to the Association of Intercollegiate Athletics for Women (AIAW) national championship. When she graduated in 1980, she had been an all-American for three years.

The Emerging Champion

In 1979, the women's national team qualified for the Olympics in a zonal contest against Cuba. Even though the U.S. team came in second, Flo was named the most valuable player for the tournament. The individual award did not mean as much

---

Honors, Awards, and Milestones

Year	
1974	AIAW National Championship Team
1974-76	College All-American
1976	Outstanding U.S. College Player
1979	Most valuable player, Women's U.S. National Team versus Cuba
1980	Women's U.S. Olympic Volleyball Team
1981	World Cup Best Hitter
	All-World Cup Team
1984	U.S. Olympic silver medalist
1985	Volleyball Hall of Fame All-Time Great Volleyball Player
1986	Inducted into Sudafed International Women's Sports Hall of Fame
1988	Inducted into Volleyball Hall of Fame
	Volleyball Hall of Fame Court of Honor
1989	Volleyball Hall of Fame Medal of Honor
	Flo Hyman Memorial Award established and presented yearly to a top U.S. female athlete

---

to her, however, as the chance to compete in the Olympics. However, the United States boycotted the 1980 Moscow Olympics, and the hardworking national team could not reach its goal of earning an Olympic medal.

Flo was one of seven players who dedicated four more years to the pursuit of an Olympic medal in volleyball. Under the guidance of Coach Arie Selinger, the team trained six to eight hours a day for the 1984 Olympic Games in Los Angeles.

Flo was the team leader and spokesperson. If Flo played well, so did the team. She was the oldest woman volleyball player in the 1984 Olympics, turning thirty years old on the first day of competition. In Los Angeles, the U.S. women's team won the silver medal, losing to a talented team from China in the finals. Flo's leadership on the Olympic team inspired more African American women athletes to play volleyball.

Continuing the Story

Flo Hyman was a major force in turning the women's national team from a recreational to an international competitor. Many athletes would be disappointed with winning a silver medal instead of a gold medal, but Flo was proud of her silver medal. The license plate holder on her car read "1984 Olympian: A Silver Lined With Gold." She had set a goal to win an Olympic medal and worked for ten years in pursuit of it.

In 1985, Flo retired from the national team. She was not satisfied to rest on her accomplishments in volleyball. She tried a brief acting career. In the 1985 movie *Order of the Black Eagle,* she played a warrior named Spike. She felt she had some experience for acting from all of her interviews about volleyball. Then she decided to go play volleyball in Japan for a year.

On January 24, 1986, Flo's Japanese team Daiei was playing a match against Hitachi in Matsue, Japan. In the third game, Flo came out of the game during a normal substitution. She sat down on the bench and started cheering for her team. In a few moments, she collapsed. She was taken to the Red Cross Hospital, where she was pronounced dead at 9:30 P.M. Flo had died of a rare disease known as Marfan Syndrome, which strikes tall, slender people. She was 6 feet 5 inches tall and weighed 180 pounds. With Marfan Syndrome, a person's heart enlarges and forces weak spots in the aorta to burst. In most cases, there is no method of detecting the disease. Because of Flo's death, awareness of the symptoms of Marfan Syndrome has increased. Many tall, slender athletes in volleyball and basketball have been tested for the disease.

Summary

Flo Hyman will always be considered one of the best women volleyball players in the world. She always represented a dedication to excellence. Several awards and scholarships have been given to women athletes in memory of Flo's determination to work and her will to succeed.

Kathy Davis

Additional Sources

Markel, Robert, Susan Waggoner, and Marcella Smith, eds. *The Women's Sports Encyclopedia.* New York: Henry Holt, 1997.

Miller, Ernestine G. *Making Her Mark: Firsts and Milestones in Women's Sports.* Chicago: Contemporary Books, 2002.

Wallechinsky, David, and Jaime Loucky. *The Complete Book of the Olympics: 2008 Edition.* London: Aurum Press, 2008.

Woolum, Janet. *Outstanding Women Athletes: Who They Are and How They Influenced Sports in America.* Phoenix, Ariz.: Oryx Press, 1998.

Nick Hysong

Born: December 9, 1971
Winslow, Arizona

Early Life

Born in Winslow in northern Arizona in 1971, Nick Hysong grew up as a second-generation pole-vaulter. His father, Cranston Hysong, had been a pole-vaulter at Northern Arizona University in nearby Flagstaff and was also a track coach in Winslow. Early in his life, Nick accompanied his father to track practices. From as early as age three, Nick remembered watching men soar gracefully over the bar. By the age of nine, Nick was trying to emulate their feats by pole-vaulting with a broomstick.

Nick began competing in the pole vault as soon as he entered high school and qualified for his school's track and field team. His father coached him during these years. After continuously honing his skills and agility through high school, Nick was recruited by Arizona State University in 1990. He eagerly joined the team there and continued perfecting his form and raising his height.

The Road to Excellence

During his freshman year at college, Nick finished eleventh in pole-vaulting in the 1991 National Collegiate Athletic Association (NCAA) championships. He continued working diligently. Over the ensuing years, he improved his place in the NCAA competitions from eleventh, to seventh, to fifth. Finally, during his senior year, Nick won the pole-vaulting event during the 1994 NCAA championships. He graduated from Arizona State a six-time all-American in both indoor and outdoor track. The Arizona State outdoor pole-vault record of 18 feet 8¼ inches that he set at the 1994 NCAA championships still remained in 2008, as did his school indoor record of 18 inches 7¼ inches.

The Emerging Champion

Nick graduated from college with a degree in marketing, but he wanted to focus on his dream of competing in the Olympics, so he continued to train and compete in the pole vault. In 1994, he placed fourth at the Olympic Festival and was ranked seventh in the event in the United States by *Track and Field News.* The following year he finished only thirteenth in the qualifying trials for the 1996 Olympics in Atlanta. His best vault of 18 feet 8¾ inches was better than his college record but not high enough for him to qualify for the U.S. Olympic team.

Nick's resolve only grew as he had to sit out the 1996 Olympics. The next four years were filled with hard work as he continued training and competing. In 1997, *Track and Field News* ranked him ninth in the pole vault. By 1999, he ranked sixth in the world and second in the United States. During that year, he tied for second at the USA Outdoor Track

Nick Hysong competing in the 2000 U.S. Olympic team trials. (Andy Lyons/Getty Images)

and Field Championships with a mark of 18 feet 6½ inches. He also tied for fourth at the World Track and Field Championships with a mark of 18 feet 8¼ inches. His hard work caused him to climb in the rankings, while vaulting ever higher.

Continuing the Story

Nick experienced his greatest success in 2000. Although his focus was on the Olympics, he competed in other important meets throughout the year. In June, 2000, he faced heavy competition at a meet in Rome. There he placed second behind world champion Maksim Tarasov of Russia, who had won the gold in the 1992 Olympics. Later that year, Nick arrived at the Olympic trials, again competing in an extremely strong field. The favorite, Jeff Hartwig, did not qualify, however, creating spots on the team for Nick and Lawrence Johnson.

With Hartwig's failure to qualify, many felt that the United States was out of medal contention. The Americans had dominated the sport of pole-vaulting from 1896 through 1968, winning sixteen consecutive pole-vault titles. Bob Seagren's 1968 gold medal in Mexico City had been the end of domination, however, and the United States had not won a gold medal in the event after that. Consequently, Nick faced great pressure as he headed to Sydney, Australia, for the 2000 Summer Games. He came to the Olympics hoping to show the world that Hartwig was not the only great American pole-vaulter and that he and Johnson were ready to jump.

After arriving in Sydney and starting to practice his vaults, Nick injured his foot when he missed the pit during a landing. For two days, he could not even walk. He was already considered a long shot for a medal, but after the injury, his chances seemed even more remote. However, in a close field, Nick, Johnson, and Tarasov, as well as Michael Stolle of Germany, all cleared the same height of 19 feet 4¼ inches. In such situations in the pole vault, places are determined by how many attempts each athlete needs to make the height. Because Nick cleared the bar on his first try, he earned the gold medal. Johnson cleared the height on his second attempt, so he won silver. Tarasov cleared the bar on his third try, so he got bronze.

Nick and Johnson's one-two finish in the pole vault was considered a stunning upset, as neither pole-vaulter had been expected to medal. In addi-

Major Pole Vault Championships

Year	Competition	Place	Height
1990	World Junior Championships	6th	17' 4¾"
1994	NCAA Championships	1st	18' 8¼"
1999	World Championships	4th	18' 8¼"
	USA Outdoor Championships	2d	18' 6½"
2000	USA Indoor Championships	5th	18' 4¾"
	Olympic Trials	2d	18' 9½"
	Olympic Games	Gold	19' 4¼"
2001	World Championships	3d	19' 2¼"
	USA Outdoor Championships	3d	19' 2½"
2002	USA Outdoor Championships	3d	18' 10"
2003	USA Outdoor Championships	5th	18' 6½"
2004	USA Indoor Championships	4th	18' 4½"
2005	USA Outdoor Championships	2d	18' 6½"
	World Championships	5th	18' ½"

tion to winning the gold medal, Nick had set a personal best.

After the Sydney Olympics, Nick continued competing. In 2001, he won a bronze medal in the USA Outdoor Track and Field Championships with a vault of 19 feet 2½ inches—less than 2 inches below his winning Olympic mark. Over the next several years, his marks kept him near the top of the U.S. and world pole-vault rankings, but he narrowly missed making the 2004 Olympic team.

Summary

Pole-vaulters are notorious among track and field athletes for their inconsistency. Vaulting is a highly technical event that allows little margin for error. Moreover, because vaulters must clear fixed heights, they often adopt complex strategies to conserve their strength during competitions, which can last many hours. As a result, things often go wrong for them. Even the greatest vaulters are sometimes eliminated from competitions for failing to clear a single height. Nick Hysong is no exception. However, vaulting seems to have been in his blood, and he has repeatedly shown an ability to bounce back from defeat and disappointment—the true tests of champion athletes.

Becoming a champion was a dream that Nick pursued from an early age. Succeeding took years of hard work and the patience to overcome severe disappointments. Each year, Nick inched up the rankings in his event, while continuing to vault ever higher. From the time he was in high school he practiced and became steadily better. Even when he was not expected to succeed, Nick used his determination to improve his marks—and bring home the medals. When the United States succeeded at the 2000 Olympics, he proved to himself and showed the world that he was the best.

Deborah Service, updated by the Editors

Additional Sources

Huebner, Barbara. "Hysong Gets High Honors." *Boston Globe*, September 30, 2000, p. G12.

Johnson, Jan Eric, and Russ Versteeg. *Illustrated History of the Pole Vault*. Atascadero, Calif.: Sky Jumpers, 2008.

Looney, Douglas S. "Olympics 2000 Notebook." *The Christian Science Monitor*, October 2, 2000, p. 10.

Rosen, Karen. "Track and Field: Bar Wobbles but Holds." *The Atlanta Journal-Constitution*, September 30, 2000, p. C4.

Wallechinsky, David, and Jaime Loucky. *The Complete Book of the Olympics: 2008 Edition*. London: Aurum Press, 2008.

Imre Földi

Born: May 8, 1938
Kecskemét, Hungary

Early Life

Imre Földi, who added weightlifting to his nation's list of serious Olympic triumphs, was born in the town of Kecskemét in central Hungary. As a boy, he dreamed of becoming a goalkeeper in professional soccer like his hero Gyula Grosics, who played for the Hungarian national soccer team, known as the Golden Elves. Imre explored various areas of gymnastics, such as the rings and parallel bars, before deciding at the age of fourteen to pursue weightlifting. To support himself, he went to the town of Tatabánya and learned the trade of locksmith. Later, he joined the Hungarian army. At an early stage of his career, Imre lost a portion of the ring finger on his right hand in a machine-shop accident. The injury permanently affected his abilities in snatch lifting but not in the press lift, in which he set numerous records. When Imre was a young man, weightlifting, though not commonly practiced in amateur clubs at the university level, was one of the forty-one sports recognized by the Hungarian government's sports agency.

The Road to Excellence

Imre's first appearance on the international weightlifting competitive circuit came in 1959, when he was twenty-one years of age. He competed in the World Masters and European Masters Championship contests in Warsaw, Poland, in the bantamweight category and took third place. The following year, he returned to the European Masters, finishing second, and participated in his first Olympic Games. In Rome as part of the Hungarian contingent, he was ranked sixth. In the early 1960's, he became an established figure on the European weightlifting circuit in the bantamweight and featherweight classes. He came in second place at the Grand Prix of Moscow, Soviet Union (now in Russia); the European Masters in Vienna, Austria; and the World Masters in Budapest, Hungary.

In 1964, Imre placed first at the Danube Cup held in Ljubljana, Yugoslavia (now Slovenia), and third in the featherweight category at the European Masters in Moscow. He won a silver medal at his second Olympic appearance, in Tokyo in 1964. In the years between the

Imre Földi competing in the 1968 Olympic Games at Mexico City, where he set a world record in the bantam weightlifting division. (Hulton Archive/Getty Images)

467

Major Weightlifting Championships

Year	Competition	Place
1959	World Championships	3d
1961	World Championships	2d
1962	World Championships	2d
1964	Olympic Games	Silver
1966	World Championships	2d
1968	Olympic Games	Silver
1970	World Championships	2d
1972	Olympic Games	Gold

Tokyo Games and the Mexico City Olympics of 1968, Imre compiled four successive first-place finishes at the yearly Danube Cup. In 1965, he won the World Masters contest in Tehran, Iran. At the 1968 Olympic Games in Mexico City, he garnered a silver medal.

The Emerging Champion

In 1970, at the World Masters in Columbus, Ohio, Imre was first exposed to American followers of international weightlifting. In the 1970's, Imre entered competitions in sites as varied as Lima, Peru; Montreal, Canada; Havana, Cuba; and Japan. At the 1972 Olympics in Munich, he won the gold medal in the bantamweight class, an accomplishment matched by his first-place finish the same year in the Danube Cup. Until 1972, he competed in the Olympic weightlifting triathlon: the clean, snatch, and jerk. After 1973, he competed in only the snatch and jerk.

From 1972 until the Montreal Olympics of 1976, Imre continued to compete in the flyweight and bantamweight classes and consistently placed in the top five on the Masters circuit. However, he was unable to match his earlier performances. Montreal marked the fifth Olympic Games in which Imre participated, a record not equaled by other weightlifters until the 2004 Games in Athens, Greece, when two Germans, Ingo Steinhöfel and Ronny Weller, also became five-time Olympians.

Continuing the Story

Beginning in 1964, the Masters tournaments awarded medals in the same manner as the Olympic Games. In his career, Imre received five gold, five silver, and two bronze medals from the World Masters competition.

Imre retired from competition in 1978 and became a trainer, helping his daughter Csilla become a competitive weightlifter. Continuing her father's weightlifting legacy, Csilla held the European women's title in the 44-kilogram weight class from 1989 to 1993 and was a member of Hungary's first women's weightlifting team, at the 2000 Olympics in Sydney, Australia.

Summary

Imre Földi was the first Olympic weightlifter to represent Hungary and one of only three athletes to compete in five successive Summer Olympics between 1960 and 1976. He also set numerous world records for weightlifting between 1961 and 1972 and was a Hungarian national champion thirteen times in the bantamweight and featherweight classes. In February, 2007, his influence on Hungarian sports was recognized when he was named one of Hungary's twelve "Athletes of the Nation," an honor initiated in 2004 that carried with it a lifetime pension.

Robert B. Ridinger

Additional Sources

Kiado, Corvina. *The History of Hungarian Sport*. Budapest: Egyetemi Nyomda, 1983.

Wallechinsky, David, and Jaime Loucky. *The Complete Book of the Olympics: 2008 Edition*. London: Aurum Press, 2008.

Yelena Isinbayeva

Born: June 3, 1982
     Volgograd, Soviet Union (now in Russia)
Also known as: Yelena Gadzhievna Isinbayeva
    (full name)

Early Life

Yelena Gadzhievna Isinbayeva was born into modest circumstances in Volgograd, Soviet Union (now in Russia), on June 3, 1982. She was born one of two daughters of Gadzhi Gadzhiyevich Isinbayeva, a plumber of Tabasaran ethnicity and a Sunni Muslim from Dagestan, a mountainous republic located in the extreme southwest of the Russian confederation. The girls' mother, a Russian, was a shop assistant.

Yelena attended nursery school from 1985 to 1987, where she took up artistic gymnastics. Her parents enrolled her in preschool from 1987 to 1989. She studied at a technical high school until 1997, earning the title master of sport for artistic gymnastics. Having grown too tall to become competitive in international gymnastics—she eventually grew to more than 5 feet 8 inches—Yelena entered a special training facility in her hometown, where she began learning to pole-vault under Coach Evgenii Vasilievich Trofimov.

The Road to Excellence

By 1998, Yelena had perfected her pole-vaulting techniques enough to begin competing. At her first major meet that year, the 1998 World Junior Track and Field Championships in Annecy, France, she cleared 4 meters (more than 13 feet) but was about 4 inches short of earning a medal. The following year, at the World Youth Championships in Poland, she soared 4.1 meters (13 feet 5 inches) to win her first gold medal and set a record for the event. At the 2000 World Junior Track and Field Championships competition in Santiago, Chile, Yelena improved to 4.2 meters (13 feet 9 inches) to again capture gold and set another youth record. That same year—when women's pole vault debuted as an Olympic event—Yelena graduated from her local school and began studying at the Volgograd State Academy of Physical Culture.

Throughout the early years of the twenty-first century, Yelena continued to improve while excelling at competition. She took first at the 2001 European Junior Championships in Athletics, won silver at the 2002 European championships in Athletics, earned bronze at the 2003 World Track

Yelena Isinbayeva breaking the world record in the pole vault at the 2004 Olympic Games in Athens. (Eric Feferberg/AFP/Getty Images)

469

and Field Championships, and captured gold at the 2003 European Athletics Under-Twenty-three Championships.

The year 2004 was especially memorable for Yelena. She captured first place at the World Indoor Track and Field Championships at Budapest, Hungary, setting a new world record of 4.86 meters (15 feet 11 inches). At the Summer Olympics, she won the women's pole-vault gold medal with another world record, 4.91 meters (16 feet 1 inch). She capped off an outstanding season with another first-place finish at the International Association of Athletics Federations (IAAF) World Athletics Final at Monte Carlo, Monaco, where she was named female athlete of the year.

The Emerging Champion

As outstanding as Yelena's early years as a pole-vaulter had been, even greater glory lay ahead of her. In 2005, when she earned a degree in physical education at Volgograd State Academy and began studying for her master's degree, she swept to gold medals at a series of events. She captured the European Indoor Championships in Athletics, the World Track and Field Championships, and the IAAF World Athletics Final, where she was again named IAAF female athlete of the year. Later in 2005, Yelena, an officer in the Russian army who represented the railroad military team in club competitions, was promoted to the rank of senior lieutenant.

Yelena continued her winning ways in 2006. She dominated her sport, winning the World Indoor Track and Field Championships; the European championships in Athletics, setting a new event record; the IAAF world event; and the World Cup, setting another new world record. For the 2006 season, Yelena was honored as Laureus world sportswoman of the year. She did not slow down the following year, either. In 2007, she again finished first at the World Track and Field Championships and

Major Pole Vault Championships

Year	Competition	Place
1999	World Youth Championships	Gold
2000	World Junior Championships	Gold
2002	European Championships	Silver
2003	World Championships	Bronze
	World Indoor Championships	Silver
2004	Olympic Games	Gold
	World Indoor Championships	Gold
2005	World Championships	Gold
	European Indoor Championships	Gold
2006	World Indoor Championships	Gold
	European Championships	Gold
2007	World Championships	Gold
2008	Olympic Games	Gold
	World Indoor Championships	Gold

the IAAF Golden League. She won the World Athletics Final with a new event record.

Continuing the Story

Virtually unbeaten in the women's pole vault after taking the gold medal at the 2004 Athens Olympics, Yelena solidified her claim as the world's best at her sport. She set a new world record—her twenty-first—at the 2008 World Indoor Track and Field Championships in Valencia, Spain, and raised the world indoor mark to 5.03 meters (16 feet 6 inches) at the Golden Gala meet in Rome, Italy. After conquering the competition at the 2008 Super Grand Prix in Monte Carlo, with another 5-meter-plus effort, she defended her title at the 2008 Olympics in Beijing, China, raising the women's world pole vault record to 5.05 meters (about 16 feet 7 inches). She also claimed first place at the competition she owned over the previous several seasons, the IAAF World Athletics Final.

Late in 2008, Yelena was promoted to captain in the Russian army. At the height of her athletic abilities and already with two dozen indoor and outdoor world records to her credit, she was still young enough to conquer new heights while narrowing the margin between the men's and the women's best pole-vaulting efforts. After the 2008 Olympics, she finally gained tangible recognition for her unparalleled success in a sport in which women have been allowed

Honors and Awards

2004-05, 2007	*Track and Field News* women's track and field athlete of the year
2007	Laureus World Sports Award: sportswoman of the year
2008	Waterford Crystal European athlete of the year
	Glamour (Russia) woman of the year
	European Athletics Association best European female athlete

to participate only since the late 1990's. She was featured in a series of Toshiba advertisements that promoted the company's products across Russia.

vaulter in history, even as she continued to break her own world records.

Jack Ewing

Summary

A tall, powerful, graceful athlete who benefited from early training in gymnastics, Yelena Isinbayeva dominated women's pole-vaulting starting in the late 1990's and continuing through the first decade of the twenty-first century. With a technique that was favorably compared to that of the best male competitors in the sport, she became almost unbeatable in international competitions. A champion on every major stage—European, world, and Olympics—and at both indoor and outdoor events, Yelena established herself as the best female pole-

Additional Sources

Findling, John E., and Kimberly D. Pelle. *Encyclopedia of the Modern Olympic Movement.* Champaign, Ill.: Sports, 2004.

Jacoby, Ed. *Winning Jumps and Pole Vault.* Champaign, Ill.: Human Kinetics, 2008.

Johnson, Jan Eric, and Russ Versteeg. *Illustrated History of the Pole Vault.* Atascadero, Calif.: Sky Jumpers, 2008.

Wallechinsky, David, and Jaime Loucky. *The Complete Book of the Olympics: 2008 Edition.* London: Aurum Press, 2008.

Midori Ito

Born: August 13, 1969
     Nagoya, Japan

Early Life
Midori Ito was born on August 13, 1969, in Nagoya, Japan's fourth-largest city. When she was four years old, her family began going to the nearby Osumo ice-skating rink for recreation. Captivated, Midori watched other young children practice their spins and jumps. She asked her parents if she, too, could take lessons from Osumo's experienced figure skating coach, Machiko Yamada. Midori's formal training in the sport began one year later.

At the age of ten, Midori moved into Yamada's home. She became part of her coach's family, but she was expected to focus all of her energy on her athletic development. From that point, she had little contact with her own parents and her brother and sister. Midori's daily schedule centered on the ice: She practiced from 6:00 to 7:30 A.M., stopped long enough to go to school, and then returned to the rink from 5:00 to 8:00 P.M. every evening.

The Road to Excellence
Midori's dedication was gradually rewarded in competition. In 1980, she placed eighth in the Junior World Figure Skating Championships; in 1983, she moved up to third place. At the age of fifteen, she competed as a senior, or adult, in the 1984 World Figure Skating Championships.

Just 4 feet 9 inches in height and weighing less than 100 pounds, Midori exhibited enormous power when she skated. The height and consistency of her jumps were particularly noticable. Her best jump was the triple axel, a move named after Norwegian skater Axel Paulson, a star skater of the early 1900's. One of the most difficult jumps to complete, the triple axel demands that the skater take off while moving forward and land skating backward—after rotating three and one-half times in the air. While several men had been successful with this jump, no woman had ever before attempted the triple axel in competition because of its difficulty. Midori wanted to be the first, planning to astonish the crowd at the 1985 World Figure Skating Championships in Tokyo. The day before the competition, however, she fell and broke her leg during practice.

It took three years of recovery and additional training before Midori gained worldwide recognition. She gave a dazzling performance at the 1988 Olympic Games in Calgary, but she finished in fifth place. Her standing improved when she won the All-Japan Figure Skating Championships several months later and captured her country's attention by becoming the first woman ever to land the triple axel in competition.

The Emerging Champion
The 1989 World Figure Skating Championships in Paris were another milestone for Midori. She managed to overcome a longtime weakness in the compulsory part of the competition, which involved tracing assigned "figures," or patterns, on the ice without creating unnecessary lines. She finished sixth after these exercises. For her short program, a two-minute original routine, two of the judges gave Midori the day's only perfect scores of 6.0. This achievement advanced her to third place. Midori's four-minute-long program contained six different jumps, including a beautiful triple axel. Her dynamic performance earned her the gold medal, along with the title of 1989 women's figure skating world champion.

In addition to her status as the first woman to include a triple axel in her program, Midori was the first Asian to win the world championship title. Unlike some skaters who emphasized grace and elegance in their routines, Midori represented an

---

Major Figure-Skating Championships

Year	Competition	Place
1983	World Junior Championships	3d
1988	All-Japan Championships	1st
1989	World Championships	1st
1990	World Championships	2d
1991	World Championships	3d
1992	Olympic Games	Silver

aggressive and creative approach to the sport. Her triumph in Paris signaled a stylistic change in women's figure skating. Midori set a new standard for athletic achievement on the ice.

However, not every competition after this point brought Midori the top honor. In the 1990 World Figure Skating Championships held in Halifax, Nova Scotia, she finished in second place, behind Jill Trenary of the United States. Though Midori received three perfect scores for her triple jumps during the freestyle routines, Trenary performed better during the compulsories and won the event.

At the 1991 World Figure Skating Championships in Munich, Midori met further frustration. During practice, she collided with another skater and was badly bruised. Still shaken as she began her short program, she miscalculated the landing of a jump too close to the rink's edge. When her blade hit the barrier, she lost her balance and crashed into a cameraman on the other side. She fell again during the long program, managing to complete only four of the eight triple jumps she had planned. American Kristi Yamaguchi won the championship, and Midori received the bronze medal.

Continuing the Story

Despite these frustrations, Midori went to the 1992 Olympic Games in Albertville, France, hoping to finish first. All of Japan was watching; no Japanese woman had ever won a gold medal in the Winter Games, and no Japanese man had won one in twenty years. She also faced a new rival, America's Tonya Harding, who had performed a triple axel in competition one month earlier. Emotional strain, combined with chronically sore knees from years of jumping, caused Midori to fall on an easy triple lutz jump.

Midori's embarrassment was great, but her spirit was greater: "I was never disappointed for myself, only that I had let down the people of Japan. I have no regrets because I know I did my best—all I could do," she said. This determination led Midori to another triumphant accomplishment. In the final moment of her long program, she landed a triple axel after falling on the same jump just minutes before. Everyone recognized the courage this effort demanded. The jump propelled her from fourth place to the silver-medal spot, and Midori became the first woman ever to land a triple axel in the Olympic Games.

At twenty-three years old, Midori retired from amateur competition after Albertville. Her physical strength and stamina had suffered from years of strenuous practice. With a degree in home economics from a junior college, she was hired as a spokesperson for a prominent Japanese hotel chain. She also appeared in commercials for Japanese television. Performing in a few professional figure skating championships, Midori became the first woman to successfully complete the triple axel in professional competition. She also began to coach skaters on the Japanese national team. At the 1998 Winter Games in Nagano, Japan, she had the honor of lighting the Olympic flame. Her legacy on the rink endures as generations of skaters attempt to match the mighty Midori on the ice.

Summary

Midori Ito, winner of the 1989 world figure skating championship title and the silver medalist at the 1992 Winter Olympics, was the first woman to complete the difficult triple axel in competition. Her powerful, aggressive style of skating helped to redefine the sport.

Alecia C. Townsend Beckie

Additional Sources

Hines, James R. *Figure Skating: A History.* Urbana: University of Illinois Press, 2006.

Ryan, Joan. *Little Girls in Pretty Boxes: The Making and Breaking of Elite Gymnasts and Figure Skaters.* New York: Warner Books, 2000.

Smith, Lissa, ed. *Nike Is a Goddess: The History of Women in Sports.* New York: Grove Atlantic, 2001.

Wallechinsky, David, and Jaime Loucky. *The Complete Book of the Winter Olympics.* Wilmington, Del.: Sport Media, 2005.

Jaromir Jagr

Born: February 15, 1972
Kladno, Czechoslovakia (now in Czech Republic)
Also known as: Jags; Puff Nuts

Early Life

Jaromir Jagr was born on February 15, 1972, in Kladno, Czechoslovakia (now in Czech Republic). He began skating on his family's farm when he was three years old. By the time Jaromir was six, he was playing hockey against other boys who were two to four years older than he. From 1988 to 1990, he played on a professional hockey team in his hometown. In 1990, he also played for Czechoslovakia in the Junior Hockey World Cup tournament, in which the team placed second, and made the tournament's all-star team.

Jaromir Jagr after scoring a goal during the 2008 NHL playoffs. (Bruce Bennett/Getty Images)

The Road to Excellence

In the 1990 NHL draft the Pittsburgh Penguins chose Jaromir fifth overall in the first round. When Jaromir joined the Pittsburgh team, he wore the number 68 on his jersey, the same number he had worn when he played in his home country. This number was a tribute to his grandfather, who was killed in 1968 when Soviet troops invaded Czechoslovakia. Jaromir was making a political statement, showing his displeasure with the Soviet invasion.

Jaromir was the first Czech player to play hockey in the United States without having to defect from his country. He was only eighteen years old when he was drafted by the NHL. Soon after Jaromir began his professional career, his mother came to the United States to live with him in Pittsburgh. Homesick and experiencing trouble speaking English, Jaromir showed he was destined for greatness during his first season with the Penguins. He set an NHL record for assists by a rookie during the playoffs, with 5, against Minnesota. He was named to the all-rookie team and helped Pittsburgh win the Stanley Cup in 1990-1991 during his first NHL season.

Jaromir continued his outstanding play during the 1991-1992 season, but in January, 1992, he received a ten-game suspension for abusive behavior toward a game official. During the 1991-1992 season, the Penguins won the Stanley Cup again. Jaromir played in the all-star games in both the 1991-1992 and the 1992-1993 seasons. He continued playing exceptionally well for Pittsburgh for the next several years, compiling close to 100-point seasons each year.

The Emerging Champion

In the 1995-1996 season, Jaromir scored 62 goals and made 87 assists for 149 points in eighty-two games, setting an NHL record for scoring and assists by a player in the right-wing position. During that season, Jaromir made the all-star first team.

Injuries plagued Jaromir during 1996-1997. He made the second team all-stars but was physically unable to play in the game. In 1997-1998, Jaromir rebounded and won his second Art Ross Trophy as

NHL Statistics

Season	GP	G	Ast.	Pts.	PIM
1990-91	80	27	30	57	42
1991-92	70	32	37	69	34
1992-93	81	34	60	94	61
1993-94	80	32	67	99	61
1994-95	48	32	38	70	37
1995-96	82	62	87	149	96
1996-97	63	47	48	95	40
1997-98	77	35	67	102	64
1998-99	81	44	83	127	66
1999-00	63	42	54	96	50
2000-01	81	52	69	121	42
2001-02	69	31	48	79	30
2002-03	75	36	41	77	38
2003-04	77	31	43	74	38
2005-06	82	54	69	123	72
2006-07	82	30	66	96	78
2007-08	82	25	46	71	58
Totals	1,273	646	953	1,599	314

Notes: GP = games played; G = goals; Ast. = assists; Pts. = points; PIM = penalties in minutes. 2004-05 NHL season canceled because of lockout.

NHL Records

Most points by a right winger in a single season, 149 (1996)
Most assists by a right winger in a single season, 87 (1996)
Most consecutive seasons with at least 30 goals, 15 (1991-2007)
Most consecutive seasons with at least 70 points, 16 (1991-2008)
Most assists by a rookie, Stanley Cup Finals, 5 (1991)
Most overtime goals, career, 15 (record shared)

the leading NHL point scorer. During that season he scored 102 points in seventy-seven games. He was runner-up for the Hart Trophy, the most valuable player award. The winner of the award that year was his fellow countryman Dominik Hasek, goaltender for the Buffalo Sabres. Again, Jaromir was a starter in the all-star game.

Continuing the Story

In 1998-1999, Jaromir became captain of the Penguins. This honor followed a decade of records and awards despite constant injuries. As captain of the Penguins, Jaromir played in the all-star game and won both the Hart and Lester B. Pearson Trophies. For the third time he won the Art Ross Trophy, scoring 127 points in eighty-one games. During the 1999-2000 season, he was seriously injured again. In March, 2000, about two months before the playoffs, he had to have a blood clot removed from his thigh and missed the last two months of regular play. During the playoff series between the Penguins and the Philadelphia Flyers, Jaromir struggled.

Nevertheless, even though he had missed nineteen games, managing to play in only sixty-three, he led the NHL in scoring. He won the Art Ross Trophy, as leading scorer, with 96 points. During the 1999-2000 season he became the first NHL player to garner more than one million all-star votes and won both the Hart and Pearson Trophies.

In 2000-2001, Penguin superstar Mario Lemieux returned to the team, and Mario quickly took over as the team leader, although Jaromir kept the captaincy. With two large salaries in Pittsburgh's small market, Jaromir was traded to Washington for the beginning of the 2001-2002 season. Washington paid Jaromir $77 million for seven seasons, the largest NHL contract in history at that time. He played with Washington for three seasons and averaged a respectable one point per game, but Washington failed to have any success. In the middle of the 2003-2004 season, he was traded to the New York Rangers. In 2005-2006, Jaromir broke every Rangers scoring record, recording 54 goals and 123 points and finishing second in the league in scoring.

As of 2008, Jaromir was second in all-time points among active NHL players, with 1,600. He won the Stanley Cup twice with Pittsburgh and won the Art Ross Trophy, as the league's scoring leader, five

Honors and Awards

1990	Czechoslovakian League Junior All-Star team
1991	NHL All-Rookie team
1992-96, 1998-2001	NHL First Team All-Star
1995-96	*Sporting News* All-Star first team
1995-96, 1999-2000, 2002, 2005-07	Golden Stick Award (Czech Republic)
1995-2001, 2006	NHL All-Star
1995, 1998-2000	Pittsburgh Penguins team most valuable player
1995, 1998-2001	Art Ross Trophy
1997	NHL Second Team All-Star
1998	Gold medal, Olympic games
1999-2000	Hart Trophy
	First NHL player to top one million All-Star votes
1999-2000, 2006	Lester B. Pearson Trophy
2005	Czech Sportsman of the Year
2006	Bronze medal, Olympic games

times. He won the Lester B. Pearson Trophy, given to the NHL's most outstanding player, three times and the Hart Trophy, as the player in the league most valuable to his team, once. He was a finalist for the latter award five other times. Jaromir was an eight-time NHL all-star. He set eight Rangers records and twelve league records, including most consecutive 30-goal and 70-point seasons at fifteen. He set virtually all the records for European-born players. Furthermore, he won Winter Olympic gold and bronze medals while playing for the Czech Republic.

Summary

Jaromir Jagr began skating in early childhood in the Czech Republic. During his tenure with the Pittsburgh Penguins he brought glory to himself and to his team. During his eleven seasons in Pittsburgh, he won the Stanley Cup twice. After the 2007-2008 NHL season, he signed a two-year contract to play for a Russian professional team. He established himself as one of the greatest European-born players to ever play in the NHL and is a likely candidate for the Hockey Hall of Fame.

Annita Marie Ward, updated by Timothy M. Sawicki

Additional Sources

Gilbert, John, and Vartan Kupelain. *Pittsburgh Penguins.* Buffalo, N.Y.: Creative Education, 1995.

Jagr, Jaromir. *Jagr: An Autobiography.* Pittsburgh, Pa.: 68 Productions, 1997.

Leonetti, Mike. *Hockey Now.* Richmond Hill, Ont.: Firefly Books, 2006.

Morrison, Scott. *By the Numbers.* Toronto: Key Porter Books Limited, 2007.

Podnieks, Andrew, and Anthony Jenkins. *The Little Book of Hockey Sweaters.* Toronto: Key Porter Books Limited, 2005.

Dan Jansen

Born: June 17, 1965
West Allis, Wisconsin
Also known as: Daniel Erwin Jansen (full name)

Early Life

Daniel Erwin Jansen was born on June 17, 1965, in West Allis, Wisconsin, to Harry Jansen, a police lieutenant, and Gerry Jansen, a nurse. Dan was the youngest of nine children, including five sisters and three brothers. The family lived close to where the annual North American Speedskating Championships were held, and Dan's parents introduced all of their children to skating at an early age. Instead of staying with a babysitter, Dan was taken to

Dan Jansen preparing to start a speed-skating race in the 1994 Winter Olympic Games in Lillehammer. (CBS Photo Archive/ Hulton Archive/Getty Images)

the West Atlas skating oval, where his father first laced him into a pair of skates at the age of four. Dan had to work hard to keep up with the rest of the family at the skating oval, but eventually he showed a true aptitude for skating. When he was eight, Dan began winning regional speed skating meets. By the time he was twelve, he was winning at the national level.

The Road to Excellence

In high school, Dan was a good all-around athlete. He played football for his first two years of high school, and he played baseball for all four years. Speed skating was the sport in which Dan excelled, though. In 1983, he competed in the World Sprint Championships, placing twelfth overall. Dan concentrated on the 500-meter and 1,000-meter races, and he was chosen to be a member of the U.S. Olympic team that would compete in the 1984 Winter Olympics at Sarajevo, Yugoslavia. Dan was still eighteen when he finished fourth in the 500-meter race at Sarajevo in a time of 38.55 seconds. He barely missed finishing third and earning a bronze medal. He had also skated in the 1,000-meter race, placing sixteenth with a time of 1:18.73.

With his first Olympic experience behind him, Dan began preparing for World Cup competition and attending the University of Wisconsin at Milwaukee. Dan felt close to his family and to the people of Wisconsin who rooted for him, and he wanted to do well in order to live up to their expectations. At the 1985 World Sprint Championships, Dan finished third overall, a striking improvement over his finish only two years earlier. He continued to work diligently to refine his skating techniques, and he moved up to second overall at the 1986 World Sprint Championships. At 6 feet and 190 pounds, Dan was capable of a powerful start to his 500-meter race, but he needed to train properly in order to have enough energy to finish a race strongly.

477

The Emerging Champion

Dan slipped to twelfth overall at the 1987 World Sprint Championships, but in 1988, he made a remarkable comeback and finished in first place in the World All-Around Championships. Dan seemed to be in top form for the 1988 Winter Olympics in Calgary, Alberta, Canada. In January, 1987, however, his sister, Jane Beres, had been diagnosed with leukemia. She and her husband, Rich Beres, had been married for five years, and Jane had given birth to their third child only twenty-four hours prior to learning that she suffered from cancer. She refused to let Dan donate his bone marrow for a transplant, because she did not want him to be too weak to compete in the upcoming Olympics. In September, 1987, Jane underwent a bone-marrow

---

Records

First skater to break 36-second barrier in 500 meters
Set world record in 500 meters, 35.92 seconds

Award

1988   Olympic Spirit Award

---

transplant with marrow from her sister, Joanne. She had to return to the hospital in December.

On February 14, 1988, as he was in Calgary preparing to compete in the Olympics, Dan was awakened early in the morning by a phone call from Wisconsin. Dan's mother informed him that his sister was dying and that she wanted to say good-bye.

Since she was on a respirator, it was impossible for her to talk, so Dan did all of the talking, but his mother reassured him that Jane understood what he had said. Merely four hours after the first call, Dan received another call stating that his sister had died. Dan was scheduled to skate that night, but he was unsure whether he could go through it.

With the support of his family, Dan decided that he would try to win the 500-meter race for Jane. However, he did not skate his best. Only two strokes into the first turn, Dan fell, and all of his hopes of winning a medal for Jane were dashed. For Dan and his supporters, the agony was almost too much to bear. Four days later, during his 1,000-meter race, Dan fell again, and all of his Olympic dreams seemed to be crushed. After the race, he flew to Milwaukee to attend Jane's funeral, and he received an outpouring of sympathy from thousands of well-wishers. Dan may not have won a medal at Calgary, but in the hearts of his supporters, he had proven to be a consummate champion who had handled adversity with great dignity.

Continuing the Story

Although it was difficult for Dan to bounce back, over the next few years he was one of the best speed skaters in the history of World Cup competition. He was helped enormously by coach Paul Mueller, who designed a tough off-season workout plan that focused on increasing Dan's stamina. From 1991 to 1993, Dan was World Cup Series champion in the

---

Major Speed-Skating Championships

Year	Competition	Event	Place
1984	Olympic Games	500 meters	4th
		1,000 meters	16th
1985	World Sprint Championships	Overall	3d
1986	World Sprint Championships	Overall	2d
1987	World Sprint Championships	Overall	12th
1988	Olympic Games	500 meters	—
		1,000 meters	—
	World All-Around Championships	500 meters	2d
		1,500 meters	2d
		Overall	1st
	World Sprint Championships	Overall	3d
1989	World All-Around Championships	500 meters	2d
		1,500 meters	9th
		5,000 meters	11th
		10,000 meters	9th
		Overall	4th
	World Sprint Championships	500 meters #1	11th
		500 meters #2	9th
		1,000 meters #1	3d
		1,000 meters #2	11th
		Overall	7th
1990	World All-Around Championships	500 meters	3d
		1,500 meters	19th
		5,000 meters	25th
	World Sprint Championships	500 meters #1	22d
		500 meters #2	17th
		1,000 meters #1	13th
		1,000 meters #2	14th
		Overall	16th
1991	World Cup	500 meters	1st
1992	Olympic Games	500 meters	4th
		1,000 meters	26th
	World Cup	500 meters	1st
1993	World Cup	500 meters	1st
1994	Olympic Games	500 meters	8th
		1,000 meters	Gold

---

500 meters. In April, 1990, he had married Robin Wicker; from that point on, Dan was determined not to allow his skating to overshadow life with his wife.

Dan went into the 1992 Winter Olympics at Albertville, France, hoping to erase his prior Olympic memories. Dan was able to finish only fourth in the 500-meter race and twenty-sixth in the 1,000 meters. In 1993, however, he captured the World Cup championship in the 500 meters, and in March of that year, he set a world record in the 500 meters with a time of 36.02 seconds. He was even happier in May, 1993, when his wife had a daughter, Jane Danielle, who was named in memory of Dan's sister. On December 4, 1993, Dan broke his world record and became the first speed skater to break the 36-second barrier with a time of 35.92.

In 1994, Dan competed in his fourth Winter Olympic Games, in Lillehammer, Norway. With his family there to root for him, Dan realized that this probably would be his last chance to capture an Olympic medal; he had already won everything else there was to win in speed skating. On February 14, 1994, Dan slipped in the 500-meter race and finished in eighth place. He had only the 1,000 meters left. Igor Zhelezovsky of Belarus was considered the favorite in the 1,000 meters, but in dramatic fashion, Dan skated through a slight slip and won the race in the world-record time of 1:12.43. Dan had finally won an Olympic gold medal. He retired from skating after the 1994 Games.

Summary

Dan Jansen combined power, technique, and determination to rise to the top ranks of speed skating. He fought through tragedy and never gave up his dreams or surrendered his integrity. Dan proved to be a true champion both on and off the ice.

Jeffry Jensen

Additional Sources

Jansen, Dan, and Jack McCallum. *Full Circle: An Autobiography.* New York: Villard Books, 1994.

Publow, Barry. *Speed on Skates.* Champaign, Ill.: Human Kinetics, 1999.

Wallechinsky, David, and Jaime Loucky. *The Complete Book of the Winter Olympics.* Wilmington, Del.: Sport Media, 2005.

Chet Jastremski

Born: January 12, 1941
     Toledo, Ohio
Also known as: Chester Andrew Jastremski (full name); the Jet

Early Life

Chester Andrew Jastremski was born on Giant Street in Toledo, Ohio, on January 12, 1941. Throughout his later career, he had to struggle to live up to the name of his street. He was of Polish American parentage and soon established himself as an all-American boy, participating in YMCA athletic programs, where he was called "Chet the Jet" and admired for his cheerful smile and hardworking style.

The Road to Excellence

Chet's first national fame came as a butterfly champion in the YMCA National Swimming Championships. He was a good all-around swimmer. However, he was not a great swimmer until James "Doc" Counsilman gave him a scholarship to Indiana University and turned him into a breaststroker, something Chet's previous coaches had considered too difficult for him.

Even though he became the world's best breaststroker and the founder of a style copied around the world, Chet thought of himself as a butterflyer right to the end of his long and monumental career. He was the first modern breaststroker; he invented the "jump stroke." With a narrow whip kick and a fast sculling pull, Chet revolutionized the breaststroke and set the records to prove it.

The Emerging Champion

After Doc Counsilman changed Chet's stroke, Chet quickly became the world's premier breaststroker. In six weeks in 1961, he lowered the world record for the 100-meter breaststroke six times, from 1 minute 11.1 seconds to 1 minute 07.5 seconds. Chet was not eligible for the National Collegiate Athletic Association (NCAA) Championships because Indiana was on probation for football recruiting violations, but he proved his competitiveness by winning several Amateur Athletic Union (AAU) National Championships.

Chet's Olympic record was one of continuous misfortune. He missed the 1956 Olympic team headed for Melbourne when he was disqualified on a disputed judges' decision in the finals of the Olympic trials. In 1960, he made the team and then was removed, again by rules and an arbitrary official decision. The rule had been changed to include only two breaststrokers picked by a controversial point system. In 1964, he refused to taper, going into the pool to swim extra laps because he felt he was getting out of shape and losing his competitive edge. He held the world record but finished third in Tokyo. In 1968, he allowed too little time for his training comeback from medical school studies and made alternate by finishing fourth in the trials. Then, still getting into shape, he was allowed to swim in the heats for the U.S. med-

Chet Jastremski. (Courtesy of International Swimming Hall of Fame)

ley relay team when they reached Mexico. His time was two hundredths of a second faster than the eventual Olympic champion swam the event in the finals.

Continuing the Story

In spite of his bad luck at the Olympics, Chet's prowess was recognized, and he was selected world breaststroker of the year a record four times. Chet broke world records nine times and American records seventeen times; these records were actually world's best times but were swum in the 25-yard short course format rather than in the 50-meter pool. He was the first man in the world to break the one-minute barrier for the 100-yard breaststroke, something equivalent to Roger Bannister's four-minute mile in track and field. Altogether, Chet won sixteen U.S. national championships. He was the second man in the world to beat two minutes for the four-stroke 200-yard individual medley. The first was Chet's Indiana University teammate, Teddy Stickles. Chet was also on three world-record relay teams. Two of his national championships were in the four-stroke medley, where Chet had a chance to prove his contention that he was also a butterflyer.

Perhaps his greatest thrill came when he was first introduced to Catie Ball, the world's greatest woman breaststroker, who shared his stroke and his bad luck in the Olympics. "Chet Jastremski!" exclaimed Catie in her best southern drawl, "You are my hero. I've tried to swim like you since I was a little girl."

Summary

Chet Jastremski went on to become a medical doctor and the women's swim coach at Indiana University. He served on the 1976 Olympic medical team and was the team doctor on several U.S. national and international swimming trips. Chet is often called the father of the modern breast-

stroke. He was inducted into the International Swimming Hall of Fame in 1977.

Buck Dawson

Additional Sources

Gonsalves, Kelly, and Susan LaMondia. *First to the Wall: One Hundred Years of Olympic Swimming.* East Longmeadow, Mass.: FreeStyle, 1999.

Levinson, David, and Karen Christensen, eds. *Encyclopedia of World Sport: From Ancient Times to the Present.* Santa Barbara, Calif.: ABC-Clio, 1996.

Wallechinsky, David, and Jaime Loucky. *The Complete Book of the Winter Olympics.* London: Aurum, 2006.

Major Swimming Championships

Year	Competition	Event	Place	Time
1960	AAU Outdoor Championships	100-meter breaststroke	1st	1:12.4
1961	AAU Outdoor Championships	100-meter breaststroke	1st	1:07.5 WR
		200-meter breaststroke	1st	2:29.6 WR
	AAU Indoor Championships	100-yard breaststroke	1st	59.6
		220-yard breaststroke	1st	2:26.8
1962	AAU Outdoor Championships	100-meter breaststroke	1st	1:08.2
		200-meter breaststroke	1st	2:30.0
	AAU Indoor Championships	100-yard breaststroke	1st	59.1
		220-yard breaststroke	1st	2:25.3
		200-yard individual medley	1st	1:59.4
1963	Pan-American Games	200-meter breaststroke	1st	2:35.4
	AAU Indoor Championships	100-yard breaststroke	1st	58.5
		200-yard breaststroke	1st	2:09.0
		200-yard individual medley	1st	1:58.2
1964	Olympic Games	Breaststroke	Bronze	—
	AAU Outdoor Championships	100-meter breaststroke	1st	1:10.0
		200-meter breaststroke	1st	2:31.8
1965	AAU Outdoor Championships	200-meter breaststroke	1st	2:30.1

Note: WR = World Record

Records

First man to break 1 minute for the 100-yard breaststroke (59.6)
Set nine world records and was on three world-record relay teams
Set seventeen American records and was on four American-record relay teams

Honors and Awards

1965-66, 1970-71   World Breaststroker of the Year
1977   Inducted into International Swimming Hall of Fame

David Jenkins

Born: June 29, 1936
    Akron, Ohio
Also known as: David Wilkinson Jenkins (full
    name)

Early Life

David Wilkinson Jenkins was born on June 29, 1936, in Akron, Ohio, to Hayes R. Jenkins, an attorney, and Sara W. Jenkins, a figure skating judge. David began figure skating at the age of eight, following in a family tradition. Soon, he joined his older brother Hayes Alan and sister Nancy Sue as representatives of the Akron Skating Club in local competitions. Three years younger than his brother, David strove to match Hayes's many accomplishments on the ice. Hayes had earned his first title, the United States Junior Men's Figure Skating Championship, at the age of fifteen. As partners, Hayes and Nancy Sue also won awards in pairs skating and ice-dancing events. David showed great promise as a skater as well. In particular, he was able to execute jumps with great strength and consistency. He also interpreted the music that accompanied his freestyle, or original, routines with sensitivity—a trait that his brother shared.

The Road to Excellence

Like his brother, David spent many years preparing for increasingly important championships. His long apprenticeship in the sport was guided first by coach Walter Arian in Cleveland and then by Gustave Lussi in Lake Placid, New York. In 1947, eleven-year-old David competed in his first sectional, or regional, competition. His first national competition was two years later. However, David did not win a title until 1953, when he earned the Senior Men's gold medal at the Midwestern Sectional.

That same year, David won the U.S. Junior Men's Figure Skating Championship held in Hershey, Pennsylvania. In 1954, he moved to Colorado Springs, Colorado, with his mother and Hayes. Both brothers began working with coach Edi Scholdan at the Broadmoor, a well-known resort and training facility for winter

sports. In addition to his practice on the ice, David attended the local high school. After graduation, the blond-haired skater enrolled in Colorado College.

David continued to compete nationally and internationally, winning two silver medals and one bronze in the U.S. Men's Championships. In his first World Figure Skating Competition, in 1954, David finished in fourth place. In the 1955 North American Figure Skating Championships, David took second place behind Hayes.

The 1956 World Figure Skating Championships in Germany and the 1956 Winter Olympic Games in Italy were memorable for the U.S. figure skating teams and for the Jenkins family. In both competitions, the top medals were won by Americans. David took the third-place bronze, Californian Ronald Robertson finished second, and Hayes won the gold. After his Olympic victory, Hayes retired from amateur competition in order to attend law school. The way was clear for David to follow his brother as the top man in figure skating.

The Emerging Champion

David quickly proved to be a worthy successor to Hayes, distinguishing himself by often performing more than one triple jump during his freestyle program. Skaters did not routinely include one or

---

Major Figure-Skating Championships

Year	Competition	Place
1953	U.S. National Junior Men's Championships	1st
1955	North American Championships	2d
	World Championships	3d
1956	Olympic Games	Bronze
	U.S. National Senior Men's Championships	3d
	World Championships	3d
1957	North American Championships	1st
	U.S. National Senior Men's Championships	1st
	World Championships	1st
1958	U.S. National Senior Men's Championships	1st
	World Championships	1st
1959	U.S. National Senior Men's Championships	1st
	World Championships	1st
1960	Olympic Games	Gold
	U.S. National Senior Men's Championships	1st

Honors and Awards

1976	Inducted into U.S. Figure Skating Association Hall of Fame
	Inducted into World Skating Hall of Fame

more of the difficult triple jumps in their performances until many years after David's retirement. He not only was able to execute several difficult jumps in one program but also helped to develop and refine the athletic technique of the triple jump.

In 1957, David won his first national and world titles. He received the gold medal at the North American Championship in February. Also that month, the World Figure Skating Championships were held at the Broadmoor, the first time the competition had been held in the United States in twenty-five years. David took first place out of seventeen competitors from nine countries. One month later, at the U.S. Figure Skating Championships, David again earned the gold medal.

David won the U.S. skating title for four consecutive years, 1957 through 1960. He defended his world title in 1958, in Paris, closing the competition with a dazzling freestyle performance after having trailed the second-place winner in the compulsory exercises. The compulsories were a difficult event, requiring skaters to trace patterns, or figures, on the ice repeatedly without making unnecessary lines.

In 1959, David won his third world title, back in Colorado Springs. Again, his spectacular free-skating program pulled him ahead of the fourteen contestants to help him retain his crown. The performance of each of the two skaters before David had brought the audience to its feet with wild applause. However, David met the challenge, receiving a standing ovation from the crowd of thousands as he executed a high-flying triple toe-loop jump. One reporter called him "a human top" because he whirled around the ice with such speed and daring.

The 1960 Winter Olympic Games, held in Squaw Valley, California, were the climax of David's competitive career. Again falling behind after the compulsory exercises, twenty-three-year-old David managed to gain the lead with his flawless freestyle performance. His high double and triple jumps, combined with dizzying spins, were unbeatable by any of his competitors. Leaving the audience breathless after his five-minute routine, David won the Olympic gold. For the only time in history, brothers had won consecutive gold medals in an Olympic figure skating event.

Continuing the Story

After winning his fourth U.S. championship and the Olympic crown, David decided not to defend his world title again. Instead, he announced his retirement from amateur figure skating in order to concentrate on medical school at Western Reserve University in Cleveland. To finance his medical education, he skated briefly with the Shipstads and Johnson Ice Follies; however, this professional stint was simply a means to an end. During all of his years of training and competing, David had been simultaneously carrying a complete academic load. His accomplishments in school were no less important to him than his athletic achievements. David became a successful surgeon in Tulsa, Oklahoma, where he and his wife reared three children. In 1976, the U.S. Figure Skating Association elected David to the Figure Skating Hall of Fame in recognition of his achievements and artistry.

Summary

David Jenkins won the U.S. Figure Skating Championship four times, the World Figure Skating Championship three times, and the Olympic gold medal in 1960. Following the lead of his older brother, David helped to refine the athletic nature of figure skating.

Alecia C. Townsend Beckie

Additional Sources

Hines, James R. *Figure Skating: A History*. Urbana: University of Illinois Press, 2006.

Nichols, Nikki. *Frozen in Time: The Enduring Legacy of the 1961 U.S. Figure Skating Team*. Cincinnati: Emmis Books, 2006.

Wallechinsky, David, and Jaime Loucky. *The Complete Book of the Winter Olympics*. Wilmington, Del.: Sport Media, 2005.

Hayes Jenkins

Born: March 23, 1933
Akron, Ohio
Also known as: Hayes Alan Jenkins (full name)

Early Life

Hayes Alan Jenkins was born on March 23, 1933, in Akron, Ohio, to a unique skating family. His mother, Sara W. Jenkins, was a figure skating judge; his father, Hayes R. Jenkins, was an attorney. Hayes began training intensively in the sport at an early age together with his younger brother David and sister Nancy Sue. As children, they represented the Akron Skating Club and later the Cleveland Skating Club in local and national competitions. Hayes was an all-around skater, performing not only as a soloist but also as a pairs and ice dancing competitor with Nancy Sue. In 1945, twelve-year-old Hayes and Nancy Sue were the Midwestern Junior Dance champions. That same year, they made their first appearance at the U.S. championships. Competing in the junior pair event, Hayes and Nancy Sue finished eighth. They were the Silver Dance champions for two consecutive years, 1947 and 1948, and also the 1948 Midwestern senior pair champions.

The Road to Excellence

At the same time, Hayes perfected his performance as a single skater. In 1947, he won the bronze medal at the U.S. novice men's competition. One year later, Hayes won his first national gold medal at the U.S. Junior Men's Championships. As the junior champion, in 1949, Hayes entered his first World Figure Skating Championship, held in Paris. He placed sixth, leaving him out of contention for a medal. Also that year, he competed in the U.S. Figure Skating Championships in Colorado Springs,

Hayes Jenkins in 1955. (AFP/Getty Images)

Colorado, and won the bronze medal in the senior men's event.

Hayes continued to compete at the national and international levels as a soloist. He earned the silver medal at the U.S. championships in 1950 and bronze medals in 1951 and 1952. Hayes was also a medalist at the 1949 and 1951 North American Championships. He was third in the 1950 World Figure Skating Championships, fourth in 1951, and third again in 1952. In 1952, at his first Olympic Games in Oslo, Norway, Hayes took fourth place.

The Emerging Champion

The experience that Hayes gained through these years of training and steady competition helped him rise to the top of the sport. In 1953, he won his first world championship title, the highest honor outside the Olympics for amateur ice skaters. This was the year after Dick Button, a talented and popular skater, had retired. In this competition, Hayes also defeated American skater Jimmy Grogan, a favorite for the title.

Two significant figure skating instructors helped to propel Hayes to his many victories. At Lake Placid, New York, Gustave Lussi coached Hayes early in his career on the athletic content of his routines. Lussi was a great teacher of jumps. In 1954, Hayes moved to Colorado Springs with his mother and David. Both brothers were able to train full time with Edi Scholdan at the Broadmoor, a well-known resort and training facility for winter sports. Scholdan worked with Hayes on his freestyle program, particularly helping him to combine his unique understanding of music and style with the necessary level of technical ability. Few skaters could better perform Hayes's trademark high-flying sit spin, a move that began with a jump and ended in a low spin with one leg parallel to the ice.

Hayes continued to earn championship titles at the major figure skating competitions both at home and abroad. He was U.S. champion and gold-medal winner for four consecutive years, 1953 through 1956. During those same four years, Hayes also repeatedly earned the world champion title and gold medal. He won the North American Championship twice, in 1953 and 1955. The 1956 Winter Olympic Games were held in Cortina d'Ampezzo, Italy, one month before Hayes's twenty-third birthday. This event was the culmina-

Year	Competition	Place
1948	U.S. National Junior Men's Championships	1st
1949	North American Championships	3d
	U.S. National Senior Men's Championships	3d
1950	U.S. National Senior Men's Championships	2d
	World Championships	3d
1951	North American Championships	3d
	U.S. National Senior Men's Championships	3d
1952	U.S. National Senior Men's Championships	3d
	World Championships	3d
1953	North American Championships	1st
	U.S. National Senior Men's Championships	1st
	World Championships	1st
1954	U.S. National Senior Men's Championships	1st
	World Championships	1st
1955	North American Championships	1st
	U.S. National Senior Men's Championships	1st
	World Championships	1st
1956	Olympic Games	Gold
	U.S. National Senior Men's Championships	1st
	World Championships	1st

tion of Hayes's skating career and also a significant moment in figure-skating history. The 1956 Games were the first Winter Olympics to be internationally televised, and the exciting events in men's figure skating received much attention.

During the men's free-skating event, a trio of Americans dominated the competition and captured all three medals. Third place went to Hayes's younger brother David. The second-place silver medalist was Ronald Robertson, a daring and acrobatic skater from California. After an excellent long program, the judges awarded Hayes the gold medal and title of Olympic figure skating champion. Following this victory, Hayes retired from amateur competition.

Continuing the Story

Hayes's dedication to figure skating earned him many top honors around the world; however, his quest for excellence did not end when he unlaced his skates. While training at the Broadmoor, Hayes attended Colorado College in Colorado Springs; he graduated Phi Beta Kappa with a B.A. degree in

Honors and Awards

1976	Inducted into U.S. Figure Skating Association Hall of Fame
	Inducted into World Skating Hall of Fame

economics. Following his retirement from amateur skating, Hayes appeared as a professional performer in order to pay for his continued education at Harvard University Law School.

Hayes's lifelong international profile was not limited to athletic competition, either. Hayes became a successful international lawyer for the Goodyear Tire and Rubber Company in his original hometown of Akron, Ohio. His father had also been an attorney and officer of the company. Hayes married another Olympic figure skating champion, Carol Heiss, and together they had three children. In 1976, Hayes was elected to the U.S. Figure Skating Association's Hall of Fame and World Skating Hall of Fame in recognition of his many accomplishments.

Summary

Hayes Jenkins combined athletic skill with artistry to earn four world championship titles and an Olympic gold medal. Together with his brother and his wife, he was part of a unique family of figure skating champions.

Alecia C. Townsend Beckie

Additional Sources

Hines, James R. *Figure Skating: A History.* Urbana: University of Illinois Press, 2006.

Lipoński, Wojciech. *World Sports Encyclopedia.* St. Paul, Minn.: Motorbooks International, 2003.

"Olympic Update: A Look at a U.S. Olympic Champion, Hayes Alan Jenkins." *Skating* 78, no. 6 (June/July, 2001): 59.

Bruce Jenner

Born: October 28, 1949
     Mount Kisco, New York
Also known as: William Bruce Jenner (full
   name); Bruiser

Early Life

William Bruce Jenner was born on October 28,
1949, in Mount Kisco, New York, the second of four
children of William and Estelle Jenner. His father
was a descendant of the famous English physician
Edward Jenner (1749-1823), who discovered the smallpox virus. The family mi-
grated to the middle-class suburb of Newton, Connecticut, where Bruce's father
ran a tree and shrubbery landscaping
business. Here Bruce showed a propen-
sity for many different sports, including
waterskiing, which he practiced at his
family's lakefront home. When he got to
high school, he played football and basketball and excelled in a number of track
and field events. He earned letters in all
three sports and also won the East Coast
waterskiing championship three times,
in 1966, 1969, and 1971. He also placed
well in the high jump and pole-vaulting
events at the Connecticut high school
track championships his senior year. As
an all-around athlete, he hoped for a college sports career in at least one of his
personal favorites.

The Road to Excellence

After he graduated, Bruce accepted a
$250-a-year football scholarship from tiny
Graceland College in Lamoni, Iowa.
Graceland was an institution affiliated
with the Reorganized Church of Jesus
Christ of Latter-day Saints. That was the
best offer Bruce received, despite his high
school achievements. Surprised by the
strict moral code of the church-related
school, Bruce nevertheless thrived under its discipline and there met his future
wife, Chrystie. After missing his freshman football season because of an injury, Bruce
was encouraged by Graceland's track coach, L. D.
Weldon, to compete in the decathlon at the Drake
University Relays.

To Bruce's surprise and delight, Bruce amassed
6,991 points, breaking a school record and finishing sixth. Impressed by his potential, Bruce decided to concentrate full time on the decathlon.
He was determined to excel in the sport to the
same degree he had in waterskiing. Bruce began a

*Bruce Jenner celebrating his victory in the Olympic decathlon in
Montreal in 1976.* (Tony Duffy/Getty Images)

487

Major Decathlon Championships

Year	Competition	Place	Points
1972	Olympic Games	10th	7,722
1974	National AAU Outdoor Championships	1st	8,245
1975	Pan-American Games	1st	8,045
1976	Olympic Games	Gold	8,618 WR, NR, OR
	National AAU Outdoor Championships	1st	8,542

Notes: OR = Olympic Record; WR = World Record; NR = National Record

year-round program of conditioning and endurance to prepare for Olympic competition. He was an unknown when he competed in the Olympic trials at Eugene, Oregon, in 1972. After seven of the ten events, Bruce was in seventh place in a field of twenty-two. He performed so strongly in the last three events—the pole vault, the javelin throw, and the 1,500-meter race—that he won the third spot on the Olympic team.

The Emerging Champion

In the 1972 Munich Olympics, Bruce got his first taste of world-class decathlon competition and placed a respectable, but to him disappointing, tenth, achieving 7,722 points, far below the world-record 8,454 points of the Soviet champion, Nikolai Avilov. Bruce congratulated Avilov on his gold medal but vowed to win the decathlon in the 1976 Olympics in Montreal. Soon after the Munich Olympics, Bruce married his college sweetheart, Chrystie Crownover, who put aside her own dreams and goals to work full time as a flight attendant to support her husband's year-round pursuit of decathlon excellence.

Temporarily slowed by a back injury and a broken foot, Bruce moved to San Jose, California, in 1973, to train with the dozens of world-class athletes who lived in the area. He wanted to train not with other decathlon athletes but also with the most accomplished athletes in each of the specific events: America's best shot-putter, discus thrower, pole-vaulter, and so on. Between 1973 and 1976, Bruce won the decathlon in all but one of thirteen competitions. His loss in the 1975 national Amateur Athletic Union (AAU) meet, in which he failed to complete the pole-vault event, drove him to tears. He was determined that he would never lose his concentration again.

Continuing the Story

The following August, Bruce eclipsed the world record for the decathlon in the United States-Soviet Union-Poland meet at Eugene, Oregon, by achieving 8,524 points. After his victory, Bruce was considered a 1976 Olympic favorite, with all the pressure that implied. Bruce's personal strategy was to stay within two hundred points of his most likely nemesis, Nikolai Avilov, on the first day's events and then catch him on the second day in the events in which he excelled, including the 1,500-meter race, his strongest event.

As it turned out, Bruce performed so well on the first day—scoring personal bests in every event except the 110-meter hurdles—that by the third event of the second day, he had already clinched the gold medal. Nevertheless, he ran the decathlon's most grueling event, the 1,500-meter race, in his fastest time ever, finishing with 8,618 points, both a world and an Olympic record. His single-minded devotion to the task of winning the decathlon had paid off.

Bruce's Olympic victory brought him instant adulation and fame in the United States. He had hundreds of opportunities for endorsements as well as television and motion picture roles. He virtually abandoned athletic competition soon after his Olympic triumph to become a media spokesperson and sports broadcaster.

The strain and pressures of his newfound fame eventually caused the breakup of his marriage to Chrystie, who had been such a part of his success. Bruce later remarried and began competing in professional auto racing. He remained a popular and winsome sports personality. He appeared on a number of reality-based television shows, as have his sons and stepchildren.

Honors, Awards, and Records

1973-76	Won twelve of thirteen decathlons entered
1976	James E. Sullivan Award
	Associated Press Male Athlete of the Year
	Sport magazine Track and Field Performance of the Year award
1980	Inducted into USA Track and Field Hall of Fame
1986	Inducted into U.S. Olympic Hall of Fame

Summary

Bruce Jenner is remembered for his resounding victory in the decathlon. Few athletes have ever dominated an event with such decisiveness as Bruce exhibited in the 1976 Olympics in Montreal. Because of his victory in arguably the most strenuous event in the Olympics, he earned the title "World's Greatest Athlete" and became one of American sports' most recognizable personalities.

Bruce L. Edwards

Additional Sources

Greenberg, Stan. *Whitaker's Olympic Almanack: An Encyclopaedia of the Olympic Games.* Chicago: Fitzroy Dearborn, 2000.

Jenner, Bruce, and Mark Seal. *Finding the Champion Within: A Step-by-Step Plan for Reaching Your Full Potential.* New York: Simon & Schuster, 1996.

Wallechinsky, David, and Jaime Loucky. *The Complete Book of the Olympics: 2008 Edition.* London: Aurum Press, 2008.

Kathy Johnson

Born: September 13, 1959
       Indialantic, Florida
Also known as: Kathy Johnson Clarke (full name)

Early Life

Kathy Johnson was born on September 13, 1959, in Indialantic, a small town on the central coast of Florida, below Cape Canaveral. She began learning gymnastics at the age of twelve, when a friend's mother, who assisted a high school gymnastic team coach, encouraged Kathy to join the team. By age fourteen, Kathy was attending summer gymnastics camps and had the good fortune to learn the fundamentals from coach Fred Martinez at his camp in Atlanta, Georgia. The basics Kathy learned from

Kathy Johnson performing a floor exercise routine. (LAOOC Collection, Department of Special Collections, University Research Library, UCLA)

Martinez remained with her for her entire career. She quickly tried out for a number of national meets and qualified for the 1976 Olympic trials.

The Road to Excellence

Kathy was awed by the Olympic trials, the first time she had seen any of the prominent U.S. gymnasts. She performed poorly in the compulsory events but finished third in the optional events. Coaches began to notice her.

At the Olympic trials, Kathy met Vannie Edwards, the U.S. women's Olympic coach. Edwards invited Kathy to come to his Olympia Training Center, a club in Belcher, Louisiana. Edwards's team-oriented club was influential in Kathy's development as an elite gymnast. She won the first United States Gymnastics Federation (USGF) Elite National Championships and the American Cup in 1977. In the latter competition, Kathy won all four individual events—she tied for first on the balance beam with Donna Turnbow—and was the all-around champion. Later, in Los Angeles, she placed second to Turnbow in the USGF Nationals.

In the fall of 1977, Kathy entered Centenary College on a gymnastics scholarship. She was among the first of a group of women awarded an athletic grant at this institution. Edwards was the coach at Centenary College. In 1978, Kathy won the all-around championship in the first-ever National Small College Meet sponsored by the Association of Intercollegiate Athletics for Women (AIAW). Thus she was a witness to the early evolution of women's collegiate athletics in the United States.

The Emerging Champion

Kathy's first big meet was the 1976 Olympic trials; she was so nervous and distracted that she did not place prominently. Coach Edwards guided her development through the first high point of her career,

Major Gymnastics Championships

Year	Competition	Event	Place	Event	Place
1977	Elite National Championships	All-around	1st	Balance beam	1st
		Floor exercise	1st	Vault	1st
	American Cup	All-around	1st		
1978	U.S. National Championships	All-around	1st		
	World Cup	All-around	14th		
	World Championships	All-around	8th	Team	5th
		Floor exercise	3d		
1979	World Championships	All-around	18th	Team	6th
	World Cup	All-around	6th	Uneven bars	3d
		Floor exercise	7th	Vault	6th
1980	U.S. National Championships	All-around	2d		
1981	U.S. National Championships	All-around	2d	Balance beam	3d
		Floor exercise	2d		
	World Championships	All-around	15th	Team	6th
1982	U.S. National Championships	All-around	8th	Vault	3d
		Balance beam	4th		
1983	U.S. National Championships	All-around	5th	Uneven bars	5th
		Floor exercise	4th	Balance beam	2d
	World Championships	All-around	11th	Team	7th
		Floor exercise	8th		
1984	U.S. National Championships	All-around	4th	Vault	3d
		Balance beam	3d		
	Olympic Games	Balance beam	Bronze	Team	Silver

a bronze medal in the 1978 World Gymnastics Championships in Strasburg, France. Kathy also finished eighth all-around. This was the highest placement ever for an American woman at that time. She had tasted international glory, and it would remain with her through the difficult years that were to follow.

Kathy felt that she needed further technical training and routine upgrading after the World Gymnastics Championships, as she was not fully satisfied with collegiate, team-oriented gymnastics. She enrolled with Bill Sand's Mid-American Twisters in Chicago. Although she spent less than a year with Sand, his training methods brought her to a new level of individual development.

Experts predicted that Kathy would dominate the 1979 American Cup championships, but she had a series of falls and minor injuries. She placed fourth and lost the bronze medal to a twelve-year-old newcomer named Tracee Talavera. Kathy's left foot was to give her constant problems during the

remainder of her career, but she overcame this handicap. After 1979, she was frequently seen icing her troublesome foot.

Following the American Cup, Kathy dropped out of competition for almost a year. She was unhappy in Chicago and did not have many friends there. In 1980, she returned to Tucker, Georgia, near Atlanta, where she had begun learning gymnastics with Fred Martinez in the early 1970's, and began training with Tom and Bunny Cook. She had been away from her Florida home and from her parents since she was fifteen, and she needed time for reflection. Coach Sand referred to her action as a "strategic retreat." There was, however, more to her story. She was physically ill and was trying to overcome a lack of feeling in one of her arms, which had been broken previously. In addition, before the 1979 World Gymnastics Championships, she had knee surgery.

Despite nagging pain, Kathy placed second at the 1980 Olympic trials. Her Olympic dream, however, was shattered by the U.S. boycott of the Moscow games. Kathy's love of the sport and the need to satisfy her competitive spirit made her continue training for the next Olympics.

Kathy identified with her gymnastics hero, Nelli Kim of the Soviet Union. In a sport dominated by teenagers, Kim continued to surprise the world with routines more associated with younger performers. Kathy's first encounter with a child star had been in 1979. During her reentry to national

Honors, Awards, and Records

1977	First USGF Elite National Champion
	U.S. Gymnast of the Year
1978-79, 1981, 1983	Women's U.S. World Championships Team
1980, 1984	Women's U.S. Olympic Team (a member of the U.S. National Team for nine years)
1982	U.S. Olympic Committee Olympia Award

gymnastics competition, she found that she was capable of competing with the younger girls. At the age of twenty-two, long after her contemporaries had retired, Kathy frequently bested the younger women in competition. For example, she tied with fourteen-year-old Dianne Durham at an international invitational sponsored by the USGF in 1982.

In 1983, Kathy joined the nationally prominent SCATS (Southern California Acro Teams), where she completed her career under the guidance of yet another Olympic coach, Don Peters. Kathy was fifth at the 1983 U.S. National Championships, barely beaten by another rapidly developing youngster named Mary Lou Retton—who would eventually become the United States' first Olympic all-around champion.

At the Pre-Olympics in August, 1983, Kathy advanced to third all-around. Later, at the World Gymnastics Championships in Budapest, Kathy placed eleventh, proving once again her ability as a world-class gymnast. She was timing her training carefully, placing second to Mary Lou Retton at the American Classic in March, 1984. She barely made the Olympic team in June, scoring poorly because of a fall from the beam, but she performed flawlessly during the remainder of the trials. Finally, at the 1984 Los Angeles Games, she realized her dream of winning an Olympic medal—a bronze on the balance beam. Just shy of her twenty-fifth birthday, Kathy was the oldest member of the team.

Continuing the Story

Kathy stayed involved in the gymnastics world as a motivational speaker and commentator for ABC and ESPN sports. She became active in the Los Angeles area dance community, took up running as a sport, married actor Brian Clarke (becoming Kathy Johnson-Clarke), and gave birth to a son in March, 1998. She continues to speak out for the rights of athletes and has served as an athletic ambassador for the Culture, Education, Sports and Ethics Program (CESEP).

Summary

Kathy Johnson is living proof that physical maturity is not necessarily the end of a female gymnast's career. She entered the world of elite gymnastics in 1979 and stayed near the top, despite injuries, until her Olympic medal performance in 1984. Kathy's elegant walk to and from the floor exercise area was illustrative of her quest to produce a positive view of her gymnastic artistry.

A. Bruce Frederick

Additional Sources

Greenberg, Stan. *Whitaker's Olympic Almanack: An Encyclopaedia of the Olympic Games.* Chicago: Fitzroy Dearborn, 2000.

Wallechinsky, David, and Jaime Loucky. *The Complete Book of the Olympics: 2008 Edition.* London: Aurum Press, 2008.

Michael Johnson

Born: September 13, 1967
  Dallas, Texas
Also known as: Michael Duane Johnson (full
  name)

Early Life

Michael Duane Johnson was born in Dallas, Texas, on September 13, 1967. His parents—truck driver Paul Johnson and elementary school teacher Ruby Johnson—emphasized education. Michael was always the fastest child on the block. In junior high, he participated in track and football but quit the latter because of the aggressive nature of the sport. He placed second in the 200 meters in his first junior high school race. After taking off two years from athletics to concentrate on academics, he returned to running during his junior year at Skyline High School in Dallas. As a senior, his second-place finish in the 200 meters at the Texas state meet and his outstanding academic achievements helped him earn a scholarship to Baylor University in Waco, Texas.

The Road to Excellence

With an erect, statuesque running style, Michael did not look like a speedster, but Baylor coach Clyde Hart recruited Michael for his relay teams. To Hart's surprise, Michael set a new Baylor record in the 200 meters, at 20.41 seconds, in his first collegiate competition. A pulled hamstring reduced his participation during his freshman year to relay events at the National Collegiate Athletic Association (NCAA) Championships. In 1988, he gained the track world's attention with times of 20.07 seconds in the 200 meters and 43.5 seconds in a 4×400-meter relay leg.

Michael suffered a stress fracture in his left leg in the NCAA 200-meter finals. The injury hindered

Sprinter Michael Johnson next to a scoreboard showing his world-record time in 200 meters at the 1996 Olympic Games in Atlanta. (Mike Powell/Getty Images)

his effort in the 1988 Olympic trials, where he finished seventh in his 400-meter heat; he skipped the 200 meters. The following track season he won the 200 meters at the NCAA Indoor Championships with an American record of 20.59 seconds. However, he pulled a hamstring, which ruined his chances of capturing the NCAA Outdoor and the U.S. Championship titles.

The Emerging Champion

In his senior year, 1990, Michael won in the 400 meters at the U.S. Indoor Championships and in the 200 meters at the NCAA Indoor and Outdoor Championships and U.S. Outdoor Championships. These finishes earned him the number-one ranking in the world in both events. Michael not only was the first athlete to hold both of these rankings in a career but also accomplished this feat in the same year. He graduated from Baylor with a bachelor's degree in business in 1990. Wins in the 400 meters at the U.S. Indoor Championships and the 200 meters at the U.S. Outdoor and World Track and Field Championships helped him retain his number-one ranking in the world in both events in 1991.

Michael decided to concentrate on the 200 meters in the 1992 Olympics. Although he was the heavy favorite to win, he suffered from food poisoning. He did not qualify for the 200-meter finals, but he won a gold medal as part of the 4×400-meter relay team. The following year, Michael slipped to number four in world rankings in the 200 meters, but his dominance of the 400 meters continued. He won at the U.S. and World Track and Field Championships. He also anchored the U.S. men's 4×400-meter relay team at the latter event with the fastest leg in history: 42.79 seconds. The 1995 season was a precursor to the coming Olympics: He won the 200 meters, in 19.79 seconds, and 400 meters, 43.39 seconds, at the World Track and Field Championships.

Continuing the Story

At the 1996 Olympics in Atlanta, Georgia, Michael made track history: He became the first man to win the gold medal in both the 200 and 400 meters. In the process, he set a world record of 19.32 seconds in the 200 meters and an Olympic record of 43.49

Major Sprint Championships

Year	Competition	Event	Place
1990	U.S. Championships	200 meters	1st
1991	U.S. Championships	200 meters	1st
	World Championships	200 meters	1st
1992	Olympic Games	4×400-meter relay	Gold
1993	U.S. Championships	400 meters	1st
	World Championships	400 meters	1st
		4×400-meter relay	1st
1995	U.S. Championships	200 meters	1st
		400 meters	1st
	World Championships	200 meters	1st
		400 meters	1st
		4×400-meter relay	1st
1996	Olympic Games	200 meters	Gold OR
		400 meters	Gold OR, WR
1997	World Championships	400 meters	1st
1999	World Championships	400 meters	1st WR
		4×400-meter relay	1st
2000	Olympic Games	400 meters	Gold
		4×400-meter relay	Gold*

*Later nullified by the International Olympic Committee (IOC)

Notes: OR = Olympic Record; WR = World Record

seconds in the 400 meters. Afterward, he admitted that he had shocked even himself. However, he also felt that he might have been able to run the 200 meters even faster because he had not run perfectly. According to Michael, the clock, more than any other runner, was always his biggest rival.

After the Olympics, Michael signed many lucrative endorsement contracts, including a $12 million deal with Nike. He continued his dominance of the 400 meters through the year 1999. He won the 400 meters at the 1997 and 1999 World Track and Field Championships and the 1998 Goodwill Games and anchored the world-record-setting 4×400 meter U.S. relay team at the Goodwill Games. His time of 43.18 seconds at the 1999 World Track and Field Championships broke the world record.

At the 2000 Olympic trials, Michael won the 400 meters, but an injury during the 200-meter finals prohibited him from finishing the race. He could not repeat his 1996 feat, but he did win the 400 meters at the 2000 Olympics in Sydney, Australia, to become the first man to successfully defend a 400-meter Olympic title. He also won a gold medal in the 4×400 relay. The International Olympic Committee later stripped him of the medal because one of his teammates admitted to using illegal performance-enhancing drugs at the time of the event.

While competing at the 2000 Summer Olympics, Michael began a career working as a sports commentator in television broadcasts. Prior to his retirement from track and field, he spent several months promoting public interest in his sport, talking with young people and holding coaching clinics for them in thirteen different cities. In 2004, he was inducted into the USA Track and Field Hall of Fame. At that time, his 19.32 finish in the 200 meters at the 1996 Olympics was declared the greatest moment in U.S. track and field during the previous quarter-century.

Although Michael retired from competition, he remained involved in track and field. He worked as an agent for Jeremy Wariner, who won the gold medal in the 400 meters at the 2004 Olympics and the silver medal in the same event at the 2008 Olympics. Michael also served as a consultant for track and field athletes at his alma mater, Baylor University.

Summary

Rarely does one person possess both the speed required to win the 200 meters and the endurance necessary to win the 400 meters, but Michael Johnson had both attributes. For eight years, from 1993 to 2000, he was the premier 400-meter runner in the world. Furthermore, for several years during the 1990's, he was the world's best 200-meter sprinter. His dominance of these events culminated in gold medals in both events at the 1996 Olympics; he became the first man to accomplish such a feat. Along with Jesse Owens and Carl Lewis, he will be known as one of the greatest American sprinters of the twentieth century.

Marlene Bradford, updated by Caroline Collins

Additional Sources

Johnson, Michael. *Slaying the Dragon: How to Turn Your Small Steps to Great Feats.* New York: Regan Books, 1996.

Porter, David L. *Latino and African American Athletes Today.* Westport, Conn.: Greenwood Press, 2004.

Rosenthal, Bert. *Michael Johnson: Sprinter Deluxe.* St. Charles, Mo.: GHB, 2000.

Nancy Johnson

Born: January 14, 1974
    Downers Grove, Illinois
Also known as: Nancy Lynn Napolski (birth
    name)

Early Life

Nancy Johnson was born Nancy Lynn Napolski on January 14, 1974, in Downers Grove, Illinois, a suburb of Chicago. When Nancy was ten, she watched on television as gymnast Mary Lou Retton won the all-around gold medal at the 1984 Olympic Games. At that moment, she became determined to go to the Olympics. Five years later, she thought she had found the sport that was to fulfill this dream. She told her parents, Ben and Diane, that she wanted to learn archery so she could go deer hunting with her father. According to family lore, her father told her that she would not be a good hunter because she could not remain quiet long enough. While her home in Illinois did not have a local archery range, there was a nearby shooting range and the Downers Grove Junior Rifle Club. Initially, Nancy did not have any interest in the rifle; however, her father prevailed and talked her into trying the sport.

The Road to Excellence

Although Nancy found shooting difficult, she loved it from the beginning. Her high school, Benet Academy in Lisle, Illinois, had no shooting club, but Nancy was able to compete at private clubs and against the teams of other high schools, shooting a .22-caliber long rifle, rather than the .177-caliber pellet rifle used in the Olympics. A natural at the sport, Nancy soon began winning local shooting prizes. In 1991, she began losing feeling along the left side of her body, which made holding a rifle for any length of time difficult for her. Originally thought to be multiple sclerosis—a nerve disease that can lead to paralysis—the numbness left her after about six months, as mysteriously as it had come. It required a year of physical therapy before Nancy completely regained her strength.

After high school graduation, Nancy enrolled at the University of Kentucky, where, in addition to firing the .22-caliber rifle, she also began practicing with the air rifle. In competition, the .22 is fired at targets set at a distance of 50 meters (more than 150 feet) from three positions: standing, kneeling, and prone. The air rifle, however, is shot from only 10 meters (about 33 feet) away from targets. Nancy practiced hard in both disciplines, learned well, and began to earn victories while in college. She won a National Collegiate Athletic Association (NCAA) air-rifle championship in 1994. She earned a bronze medal in air rifle at the 1995 national championships. A three-time collegiate all-American, she took gold in air rifle at the 1996 World Cup and earned a berth on the 1996 U.S. Olympic team and the opportunity to compete in Atlanta, Georgia.

The Emerging Champion

The 1996 Olympics represented only the fourth competition at the international level for Nancy, and she later admitted that she was not ready for the intense pressure she faced. Though she finished only thirty-sixth in her event, she had the chance to fulfill her youthful dream of participating in the Olympics.

After the Olympics, Nancy began dating Kenneth Alden "Ken" Johnson, a marksman whom she had met two years earlier at the U.S. national shooting competition. The following year, in 1997, they married and moved to Phoenix City, Alabama, where Ken was an Army sergeant. His specialty as a

Major Shooting Championships

Year	Competition	Event	Score	Place
1994	World Shooting Junior Championship	Junior Female 10m Air Rifle	389.0	8th
1996	Olympic Games	Women's 10m Air Rifle	386.0	36th
	World Cup	Women's 10m Air Rifle	500.0	1st
1997	World Cup	Women's 10m Air Rifle	494.0	3d
1998	World Cup	Women's 50m Sport (Std) Rifle	675.9	3d
	World Shooting Championship	Women's 10m Air Rifle	493.0	7th
1999	Pan-American Games	Women's 50m Sport (Std) Rifle	661.0	2d
2000	Olympic Games	Women's 10m Air Rifle	497.7	Gold

marksman and his place in an elite competition unit allowed him to serve in the Army and train to compete in national and international competitions at the same time.

Nancy also continued training, rising early six days a week in order to be at the rifle range from 7:30 A.M. until 3:00 P.M. Her regime also included 2 hours of exercising and weightlifting. She needed to build both stamina and a slow, steady heartbeat. In order to be precise enough to hit the target, shooters have to squeeze off their shots between heartbeats. This training helped her make all of the international finals in her sport. She won a bronze medal in air-rifle competition at the 1997 World Cup, before a wrist injured in a car accident left her unable to compete in that year's national championships. She had recovered enough the following year to win bronze at the 1998 national championships. Nancy also picked up a gold medal with the air rifle at the 1999 national championships and a silver medal at the 2000 Pan-American Games in Winnipeg, Manitoba, Canada. Meanwhile, her husband won gold medals in air rifle and three-position rifle at the 1999 Pan-American Games, a silver medal in three-position rifle at the World Cup, and an air-rifle bronze at the 2000 U.S. championships. Nancy and Ken hoped that extensive training and competition experience would ultimately pay off, allowing them both to compete in the 2000 Olympics in Sydney, Australia.

Continuing the Story

That dream came true when Nancy and Ken became the first husband and wife to make the same U.S. Olympic team. When Nancy arrived in Sydney, she decided not to participate in the parade of athletes in the Opening Ceremony and the partying that followed. Nancy stayed in the athletes' village, missing all the festivities, because she had to be ready to compete at 9:00 A.M. the following morning in the first event of the Games.

Nancy finished the qualifying round in a disappointing fifth place. However, after receiving advice from her husband, she adjusted her technique and narrowly defeated Kang Cho-hyun of South Korea to win the gold medal. She not only captured the first gold medal to be awarded in the Sydney Olympics but also became the first American to win the shooting event since 1984. Although Ken could not match his wife's performance and tied for thirty-eighth place, he said that the pressure was off him because someone in the family was bringing home the gold.

Apparently, that gold medal was a sufficient reward for Nancy and Ken Johnson in the years after her triumph at Sydney. While the couple mused about competing in the 2004 Olympics, and Nancy took up archery and considered running a marathon, neither Nancy nor Ken participated at the 2004 or the 2008 Olympics. Instead, Nancy was using her B.S. degree in horticulture in the nursery of a Home Depot in Columbus, Georgia. Ken, meanwhile, finished his stint in the Army. Both contemplated entering graduate school at nearby Auburn University, where Nancy thought of pursuing a master's degree in nutrition. Together, they often practiced their shooting skills in hunting for deer, duck, and wild boar.

Summary

Nancy Johnson knew from an early age she wanted to compete in the Olympics but did not have a direction until she was introduced to the rifle range. Once she began shooting, she knew she had found a sport that she loved. She overcame a mysterious and debilitating ailment to devote thousands of hours to training and competing. She had such a love of the sport that not even a disappointing finish in the 1996 Olympics deterred her. She trained with her husband, and the couple pushed each other to compete harder. This partnership worked well for Nancy, who won a gold medal in women's air rifle at the 2000 Olympics—the first American since 1984 to capture the gold in that event.

Deborah Service, updated by Jack Ewing

Additional Sources

Derocher, Robert. "Dupage Native Shoots for Olympics." *Chicago Tribune*, August 6, 1999, p. 3.

Findling, John E., and Kimberly D. Pelle. *Encyclopedia of the Modern Olympic Movement*. Champaign, Ill.: Sports, 2004.

Hirsley, Michael. "Air Rifle's First Family Has to Settle for Single Gold." *Chicago Tribune*, September 18, 2000, p. S12.

Pennington, Bill. "Well-Rested, American Wins the First Gold." *The New York Times*, September 16, 2000.

Wallechinsky, David, and Jaime Loucky. *The Complete Book of the Summer Olympics: 2008 Edition*. London: Aurum Press, 2008.

Rafer Johnson

Born: August 18, 1935
Hillsboro, Texas
Also known as: Rafer Lewis Johnson (full name)

Early Life
Rafer Lewis Johnson was born on August 18, 1935, in Hillsboro, Texas, about fifty-five miles south of Dallas. Rafer was one of six children. In the hope of bettering their living conditions, the Johnson family moved to Kingsburg, in California's San Joaquin Valley, when Rafer was nine years old. The family lived in a railroad boxcar, which they had modified into a home. Rafer's athletic career nearly ended before it began when, as a young boy, his left foot was severely cut when it was caught in a conveyor belt.

The Road to Excellence
At Kingsburg High School, Rafer served as student body president and won a total of thirteen varsity letters in basketball, track, football, and baseball. As a halfback, Rafer averaged more than nine yards every time he carried the football and led his team to three league championships. He was also an outstanding basketball player, averaging seventeen points per game. Rafer was the center fielder in baseball, where he batted more than .400, including a .512 average in his junior year.

Rafer's talent in football earned him a scholarship offer from the University of California at Los Angeles (UCLA), but his favorite sport was track. He was concerned that football injuries might affect his track career, so he eventually stopped playing football.

Track and field became Rafer's sport. He won state championships in the 110-yard hurdles and the decathlon, a single competition composed of ten separate events. Rafer excelled in decathlon events such as the 100-meter and 400-meter runs, the shot put, the discus, and the javelin. Other decathlon events such as the pole vault, high jump, and broad jump were more difficult for him, but

Rafer dreamed about qualifying for the Olympic Games.

Because Rafer had been a state track champion and because he had also won all-league honors in every sport, he was inducted into the National High School Sports Hall of Fame on July 6, 1990, in Minneapolis. However, Rafer's high school greatness was only the first chapter of a championship story.

The Emerging Champion
While still a freshman at UCLA, Rafer began his famous decathlon career by winning the event at the

Rafer Johnson carrying the torch at the opening ceremony of the 1984 Los Angeles Olympic Games, for which he lit the stadium torch. (Courtesy of Rafer Johnson)

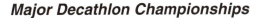

1955 Pan-American Games in Mexico City, with 6,994 points. In June of that year, he set a new world decathlon record of 7,758 points. In 1956, Rafer won his first national decathlon championship at the Amateur Athletic Union (AAU) meet. In his enthusiasm to prepare himself for the 1956 Olympics in Melbourne, Australia, Rafer tore a stomach muscle. The old football injuries that he feared had caught up with him. Rafer was still able to win a silver medal at Melbourne with a second-place finish in the decathlon. He was forced to withdraw from the long jump, for which he had also qualified.

Rafer had four years to prepare for the 1960 Olympics, and he trained like a true champion. In the 1958 "Little Olympics" in Moscow, where track athletes from the United States and the Soviet Union competed, Rafer won the decathlon. He also set a world decathlon record of 7,896 points and defeated Vasiliy Kusnyetsov—whom the Soviets called their "Man of Steel"—by 505 points.

A young man of great overall character, Rafer excelled as both a citizen and a student while at UCLA. He maintained nearly an A average, headed three campus honor societies, was president of the student body, and was the university's first black student to pledge a white fraternity.

A car accident one year before the 1960 Rome Olympics left Rafer with a severely injured back. He spent several weeks in the hospital but recovered enough to win the Olympic trials. The ten-event decathlon in Rome was completed in a twenty-six-hour span. Rafer compiled a world record 8,392 points and earned the title of the greatest all-round athlete in the world. At the age of twenty-five, he had fulfilled his high school dream.

Major Decathlon Championships

Year	Competition	Place	Points
1955	Pan-American Games	1st	6,994
1956	Olympic Games	Silver	7,587
	National AAU Championships	1st	7,754
1958	National AAU Championships	1st	7,754
1960	National AAU Championships	1st	8,683
	Olympic Games	Gold	8,392 OR, WR

Notes: OR = Olympic Record; WR = World Record

Continuing the Story

In 1960, Rafer was voted *Track and Field News* world athlete of the year and also won the James E. Sullivan Memorial Award as the outstanding amateur athlete of the year. More honors were to follow as Rafer was named to the Helms Hall of Fame as Hall of the Athlete Foundation athlete of the year, *Sports* magazine athlete of the year, and Associated Press male athlete of the year, and was given the Junior Chamber of Commerce Award as one of the ten outstanding young men in the United States. He was subsequently inducted into both the USA Track and Field Hall of Fame and the Black Athletes Hall of Fame.

Rafer later worked in a number of diverse fields, including films, network television sportscasting, and politics; he also served as a goodwill ambassador for the U.S. State Department. This talented man also sang baritone in two church choirs and served on both California's State Recreation Committee and the board of directors of the National Recreation and Park Association. Other boards of directors on which Rafer has served are the Close Up Foundation and the California Special Olympics, the national advisory board of the United States Association for Blind Athletes, and the advisory board of the

Honors, Awards, and Records

1955, 1958, 1960	Set three world records in the decathlon: 7,758 points in 1955, 7,896 points in 1958, and 8,392 points in 1960
1958	*Sports Illustrated* Sportsman of the Year
	World Trophy
1960	Helms Hall of Fame Hall of the Athlete Foundation Athlete of the Year
	Track and Field News World Athlete of the Year
	James E. Sullivan Award
	Associated Press Male Athlete of the Year
	Sports magazine Athlete of the Year
1974	Inducted into USA Track and Field Hall of Fame
1975	Inducted into Black Athletes Hall of Fame
1983	Inducted into U.S. Olympic Hall of Fame
1990	Inducted into National High School Hall of Fame

499

U.S. Department of Health and Human Services Physically and Mentally Handicapped Committee.

One of the most respected, articulate, and socially conscious athletes of his time, Rafer served on the board of directors of the Los Angeles Athletic Foundation (LAAF). The LAAF developed out of the 1984 Los Angeles Olympic Committee and has been responsible for distributing more than $200 million raised at the 1984 Olympic Games to youth sports programs.

Rafer again participated in the Olympics twenty-four years after winning his gold medal when, as the final torchbearer, he ran up the giant stairway at the Los Angeles Coliseum to light the flame that symbolized the opening of the 1984 Olympic Games. The torch was passed to Rafer by the granddaughter of Jesse Owens, the African American sprinter who won four gold medals for the United States at the 1936 Berlin Olympics. One of Rafer's greatest Olympic thrills, however, came in the 2000 Games at Sydney, Australia, when he watched his daughter, Jenny Johnson Jordan, represent the United States in beach volleyball.

Summary

Rafer Johnson had the unique ability to overcome both childhood poverty and severe injury to fulfill his dream of becoming an Olympic champion. He has given of himself to others, especially in representing the Special Olympics and promoting recreational activities for youngsters. He remains an exemplary role model for athletes and nonathletes alike.

Ronald L. Ammons

Additional Sources

Cazeneuve, Brian. "Rafer Johnson, Olympic Hero." *Sports Illustrated* 93, no. 10 (September 11, 2000): 20.

Johnson, Rafer, and Philip Goldberg. *The Best That I Can Be: An Autobiography.* New York: Galilee, 1999.

"Power Play: Rafer Johnson, Olympic Gold Medalist." *Parks and Recreation* 38, no. 5 (May, 2003): 84.

Wallechinsky, David, and Jaime Loucky. *The Complete Book of the Olympics: 2008 Edition.* London: Aurum Press, 2008.

Shawn Johnson

Born: January 19, 1992
    West Des Moines, Iowa
Also known as: Shawn Machel Johnson (full
   name); Peanut

Early Life

Shawn Machel Johnson was born on January 19,
1992, to junior high school sweethearts Doug and
Teri Johnson, in West Des Moines, Iowa. Her father
worked as a carpenter, and her mother was an ac-
counting clerk for the West Des Moines School
District. At birth, Shawn had an Activity, Pulse,
Grimace, Appearance, and Respiration (APGAR)

Shawn Johnson performing on the balance beam at the 2008 Olympic Games in Beijing. (Cameron Spencer/Getty Images)

score of zero. This test rates a baby's physical condition on a scale of zero to two; Shawn received the
lowest score possible.

Shawn quickly improved, however, and proved
to be highly active and energetic. She was walking
by nine months old, after skipping the crawling
stage, and began pulling herself up and climbing
out of her crib shortly thereafter. Desperate for a
release for their daughter's energy, Shawn's parents enrolled her in a dance class and a tumbling
class when she was three. These classes were too slow
for the energetic toddler, so her mother turned to
gymnastics. Shawn immediately took to the sport
and, at six years old, transferred from
her local gymnasium to the newly opened
Chow's Gymnastics, owned and operated
by former Chinese gymnastics stars Liang
Chow and Liwen Zhuang. Upon her
first visit to Chow's, Shawn immediately
jumped onto the uneven bars, showing
no inhibition.

The Road to Excellence

Because the gym had opened recently,
it had no gymnastics team; therefore,
Shawn was able to train with Chow in the
basics of the sport. Chow quickly realized Shawn's talents and sent a tape of
her performances to former Romanian
coaches Béla and Martha Károlyi. The
Károlyis compared Shawn to Kim Zmeskal, who earned an all-around gold
medal at the 1991 World Gymnastics
Championships. Shawn and Zmeskal had
identical body types and confidence levels; Béla Károlyi said that in his forty
years of teaching, he had never seen two
athletes so similar. The Károlyis began
coaching Shawn in 2005.

When Shawn debuted in the competitive arena, she was viewed as a fierce and
emerging gymnast. In 2005, she began
to receive attention when she placed
third at the U.S. Classic after qualifying
for junior international elite status on

Major Gymnastics Championships

Year	Competition	Event	Place
2005	U.S. Gymnastics Championships	All-around	10th
		Vault	4th
		Uneven bars	9th
2006	U.S. Gymnastics Championships	All-around	1st
		Vault	1st
		Balance beam	1st
		Floor exercise	1st
		Uneven bars	2d
	Pan-American Gymnastics Championships	Team	1st
		Balance beam	1st
		All-around	1st
		Uneven bars	2d
		Floor exercise	2d
	Pacific Alliance Gymnastics Championships	All-around	1st
		Team	1st
		Vault	1st
		Floor exercise	1st
		Balance beam	2d
2007	American Cup	All-around	1st
	World Championships	Team	1st
		All-around	1st
		Floor exercise	1st
	Pan-American Games	Team	1st
		All-around	1st
		Uneven bars	1st
		Balance beam	1st
		Floor exercise	2d
2008	American Cup	All-around	2d
	Olympic Games	Balance beam	Gold
		All-around	Silver
		Team	Silver
		Floor exercise	Silver

her first attempt. Shawn had an impressive junior career: In 2006, in St. Paul, Minnesota, she won the all-around U.S. Junior Gymnastics Championships with a higher score than any senior elite competitors. That same year, she also captured the all-around titles at the Pan-American Championships in Gatineau, Quebec, Canada, and the Pacific Alliance Championships in Honolulu, Hawaii.

The Emerging Champion

In 2007, Shawn entered the senior division and won all-around titles at the United States versus Great Britain International Competition; the Pan-American Games, in Rio de Janeiro, Brazil; the World Gymnastics Championships in Stuttgart, Germany; the American Cup in Jacksonville, Florida; and the U.S. Gymnastics Championships in San Jose, California. In 2008, Shawn continued her

winning streak, placing first in the all-around at the U.S. Gymnastics Championships for the second consecutive year. Also, she was second in the all-around competition at the 2008 American Cup.

At the age of sixteen, Shawn became possibly the only gymnast in the world to incorporate three "G-level" elements in her competitions—judges award points based on degree of difficulty; "A" is basic skill level and "G" is the most difficult. Shawn's advanced-level skills included a double twisting double layout dismount on the uneven bars, a full twisting double tuck dismount on the balance beam, and her tucked double twisting double tumbling pass on floor exercises. Shawn became one of only three women in the world to perform a two and one-half twisting layout Yurchenko on the vault.

Continuing the Story

In June of 2008, Shawn finished first in the trials for the U.S. women's Olympic team and traveled to the Olympic Games in Beijing, China. Under increased pressure, Shawn pushed herself to her limits and qualified in all four events: balance beam, floor exercise, uneven bars, and the vault. Shawn received the silver medal in the individual all-around competition, while Nastia Liukin, Shawn's teammate and Olympic Village roommate, took the gold medal. Shawn won the silver medal in floor exercises, while Liukin received the bronze medal. Shawn captured the gold medal on the balance beam, while Liukin earned the silver medal. The 2008 Olympics represented the first time the United States, and the fourth time any country, had won both gold and silver medals in the individual all-around competition. The U.S. women received the silver medal in the team competition, while China earned the gold medal.

After the Olympics, Shawn began her junior year at Valley High School. Unlike other elite gymnasts who train 40 or more hours a week and are tutored privately, Shawn trained for 25 hours to leave time for her homework and social life. She maintained a 4.0 grade point average, which placed her on the honor roll, and had aspirations of attending an Ivy League university.

Summary

Shawn Johnson had an amazing career at a young age. Her athletic talents earned her medals, titles, and the admiration of gymnastics enthusiasts across the globe. Shawn helped her team win the silver medal in the 2008 Olympic Games and gold medals at the Pan-American Games and the World Gymnastics Championships in 2007. She joined the ranks of Kim Zmeskal, Chellsie Memmel, and Shannon Miller as American female world champions and Carly Patterson and Mary Lou Retton as American Olympic gold medalists.

Shawn's accomplishments did not go unnoticed by those outside gymnastics. Governor Chet Culver pronounced October 17 Shawn Johnson Day in Iowa, and, in July of 2008, a bronze statue of Shawn was erected in the Iowa Hall of Fame. The spirit, excitement, and passion that Shawn brought to gymnastics, and her ability to introduce a new generation of fans and future competitors to the sport, was as impressive and important as her medal count.

Sara Vidar

Additional Sources

Layden, Joe. *Superstars of USA Women's Gymnastics (Women Athletes of the 2000 Olympics)*. New York: Aladdin Paperbacks, 2000.

Morley, Christine. *The Best Book of Gymnastics*. Boston: Kingfisher, 2003.

Olsen, Leigh. *Going for Gold: The 2008 Women's Gymnastics Team*. New York: Penguin, 2008.

Colleen Jones

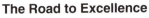

Born: December 16, 1959
Halifax, Nova Scotia, Canada
Also known as: Colleen P. Jones (full name)

Early Life

Colleen P. Jones was born into a family of curlers. She grew up with seven older sisters, all of whom participated in the winter sport. Every Saturday morning, Colleen and her sisters went to the Mayflower skating rink in Halifax to practice curling. Watching her sisters compete instilled in Colleen a desire to become as good as or better than her sisters. With eight girls, there were always two curling teams and plenty of competition. Colleen practiced with a kitchen broom and skated in her stockinged feet on the kitchen floor when she could not go to the ice rink. She spent all of her time away from school practicing to be a great curler. Curling became her life's passion, but the sport was not a career, so Colleen went to Dalhousie University in Halifax.

Colleen Jones competing at the World Curling Championships in Sweden in 2004. (Jack Mikrut/AFP/Getty Images)

The Road to Excellence

In 1982, Colleen became the youngest curling skip to win a Canadian Curling Championship. In curling, the skip is the team captain and directs each of the throwers where to aim the stones, or smooth granite rocks, by holding a broom and hollering "hurry hard" to the team. The skip also throws the last two stones as the vice-skip holds the broom and hollers at the rest of team sweeping ahead of the stone, ensuring the proper direction of the stone. Each member of the team sweeps the ice ahead of the stone to determine the path toward the house, which is composed of concentric, painted circles at the end of the strip of ice. In 1982, Colleen hollered her team to the first of seven national Canadian Curling Championships. She graduated from college the following year.

For half of the year, curlers have regular lives with jobs and families; for the other half of the year, they become athletes. Therefore, in 1982, Colleen started her broadcasting career with the CHUM radio group, doing morning sports reports and local sports stories. In 1984, she moved to television in Halifax. Her dedication to her career landed her a job with the Canadian Broadcasting Corporation (CBC) out of Nova Scotia with the evening news. Less than ten years later, in 1993, Colleen joined the morning edition of CBC Newsworld. In addition, Colleen covered five Olympic Games for CBC beginning in 1988.

The Emerging Champion

In 1990, Colleen was inducted into the Curling Hall of Fame as the youngest skip to ever win a Canadian Curling Championship. In 1999, she brought a team together—that included Kim Kelly, Mary Anne Wayne-Arsenault, and Nancy Delahunt—and won the

Honors and Awards

1982	Youngest curling skip to win a Canadian Curling Championship
1982, 1999-2004	Canadian Curling Championship
1990	Inducted into Curling Hall of Fame
1993, 1999	Canadian Mixed Curling Champion
2001, 2004	World Curling Championship

Canadian Curling Championship. From 1999 to 2004, her team won the Canadian Curling Championship a record-breaking five times and won the World Curling Championship in Switzerland in 2001 and 2004. Colleen and her team members became household names in Canada. Although the team was winning, it was unwilling to make the sacrifices to go to the Olympics in 2006. The team members wanted to have fun curling and did not want the extra practice time, traveling, and fast-paced life required for inclusion on the Olympic team.

Continuing the Story

In 2007, Colleen's longtime team split apart. Colleen and the rest of the team no longer got along. The team hired a skip to replace Colleen. Though Colleen found it difficult to watch her old team play without her, she was determined to start fresh with a new team, which included her sister, Monica Moriarty, as lead. At the age of forty-six, Colleen played the third position for the first time in her career. She stated that since she was starting fresh, she should choose a new position on the team. She and her team practiced with hopes of competing in the 2010 Olympics.

Summary

Colleen Jones was the youngest skip to ever win the Canadian Curling Championship. She was inducted into the Curling Hall of Fame at the age of thirty, only ten years after taking her first national title. Beginning in 1999, she won six Canadian Curling Championships and two world titles. She did not quit curling when her team of five years did not want to make the Olympics; instead, she forged ahead and brought a new team together. At the age of forty-six, she started playing a new position, which meant learning a new skill. Colleen showed that with practice and determination, she could become a successful journalist and champion curler.

Pamela D. Doughty

Additional Sources

Jones, Colleen. *Curling Secrets: How to Think and Play Like a Pro.* Halifax, N.S.: Nimbus, 2007.

Walling, Alex J. *Golden Gushue: A Curling Story.* Halifax, N.S.: Nimbus, 2006.

Marion Jones

Born: October 12, 1975
  Los Angeles, California
Also known as: Marion Lois Jones (full name);
  Marion Jones-Thompson

Early Life
Marion Lois Jones was born in Los Angeles, California, in 1975. Inspired by the 1984 Los Angeles Olympic Games, she wanted to become an Olympic champion. Her early athletic promise blossomed while she was in high school, where she was an all-star basketball player and track athlete. In fact, she never lost a track event after her freshman year and was a four-time state champion in the 100-meter dash. During her senior year, she failed to take a mandatory urine test for performance-enhancing drugs, but the charges were dropped. Accepting a scholarship to the University of North Carolina, as a freshman, she starred on the women's basketball team, which won the 1994 national championship. However, she decided to concentrate on track and field, stating that she wanted to be the fastest woman in the world.

The Road to Excellence
An injury kept Marion out of the 1996 Atlanta Olympics, but at the 1997 World Track and Field Championships at Athens, Greece, she won the 100-meter race. At the World Track and Field Championships in Johannesburg, South Africa, in 1999 she long-jumped 7.3 meters (23 feet 11¾ inches) and ran the 100 meters in 10.65 seconds and the 200 meters in 21.62 seconds. That year, she was victorious in thirty-five out of the thirty-six sprint races that she entered. By the eve of the 2000 Sydney Olympic Games, Marion had become an international celebrity and was featured in numerous advertising campaigns with Nike, Gatorade, General Motors, Kellogg's cereals, and Panasonic. An official of the U.S. track and field federation claimed that Marion had received more attention from the media and advertising sources than any athlete in history. Before the Games, Marion said she wanted to win five gold medals: two in the sprints, two in the relays, and one in the long jump.

The Emerging Champion
Marion was only twenty-four years old in 2000. Many commentators were already looking ahead to the 2004 and 2008 Olympics and the possibility that Marion could surpass Carl Lewis's nine gold medals. C. J. Hunter, Marion's husband, was the reigning world champion in the shot put, which added to the drama. If Marion did not entirely reach her goal, her achievements at Sydney were outstanding. Although she failed in her quest for five gold medals, she won three, running 10.75 in the 100 meters and 21.8 in the 200 meters and anchoring the 4×400-meter relay team. She won bronze medals in the long jump and the 4×100-meter relay. She was the first woman to win five medals in a single Olympics. Her achievements

Major Track and Field Championships

Year	Competition	Event	Place
1997	World Championships	100 meters	1st
1998	Goodwill Games	100 meters	1st
		200 meters	1st
	World Cup	100 meters	1st
		200 meters	1st
	U.S. Nationals	100 meters	1st
		200 meters	1st
		Long jump	1st
1999	World Championships	100 meters	1st
		Long jump	3d
2000	Olympic Games	100 meters	Gold*
		200 meters	Gold*
		4×400-meter relay	Gold*
		Long jump	Bronze*
		4×100-meter relay	Bronze*
2001	World Championships	100 meters	2d**
		200 meters	1st**
		4×400-meter relay	1st**
2002	World Cup	100 meters	1st**

*Later nullified by the International Olympic Committee (IOC) and the International Association of Athletics Federations (IAAF). Jones returned medals to the IOC.

**Later nullified by the IAAF.

were slightly clouded when Hunter pulled out of the Games, supposedly because of an injured knee. However, he reportedly failed several drug tests that summer and was accused of using anabolic steroids.

Marion's Olympic triumphs in 2000 made her the most famous female athlete in the world. She commanded as much as $80,000 per race to compete in track and field meets, and her commercial endorsements made her a millionaire. She graced the covers of *Time* magazine, pictured in her running garb, and *Vogue* magazine, for which she glamorously wore a stunning red evening dress. She was featured in the popular "Got Milk" advertising campaign.

Continuing the Story

However, rumors had long circulated about Marion's possible use of performance-enhancing drugs. Hunter, whom Marion divorced in 2002, had used steroids. Her coaches, including Trevor Graham, Charlie Francis, and Steve Riddick, were allegedly involved with performance-enhancing drugs. Francis admitted giving his athletes steroids. Some of Riddick's runners were suspended for illegal drug use, while Graham was investigated by grand juries and convicted of lying to federal agents. In 2003, Victor Conte, whose Northern California Bay Area Laboratory-Cooperative (BALCO) became notorious for providing illegal substances to many athletes, testified on television that he personally gave Marion performance-enhancing drugs before, during, and after the Sydney Olympics. Also, sprinter Tim Montgomery, the father of Marion's first child, was suspended for using steroids. Furthermore, Hunter testified that Marion had used steroids, acquired from Conte, before the 2000 Olympics.

When interviewed by federal authorities in 2003, Marion denied using steroids knowingly, asserting she assumed she was simply using a flaxseed-oil substance, a claim also made by other athletes implicated in the scandal. Because of pregnancies and injuries, Marion competed only occasionally after 2001. In 2006, she won the 100-meter race at the USA Outdoor Track and Field Championships. Although an initial urine test indicated that she had used the blood-enhancing substance Erythropoietin, the second test came back negative.

In spite of her years of denials about drug use, on October 5, 2007, Marion confessed in court that she had used "the Clear," the anabolic steroid Tetrahydrogestrinone, in 2000 and 2001. Other court documents indicated that she had used several additional illegal substances, including human growth hormones. The International Olympic Committee immediately stripped Marion of her five Olympic medals.

Summary

On January 11, 2008, Marion Jones was sentenced to six months in prison and two years of community service, both for her involvement in a check-fraud scheme with Montgomery and for lying under oath about steroid use. The millions of dollars she had made through her competitions and endorsements had dissipated, and her reputation lay in tatters. Some hoped that she could redeem herself in the future as a repentant role model, but others, among them former Olympic track and field athletes, harshly condemned her actions as compromising the integrity of her sport.

Eugene Larson

Additional Sources

Cazeneuve, Brian. "Running on Empty." *Sports Illustrated* 108, no. 1 (January 14, 2008).

Jones, Marion, with Kate Sekules. *Marion Jones: Life in the Fast Lane.* New York: Warner Books, 2004.

Rapoport, Ron. *See How She Runs: Marion Jones and the Making of a Champion.* Chapel Hill, N.C.: Algonquin Books, 2000.

Smith, Stephen A. "Falls from Grace." *Ebony* 63, no. 3 (January, 2008).

Jackie Joyner-Kersee

Born: March 3, 1962
      East St. Louis, Illinois
Also known as: Jacqueline Joyner (birth name)

Early Life

Jackie Joyner-Kersee was born Jacqueline Joyner on March 3, 1962, in East St. Louis, Illinois, the second of Alfred and Mary Joyner's four children. Her grandmother named her after President John F. Kennedy's wife, Jacqueline Kennedy, saying, "this girl will be the first lady of something." The family had to struggle for economic survival and suffered many hardships, particularly in the severe winters. The area of East St. Louis where Jackie grew up was depressed and crime-ridden. By the time Jackie was eleven, she had witnessed a murder near her home.

The Road to Excellence

Jackie entered her first competitive race at the age of nine and finished last. The defeat inspired her to work harder, and her natural talent and strong determination to succeed set the foundation for the remainder of her career. Her rapid improvement was phenomenal; she soon began to win, and one day had five first-place finishes. Her parents initially thought that track was not a good choice for a girl but were eventually persuaded otherwise. When Jackie tried the long jump, her natural ability was obvious; she leaped more than 17 feet when she was only twelve years old. A coach advised her that if she wanted to make it to the Olympics, it was best to be good at several events. He suggested that she train for the pentathlon, an Olympic event for women that consisted of five events: long jump, javelin throw, 200-meter dash, discus throw, and 1,500-meter run. Jackie understood her coach's logic, and, at the age of fourteen, she won the National Junior Pentathlon championship for the first time. She also won it in each of the next three years.

Jackie's older brother Al was also involved in track, though he was not initially as dedicated as Jackie. When he began to be teased about Jackie's frequent wins, Al became more serious and later became a master of the triple jump and won an Olympic gold medal.

The Emerging Champion

Jackie was disappointed by U.S. decision to boycott the 1980 Olympics; she had improved her own personal record in the long jump during the Olympic trials, jumping 20 feet 9¾ inches. College was still before her, however, and she looked forward to the opportunity to compete at the University of California at Los Angeles (UCLA), where she was granted a basketball scholarship. In the same year, Jackie's mother died suddenly at the age of thirty-eight. Although grief-stricken, Jackie honored her

Jackie Joyner-Kersee competing in the long jump at the 1996 Olympic Games in Atlanta. (Mike Powell/Allsport/ Getty Images)

Major Track and Field Championships

Year	Competition	Event	Place	Distance/Points/Time
1981	U.S. Nationals	Heptathlon	2d	5,827
1982	U.S. Nationals	Heptathlon	1st	6,041
1983	U.S. Nationals	Heptathlon	2d	6,418
		Long jump	4th	21′ 9″
1984	Olympic Games	Heptathlon	Silver	6,385
		Long jump	5th	22′ 2½″
1986	Goodwill Games	Heptathlon	1st	7,148 WR
	Olympic Festival	Heptathlon	1st	7,161 WR
1987	World Championships	Heptathlon	1st	7,128
		Long jump	1st	24′ 1¾″
	Pan-American Games	Long jump	1st	24′ 5½″
	USA/Mobil Indoor Championships	55-meter hurdles	1st	7.64 sec
	U.S. Nationals	Heptathlon	1st	6,979
		Long jump	1st	23′ 4½″
1988	Olympic Games	Long jump	Gold	24′ 3½″ OR
		Heptathlon	Gold	7,291 WR, OR
1990	Goodwill Games	Heptathlon	1st	6,783
1991	World Championships	Long jump	1st	24′ ¾″
1992	Olympic Games	Heptathlon	Gold	7,044
		Long jump	Bronze	23′ 2½″
1993	World Championships	Heptathlon	1st	—
1996	Olympic Games	Long jump	Bronze	22′ 11¾″
1998	Goodwill Games	Heptathlon	1st	6,502

Notes: OR = Olympic Record; WR = World Record

mother with her own determination to succeed. She improved her skills in both basketball and the long jump and maintained a B average in her academic work.

Bob Kersee, an assistant track coach at UCLA, noticed Jackie's incredible potential and convinced both Jackie and the school's athletic staff of her ability. He began training her for the heptathlon, a category made up of seven events: 100- and 200-meter runs, shot put, high jump, long jump, javelin throw, and 800-meter run. In 1983, Jackie and her brother Al both represented the United States at the World Track and Field Championships in Helsinki, Finland. Jackie suffered a pulled hamstring and was unable to compete, but she qualified for the Olympics the following year. Jackie again lost because of injuries, but for many fans the sight of Al racing alongside the track to support and encourage his sister was the most inspiring moment of the Games.

Continuing the Story

In 1986, Jackie and Bob Kersee were married. Jackie seemed to reach a turning point and her

determination to win peaked. In July, 1986, at the Goodwill Games in Moscow, she set a number of records and personal bests. Less than a month later, at the U.S. Olympic Festival in Houston, Texas, Jackie broke more records. Finally, in 1988, she achieved one of her most important goals—she won Olympic gold medals in the long jump and the heptathlon, setting records in both events.

In 1992, at the Barcelona Olympics, Jackie won another gold in the heptathlon, scoring well below her world-record mark with 7,044 points. She also won the bronze in the long jump. Leading up to the 1996 Olympic Games in Atlanta, she continued to dominate the heptathlon and long-jump events. She won the heptathlon event at the 1993 World Track and Field Championships and, in 1994, set a world record in the long jump (24 feet 7 inches). In Atlanta, she had to withdraw from the heptathlon when she injured her ankle. However, she still competed in the long jump, in which she won a bronze medal. At the 1998 Goodwill Games, she scored well below her world-

Records

World heptathlon record in 1988 (7,215)
American indoor record in long jump in 1994 (23′ ¾″)
American outdoor record in long jump in 1994 (7.49 meters) (24′ 7″)
American record twice in 55-meter hurdles in 1989 (7.37 sec)

Honors and Awards

1986	James E. Sullivan Award
1986-87	*Track and Field News* Athlete of the Year
	Jesse Owens Award
1987	Associated Press Female Athlete of the Year
	McDonald's Amateur Sportswoman of the Year
1987-88	Women's Sports Foundation Sportswoman of the Year
1988	Flo Hyman Award
2000	Received Library of Congress Living Legend Award
2003	Inducted into Women's Sport Hall of Fame
2004	Inducted into USA Track and Field Hall of Fame
	Inducted into U.S. Olympic Hall of Fame

record mark in the heptathlon but still took the gold. She announced her retirement but did not officially retire.

In 2000, Jackie attempted to compete in her fifth Olympics but was unable to qualify. Having set the world record in the heptathlon and the American record in the long jump, she officially retired in 2001. *Sports Illustrated* named her the greatest female athlete of the twentieth century.

Summary

The basis for Jackie Joyner-Kersee's success was that she concentrated on challenging but realistic goals throughout her career. She ranks with the great female athletes of all time. She won six Olympic medals, three of them gold. She has garnered many accolades for her athletic endeavors and, in 2001, was named top woman collegiate athlete of the previous twenty-five years by a panel comprising members from nearly one thousand National Collegiate Athletic Association (NCAA) schools.

Mary Johnson

Additional Sources

Buren, Jodi, and Donna A. Lopiano. *Superwomen: One Hundred Women, One Hundred Sports.* New York: Bulfinch Press, 2004.

Joyner-Kersee, Jacqueline, and Sonja Steptoe. *A Kind of Grace: The Autobiography of the World's Greatest Female Athlete.* New York: Warner Books, 1997.

O'Neil, Dana Pennett, and Pat Williams. *How to Be Like Women Athletes of Influence: Thirty-one Women at the Top of Their Game and How You Can Get There Too.* Deerfield Beach, Fla.: Health Communications, 2007.

Rutledge, Rachel. *Women of Sports: The Best of the Best in Track and Field.* Brookfield, Conn.: Millbrook Press, 1999.

Wallechinsky, David, and Jaime Loucky. *The Complete Book of the Olympics: 2008 Edition.* London: Aurum Press, 2008.

Woolum, Janet. *Outstanding Women Athletes: Who They Are and How They Influenced Sports in America.* Phoenix, Ariz.: Oryx Press, 1998.

Alberto Juantorena

Born: December 3, 1950
    Santiago, Cuba
Also known as: Alberto Juantorena Danger (full
    name); El Caballo; the Horse

Early Life

Alberto Juantorena Danger was born in Santiago, Cuba, on December 3, 1950. Like many youngsters, he was always interested in sports. Alberto grew up during difficult times in Cuba. His nation was going through a bloody and dangerous revolution. In 1959, after years of fighting, Fidel Castro came to power and changed Cuban society dramatically. Castro put Cuba's sports program under the control of the government. Athletes were given a special place in the new revolutionary society. Sports became a way of uniting the Cuban people behind the new society.

Throughout the Caribbean, and especially in Cuba, baseball is the most popular sport. The Cuban government also began to pay more attention to other sports that were included in the Olympic Games, like boxing, basketball, and track and field. Sports became a way of advertising how successful Castro's revolution was in Cuba, and victories in the Olympics were a source of tremendous national pride for the Cuban people.

The Road to Excellence

In 1961, the Cuban government created the National Institute of Sports, Physical Education, and Recreation (INDER) to help athletes excel in competitive sports. INDER enabled Cuba to become an international sports power by the 1970's. For a poor country like Cuba this was a tremendous achievement. All of the attention to Olympic sports paid off. In the 1964 Summer Olympics, Cubans won only one medal. They earned ten medals in

Alberto Juantorena winning the 800-meter race at the 1976 Olympic Games in Montreal. (Bob Thomas/Getty Images)

the next Olympiad, in 1968, twenty-two medals in 1972, thirteen in 1976, and twenty in 1980. Alberto Juantorena played a prominent role in the Cuban success story.

INDER built a sports complex on the outskirts of the capital, Havana, and the best athletes from all over the country were brought there to live and train. Alberto was tall and strong as a teenager and was so good at basketball that he became a member of the Cuban national basketball team that represented the nation in international tournaments and the Olympic Games. Alberto's talent in basketball was limited, however, and in 1971, at the age of twenty, he lost his place on the national team. A Cuban coach suggested that he try track. The coach felt that Alberto, at 6 feet 2 inches and a muscular 185 pounds, was perfect for the 400-meter run.

The 400 meters is one of the toughest events in track and field. To excel in this event, an athlete needs both strength and speed. Alberto made remarkable progress. Most runners begin serious training at an early age, but Alberto's late start did not seem to hamper him. Within one year, Alberto had made the Cuban national team in track and field, and he ran the 400 meters in the 1972 Olympic Games in Munich, West Germany. Although he did not win a medal, Alberto's rapid improvement encouraged him to train seriously for the next Olympics, four years later in Montreal.

The Emerging Champion

United States runners had a monopoly on the 400 meters. In Munich, Vincent Matthews won the 400, the fifth victory in a row for a U.S. runner in this event at the Olympics. Alberto was determined to end the U.S. domination of this event. In 1973 and 1974, Alberto was undefeated in international competition and, by the end of 1974, he was ranked the world's number one runner in the 400 meters.

In 1975, Alberto suffered a serious foot injury. His leg was in a cast from his foot to his thigh. When

Major Running Championships

Year	Competition	Event	Place	Time
1976	Olympic Games	400 meters	Gold	44.26
		800 meters	Gold	1:43.50 WR
1977	World Cup	400 meters	Gold	45.56
		800 meters	Gold	1:44.0
1980	Olympic Games	400 meters	4th	45.09

Note: WR = World Record

the cast finally was removed, Alberto immediately went back to serious training to prepare for the upcoming Olympics. To help him regain his leg strength, Cuban coaches recommended that Alberto run 800 meters as fast as he could several times a week. By the end of the year, Alberto was running the 800 meters at very high speeds. Early in 1976, Alberto entered races at both 400 and 800 meters, but no observer believed that he would run both races at the Olympics. Coaches counsel runners to devote all of their efforts to preparing for one event at the Olympics. Because runners have to enter qualifying heats before the final race for the gold, coaches do not want their runners tiring themselves out by running in heats for more than one event.

Less than two weeks before the Montreal Olympiad, however, Alberto ran an 800-meter race in 1 minute 44.9 seconds, only a half a second above the Olympic record. Alberto decided to enter both the 400- and 800-meter races. Many great runners had attempted to win gold medals in both these races but no one had ever succeeded before. Runners who specialize in the 800 often have to devote themselves to long-distance training, whereas speed is much more important in the 400.

In Montreal, the 800 was scheduled first. The world record holder, American Rick Wohluter, was favored to win. Alberto took the lead during the first lap, but Wohluter followed him in second place. The two ran stride for stride for the entire race. During the last lap, it appeared that Wohluter was gaining on Alberto, but the Cuban gave his all at the end and won the race, also setting a new world record of 1 minute 43.5 seconds. Alberto had one day to rest and regroup for the 400. Alberto's two greatest rivals were Americans Herman Frazier and Fred Newhouse. In

Honors, Awards, and Milestones

1974	Ranked number one in the world in the 400 meters
1976	World Trophy
	First runner in history to win both 400 meters and 800 meters at one Olympiad
1976-77	*Track and Field News* World Athlete of the Year
1977	*Athletics Weekly* World Athlete of the Year

this race, Alberto did not take the lead, but as the runners pounded into the final turn, Alberto passed Frazier and then Newhouse to win his second gold medal of the Games.

Continuing the Story

Alberto became the first runner in Olympic history to win both races. After his glorious triumphs, he dedicated his victories to Fidel Castro and the Cuban Revolution. His message was both emotional and patriotic. Alberto became a national hero on his native island, where he earned the nickname, "El Caballo," or "The Horse."

Alberto continued to run successfully. The year after the Olympics, he performed another "double," winning both the 400 and 800 at the World Cup. He also set another world record in the 800 meters that year. In 1978, Alberto won every race he entered in the 400 and lost only once in six 800-meter races. To keep himself in peak physical condition, Alberto trained six days a week, three days on speed work and three days of distance running. The combination of different training methods helped him to stay a champion.

More than anything, Alberto wanted to repeat as Olympic champion in 1980, in Moscow. Sadly, injuries kept him from duplicating his sensational performances in Montreal. In March of 1980, Alberto underwent Achilles tendon surgery, a very serious operation for a runner. Even though he did not have enough time to properly train for the Olympics, he entered the 400-meter race and val-iantly came in fourth. In defeat, Alberto proved his courage and determination.

Injuries continued to beset Alberto's career. Back problems and a fractured foot kept him from performing at his best during the early 1980's. To make matters worse, Alberto was denied an opportunity to participate in the 1984 Olympics in Los Angeles because Cuba boycotted the Olympics that year. In September of 1984, at the age of thirty-four, Alberto announced his retirement from track.

Summary

No runner has ever dominated the 400 and 800 meters like "El Caballo." After his athletic career, Alberto became the vice minister of Sports for Cuba. Despite the injuries in his later years, in victory or defeat, Alberto Juantorena was always a shining example of a champion who brought great honor to his country.

Allen Wells

Additional Sources

Lawson, Gerald. *World Record Breakers in Track and Field Athletics.* Champaign, Ill.: Human Kinetics, 1997.

Sandrock, Michael. *Running with the Legends.* Champaign, Ill.: Human Kinetics, 1996.

"Victory Lap: Alberto Juantorena's 1976 Olympic Win." *Runner's World* (March, 1999): 122.

Wallechinsky, David, and Jaime Loucky. *The Complete Book of the Olympics: 2008 Edition.* London: Aurum Press, 2008.

Duke Kahanamoku

Born: August 24, 1890
Honolulu, Territory of Hawaii (now in
Hawaii)
Died: January 22, 1968
Honolulu, Hawaii
Also known as: Duke Paoa Kahinu Mokoe
Hulikohola Kahanamoku (full name); the Big
Kahuna
Other major sport: Surfing

Early Life
Duke Kahanamoku was born on August 24, 1890, close to the shores of Waikiki Beach in Honolulu, then part of the territory of Hawaii. Duke was the eldest of six brothers and one sister. He grew up in the Royal Palace because his grandfather was a Hawaiian high chief. This played a part in his surfing because, traditionally, surfing was the exclusive sport of island royalty. Duke was named after his father, who was named after the Duke of Edinburgh, who visited Hawaii.

Even as a child, Duke was a graceful and strong swimmer. When he was a young boy, he went on a Sunday school excursion. The group had gone sailing and the boat capsized. The Sunday school group and Duke paddled the two miles back to shore and safety. Many say this distance was nothing to Duke because he could swim as easily as walk.

The Road to Excellence
Duke had an inherent swimming ability. His tropical upbringing, natural buoyancy, and physical structure made him a natural swimmer. He took good care of his body, never smoking or drinking and training consistently. Duke's peculiar method of swimming contributed to his success. He was able to get the maximum push from each stroke and thus wasted no energy. He swam with his head out of the water and was able to keep a close eye on his competitors. He used a typical American "crawl" stroke perfected by the "Kahanamoku kick" he had mastered as a better means of propelling his surfboard. His style made him practically unbeatable in his favorite distances, from 50 to 200 yards.

It seemed that everyone wanted to take credit for Duke's swimming success—except for Duke himself. Mainland Americans claimed he was "Made in America"—Hawaii was not a state at this time—because he had to be retaught everything significant concerning swimming. In reality, all he did in the United States was fine-tune his style to fit the restraints of the swimming pool. He learned how to start and turn more quickly, because this was where seconds were won or lost in competition.

The Emerging Champion
Duke's road to excellence led him to victories at the Olympics and subsequent worldwide fame. It all started in his native Hawaii. Swimming in the open water of Honolulu Harbor, he surpassed the

Duke Kahanamoku. (Courtesy of Amateur Athletic Foundation of Los Angeles)

514

100-yard world record by 4.6 seconds at 55.4 seconds. The swimming world was astounded. Officials on the mainland refused to believe it and would not recognize the effort. He was offered a chance to come to the mainland to compete. In meets in Pittsburgh and Philadelphia, he beat records in the 50-, 100-, and 220-yard freestyle events. He was justly awarded the 100-yard open water record and, most important, a spot on the 1912 U.S. Olympic team. The Olympic Games were to be held at Stockholm, Sweden, that year, and United States officials were confident that Duke would take first place, provided the cold water did not slow him down. He won the 100-meter race easily in a time of 1 minute 3.4 seconds and claimed a gold medal.

Duke won the gold medal in the 100 meters at the 1920 Olympic Games and the silver at the 1924 Games. He switched to water polo for the 1932 Olympics because he said he was too slow for competitive swimming. Through those years, he worked on shaving fifths of a second off his world records. His personal bests for the 100 and 50 yards ultimately would be 53 seconds and 24 seconds, respectively.

Major Swimming Championships

Year	Competition	Event	Place	Time
1912	Olympic Games	100-meter freestyle	Gold	1:03.4
	AAU Indoor Championships	100-yard freestyle	1st	57.8
1916	AAU Outdoor Championships	100-yard freestyle	1st	53.2
1917	AAU Outdoor Championships	100-yard freestyle	1st	54.0
1920	Olympic Games	100-meter freestyle	Gold	1:00.4 WR, OR
		4×200-meter freestyle relay	Gold	10:04.4 WR, OR
	AAU Outdoor Championships	100-yard freestyle	1st	55.4
1924	Olympic Games	100-meter freestyle	Silver	—

Notes: OR = Olympic Record; WR = World Record

Records and Milestones

Olympic champion and record holder for 12 years

Set three universally recognized world records in the 100-yard freestyle between July 5, 1913, and Sept. 5, 1917 (53 seconds; broken by Johnny Weissmuller in 1922)

Competed for the United States in water polo at the 1932 Olympic Games

Introduced surfing to Australia

His life-size wax figure and a recorded eulogy are part of a permanent exhibit at the International Swimming Hall of Fame

Sheriff of Honolulu from 1932 to 1961

Hawaii's official greeter from 1961 until his death at 77 years of age

Honors and Awards

1965	Inducted into International Swimming Hall of Fame
1966	Inducted into International Surfing Hall of Fame
1984	Inducted into U.S. Olympic Hall of Fame

Continuing the Story

Duke was also the prime catalyst for surfing's rebirth. He reintroduced surfing to Hawaii, New Zealand, Australia, and the United States. Some of Duke's surf rides had become so exaggerated that there were no actual statistics to verify them. Duke was instrumental in the development and manufacture of the giant hollow surfboards more than ten feet tall that became popular—especially for lifesaving work—during the 1930's.

In 1925, Duke started an acting career in Hollywood that lasted fourteen years. He mostly played roles of chiefs—Polynesian, Aztec, and Indian—and he appeared in *Gone with the Wind* (1939). He was physically well qualified for these chief roles because he was 6 feet 3 inches tall and had a majestic bearing and posture.

In 1932, Duke ran for sheriff in Honolulu as a Democrat and was unopposed. Several years later, he switched to the Republican party. He was the most popular political figure on the island and served as sheriff until 1961. While he was sheriff, he acted as an unofficial greeter for the island. Then, in 1961, he was appointed Hawaii's official greeter, welcoming film stars, politicians, and royalty. He even had the privilege of teaching Queen Mother Elizabeth of Britain how to do the hula.

Duke was a staff member of the Public Works Department of the Territory of Hawaii. As an inspector of wharf building, he was constantly at the waterfront. This helped him become an expert diver. He used to dive to the bottom of the harbor to inspect piers and other features in connection with wharf construction.

515

Duke continued to swim and sail almost to the day of his death, even after he suffered several heart attacks and had survived a brain operation. He never actually trained anyone but often gave out advice to young men and women on how to improve their style.

On January 22, 1968, Duke collapsed at the Waikiki Yacht Club and was rushed to Kaiser Foundation Hospital, where he died. He was seventy-seven years old at the time.

Summary

Duke Kahanamoku was a man of many talents. He was an Olympic gold medalist, father of modern surfing, a Hollywood actor, a sheriff, and an official greeter in Honolulu. King Kamehameha once prophesied that Hawaii would be completely run by the white man, but before that happened, one Hawaiian man would bring it fame. Duke fulfilled the prophecy.

Rodney D. Keller

Additional Sources

Crowe, Ellie, and Richard Waldrep. *Surfer of the Century: The Life of Duke Kahanamoku.* New York: Lee & Low Books, 2007.

Hall, Sandra Kimberley. *Duke: A Great Hawaiian.* Honolulu, Hawaii: Bess Press, 2004.

Horwitz, Tony. *The Devil May Care: Fifty Intrepid Americans and Their Quest for the Unknown.* New York: Oxford University Press, 2003.

Osmond, Gary, Murray Phillips, and Mark O'Neill. "'Putting up Your Dukes': Statues, Social Memory, and Duke Paoa Kahanamoku." *The International Journal of the History of Sport* 23, no. 1 (2006): 82-103.

Akakios Kakiasvilis

Born: July 13, 1969

      Tiflida, Soviet Union (now in Georgia)

Also known as: Kakhi Kakhiachvili (birth name); Akakide Kakiachvilis; Kaki

Early Life

Akakios "Kaki" Kakiasvilis was born Kakhi Kakhiachvili on July 13, 1969, in Tiflida, Soviet Union (now in Georgia). His mother, Maria Labrianidi, was of Greek origin. Little is known about Kaki's early life in Georgia; at some point, he discovered a love of weightlifting and began pursuing his passion. While beginning his weightlifting career, he also obtained a degree in economics at Tiflida's national polytechnic institute.

The Road to Excellence

By 1992, Kaki had perfected his abilities and won a spot on the Georgian Olympic weightlifting team as a middle heavyweight. He traveled to Barcelona, Spain, to represent his country. Although he was an excellent competitor, early in the event, he appeared to be out of the medal race. He trailed by 22 pounds prior to attempting his final lift. In a dramatic turnaround, he made his final lift and set a world record with a total weight of 412.5 kilograms (909 pounds). His lift tied that of another athlete, his countryman Sergey Syrtsov. However, Kaki earned the gold medal because his body weight was lower than Syrtsov's.

Shortly after returning to Georgia in triumph, Kaki discovered that both his mother and his grandmother had been born in Greece. In 1994, he made the decision to leave Georgia and reestablish his Greek roots. When he first moved to Greece and before he adopted Akakios Kakiasvilis as his name, he was known by the Georgian-Greek hybrid Akakide Kakiachvilis.

The Emerging Champion

Greece, which was in the process of building a first-class weightlifting team, welcomed Kaki. Kaki found himself on the same team as Albanian-born Pyrros Dimas, a fellow Greek immigrant and Olympic gold medalist. Kaki joined the Milon Club to train

and began to show the world that his victory at the 1992 Olympics had not been a fluke. He also joined the Greek air force and later rose to the rank of first lieutenant.

In 1994, Kaki excelled at the World Cup, winning a silver medal, and he reigned as world champion the following year. In 1996, four years after his upset win in Barcelona, Kaki again struggled to win a medal, this time in the 99-kilogram (218-pound) class at the Olympics in Atlanta, Georgia. He trailed Anatoly Khrapaty of Kazakhstan going into the final round. For Kaki to win the gold medal, he had to make a world-record lift in the clean and jerk. He composed himself and overcame his nervousness to break the world record and win a gold medal in his second consecutive Olympics. Like

Akakios Kakiasvilis lifting in the 94-kilogram weight division during the 2004 Olympic Games in Athens. (Ramzi Haidar/AFP/Getty Images)

Major Weightlifting Championships

Year	Competition	Snatch in kg.	Place	Clean & Jerk in kg.	Place	Total kg	Place
1992	European Championships	175.0	3d	225.0	1st	400.0	1st
	Olympic Games	177.5		235.0		412.5	1st
1993	European Championships	180.0	1st	222.5	1st	402.5	1st
	World Championships	180.0	3d	222.5	1st	402.5	2d
1994	European Championships	180.0	3d	220.0	2d	400.0	2d
	World Championships	180.0	3d	230.0	2d	397.5	2d
1995	European Championships	180.0	1st	227.5	1st	407.5	1st
	World Championships	187.5	3d	230.0	1st	410.0	1st
1996	European Union Championships	172.5	2d	215.0	1st	382.5	1st
	European Championships	175.0	3d	222.5	1st	392.5	1st
	Olympic Games	187.5		235.0		420.0	Gold
1998	European Union Championships	167.5	3d	210.0	1st	372.5	1st
	European Championships	172.5	4th	212.5	3d	380.0	3d
	World Championships	182.5	3d	220.0	1st	400.0	1st
1999	European Championships	180.0	3d	225.0	1st	402.5	2d
	World Championships	188.0	1st	230.5	1st	412.5	1st
2000	Olympic Games	187.5		220.0		405.0	Gold

teammate Dimas, he was celebrated when he returned to Greece. He and the other gold medalists were awarded a second gold medal by the mayor of Athens, and Greek sports journalists selected Kaki as the athlete of the year.

Kaki trained harder than ever while working toward the 2000 Olympics in Sydney, Australia. He repeated as world champion in 1998. In 1999, he was crowned world champion in his 94-kilogram (207-pounds) weight class. In November, in Athens, he set two world records, lifting 188 kilograms (415 pounds) in the snatch and hoisting a total of 412½ kilograms (909 pounds). He again earned athlete of the year honors in Greece.

Continuing the Story

Despite suffering a torn rotator cuff early in the season, Kaki entered the 2000 Olympics as the favorite. In 1999, he was one of only three weightlifters who had lifted more than 400 kilograms (882 pounds), and he had cleared 7.5 kilograms (16.5 pounds) more than any of the others. Unlike his prior two Olympic experiences, he had a much easier time. He lifted 220 kilograms (485 pounds) in his first try at the clean and jerk. The European champion, nineteen-year-old Szymon Kołecki of Poland, then lifted 222.5 kilograms (490 pounds 8 ounces), leaving both athletes at 405 kilograms (893 pounds) with two lifts remaining.

Kaki realized that, although he was tied with Kołecki, he was in gold-medal position because of his lower body weight; he weighed about 3 pounds less than Kołecki. Kaki then devised a strategy to bluff Kołecki. He asked for weight to be added to the bar but then declined his lift at the last minute, forcing Kołecki to decide whether or not to accept the challenge. Kołecki tried to lift the bar loaded with 227 kilograms (500 pounds). He was unable to complete the lift, injured his ankle, and had to decline his final attempt. Kaki not only won the gold medal but also joined an elite group of weightlifters, including teammate Dimas, in winning three consecutive gold medals in weightlifting. He also won his third Greek athlete of the year award.

With three consecutive gold-medal wins under his belt, Kaki already began thinking about the 2004 Games in Athens. However, at the age of thirty-five, he was demanding too much of his body. For the first time in his career, he failed to complete a valid lift in the clean and jerk and finished out of the medals. Hoping to redeem himself, he trained for the 2008 Olympics in Beijing, China, but at the age of thirty-nine, was unable to make the qualifying round.

Summary

Not as colorful a character nor as well known as teammate Pyrros Dimas, Akakios Kakiasvilis nonetheless equaled Dimas's winning record and is considered one of the best weightlifters of the modern era. Kaki persevered despite cultural adjustments, bouts of nervousness, and serious injuries. He set several world records and captured three world titles. He won weightlifting gold medals in three consecutive Olympics on three different continents. In 2004, at the age of thirty-five, he participated in a fourth Olympics, in his adopted homeland, but failed to medal, much to the disappointment of his fans at the host venue of Athens. Kaki is one of only a handful of athletes to win gold medals for two different countries, and he joined an elite club of weightlifters that have taken gold medals in three consecutive Olympics: Yhe other three are Dimas, Naim Süleymanoğlu, and Halil Mutlu.

Deborah Service, updated by Jack Ewing

Additional Sources

Everett, Greg. *Olympic Weightlifting: A Complete Guide for Athletes and Coaches.* Bonsall, Calif.: Catalyst Athletics, 2008.

Findling, John E., and Kimberly D. Pelle. *Encyclopedia of the Modern Olympic Movement.* Champaign, Ill.: Sports, 2004.

Wallechinsky, David, and Jaime Loucky. *The Complete Book of the Olympics: 2008 Edition.* London: Aurum Press, 2008.

Valerie Kanavy

Born: July 9, 1946
   California

Early Life

Valerie Kanavy was born on July 9, 1946, in California. Her family soon moved to Wichita, Kansas. Valerie babysat and delivered newspapers to amass enough money to buy a horse, which she did at twelve years old. Her first horses were Quarter horses. She rode for pleasure and entered some Western horse-riding competitions in the areas of showing and barrel racing.

In 1967, Valerie moved to West Chester, Pennsylvania, with her husband Larry. They became interested in foxhunting, and Valerie purchased her first Arabian horse, a mare named Jameel Abyad. Preparing a horse for a long, grueling day of foxhunting was much different from the pleasure riding Valerie had done in Kansas. In 1972, she took part in her first competitive trail ride and won the competition.

Larry began riding in endurance races, while Valerie acted as trainer and crewed for him. Although she competed in a few events, Valerie primarily stayed behind the scenes until the 1980's, when her husband started his own business and no longer had time to practice and compete. He felt that Valerie was capable of developing the skills to compete at a high level and persuaded her to pursue competitive equestrian endeavors. She trained and competed with Ramegawa Tomano in the Northeast region and won the championship.

Championships and Honors

1994, 1998	Gold medal, World Endurance Championship
1996	Silver medal, World Endurance Championship
1999	USA Equestrian horsewoman of the year
	Virginia horsewoman of the year
	United States Equestrian Team Whitney Stone Award
2003	World Champion Master
	Arabian Horse Association National Championship Endurance Ride (winner: 100-mile and 50-mile race)

She also entered the national top twenty-five senior division.

The Road to Excellence

In 1992, Valerie tried for a position on the U.S. team scheduled to compete in the 1994 world championship competition. In order to earn a place on the team, she needed to accumulate a consistent record of success with one horse. While trying to decide which of her horses—Ramegawa Rhodora, also known as Dory, or Pieraz, also known as Cash—to use in her attempt to make the U.S. team, she had an opportunity to sell one of them. The buyers chose Dory, and Cash became the horse with which Valerie competed.

Cash had finished in the top ten in 100-mile races several times. In 1992, the horse placed eighth in the Race of Champions. However, Valerie's best chance to make the U.S. team came when she and Cash were chosen to compete in the 1993 North American Championship in Calgary, Alberta, Canada. Valerie and Cash finished sixth in Calgary, but Valerie left the competition with doubts about continuing to compete in endurance races. Cash experienced an upper respiratory problem on the way to Calgary. His antibiotic treatment had to be suspended five days before the competition; he cramped and was lame immediately after the race.

The Emerging Champion

Once home, Cash was sound again, and Valerie's husband persuaded her to keep trying. She rode Cash to a fifth-place finish in the International Arabian Horse Association competition. Cash also won the award for best condition. Then, Valerie entered eight 100-mile endurance races and placed first in all but one, in which she finished second.

In 1994, Valerie and Cash qualified for the World Endurance Championship in The Hague, Netherlands. The race required all of their skills and competitive spirit, especially in the last leg over cobblestone streets. They had to negotiate the rough footing at a gallop in order to win the individual gold medal. In 1996, Valerie, riding TK Fire N

Gold, took the silver medal at the World Endurance Championship. Her daughter Danielle, riding Cash, won the gold medal. Valerie also received a team gold medal at Kansas City. In 1998, riding High Winds Jedi, Valerie again won the individual gold medal at the World Endurance Championship in the United Arab Emirates. In 1999, she was named horsewoman of the year by the American Horse Show Association (now United States Equestrian Federation) and also received the United States Equestrian Team (USET) Whitney Stone Award.

Continuing the Story

In 2000 and 2001, Valerie, riding Bearcat O'Reilly, won the USET Endurance Championship. In 2002, she was invited to participate in the Endurance World Cup in the desert of Dubai and Abu Dhabi in the United Arab Emirates. Riding Bearcat O'Reilly, she finished seventh and was the only foreign rider to finish in the top ten. This accomplishment earned her recognition as the USET March athlete of the month. In 2003, she won the Féderation Equiste Internationale Masters World Championship and the Arabian Horse Association Endurance Ride Championship.

Summary

Valerie Kanavy played a significant role in endurance riding both as a competitor and as a trainer. She competed throughout the United States and Canada, and in more than twenty other countries. Of the nearly thirty horses that she has trained and ridden in 100-mile races, twenty have been winners. She has lectured throughout the world on endurance riding and served on committees in all of the major organizations involved with the sport. Her induction into the American Endurance Ride Conference Hall of Fame enabled her to be a spokeswoman, instructor, and ambassador for endurance riding.

Shawncey Webb

Additional Sources

Kanavy, Valerie, and Donna Snyder-Smith. *The Complete Guide to Endurance Racing and Competition.* New York: Howell Book House, 1998.

Ridgway, Kerry J., and Nancy S. Loving. *Go the Distance: The Complete Source for Endurance Horse Racing.* North Pomfret, Vt.: Trafalgar Square Books, 2006.

Wild, Clare. *Endurance Riding: From First Steps to One Hundred Miles.* Newton Abbot, Devon, England: 2006.

Jigoro Kano

Born: October 28, 1860
    Mikage, Japan
Died: May 4, 1938
    aboard Japanese passenger ship *Hikawa Maru*
Also known as: Dr. Kano; Grandmaster Kano

Early life

Jigoro Kano was born October 28, 1860, to a reasonably wealthy family in the small village of Mikage, near Kobe, Japan. His family's wealth came from his grandfather's sake business. Jigoro's father did not inherit the family business but was successful as a Shinto priest and a ranking Japanese government official.

Jigoro was the third son in a family of three boys and two girls. He was physically small into his late teen years. In fact, he stood a mere 5 feet 2 inches tall and weighed a meager 90 pounds. Because he was so physically small and weak, he became an easy target for local town bullies. Therefore, Jigoro became determined to further his education and training in the dojo, or martial arts center, to better defend himself from his attackers.

At the age of seventeen, Jigoro began studying the ancient Japanese martial art known as jujitsu: *ju* translates as "gentle" or "giving way," and *jitsu* means "art" or "technique." His instructor at the time believed Jigoro was too young and small to train, so he only gave him basic exercises to learn. This only heightened Jigoro's desire to study more about this ancient form of empty-handed combat.

The Road to Excellence

At the age of eighteen, Jigoro enrolled in the prestigious Tokyo Imperial University, from which he earned degrees in both political science and economics. In his spare time, Jigoro searched the local area for "bonesetters," or doctors of osteopathic medicine. These doctors were thoroughly trained in jujitsu and provided Jigoro advice on where to obtain the best martial arts tutelage. During these early college years, Jigoro met a "bonesetter" who introduced him to a series of jujitsu teachers, or sensei. For the next three years, Jigoro trained and studied rigorously with these jujitsu masters, learning their various styles and techniques.

Jigoro's desire for knowledge grew, and he attempted to discover the spirituality behind the martial art. Thus, he traveled to dojos of other masters to study their techniques and learn the secret doctrines behind the various styles. Specifically, he wanted to learn the techniques of mental preparation his masters had acquired during the years of their training. This led Jigoro to study the teachings of various ancient Chinese philosophers and religions like Zen Buddhism.

Jigoro believed that the all jujitsu styles could be combined into one system that could be taught not only as a sport or exercise but also as a way of life.

Jigoro Kano (right) demonstrating one of his judo moves.

Awards and Milestones

Founder of Judo
First Asian to serve on the International Olympic Committee
Japan's Order of Merit
Japan's Order of the Rising Sun
Japan's "Father of Sport" (1935)
Inducted into International Judo Federation Hall of Fame (1999)

Jigoro's new martial art merged a variety of traditional jujitsu techniques with a strong philosophical component that combined meditation with physical exercise. He purposely discarded some of the ancient lethal techniques to make his art more peaceful and egalitarian. This new art was a form of self-defense that forged consistent training of the mind and body.

The Emerging Champion

The outcome of Jigoro's efforts was a martial art that he called judo: *ju* means "gentle" or "giving way," and *do* translates as "the way" or "path." Jigoro stated openly that judo encouraged passivity until the right moment arrived to act, whether with words or physical actions. In fact, Jigoro taught that true warriors did not have to act physically but could use their minds to diffuse a potential attack by calmly and verbally outsmarting their opponents. However, his methodology stated that if attacked, one should use the force and negative emotion of the attacker to an advantage.

In 1882, Jigoro founded the Kodokan Judo Institute in Tokyo, Japan. The term *kodokan* is made up of three words: *ko* meaning "to preach" or "lecture," *do* meaning "the way," and *kan* meaning "hall." Jigoro explained that the art of judo was centered on two key principles: *seriyoku-zenyo*, or "maximum efficient use of mental and physical energy," and *jita-kyoei*, or "mutual benefit and welfare." Practitioners of judo engaged in two types of physical training: *randori*, or free practice, and *katas*, prearranged forms. As the student progressed, the training was combined with guided meditations to strengthen the mind and spirit. The ultimate goal of judo was to develop athletes who discovered and developed their true potential not only on the judo mat but also in every aspect of life. A true Judoist, according to Jigoro, was a person who learned, through training, to live a healthy life centered on the values of respect, goodwill, sacrifice, self-control, and mercy.

Continuing the Story

Over the next several decades, Jigoro not only trained students at the Kodokan, but he also traveled to share his martial art with people around the world. During this time, Jigoro maintained his occupation as teacher, professor, and head master at various schools and colleges throughout Japan. Jigoro was also appointed as the first Japanese member of the International Olympic Committee and became an ambassador and spokesmen for all Japanese sports throughout the world. Furthermore, Jigoro played an integral role in Japan's selection as the sight of the twelfth Olympics, which were canceled because of World War II. On May 4, 1938, while journeying home from this particular Olympic meeting, Jigoro died from complications of pneumonia aboard a Japanese passenger ship.

After its inception in 1882, judo gained international acclaim as one of the most frequently studied martial arts of all time. Millions of people throughout the world practice judo not only as a sport but also as a way of life. Furthermore, in 1964, judo became an official Olympic sport, one of the few competitive martial arts showcased during the Olympic Games.

Summary

Jigoro Kano was an educator, sportsman, and martial arts pioneer. His invention became known as judo. Jigoro sought to create not only physically prepared warriors but also educated individuals who attempted to help others by teaching and sharing wisdom through meditation and physical exercise.

Paul M. Klenowski

Additional Sources

Harrington, Pat. *Judo: A Pictorial Manual.* Rutland, Vt.: Charles E. Tuttle, 1992.

Kano, Jigoro. *Kodokan Judo.* Reprint. New York: Kodnansha International, 1994.

Watanbe, Jiichi, and Lindy Avakian. *The Secrets of Judo: A Text for Instructors and Students.* Rutland, Vt.: Charles E. Tuttle, 1960.

Aleksandr Karelin

Born: September 19, 1967
      Novosibirsk, Siberia, Soviet Union (now in
      Russia)
Also known as: Aleksandr Aleksandrovich Karelin
    (full name); World's Meanest Man; King Kong;
    the Experiment

Early Life

Aleksandr Aleksandrovich Karelin was born September 19, 1967, in Novosibirsk, 1,750 miles east of Moscow in southern Siberia. His father, Aleksandr, was a truck driver; his mother, Zineida, was an office worker. From the beginning, Aleksandr displayed unusual size and strength. He reportedly weighed 15 pounds at birth. Young Aleksandr—called "Sasha" by friends and family—attracted the attention of local wrestling coaches as a young boy but preferred hunting, skiing, and swimming to wrestling and did not enjoy the sport when he first tried it at the age of thirteen. Later that year, he was discovered by wrestling coach Victor Kusnetzov, an expert in the Greco-Roman style of wrestling who instilled in Aleksandr an affection for the sport. Aleksandr decided to continue wrestling and improved steadily under the tutelage of Kusnetzov.

The Road to Excellence

Aleksandr suffered a setback at the age of fifteen, when he broke his leg in a junior tournament match. Despite his mother's request that he quit wrestling, he continued training and returned to the sport within a year. During his recovery, Aleksandr also exercised his mind by reading the works of Russian novelists, intellectuals, and poets, and listening to opera and ballet music. His favorite author was Dostoevsky, and his favorite operatic composer was Mussorgsky. Although his formal education was a typical one for a Soviet athlete—he received college degrees in automotive mechanics and physical education—the interest in fine arts and literature that he cultivated as a youth remained with him throughout his adult life and motivated him to approach wrestling as an art form. Aleksandr taught himself to read English so that he might read Shakespeare's work in its original language.

Aleksandr returned from his teenage injury stronger and with renewed enthusiasm for wrestling, rising quickly to the top of the ranks of junior wrestlers in the Soviet Union. In 1986, he lost in the finals of the Soviet National Wrestling Championships to two-time world champion Igor Rostorotsky. Devastated by the loss, the nineteen-year-old Aleksandr established a rigorous training routine that involved rising early, drinking a one-half gallon of milk, and running for two hours in thigh-deep snow while carrying an armload of logs. Working with Kusnetzov, he de-

Aleksandr Karelin (right) wrestling American Siamak Ghaffari during the 1996 Olympic Games at Atlanta. (Pascal Rondeau/Getty Images)

veloped the reverse body lift, a move that made him the most feared Greco-Roman wrestler in the world. The maneuver, in which a wrestler lifts his opponent off the mat and throws him over his shoulder back to the mat, had previously been employed by lighter Greco-Roman wrestlers but never by competitors in the heavier weight classes of the sport. With the help of this move, Aleksandr did not lose another match for fourteen years.

Major Wrestling Championships

Year	Event	Place	Year	Event	Place
1988	Olympic Games	Gold	1993-2000	Russian Championships	1st
1988-92	Soviet Championships	1st	1996	Olympic Games	Gold
1989-2000	European Championships	1st	2000	Olympic Games	Silver
1992	Olympic Games	Gold			

The Emerging Champion

A series of high-profile victories, including several over Rostorotsky, earned Aleksandr a world junior championship and spots on the 1988 Soviet national and Olympic teams. Aleksandr's Olympic teammates chose him to bear the Soviet flag in the Opening Ceremony of the 1988 Games in Seoul, South Korea—an honor usually reserved for veterans of the Games. In Seoul, the world got its first glimpse of Aleksandr and his powerful wrestling style. His only serious challenge came in the superheavyweight final when, down by a point to Rangel Gerovski with only 30 seconds left, he reverse-body-lifted the Bulgarian to win the gold medal.

Aleksandr's victory in Seoul was the beginning of his dominance of international competition in Greco-Roman wrestling. At 6 feet 4 inches tall and approximately 290 pounds, Aleksandr gained a reputation for incomparable strength. In one often-told story, he carried a refrigerator that was more than twice his weight up eight flights of stairs by himself. Competing for the Unified Team in the 1992 Olympics in Barcelona, Spain, Aleksandr defeated his opponents in the semifinals and finals while barely breaking a sweat and without resorting to his fearsome reverse body lift. An observer noted that the wrestlers appeared to be so frightened of the maneuver that "they practically let themselves be pinned."

Aleksandr continued his dominance of Greco-Roman wrestling throughout the 1990's, amassing nine consecutive world titles between 1991 and 1999 and winning a third Olympic gold medal while wrestling for Russia at the Atlanta Games in 1996. To win the gold at Atlanta, Aleksandr had to defeat American Matt Ghaffari, his most serious challenger. Aleksandr had suffered a broken rib in a match with Ghaffari at the 1993 world championships and had struggled to defeat the American by decision in overtime. In Atlanta, he bested Ghaffari 1-0 by scoring the only point nearly 2 minutes into the match. Aleksandr was Ghaffari's nemesis. Despite his best efforts, Ghaffari could never defeat Aleksandr, going 0-22 against the Russian.

Continuing the Story

The 1996 Games marked the high point of Aleksandr's wrestling career. Although he continued to dominate international Greco-Roman competition during the late 1990's, rumors began to circulate that he was becoming vulnerable, and his opponents noted that his margins of victory were growing smaller. In March, 2000, on the eve of his fourth Olympic Games, Aleksandr withdrew from a meet in Sweden, prompting speculation that he had suffered a career-ending back injury. He returned to win the 2000 European championships with apparent ease. However, after easy victories in early matches at the 2000 Olympics in Sydney, Australia, Aleksandr suffered the second defeat of his wrestling career at the hands of American Rulon Gardner. Aleksandr was such an overwhelming favorite, such an intimidating force, that Gardner's victory was considered by many to be the single greatest individual upset in Olympic history. His winning streak dashed, a clearly disappointed Aleksandr came away from the Games with a silver medal, which he afterward ripped from his neck. Aleksandr never publicly discussed his match against Rulon Gardner.

Both competitors and admirers have given Aleksandr numerous nicknames, calling him "The World's Strongest Man," "The World's Meanest Man," "King Kong," and "The Experiment." Aleksandr exhibited a rare combination of physical and mental strength, realizing that the mind and body can both be trained to achieve the desires of one's ambition. No athlete in any sport achieved such complete domination in the arena for as many years. When asked how many consecutive matches he had won, Aleksandr claimed not to know, not to keep track of such statistics. A victory over an opponent did not bring a celebration or a rest. "I'm not one for passive relaxation," Aleksandr once said. "If you sit back and relax, you become kind and passive, and it's not good."

Prior to his loss at the Sydney Games, Aleksandr had announced that the 2000 Olympics would be his last. Having earned every title and accolade his sport had to offer, Aleksandr had begun preparing for life after wrestling. In 1999, he ran for the Duma, the Russian legislative body, and won on the strength of his enormous popularity in his hometown of Novosibirsk. Despite rumors that he planned to run for president of Russia or pursue freestyle or professional wrestling, Aleksandr kept a low profile after his Olympic defeat.

Summary

Aleksandr Karelin dominated Greco-Roman wrestling from 1987 through 2000. Unbeaten at major international competitions until his defeat at Sydney, he won nine consecutive world championships and three consecutive Olympic titles. His silver medal in the 2000 Games gave him thirteen world and Olympic medals, tying him with American heavyweight Bruce Baumgartner for the most medals won by any wrestler. From the 1993 world championships through 1998, he did not surrender a single point at championship-level events.

In addition, Aleksandr developed a reputation as a well-rounded individual whose interests included music, literature, poetry, and politics. He attained the status of a *bogatyr*, or folk hero, in Russia and is perhaps the most famous athlete in the history of his homeland of Siberia. Although his loss to Rulon Gardner in the 2000 Olympics cast doubt upon his future as an athlete, his future as a legend of Russian sport was assured.

Michael H. Burchett, updated by Randy L. Abbott

Additional Sources

Dawidoff, Nicholas. "A Bruiser and a Thinker." *Sports Illustrated* 74 (May 13, 1991): 66-71.

Greenwald, John. "Alexander Karelin." *Time* 156 (September 11, 2000): 80-81.

Lavrikov, Mikhail. "Self-Made." *The Current Digest of the Post-Soviet Press* 51, no. 42, p. 11.

Pertti Karppinen

Born: February 17, 1953
    Vehmaa, Finland
Also known as: Pertti Johannes Karppinen (full
   name)

Early Life
Pertti Karppinen was born on February 17, 1953, in Vehmaa, Finland. Vehmaa is near Turku, one of Finland's largest cities. Turku was once the capital of Finland and the center of its Swedish-speaking community. Pertti's early life was a simple one and remained so. When he won the 1976 Olympics, friends had to go to his house to congratulate him because he did not have a telephone. He and his five brothers and one sister grew up in a small

Pertti Karppinen rowing a skiff during the 1980 Olympic Games at Moscow. (Jean-Claude Delmas/AFP/Getty Images)

house near the lake where he learned to row. Pertti became interested in rowing and learned how to race from watching his older brothers. He was by far the most successful, however, owing to his great physical talent. At 6 feet 7 inches tall and 230 pounds, Pertti was large even for a rower.

The Road to Excellence
Pertti started sculling as a boy. At first, he was tall and weak, unable to balance the narrow rowing shells. These boats are only twelve inches wide and require a great deal of sensitivity to balance. In addition, it took Pertti a long time to develop the endurance to race 2,000 meters, the standard race distance. He worked hard at getting stronger, lifting weights to grow as strong as he was big. He also learned how to take advantage of his size by rowing many miles to develop his sense of balance. By 1973, he was ready to challenge the great rowers in the European championships.

When Pertti reached the European championships he did not resemble the awkward, tall boy of a few years earlier. Rather, he had become a towering man with a huge chest and shoulders built by hours of rowing and weightlifting. Pertti was only twenty years old and in his first major competition; he placed seventh in the single sculls.

The Emerging Champion
The 1973 European championships set the stage for Pertti's growth as a great single sculler. Each year, he placed a little higher in the World Championships. In 1974, he made the finals and placed sixth. In 1975, he made the finals again and placed fourth. Although these races were exciting, they were nothing like the 1976 Olympics in Montreal.

The rower Pertti had to beat was a West German named Peter Kolbe, who was also known as the *Wunderkind*, or "wonderchild," of sculling. Kolbe was physically impressive—standing 6 feet 4 inches tall—and he was a wonderful technical rower. He had beaten Pertti in every world championship competition in which they had competed, and he was the favorite to win the Montreal Olympics.

The race started like everyone expected, with

Major Rowing Championships

Year	Competition	Event	Place
1973	European Championships	Single sculls	7th
1974	World Championships	Single sculls	6th
1975	World Championships	Single sculls	4th
1976	Olympic Games	Single sculls	Gold
1977	World Championships	Single sculls	1st
1978	World Championships	Single sculls	6th
1979	World Championships	Single sculls	1st
1980	Olympic Games	Single sculls	Gold
1981	World Championships	Double sculls	2d
1982	World Championships	Double sculls	5th
1983	World Championships	Double sculls	4th
1984	Olympic Games	Single sculls	Gold
1985	World Championships	Single sculls	1st
1986	World Championships	Single sculls	2d
1987	World Championships	Single sculls	3d
1988	Olympic Games	Single sculls	7th

Kolbe jumping out to an eight-second lead by the 1,000-meter, or halfway, mark. Pertti, however, rowed his own race plan, one that used the latest methods of exercise science. He knew that the human body is most efficient if it paces itself evenly and does not start out too fast. The problem in rowing with this strategy is that rowers sit in their boats facing the starting line. This means that a quick start gives the leader a psychological advantage because of the ability to see the competition trying to catch up.

Pertti had practiced his race plan diligently. He knew he was fastest over the entire distance of 2,000 meters if he broke the race into four equal parts of 500 meters each and rowed each part at the same speed. The hardest part of his plan was having the confidence to do it. Pertti's race plan was perfect. In the last 500 meters, Kolbe tired from starting too fast, and Pertti had much more energy left because he had paced himself perfectly. In the last 100 meters, Pertti passed Kolbe, winning by 1.64 seconds in the most exciting single scull final in the history of the Olympics.

Continuing the Story

Pertti continued his racing technique and used it with great success. He won the 1977 World Cham-

pionships in Amsterdam but had a disappointing year in 1978 when he placed sixth. He bounced back in 1979 and 1980, winning the World Championships and the Moscow Olympics.

In 1981, Pertti decided to try the double sculls, teaming with his brother Reina. The two were moderately successful at the World Championships, placing second in 1981, fifth in 1982, and fourth in 1983. For 1984, however, Pertti decided to go back to the single scull. He wanted to match the great Soviet sculler Vyacheslav Ivanov's record of three consecutive Olympics in the single scull.

To do this, Pertti had to beat Kolbe again. The race started out just like the 1976 Olympic race. Kolbe jumped out to a big lead and appeared to be in the midst of the best race of his life. Pertti used his same plan, pacing himself evenly and not using too much energy by trying to get ahead early. With only 250 meters left in the race, Kolbe was ahead by almost one second, but it was not enough. Pertti continued his relentless pace and passed Kolbe to win by 1.95 seconds. He had his third consecutive Olympic victory, tying him with the great Ivanov.

Summary

Pertti Karppinen tried for an unprecedented fourth consecutive win in the Seoul Olympics but finished seventh. He remains, however, one of the great scullers of all time. Pertti showed how using science can help determine a race plan, but more important, he showed how belief in oneself makes the plan work. Pertti remains an inspiration to all of those who start slowly and who have to work hard for success.

Steven G. Estes

Additional Sources

Findling, John E., and Kimberly D. Pelle, eds. *Historical Dictionary of the Modern Olympic Movement.* Westport, Conn.: Greenwood Press, 2004.

Greenberg, Stan. *Whitaker's Olympic Almanack: An Encyclopaedia of the Olympic Games.* Chicago: Fitzroy Dearborn, 2000.

Noden, Merrell. "Knocking Sculls." *Sports Illustrated* 69 (September 14, 1988): 120-121.

Sawao Kato

Born: October 11, 1946
Niigata, Japan

Early Life

Sawao Kato was born on October 11, 1946, in Niigata, a city on the north coast of the island of Honshu. Sawao did not begin gymnastics until the age of fourteen, relatively late even for a male gymnast. His first interest was in the horizontal bar, and from there he was determined to become an all-around competitor. Sawao continued his development through his teen years and studied at Tokyo Educational University in 1965. Sawao was a dedicated student who embodied the classical Japanese samurai tradition of discipline, teamwork, and obedience to superiors. He was trained by and developed a long-standing relationship with Olympic veteran Akitomo Kaneko.

The Road to Excellence

Sawao's first major international triumph was at the 1967 World University Games, where he placed third in the all-around and took medals in five of six individual events, including a tie for gold on the horizontal bar.

Sawao's performance prepared him to succeed 1964 Olympic champion Yukio Endo as leader of the Japanese team. Sawao was a twenty-two-year-old university senior during the 1968 Mexico City Olympics. At 5 feet 3 inches tall, he was of perfect stature for gymnastics, and his smooth style was already among the most elegant in the world. In Mexico City, Sawao performed to potential and became the all-around Olympic champion, with a gold medal in the floor exercise and a bronze in the rings. In addition, his gold medal as a member of the Japanese team began his participation in the so-called "V-10" dynasty—a series of ten successive Japanese team titles in Olympic and world championship competitions stretching from the 1960 Rome Olym-

pics to the 1978 World Gymnastics Championships in Strasbourg, France.

Becoming an international champion is difficult enough; remaining one is even harder. Beset by injuries after his success in Mexico City, Sawao was unable to attend the 1970 World Gymnastics Championships in Ljubljana, Yugoslavia, as a result of a torn Achilles tendon. He healed enough to come to the United States in January, 1972, for a tour of meets and exhibitions in California, Denver, Chicago, and Philadelphia, in anticipation of the upcoming Olympics.

The Emerging Champion

Through 1972, Sawao's injuries continued to interfere, but Sawao the competitor always had a positive mental attitude; he loved gymnastics and strove for perfection. In the qualifying competition, he overcame teammate Eizo Kenmotsu in the eighteenth exercise to make the Japanese Olympic team. He came to Munich with a bad shoulder and a bandaged elbow, but he never questioned his decision to compete.

As reigning Olympic champion, Sawao was closely watched, and he did not disappoint. Rather, in Munich, he improved upon his record in the

Major Gymnastics Championships

Year	Competition	Event	Place	Event	Place
1967	World University Games	All-around	3d	Pommel horse	3d
		Floor exercise	5th	Rings	2d
		Horizontal bar	1st	Vault	3d
		Parallel bars	3d	Team	1st
1968	Olympic Games	All-around	Gold	Rings	Bronze
		Floor exercise	Gold	Team	Gold
1972	Olympic Games	All-around	Gold	Pommel horse	Silver
		Floor exercise	6th	Rings	4th
		Horizontal bar	Silver	Vault	4th
		Parallel bars	Gold	Team	Gold
1976	Olympic Games	All-around	Silver	Pommel horse	5th
		Floor exercise	5th	Rings	6th
		Parallel bars	Gold	Team	Gold
1977	World Cup	All-around	4th	Parallel bars	3d
		Floor exercise	4th	Pommel horse	6th
		Horizontal bar	8th	Vault	8th

previous Olympics: He was in the top six in each event and took three medals as well as another team-gold. More important, he repeated as all-around champion, the first to do so since Soviet Victor Tchoukarine took titles in 1952 and 1956.

With two Olympic championships, Sawao's claim to eminence was clear, but his life was far from simple. Shortly after Munich, he was in an automobile accident; personal and legal complications forced him to miss a year of training. In addition, he continued to fight against injury and was unable to compete at the 1974 World Gymnastics Championships in Varna, Bulgaria. Meanwhile, on April 2, 1973, Sawao married Makiko Matsubara, and, in 1975, the first of three daughters, Tomoko, was born to the couple. The couple had two other daughters: Yuki, born in 1978, and Mayuko, born in 1982.

Sawao was back in shape for the 1976 Montreal Olympics. Though twenty-nine years old, older than many of his competitors, and suffering ankle problems, he continued to show his championship qualities. He was unable to capture his third successive championship, taking second place in the all-around competition to Soviet gymnast Nikolai Andrianov; however, he placed among the top six in four events and took his second successive Olympic title on the parallel bars. In addition, the quiet, reserved gymnast was the center of a controversy over the score given him by a Soviet judge in the rings competition during the final hours of the competition. In spite of the controversy, and in spite of the Japanese team handicap—a member was sidelined with appendicitis—Sawao received his third Olympic team gold medal. In Montreal, Sawao became the first gymnast ever to win gold medals in three successive Olympics.

Continuing the Story

Travel fatigue from a twenty-four-hour journey from Japan to Oviedo, Spain, accounted for Sawao's mediocre showing at the 1977 World Cup, where he placed fourth all-around and third on the parallel bars. By then he was thirty-one years old and ripe for retirement. In 1978, he left the competitive circuit and turned to coaching and writing.

Records

Set record for the most Olympic gold medals won to date (8)
First gymnast to win gold medals in three successive Olympic games

---

In March of 1979, Sawao joined his friend and mentor Kaneko at Tsukuba University, a modern institution in the Ibaraki region north of Tokyo. Following Kaneko's example, in the early 1980's, Sawao began writing special articles on gymnastics and, in 1983, published a manual on the sport. By the end of the decade, he had published three such volumes. In his writing he demonstrated the same appreciation for technique and precision that characterized him as a performer and competitor. He continued to write, coach, and lecture through the 1990's. He was inducted into the International Gymnastics Hall of Fame in 2001 and served as a gymnastics judge at the 2004 Athens Olympics.

Summary

Sawao Kato was a sure, dedicated, and elegant performer who overcame many difficulties to achieve one of the best records in Olympic history. With his calm exterior, his technical expertise, his perseverance, his team spirit, and his love of form, he embodied many of the finest qualities of gymnastics competition.

Barry Mann

Additional Sources

Conner, Floyd. *The Olympics' Most Wanted: The Top Ten Book of the Olympics' Gold Medal Gaffes, Improbable Triumphs and Other Oddities.* Washington, D.C.: Brassey's, 2002.

Greenberg, Stan. *Whitaker's Olympic Almanack: An Encyclopaedia of the Olympic Games.* Chicago: Fitzroy Dearborn, 2000.

Normile, Dwight. "Classic Class." *International Gymnast* 43, nos. 8/9 (August/September, 2001): 8-11.

Wallechinsky, David, and Jaime Loucky. *The Complete Book of the Olympics: 2008 Edition.* London: Aurum Press, 2008.

Tatyana Kazankina

Born: December 17, 1951
 Petrovsk, Soviet Union (now in Russia)
Also known as: Tatyana Vasilyevna Kazankina
 (full name)

Early Life

Tatyana Vasilyevna Kazankina was born on December 17, 1951, in Petrovsk, Soviet Union. In her early years, Tatyana enjoyed running, despite the fact that she looked frail and fragile. In the Soviet Union in the 1960's, the great national women's champions were in the strength events such as the high hurdles, the long jump, the discus, the javelin, and the shot. Tatyana ran and trained hard at school in spite of receiving mixed messages. In the Soviet Union, although female involvement in sport was encouraged, it tended to be focused narrowly. For example, gymnastics received the greatest state assistance in terms of funds allocated for coaching and facilities. By the 1970's, however, women's track and field had come of age in the Soviet Union. At the 1972 Olympics, twenty-nine-year-old Lyudmila Bragina won the gold medal and set a world record in the 1,500-meter run.

The Road to Excellence

Melvin Watman, in *The Encyclopedia of Track and Field Athletics* (1981), summarizes the contrast between Tatyana's body type and her feats of speed and stamina. Photographs show a slight figure, yet there was enormous power and elasticity in her legs: "Small, skinny and pale, Tatyana Kazankina may not look like a superwoman, but . . . no female distance runner in history has achieved so much."

Up to 1976, Tatyana was seen as a good, hard-training distance runner. She had represented her country on several occasions and, although she was fit and strong, critics dismissed her as a one-speed athlete: an 800- and 1,500-meter runner who would never give up, but one who had neither the speed nor the acceleration to change gears in a race and finish off the opposition. Her best race had been a

fourth place in the 1974 1,500-meter European championships.

In the summer of 1976, Tatyana proved that her training regimen was working. It gave her the necessary stamina to win punishing preliminary races as well as the pace to turn a race, especially the 1,500 meters, into a quality run, rather than the traditional tactical race for three and a half laps climaxed with a burst to the finish line.

The Emerging Champion

In 1976, in perhaps the greatest ever series of non-Olympic women's races, Tatyana completed her training plan with a world record in the 1,500 me-

Tatyana Kazankina immediately after winning the 1500-meter race in the 1980 Olympic Games at Moscow. (Tony Duffy/ Getty Images)

Honors, Awards, and Records

1976	*Track and Field News* World Athlete of the Year
1976, 1980	*Athletics Weekly* World Athlete of the Year
1980	Set world record at 1,500 meters (3:52.47)
1984	Set world record at 3,000 meters (8:22.62)
	Set world record at 2,000 meters (5:28.72)

ters in a time of 3 minutes 56 seconds. Weeks later, she lowered her best performance in the 800 meters to 1 minute 56.6 seconds. In track, even at middle distances, records are normally broken by small margins—frequently, only a fraction of a second. In this instance, Tatyana smashed the world record by an amazing 5.4 seconds.

European and American coaches wondered if Tatyana had peaked too soon. Had she taken too much out of her physical system? Could she possibly withstand the grind and tactical perils of heats, semifinals, and finals in the 800/1,500 meters? No female athlete had ever pulled off such a feat.

At the Montreal Olympics, Tatyana started similarly to her earlier 1976 runs. In the 800 meters, she was a distant fifth coming into the home straight. Then she changed gears and moved past the rest of the field to win in a world and Olympic record of 1 minute 54.94 seconds. However, the competition in this event was diluted because the 1968 Olympic champion, the world record holder, and the European champion were eliminated prior to the finals.

In the Montreal 1,500-meter finals, Tatyana, although favored because of her 1976 world record in the event, faced a seasoned campaigner in Soviet teammate Lyudmila Bragina, the 1972 Olympic champion. Tatyana bided her time in a relatively slow-paced race. She stayed sheltered in the field, avoided an elbowing charge of runners on the last bend, and broke free less than one hundred meters from the finishing tape. Her time of 4 minutes 5.48 seconds was four seconds slower than Bragina's then-world record.

At the 1976 Olympics, it was her competitive focus, built on a solid foundation of quality running, that saw her through. She and her coach, Nikolai Malyshev, had planned on concentrating on only the 1,500 meters. The 800 meters was to be a training run. Then the Soviet team officials indicated that she would run in both. A lesser athlete might have failed the challenge.

Tatyana was quoted on her feelings prior to the 1,500-meter race: "I was afraid of letting the team down. But that was only before the race. Once I was on the track my fears vanished." Her achievements made her *Track and Field News* and *Athletics Weekly* world athlete of the year for 1976.

Continuing the Story

Tatyana and her husband, Alexander Kovalenko, the holder of an advanced degree in mathematics, had a daughter in 1978. It is an interesting physiological quirk that layoffs, in this case to have a baby, can consolidate rather than weaken long-term athletic fitness. Tatyana found that, as the 1980 Olympics approached, her reduced speed precluded her from repeating her 800-meter success, but her pace at the longer event—the 1,500 meters—was undiminished.

In front of an ecstatic home crowd in the Lenin Stadium in Moscow, Tatyana won the Olympic 1,500 meters in a time of 3 minutes 56.6 seconds. In that race, she ran the final 800 meters in less than 2 minutes. Her 1,500-meter time was faster than that of the men's champion Paavo Nurmi of Finland at the 1924 Olympics.

Tatyana continued running during the early 1980's and in 1983 ran competently in the World Track and Field Championships, but lost to American Mary Decker in the 3,000 meters. During competitions in Paris in 1984, Tatyana refused to take a drug test. The ban that followed effectively ended her competitive career. She went on to have a successful career as a scientist, publishing numerous works.

Summary

Tatyana Kazankina finished her career as a three-time Olympic gold medalist. Her most amazing

Major Running Championships

Year	Competition	Event	Place	Time
1974	European Championships	1,500 meters	4th	—
1976	Olympic Games	800 meters	Gold	1:54.94 WR, OR
		1,500 meters	Gold	4:05.48
1977	European Cup	1,500 meters	1st	4:04.4
	World Cup	1,500 meters	1st	4:12.7
1980	Olympic Games	1,500 meters	Gold	3:56.6 OR

Notes: OR = Olympic Record; WR = World Record

performance was her 1,500-meter run of 3 minutes 52.47 seconds set at Zurich, Switzerland, on August 13, 1980. This world-record performance, only twelve days after her Olympic success, was the equivalent of a mile in 4 minutes 10 seconds. In other words, only twenty-six years after women broke the five-minute barrier, this outstanding Soviet athlete showed, in a dramatic fashion, that women would soon break the four-minute barrier for the mile.

Scott A. G. M. Crawford

Additional Sources

Lipoński, Wojciech. *World Sports Encyclopedia*. St. Paul, Minn.: Motorbooks International, 2003.

Rutledge, Rachel. *Women of Sports: The Best of the Best in Track and Field*. Brookfield, Conn.: Millbrook Press, 1999.

Smith, Lissa, ed. *Nike Is a Goddess: The History of Women in Sports*. New York: Grove Atlantic, 2001.

Wallechinsky, David, and Jaime Loucky. *The Complete Book of the Olympics: 2008 Edition*. London: Aurum Press, 2008.

Kip Keino

Born: January, 1940
      Kipsamo, Nandi District, British East Africa
        (now in Kenya)
Also known as: Hezekiah Kipchoge Keino (full
  name)

Early Life

Hezekiah Kipchoge "Kip" Keino was born in Kipsamo, Nandi District, British East Africa (now in Kenya), near the equator in east Africa, in January, 1940. Kip was born in a mud hut in the village of his tribe, the Nandi. Because birth records were not kept by his tribe, no one knows exactly what Kip's birthday was. Kip grew up speaking Swahili, his native tongue, but he learned English at a Protestant missionary school in his village. He began his career as a runner at the school. He set records in the small village's school sports program.

At the time of Kip's birth, Kenya was a British colony; sports competition was generally discouraged by the colonial leadership. They feared that attention to personal achievement of this kind might eventually pose problems of unrest for the government. Kip lived in a nation where there was little athletic tradition to inspire its people to strive for competitive excellence, and Olympic stardom was the furthest thing from his mind.

The Road to Excellence

After finishing school, Kip worked as a cattle herdsman for his father before enrolling in the police academy in Kiganjo, more than two hundred miles from his home. At the police academy, Kip excelled in the intramural sports program.

Kip was such an outstanding talent that, in 1962, he was chosen to be the physical fitness instructor for the academy, and he began racing in national competitions. In his first few races for his country, Kip set records for the one- and two-mile events, and later met and defeated the then-Kenyan champion, Pius Talam, in the three-mile event.

In 1962, Kenya, on the verge of receiving its independence as a nation, made plans to develop its athletics programs, particularly in track and field events. An Englishman by the name of John Velzian, a consultant developing Kenya's expanding athletic program, spotted Kip's potential as a long-distance runner and soon became his coach. After training Kip for several months, Velzian realized that Kip could discipline and pace himself well enough without the assistance of a coach and "turned him loose" on the world of international track and field competition.

The Emerging Champion

Kip represented his country in the British Commonwealth Games in Perth, Australia, in November, 1962. He finished in fifth and eleventh place in the one-mile and three-mile contests, disappointing finishes after he had taken the lead from the start in both races.

Kip's determination to increase his endurance and his new confidence in his ability to compete with the world's best runners spurred him on, and

Kip Keino winning the steeplechase at the Olympic Games in 1972. (AFP/Getty Images)

he tried out for the 1,500-meter and 5,000-meter runs in the 1964 Summer Olympic Games in Tokyo. He hoped to become the first Kenyan athlete to win a gold medal. Kip failed to qualify in the 1,500-meter event but placed fifth in the 5,000-meter run at the Games. His performance disappointed him but again convinced him he belonged in the company of the great mile and 1,500-meter runners, such as the American Jim Ryun.

In August, 1966, Kip won both the mile and three-mile contests in the British Commonwealth Games, and the public began clamoring for a showdown with Jim Ryun, at that time regarded as the world's fastest man and record holder in the mile.

In July, 1967, track and field fans got their wish as Kip and Ryun competed in the United States-British Commonwealth Games in Los Angeles, foreshadowing the epic duels the two runners shared in the Olympic Games. In the one face-off they had, Ryun won the 1,500-meter competition, but he had to break the world record to do it.

Continuing the Story

This 1,500-meter race in Los Angeles was a precursor to the famous Olympic races between Kip and Ryun in 1968 and 1972. The 1968 Olympics were held in Mexico City, at an elevation of seven thousand feet above sea level. This gave the advantage to Kip because he had spent most of his life training and running in Kenya at six thousand feet above sea level. Kip entered Olympic competition in relays and several individual events but kept his focus on Ryun, who he would meet in the 1,500-meter race.

Ryun won the qualifying heat for the 1,500 meters at a pace most observers regarded as surprisingly slow, but Kip knew what he was doing. He was, however, unprepared for the physical obstacle he would face on the day of the finals. Caught in a traffic jam before the scheduled competition, Kip got out of his cab and jogged the final mile to the stadium. Nevertheless, in the race, he set a blistering pace for his opponent and set an Olympic record of 3 minutes 34.9 seconds—a pace that would have been a record mile of 3 minutes, 50 seconds.

Major Running Championships

Year	Competition	Event	Place	Time
1964	Olympic Games	5,000 meters	5th	13:50.4
1966	Commonwealth Games	1 mile	Gold	3:55.3
		3 miles	Gold	12:57.6
1968	Olympic Games	1,500 meters	Gold	3:34.9 OR
		5,000 meters	Silver	14:05.2
		4×400-meter relay	Silver	—
1970	Commonwealth Games	1,500 meters	Gold	3:36.6
		5,000 meters	Bronze	—
1972	Olympic Games	1,500 meters	Silver	3:36.8
		3,000-meter steeplechase	Gold	8:23.6 OR
	Commonwealth Games	3,000-meter steeplechase	Gold	—

Note: OR = Olympic Record

The beleaguered Ryun could not overcome Kip's pace. Even in 1972, in the more hospitable Munich Olympics, Ryun was destined to lose to his Kenyan nemesis. These two great athletes both ended their illustrious Olympic careers with the Munich Games. Facing each other in the fourth heat of the first round of the 1,500 meters, Kip won easily; Ryun was knocked out of the race literally when he tripped on the heel of Ugandan runner Vitus Ashaba. In the final, no longer challenged by the presence of Ryun, Kip lost to Finland's Pekkha Vasala by just five-tenths of a second.

Kip made up for this disappointing and unexpected loss by surprising everyone with a gold medal in the 3,000-meter steeplechase, a race in which he had little experience and that he had entered only as a personal challenge.

Summary

Kip Keino was a pioneer and an inspiration to Kenyan and other African athletes. Virtually self-trained

Records

World record at 3,000 meters and 5,000 meters in 1965
First man to set Olympic records in two different running events

Honors and Awards

1965	World Trophy
1987	*Sports Illustrated* Sportsman of the Year (shared)
1996	Inducted into World Sports Humanitarian Hall of Fame
1999	Made president of Kenya Olympic Committee
2007	Honorary Doctor of Law, Bristol University

and self-motivated, Kip proved what could be accomplished with personal discipline and pride.

Following his Olympic and international career in long-distance running, Keino returned to his homeland and to the police force, where he continued to keep his students in good shape while contributing his formidable knowledge of running to a new generation of Kenya's athletes. In 1984, Kip and his wife established a children's home to care for and educate abandoned children.

In 1999, Kenya honored Kip by making him the president of its national Olympic committee. The post also made Kip—whose name was probably as well known throughout the world as that of any Kenyan who ever lived—a member of the International Olympic Committee. Illustrating his commitment to education, his secondary school opened in 2008.

Bruce L. Edwards

Additional Sources

Noakes, Timothy. *Lore of Running*. Champaign, Ill.: Human Kinetics, 2003.

Sandrock, Michael. *Running with the Legends*. Champaign, Ill.: Human Kinetics, 1996.

Wallechinsky, David, and Jaime Loucky. *The Complete Book of the Olympics: 2008 Edition*. London: Aurum Press, 2008.

Johnny Kelley

Born: September 6, 1907
West Medford, Massachusetts
Died: October 6, 2004
Cape Cod, Massachusetts
Also known as: John Adelbert Kelley (full name)

Early Life
Born on September 6, 1907, John Adelbert Kelley was one of ten children. He first competed in track and cross-country at Arlington High School in Massachusetts. After finishing high school, Johnny worked at Boston Edison as a mechanic—there were no professional track athletes at that time. He still found time to run, however, devoting evenings after work to his sport. He once said, "All day long, I did what my boss told me to do. But when I ran at night, I felt free. I ran till I was exhausted." His flexible work schedule allowed him time to train: Every other week he worked Sundays, which gave him a three-day weekend the following week. This allowed him to run two to three hours on Saturday as well as his normal 4-5 miles every other day.

The Road to Excellence
In 1928, at the age of 20, he first entered the Boston Marathon, the competition for which he became famous. Tired from running a marathon in Rhode Island shortly before the Boston race, he failed to finish the marathon when exhaustion took its toll; he accepted a ride from someone who offered him a lift to the finish.

Johnny did not attempt the Boston run again for another four years. He did not have running shoes and was forced to use a pair of black leather high-jumping shoes that he cut open at the toes with a razor blade. Even so, he was among the leaders for several miles of the race until his feet became so badly blistered he withdrew from the competition.

Not one to give up, Johnny ran again the following year. Although recovering from the flu, he finished thirty-seventh in a field of two hundred. In 1934, he ran again and finished second. He battled head-to-head with Dave Komonen of Canada before he watched his competition pull away. Finally, in 1935, Johnny achieved his dream when he fin-

ished first, more than two minutes ahead of Pat Dengis of Maryland. After the race, at the finish line, he collapsed in his father's arms.

The Emerging Champion
In 1936 a portion of the Boston Marathon's route was named after Johnny. He was the defending champion and, by his own admission, was a little cocky. When he was nearing a series of hills near Newton, Massachusetts, he came up behind Tarzan Brown, who was struggling to maintain a lead. Johnny lightly tapped Brown on the back, which only served to redouble his competitor's effort. Brown went on to win the race. A reporter saw that

Boston Marathon Competitions

Year	Time	Place	Age	Year	Time	Place	Age
1928	DNF		20	1962	2:44:36	25th	54
1932	DNF		24	1963	3:14:00	84th	55
1933	3:03:56	37th	25	1964	2:49:14	48th	56
1934	2:36:50	2d	26	1965	2:48:00	58th	57
1935	2:32:07	1st	27	1966	2:55:00	59th	58
1936	2:38:49	5th	28	1967	3:13:00	135th	59
1937	2:39:02	2d	29	1968	Injured		60
1938	2:37:34	3d	30	1969	3:05:02	186th	61
1939	2:41:03	13th	31	1970	3:03:00	163d	62
1940	2:32:03	2d	32	1971	3:45:47	977th	63
1941	2:31:26	2d	33	1972	3:35:12	890th	64
1942	2:37:55	5th	34	1973	3:35:02	1,105th	65
1943	2:30:00	2d	35	1974	3:24:10	1,266th	66
1944	2:32:03	2d	36	1975	3:22:48	1,633d	67
1945	2:30:40	1st	37	1976	3:28:00	1,094th	68
1946	2:31:27	2d	38	1977	3:32:12	1,892d	69
1947	2:40:00	13th	39	1978	3:42:36	3,729th	70
1948	2:37:50	4th	40	1979	3:45:12	3,577th	71
1949	2:38:07	4th	41	1980	3:35:21	3,444th	72
1950	2:43:45	5th	42	1981	4:01:25	5,074th	73
1951	2:39:09	6th	43	1982	4:01:30	NA	74
1952	3:04:59	12th	44	1983	4:23:22	NA	75
1953	2:32:46	7th	45	1984	sub-5:00	NA	76
1954	2:50:25	16th	46	1985	4:31:00	NA	77
1955	2:45:22	24th	47	1986	4:27:00	NA	78
1956	DNF		48	1987	4:19:56	NA	79
1957	2:53:00	13th	49	1988	4:26:36	NA	80
1958	2:52:12	9th	50	1989	5:05:15	NA	81
1959	2:47:52	23d	51	1990	5:05:00	NA	82
1960	2:44:39	19th	52	1991	5:42:54	NA	83
1961	2:44:53	17th	53	1992	5:58:00	NA	84

Notes: NA = Place not available; DNF = Did not finish

touch as the turning point of the race and the beginning of Johnny's defeat and so named it Heartbreak Hill. In 1993, a bronze statue of Johnny was erected at the foot of Heartbreak Hill.

Not content to run the Boston Marathon only, Johnny qualified to become a member of the 1936 U.S. Olympic team and compete at the Berlin Games. These games became known for Jesse Owens's incredible victories and Adolf Hitler's snub of Owens. Johnny finished eighteenth in the marathon. Although never really in contention for a medal, Johnny was content merely to be part of the Games.

Johnny continued running the Boston Marathon and competing in other races. He made the 1940 U.S. Olympic team but lost his chance to compete when Hitler's army invaded Norway and the Games were canceled. After the war Johnny competed in one final Olympics. He ran the marathon in London, finishing twenty-first at the age of forty.

Continuing the Story

Johnny was not about to give up running despite having reached an age when most runners stop competing. The Boston Marathon was Johnny's race, and he intended to run it as long as he could. Throughout the 1940's and 1950's he ran the twenty-six miles. In 1941, 1943, and 1944 he placed second. In 1945, he took the advice of a reporter and used his head to run a smarter, more evenly paced race and took first place. The following year he again placed second. After 1946, however, he began slowing down.

Despite slower times, every year Johnny stood at the starting line, waiting to run his race. In 1972, he retired from his job at Boston Edison but not from running. In 1992, at the age of eighty-four, Johnny ran his last Boston Marathon. He was the oldest man to have run the race. Famous for the number

of times he had run it, he was made the 1995 Grand Marshal of the marathon. He attended the race every year until 1999, when he was sidelined by abdominal surgery. Although he ceased to run the marathon, Johnny refused to give up running. He and his wife retired to Cape Cod, where he was often seen running along the country roads or on the beach. In 2000, the magazine *Runner's World* named him the runner of the century. Johnny died in 2004.

Summary

Johnny Kelley ran because he loved it, not because it paid him a lot of money. He began running at a time before professional athletics and lucrative endorsements made participating in sports profitable. Instead, Johnny worked as a mechanic and trained in his spare time. He also persevered and ran in the Boston Marathon every year from 1932 until 1992, ultimately becoming a legend. He used his fame to help a number of charities, including the Special Olympics. He established a Memorial Day race to raise money for his favorite charity, the Cape Cod Hospital.

Deborah Service

Additional Sources

Connelly, Michael. *Twenty-six Miles to Boston: The Boston Marathon Experience from Hopkinton to Copley Square.* Guilford, Conn.: Lyons Press, 2003.

Derderian, Tom. *The Boston Marathon: A Century of Blood, Sweat, and Cheers.* Chicago: Triumph Books, 2003.

Lewis, Frederick, and Dick Johnson. *Young at Heart: The Story of Johnny Kelley, Boston's Marathon Man.* Cambridge, Mass.: Rounder Books, 2005.

Martin, David E., and Roger W. H. Gynn. *The Olympic Marathon.* Champaign, Ill.: Human Kinetics, 2000.

John Kelly, Sr.

Born: October 4, 1889
  Philadelphia, Pennsylvania
Died: June 20, 1960
  Philadelphia, Pennsylvania
Also known as: John Brendan Kelly, Sr. (full
  name); Jack Kelly

Early Life

John Brendan Kelly, Sr., was born October 4, 1889, in Philadelphia, Pennsylvania. His parents were John Henry Kelly, an Irish immigrant millworker, and Mary Ann Costello. John had four older brothers, all of whom became famous in either sports, business, or the theater.

John was a self-made man. He attended public school for eight years and then worked days laying bricks while he went to school at night. In 1919, he borrowed money to start his own construction firm; eventually, he became a millionaire. John's children were as famous as he was. One daughter, Grace, became a film star and married the prince of Monaco. John B. Kelly, Jr., won the Diamond Sculls at the Royal Henley Regatta twice and a bronze medal in the 1948 Olympics, and he also became president of the United States Olympic Committee.

The Road to Excellence

John was an all-around athlete, competing in boxing, swimming, football, and basketball in top-level competition. He enlisted in the U.S. Army as a private in World War I and boxed to pass the time. He defeated twelve heavyweight boxing opponents and was scheduled to fight heavyweight champion Gene Tunney until a broken ankle canceled the fight.

John's first love, however, was rowing. He began rowing in 1909, at the age of twenty, and competed in singles, doubles

(two-person), and four-person boats. That year, he won the first of 124 sculling victories, a total that was not surpassed until many years later. In 1913, he won nine races, including the single at the United States Henley in Boston, Massachusetts. After this race, he was acclaimed as the best rower in America.

The Emerging Champion

In 1914, John was equally successful; he won the U.S. Nationals Association single and double sculls. After discharge from the U.S. Army, John started his construction business and resumed rowing. He won the elite single scull championship in 1919 and the double scull in 1920. Perhaps his most difficult race of this period was against Bob Dibble, the longtime Canadian champion. John defeated Dibble by a half length in one-hundred-degree heat to become the undisputed American champion.

Although John had considerable success before and during 1919, it was nothing like what was to follow. In 1920, John tried to enter the Diamond Sculls event at the Royal Henley Regatta in

John Kelly, Sr., rowing during the 1924 Olympic Games in Paris. (Courtesy of Amateur Athletic Foundation of Los Angeles)

Thames, England, but the Regatta officials would not let him race. No official explanation was ever given, but John believed that the Regatta officials did not like him because he was a "professional." By professional, the Regatta officials meant that Kelly had more muscles because he worked with his hands as a bricklayer, and this gave him an unfair advantage. John's feelings were hurt by this snub, and he claimed that he would come back one day and win the Diamond Sculls.

John trained harder than ever after the snub by the Regatta officials. During this time, he came up with the idea of racing against the Royal Henley winner in the Olympics. He entered two events in the Olympic trials and won them both. First he won the single, which gave him the chance to race against the great Jack Beresford of England. Then he won the double sculls, teaming with his cousin, Paul Costello. Rowing in two events in the Olympics is difficult because there is so little time to rest between races. Nonetheless, John was at his best. First he beat Beresford; this victory was especially sweet. Beresford, the winner of the Diamond Sculls at the Royal Henley, was just beginning a great rowing career. In a tough race, John beat him by only one second. Then John and his cousin Paul teamed up to win the gold medal in the double, defeating a fine French team. Thus, John left his mark in the world of rowing, becoming the first rower to win two gold medals in the same Olympic Games.

Continuing the Story

John continued to train in Philadelphia, winning the Elite double with his cousin Paul in 1921, for the Vesper Boat Club. John and Paul were the best combination in the world for four years, and the two displayed their speed again in the 1924 Olympics. During the finals of the Olympics, John and

Major Rowing Championships

Year	Competition	Event	Place
1913-16, 1919	Schuylkill Navy Championship	Senior single sculls	1st
1914	U.S. Nationals Association Championship	Single sculls	1st
		Double sculls	1st
1919	U.S. Nationals	Elite single sculls	1st
1920	Olympic Games	Single sculls	Gold
		Double sculls	Gold
1920-21	U.S. Nationals	Elite double sculls	1st
1924	Olympic Games	Double sculls	Gold

Paul stayed behind until 1,000 meters, or halfway through the race; at this point, they sprinted by the French team to take the lead and held it to the end to win by four seconds.

After the Olympics, John retired, but his heart was still in the sport. He taught his son to row at the age of nine. Much like his father, John Jr., or "Kell," was an all-around athlete who loved the sport. Unlike his father, however, Kell was allowed to enter the Diamond Sculls event, winning the coveted title in 1947 and 1949 and racing in three Olympics in the single. Kell's best performance came in 1956, when he won a bronze medal.

Summary

After retiring from rowing, John Kelly, Sr., had a successful career as a businessman and politician. He had an incredible impact on rowing in later life. His contributions included rebuilding the Vesper Boat Club, home of many Olympic and world champion rowers. His famous "Kelly For Brickwork" shirts are still worn by rowers in Philadelphia. These shirts symbolize what John stood for: Anyone should be able to race if he or she wishes to do so. Most important is the standard John set for rowers: two gold medals in one Olympics.

Steven G. Estes

Additional Sources

Churbuck, D. C. *The Book of Rowing*. Rev. ed. Woodstock, N.Y.: Overlook Press, 2003.

Wallechinsky, David, and Jaime Loucky. *The Complete Book of the Olympics: 2008 Edition*. London: Aurum Press, 2008.

Honor

1990	Inducted into U.S. Olympic Hall of Fame

Lee Kemp

Born: December 24, 1956
   Cleveland, Ohio
Also known as: Leroy Percy Kemp, Jr. (full
   name); Darnell Freeman (birth name)

Early Life

Leroy Percy Kemp, Jr., was born on the day before Christmas in 1956, in Cleveland, Ohio. His first love was playing basketball on the playgrounds of Cleveland. When he was twelve years old, the family moved to the small farming community of Chardon, Ohio. Lee continued to enjoy basketball and eventually tried out for his school's eighth-grade team, but he was cut from the team.

The Road to Excellence

The next year, Lee happened to see his school's wrestling team practicing. He thought it was inter-

Lee Kemp (left) grappling a German wrestler during the 1978 World Wrestling Championships. (AP/Wide World Photos)

esting, as everyone was involved in the practice—not just the top wrestlers. He decided to try out for the ninth-grade team. At first, he did not like the sport because it was tough, but he enjoyed winning and won enough bouts that first year to remain interested. By all standards, Lee was a late starter, yet he became devoted to wrestling because of the thrill he experienced whenever he defeated an opponent.

The next year, Lee made the varsity team; his record was 11-8. There were no signs that Lee would eventually become a dominant force in the field of wrestling.

The summer between Lee's tenth and eleventh grades was memorable. He attended a wrestling clinic, where he met Dan Gable, the highly successful wrestler from Iowa State University and equally successful coach of the Iowa Hawkeyes. Dan had an immediate impact on Lee. Dan's message was simple: If you are willing to work hard and have an interest in what you are doing, success will follow. Lee became motivated to work hard; he worked diligently, always trying to learn and improve. He was never satisfied. He asked every wrestler with whom he came in contact to teach him; he became a great student of the sport.

No one could have guessed the turnaround in Lee's wrestling. Lee went undefeated the next year, an incredible record in comparison to his mediocre previous year. He also won the Ohio state championship by beating the defending champion. His winning ways continued in his senior year; he went undefeated again and repeated as the state champion.

The Emerging Champion

After graduation from high school, the two-time Ohio state champion continued his education and wrestling at the University of Wisconsin.

NCAA Record

Most victories in national tournaments, 20

Honors, Awards, and Milestones

1974	U.S. junior freestyle champion
1974-75	Ohio State high school champion
1976-78	NCAA champion
1978-79, 1982	World Championships gold medalist
1979-82	World Cup freestyle champion
1979-83	U.S. freestyle champion
1979, 1983	U.S. Pan-American Games gold medalist
1980	U.S. Olympic team
1981	World Championships bronze medalist
1990	Inducted into National Wrestling Hall of Fame

He set a high goal—to be the first four-time National Collegiate Athletic Association (NCAA) wrestling champion. Lee had a successful first year in college wrestling and was on his way to reaching his goal. In the finals of the NCAA Tournament, his bout ended in a tie and was forced into overtime. After an additional three minutes of wrestling, the score was still tied. The referees had to choose a winner. Lee lost by a 2-1 vote. Because he could not be a four-time champion, Lee set another difficult goal—never to lose again. This goal he reached. After the narrow defeat in the NCAA finals in his freshman year, he did not lose another match in college. In the next three years, he won 108 matches and tied one for a career record of 143-6-1, with an unbeaten string of 109 bouts.

Continuing the Story

Lee dominated his weight class in collegiate wrestling. Now it was time to move on to the world. A few months after graduating from Wisconsin, Lee was the U.S. representative in the World Wrestling Championships. On August 27, 1978, he defeated his Bulgarian opponent to become the youngest American to ever win a gold medal and a world freestyle championship.

Lee's success at this first tournament was only the beginning of his dominance of the international scene. He repeated as world champion in 1979 and 1982, becoming the first American to win three championships. He was third in 1981. He was the pan-American champion in 1979 and 1983, and he led the American team to its first two team trophies in the World Cup championships in 1980 and 1982, by defeating the highly favored team from the Soviet Union.

Lee also made the 1980 Olympic team and was heavily favored to win a gold medal. The United States, however, boycotted the Olympics because of the Soviet Union's military action in Afghanistan. This was a terrible letdown to Lee. He was unable to make the 1984 team, finishing second.

After ending his wrestling career, Lee returned to school to receive his master's degree in business administration and to redirect his philosophy of winning to the world of business. His philosophy was quite simple: Pursue what you enjoy doing. Lee loved wrestling, which made the hard work that was required to be a champion easier. He felt that if one finds something that one loves, the work will be easier and fulfillment will result. Lee later became a wrestling coach. He was a member of the coaching staff for the U.S. team in 2006 and for the junior world team in 2007. In 2008, he was the Olympic freestyle wrestling coach.

Summary

Lee Kemp was cut from basketball and barely had a winning season his first varsity year of high school wrestling. Then he discovered that success takes hard work. Because he loved wrestling, the hard work was bearable. The end result of his hard work and love for his sport was a world championship.

Michael J. Welch

Additional Sources

Chapman, Mike. *Wrestling Tough.* Champaign, Ill.: Human Kinetics, 2005.

Kopriva, Don, and Jim Mott. *On Wisconsin! The History of Badger Athletics from 1896-2001.* Champaign, Ill.: Sports, 2001.

Wallechinsky, David, and Jaime Loucky. *The Complete Book of the Olympics: 2008 Edition.* London: Aurum Press, 2008.

Nancy Kerrigan

Born: October 13, 1969
      Woburn, Massachusetts
Also known as: Nancy Ann Kerrigan (full name);
      Nancy Solomon

Early Life

Nancy Ann Kerrigan was born in Woburn, Massachusetts, to Daniel and Brenda Kerrigan on October 13, 1969, and grew up in nearby Stoneham. The younger sister of two hockey-playing brothers, Nancy began skating at the age of six with an apparently inborn aptitude, and her parents encouraged her to pursue figure skating. Daniel, a welder, worked odd jobs and took out loans to pay the expenses involved in competitive skating. Brenda, whose sight had been severely impaired by a rare virus when Nancy was two years old, could not see her daughter's progress except by sitting close to a television screen.

The Road to Excellence

By the time Nancy was in high school, she was practicing at 4:00 A.M. each day. The Kerrigans went without typical family vacations, instead attending Nancy's competitions. Able to do a triple-toe jump as a novice, she was quickly pegged as a future Olympian.

Nancy rose quickly through the ranks of amateur competitions. She finished third in the New England Junior Championships in 1987; the following year, she won the more competitive New England Senior Championships. Her dedication earned Nancy a place on the 1992 U.S. Olympic team. She skated well at the Winter Games in Albertville, France, but a slight stumble hurt her score, and she earned a bronze medal.

The Emerging Champion

At the 1993 World Figure Skating Championships in Prague, Czechoslovakia, Nancy did not skate up to her potential. She fell and placed fifth. Her coach blamed her heavy schedule, which included a flurry of personal appearances and commercial endorsements.

In response, she began practicing four hours a day, working toward the 1994 Winter Olympics.

At the 1993 U.S. National Championships, she performed with grace and maturity to earn her first national title. After placing first at competitions in Norway and in Philadelphia, she began preparing for the 1994 U.S. National Championships in Detroit—the competition that would determine the U.S. team for the Olympics in Lillehammer, Norway.

On January 6, 1994, after finishing practice at the Detroit, Michigan, rink where the championships would be held, Nancy was bludgeoned on the

Nancy Kerrigan skating in 1994. (AP/Wide World Photos)

knee by an assailant. The injury was not permanently disabling, but she was not be able to compete in the championship the next day. U.S. Olympic Committee rules required prospective team members to compete in the event; Nancy, however, was soon granted a waiver, in deference to her ability and the viciousness of and suspected motives for the crime.

Suspicion fell almost immediately on Tonya Harding, Nancy's Olympic teammate, who won the championship in Nancy's absence. The assailant was soon identified as a man with links to Harding's former husband, and the blitz of publicity that followed was unrelenting. With reporters following her every move, Nancy conducted a hurried physical rehabilitation.

By the time the Lillehammer Games began several weeks later, the strength of Nancy's landing knee was still in doubt; yet in the short program, she skated with assurance and placed first. The long program, however, would determine who would win the gold. Nancy gave a stunning performance. Her program included five triple jumps—two in combination—and her trademark spiral, a graceful move in which she glided while grasping her right leg and holding it behind her. Her scores reflected the judges' approval of her flawless performance. The gold seemed to be hers.

Then Oksana Baiul, a Ukrainian orphan with a heartbreaking story of her own, skated onto the ice seemingly unconscious of the slash in her leg, the result of a collision during practice. Her program was not as technically difficult as Nancy's; in figure skating, however, artistic merit counts, and in this case it tipped the score in Baiul's favor.

Nancy was visibly disappointed by the sudden and unexpected loss of the gold medal, yet she expressed satisfaction with her performance and with the silver medal. The decision had been made on artistic merit, a matter of taste. Many observers believed that Nancy had given a performance worthy of a gold medal.

Continuing the Story

Nancy was bombarded with offers for endorsement contracts and personal appearances, and she was also deluged with bids for the film and television rights to her story. This time, however, Nancy could handle such a schedule, as her competitive

Major Figure-Skating Championships

Year	Competition	Place
1989	U.S. National Senior Ladies Championships	5th
	World University Games	3d
1990	U.S. National Senior Ladies Championships	4th
	Goodwill Games	5th
1991	U.S. National Senior Ladies Championships	3d
	Nations Cup	1st
1992	U.S. National Senior Ladies Championships	2d
	Olympic Games	Bronze
	World Championships	2d
1993	U.S. National Senior Ladies Championships	1st
	World Championships	5th
1994	Olympic Games	Silver

career was winding down. In addition to her devotion to charities for the blind, in which she had been involved for many years, she became a spokesperson for Revlon Cosmetics and signed a deal with the Walt Disney Company that included several projects. A year later, in 1995, Nancy married Jerry Solomon, a sports agent, and she gave birth to their son, Matthew, in 1996. She was back on the professional circuit, in excellent condition, by 1997. Her skating was strong enough for her to win the bronze medal at the 2000 Winter Goodwill Games. Nancy and her husband also established the Nancy Kerrigan Foundation to help fund organizations that support the vision-impaired. In 2005, Nancy gave birth to her second son, Brian. In May, 2008, Nancy had her third child, a girl named Nicole.

Summary

Nancy Kerrigan overcame injury, opposing skaters, and the pressures imposed by the media on her way to a memorable Olympic performance. Her calm confidence and grace under pressure won her countless admirers.

Janet Long

Additional Sources

Hines, James R. *Figure Skating: A History.* Urbana: University of Illinois Press, 2006.

Kerrigan, Nancy, and Eric Roston. "The Rules Need to Be Changed." *Time* 159, no. 8 (February 25, 2002): 32.

Kerrigan, Nancy, and Mary Spencer. *Artistry on Ice: Figure Skating Skills and Style.* Champaign, Ill.: Human Kinetics, 2003.

Svetlana Khorkina

Born: January 19, 1979
      Belgorod, Soviet Union (now in Russia)
Also known as: Svetlana Vasilievna Khorkina (full
    name); Sveta; Queen of the Bars

Early Life

Svetlana Vasilievna Khorkina was born to Vassily and Lyubov Khorkina in Belgorod, Soviet Union (now in Russia), on January 19, 1979. Svetlana became interested in gymnastics at the age of four while watching the Soviet gymnastics team win the 1983 World Gymnastics Championships. When Svetlana was six years old, her interest in the sport

Svetlana Khorkina on the balance beam during the 2000 Olympic Games at Sydney. (Popperfoto/Getty Images)

turned serious after she saw champion Oksana Omelianchik perform on television. Even at this young age, Svetlana had obvious talent and ambition. She grew taller than the other gymnasts and developed a body unlike the classic pixieish shape associated with most gymnasts. She did, however, have the spirit, stubbornness, and competitive drive of a champion.

The Road to Excellence

As Svetlana continued to grow, her trainers tried to persuade her to concentrate on rhythmic gymnastics. However, she longed to return to artistic gymnastics. Her coach, Boris Pilkin, encouraged her and helped tailor her routines to complement her long limbs and slim build, to make her height an advantage, not a disadvantage.

In 1992, Svetlana joined the new Soviet junior national team at the age of thirteen. She progressed quickly through the Russian gymnastics program. Her first big event was the Moscow World Stars competition, in which she placed fifth in the all-around. Within a year, her natural brilliance began to show. She took five individual gold medals in the Baltic Sea Games and at the Russian Gymnastics Championships in 1993. She earned two of these medals on the uneven bars, the event that best complemented her elegant frame.

In 1994, Svetlana found added success. She finished second at the European Gymnastics Championships and won a gold medal on the uneven bars. She won two more individual medals at the World Gymnastics Championships in Brisbane, Australia, and three at the Goodwill Games.

Svetlana continued to impress gymnastics fans with her talent and consistency while working toward the 1996 Olympics. In almost all of the competitions Svetlana entered, she managed to place in all-around and the uneven bars. Svetlana made a name for herself in this event and even had three original moves named after her.

Major Gymnastics Championships

Year	Competition	Event	Place	Event	Place
1992	Moscow Stars of the World	Vault	5th	Uneven bars	3d
1993	Junior European Championships	All-around	7th	Vault	8th
		Uneven bars	4th	Floor exercise	4th
1994	World Team Championships		3d		
	Goodwill Games	Team	1st	Vault	3d
		Uneven bars	1st		
	World Championships	All-around	9th	Vault	2d
		Uneven bars	2d		
	European Championships	All-around	2d	Uneven bars	1st
1995	European Cup	All-around	1st	Vault	3d
		Uneven bars	2d	Floor exercise	3d
	World Championships	Team	4th	All-around	2d
		Vault	5th	Uneven bars	1st
	Russian National Championships	All-around	1st		
1996	World Championships	Vault	5th	Uneven bars	1st
	Russian National Championships	All-around	3d		
	European Championships	Team	2d	All-around	6th
		Vault	4th	Uneven bars	1st
	Olympic Games	Team	Silver	All-around	15th
		Uneven bars	Gold		
1997	World Championships	Team	2d	All-around	1st
		Vault	8th	Uneven bars	1st
		Balance beam	2d	Floor exercise	2d
	Russian National Championships	All-around	1st		
1998	World Cup	Vault	5th	Uneven bars	2d
		Balance beam	4th	Floor exercise	4th
	European Championships	Team	2d	All-around	1st
		Uneven bars	1st	Floor exercise	1st
1999	France Telecom International	All-around	1st	Uneven bars	1st
		Floor exercise	1st		
	European Championships	Team	1st		
	World Championships	Team	2d	All-around	12th
		Uneven bars	1st	Floor exercise	3d
2000	European Championships	Team	1st	All-around	1st
		Uneven bars	1st	Balance beam	1st
	Olympic Games	Team	Silver	All-around	10th
		Uneven bars	Gold	Floor exercise	Silver
2001	World Championships	All-around	1st	Floor exercise	3d
		Vault	1st	Team	2d
		Uneven bars	1st		
2002	European Championships	All-around	1st	Floor exercise	5th
		Uneven bars	1st	Team	1st
		Beam	2d		
2003	World Championships	All-around	1st	Team	6th
2004	European Championships	All-around	4th	Floor exercise	7th
		Uneven bars	1st	Team	3d
		Beam	3d		
	Olympic Games	Team	Bronze	All-around	Silver

The Emerging Champion

At Svetlana's first Olympics in Atlanta in 1996, she earned gold for her performances on the uneven bars and silver in team competition. However, the remainder of the Olympic competition was a disaster for her. She finished a disappointing fifteenth in all-around and the Unified Team, athletes from Russia and other former Soviet countries, finished second behind the United States.

Svetlana used her experience in Atlanta to improve her skills on the floor exercises and vault in preparation for the 1997 World Gymnastics Championships. Her hard work paid off: She received gold medals in the all-around and in the uneven bars and collected three silver medals. Later that year, the blond, gray-eyed Svetlana caused a sensation in her country by posing nude for the Russian edition of *Playboy*.

After winning a gold medal in the uneven bars, a silver medal in the team competition, and a bronze medal in the floor exercise at the World Gymnastics Championships at Tianjin, China, Svetlana prepared for the 2000 Olympics in Sydney, Australia. Although one of the favorites to win the all-around, she finished a disappointing eleventh after falling on the vault and the uneven bars. The psychological damage done by the fall on the vault affected her other routines, dropping her in the standings. In the event finals, however, she took a gold medal in uneven bars and captured silver medals in the team competition and floor exercise.

Svetlana gained popularity

outside gymnastics as well. Her engaging personality and quick wit captivated the media. She granted interviews to journalists and answered their questions with honest and candid responses. When she reached her twenties, considered old for a gymnast, Svetlana was determined to continue competing.

Continuing the Story

At the 2001 World Gymnastics Championships, Svetlana had one of her best performances. She captured gold medals in vault, uneven bars, and all-around; took silver in the team competition; and won bronze in the floor exercise. Having won five consecutive world crowns and two Olympic gold medals on uneven bars, Svetlana had laid claim as the best gymnast ever on a single apparatus. She won the all-around competition at both the 2002 European Gymnastics Championships and the 2003 World Gymnastics Championships. At the latter, she had won her third all-around world title, more than any female gymnast ever.

A favorite going into the 2004 Athens Olympics, Svetlana did not perform to expectations, though she qualified for the finals in uneven bars and all-around. She won silver in all-around and afterward claimed she had been robbed of gold. She also helped a relatively weak Russian squad to the bronze medal in team competition.

Retiring after the 2004 Olympics, Svetlana married and gave birth to a son. In 2003, she had become interested in politics after joining the United Russian political party, and in 2007, she was elected as a delegate to the Duma, the lower branch of the Russian legislature. In 2008, she published an autobiography. Svetlana maintained close contact with her sport: At the 2008 Olympics, she served as commentator for NTV, a Russian television channel.

Summary

A world-class competitor for more than a decade in a sport that takes considerable toll on an athlete's body, Svetlana Khorkina was one of the most accomplished female gymnasts ever. Recognized for attempting difficult and creative routines, she had eight moves in four different disciplines, more than any other gymnast of either gender. Winner of nine gold, eight silver, and three bronze medals at World Gymnastics Championships, Svetlana overcame her unusual height for a female gymnast and took advantage of her slender elegance to become a popular performer. The first to win three all-around world titles, she also collected seven Olympic medals.

Maryanne Barsotti, updated by Jack Ewing

Additional Sources

Hofstetter, Adam B. *Great Moments in Olympic History: Olympic Gymnastics.* New York: Rosen Central, 2007.

Khorkina, Svetlana. *Somersault on High Heels.* Moscow, Russia: Olma-Press, 2008.

"Update: Olympian Svetlana Khorkina Becomes a Mom." *People Weekly,* June 20, 2005, 112.

Billy Kidd

Born: April 13, 1943
     Burlington, Vermont
Also known as: William Winston Kidd, Jr. (full name)

Early Life

Born in Burlington, Vermont, on April 13, 1943, William Winston Kidd, Jr., grew up skiing. His father, William Sr., was an avid skier. He began taking his son Billy skiing when Billy was four. Billy was not a natural athlete. He played Little League baseball for several years but was not a good player and rarely got to play. When he began skiing, he fell frequently. He stayed with the sport, however, and by the time he was eleven, he could ski faster than his father.

The Road to Excellence

In his first ski race, at the age of eleven, Billy placed second in a field of sixty. The next year, he entered a race at Mad River Glen, Vermont, and defeated many college skiers in the race. He was later disqualified because he was underage.

Almost every winter weekend, Billy and his father drove to Stowe, Vermont, a center of skiing activity and the home of the Mount Mansfield Ski Club, a club known for developing outstanding ski racers. In Stowe, Billy learned from some of the best coaches in the country. When Billy was fourteen, his family moved to Stowe and built a motel so that Billy could devote himself to skiing. That year, Billy began competing in Junior National competition.

The Emerging Champion

In 1961, Billy left the junior ranks and competed successfully in several American races. The following year, at the world championships in France, he finished eighth in the slalom event and twelfth in the giant slalom.

Throughout his career, Billy was plagued by injuries. The most serious problem was an ankle injury that kept him out of competition for much of the 1963 season. That injury continued to bother him for the rest of his career. Because of his inju-

ries, Billy was not able to train as hard for his sport as other top skiers. To compensate for his lack of training time, Billy carefully studied his sport, sometimes spending six hours a night viewing films.

The greatest achievement of Billy's ski career came at the 1964 Winter Olympic Games in Innsbruck, Austria. Before 1964, no American man had ever won an Olympic medal in alpine skiing. The U.S. Olympic coach Bob Beattie was determined that the American men would win a medal. Billy and the other members of the U.S. team shared his dedication.

As the 1964 Olympic Games approached, Billy and his coach realized that it would be almost impossible to win a medal unless the American skiers had good starting positions in the Olympic races. In ski racing, skiers go down the hill one at a time. The competitors who get to start first usually have

Billy Kidd. (Courtesy of Amateur Athletic Foundation of Los Angeles)

faster times than those who go last. This is because the snow on the race course is smooth for the early starters but becomes bumpy and icy for the later skiers.

Beattie believed that the European officials, who controlled ski racing, discriminated against American skiers when assigning starting positions. In the months before the Innsbruck Games, he argued constantly with these officials so that Billy and his teammates would not be among the last racers to ski. Beattie's pressure and some good performances by the Americans in pre-Olympic races finally resulted in a starting position Billy needed to do well at Innsbruck.

In the first two alpine skiing events at Innsbruck, the giant slalom and the downhill, the American men failed to win a medal. Going into the final event, the slalom, there was tremendous pressure on the U.S. men's team to do well. The slalom consists of two runs. After the first run, Billy was in sixth place. He skied so well on the second run that he moved up in the standings to second place to take a silver medal. His teammate Jimmie Heuga finished in third place, winning a bronze medal. They became the first American men to win Olympic medals in skiing.

Continuing the Story

Billy continued competitive skiing through the 1972 season. During that time, he attended the University of Colorado. In 1969, he graduated with a degree in economics.

Although Billy did not win any more Olympic medals after 1964, he remained one of the best skiers in the world. He defeated the great French skier Jean-Claude Killy several times in 1966 and 1968. He missed the 1967 season because of a broken leg

Records

First American man, with Jimmie Heuga, to win an Olympic medal in skiing (a silver in slalom in 1964)

First American skier to win the World Championships

First American skier to win the World Professional Championships

Honor

1976 Inducted into National Ski Hall of Fame

Major Skiing Championships

Year	Competition	Event	Place
1962	World Championships	Slalom	8th
1964	Olympic Games	Downhill	16th
		Slalom	Silver
		Giant slalom	7th
1968	World Cup	Overall	7th
	Olympic Games	Downhill	18th
		Slalom	Did not finish
		Giant slalom	5th
1970	World Championships	Downhill	5th
		Slalom	3d
		Giant Slalom	15th
		Combined	1st
	World Professional Championships	Combined	1st

and then sprained his ankle before the 1968 Winter Olympic Games in Grenoble, France. Despite his ankle injury, Billy skied well. He finished eighteenth in the downhill and fifth in the giant slalom. In the giant slalom, he missed winning a medal by .54 of a second.

In 1970, Billy established two more historic firsts. He became the first American to win the International Ski Federation World Championships title for the best all-around performance at the championships. He then joined the professional skiing circuit. Two weeks after turning professional, Billy won the World Professional Championships, becoming the first person to win both the amateur and professional championships in the same year.

Injuries and a desire to spend more time on other interests convinced Billy to retire from competitive skiing after the 1972 season. However, he remained deeply involved in skiing. For several years, he served as the director of skiing at the Steamboat Ski Area in Colorado. In addition, he became a television commentator and a design consultant to ski equipment manufacturers. He wrote several ski books, ran ski racing camps, and made an instructional ski series for television. Billy also served on the President's Council on Physical Fitness and Sports and on the board of directors of the International Special Olympics.

Summary

Billy Kidd proved that America's male skiers could be top international competitors. He set a standard of excellence that influenced later American ski racers. He will be remembered as the first American to win a world championship and the first American man, along with Jimmie Heuga, to win an Olympic skiing medal.

Wayne Wilson

Additional Sources

Fry, John. *The Story of Modern Skiing.* Hanover, N.H.: University Press of New England, 2006.

Hickok, Ralph. *A Who's Who of Sports Champions: Their Stories and Records.* Boston: Houghton Mifflin, 1995.

Kidd, Billy, and Bill Grout. *Billy Kidd's Ski Racing Book.* Chicago: Contemporary Books, 1984.

Tejada-Flores, Lito. *The Unofficial Guide to Skiing and Snowboarding in the West.* Hoboken, N.J.: John Wiley & Sons, 2003.

Wallechinsky, David, and Jaime Loucky. *The Complete Book of the Winter Olympics.* Wilmington, Del.: Sport Media, 2005.

Jean-Claude Killy

Born: August 30, 1943
       Saint-Cloud, France
Also known as: Toutoune

Early Life

The son of Robert and Elaine (Fidelaire) Killy, Jean-Claude Killy was born on August 30, 1943, in Saint-Cloud, a suburb of Paris, France. Jean-Claude was the eldest of three children, all of whom were raised by their father after Robert and Elaine were divorced. Growing up without his mother, Jean-Claude suffered immeasurably from a lack of affection.

Later in Jean-Claude's childhood, Robert Killy moved the family to Val d'Isere, a ski resort in the French Alps, where he owned and managed a seventeen-room ski lodge. Known as La Bergerie, the lodge was not only Jean-Claude's boyhood home but also his home base throughout later life as a famous skiing athlete.

When Jean-Claude was three years old, his father put him on his first pair of skis and began to teach him the sport. Within three years, the boy was able to follow and keep up with his father on the slopes. Often he fell, but he was as fast on skis as his father. By the time he was a teenager, there were few skiers at Val d'Isere who were as good.

The Road to Excellence

Skiing gave Jean-Claude confidence and made him a rebel at school. Often he was absent from classes in order to attend skiing meets nearby. Finally, when he was fifteen years old, he was expelled from school for his excessive absences.

In 1958, Jean-Claude broke a bone in his leg. X rays showed signs of tuberculosis in his lungs. He was sent to a sanatorium for treatment. When, at last, he was released and able to return to skiing competition, Jean-Claude lost no time in winning three events on the French national junior team. As a result, the following year, he was invited to become a senior member of the French ski team. Still, he had some hurdles to overcome. In 1962, he had to stop skiing when he broke his ankle. Next, he was required to serve with the French army as a truck driver in Algeria, where he came down with a case of jaundice.

In 1964, Jean-Claude was able to rejoin the French national team, but his health was not up to par, and his skiing was a disappointment to all. Also, before he could begin to turn himself into a champion, he had a major handicap to overcome:

Jean-Claude Killy skiing in a slalom event. (Courtesy of Amateur Athletic Foundation of Los Angeles)

Major Skiing Championships

Year	Competition	Event	Place
1964	Olympic Games	Giant slalom	5th
1965	World Championship	Combined	1st
1966	High Sierra Cup	Overall	1st
	World Championship	Combined	1st
1967	World Cup	Overall	1st
1968	Olympic Games	Giant slalom	Gold
		Downhill	Gold
		Slalom	Gold

By nature, he was a despondent, nervous young man. He deliberately worked on this problem, since it undermined his ability as an athlete. He went to the United States and noticed how American skiers enjoyed themselves because they did not take the sport as seriously as the French did. Jean-Claude decided to become his team's light-hearted clown. He played pranks on his teammates. His ski helmet bore the picture of a skull. His antics gave him a needed sense of nonchalance and self-confidence, and his skiing at last began to reflect the inward changes he had made.

The Emerging Champion

By 1965, Jean-Claude was a new man on the slopes. He won nearly every event he skied in that year, both major and minor alpine competitions. He was rated first in the giant slalom and sixth in the downhill by the International Ski Federation (FIS), and he was named European champion.

The following year he dominated slalom skiing in both the United States and Europe. In March, he led the French team to victory at the U.S. Alpine Championships at Stowe, Vermont. Later, he claimed the Werner Cup for France with his success in the men's slalom at Sun Valley, Idaho. The next month, April, he won the High Sierra Cup at Heavenly Valley, California. He spent the months after that preparing in earnest for the FIS World Championships at Portillo, Chile.

Jean-Claude skied the Portillo downhill in record time—in just a little more than eighty seconds—and his scores in the giant slalom and slalom earned him the combined alpine world championship. The French did well in Chile, and they were proud of it.

By the next season, 1967, Jean-Claude topped all records. He accumulated 225 points, the maximum possible score, and won the World Cup from the FIS. When the Winter Olympics were held the next year in Grenoble, France, Jean-Claude was ready. He came away from the event with three gold medals—in the downhill, the slalom, and the giant slalom. Only once before, had anyone swept all three Olympic events.

Continuing the Story

Jean-Claude—who was able to reach a speed of up to 80 miles per hour on the downhill, skiing's most dangerous event—claimed he never experienced physical fear. Skiing came so naturally to him that he skied mainly by instinct. He never tried to look stylish while racing, and often flew down the slopes with legs splayed and arms waving around. He was too busy racing to care about appearance. He used the "egg" position when skiing, as well as a slalom technique called the "serpent." The French government doted on Jean-Claude and on all members of the national team, designing their aerodynamic clothes and giving them nominal posts in customs inspection, so they could have some income without jeopardizing their amateur status.

Jean-Claude returned to La Bergerie, spending his free time motorbike riding, parachuting, and even bullfighting. He began auto racing, entering the Paris Dakar Rally. Auto racing requires the same skills he used in skiing: The will to win, reflexes, and instinct. He signed a contract with General Motors to promote its cars and he also planned to develop and retail a line of ski equipment and clothing.

Jean-Claude is idolized by the French and received up to five hundred letters from fans in a day—quite a change from the motherless years when he was growing up, aching for affection and attention. He remained active in the Olympic com-

Honors and Awards

1965	European Champion
1966	Member of the French team that won the U.S. Alpine Championships
	Member of the French team that won the Werner Cup
1968	Second man ever to win Olympic gold medals in all three alpine events
	World Trophy

munity as a member of the International Olympic Committee. In 2000, he became a Grand Officer in the French Legion of Honor.

Summary

Jean-Claude Killy dominated the European skiing scene and world competition in the late 1960's and was responsible for the French national team's rise to prominence in alpine racing. He won the World Cup and was the second man in history to win the triple Olympic crown.

Nan White

Additional Sources

Seibert, Peter W., William Oscar Johnson, and Jean Claude Killy. *Vail: Triumph of a Dream.* Boulder, Colo.: Mountain Sports Press, 2000.

Singer, Barnett. "Jean-Claude Killy: France's King of the Ski Slopes." *The Contemporary Review* 286, no. 1670 (2005): 170.

Uschan, Michael V. *Male Olympic Champions.* San Diego, Calif.: Lucent Books, 2000.

Wallechinsky, David, and Jaime Loucky. *The Complete Book of the Winter Olympics.* Wilmington, Del.: Sport Media, 2005.

Chris Kinard

Born: November 8, 1950
   Pasadena, California
Also known as: John Christopher Kinard (full name)

Early Life

John Christopher Kinard was born on November 8, 1950, in Pasadena, California. Chris and his twin brother were the oldest of four children. Chris attended Pasadena schools, graduating from Pasadena High School. His college years at Pasadena City College, California State University, Los Angeles, and the University of California at Los Angeles (UCLA) were frequently interrupted by the travel involved in badminton training and compe-

Chris Kinard. (Courtesy of South African Badminton Union)

tition, yet he persevered in college studies, receiving his B.A. from UCLA in 1977.

Chris was an all-star player in Little League baseball and was a long jumper in junior high and high school. For two successive years in junior high he received the Presidential Fitness Award, presented to those students scoring the most points in a physical fitness competition sponsored by the President's Council on Physical Fitness and Sports. Chris earned this distinction by placing among the top five scorers out of 350 boys in his class.

Although he had played in his first badminton tournament at the age of eleven, it was not until high school that he decided that badminton was the sport in which he most wanted to excel. In 1969, at the age of eighteen, Chris was chosen for the U.S. Thomas Cup badminton team to play against the Peruvian national team in Lima, Peru. The experience convinced him that badminton was worth his full concentration.

The Road to Excellence

After winning the U.S. National 18-and-under Championships doubles title with Mike Walker in 1967 and 1968, Chris decided to concentrate on singles. In 1972, he won his first U.S. national championship in singles at the age of twenty-one. He followed that with five other U.S. singles titles and was ranked number one in U.S. singles for seven years from 1972 to 1981. When asked what had helped him achieve his decade-long dominance of the sport, Chris replied that he had the good fortune to grow up in Pasadena and belong to the Pasadena Badminton Club, which produced more U.S. champions than any other club in the United States. He could watch U.S. and world champions like Joe Alston and Wynn Rogers, and, when still a junior, play doubles with his father against older, more experienced players.

Additionally, following his first U.S. singles championship, Chris toured the

United States with the Indonesian team, playing against the nine-time world champion, Rudy Hartono. On the 1972 tour, Chris met Rudy's sister, Utami Dewi, the Indonesian and all-Asian champion; they married in Indonesia, in 1977. Subsequently, Chris became the first foreign badminton player ever to be invited to train with the Indonesian national team at its main complex, the World Championship Training Center, in Indonesia. Chris spent 1973 practicing with nine of the world's best players. As he recalled, "It was there that I learned that confidence in yourself in a match comes from knowing that you have trained harder and prepared yourself more completely than your opponents have."

The Emerging Champion

During his ten years as the dominant U.S. singles player, Chris traveled throughout the world, winning singles and doubles titles in South Africa and Peru, defeating the champions of England, Japan, Taiwan, and Mexico, and reaching the Round of 16 in the World Badminton Championships in Jakarta, Indonesia, before losing to eventual winner Rudy Hartono. He also competed in national championships in other countries, including Denmark, Sweden, Germany, Ireland, Canada, and Singapore.

In 1979, Chris became the first U.S. badminton player ever to play in the World Racquets Championships when he competed against John McEnroe (tennis), Marty Hogan (racquetball), Sharif Khan (squash), and Dan Seemiller (table tennis). Each of the five competitors gave an exhibition of his own particular sport and then competed against the others in each of the sports except his own.

When asked why he had chosen badminton and what advice he has for others who make the same choice, Chris answered that he believed badminton was the most physically demanding of all the sports that were reasonable choices, adding that the size that is now required for a career in football or basketball is a disadvantage in badminton, which

demands quick reactions and the ability to get to any part of the court in a fraction of a second. Badminton presented a real physical challenge which a person his size could attempt to meet. Further, the sport is played all over the world—and thus offered interesting travel experiences as a reward for playing well enough to be invited to foreign championships.

Continuing the Story

Chris's string of championship tournament victories is extensive. He won the U.S. Intercollegiate Badminton Championships in singles and doubles while earning his undergraduate degree from UCLA—becoming the first player to capture both of those titles while simultaneously holding the U.S. national singles title. In 1986, Chris was inducted into the Athletic Hall of Fame at California

---

Major Badminton Championships

1971	South African Open Championships doubles (with Don Paup)
1971-72	U.S. National Championships doubles finalist (with Joe Alston; with Charles Coakley)
1972, 1974, 1976-77, 1979, 1981	U.S. National Championships
1974	Peruvian Open Championships mixed doubles (with Cindy Baker)
1976	Peruvian Open Championships
	Peruvian Open Championships doubles (with Mike Walker)
1977	U.S. Intercollegiate Championships
	U.S. Intercollegiate Championships doubles (with Mike Kelly)
1979	Mexican Open Championships mixed doubles (with Utami Dewi Kinard)
1980	U.S. National Championships finalist
	South African Open Championships
	South African Open Championships doubles finalist (with Coakley)

Other Notable Victories

1967-68	U.S. National 18-and-under Championships doubles (with Walker)
1971, 1974, 1977, 1979, 1981	Western States Open Championships
1972-74, 1976-77, 1979, 1981	Dave Freeman Open Championships
	Pacific Southwest Open Championships
1973	Yonex Invitational Challenge Cup Championships
1977	California State Collegiate Championships

State University, Los Angeles, the school he had attended before transferring to UCLA.

Although retired from competition, Chris remained active in badminton in promotion and coaching. He was tournament director and promoter of the 1988 U.S. Open Championships, the first International Grand Prix Championship held in the United States. He conducted a clinic with Rudy Hartono in Taipei for Taiwan's national team in 1986. In 1984, with Flemming Delfs, former world champion from Denmark, Chris conducted clinics throughout South Africa for the South African national team and provincial teams. At numerous national universities and high schools, Chris has conducted clinics for players and coaches focusing on competitive strategy, tactics, and conditioning.

Chris also served as vice president of a manufacturing company in Southern California and was an associate professor at California State University, Los Angeles, teaching badminton in the physical education department.

Summary

Chris Kinard's high school decision to remain in badminton was a fortunate one for the sport. Chris became one of the outstanding athletes in the United States, creating a record unmatched by any

Honors, Awards, and Milestones	
1964-65	Presidential Fitness Award, the President's Council on Physical Fitness and Sports
1969-82	U.S. Thomas Cup team
1972-74, 1976-77, 1979, 1981	Ranked the number one U.S. player
1973	First foreign player to train with the World Champion Indonesian national team at its World Championship Training Center
1976	Men's U.S. Devlin Cup team
1978	U.S. Sportsmanship Award (Ken Davidson Award)
1979	Men's U.S. Pan-American Games badminton team
	First U.S. badminton player to compete at the World Racquets Championships
1986	Inducted into Athletic Hall of Fame, California State University, Los Angeles

U.S. player for national and international badminton titles.

Wynn Rogers

Additional Sources

Bloss, Margaret Varner, and R. Stanton Hales. *Badminton*. Boston: McGraw-Hill, 2001.

International Badminton Federation. *Sixty Years, 1936-1996: Sixtieth Jubilee Factbook.* Colorado Springs, Colo.: United States Badminton Association, 1996.

Levinson, David, and Karen Christensen, eds. *Encyclopedia of World Sport: From Ancient Times to the Present.* Santa Barbara, Calif.: ABC-Clio, 1996.

Micki King

Born: July 26, 1944
  Pontiac, Michigan
Also known as: Maxine Joyce King (full name);
  Micki King Hogue

Early Life

Maxine Joyce King was born in Pontiac, Michigan, near Detroit, on July 26, 1944. One of Leonard and Olga King's three children, she was active and athletic. She learned to swim and to play ball games while very young. She was soon playing softball with the neighborhood boys, who often picked her first when choosing teams. At an early age, she was nicknamed Micki—a name that stuck.

Micki King showing off the gold medal she won in the 3-meter springboard competition at the 1972 Olympic Games in Munich. (Courtesy of International Swimming Hall of Fame)

The most important person in Micki's life was her father, who worked nights at the General Motors factory. He convinced her that girls could do anything. He also taught her to dive by throwing her over his shoulder as they played in the lakes. To keep her active in the winter, the family enrolled her in the YMCA, which had two "girl's nights" and one "family night" weekly. She found indoor swimming boring and was soon playing on the diving board. When she was ten, boys at the YMCA challenged her to play follow-the-leader from the diving board. Like the great 1948 and 1952 Olympic champion Sammy Lee, Micki learned to dive and to love the sport while playing that game.

The Road to Excellence

When Micki was fifteen, YMCA coach John La-Monte began coaching her and teaching her the names of the dives. He took Micki to her first meet at Toledo, Ohio. That was a frightening experience, but she won the meet. She promised herself that next time she would be more prepared. That was not easy, for during those years there were no high school or college teams for women. When Coach LaMonte left Pontiac, Micki had to drive to Detroit to practice with her new coach, Jim Ottinger. He filled a big need in her life.

After graduating from Pontiac Central High in 1962, Micki enrolled at the University of Michigan. She asked the men's diving coach, Dick Kimball, to be her coach. He agreed and let her practice with the men's team, giving her the same workouts and the same tough dives as the men. In 1965, Micki won her first major titles. She won the Amateur Athletic Union (AAU) National Indoor Championships in both the ten-meter platform and three-meter springboard. For this she was named 1965 AAU diver of the year.

The Emerging Champion

When she graduated from college in 1966, Micki joined the United States Air Force. Because she was aiming for the 1968 Olympics, this was a good choice. The armed forces allowed Olympic hopefuls time off to train and compete, while other em-

Major Diving Championships

Year	Competition	Event	Place	Points
1965	AAU National Indoor Championships	3-meter springboard	1st	—
		10-meter platform	1st	—
1967	World University Games	3-meter springboard	—	698.65
1971	Pan-American Games	3-meter springboard	—	432.51
		10-meter platform	—	337.77
1972	Olympic Games	3-meter springboard	Gold	450.03

ployers often forced athletes to choose between sports and a job.

Micki was the first woman with the Air Force Reserve Officers Training Corps (ROTC) at the University of Michigan. This allowed her to keep training with Coach Kimball. She worked full time until a month before the Olympic trials, practicing three to four hours a day after work.

At the Olympics, it seemed that all of her hard work had paid off. She led the three-meter springboard competition after eight dives. On the ninth, misfortune struck when she hit the board, breaking her arm. Despite the pain, she did her last dive, which made the pain even worse. She came home with her arm in a cast and a fourth-place finish instead of a medal. It took her more than a year to recover.

Micki was transferred to the Los Angeles Air Force Base in California, far from home and Coach Kimball. She was about to quit diving for good when the Air Force asked her to compete at the World Military Games (WMG), something no woman had ever done. Although not fully recovered from her injury, she started practicing. The only woman in the WMG, she won a bronze medal. She decided to go for the Olympic gold again. After work each day, she drove forty miles round trip to work out three hours at a pool.

By the time she made the 1972 Olympic team, twenty-eight-year-old Micki was an Air Force captain. She had won eight more AAU championships and three more diver of the year awards. At the Munich Olympics, she finally won the gold medal on the three-meter springboard, and retired happily from competitive diving.

Continuing the Story

In 1973, Micki became diving coach and physical education teacher at the Air Force Academy. There were no women students at the Academy then. She was the first woman coach of a men's college team anywhere. However, she had practiced with men for years and was confident of success. It came quickly. She became the first woman to coach a National Collegiate Athletic Association (NCAA) champion when Cadet Rick McAllister won the 1974 title.

Micki did television commentary and made international goodwill tours for diving and the Olympics. In 1976, she married a fellow officer, Major James Hogue. They served in several places during the next ten years. They also had two children, Kevin and Michelle.

Micki earned a M.A. in communications and became one of the leaders of United States Diving, Incorporated (U.S. Diving), formed in 1980 to regulate diving in place of the AAU. By 1988, she was one of 108 female colonels in the Air Force, vice president of U.S. Diving, and manager of the Olympic diving team.

After another tour at the Air Force Academy, she and the family moved to her new job as professor and Air Force ROTC Commander at the University of Kentucky. Despite her busy career and family life, in 1990, Micki accepted the challenge of running for president of U.S. Diving. Her opponent had been president for four years. In winning the election, she became the first woman president of the organization and one of the top women among American Olympic leaders. She became the assis-

Record

Won 10 AAU National Diving Championships

Honors and Awards

1965, 1969, 1972	AAU Diver of the Year, Springboard
1969	AAU Diver of the Year, Platform
1973	Inducted into Helms Athletic Foundation Hall of Fame
1978	Inducted into International Swimming Hall of Fame
1983	Inducted into Sudafed International Women's Sports Hall of Fame

tant athletic director for the University of Kentucky and, in 2005, was elected vice president of the U.S. Olympians Association.

Summary

Micki King was a daring, athletic youngster who chose diving because she loved a challenge, and who finally became an Olympic champion. Throughout her career as athlete, coach, and official, Micki was often the first and only woman in her field. This not only made her stronger but also helped open new opportunities for women. Even with the hectic schedule of an Air Force officer, she found time to be a wife, mother, and volunteer for the Olympic movement and women's sports. With all of her achievements, it is no surprise that Micki King Hogue rose to prominent positions in a num-

ber of organizations and was named to multiple halls of fame.

Mary Lou LeCompte

Additional Sources

Greenberg, Stan. *Whitaker's Olympic Almanack: An Encyclopaedia of the Olympic Games.* Chicago: Fitzroy Dearborn, 2000.

Miller, Ernestine G. *Making Her Mark: Firsts and Milestones in Women's Sports.* Chicago: Contemporary Books, 2002.

Wallechinsky, David, and Jaime Loucky. *The Complete Book of the Olympics: 2008 Edition.* London: Aurum Press, 2008.

Woolum, Janet. *Outstanding Women Athletes: Who They Are and How They Influenced Sports in America.* Phoenix, Ariz.: Oryx Press, 1998.

Roger Kingdom

Born: August 26, 1962
Vienna, Georgia

Early Life
Roger Kingdom was born on August 26, 1962, in Vienna, Georgia, near the city of Savannah. Life in Vienna was simple for Roger and his brothers and sisters, who helped their parents with farming chores. Helping the family with the crops led Roger to realize the importance of discipline and diligent effort. Later in life, he found out just how important those character traits were in his athletic endeavors. Like many of the families in the Southern town, the Kingdoms relied on farming as a way of living, growing cotton, peanuts, and watermelon. Roger was athletic at a very young age, but he was not the best athlete in the family.

The Road to Excellence
Roger's athletic ability was always apparent, but it was not until he attended Vienna High School and started playing football and competing in track and field that he began to transform into something special.

Football was his favorite sport, and he was one of the top high school players in the state of Georgia. However, track and field, in which athletes are judged on an individual basis, was something that

Roger did well naturally. As a junior and senior in high school, he won the state Class AA titles in the discus, 120-yard hurdles, and high jump events.

Roger received hundreds of scholarship offers for football and track before deciding to accept a football scholarship from the University of Pittsburgh in 1981. Roger was also able to run on the Pittsburgh Panthers' track team. He excelled, especially in the 110-meter high hurdles, which took him all the way to Olympic stardom in 1984. While at Pitt in the 1980's, Roger was considered one of college track's best hurdlers. Still, he was not an outright favorite to become king of the 110-meter high hurdles.

The Emerging Champion
Roger's best moments in the 1980's came after making the U.S. track and field team. That was the first hurdle of many that he successfully cleared in his pursuit of greatness in the track and field circle. Inspired most of his life by his grandfather, Matt Wallace, who helped raise him, Roger applied the same amount of drive to his track career as his grandfather had to working farmland. Matt showed Roger that with work comes reward.

Roger raced to a third-place finish in the U.S. Olympic trials by running a time of 13.57 seconds in the 110-meter hurdles. At the 1984 Olympics, held in Los Angeles, Roger finally stood atop the 110-meter high hurdles competition. Roger shocked the world by winning the race in an Olympic record time of 13.20 to claim the gold medal.

From 1984 to 1985, Roger held a number-one world ranking. In 1985, he finished first in the U.S. Nationals by dashing to a winning time of 13.37. Roger's road to glory continued up to the 1988 Olympics in Seoul, South Korea. After taking first in the 1988 U.S. Nationals with a time of 13.15 seconds, Roger won his second straight gold medal to become only the second man to repeat as an Olympic 110-

Major Hurdles Championships

Year	Competition	Event	Place	Time
1983	Pan-American Games	110-meter hurdles	1st	13.44
1984	Olympic Games	110-meter hurdles	Gold	13.20 OR
	NCAA Championships	55-meter high hurdles	1st	7.08
	U.S. Nationals	110-meter hurdles	2d	13.62
1985	U.S. Nationals	110-meter hurdles	1st	13.37
1988	Olympic Games	110-meter hurdles	Gold	12.98 OR
	U.S. Nationals	110-meter hurdles	1st	13.15
1989	IAAF World Indoor Championships	60-meter hurdles	1st	7.43
	World Cup	110-meter hurdles	1st	12.87
1990	Goodwill Games	110-meter hurdles	1st	13.47
1995	Pan-American Games	110-meter hurdles	1st	
	World Cup	110-meter hurdles	3d	
	U.S. Nationals	110-meter hurdles	1st	

Note: OR = Olympic Record

Honors, Awards, and Records

1989	Jesse Owens Award
	Set a world record and the American outdoor record in the 110-meter high hurdles (12.92)
	Set an American indoor record in the 60-meter hurdles (7.36)
2002	Inducted into Georgia Sports Hall of Fame

---

meter hurdles champion. American Lee Calhoun achieved the same feat by taking the gold medals in the 1956 and 1960 Olympics.

Continuing the Story

In 1989, Roger's success on the track continued; he set a world record with a time of 12.92 seconds, beating Renaldo Nehemiah's old record of 12.93. Still, a world record and Olympic gold medals did not make Roger complacent. He continued running after his Olympic success. However, his attempt to qualify for the 1991 World Track and Field Championships was stopped after he could not compete in the U.S. Nationals because of a leg injury suffered while playing a pickup game of basketball.

Roger still had a track career of which to be proud. After winning the Olympic gold medal in Los Angeles in 1984, Roger was one of the U.S. top track and field performers. Among the many other awards that Roger won were first place at the 1983 Olympic trials and the Pan-American Games. Roger also won the 1988 Athletic Club Championships.

In 1991, following surgery to repair his knee, Roger began to prepare for the 1992 Olympics in Barcelona. He made it to the finals of the Olympic trials but crashed at the ninth hurdle. Many thought that his career was over. Roger's performances in 1993 and 1994 seemed to confirm that his best days were behind him. In 1995, however, Roger surprised everyone by winning the 110-meter hurdles at the U.S. nationals with a time of 13.09. The following year, Roger made the U.S. Olympic team but won no medals in Atlanta.

Roger continued to compete in both national and international events through the late 1990's, though he rarely finished in the top five. In 1998, as his track career came to a close, Roger turned his attention to professional bowling. He later became the track and field coach at the California University of Pennsylvania.

Summary

During the 1980's, Roger Kingdom proved to be one of the greatest hurdlers of all time, capturing gold medals in the 110-meter high hurdles in two successive Olympics. Roger also set a world record, breaking a mark that had stood for nearly a decade.

Don Emmons

Additional Sources

Greenberg, Stan. *Whitaker's Olympic Almanack: An Encyclopaedia of the Olympic Games.* Chicago: Fitzroy Dearborn, 2000.

Wallechinsky, David, and Jaime Loucky. *The Complete Book of the Olympics: 2008 Edition.* London: Aurum Press, 2008.

Wilson Kipketer

Born: December 12, 1972
      Kapchemoiywo, near Kapsabet, Kenya
Also known as: Wilson Kosgei Kipketer (full
  name)

Early Life
A member of East Africa's Kalenjin ethnic group, Wilson Kipketer (no relation to Wilson Boit Kipketer, another Kenyan runner) was born in Kapchemoiywo, near Kapsabet, Kenya, and later became a citizen of Denmark, settling in Copenhagen. He was born on December 12, 1972.

Wilson was born at a time when Kenya was starting to win renown for the emergence of a growing number of great middle-distance runners, such as Kip Keino, in world competitions. Thus, that a Kenyan boy such as Wilson would want to be a runner seemed natural. Wilson began his running training in the village of Item under Colm O'Connell, a member of the Patricians, the Irish teaching brotherhood that has nurtured many Kenyan champions.

O'Connell was also Wilson's headmaster and confidant and had bigger hopes for him as a pupil than as an athlete, believing Wilson to be a profound learner and great initiator. In 1990, Wilson went to Denmark to study electrical engineering in Copenhagen. While in Denmark, he trained rigorously for his favorite race, the 800 meters.

The Road to Excellence
During his first years in track and field competitions, Wilson represented his homeland, Kenya, in middle-distance events ranging from 800 meters to 5,000 meters. In 1995, Wilson decided to represent his new country, Denmark, in his first major world-level event, so he applied for Danish citizenship despite Denmark's seven-year residency requirement. At the 1995 World Track and Field Championships, competing for Denmark, he won the first of his three consecutive titles.

The Emerging Champion
Wilson dominated the men's 800 meters through the late 1990's, winning three world titles, in 1995, 1996, and 1997. He was not able to participate at the 1996 Atlanta Olympics, however, because he had not yet been granted Danish citizenship, which was required to represent that country in the Olympics. After fulfilling his residency requirement, he became a Danish citizen in 1997. That same year he set several world records in the 800 meters. In March, 1997, the International Association of Athletics Federations president congratulated him for stunning the public and performing "beyond the most optimistic expectations."

Wilson was the star of the World Indoor Track and Field Championships held in Paris in March, 1997. He was the 800 meters champion. He made his mark in the first of three rounds of competition, with a time of 1 minute 43.96 seconds, which lowered the previous world record by .88 seconds.

Wilson Kipketer (left) with Swiss runner Andre Bucher running the 800-meter event at the 2004 Olympics. (Andy Lyons/Getty Images)

After finishing the semifinal race in 1 minute 48.49 seconds, Wilson ran the final in 1 minute 42.67 seconds. Only five other men had ever run the race in better times, and they had done so on outdoor tracks, which are almost always faster.

Continuing the Story

Long residence outside Africa weakened Wilson's resistance to the tropical disease malaria. While visiting his native Kenyan village of Kapchemoiwa in December, 1997, he contracted a severe strain of malaria and spent ten days in a Portuguese hospital. Afterward, he was unable to resume serious training until late May. As a result, he suffered his first loss in twenty-nine races the following August. Two weeks later, Wilson struggled to make a comeback and finished last in the 800-meter final at his European Championships in Athletics debut. For the first time since 1993, he did not hold the world's number-one ranking in the 800 meters at the end of the year.

Despite this setback, Wilson worked his way back into the international spotlight. In July, 1999, he won the 800-meter events at all seven Golden League meets. He secured a share of the $1 million jackpot given to athletes who complete the series undefeated and won $500,000.

After setting a world record of 2 minutes 14.96 seconds in the rarely run 1,000-meter race in early 2000, Wilson was the favorite to win a gold medal in the 800-meter event in Summer Olympic Games in Sydney, Australia. However, his time of 1 minute 45.57 seconds was not fast enough to win. Nils Schumann of Germany beat Wilson by less than one-half second, forcing Wilson to settle for the silver medal. Though disappointed, Wilson said, philosophically, that was what competitions were all about: One person wins, and the others lose.

After the disappointment of the 2000 Olympics, Wilson bounced back nicely. Two years later, in Munich, Germany, he won the gold medal for the 800 meters at the European championships in Athletics by defeating both Schumann and Andre Bucher, who was then the reigning world champion. In 2002, he won all but one of the races in which he competed and ran the fastest 800-meter race in the world that year with a time of 1 minute 42.32 seconds. Furthermore, he became the first 800-meter runner to rank number one in the world in the event six times.

Major 800-Meter Championships

Year	Competition	Place	Time
1990	World Junior Championships	4th	1:48.13
1995	World Championships	1st	1:45.08
1997	World Championships	1st	1:43.38
	World Indoor Championships	1st	1:42.67
1998	European Championships	8th	1:50.13
1999	World Championships	1st	1:43.30
	World Indoor Championships	2d	1:45.49
2000	Olympic Games	Silver	1:45.57
2002	European Championships	1st	1:47.25
2003	World Championships	4th	1:45.23
	World Indoor Championships	2d	1:45.87
2004	Olympic Games	Bronze	1:44.65

After 2002, injuries began interfering with Wilson's racing. In 2003, his best performance was a second-place finish in the World Indoor Track and Field Championships. A year later, he won a bronze medal in the 800 meters at the Athens Olympics. In August, 2005, he announced his retirement from racing.

Summary

Born in a small African nation with a seemingly inexhaustible supply of great middle-distance runners, Wilson Kipketer went to Europe to study engineering and ended up becoming the greatest runner in Danish history. He became a citizen of Denmark not because he loved Kenya less, but because he came to love Denmark even more. With his long string of championships, records, and honors, he managed to bring glory to countries in two continents.

Alex Mwakikoti, updated by the Editors

Additional Sources

Bale, John, and Joe Sang. *Kenyan Running: Movement, Culture, Geography, and Global Change.* Portland, Oreg.: F. Cass, 1996.

Cazeneuve, Brian. "A Mysterious Warrior." *Sports Illustrated* 91 (August 23, 1999): R6.

Cheever, Benjamin. *Strides: Running Through History with an Unlikely Athlete.* New York: Rodale Books, 2007.

"Great Dane." *Sports Illustrated* 87 (August 25, 1997): 22.

Wallechinsky, David, and Jaime Loucky. *The Complete Book of the Olympics.* London: Aurum Press, 2008.

Karch Kiraly

Born: November 3, 1960
  Jackson, Michigan
Also known as: Charles Frederick Kiraly (full name); Thunderball in Volleyball

Early Life

Charles Frederick "Karch" Kiraly (pronounced Keer-i) was born on November 3, 1960, to Laszlo Kiraly and Toni Iffland Kiraly, in Jackson, Michigan. The family moved to California when Karch was a child. He grew up on the beaches of Santa Barbara playing volleyball. Beach volleyball is played throughout Southern California, and Karch learned the game at an early age from his father, Laszlo, a former Hungarian junior national team player. Although Karch was talented athletically and participated in a variety of sports as a youngster, his love for volleyball, and his father's influence and encouragement, contributed to his specialization in that sport. Growing up near the beach meant a game was always available, and from an early age, Karch was an intense competitor. He pushed himself to improve and began learning game strategies that helped him perfect his skills.

The Road to Excellence

At the age of six, Karch was already a student of volleyball. He learned from his father, practiced hard, and played year-round with his friends. When he was ten, he read an article about an eleven-year-old who was the youngest player ever to compete in a beach tournament. Karch decided that he wanted to break that record. His father made him wait another year, but during that time, he and his father practiced together and became a formidable team. They entered a beach tournament when Karch was eleven years old. Although they lost consecutive games, Karch was hooked on tournament volleyball. This tournament was the only one in which he lost two consecutive games.

Karch concentrated on volleyball in high school even though he was also an excellent basketball player. By the time he was in the tenth grade, he was already more than 6 feet tall and had amazing vertical jumping ability. He was a successful high school volleyball player and was the star of the Santa Barbara High School team. In 1978, he was voted the prep player of the year in the California Interscholastic Federation and led his school to an undefeated season and a league championship. Although he preferred playing on the front line and was a great spiker, his real ability was in setting the ball. College coaches wanted to recruit him not only because he was a great athlete but also because he was an exceptional student.

Karch Kiraly in a beach volleyball game during the 1996 Olympic Games in Atlanta. (Doug Pensinger/Getty Images)

Major Volleyball Competitions

Year	Competition
1977-78	U.S. Men's Junior National Team Pacific Rim Championship
1979	Won first professional open beach volleyball tournament as an amateur
1979, 1981, 1988	World Championship of Beach Volleyball
1980-82	Men's NCAA Championship Team
1984, 1988, 1996	U.S. Olympic gold medalist
1985	U.S. World Cup gold medalist
1986	U.S. World Championships gold medalist
1987	U.S. Pan-American Games gold medalist
1988	Fédération Internationale de Volleyball Beach Volleyball World Championships

AVP Tour Victories

Year	Competition
1990	Miller Lite Open, Ft. Lauderdale, Fla.
	Miller Lite Open, New Orleans, La.
	Miller Lite Open, Venice, Calif.
	Miller Lite Open, Cape Cod, Mass.
	Off Shore Manhattan Beach Open, Calif.
	Miller Lite Open, Grand Haven, Minn.
	Miller Lite Open, Seattle, Wash.
1991	Miller Lite Open, New Jersey
	Off Shore Manhattan Beach Open, Calif.
	Miller Lite Open, Grand Haven, Mich.
	Miller Lite Open, Chicago, Ill.

Records and Milestones

World championships in both indoor (an Olympic gold medal) and open beach (the World Championship of Beach Volleyball) competition

U.S. Olympic Committee Male Volleyball Athlete of the Year

USA volleyball team most valuable player, four consecutive seasons

Honors and Awards

Year	Award
1978	CIF Prep Player of the Year
1979-82	NCAA All-American
1980-82	NCAA All-Tournament Team
1981-82	NCAA Tournament most valuable player
1982	USVBA National Tournament most valuable player
	World Championships most valuable player (consolation bracket)
1983	NCAA Today's Top Five Award
1984	Olympic volleyball competition Best Sportsman
	Inducted into Volleyball Hall of Fame Court of Honor
1985	World Cup most valuable player
	NCAA Salute to the 1984 Olympians
1986, 1988	Fédération Internationale de Volleyball World's Best Player
	USA Cup most valuable player
1988	Olympic Games most valuable player
	Southland Corporation Olympia Award
1990	AVP most valuable player
	AVP best offensive player
1990, 1992-95, 1998	AVP Most Valuable Player
1990, 1993-94	AVP Best Offensive Player
1995, 1997-98	AVP Sportsman of the Year
1996	AVP Miller Lite Cup Champion
1997	AVP Comeback Player of the Year
1998	AVP Most Inspirational
2001	Inducted into Volleyball Hall of Fame
2002	AVP Best Defensive Player
	AVP Special Achievement Award
2004	AVP Outstanding Achievement Award
	AVP Team of the Year (with Mike Lambert)

The Emerging Champion

Although Karch had more than fifty college scholarship offers, he wanted to stay in Southern California. He wanted to attend a school that offered the science courses that he desired to study. He knew that his athletic days would end at some point, and he wanted to be a physician. He chose the University of California at Los Angeles (UCLA), which was close to home and had a premier volleyball program.

Karch was so dominating as a player at UCLA that he was asked to join the U.S. national volleyball team at the age of nineteen. He had grown to 6 feet 3 inches and had a forty-inch vertical jump. His ball control abilities were phenomenal, and his intensity about winning every point soon became legendary. Al Skates, the UCLA volleyball coach, called him the most dominating volleyball player ever to play the sport. He led UCLA to consecutive national championships in 1980, 1981, and 1982 and was a first-team all-American selection from 1979 through 1982.

The rise of the U.S. team in international rankings coincided with Karch's addition to the team.

The U.S. squad toured the world preparing for the 1984 Olympics, and Karch was elected team captain because of his abilities and leadership. He guided the United States to a gold medal in volleyball in the Olympic Games and became a celebrity, along with teammate Steve Timmons. Karch was the youngest member of the Olympic team and decided to stay on through 1988 and another Olympic Games.

Continuing the Story

Karch had an honor-packed career, and his commitment to the United States Volleyball Association was a primary reason volleyball became a popular spectator and participant sport in the United States. As a senior in college, Karch received the National Collegiate Athletic Association Today's Top Five Award, a postgraduate scholarship. This award is given to athletes who are also outstanding students. He was also nominated four years in a row for the Sullivan Award,

which is given to the nation's most outstanding amateur athlete. In 1983, Karch showed his versatility as an athlete when he competed in the popular Superstars competition and took second place behind Mark Gastineau, who at that time was a member of the National Football League's New York Jets.

While competing for the U.S. volleyball team in preparation for the 1988 Olympics, Karch continued to play beach volleyball. He became the first athlete ever to win both a Beach Volleyball World Championship and an Olympic gold medal. He turned down the huge salaries offered by professional teams in Europe to stay in the United States and help the team prepare for the Olympics in Seoul, South Korea.

In 1988, Karch led the United States to its second consecutive Olympic gold medal in volleyball and was deservedly named the best player of the game by several organizations. After the 1988 Olympics, he retired from international competi-

AVP Tour Highlights

Year	Competition
1989	Miller Lite Fort Myers Open, Fort Myers, Fla.
	Miller Lite Venice Open, Venice Beach, Calif.
1992	Miller Lite Austin Open, Austin, Tex.
	Miller Lite San Diego Open, San Diego, Calif.
	Jose Cuervo Gold Crown Boulder, Boulder, Colo.
	AVP/Miller Lite Chicago Open, Chicago, Ill.
	AVP/Miller Lite Cape Cod Open, Cape Cod, Mass.
	Miller Lite U.S. Championships, Hermosa Beach, Calif.
	Miller Lite Tournament of Champions, Santa Barbara, Calif.
	Old Spice King of the Beach Invitational, Various Locations
1993	Hawaii Open Molokai, Hawaii
	Evian Indoor New York, New York, N.Y.
	Jose Cuervo Gold Crown, Clearwater, Fla.
	Miller Lite Milwaukee Open, Milwaukee, Wis.
	Miller Lite Grand Haven Open, Grand Haven, Mich.
	Jose Cuervo Gold Crown Santa Cruz, Santa Cruz, Calif.
	Miller Lite U.S. Championships, Hermosa Beach, Calif.
	Old Spice Tournament of Champions, Cincinnati, Ohio
	Old Spice King of the Beach, various locations
1994	Evian Indoor New York, New York, N.Y.
	Old Spice Boca Raton Open, Boca Raton, Fla.
	Miller Lite Miami Open, Miami, Fla.
	Jose Cuervo Gold Crown Clearwater, Clearwater, Fla.
	Miller Lite Jacksonville Open, Jacksonville, Fla.
	Nestea Atlanta Open, Atlanta, Ga.
	Nestea Dallas Open, Dallas, Tex.
1995	Evian Indoor Minneapolis, Minneapolis, Minn.
	Nestea Singer Island Open, Singer Island, Fla.
	Miller Lite Fort Myers Open, Fort Myers, Fla.
	Miller Lite Mesa Open, Mesa, Ariz.

Year	Competition
1995 (cont.)	1-800-COLLECT San Diego Open, San Diego, Calif.
	Nestea Atlanta Open, Atlanta, Ga.
	Miller Lite Chicago Open, Chicago, Ill.
	Miller Lite Boston Open, Boston, Mass.
	Jose Cuervo Gold Crown Santa Cruz, Santa Cruz, Calif.
	Jose Cuervo Gold Crown Boulder, Boulder, Colo.
	AVP Player's Championships, Newport, R.I.
1996	Evian Indoor Fairfax, Fairfax, Va.
	Swatch King of the Beach Invitational, various locations
	Miller Lite Riviera Beach Open, Riviera Beach
	Miller Lite U.S. Championships, Hermosa Beach, Calif.
1997	Miller Lite U.S. Championships, Hermosa Beach, Calif.
	Golden State Open, Sacramento, Calif.
	AVP Vail Open, Vail, Colo.
1998	Miller Lite Tucson Open, Tucson, Ariz.
	Golden State Open, Sacramento, Calif.
	Miller Lite U.S. Championships, Hermosa Beach, Calif.
1999	AVP Miller Lite New Orleans Open, New Orleans, La.
	AVP/Sunkist Tournament of Champions, Dallas, Tex.
	AVP Karch Kiraly Classic, Santa Barbara, Calif.
2000	Paul Mitchell AVP Virginia Beach Open, Virginia Beach, Va.
2002	Michelob Light Santa Barbara Open, Santa Barbara, Calif.
2003	Huntington Beach Open, Huntington Beach, Calif.
2004	Manhattan Beach Open, Manhattan Beach, Calif.
	San Diego Open, San Diego, Calif.
	Aquafina AVP Shootout, Las Vegas, Nev.
2005	Huntington Beach Open, Huntington Beach, Calif.

tion and pursued his professional beach volleyball career, accumulating an impressive string of victories as part of a two-man team.

In 1996, Karch won his third gold medal, this time in the two-man beach volleyball competition, hich debuted as an Olympic sport in Atlanta. However, he and his partner, Adam Johnson, did not qualify for the 2000 Olympics in Sydney. The two were beaten by the eventual gold-medal winners Dain Blanton and Eric Fonoimoana.

Karch continued to impress on the sand as he did indoors. In 2004, he and his partner Mike Lambert won three titles and were named Association of Volleyball Professionals team of the year. With a win in 2005, Karch increased his record of total career wins to 148. Sinjin Smith held the previous record with 139 career wins. Karch also became the all-time leader in career earnings, with more than $3 million. He was inducted into the Volleyball Hall of Fame in 2001 and the American Volleyball Coaches Association Hall of Fame in 2005. He retired from competitive beach volleyball at the end of the 2007 season.

Apart from his success as a competitor, Karch became an author, publishing several books on beach volleyball as well as his autobiography, *The Sand Man* (1999). He also covered beach volleyball as a broadcaster for ESPN and for NBC. With his wife, Janna, and their two sons, Karch settled in San Clemente, California.

Summary

Volleyball players and coaches rarely argue over who was the most dominant United States volleyball player ever to play the game: Karch Kiraly. His knowledge of the game, his desire to win, and his incredible athletic skill captured the attention of a nation in three Olympic Games. He was paid the ultimate compliment when the junior players in Europe and the Soviet Union tried to pattern their play and their court mannerisms after him, evidence that he was the most recognizable volleyball player in the world.

Henry A. Eisenhart, updated by Jeffry Jensen

Additional Sources

Anderson, Kelli. "Let Us Now Praise Karch Kiraly." *Sports Illustrated* 107, no. 13 (October 1, 2007).

Couvillon, Arthur R. *Karch Kiraly: A Tribute to Excellence.* Hermosa Beach, Calif.: Information Guides, 2008.

Hickok, Ralph. *A Who's Who of Sports Champions: Their Stories and Records.* Boston: Houghton Mifflin, 1995.

Kiraly, Karch. *Karch Kiraly's Championship Volleyball.* New York: Simon & Schuster, 1996.

Kiraly, Karch, with Byron Shewman. *The Sand Man: An Autobiography.* New York: St. Martin's Press, 1999.

Reisgies, Tess. "A King and His Courts." *Sports Illustrated for Kids* 8, no. 2 (1996).

Franz Klammer

Born: December 3, 1953
      Mooswald, Austria

Early Life

Franz Klammer was born in Austria, on December 3, 1953. He grew up in Mooswald, a small mountain town near the Yugoslavian border. The Klammer family lived in a two-hundred-year-old farmhouse. Franz grew up with two brothers, Klaus and Michael, and a sister, Barbara. Franz's parents ran a small inn and an eighty-nine-acre farm. Franz was expected to help with the chores on the farm. Sometimes, work on the farm would last from 6:00 A.M. until 8:00 P.M. Later in his career, Franz credited his skiing success to the hard physical labor that he did on the farm.

Franz Klammer in 1983. (AFP/Getty Images)

The Road to Excellence

Unlike many top racers, Franz did not begin ski racing at an early age. Although he learned to ski before he was ten, Franz did not begin racing until he was a teenager. His first coach was a local ski champion named Karl Posauz. When he was fifteen, Franz enrolled in a special ski school. Students attended classes in the morning and practiced skiing in the afternoon. In 1972, Franz was named to the national C team. The C team was for promising skiers who were not yet the best skiers in Austria.

Two characteristics were important in Franz's development as a skier. One was a single-minded dedication to becoming a champion racer. The other was his ability to ski at high speeds without losing his nerve. His love of fast skiing made him especially good at the downhill event. The downhill was faster than the other two alpine events at that time—the slalom and giant slalom. Downhill racers sometimes reached speeds of more than 80 miles per hour.

Although later in his career Franz became an all-around sportsman who played tennis, windsurfed, and water-skied, he concentrated almost entirely on skiing early in his life. When he was not skiing or doing farmwork, his two favorite kinds of recreation were motorcycle and horseback riding in the mountains near his home.

The Emerging Champion

In 1973, Franz won his first World Cup downhill race. By the end of 1974, Franz was one of the best downhill skiers in the world. He placed second at the Alpine World Ski Championships in the downhill. He also was first in the combined scoring, with a tenth-place finish in the giant slalom and a twentieth in the slalom. The following year, Franz amazed the skiing world by winning eight out of the nine World Cup downhill races he entered. Franz's eight World Cup victories in 1975 set a new record for World Cup wins in a single season. The previous record of five had been set by the great French skier Jean-Claude Killy in 1967.

The 1975 season marked the beginning of a

Major Skiing Championships

Year	Competition	Event	Place
1973	World Cup	Overall	8th
1974	World Championships	Downhill	2d
		Slalom	20th
		Giant slalom	10th
		Overall	1st
	World Cup	Overall	5th
		Downhill	3d
1975	World Cup	Overall	3d
		Downhill	1st
1976	Olympic Games	Downhill	Gold
		Giant slalom	Did not finish
	World Cup	Overall	4th
		Downhill	1st
1977	World Cup	Overall	3d
		Downhill	1st
1978	World Championships	Downhill	5th
	World Cup	Overall	5th
		Downhill	1st
1979	World Cup	Overall	50th
		Downhill	19th
1984	Olympic Games	Downhill	10th

long string of victories for Franz. In fact, between 1975 and 1977, he won nineteen World Cup races. This was a remarkable accomplishment because, in ski racing, the difference between winning and losing is often less than one tenth of a second. By the mid-1970's, Franz was a sports star in Austria. Some days he would receive more than four hundred letters and cards from fans.

Continuing the Story

Franz solidified his place in sports history with his performance at the 1976 Winter Olympic Games in Innsbruck, Austria. Austrians view skiing as a major sport and follow the progress of their skiers with great interest. Many Austrians believed that the success of their country's winter tourist industry depended on the success of their ski team in international competition. Austrian sports fans expected their ski team to win several medals at the 1976 Olympic Games. However, in the opening days of competition, not a single Austrian won a medal. The downhill was the last event on the men's schedule. Franz, a national hero, was under great pressure to win.

Franz drew the fifteenth starting position. All of the other top skiers raced before him. Bernard

Russi of Switzerland and Italy's Herbert Plank had excellent runs. As Franz entered the starting gate, everyone knew that only a great run would win the gold medal. What followed was one of the most dramatic moments in Olympic history. Before sixty thousand cheering spectators, Franz attacked the course. He took chances at every turn. Several times he almost fell. Two-thirds of the way down the hill, his time was slower than Russi's. In the final part of the course, his great strength paid off, and he flashed across the finish line .33 of a second ahead of Russi. Austria had its gold medal.

In the late 1970's, Franz's performances began to decline. Many people claimed that this was because his brother Klaus was paralyzed in a skiing accident in 1977. Others claimed that the intense pressure caused by his role as a national sports hero hurt him. In any case, Franz never again won an Olympic medal. In 1979 and 1980, his performance declined so much that Austrian team officials did not even select him to ski in the downhill at the 1980 Winter Olympic Games in Lake Placid, New York. Despite this disappointment, Franz continued to ski for the Austrian team. His last Olympics were in 1984 Games at Sarajevo, Yugoslavia. He placed tenth in the downhill.

Summary

Franz Klammer's race at Innsbruck in 1976 will always be viewed as a classic example of an athlete performing his best under great pressure. Although his career never again reached the heights of his 1976 Olympic performance, Franz was a world-class skier for more than ten years. Between 1975 and 1977, he dominated his sport in a way that few skiers have before or since.

Wayne Wilson

Additional Sources

Fry, John. *The Story of Modern Skiing.* Hanover, N.H.: University Press of New England, 2006.

Liponski, Wojciech. *World Sports Encyclopedia.* St. Paul, Minn.: Motorbooks International, 2003.

Wallechinsky, David, and Jaime Loucky. *The Complete Book of the Winter Olympics.* Wilmington, Del.: Sport Media, 2005.

Wilner, Barry, and Ken Rappoport. *Harvard Beats Yale 29-29: And Other Great Comebacks from the Annals of Sports.* Lanham, Md.: Taylor Trade, 2008.

Bill Koch

Born: June 7, 1955
     Brattleboro, Vermont
Also known as: William Koch (full name)

Early Life

William Koch was born in Brattleboro, Vermont, on June 7, 1955. He grew up in the small southern Vermont towns of Putney and Guilford. Bill's father, Fred Koch, put Bill on skis before Bill was two years old. Bill was an alpine skier and a ski jumper with the Brattleboro Outing Club before he became a cross-country skier. In 1963, he entered and won his first cross-country race. When Bill was eight, his parents separated. He later said that he used skiing as a way of dealing with the emotional stress of the separation.

The Road to Excellence

Bob Gray, a top U.S. cross-country skier and an instructor at the Putney School, was a major influence in Bill's life. When Bill was twelve, he introduced himself to Gray and asked to train with the Putney team. Gray agreed and began to teach Bill the fine points of skiing and serious training. Bill eventually enrolled at the Putney School, where he trained every day with some of the best young skiers in the country. Like most world-class cross-country skiers, Bill skied more than one hundred miles each week. In the off-season, he bicycled and roller-skied. In one summer, he roller-skied more than six hundred miles. He also kept a training diary, which he updated daily.

The Emerging Champion

In 1974, Bill achieved international success with a third-place finish in the fifteen-kilometer race at the European Junior Championships in France. He also finished second in the Holmenkollen, an important race in Norway. The following year, he did well in junior races in Norway and Finland.

Despite his successes as a junior, few people gave him a chance to win a medal in the 1976 Winter Olympic Games at Innsbruck, Austria. Bill, however, stunned the cross-country world by winning a silver medal in the men's thirty-kilometer race, fin-ishing about half a minute behind the winner, Sergei Saveliev of the Soviet Union. His second-place finish was the first time that an American had won a medal in cross-country skiing.

Bill's success in the Olympic Games was remarkable for two reasons. First, the United States did not have a tradition of excellence in cross-country skiing. Cross-country athletes received little recognition and financial support. Second, Bill suffered from a breathing problem called exercise-induced asthma, which made it difficult for him to breathe when he trained or competed. For many years, Bill relied on drugs approved by his doctors and the International Olympic Committee to control the problem. Eventually, though, following the 1976 Olympic Games, he stopped taking the drugs and was able to function well.

Bill Koch won the silver medal at the 1976 Winter Olympics in Austria. (AP/Wide World Photos)

Continuing the Story

In the three years following his medal-winning performance at Innsbruck, Bill did not ski as well as many people expected he would. He stated that his failure to win major international races was the result of his sudden fame at the age of twenty, poor training, and illness.

At the 1980 Olympic Games in Lake Placid, New York, Bill finished sixteenth in the fifteen-kilometer and thirteenth in the fifty-kilometer. Also in 1980, Bill began to use a technique that revolutionized cross-country skiing. The classic skiing technique, called the diagonal stride, was similar to running. Each ski was placed in a track and the skier slid one foot in front of the other. In 1980, in a race in Sweden, Bill was passed by a skier who looked like he was skating on skis. The skating technique was a faster way of skiing than the diagonal stride. Bill quickly copied the skating style and soon perfected it. The skating technique became so popular that now there are two kinds of races at all major competitions: classic and skating, also called freestyle.

Using the skating technique in 1981, Bill became the first man to ski fifty kilometers in less than two hours. He also discovered that, using the skating technique, he could ski a mile in about three minutes and twenty seconds. In 1982, six years after winning his Olympic medal, Bill once again rose to the top of his sport by winning the World Cup championship. The World Cup was awarded to the skier who had the best overall performance in ten international races.

Throughout his career, Bill was viewed as a maverick. He liked to train in his own way and clashed with any coach who did not give him the freedom to design his own training schedules. He also advised other athletes not to be obsessed with winning. Instead, he said, athletes should simply strive to do their best and reach their full potential.

Bill's last year of Olympic competition was 1984. Following his competitive career, Bill stayed active in cross-country skiing, often writing about the sport. He also became involved in the development of the Bill Koch Ski League, a program of instruction and competition for young skiers, and in the design of ski trails.

Summary

Bill Koch was the first American to win an Olympic medal in cross-country skiing and the

Major Skiing Championships

Year	Competition	Event	Place
1974	World Championships	15 kilometers	46th
		Team relay	12th
1976	Olympic Games	15 kilometers	6th
		30 kilometers	Silver
		50 kilometers	13th
		Team relay	6th
1978	World Championships	15 kilometers	6th
		30 kilometers	33d
		Team relay	9th
1979	World Cup	Overall	23d
1980	Olympic Games	15 kilometers	16th
		30 kilometers	Did not finish
		50 kilometers	13th
1982	World Cup	Overall	1st
1984	Olympic Games	15 kilometers	27th
		30 kilometers	21st
		50 kilometers	17th
		Team relay	

first to win a World Cup championship. He was an unusually determined athlete who overcame a medical problem to become one of the best skiers in the world. In addition to his place as the best American cross-country skier in history, he will be remembered as the athlete who popularized a new skiing technique that is now used by all leading cross-country competitors.

Wayne Wilson

Additional Sources

Fry, John. *The Story of Modern Skiing*. Hanover, N.H.: University Press of New England, 2006.

Levinson, David, and Karen Christensen, eds. *Encyclopedia of World Sport: From Ancient to Present*. Santa Barbara, Calif.: ABC-Clio, 1996.

Wallechinsky, David, and Jaime Loucky. *The Complete Book of the Winter Olympics*. London: Aurum Press, 2008.

Honors, Awards, and Records

1975-76, 1979-80	U.S. Nordic Competitor of the Year
1976	Inducted into National Ski Hall of Fame
	First American to win an Olympic medal in cross-country skiing (a silver medal)
1981	First athlete to ski 50 kilometers in under two hours
1982	First American to win the World Cup

Pavel Kolobkov

Born: September 22, 1969
     Moscow, Soviet Union (now in Russia)
Also known as: Pavel Anatolyevich Kolobkov (full name)

Early Life

Pavel Kolobkov was born on September 22, 1969, in the then-Soviet capital of Moscow. From an early age, he demonstrated an affinity for sports. His biggest problem was finding the sport that best fit his particular gifts. His parents, noting his sure-footedness and elegant sense of movement, pushed him into figure skating. However, he did not like the sport, particularly its subjective scoring system. Then, he tried swimming—but was regarded as too small to compete effectively—and ski jumping.

Pavel was introduced to épée fencing at the age of ten, relatively late for a sport that, as a major cultural fixture in Soviet athletics with a long history of premiere Olympic competition, regularly schooled its most promising athletes from a much earlier age. The sport was a perfect fit for young Pavel's grace, innate sense of balance, and wiry frame.

The Road to Excellence

Of the three modern competitive fencing events—foil and saber are the other two—épée most resembles traditional sword-fighting. Fencers of the late nineteenth century who wanted to create a more competitive and fluid style of fencing developed the épée discipline. Thus, the sword is much heavier than in the other forms, creating a more deliberate style of engagement. Important for an athlete with the nimbleness and natural grace of Pavel, the entire body is the target area for scoring, and there are no rules for regulating "right-of-way," or mandated movements after first attack. Those elements create a decidedly strategic style of play that rewards footwork and mental toughness.

Pavel, under the tutelage of Soviet coach Boris Nikolaychuk, quickly established himself as an elite competitor, winning Junior World Fencing Championship titles in both 1987 and

1988. Despite that remarkable success, by Soviet standards, Pavel was, at eighteen, something of a neophyte rather than a product of the Soviet athletic system. Thus, his place on the prestigious 1988 Soviet Olympic squad was a remarkable achievement. At Seoul, South Korea, Pavel won his first medal: He shared in the team bronze. However, given the intense focus that the sport places on the response and reflexes of the fencer, individual success is the traditional standard of great achievement. Thus, returning from Seoul, Pavel dedicated himself to raising his acumen.

The Emerging Champion

Leading up to the 1992 Olympic Games at Barcelona, Spain, Pavel established himself as the dominant figure in épée fencing by claiming the first of his five world individual championship titles in 1991. Against the often flashier play of competitors, Pavel executed a deliberate style: He was opportunistic and careful; possessed clear strategic movements; and, because of his elegant sense of balance and footwork, had an ability to anticipate scoring efforts by opponents and to control the matches. When Pavel lost in the finals in Barcelona

Major Fencing Championships

Year	Competition	Event	Place
1987	Junior World Fencing Championship	Épée team	1st
1988	Junior Fencing World Championship	Épée team	1st
	Olympic Games	Épée team	Bronze
1991	Fencing World Championship	Épée individual	1st
1992	Olympic Games	Épée individual	Silver
		Épée team	Bronze
1993	Fencing World Championship	Épée individual	1st
1994	Fencing World Championship	Épée individual	1st
1996	European Fencing Championship	Épée individual	1st
	Olympic Games	Épée team	Silver
1999	Fencing World Cup	Épée individual	1st
2000	Olympic Games	Épée individual	Gold
	European Fencing Championship	Épée individual	1st
2002	Fencing World Championship	Épée individual	1st
2004	Olympic Games	Épée individual	Bronze
2005	Fencing World Championship	Épée individual	1st
2008	Challenge Bernadotte	Épée individual	1st

and took a silver medal, the result was somewhat of an upset and testimony to how the sport is prone to the element of chance.

Undaunted, Pavel set his sights on the 1996 Olympic Games at Atlanta, Georgia, claiming the World Championships in Fencing titles in 1993 and 1994. However, Pavel's experience in Atlanta was more disappointing than his result in Barcelona: He was eliminated from the medal competition entirely. Critics said his deliberate play left him open to younger, more improvisational players who were able to take advantage of the sport's pace and element of surprise. Pavel, to his credit, offered no excuses.

Pavel returned to train for the Sydney Olympic Games in 2000, driven more than ever to capture the gold medal. Even a Fencing World Cup title in 1999 did little to quash the intensity of his focus on Olympic gold. Despite his considerable record, which included the 2000 European Fencing Championship title, he was considered a long shot in Sydney. However, in a dramatic showdown against former world champion Hugues Obry of France, Pavel took the point lead in the second period of the final match and claimed his coveted Olympic gold medal at last.

Continuing the Story

Possessing Olympic gold, at the pinnacle of his sport, and widely considered épée's most accomplished champion, Pavel did not concede to celebrity but continued to compete, claiming two additional world championship titles in 2002 and 2005. Pavel, realizing he would retire from competition eventually, drew on his celebrity to establish and manage several state-of-the-art fitness clubs in the Moscow area.

Not content with his entrepreneurial success, however, Pavel still sought the satisfaction of high-level competition. Approaching his mid-thirties, Pavel, after four Olympics, was considered the veteran anchor of the Russian team sent to compete in the Athens Olympic Games in 2004. Relying on his signature style of quiet but aggressive play, Pavel fought his way to the medal round, eventually

claiming the bronze. This Olympic performance was a classic demonstration of his style: a quiet finesse game, a refusal to concede any match, and a mental toughness that allowed him to dominate much younger and much more energetic competition.

Pavel continue to compete, but his come-from-behind championship run in the prestigious Challenge Bernadotte in Stockholm, Sweden, in 2008, was widely regarded as his last major competitive effort. Close to forty, he had become a finesse coach for promising young Russian fencers who admired his old-school style of mental discipline and deliberate play.

Summary

To a sport not given to flash and spectacle, Pavel Kolobkov brought a minimalist style that, despite the sport's bulky clothing, heavy sword, and cumbersome mask, emphasized lightning-quick reflexes, careful balance, alert anticipation, and agile footwork. His style was often compared to martial arts, in which mental alertness rather than physical strength determines success. Pavel possessed a keen intuitive ability to anticipate an opponent's moves and counter them with deft and wily repositionings. His fluid and cagey athleticism was often missed by those not trained in the subtle dynamics of the sport. However, experts considered him one of fencing's greatest athletes ever.

Joseph Dewey

Additional Sources

Cohen, Richard. *By the Sword: A History of Gladiators, Musketeers, Samurai, Swashbucklers, and Olympic Champions.* New York: Modern Library, 2003.

Evangelista, Nick. *The Inner Game of Fencing: Excellence in Form, Technique, Strategy, and Spirit.* New York: McGraw-Hill, 2000.

Gaughler, William M. *The History of Fencing: Foundations of Modern European Swordplay.* Egg Harbor City, N.J.: Laureate, 1997.

Pitman, Brian. *Fencing: Techniques of Foil, Épée, and Saber.* Ramsbury, Marlborough, Wiltshire, England: Crowood Press, 1988.

Tommy Kono

Born: June 27, 1930
      Sacramento, California
Also known as: Thomas Tamio Kono (full name)
Other major sport: Bodybuilding

Early Life

Thomas Tamio Kono was born June 27, 1930, in Sacramento, California, of Japanese American parents. Skinny and sickly as a child, Tommy suffered from chronic asthma. Always the smallest child on the block, he dreamed of taking a Charles Atlas correspondence course in bodybuilding but could not afford one. After the outbreak of World War II, Tommy and his family, like many Japanese Americans, were forced to enter a detention camp. They spent three and a half years in the Tule Lake camp in Northern California. At Tule Lake, Tommy took up weightlifting to improve his health and occupy his time. He was a natural at the sport. In the span of seven years, he developed into an Olympic champion and, according to most experts, the greatest competitive weightlifter of all time.

Tommy Kono performing during a bodybuilding competition. (Courtesy of Amateur Athletic Foundation of Los Angeles)

The Road to Excellence

Tommy continued to train on his own until 1952, when he entered the United States Army. With Army support, he began training for the Olympic trials. That year he won the lightweight division Olympic gold medal at Helsinki, Finland. He continued to dominate the sport for the next thirteen years.

Competitive weightlifting requires both enormous strength and close attention to technique. Divided into weight classes, lifters competed in three categories: snatch, clean and jerk, and press (discontinued after the 1972 Olympics). In case of a tie, the lifter with the lowest body weight wins. It is thus to the lifter's advantage to be at the lowest weight possible while competing in the heaviest class possible.

Tommy's unique talent was his ability to use his body weight to full advantage. While setting records in world competitions, he moved up and down through four different weight classes (148, 165, 181, and 198 pounds). His three Olympic medals were each won in different weight categories: a gold medal in the lightweight class (148 pounds; Helsinki, 1952) and in the light-heavyweight class (181 pounds; Melbourne, 1956); and a silver medal in the middleweight class (165 pounds; Rome, 1960).

To control his weight, Tommy relied principally on diet. He had to eat six to eight meals a day just to maintain his weight. To lose weight he would "diet" by eating only three or four meals a day. Sometimes he would resort to force-feeding himself in order to gain weight for competition.

The Emerging Champion

Tommy became the most successful lifter of all time, winning Olympic and World Weightlift-

Major Weightlifting Championships

1952	U.S. lightweight champion
	U.S. Olympic gold medalist (lightweight division)
1953, 1957-59	World middleweight champion
1953, 1958-60	U.S. middleweight champion
1954-55	World light-heavyweight champion
1954-56, 1961-63	U.S. light-heavyweight champion
1955, 1963	U.S. Pan-American Games gold medalist (light-heavyweight division)
1956	U.S. Olympic gold medalist (light-heavyweight division)
1959	U.S. Pan-American Games gold medalist (middleweight division)
1960	U.S. Olympic silver medalist (middleweight division)

World Bodybuilding Titles

1954	Mr. World
1955, 1957, 1961	Mr. Universe

ing Championships for eight consecutive years from 1952 to 1959. He established world records in four different body weight classes and held World and Olympic titles in three different body weight classes. He won the World Middleweight Championship in 1953 and 1957 through 1959, and the World Light-Heavyweight Championship in 1954 and 1955.

Although a keen individual competitor, Tommy was always respected for his commitment to his team and to the sport in general. He enjoyed the excitement of the competition as much as winning. He often remarked that he felt as satisfied if he came in second instead of first, if he knew that he had fought hard and done his best. Always humble in victory and gracious in defeat, he was a true gentleman champion in the sport.

Tommy took seriously the advice of his mentor and friend, Charles Davis: "Be prepared to perform under any conditions because people will always be looking at you as a champion." He never forgot these words and lived by them. Once, while giving exhibitions in France in the 1950's, he arrived at a gymnasium that had a dirt floor and a

badly balanced set of weights. He performed without complaint, aware of his responsibility to present himself as a true champion under any circumstances.

Continuing the Story

Tommy was one of the early innovators in developing effective weightlifting routines. In order to maximize muscle growth and avoid becoming stale, he would change training programs on a regular basis, usually every six weeks. To give his body plenty of rest, he alternated the heavy weight-training routines needed to prepare for competitions with bodybuilding routines that involved light weights and many repetitions. As a result of his varied training, Tommy competed in world-class bodybuilding events, winning the titles of Mr. World in 1954, and Mr. Universe in 1955, 1957, and 1961.

Tommy earned international respect for his knowledge of his sport. From 1966-1968, he was engaged as the national and Olympic weightlifting coach for Mexico. He introduced the Mexican team to the routine of recording every lift, even during practice, so that each member could monitor individual progress. At the time, this method was a significant innovation in weight training and has now become common practice.

After his success with the Mexican team, Tommy served as the national and Olympic weightlifting coach for West Germany in preparation for the Munich Olympics in 1972. After the Munich Olympics, Tommy served as the U.S. Olympic coach, in 1976, as a volunteer, coaching for love of the sport. He later also coached the U.S. women's team.

In 1955, Tommy moved permanently to Hawaii, where he married Florence Rodrigues, a native of the islands, and raised three children, Jameson, JoAnn, and Mark. In 1973, he took a position with the Department of Parks and Recreation in Honolulu. In 1990, he was inducted into the U.S. Olympic Hall of Fame.

Honors, Awards, and Records

Awarded the International Weightlifting Federation's Fifteen-Year Service Medal
Awarded the International Weightlifting Federation's Twenty-five-Year Service Medal
Set forty-one international records
Set twenty-six world records in four weight classes
Set seven Olympic records
Set eight Pan-American Games records
Inducted into U.S. Olympic Hall of Fame (1990)

Summary

After retiring from competition in 1965, Tommy Kono continued to train regularly; he considered weightlifting to be a sport, a hobby, and a way of life. He left the sport a winner, having set forty-one international records, twenty-six world records, seven Olympic records, and eight Pan-American Games records. In 1988, the International Weightlifting Federation ranked him first among the thirty greatest lifters of all time. The skinny child had come a long way since the days when he yearned to look like Charles Atlas.

William C. Griffin

Additional Sources

Kim, Hyung-chan, ed. "Tommy Tamio Kono." In *Distinguished Asian Americans: A Biographical Dictionary*. Westport, Conn.: Greenwood Press, 1999.

Kono, Tommy. *Weightlifting, Olympic Style*. Honolulu: Hawaii Kono Company, 2001.

Wallechinsky, David, and Jaime Loucky. *The Complete Book of the Olympics: 2008 Edition*. London: Aurum Press, 2008.

John Konrads

Born: May 21, 1942
Riga, Latvia

Early Life

John Konrads, of the brother-and-sister combination known as "the Konrads Kids," was born on May 21, 1942, in Riga, Latvia. His sister, Ilsa, was born on March 29, 1944. When John was three years old, his parents fled the Soviet-occupied Latvia to Germany and then immigrated to Australia in 1949. John's swimming story is even more dramatic in that he contracted polio while his family was living in a refugee camp near Stuttgart, Germany, before they moved to Sydney, New South Wales, Australia. To help John's polio, the "Konrads Kids" first started swimming.

The Road to Excellence

In Australia, the "Konrads Kids" were discovered by the famous Australian Olympic coach Don Talbot, who found them to be remarkable young swimmers, both coachable and willing to work hard. They quickly became child prodigies in swimming.

Ilsa was the first to set world records, at the age of thirteen, on January 9, 1958. She set two world records in the same race, in the half-mile and the 800 meters. The first was an English yards measurement, and the second, a metric measurement; world records were measured in both yards and meters at that time. Two days later, as if prompted by his little sister, John broke the men's world records at the same distances and then added four more world records before another week had passed. The new world records were in the furlong (220 yards), the 200 meters, the quarter-mile, and the 400 meters.

The Emerging Champion

The world was excited about these wonder children from Lativa, via Australia, who had smashed so many records. They were called the "Concrete Kids" because of their toughness, the "Kindergarten Kids" because of their youth, and the Konrads Kids because that was their name. In 1956, John was a standby on the Olympic team.

In 1958, the brother-and-sister duo performed in front of Queen Elizabeth and Prince Philip, who was chairperson of the British Commonwealth Games at Cardiff, Wales. Ilsa won the 440 yards (quarter-mile), and John was a triple gold medal winner in the three longest freestyle races. The Konrads became the only brother-and-sister combination in the history of the Commonwealth Games to win gold medals. Between them, the Konrads set seven world records in the twenty-five months between January, 1958, and February, 1960, all before John was eighteen years old and Ilsa, fifteen.

Continuing the Story

John made his biggest mark in the world of swimming at the 1960 Olympics in Rome, Italy. He won not only a gold medal in the 1,500 meters but also two bronzes in the 4×100- and 4×200-meter freestyle relays. John was also a member of the 1964 Olympic team in Tokyo and was the first man to

John Konrads. (Courtesy of International Swimming Hall of Fame)

swim the 800-meter freestyle and the 880-yard freestyle in less than 9 minutes (8 minutes 59.6 seconds).

After the Rome Olympics, John took a job as promotional manager of a large ten-pin bowling enterprise with alleys in three of Sydney's suburbs. He decided to give his bowling career up, however, to accept a scholarship from Peter Daland at the University of Southern California (USC), where he swam on the same team with future hall-of-famers Murray Rose, Roy Saari, and Tsuyoshi Yamanaka, all world-record holders in the distance freestyle. These four did not all graduate together, but they did compete together as the most dominant distance freestyle group ever assembled on one team. In 1971, John and Ilsa were both inducted into the International Swimming Hall of Fame.

Major Swimming Championships

Year	Competition	Event	Place	Time
1958	Commonwealth Games	400-yard freestyle	1st	4:25.9
		1,650-yard freestyle	1st	17:45.4
		220-yard freestyle	1st	8:33.4
1960	Olympic Games	1,500-meter freestyle	Gold	17:19.6
		4×100-meter freestyle relay	Bronze	—
		4×200-meter freestyle relay	Bronze	—
1963	NCAA Championships	500-yard freestyle	1st	4:50.7
		1,650-yard freestyle	1st	17:24.0

Records

Set 25 world records in his career

Best times: 200-meter freestyle (2:02.2), 220-yard freestyle (2:01.6), 400-yard freestyle and 440-yard freestyle (4:15.9), 1,500 and 1,650-yard freestyle (17:11.0)

First man under 9 minutes for the 800-meter and 880-yard freestyle (8:59.6)

Honors and Awards

1956, 1960, 1964	Men's U.S. Olympic swimming team
1971	Inducted into International Swimming Hall of Fame

Summary

The Konradses' stay at the top of competitive swimming was brief but brilliant. They were among the first of the very young swimmers to achieve excellence. Altogether, John Konrads set twenty-five records during his career, made three Olympic teams, and won three medals in Olympic competition. After serving as the president and chief executive officer of several large companies in Australia, John became a successful international marketing consultant.

Buck Dawson

Additional Sources

Colwin, Cecil. *Breakthrough Swimming*. Champaign, Ill.: Human Kinetics, 2002.

Gonsalves, Kelly, and Susan LaMondia. *First to the Wall: One Hundred Years of Olympic Swimming*. East Longmeadow, Mass.: FreeStyle, 1999.

Wallechinsky, David, and Jaime Loucky. *The Complete Book of the Olympics: 2008 Edition*. London: Aurum Press, 2008.

Olga Korbut

Born: May 16, 1955
      Hrodno, Byelorussia, Soviet Union (now in Belarus)

Also known as: Olga Valentinovna Korbut (full name)

Early Life

Olga Valentinovna Korbut was born on May 16, 1955, in Hrodno, Byelorussia, Soviet Union (now in Belarus), an industrial city not far from the Polish border. The daughter of a civil engineer and a cook, Olga was the youngest of four girls. Her oldest sister, Ludmila, was also a gymnast and was awarded the title Master of the Sport.

At the age of nine, Olga entered a sports school headed by Renald Knysh and was put under the tutelage of former Olympic gymnast Elena Volchetskaya. At 4 feet 11 inches and 98 pounds, her size was ideal for gymnastics, and her coaches stressed back exercises to increase her spine flexibility.

The Road to Excellence

Training through her adolescence, Olga developed a daring and original style, incorporating lively, insect-like rhythms into her floor exercises. She collaborated with Knysh on complicated choreography and developed a daring backward flip on the balance beam. Her pert, charismatic individuality was a departure from the subdued balletic form of most Soviet gymnasts.

During these developmental years, Olga studied at the Grodno Pedagogical Institute, where she was named an Honored Master of Sports in 1972. She was a diligent student but still managed to spend hours in the gymnasium, practicing a given move as many as four hundred times a day.

Olga's first major competition was the 1969 Soviet Championships, where she took fifth place in the all-around and introduced her backflip; the following year she took a gold medal in the vault. At these national championships, Olga developed the major rivalry of her career, with teammate Ludmila Turishcheva, whose quiet technical expertise was in direct contrast to Olga's joyful artistry. A great personal triumph for Olga was her defeat of Turishcheva at the 1972 Union of Soviet Socialist Republics (U.S.S.R.) Cup.

Olga Korbut performing on the uneven bars during a Soviet gymnastics team tour of the United States in 1973. (Courtesy of Amateur Athletic Foundation of Los Angeles)

The Emerging Champion

The true test of a gymnast is international competition, and Olga's opportunity came with the 1972 Munich Olympics. She made the team as an alternate, only after another gymnast withdrew because of injury. Nevertheless, she performed excellently, and her entire Olympic experience was marked by drama and excitement. A week before the Games she changed her floor exercise music, selecting a piece entitled "Java," from a German wartime film, calculated to heighten crowd appreciation. She won a gold medal in that event, as well as on the balance beam, where her backward aerial thrilled audiences. However, the backward aerial created controversy; the International Gymnastics

Major Gymnastics Championships

Year	Competition	Event	Place	Event	Place
1972	Olympic Games	All-around	7th	Balance beam	Gold
		Floor exercise	Gold	Vault	5th
		Uneven bars	Silver	Team	Gold
1973	European Championships	All-around	2d		
	World University Games	All-around	1st	Balance beam	1st
		Floor exercise	1st	Vault	3d
		Uneven bars	1st	Team	1st
1974	World Championships	All-around	2d	Balance beam	2d
		Floor exercise	2d	Vault	1st
		Uneven bars	2d	Team	1st
1976	Olympic Games	All-around	5th	Balance beam	Silver
		Uneven bars	5th	Team	Gold

Federation attempted to outlaw the move as unsafe. Eventually, increased padding was added to the beam. On the uneven bars, Olga successfully attempted a backward somersault, an unprecedented move; but a sudden loss of balance dropped her score and dashed her hopes of eclipsing Turishcheva and East German Karin Janz as the successor to the 1968 Olympic champion Vera Cáslavská of Czechoslovakia. After the spill, Olga, the little redhead from Grodno, openly burst into tears on the sidelines.

While she left Munich without the all-around gold medal, Olga had won the hearts of fans worldwide. Her personality was perfect for television, and her performance at Munich, monumental and unanticipated, revolutionized the world of gymnastics. Young girls everywhere, especially in Europe and the United States, flocked to gymnastics schools to follow Olga's example. Her name became a household word. In the coming years, she frequently visited the United States and England: President Richard Nixon invited her to the White House; Chicago Mayor Richard Daley declared an "Olga Korbut Day"; an "Olga Korbut Fan Club" sprang up in Beverly Hills, California; the Faberge company sponsored a major Soviet team tour headlined by Olga; a personal bodyguard was assigned to her; and she satisfied her desire for a car and acquired a taste for Western goods such as ketchup, miniskirts, and tape recorders. At the same time, she openly criticized her teammates, questioned Soviet socialist policy, and was often surrounded with controversy and always with publicity.

Professionally, her relationship with Knysh

soured, and the two fought constantly. She experienced back ailments and fatigue, which forced her to recuperate at a spa in the Caucasus of southern Russia. An ankle injury forced her to limp away from the individual events competition at the 1973 European Gymnastics Championships in London. At that year's World University Games in Moscow and the 1974 World Gymnastics Championships in Varna, Bulgaria, she excelled with six—of a possible six—medals at each tournament.

Korbut's experiences matured her, and a stronger and more stable young woman came, under the pressure of worldwide scrutiny, to the 1976 Olympics in Montreal. She had little competition during the pre-Olympic year, and though her bright red tights showed her characteristic spunk, they could not hide a slight limp. She performed well, but the limelight that she had seized in 1972 shifted to the little Romanian Nadia Comăneci, to whom Olga took second place on the balance beam, her own best event.

Continuing the Story

By her 1977 graduation from the Grodno Pedagogical Institute, where she had studied history and English, the twenty-two-year-old Olga was ready to retire from competitive gymnastics. On New Year's Day, 1978, Olga announced her engagement to Leonid Bortkevich, a Soviet rock musician she had met in 1976, on a plane to the United States. Olga was married in a wedding dress she had bought, under great media coverage, at a department store in St. Louis, Missouri; the wedding took place in the Belarus capital of Minsk, and the couple honeymooned in Cuba. In 1978, Olga's official farewell to competitive gymnastics was made during an honorary ceremony at the Moscow News Meet.

Though she continued training and considered

Honors and Awards

1972	Honored Master of Sports
	Badge of Honor
	ABC *Wide World of Sports* Athlete of the Year
	Associated Press Female Athlete of the Year
1988	Inducted into International Gymnastics Hall of Fame

a comeback in 1979 for the 1980 Moscow Olympics, she never came out of retirement. In March of 1979, a son, Richard, was born to Olga. In the years to come, Olga became the Belarus's women's gymnastics coach and took time to explore new interests, including graphic arts, acting, singing with her husband's band, equestrian competition, and spending time with her family.

Still fit, Olga joined tours and exhibitions as tensions between the East and West eased. Olga, living in Minsk in 1986, was a victim of the Chernobyl nuclear disaster. In 1989, she sought medical help in the United States and continued for many years to suffer from a thyroid problem caused by exposure to the radiation. Using her international status, Olga raised money to help other victims and became a spokesperson for their plight. In 1991, she moved to Atlanta, Georgia, with her son, returned to coaching and making public appearances, and continued her work on behalf of Chernobyl victims. In 2000, she remarried but divorced in 2007. She eventually moved to Scottsdale, Arizona, where she worked with adults, incorporating gymnastics techniques into fitness routines.

Summary

Olga Korbut was a world-class gymnast whose captivating personality helped to establish a new age in international gymnastics. Her originality and daring changed the sport, and her audience appeal inspired millions to love and participate in the sport.

Barry Mann

Additional Sources

Beecham, Justin. *Olga.* New York: Paddington Press, 1974.

Korbut, Olga, and Ellen Emerson-White. *My Story: The Autobiography of Olga Korbut.* London: Century, 1992.

Orecklin, Michele. "Innocence Lost." *Time Europe* 159, no. 7 (February 18, 2002): 67-72.

Simons, Minot. *Women's Gymnastics, a History: Volume 1, 1966-1974.* Carmel, Calif.: Welwyn, 1995.

Woolum, Janet. *Outstanding Women Athletes: Who They Are and How They Influenced Sports in America.* Phoenix, Ariz.: Oryx Press, 1998.

Yaeger, Don, Albert Kim, and Kostya Kennedy. "Olga's Woes." *Sports Illustrated* 96, no. 7 (February 18, 2002): 28.

Janica Kostelić

Born: January 5, 1982
     Zagreb, Yugoslavia (now in Croatia)
Also known as: Snow Queen of Croatia; Croatian
  Sensation

Early Life

Janica Kostelić was born January 5, 1982, in Zagreb, Yugoslavia (now in Croatia), into a family dedicated to winter sports. Janica grew up with elder brother Ivica, who was also a skier and won the 2003 World Cup and a silver medal at the 2006 Olympics. Janica's father became her coach.

Janica began skiing at the age of three. When war came to Yugoslavia during the early 1990's, the Kostelićs left Zagreb and lived transitorily in central and Eastern Europe. Janica's family was not wealthy and camped overnight in cars or tents during tournaments. However, her parents encouraged her to compete. By the age of thirteen, she had become proficient enough to win a handful of gold and silver medals in slalom and giant slalom competitions at a number of junior European competitions; her brother achieved similar results. In 1995, on the recommendation of the national Olympic committee, the Kostelić siblings were granted scholarships as promising young athletes, which provided financial assistance to pay for training, coaching, and travel.

The Road to Excellence

Between 1995 and 1997, Janica continued her high school education around training sessions and various competitions and recorded excellent grades. During the 1996-1997 season, Janica entered twenty-two junior races and won every contest. By the 1997-1998 season, she had begun to enter senior competitions and the International Ski Federation (FIS) World Cup events. Just two months after transferring to senior status, she had accumulated sufficient FIS points to qualify for all five alpine disciplines—slalom, giant slalom, downhill, super giant slalom (super-G) and combined—at the 1998 Winter Olympics in Nagano, Japan.

At sixteen, Janica was the youngest alpine competitor at the 1998 Olympics and performed respectably among world-class competitors. Though she fell in the slalom, she finished twenty-fourth in giant slalom, twenty-fifth in downhill, twenty-sixth in super-G, and eighth in combined. Following the Games, Janica's Olympic scholarship expired. However, her potential had attracted attention, and she gained sponsorships from national and international companies that provided financial support to continue her athletic career.

The sponsor's backing began to pay off in 1999, when Janica won three World Cup events. Not long afterward, she suffered a major setback: damage to a knee ligament that kept her out of competition until late in 2000.

The Emerging Champion

Returning to the slopes after recovering from knee surgery, Janica soon took up where she had left off. Between November, 2000, and February, 2001, she earned nine World Cup slalom and combined victories to finish first in slalom and capture the overall World Cup title. She was the youngest world champion in twenty years.

All of Zagreb turned out to greet the conquering heroine. She was presented with a huge bouquet of roses, 1,256 in all, one blossom for each point she had accumulated in winning the World Cup title. Janica also had the honor of becoming the first athlete to be portrayed on a Croatian postage stamp.

Major Skiing Championships

Year	Competition	Event	Place
2002	Olympic Games	Slalom	Gold
		Giant slalom	Gold
		Combined	Gold
		Super-G	Silver
2003	World Championships	Slalom	1st
		Combined	1st
2005	World Championships	Slalom	1st
		Downhill	1st
		Combined	1st
2006	Olympic Games	Combined	Gold
		Super-G	Silver

The 2001-2002 season began badly for Janica, who underwent another knee operation. However, she recovered sufficiently to perform outstandingly at the 2002 Winter Olympics in Salt Lake City, Utah. She was unbeatable in the combined event, recording the fastest time in each of three runs. Then she finished second in the super-G, just .05 seconds behind the gold-medal winner. Next, she took the gold in slalom by a margin of .07. Finally, she capped off her domination by winning both runs of the giant slalom to earn her fourth medal and third gold. She became the first woman to win three alpine gold medals in a single Olympics competition. At the age of twenty, Janica had become a Croatian national icon.

Continuing the Story

Not content, Janica put her Olympic medals away to focus on the 2003 skiing season. Once again, with World Ski Championships in slalom and combined, she proved she was the world's best women slalom skier, winning her second overall World Cup title. Her brother took the 2003 World Cup title for men. Early in 2004, Janica suffered yet another knee injury. She came back the following winter to narrowly miss taking her third World Cup. With World Ski Championships in slalom, combined, and downhill, she finished only three points behind winner Anja Pärson in the most hotly contested World Cup overall title in the event's history.

In the 2005-2006 season, Janica left no doubt who was the strongest women's skier: She handily won the World Cup overall championship for the third time. She also was ranked in the top-five competitors in four alpine disciplines. She was number one in slalom, her best event.

Janica's performance perfectly positioned her for the 2006 Winter Olympics in Turin, Italy. There,

Honors and Awards

2001	Croatian postage stamp made in her honor
2001, 2003, 2006	World Cup overall champion
2006	Laureus World Sports Award: sportswoman of the year

she took the gold in women's alpine combined to become the most successful female skier in Olympic history with four gold medals. She also captured the silver in the super-G to run her Olympic medal count to six; her brother likewise won a silver medal at the Games.

With still another knee injury with which to contend, and nothing left to prove, Janica announced her retirement from competition in 2007.

Summary

Despite a series of knee injuries, Janica Kostelić became the most successful women's alpine skier in Olympic history with four gold and two silver medals earned in two Games. A national heroine in Croatia, she skied to victory in thirty World Cup events while winning overall World Cup championships in 2001, 2003, and 2005.

Jack Ewing

Additional Sources

Fry, John. *The Story of Modern Skiing*. Lebanon, N.H.: University Press of New England, 2006.

Macy, Sue. *Freeze Frame: A Photographic History of the Winter Olympics*. Des Moines, Iowa: National Geographic Children's Books, 2006.

Miller, Ernestine. *Making Her Mark: Firsts and Milestones in Women's Sports*. New York: McGraw-Hill, 2002.

Wallechinsky, David, and Jaime Loucky. *The Complete Book of the Winter Olympics*. Toronto: Sport-Classic Books, 2005.

Lenny Krayzelburg

Born: September 28, 1975
     Odessa, Soviet Union (now in Ukraine)

Early Life

Lenny Krayzelburg was born on September 28, 1975, in Odessa, Ukraine, then part of the Soviet Union. His parents, Oleg and Yelena, took a great interest in Lenny's swimming when, at the age of five, he began practicing with a Red Army club.

Lenny's coach told his father that Lenny had the potential to be an Olympic backstroker. Lenny, who at eight years old was tall and lean, with almost double-jointed elbows, began training sessions. He swam for five hours a day under the government-

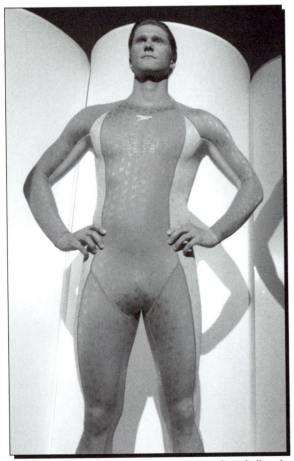

Lenny Krayzelburg modeling a new swimsuit line in 2004. (Peter Morgan/Reuters/Landov)

sponsored program, which also incorporated running and weightlifting. At the age of ten, Lenny took second place in his Soviet age-group championships. He earned silver medals the following two years as well.

The Road to Excellence

Lenny was not to become a star athlete in his homeland. Suddenly, years after Oleg and Yelena had applied for exit visas, the Russian government issued the documentation for the Krayzelburg family. "Russia [had] a lot of problems," said Yelena. "We are Jewish, and they have discrimination. [And] we were afraid Lenny would [have to] go to the Russian army." In 1989, the family, including Lenny's younger sister, Marsha, departed for the United States.

Upon their arrival in West Hollywood, California, none of the Krayzelburgs spoke English. Months passed before Oleg and Yelena could find work. To help his family make ends meet, Lenny worked thirty hours a week as a lifeguard and maintenance worker at the West Hollywood recreational department pool. His busy schedule of school and work, and his family's lack of a car, meant that he had to train close to home. He joined the swim team at the Westside Jewish Community Center.

By Lenny's senior year of high school, he had not received replies from any college swimming coaches to whom he had sent personal information. Without a scholarship, he would have been unable to continue his education or his swimming career. Even though he swam only about four hours a week at the community center, he posted impressive times in the 100-meter and 200-meter backstroke events. His talent was recognized by Gerry Rodrigues, a coach of a local swim team. Gerry introduced Lenny to Stu Blumkin, the swimming coach at Santa Monica College. Lenny began swimming there, and he won California junior college titles in the 100-meter and 200-meter backstroke that season. Lenny credited Blumkin with hastening his breakthrough: "Even having swum for fourteen years, I was pretty ignorant about some things,"

Major Swimming Championships

Year	Competition	Event	Time	Place
1997	Pan-Pacific Championships	100-meter backstroke	54.43	1st
		200-meter backstroke	1:57.87	1st
1999	Pan-Pacific Championships	100-meter backstroke	53.60	1st
		200-meter backstroke	1:55.87	1st
	U.S. Open Championships	100-meter backstroke	54.62	1st
		200-meter backstroke	1:57.74	2d
2000	Janet Evans Invitational	100-meter backstroke	54.60	1st
		200-meter backstroke	1:59.34	2d
	U.S. Olympic Swimming Trials	100-meter backstroke	53.84	1st
		200-meter backstroke	1:57.31	1st
	Olympic Games	100-meter backstroke	53.72	Gold
		200-meter backstroke	1:56.76	Gold
		4×100-meter medley relay	n/a	Gold
2001	Maccabiah Games	100-meter backstroke	55.24	1st
		4×100-meter medley	3:22.83	1st
2004	Olympic Games	4×100-meter medley	3:30.68	Gold

he said. "Pacing, racing, developing a consistent workout pattern; these were all things Stu worked with me on."

The Emerging Champion

Meanwhile, Blumkin was working on additional things for Lenny. Understanding that the swimmer needed a more challenging program to develop his full potential, he introduced Lenny to University of Southern California (USC) swimming coach Mark Schubert. Lenny had Schubert's attention after one workout and was offered a full scholarship to USC. Schubert later cited Blumkin's unselfishness in giving away the kind of swimmer a coach sees once in a lifetime.

Again, Lenny flourished in a new atmosphere. At the 1995 U.S. summer nationals, he was named rookie of the meet and subsequently turned down an offer to swim for Ukraine in the 1996 Olympics. He became a United States citizen that year.

Six months later, he traveled to Indianapolis, Indiana, for the U.S. Olympic trials. Though he failed to make the team, he swam a lifetime best of 2:00.49 in the 200-meter backstroke. That summer, his momentum continued to build as he won gold medals in both the 100- and the 200-meter backstroke events at the U.S. summer nationals.

In 1997, his junior year at USC, he won the 200-meter backstroke at the National College Athletic Association championships, swimming the third-

fastest time ever recorded in his fourteenth swim in three days. At the summer nationals that year, he swept the 100- and 200-meter backstroke events, becoming the national record holder in the latter. Two weeks later, at the Pan-Pacific Championships in Japan, he repeated his performance, winning the 100 meters with a time of 54.53 and lowering the record time he had set for the 200 meters to 1:57.87.

Continuing the Story

At the 1998 World Swimming Championships in Australia, Lenny's family, together with his mentor Gerry Rodrigues, cheered on Lenny as he won gold medals in the two backstroke events. That year, Lenny graduated from USC with a degree in finance.

Lenny again struck gold at the 1999 Pan-Pacific Championships in Sydney. Both his 100- and 200-meter backstroke times set world records. Organizers of the Pan-Pacific Championships set up a special time trial for the 50-meter backstroke; Lenny set a record in that event as well.

Lenny took first and second place at the U.S. Open Swimming Championships for 100- and 200-meter backstroke, respectively. In 2000, when the Olympic trials came around, Lenny was ready. He swept the backstroke events. The national governing body for the sport, USA Swimming, named him swimmer of the year in 1999 and 2000. Many anticipated Lenny's performances at the Sydney Olympic Games. The swimming-gear company Speedo paid more to sponsor him than it had for any non-Olympian. The competition was intense: Australian star Ian Thorpe, Dutch swimmer Pieter van den Hoogenband, and Russia's Alexander Popov all lost at least one event. Nobody, however, beat Lenny, as he swam a time of 53.72 to win the 100-meter backstroke. He won the 200-meter backstroke in 1:56.76, with U.S. teammate Aaron Peirsol taking the silver medal. The U.S. team finished first in the 4×100-meter medley relay, as Lenny earned his third gold medal of the Games.

Lenny, a triple-gold medalist, returned home to multiple television appearances. Though plagued by shoulder and knee pain, he never lost his desire to swim. In 2001, he won gold medals in the 100-

meter backstroke and 4×100-medley relay at the World Maccabiah Games in Israel. Afterward, he was forced to take some time off for shoulder and knee surgeries. When he got back into the pool, he concentrated on the 100-meter backstroke and switched training programs. He chose to train with Dr. Dave Salo, who had coached several Olympians, including Peirsol, to success.

Lenny made the 2004 Olympic team. He was team captain and Michael Phelps's roommate at the Olympic Village in Athens, Greece. Despite shoulder pain, Lenny swam to a fourth-place finish in the 100-meter backstroke, missing the bronze medal by just two one-hundredths of a second. Peirsol took the gold medal and set a new world record. Lenny earned his fourth Olympic gold as a member of the 4×100-meter medley relay team.

After Athens, Lenny had another shoulder surgery and turned his attention to other pursuits. He had always wanted to give back to the Los Angeles community that had embraced him as an immigrant. In 2003, he established the Lenny Krayzelburg Foundation to help teach underprivileged children in inner-city Los Angeles how to swim. In 2005, he opened the Lenny Krayzelburg Swim Schools at Los Angeles-area Jewish community centers. That same year, he and his wife, Irina, had twin daughters.

Lenny announced his retirement from competitive swimming just before the 2008 Olympic trials.

Decidedly humble, he had been honored to represent the United States in two Olympic Games. As a former Olympian, he looked forward to further promoting swimming.

Summary

Four-time Olympic gold medalist and former backstroke world-record holder, Lenny Krayzelburg worked hard to overcome obstacles the typical U.S. team athlete does not even think about. He struggled to learn English in his adopted country and to help his family financially as well as find the time and the means to train.

Elizabeth Ferry Slocum, updated by Sheri Woodburn

Additional Sources

Arenofsky, Janice. "Strokes of Genius." *Boys' Life* 90 (August, 2000): 44.

Donnelly, Sally P. "Lenny Krayzelburg: The Ukrainian-Born Backstroker Takes Three Golds, Showing the Aussies Who Rules the Pool." *Time* 156 (October 2, 2000): 84.

Gruner, Brandon. "Worlds Apart." *Sport* 91 (April, 2000): 74.

Hamilton, Erik, and Dave Salo. "A Lifetime Opportunity." *Swimming Technique,* January 1, 2004.

Michaelis, Vicki. "Krayzelburg Getting His Stroke Back." *USA Today,* January 18, 2007, C14.

Montville, Leigh. "Stroke of Luck." *Sports Illustrated* 93 (August 21, 2000): 44.

Ingrid Kristiansen

Born: March 21, 1956
Trondheim, Norway
Also known as: Ingrid Christensen (birth name)

Early Life

Ingrid Kristiansen was born on March 21, 1956, in Trondheim, Norway, approximately 240 miles north of the capital city of Oslo. Her family name was Christensen. Her father worked in the oil industry, and her mother reared the family's children. Ingrid has one older brother. From the time she was a young girl, Ingrid loved both cross-country (Nordic) skiing and running. Her parents found that the only way to keep her from running and skiing in the countryside until late at night was to lock her skis and running shoes in a special compartment after dinner. At the age of fifteen, she qualified for her national track team in the 1,500 meters in the European championships. She did not lose a Nordic ski race between the ages of twelve and sixteen. Ingrid was a truly gifted athlete as a youth.

The Road to Excellence

Ingrid continued to compete in both sports with great success for several years. Her skiing career reached its peak in 1976, when she was an alternate on the Norwegian Olympic ski team. In addition to athletics, she began working as a medical technician upon completing her formal education.

In 1981, Ingrid married Arve Kristiansen and moved with him to the town of Stavanger, on Norway's west coast. The area's milder temperatures allowed her to run year-round for the first time, and she began to concentrate solely on running. Perhaps her most remarkable asset was her versatility. Ingrid possessed both the speed to run the 5,000 meters and the endurance to run the 26.2-mile distance of the marathon.

In the early part of her career, Ingrid competed in the shadow of fellow Norwegian Grete Waitz, whose many achievements in running made her a national heroine. Ingrid finished second to Waitz more than twenty times in the Norwegian championships and began to doubt if she could ever beat her older rival. However, she did not give up.

In January, 1983, Ingrid won the women's division of the Houston Marathon. In August of the same year, she gave birth to a son, Gaute. With the Olympics just one year away, Ingrid began training intensely for the marathon, in which Waitz would run as well. As a wife and new mother, Ingrid had to work hard to meet the many demands of her family life and running career.

In April, 1984, Ingrid attained her first victories over Waitz in a series of shorter races and seemed ready to challenge for a medal at the first-ever women's Olympic Marathon in Los Angeles. However, Ingrid finished fourth in the race, while Waitz won a silver medal. American Joan Benoit was the winner. Ingrid was disappointed by the outcome,

Ingrid Kristiansen running 10,000 meters during the 1988 Olympic Games in Seoul. (Bob Thomas/Getty Images)

587

but she never lost her desire or determination to improve. As she later said, "In this sport, you can never look back; you always must look to the next one."

The Emerging Champion

By the end of 1984, Ingrid was running with renewed confidence under the guidance of a new coach. Although she believed strongly in herself, not even she could have predicted the success that was soon to follow. On April 21, 1985, all of Ingrid's years of hard training paid off in stunning fashion, as she won the London Marathon in 2:21:06, a world-record time for women. She seemed to run effortlessly over the course, displaying her trademark fluid style.

For the next two years, Ingrid dominated the women's division of her sport. She not only claimed victories in the Boston and Chicago Marathons but also set world records in the 5,000- and 10,000-meter distances on the track. She became the first runner, male or female, to hold world records simultaneously in the 5,000 meters, 10,000 meters, and marathon. In 1986, *Runner's World* magazine chose her as female runner of the year.

In 1987, Ingrid's success continued; she earned the gold medal in the 10,000 meters at the World Track and Field Championships and won the London Marathon for a second time. Once more, she looked forward to the Olympics, but her bad luck in the Olympics followed her to Seoul, South Korea, in 1988. After leading in the early stages of the 10,000-meter race, Ingrid pulled up lame with a foot injury. Even though she held the world record at the distance, she failed to win a medal.

A world-class runner must be able to rebound from defeat and disappointment. Ingrid showed

Major Marathon Competitions

Year	Competition	Event	Place	Time
1983	Houston Marathon	Marathon	1st	
1984	Houston Marathon	Marathon	1st	2:24:26
	London Marathon	Marathon	1st	2:24.26
1985	London Marathon	Marathon	1st	2:21:06 WR
1986	Boston Marathon	Marathon	1st	2:24:55
	Chicago Marathon	Marathon	1st	2:27:08
	European Championships	10,000 meters	1st	30:23.25
	Oslo	10,000 meters	1st	30:13.74 WR
	Stockholm	5,000 meters	1st	14:37.33 WR
1987	London Marathon	Marathon	1st	2:22:48
	World Championships	10,000 meters	1st	31:05.85
1988	World Championships	Cross-Country	1st	
	London Marathon	Marathon	1st	2:25:41
1989	Boston Marathon	Marathon	1st	2:24:33
	New York Marathon	Marathon	1st	2:25:3

Note: WR = World Record

that she possessed this admirable quality after the Olympics. In addition to her extraordinary physical talents, she exhibited the personal determination and resiliency of a champion in 1989. She moved to Boulder, Colorado, and undertook a grueling training schedule in the high altitudes of the Rocky Mountains. Her efforts were rewarded with victories at the Boston Marathon, where she defeated her 1984 Olympic rival Benoit, and the New York City Marathon. By the end of the year, she was once again honored as the female runner of the year.

Continuing the Story

The new decade brought a new addition to Ingrid's life. She took a break from competitive running to return to Norway and give birth to her second child. Her daughter, Marte, was born on August 1, 1990. A woman of many interests, Ingrid has said that leading a balanced life has been crucial to her athletic success. She loves to spend time at home with her family and to cook and knit. She has also worked as a medical technician at a cancer-research institute and has coached younger runners. She especially likes to visit girls' groups and to encourage young women to participate in athletics.

Despite all that she accomplished, Ingrid continually strove to better her level of performance, especially in the marathon. She has said, "As long as I will run, I will keep trying to

Records and Milestones

First runner to hold world records simultaneously in 5,000 meters, 10,000 meters, and marathon

Honors and Awards

1986-87, 1989	*Runner's World* Magazine Female Runner of the Year
1992	Abebe Bikila Award

break 2:20. It's the motivation for my training. It's something I think I can make." Despite her desire to break the 2:20 mark, Ingrid took a break from running in the early 1990's to devote more time to her family and return to her skiing roots. At the age of forty, she returned to marathon running, though for the pleasure of competing rather than for the thrill of breaking records.

Summary

Ingrid Kristiansen's record-setting performances in events ranging from the 5,000 meters to the marathon distinguished her as one of the greatest runners of all time. Her outstanding achievements helped bring a new measure of respect to women runners in what was once a male-dominated sport.

Throughout her career, she ran with the strength, speed, courage, and grace of a champion.

Mark J. Madigan

Additional Sources

Rutledge, Rachel. *Women of Sports: The Best of the Best in Track and Field.* Brookfield, Conn.: Millbrook Press, 1999.

Sandrock, Michael. *Running with the Legends.* Champaign, Ill.: Human Kinetics, 1996.

Switzer, Kathrine. *Marathon Woman: Running the Race to Revolutionize Women's Sports.* New York: Carroll & Graf, 2007.

Wallechinsky, David, and Jaime Loucky. *The Complete Book of the Olympics: 2008 Edition.* London: Aurum Press, 2008.

Petra Kronberger

Born: February 21, 1969
       Pfarrwerfen, Austria

Early Life

Petra Kronberger was born on February 21, 1969, near Pfarrwerfen, Austria. Her father, Heinrich, was a truck driver, and her mother, Waltraud, was a cleaning woman and dishwasher. The family did not have much money and was forced to live with Petra's maternal grandparents on their farm in the Austrian countryside.

When Petra was two years old, her younger brother became ill and died. She felt the loss of her brother very deeply and lost herself in physical activities, becoming something of a tomboy. At the age of two, she began to ski. Within four years, at the age of six, she won her first skiing event.

The Road to Excellence

In Austria, skiing is more than a sport. Citizens revere skiing almost as if it were a religion. In order to meet this strong interest in the sport, special Austrian schools combine ski training with academics. When Petra was ten, it was suggested to her parents that she be enrolled in the ski school at Bad Gastein. By age fourteen, Petra had transferred to a commercial school in Schladming, where she learned banking and attended a nearby ski academy. Here, she started to draw the attention of prominent leaders in Austrian skiing.

In 1984, at Schladming, legendary coach Andreas Rauch first caught sight of the tall fifteen-year-old Petra. Rauch had coached the Austrian men's downhill team in 1980 and the U.S. men's downhill team for four years. At the 1984 Sarajevo

Petra Kronberger skiing in the slalom at the 1992 Winter Olympic Games in Albertville. (Gerard Malie/AFP/Getty Images)

Major Skiing Championships

Year	Competition	Event	Place
1988	Olympic Games	Combined	11th
		Downhill	6th
1990	World Cup	Overall	1st
1991	World Championships	Downhill	1st
	World Cup	Overall	1st
		Slalom	1st
1992	Olympic Games	Combined	Gold
		Slalom	Gold
	World Cup	Overall	1st

eleventh in the combined. Her finish in the combined was a slight disappointment, since she had been expected to medal in the event.

A devoutly religious woman, Petra kept a good mental attitude toward her sport. She credited her faith and her coach with keeping her strong psychologically. "I also try to keep friends around me who will just talk plain with me and not put me in bad places," she added. In 1989, Petra excelled. She had back-to-back victories in her favorite event, the downhill. Under the advice of her coaches, Petra began to spend more time on her slalom technique. As a result, she became almost unbeatable.

Winter Olympics, the Austrian team had its worst showing ever, failing to win a single medal, and Rauch returned to his homeland to help bring Austria back to prominence in skiing. When he saw Petra ski, he was fascinated with her determination, talent, and tenacity.

By 1985, Petra was training with the Austrian national ski team under the critical eye of Rauch. In 1986, she began to race in junior meets sponsored by the International Ski Federation (FIS). By 1987, she moved up to the Europa Cup races, in which she had tremendous success and showed great promise. Rauch was bringing her along slowly, so that she would have the confidence and, therefore, success on the slopes. His thought it best for her to learn how to win before moving up to the World Cup circuit.

The Emerging Champion

Although she had one of the best coaches in the world, Petra felt that she was going nowhere, and she seriously questioned if she wanted to continue in the sport. She was plagued by the self-doubt that every teenager experiences; in addition, she was suffering from a chronic ankle injury that hampered her throughout her entire career. As she gradually started to win events, however, she gained self-confidence and began to believe in her own abilities.

Petra was strong in all five of the skiing events: the slalom, the giant slalom, the super-giant slalom, the downhill, and the combined. By the end of the 1987 season, she was on the Austrian "B" team. In 1988, she was promoted to the "A" team just in time for the Winter Olympics in Calgary. In the Olympics, she placed sixth in the downhill and

Continuing the Story

Petra won the overall World Cup title for the 1989-1990 season. As her victories mounted, she was compared to the skiing greats of the past—especially to Annemarie Moser-Pröell, who dominated women's skiing in the 1970's and who had been Austria's last great female champion. Petra seemed to only get stronger as the 1992 Albertville Winter Games approached.

In December, 1990, Petra became the first woman to win races in all of the individual events. On January 26, 1991, in front of her fellow countrymen in Saalbach-Hinterglemm, Austria, she won the world downhill championship, but an injury in the super-giant slalom at the same meet forced her to retire for the season. Even though she did not compete for the rest of the season, she still defended her World Cup overall title by more than one hundred points more than her closest challenger. By the time of the Albertville Games, Petra had won fifteen World Cup races.

Before the Winter Olympics, many experts had predicted that Petra would walk away with more than one gold medal. Characteristically, she put everything in perspective by mentioning that she would be happy with whatever came her way. Although she was the most dominant and versatile woman skier in the world, she still realized that anything could happen.

Honors, Awards, and Records

1990-93	Austrian Sportswoman of the Year
1992	Amateur Athletic Foundation World Trophy
	Austrian Golden Badge of Honor

The skiing events started with the combined competition. Petra easily won the gold medal in the event, and the media again began to predict a Kronberger Olympics. Her next event was her favorite, the downhill. Petra had a good run on the fast Meribel course, but not good enough to take over first place from Germany's Katja Seizinger. By the end of the competition—the closest women's Olympic downhill ever—Petra had finished fifth, only .18 second out of first. Petra redeemed herself with a gold medal in the slalom. Austrian women's skiing had returned, with five medals, under the leadership of Petra Kronberger. After finishing first overall in the 1992 World Cup championships, Petra decided to retire from competitive skiing.

Summary

Petra Kronberger's career was brief but spectacular. Between 1988 and 1992, she won sixteen World Cup races—including three consecutive overall ti- tles—one world championship, and two Olympic gold medals. A great champion, not only on the slopes but also in her everyday life, she always kept track of her values and placed sports in perspective. She is an example of how an athlete can be a champion and still enjoy the companionship and re- spect of opponents.

Rusty Wilson

Additional Sources

Fry, John. *The Story of Modern Skiing*. Hanover, N.H.: University Press of New England, 2006.

Levinson, David, and Karen Christensen, eds. *Encyclopedia of World Sport: From Ancient to Present*. Santa Barbara, Calif.: ABC-Clio, 1996.

Lipoński, Wojciech. *World Sports Encyclopedia*. St. Paul, Minn.: Motorbooks International, 2003.

Wallechinsky, David, and Jaime Loucky. *The Complete Book of the Winter Olympics*. Wilmington, Del.: Sport Media, 2005.

Jari Kurri

Born: May 18, 1960
　　　Helsinki, Etelä-Suomen, Finland
Also known as: Jari Pekka Kurri (full name);
　Dynamo; the Finnish Flash; Jartsi; Master of
　the One-Timer; Poika

Early Life

Jari Pekka Kurri was born on May 18, 1960, in Helsinki, Etelä-Suomen, Finland, to Ville and Liisa Kurri. While a young boy he was adept at several sports, such as soccer and track and field. However, in hockey, he demonstrated the most promise. Jari's father, a sport trainer, drove him to the local rinks, where the young athlete excelled. Jari joined the Jokerit Helsinki hockey club and dreamed of playing with his idols in the Elite Ice Hockey League and of Olympic wins on the Finnish national team. He practiced extensively and worked his way up the ranks. He advanced to the senior division of the

Jari Kurri in 1985. (Bruce Bennett/Getty Images)

Jokerit's club and made his way into the Elite League. There, he played three seasons, increasing his scoring productivity each year. The following year, Jari got his wish to play on the Finnish junior national team. Over the next three years the hockey prodigy made his mark and established a name for himself in professional hockey.

The Road to Excellence

Playing for the Finnish team against the Soviet Union at the 1978 European Junior Hockey Championship, Jari scored the winning goal in double overtime. This earned his team the gold. Jari was deemed the tournament's best forward. Two years later, Jari again led his team to success, tying for lead scorer and taking a silver medal at the 1980 world junior tournament. That same year, Jari, a right winger, was named to Finland's 1980 Olympic team. He caught the attention of Glen Sather, general manager and head coach of the Edmonton Oilers. At twenty years old, Jari received a contract from the Oilers.

The Emerging Champion

Though Jari was reticent about moving to North America because he knew little English, he was persuaded by fellow countrymen Matti Hagman and Risto Siltanen, who were playing for the Oilers, to come to Canada. Planning to stay for no more than two years, Jari was soon ensconced as the "Finnish Flash" and regarded as one of the team's most complete players. He was soon paired with the legendary center Wayne Gretzky on a line that stunned crowds with record-setting and record-breaking plays. In 1984, the Oilers captured the Stanley Cup, and Jari took the Lady Byng Trophy for sportsmanship. In 1986, he was joined by left winger Esa Tikkanen; the two became an instrumental part of "The Finnish Sandwich." From 1985 to 1988, Jari and Gretzky helped the team to three more Stanley Cups. Jari made the all-star team in each year.

　Though some doubted whether Jari could sustain his high level of play after Gretzky was traded to the Los Angeles Kings in 1988, Jari continued to

NHL Statistics

Season	GP	G	Ast.	Pts.	PIM
1980-81	75	32	43	75	40
1981-82	71	32	54	86	32
1982-83	80	45	59	104	22
1983-84	64	52	61	113	14
1984-85	73	71	64	135	30
1985-86	78	68	63	131	22
1986-87	79	54	54	108	41
1987-88	80	43	53	96	30
1988-89	76	44	58	102	69
1989-90	78	33	60	93	48
1991-92	73	23	37	60	24
1992-93	82	27	60	87	38
1993-94	81	31	46	77	48
1994-95	38	10	19	29	24
1995-96	71	18	27	45	39
1996-97	82	13	22	35	12
1997-98	70	5	17	22	12
Totals	1,251	601	797	1,398	545

Notes: GP = games played; G = goals; Ast. = assists; Pts. = points; PIM = penalties in minutes

He became the general manager of the Finnish national team. In 2001, he was inducted into the Hockey Hall of Fame, the first Finnish player to be so honored.

Summary

From the start of his career, Jari Kurri made a significant impact on hockey. At eighteen, he scored the goal that helped his country to gold medal at 1978 European Junior Hockey Championships. As the best forward of the tournament, Jari went on to help his team earn Finland's first world championship medal. By 1980, Jari's efforts earned him not only a place in the Olympics but also prompted the Edmonton Oilers to choose him in the NHL draft. With the Oilers, Jari helped his team to five Stanley Cups and led the league in goals. Furthermore, he played in four world championships and won a silver medal with Finland in 1994. In the same year he won a bronze medal at the Olympics. Jari set, tied, or broke a number of records for goals by a right winger. Jari became the first European-trained player and the eighth NHL player to record 600 career goals and was regarded as one of the best defensive forwards in the NHL.

Roxanne McDonald

break records. By the 1989-90 season, Jari, the "Master of the One-Timer," became the twenty-fifth NHL player to reach the 1,000-point mark, had led the team to a fifth Stanley Cup, and had made the all-star team again. These feats drew the attention of the owner of the Milano Devils, an Italian team, which courted Jari until he agreed to a two-year contract. His contract stipulated that he be released to play for Finland in the Ice Hockey World Championships and be permitted the year after that to return to North America.

Continuing the Story

After Jari's season in Italy, he was traded to the Philadelphia Flyers. Then, he joined the Kings, and, once again, Jari and Gretzky proved to be a formidable duo. In 1993, they led the team to its first Stanley Cup Finals appearance. Following five seasons with the Kings, Jari signed with Anaheim's Mighty Ducks, helping to mentor emerging hockey greats such as Teemu Selanne. By the end of the 1996-1997 season, Jari considered retiring from the game. Instead, he took an offer to play for the Colorado Avalanche. During this period he scored his 600th career goal. Jari, the highest-scoring European-born player in NHL history, finally ended his career in 1998.

Additional Sources

Davidson, John, and Chris McDonell. *For the Love of Hockey: Hockey Stars' Personal Stories.* Tonawanda, N.Y.: Firefly Books, 2007.

Gallo-Stenman, Patricia, and Magnus Lofving. "Breaking the Ice with Jari and Esa." *Finnish Trade Review* 8 (December, 1991): 6.

Mennander, Ari, and Jim Matheson. *Jari Kurri: An Authorized Autobiography.* n.p.: Kurri Productions, 2001.

Honors, Awards, and Milestones

1978	European Junior Hockey Championships all-star
	European Junior Hockey Championships, Best Forward
1980	World Junior Hockey Champion (with Finland)
1983-90, 1993, 1998	NHL all-star
1984-85, 1987-88, 1990	Stanley Cup Champion (with Edmonton Oilers)
1985	Lady Byng Memorial Trophy
1991, 1994	Ice Hockey World Championships all-star
1994	Silver medal, Ice Hockey World Championships
	Bronze medal, Olympic Games
1998	Highest-scoring European-born player in NHL history
2001	Inducted into Hockey Hall of Fame

Michelle Kwan

Born: July 7, 1980
    Torrance, California
Also known as: Michelle Wing Kwan (full name);
    Guan Yingshan

Early Life

Michelle Kwan was born on July 7, 1980, in Torrance, California, the youngest of three children of Chinese immigrants and restaurant owners Danny and Estella Kwan. Michelle took gymnastics lessons at a young age but became interested in ice skating after watching her older brother, Ron, play ice hockey. Soon, she was enjoying group lessons at the local rink, where she fell in love with the sensation she described as flying across the ice. Two years later, Michelle watched on television as American Brian Boitano captured the gold medal in men's figure skating at the 1988 Calgary Winter Olympics, and her own Olympic dreams were born.

The Road to Excellence

Michelle began competing successfully at the local level when she was eight years old. She quickly ascended the various skill levels within the United States Figure Skating Association, the national governing body for figure skating. The Kwan family sacrificed time and money to finance the increasingly expensive careers of Michelle and her sister Karen. The family sold its house, and the sisters competed in used skates and shared tights and homemade costumes. At times, they were forced to skate without lessons and without a coach.

When Michelle reached the junior level, she required more intensive training. The family took weekend trips to the world-renowned Ice Castle International Training Center in Lake Arrowhead, California. A family friend arranged for Michelle and her sister to audition with coach Frank Carroll, who later stated that he realized Michelle's potential at that first lesson; Carroll started coaching both sisters. They received scholarships to live and train at Ice Castle, and Michelle continued her education with private tutors.

In 1992, Michelle finished ninth at her first Junior National Figure Skating Championships and was impatient to move up to the senior level of competition. Her new coach felt that she should wait another year, but a determined Michelle passed her skills test when Carroll was out of town and became a senior skater. In 1993, she qualified for her first Senior National Figure Skating Championships and finished sixth.

Michelle Kwan skating in the 2002 World Figure Skating Championships in Japan. (Koji Aoki/AFLO/Getty Images)

The Emerging Champion

Michelle achieved national recognition at the 1994 United States Figure Skating Championship in the wake of the heavily publicized attack on skater Nancy Kerrigan and the growing scandal surrounding skater Tonya Harding. Michelle captured the silver medal and went to the 1994 Winter Olympics in Norway as an alternate. She competed at her first World Figure Skating Championship that same year and finished eighth. The following year, Michelle again won silver at the United States Figure Skating Championship and finished fourth at the World Figure Skating Championship with a flawless performance. She also began her long association with the Campbell's Soups Tour of World Figure Skating Champions (later renamed Champions on Ice).

Michelle had earned a reputation as a skilled athlete but felt her youthful appearance and athletic emphasis were impeding her. She realized that great skaters must be both athletes and artists, so she worked with her coach and Canadian choreographer Lori Nichol to improve her artistry. Michelle began the 1996 season with graceful new programs and a more mature appearance. Her transformation was rewarded when she won her

Major Figure-Skating Championships

Year	Competition	Place	Year	Competition	Place
1992	Pacific Coast Junior	3d	1997 (cont.)	Thrifty Car Rental Skate America	1st
	U.S. Junior Championships	9th		Skate Canada	1st
	Southwest Pacific Junior	1st	1998	Olympic Games	Silver
1993	Pacific Coast Senior	1st		Ultimate Four	1st
	Southwest Pacific Senior	1st		Goodwill Games	1st
	U.S. Championships	6th		Grand Slam of Figure Skating	1st
	Gardena Spring Trophy	1st		Keri Lotion Figure Skating Classic	1st
	U.S. Olympic Festival	1st		U.S. Pro Classic	1st
	Skate America	7th		Masters of Figure Skating	1st
1994	U.S. Championships	2d		World Professional Championships	1st
	World Championships	8th	1999	Skate Canada	1st
	World Junior Championships	1st		World Championships	2d
	Hershey's Kisses Pro-Am Championships	1st		Hershey's Kisses (Team)	2d
	Goodwill Games	2d		Keri Lotion Figure Skating Classic (Team USA)	2d
	U.S. Outdoor Challenge	1st			
	Skate America	2d		Masters of Figure Skating	1st
	Trophy de France	3d		Skate America	1st
	Thrifty Car Rental International Challenge	3d		Japan Open	1st
1995	Best of the Best	2d		Hershey's Kisses—USA vs. World (Team)	1st
	World Championships	4th		Skate Canada	1st
	Hershey's Kisses International Challenge	1st	2000	Grand Prix Final	2d
	World Team Challenge	4th		International Figure Skating Challenge (Team)	2d
	Skate America	1st			
	Skate Canada	1st		Japan Open	1st
	Nations Cup	1st		Skate Canada	2d
	U.S. Postal Service Challenge (Team)	1st		World Championships	1st
1995, 1997	U.S. Championships	2d	2001	World Championships	1st
1996	Trophee Lalique	1st		Skate Canada	3d
	Champions Series Final	1st		Skate America	1st
	Thrifty Car Rental Skate America	1st		National Championships	1st
	The Continents Cup	1st		Grand Prix Final	2d
	Ultimate Four	1st	2002	Grand Prix Final	2d
	U.S. Postal Service Challenge (Team)	1st		National Championships	1st
	Hershey's Kisses Challenge (Team)	1st		Skate America	1st
	Centennial on Ice	3d		World Championships	2d
1996, 1998, 2000-01	World Championships	1st		Olympic Games	Bronze
1996, 1998-2001	U.S. Championships	1st	2003	National Championships	1st
1997	World Championships	2d		World Championships	1st
	Japan Open	1st	2004	World Championships	3d
	Hershey's Kisses Challenge (Team)	1st		National Championships	1st
	Champions Series Final	2d	2005	National Championships	1st
	Nice 'N Easy Classic (Team)	2d			

first national and world championships at the age of fifteen. She had earned a reputation as one of the finest artists in figure skating without sacrificing her technical abilities.

Continuing the Story

Michelle struggled to adjust to her new role as defending world champion and lost both her national and world titles to rising young star Tara Lipinski. The experience taught Michelle the importance of self-confidence, and she triumphed over self-doubt. Michelle entered the 1998 Olympic season with a renewed love for her sport. However, she was soon diagnosed with a stress fracture in one of her toes and was forced to spend three weeks with her foot in a cast, difficult for someone who had not spent more than two consecutive days off the ice since she was five years old. She entered the 1998 United States Figure Skating Championships unsure of her recovery but recaptured the national title with two of the best performances in the event's history, earning a record total of fifteen perfect scores from the judges.

Michelle went to the 1998 Winter Olympics in Nagano, Japan, with hopes of fulfilling three childhood wishes: to go to the Olympics, to skate well, and to win the gold medal. Michelle skated two elegant, emotional, and near-flawless performances, capturing the silver medal. She showed her characteristic graciousness despite her disappointment in losing to Lipinski and won widespread acclaim for her sportsmanship. Michelle later stated in her autobiography that she cherished her silver medal as a representation of her past accomplishments as well as her plans for the future.

Michelle won a second world championship in 1998 and two more national championships, in 1999 and 2000. Despite her continued success, Michelle had doubts about her ability to keep up, because of her age, with her sport's growing technical demands. She put aside the doubts and approached the 2000 World Figure Skating Championships with determination and discipline, delivering what many reporters called the best performance of her career and claiming her third world title. She won the national title again in 2001, the fourth consecutive and the fifth of her career.

In 2002, experts predicted the Olympic gold medal would go to Michelle or Irina Slutskaya of Russia. Although leading after the short program, Michelle had a flawed performance in her free skate and received the bronze medal. She won the World Figure Skating Championship in 2003 and the United States Figure Skating Championships from 2003 to 2005. At the 2005 national championships, she finished fourth, falling one place short of receiving a medal.

In spite of a hip injury, Michelle continued to train for the 2006 Olympics. In January, 2006, she had to withdraw from the United States Figure Skating Championships because of an abdominal injury. After suffering from a groin injury during practice in Turin, Italy, Michelle was replaced on the Olympic team by Emily Hughes. Michelle underwent arthroscopic surgery in August, 2006, and did not compete during the 2006-2007 season.

Summary

Michelle Kwan's discipline, sportsmanship, and love for figure skating sustained her through a career filled with both disappointments and triumphs. Her successful blend of artistry and athleticism made her a model for younger skaters in a sport increasingly dominated by technical demands. Her gracefulness on the ice and sportsmanship off the ice left a lasting impact on the sport of figure skating.

Marcella Bush Trevino,
updated by Kathryn A. Cochran

Additional Sources

Epstein, Edward Z. *Born to Skate: The Michelle Kwan Story.* New York: Ballantine Books, 1997.

Hill, Anne E. *Michelle Kwan.* Minneapolis: LernerSports, 2004.

Koestler-Grack, Rachel A. *Michelle Kwan.* New York: Chelsea House, 2007.

Kwan, Michelle, and Laura James. *Heart of a Champion: An Autobiography.* New York: Scholastic, 1997.

_____. *The Winning Attitude! Michelle Kwan: What It Takes to Be a Champion.* New York: Hyperion, 1999.

Peterson, Todd. *Michelle Kwan: Figure Skater.* New York: Ferguson, 2006.

Guy Lafleur

Born: September 20, 1951
    Thurso, Quebec, Canada
Also known as: Guy Damien Lafleur (full name);
    the Flower

Early Life
On September 20, 1951, Guy Damien Lafleur was born in Thurso, Quebec, Canada, a paper-mill town of three thousand French-speaking inhabitants. Thurso is located twenty-five miles downriver from Canada's capital, Ottawa, and lies on the edge of a vast northern wilderness.

Guy was the only boy in a family of five children born to Rejean and Pirrette Lafleur. Guy's father, a welder at the town's huge McLaren pulp mill, bought Guy ice skates when he was four, and the boy quickly took to hockey. From age seven, the youngster's main nonschool activities were helping the priest to serve mass, and, above all else, playing hockey. Guy's chief boyhood idol was Montreal Canadiens star Jean Beliveau. Guy wore Beliveau's number 4 on his own jersey and kept a poster of the player in his room.

The Road to Excellence
At the age of eight, Guy began an accelerated advance through the organized youth hockey leagues. When he was eleven, Guy first came to the attention of scouts as he led Thurso to the Class C championship in the 1962 Quebec City International Pee Wee Tournament. In 1965, a Quebec amateur team invited Guy to play for them. Guy's father felt that he was too young at fourteen to leave home but relented the next year when a second offer came. Over the next five seasons, Guy played at center and right wing for the Quebec Junior A Remparts. Guy finished high school during this time.

Both Gaston Marcotte, who instructed Guy at Laval University's hockey school, and Rempart's coach Maurice Filion, praised Guy's determination and hard work. He was the first one to the rink and the last to leave.

Guy's 103 goals in the 1969-1970 season were a junior hockey record. The next year, in his final amateur season, Guy led Quebec to a league title and national championship with an unbelievable 130 goals and 79 assists. During these years, Guy, whose last name translates to "the flower," was treated like royalty in Quebec City and was a national hero in French Canada. The crowds that filled Quebec's ten-thousand-seat stadium just to see Guy play included National Hockey League (NHL) scouts. Guy was the first player chosen in the 1971 NHL amateur draft, going to the Montreal Canadiens.

The Emerging Champion
As early as 1968, Montreal Canadiens owner Sam Pollock schemed to acquire Guy in the 1971 draft. The Canadiens manipulated to get the first pick through frantic trades and deals with the league's poorest teams.

Guy Lafleur during his years with the Montreal Canadiens. (Courtesy of Amateur Athletic Foundation of Los Angeles)

The tremendous publicity that preceded Guy's arrival in Montreal and the NHL put great pressure on the shy, reserved rookie. Excited fans anticipated at least fifty goals per season and were calling Guy a "second Beliveau." Guy had respectable point totals in his first three seasons but fell short of expectations. In a game during his third season, however, the soft-spoken right wing gave teammates a hint of great things to come when he faked out the whole Chicago Blackhawks team and skated through them as if they were not even there. Canadiens team captain Henri Richard's astounded comment was, "Did you see that? No one can do that."

"The flower" suddenly blossomed with the 1974-1975 season; he discarded his helmet, played aggressively, and regained confidence. For six successive seasons, Guy established himself as the NHL's most exciting and dominating player. He also brought the Canadiens back to the top of the hockey world, leading them to four straight Stanley Cups from 1975-1976 to 1979-1980.

Before games, Guy was high-strung. He would arrive at the arena several hours early and sit in the dressing room breaking sticks over a tabletop to release pent-up tension. Once on the ice, the 6-foot, 175-pound wing combined relentless, blinding speed with a powerful, deadly accurate shot rated by many as the toughest to stop in hockey. He passed beautifully, moved instinctively, and played with the grace and artistry of a ballet star. Guy could stop, start, zigzag, or suddenly accelerate more quickly than opponents. His heroics frequently had adoring fans at the Forum on their feet screaming "Guy, Guy, Guy."

Continuing the Story

From 1974-1975 to 1979-1980, Guy consistently scored more than 50 goals and 100 points while

NHL Statistics

Season	GP	G	Ast.	Pts.	PIM
1971-72	73	29	35	64	48
1972-73	69	28	27	55	51
1973-74	73	21	35	56	29
1974-75	70	53	66	119	37
1975-76	80	56	69	125	36
1976-77	80	56	80	136	20
1977-78	78	60	72	132	26
1978-79	80	52	77	129	28
1979-80	74	50	75	125	12
1980-81	51	27	43	70	29
1981-82	66	27	99	84	24
1982-83	68	27	49	76	12
1983-84	80	30	40	70	19
1984-85	19	2	3	5	10
1988-89	67	18	27	45	12
1989-90	39	12	22	34	4
1990-91	59	12	16	28	2
Totals	1,126	560	835	1,353	399

Notes: GP = games played; G = goals; Ast. = assists; Pts. = points; PIM = penalties in minutes

making the all-star team six times. He was the NHL's scoring champion three times, twice its most valuable player (MVP), and once its playoff MVP. Guy was so popular that Montreal journalists considered his every utterance and gesture newsworthy.

Guy's career unexpectedly took a downward turn with the 1980-1981 season. A knee injury was followed by an auto collision in which Guy fell asleep at the wheel of his Corvette in the early morning hours. Over the next several seasons, Guy's point total dropped to roughly half his previous output and the coach reduced his playing time. In November, 1984, Guy, under pressure to quit, painfully announced his retirement at the age of thirty-three. All Quebec mourned.

Guy, one of hockey's all-time leading scorers, was inducted into the Hockey Hall of Fame in 1988, the same year he surprised the hockey world by coming out of retirement at the age of thirty-seven. He played one season with the New York Rangers and then signed with the Quebec Nordiques. Guy retired in fitting fashion. On March 30, 1991, 17,664 fans in the Montreal Forum gave him a nearly six-minute ovation. The next evening, when the Canadiens and Nordiques finished the regular season in Quebec City, 15,399 spectators clad in white honored "the flower" in an hour-long pregame ceremony.

Honors and Awards

1975-80	NHL First Team All-Star
1976-78	Art Ross Trophy
	Lester B. Pearson Award
1976, 1981	Team Canada Member
1977	Conn Smythe Trophy
	Sport magazine NHL Playoff MVP
1977-78	Hart Memorial Trophy
1988	Inducted into Hockey Hall of Fame
	Uniform number 10 retired by Montreal Canadiens

Following his final season as a player with the Nordiques, Guy joined the front office as director of corporate affairs for one season, after which he joined the private sector. When he was not piloting a helicopter, a passion that he compared to his love of hockey, Guy was a regular on the Oldtimer's Hockey Challenge tour and remained one of the most popular figures in Quebec—he became a knight in the Order of Quebec in 2005. In 1973, Guy married Quebec native Lise Barre. They had two sons, Martin and Mark.

Summary

Guy Lafleur was hockey's most popular and exciting player during the 1970's. His awesome skating and shooting ability prompted a 1980 hockey publication to refer to him as "the peerless one beyond question." The Canadiens were one of the most successful hockey teams of the 1970's and Guy was the catalyst.

David A. Crain

Additional Sources

McDonell, Chris. *For the Love of Hockey: Hockey Stars' Personal Stories.* Richmond Hill, Ont.: Firefly Books, 2004.

_____. *Hockey's Greatest Stars: Legends and Young Lions.* Richmond Hill, Ont.: Firefly Books, 2005.

MacInnis, Craig. *Remembering Guy Lafleur: A Celebration.* Vancouver, B.C.: Raincoast Books, 2004.

Bernard Lagat

Born: December 12, 1974
  Kaptel, near Kapsabet, Kenya
Also known as: Bernard Kipchirchir Lagat (full
  name)

Early Life

Bernard Kipchirchir Lagat was born in Kaptel, a small village in the Nandi District of the highlands of Kenya, a region known for producing great runners. His father, a peasant farmer, encouraged his children to get an education. For Bernard that meant 6 miles of running each day. In high school, however, he was an indifferent track competitor. His older sister, Mary Chepkemboi, overshadowed him as a runner and became an African champion in 1994. She gave Bernard his first pair of running shoes, and he always claimed her as his inspiration.

After finishing high school, Bernard entered Jomo Kenyatta University in Mangu, near the capital city of Nairobi. There a coach discovered his natural talent and encouraged him. After a year, Bernard received an invitation to study and train at Washington State University, where he followed in the steps of legendary Kenyan runners Henry Rono and Michael Kosgei.

The Road to Excellence

Between 1997 and 1999, Bernard emerged as a track phenomenon in the United States. In 1999, he won the National Collegiate Athletic Association championships in the indoor 3,000-meter and mile races and the outdoor 5,000 meters. He was an eleven-time all-American.

In 2000, Bernard ran at the Sydney Olympics under the Kenyan flag, although he had quietly received a green card for permanent residence in the United States shortly before, a fact he did not reveal publicly. To the surprise of many, he won a bronze medal in the 1,500-meter race, competing against world-class runners such as Hicham El Guerrouj of Morocco.

The Emerging Champion

In 2002, Bernard skipped the Commonwealth Games held in Manchester, England, to take part in the International Association of Athletics Federations

Bernard Lagat running in the 5,000-meter final during the 2008 Olympic Games in Beijing. (Olivier Morin/AFP/Getty Images)

(IAAF) Golden League, which awards the major prize money in track and field. Bernard was strongly criticized in his home country. However, he was openly critical of Kenyan officials for not giving more support for emerging runners and defended those who were forced into prize competitions in order to continue in their sport. Despite having gone professional, Bernard fulfilled his promise to his father, returning to Washington State to finish two degrees—in management information systems and econometrics. He continued to develop, running in a variety of races—800, 1,000, 1,500 meters—his best and preferred distance—1 mile, 2,000 meters, 3,000, 2 miles, and 5,000 meters. In 2001, Bernard set a personal best of 3 minutes 26.34 seconds in the 1,500-meters, which was the second-fastest time at that distance as of 2008. In international competition in the years after the Sydney Olympics, he won gold medals in the 2002 African Athletics Championships and the IAAF World Cup in Madrid, Spain.

Bernard was forced out of the 2003 World Track and Field Championships after he tested positive for a banned substance. A further sample cleared him, however, and he vehemently denied ever using drugs.

At the 2004 Athens Olympics, Bernard faced El Guerrouj, the world record holder, in the 1,500-meters. The race was one of the classics of track and field, as the two great competitors dueled for first place. Bernard was in the forefront in the homestretch. El Guerrouj took the gold in a final surge, which left Bernard with the silver medal. Always a gentleman, Bernard said afterward that he had no embarrassment at losing to El Guerrouj, "the best."

Bernard came to Athens as an American citizen but ran for Kenya, since international track regulations require a three-year wait before one can represent a new country. The fact that he kept his new

Major 1,500-meter Championships

Year	Competition	Place
2000	Olympic Games	Bronze
2001	World Championships	2d
2002	World Cup	1st
	African Championships	1st
2003	World Indoor Championships	2d
2004	World Indoor Championships	1st
	Olympic Games	Silver
2006	USA Championships	1st
2007	USA Championships	3d
	World Championships	1st
2008	U.S. Olympic trials	1st

citizenship secret caused some resentment later. Kenya does not accept dual citizenship, so technically, Bernard ran as a stateless person. When the American media revealed his U.S. citizenship a year after the Olympics, some critics thought he should surrender his medal, but no action was ever taken. He was penalized, however, and banned from championship events for three years. Consequently, several of his records were not ratified by American track organizations.

Bernard continued to medal at international races in the following years, especially in the mile and 1,500 meters. In 2007, he won the 1,500- and 5,000-meter races at the World Outdoor Track and Field Championships in Osaka, Japan, becoming the first athlete to win both events at the same World Championships.

Continuing the Story

Bernard qualified for the 2008 Beijing Olympics by winning the 1,500-meter and 5,000-meter trials. The three Americans who ran in the 1,500 meters were all naturalized citizens—Bernard; Leonel Manzano, who came from Mexico; and Lopez Lomong, one of the "lost boys" from Sudan. Bernard's hopes for double medals were dashed when he failed to make the final for the 1,500 meters and came in ninth in the 5,000 meters. Some observers speculated that Kenyan runners purposely boxed him in, but Bernard made no excuses.

Bernard's decision to take American citizenship was a personal one. After living in the United States for many years, he considered the country his home. He married an Ameri-

Milestones

National Collegiate Athletic Association indoor champion in the 3,000 meters and the mile (1999)

National Collegiate Athletic Association outdoor champion in the 5,000 meters (1999)

Eleven-time all-American

Became the first runner to win both the 1,500- and 5,000-meter races at the same World Outdoor Track and Field Championships (2007)

can sports trainer whom he met at Washington State, and they had a son. The family settled in Tucson, Arizona. Bernard was committed to promoting running in both the United States and the developing world. He started a foundation for poor Kenyans, which emphasized education before athletics.

Summary

Bernard Lagat became one of the greatest distance runners in track and field, especially at 1,500 meters. Though he did not win an Olympic gold medal in the event, he won gold medals in both the 1,500 meters and 5,000 meters at the World Track and Field Championships, becoming the first athlete to accomplish that feat.

Norbert Brockman

Additional Sources

Butler, Sarah. "Secrets of Olympians." *Runner's World* 43 (September, 2008): 76-79.

Layden, Tim. "A Runaway Victory." *Sports Illustrated* 107 (September 10, 2007): 54-58.

_____. "What a Country!" *Sports Illustrated* 109 (July 14, 2008): 58-60.

Wallechinsky, David, and Jaime Loucky. *The Complete Book of the Olympics: 2008 Edition*. London: Aurum Press, 2008.

Stéphane Lambiel

Born: April 2, 1985
   Martigny, Switzerland

Early Life

Stéphane Lambiel was born in Martigny, Switzerland, on April 2, 1985. Stéphane was the second child born to Jacques and Fernanda Lambiel. His father is Swiss and his mother is Portuguese. He spent his childhood in Saxon, Switzerland. He has an older sister, Silvia, who was born in 1982, and a younger brother, Christophe, who was born in 1989. His sister also skated as a child. Stéphane watched his sister and became mesmerized by the sport of skating. Soon, he began spending his evenings watching videos of figure skaters; a short time later, he started to practice jumps in the family garage. Although he was still in elementary school, Stéphane was dedicated to becoming a skater. When he was nine years old, he met Peter Grütter and Salomé Brunner. This was the beginning of Stéphane's serious work to become a world champion figure skater. Grütter became his coach and Brunner his choreographer. Every morning before school, Stéphane was driven by his mother to Geneva to take lessons and practice his skating.

The Road to Excellence

In 1997, at the World Figure Skating Championships held in Lausanne, Switzerland, Stéphane first came to the attention of the international skating world. At this time, he was already the Swiss novice men's champion, and he was asked to do an exhibition performance. He not only impressed the audience with his natural ability but also as a young skater capable of becoming a formidable competitor.

Stéphane continued competing in Switzerland and won seven consecutive senior titles. In 1998, he earned the title of Swiss junior men's champion. In 2000, he was the Swiss senior men's champion. In 2001, he placed fifth in the World Junior Figure Skating Championships and ninth in the European Figure Skating Championships. In 2002, he was old enough to enter senior international competition. The Swiss Skating Federation offered to send him to the 2002 Winter Olympics in Salt Lake City, Utah, if he placed twelfth or better in the European Figure Skating Championships.

The Emerging Champion

Stéphane earned his way to the 2002 Olympics by placing fourth in the European championships. At the Olympics, he finished fifteenth. At the World Figure Skating Championships, he placed eighteenth. In 2003, Stéphane had another successful year. He was fifth at the European Figure Skating Championships and tenth at the World Figure Skating Championships. In 2004, he placed sixth in Europe and fourth in the world. In the same year, he completed his secondary education and graduated with a concentration in biology and chemistry. Because of a knee injury, he was not able to compete in the Grand Prix of Figure Skating competition of 2004-2005; however, he sufficiently recovered from his injury to skate in the European championships in 2005 and place fourth.

In 2005, Stéphane became the world champion. Performing to the soundtrack from *King Arthur,* he dazzled the audience with two quadruple toe loops. He was the only skater at the competition to

Major Figure-Skating Championships

Year	Competition	Place
2002	Olympic Games	15th
	European Championships	4th
2003	World Championships	10th
	European Championships	5th
2004	World Championships	4th
	European Championships	6th
2005	World Championships	1st
	European Championships	4th
2006	Skate Canada	1st
	World Championships	1st
	Olympic Games	Silver
	European Championships	2d
2007	Grand Prix Italy	1st
	World Championships	3d
2008	World Championships	5th
	European Championships	2d

perform two of these difficult movements in a performance and became the first Swiss world champion since Hans Gerschwiler in 1947.

In 2006, Stéphane competed in the Olympics again. Although he did not go to the Olympics as the favorite, he did enter the event with an impressive record for the year. He went into the 2006 season as the world champion; in the Gran Prix competition, he had won two silver medals and was first in the Grand Prix final; and he finished second in the European Figure Skating Championships. Thus, although he was not viewed as the potential gold medalist, he ranked as a medal contender. Stéphane performed well overall and did a perfect quadruple-triple-double combination, earning him the Olympic silver medal. In the World Figure Skating Championships he once again took first place, thus becoming the first Swiss skater to win two world titles.

Continuing the Story

In 2006-2007, Stéphane experienced health problems and a sense of burnout. He skated successfully at Skate Canada, where he won the gold medal. However, health problems forced him to withdraw from the NHK Trophy competition. He recuperated and participated in the Swiss Figure Skating Championships, winning his seventh first-place finish in the event. He withdrew from the European Figure Skating Championships, citing exhaustion. In the 2007 World Figure Skating Championships in Tokyo, Japan, while performing his short program, he fell during his triple axel and finished in sixth place. Still, he took third place in the overall competition. Stéphane finished third in the Cup of China and second in the Cup of Russia and completed the season by winning the Grand Prix final for the second time.

In 2008, he competed in the European and World Figure Skating Championships. At the European event, he encountered some problem in his short program but impressed in his long program with an excellent flamenco routine that included a quad-double toe-loop double-loop combination. He won the silver medal. At the World event, he finished in fifth place overall.

Summary

With two World Figure Skating Championships, Stéphane Lambiel made an important contribution to the sport both in his technical expertise and in the consistency of his training and performance. He was coached throughout his career by former Olympian Peter Grütter. Salomé Brunner was his principal choreographer. Stéphane was talented technically, with the ability to spin and jump in both directions and perform double axels, changing the direction of rotation between each.

Shawncey Webb

Additional Sources

Hines, James B. *Figure Skating: A History.* Urbana: University of Illinois Press, 2006.

Kerrigan, Nancy, and Mary Spencer. *Artistry on Ice: Figure Skating Skills and Styles.* Champaign, Ill.: Human Kinetics, 2002.

Milton, Steve. *Figure Skating Now: Olympic and World Stars.* Buffalo, N.Y.: Firefly Books, 2003.

_____. *Figure Skating Today: The Next Wave of Stars.* Buffalo, N.Y.: Firefly Books, 2007.

Larisa Latynina

Born: December 27, 1934
      Kherson, Soviet Union (now in Ukraine)
Also known as: Larisa Semyonovna Latynina (full
    name); Larisa Semyonovna Dirij (birth name)

Early Life

Larisa Semyonovna Dirij was born on December 27, 1934, in Kherson, a city on the Dnieper River, about one hundred miles east of the Black Sea port of Odessa, Ukraine. She never knew her father, and her mother, a school custodian, died when Larisa was young, so Larisa grew up as an orphan. A desire for beauty amid the starkness, poverty, and war of her childhood led her to start studying ballet at the age of eleven.

Larisa Latynina on the balance beam during the 1956 Olympic Games in Melbourne. (AFP/Getty Images)

Larisa soon turned to gymnastics, bringing with her a classical balletic style, and by the age of sixteen, in 1951, she was the national girls' gymnastics champion in the schools division. She moved to the Ukraine capital of Kiev to study at the State Institute of Physical Culture. There she married Ivan Latynin, a ship engineer on Dnieper rivercraft, and from him took her professional name, Latynina.

The Road to Excellence

Unlike the majority of female gymnasts, who often begin their careers as teenagers and have only a few years of activity and prominence, Larisa began competing internationally in her early twenties and remained at the top of her field for the better part of a decade.

Larisa studied diligently through the early 1950's, earning the title of Honored Master of Sports in 1956. Given her classical background, Larisa was a graceful and conservative gymnast: She rarely attempted especially difficult routines or innovative moves. She considered athleticism and the development of complicated maneuvers to be antithetical to the elegance and femininity that lay at the core of women's gymnastics.

When Larisa appeared on the international scene, she was already of champion quality. In her first Olympic Games, in Melbourne, Australia, in 1956, she overcame the Hungarian champion Agnes Keleti and earned five medals, including golds in the team competition, the vault, the floor exercise, and the all-around competition. She set an Olympic standard that would be hard, but not impossible, to surpass.

The Emerging Champion

Reaching the top is one thing; staying there is another. Though already an Olympic champion, Larisa was yet to reach her peak. At the 1957 European championships in Bucharest, Romania, she finished in first place in every event as well and took the all-around title. She performed nearly as well at the 1958 World Gymnastics Championships in Moscow, Soviet

Major Gymnastics Championships

Year	Competition	Event	Place	Event	Place
1956	Olympic Games	All-around	Gold	Balance beam	4th
		Floor exercise	Gold	Vault	Gold
		Uneven bars	Silver	Team	Gold
1957	European Championships	All-around	1st	Balance beam	1st
		Floor exercise	1st	Vault	1st
		Uneven bars	1st		
1958	World Championships	All-around	1st	Balance beam	1st
		Floor exercise	2d	Vault	1st
		Uneven bars	1st	Team	1st
1960	Olympic Games	All-around	Gold	Balance beam	Silver
		Floor exercise	Gold	Vault	Bronze
		Uneven bars	Silver	Team	Gold
1961	European Championships	All-around	1st	Balance beam	2d
		Floor exercise	1st	Vault	4th
		Uneven bars	2d		
1962	World Championships	All-around	1st	Balance beam	2d
		Floor exercise	1st	Vault	2d
		Uneven bars	3d	Team	1st
1964	Olympic Games	All-around	Silver	Balance beam	Bronze
		Floor exercise	Gold	Vault	Silver
		Uneven bars	Bronze	Team	Gold
1965	European Championships	All-around	2d	Balance beam	2d
		Floor exercise	2d	Vault	3d
		Uneven bars	2d		

Union, with five golds and a silver. She interrupted her career during 1959 for the birth of her daughter, Tana, but came back for her second Olympic Games in Rome, Italy, in 1960.

In Rome, Larisa defended her Olympic title and improved upon her previous Olympic performance by taking medals in all the events, a feat she would accomplish again in Tokyo four years later. In 1961, she became the Soviet women's captain and led the national team to the United States for a tour of exhibitions and meets through the Northeast and Midwest. She was a devoted and disciplined gymnast: When a thunderstorm during the 1961 European championships in Leipzig caused a lighting failure in the middle of her final floor exercise, Larisa continued her routine among sporadic flashes of lightning—a thrilling and macabre spectacle that earned her a gold medal. The following year, her supremacy continued with six medals—three of them gold—at the World Gymnastics Championships in Prague, Czechoslovakia.

Larisa was always a team performer, in the finest Soviet tradition. Even as she consistently outdid her teammate, Polina Astakhova, she was always generous and never viciously competitive. Outside the gymnasium, she served as a Kiev city councillor and became a member of the Communist Party in 1963, the same year the Soviet Union boycotted the European championships in Paris for political reasons.

By the 1964 Olympics in Tokyo, Japan, Larisa was twenty-nine years old, and younger competitors were ready to challenge the unquestioned superiority she had enjoyed for eight years. Though she again placed in every event, with a gold in the floor exercise, which had always been her strongest event, it was the Czechoslovakian gymnast Vera Cáslavská who took the all-around title. For the next two years, Larisa was consistently outranked by the Czech and by the more athletic style of her own teammate Larisa Petrik, who, at the age of fifteen, upset Larisa in the 1964 Soviet National Championships in Kiev. In her final competition, the 1966 World Gymnastics Championships in Dortmund, West Germany, Larisa struggled to finish eleventh in the all-around and saw the team title slip away to the Czech women. She retired in 1966, but by then she had won more individual Olympic titles than any athlete in any sport.

Records

Most Olympic gold medals won by a woman, 9
Most individual Olympic medals won, 14 (17 medals overall)
Only gymnast to place in every event in two Olympiads (1960, 1964)

Honors and Awards

1956	Honored Master of Sports
1960	Decorated with the Order of Lenin
	Named one of the ten foremost women in the Soviet Union
1965	Badge of Honor
1985	Inducted into Sudafed International Women's Sports Hall of Fame
1998	Inducted into International Gymnastics Hall of Fame

Continuing the Story

Though no longer competing, Larisa remained active in international gymnastics for years to come. In 1966, she became the senior coach of the Soviet national women's gymnastics team. She coached the great Soviet gymnasts Ludmila Turishcheva, Olga Korbut, and Nelli Kim and witnessed the dramatic transformation of women's gymnastics in style and popularity during the 1970's. She attended the Munich and Montreal Olympics in 1972 and 1976, wrote a book entitled *Ravnovesie* (1975; balance), and, as a member of the organizing committee of "Olympia '80," oversaw the planning of the gymnastics events at the 1980 Moscow Olympics.

In 1977, Larisa resigned as head coach of the national team and opened her own club in Moscow, which she ran until 1987. In 1991, after more than forty active years, she retired from the gymnastics world. She turned to a quiet home life in Moscow with her husband Yuri Feldman, a former national cycling champion, and spent more time with her daughter, a retired ballerina, and her grandson.

Summary

Larisa Latynina was the first great female gymnast of the so-called modern era of the sport. In a career that spanned a decade, Larisa set the standard, in her athletic performances on the apparatus, in her commitment to beauty and elegance in movement, and in her personal demeanor on the sidelines, for an entire generation of women gymnasts.

Barry Mann

Additional Sources

Greenberg, Stan. *Whitaker's Olympic Almanack: An Encyclopaedia of the Olympic Games.* Chicago: Fitzroy Dearborn, 2000.

Normile, Dwight. "Living Legends." *International Gymnast* (August/September, 1998): 46-49.

Wallechinsky, David, and Jaime Loucky. *The Complete Book of the Olympics: 2008 Edition.* London: Aurum Press, 2008.

Sammy Lee

Born: August 1, 1920
Fresno, California
Also known as: Samuel Lee (full name)

Early Life

Samuel Lee was born on August 1, 1920, in Fresno, California. He and his family soon moved to Los Angeles. His father, Sonkee Lee, and his mother, Eunkee Chun Lee, owned and operated a small family restaurant. Both parents were immigrants from Korea; the family was poor but hardworking. Sonkee Lee always encouraged his son to study hard in his classes so he could become a doctor.

Sammy did not have enough money to buy tickets for the 1932 Los Angeles Olympics, but he was inspired by the Games. He decided he wanted to become an Olympic champion, but did not know what his sport would be until the next summer. His love for diving started when he was playing follow-the-leader at the local pool. Sammy taught himself to dive well enough to compete in local meets. His father supported his interest in sport as long as it did not interfere with his studies. Sammy took his father's advice to heart, studied hard, and was student body president at Luther Burbank Junior High School.

The Road to Excellence

Sammy taught himself so well that he made the high school diving team and won the California high school championship three years in a row. In 1938, he competed in the Los Angeles Invitational meet, where he caught the eye of former Pacific Coast diving champion Jim Ryan, then a coach. After watching Sammy dive, Ryan decided he could make Sammy the world's greatest diver. The two worked together every day, and Ryan soon changed Sammy from an average diver into a champion.

Sometimes at practice or meets, Sammy would hear people say: "Boy, if Sammy Lee were white, he'd be national champion." That upset him so much he would sometimes tell them that he heard their comments. He would say: "Listen, I may not look white, but I'm an American and I'm going to make it." Of course, that made him work all the harder to achieve his Olympic dream.

Sammy did make it. In 1939, he graduated first in his class from Benjamin Franklin High School. Although only 5 feet 1¾ inches tall, he was also named the most outstanding athlete in the school. He started classes at Occidental College the next fall and also continued diving. In 1940, he won the Amateur Athletic Union (AAU) junior national springboard and platform titles.

In 1942, he won the AAU senior springboard and platform championships, his first major diving titles. Then he took time off from sports to finish college and begin at the University of Southern California Medical School. However, Sammy came back to win the AAU platform title again in 1946. He graduated from medical school the next year

Sammy Lee diving from a platform. (Courtesy of International Swimming Hall of Fame)

609

and enlisted in the United States Army Medical Corps.

The Emerging Champion

In 1948, Sammy won the gold medal in platform diving at the London Olympic Games. By that time he was a twenty-eight-year-old lieutenant in the U.S. Army. He was the first Asian American diver to win the gold. For his final dive, he chose such a hard stunt that no one had ever done it before in a meet: a 3½ somersault. He said it felt like a belly flop. The dive was excellent. It got high scores of 9½ and 10 from the judges, giving Sammy the points needed for victory.

In 1950, Sammy married Rosiland M. K. Wong, a Chinese American. At that time, he was still a doctor for the U.S. Army, and the United States was involved in the Korean War. In 1952, however, Olympic diving coach Mike Peppe urged Sammy to start diving again and to try to make the Olympic team. After getting permission from his commanding officer, Sammy started practicing once more.

At the 1952 Olympics at Helsinki, Finland, Sammy won the gold in platform diving again, setting two records. He was the first athlete to win the medal in two successive Olympics and the oldest diver, at thirty-two, to win an Olympic medal. Sammy's Olympic experience was exciting, not only because of the medals and the records but also because he did it all on his birthday.

Sammy became a great champion because he was enthusiastic and willing to try things that had never been done before. He was inventive and changed diving by his courage and creativity. During his career, he added five new and difficult dives to the official lists.

Continuing the Story

Sammy retired from diving competition after the 1952 Olympics. He continued to be a successful

Major Diving Championships

Year	Competition	Event	Place	Points
1942	AAU Championships	3-meter springboard	Gold	—
		10-meter platform	Gold	—
1946	AAU Championships	10-meter platform	Gold	—
1948	Olympic Games	3-meter springboard	Bronze	145.52
		10-meter platform	Gold	130.05
1951	Pan-American Games	3-meter springboard	—	191.916
		10-meter platform	—	153.533
1952	Olympic Games	10-meter platform	Gold	156.28

physician, specializing in the ear diseases that are a big problem for swimmers and divers. He also stayed involved with diving and the Olympics. His successful medical practice made it possible to stay in touch with his first love, diving.

In 1954, he was the first American Sports Ambassador to tour Southeast Asia. He was sent by the Information and Cultural Exchange Program sponsored by the U.S. State Department. Furthermore, he was sent by three presidents, Dwight D. Eisenhower, Richard M. Nixon, and Ronald Reagan, as their personal representative to the Olympic Games of 1956, 1972, and 1988. Sammy was also appointed to the President's Council on Physical Fitness and Sports by four presidents. He served on that council from 1970 to 1980.

Sammy coached two Olympic champions. He coached Bob Webster from the beginning of his career through his gold medals in 1960 and 1964. He was also the first coach for 1984 and 1988 Olympic champion Greg Louganis, coaching Greg through his silver medal at Montreal in 1976. Sammy coached the U.S. Olympic diving team in 1960 and the Japanese and Korean Olympic diving teams in 1964. In 1968, he was an Olympic diving judge and an inductee into the International Swimming Hall of Fame. In 1979, Sammy Lee and Steve Lehrman wrote a successful book entitled *Diving*. In 1990, Sammy was inducted into the U.S. Olympic Hall of Fame.

Honors and Awards

1953	James E. Sullivan Award
1966	Named "Outstanding American of Korean Parentage" by the Korean-American Society of Southern California
1968	Inducted into International Swimming Hall of Fame
1990	Inducted into U.S. Olympic Hall of Fame

Summary

Sammy Lee was a gifted athlete who overcame racial discrimination and financial problems to become a world champion and an inspiration to other Asian Americans. By winning national titles while finishing medical school and by taking his first Olympic gold medal only a year after he graduated,

Sammy also showed that athletics and academics can go together well. Since that time, he has been a successful doctor and father of two children. He has also given his time to help other athletes in the United States and abroad to become successful in diving. He served several U.S. presidents and worked tirelessly for the Olympic movement.

Mary Lou LeCompte

Additional Sources

Lee, Sammy. *An Olympian's Oral History: Sammy Lee, 1948 and 1952 Olympic Games, Diving.* Los Angeles: Amateur Athletic Foundation of Los Angeles, 1999.

Wallechinsky, David, and Jaime Loucky. *The Complete Book of the Olympics: 2008 Edition.* London: Aurum Press, 2008.

Mario Lemieux

Born: October 5, 1965
      Montreal, Quebec, Canada

Early Life

Like most French Canadian children, Mario Lemieux developed a love for his national sport of ice hockey at an early age. Born on October 5, 1965, in Montreal, Quebec, Canada, to Jean-Guy and Pierrette Lemieux, Mario grew up in a redbrick, box-shaped house on rue Joques in Ville Emard, a working-class neighborhood on the southwest outskirts of the city. Mario's father, a retired construction worker, used to pack wall-to-wall snow in the front hallway of his house so Mario and his two older brothers, Richard and Alain, could practice skating indoors. Mario learned to skate at a rink behind the local church and began playing organized hockey at the age of three. By nine years old, he had established himself as the dominant player among his local peers. At the age of fifteen, he was playing in the Quebec Major Junior Hockey League, and at sixteen, he dropped out of school to concentrate on his athletic career. Translated from French, *le mieux* means "the best." Mario set out to prove that he deserved that label in ice hockey.

The Road to Excellence

From the start, Mario showed great timing, an eye for the net, and the ability to control the puck as if it were attached by a string to the end of his hockey stick. He emerged through the local leagues by imitating the style of his idol, hockey legend Guy Lafleur. Mario dreamed of playing in the NHL for the Montreal Canadiens. An outstanding junior career, in which he tallied 282 points in seventy games in his last season with the Laval Voisins, propelled Mario into the NHL, at the age of eighteen, as the first overall selection in the

1984 NHL entry draft. The world waited to see the player who had been praised as the next Wayne Gretzky. Not since the 1950's, when hockey fans debated whether Montreal's Maurice "Rocket" Richard or Detroit's Gordie Howe was the greatest player, had the sport had two such supremely talented players in the league. Mario even inverted Gretzky's number 99 to his now-famous 66 and emerged on the hockey scene with the hope of sharing some of Gretzky's limelight.

The Emerging Champion

With French as his first language, Mario was still learning English when the Pittsburgh Penguins acquired him in the 1984 draft. He acquired his English vocabulary partly by watching soap operas on television. If there were hockey enthusiasts who thought that the comparisons to Gretzky were premature and unfounded, Mario silenced those skeptics with an outstanding rookie season. He scored 43 goals and added 57 assists for 100 points and was awarded the 1985 Calder Memorial Trophy as the league's rookie of the year. Mario recorded at least

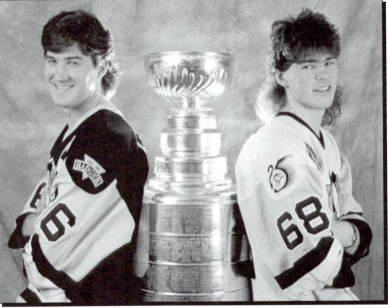

Mario Lemieux (left) and teammate Jaromir Jagr posing with the Stanley Cup the Penguins won twice during the early 1990's. (Bruce Bennett/Getty Images)

100 points in each of his next five seasons. He was honored with the 1988 Hart Trophy as the NHL's most valuable player (MVP). He captured the Art Ross Trophy, awarded annually to the league's leading scorer, in 1988 and 1989. He was named MVP in two of the first six NHL all-star games in which he played.

Mario was primarily responsible for turning around the Penguins franchise. After only six complete seasons, he topped the list of all-time Penguins scorers with 838 points, ranking first in both all-time goals, 345, and assists, 493. The year before Mario joined Pittsburgh, the Penguins averaged just 6,800 fans at forty home games. After his arrival at the Pittsburgh Civic Arena (now Mellon Arena), the Penguins' home, the team welcomed more sellout crowds than at any other time in the club's history. Pittsburghers boasted a renewed interest in the sport and a burgeoning love affair with the most gifted athlete to ever wear a Penguins uniform.

NHL Statistics

Season	GP	G	Ast.	Pts.	PIM
1984-85	73	43	57	100	54
1985-86	79	48	93	141	43
1986-87	63	54	53	107	57
1987-88	77	70	98	168	92
1988-89	76	85	114	199	100
1989-90	59	45	78	123	78
1990-91	26	19	26	45	30
1991-92	64	44	87	131	94
1992-93	60	69	91	160	38
1993-94	22	17	20	37	32
1995-96	70	69	92	161	54
1996-97	76	50	72	122	65
2000-01	43	35	41	876	18
2001-02	24	6	25	31	14
2002-03	67	28	63	91	43
2003-04	10	1	8	9	6
2005-06	26	7	15	22	16
Totals	915	690	1,033	1,723	834

Notes: GP = games played; G = goals; Ast. = assists; Pts. = points; PIM = penalties in minutes. 2004-05 NHL season canceled because of lockout.

Continuing the Story

Witnessing the explosiveness of a healthy Mario was a rare treat for hockey fans. In a sport often criticized for its brutality and violence, Mario emerged as a player of great finesse and skill. Possessing superior skating and stickhandling abilities, Mario awed teammates, opponents, and fans alike with his athletic artistry, his aggressiveness both around the net and in the corners, his ability to control the tempo of the game, and his flair for producing enviable results. His play conjured memories of all-time NHL greats Phil Esposito, Richard, and Lafleur, centers who had dominated the game. A member of the 1987 Canada Cup team, Mario was named Penguins team captain in 1988, despite his youth. In the forty-sixth game of that same year, he scored his fiftieth goal, making him the only player other than Gretzky ever to score 50 goals in fewer than fifty games.

When chronic back pain sidelined Mario near the end of the 1989-1990 season, people in hockey circles felt his absence. On July 11, 1990, Mario underwent back surgery to repair a herniated disc, and he missed a large portion of the 1990-1991 season. Hockey fans wondered if Mario's career was over.

However, late in the 1990-1991 season, Mario returned in spectacular fashion. The Penguins won the franchise's first-ever Stanley Cup, beating the Minnesota North Stars (now Dallas Stars) in six games; Mario won

Honors, Awards, and Records

1985	Calder Memorial Trophy
1985-87, 1992	NHL Second Team All-Star
1985, 1988, 1990	NHL All-Star Game MVP
1986, 1988, 1993, 1996	Lester B. Pearson Award
1988-89, 1992-93, 1996-97	Art Ross Trophy
1988-89, 1993, 1996-97	NHL First Team All-Star
1988, 1993, 1996	Hart Memorial Trophy
1989	NHL record for the most goals in a Stanley Cup Playoff game, 5 (record shared)
	NHL record for the most points in a Stanley Cup Playoff game, 8 (record shared)
1991-92	Conn Smythe Trophy
1993	Received Lou Marsh Trophy
	Received Bill Masterton Trophy
1997	Inducted into Hockey Hall of Fame
2000	Received Lester Patrick Trophy
	Selected ESPN Hockey Player of The Decade
2001	Selected to the NHL second all-star team
2004	Inducted into Canada's Walk of Fame

the Conn Smythe Trophy as the Stanley Cup most valuable player. The following season, Mario led the Penguins to a second Stanley Cup, though he still suffered from back and shoulder injuries. In the following season, he started out strong, scoring goals in each of his first twelve games.

In January, 1993, however, Mario discovered a lump on his neck and later was diagnosed with cancer of the lymph nodes, a condition known as Hodgkin's disease. After a course of radiation treatment, he returned to the Penguins' lineup in March, scoring a goal and gaining an assist in his first game back. Mario went on to win the league's scoring title that year. Injuries and complications from his cancer treatment forced Mario to miss most of the following two seasons. In 1995, however, he returned to score 69 goals and was named the league's MVP.

Mario continued to excel despite continuing health problems. After winning his sixth scoring title during the 1996-1997 season, Mario decided to retire. He finished his career with 1,494 total points, and the Hockey Hall of Fame waived its normal waiting period, inducting Mario in December, 1997.

Upon his retirement, the Penguins owed Mario millions of dollars in deferred compensation. With his former team on the brink of bankruptcy, Mario organized an ownership team and was granted primary ownership just prior to the 1999-2000 season. He decided to make a comeback in the middle of the 2000-2001 season. In his first game he scored 1 goal and made 2 assists. For the year, he scored 35 goals in forty-three games and collected 41 assists—figures comparable to his career averages.

Mario continued to play while acting as the owner of the Penguins. In the 2001-2002 season, he participated in only ten games because of injury. That winter, Mario decided to play in the 2002 Olympics for Team Canada, which won the gold medal in ice hockey. In the 2003-2004 season, at the age of thirty-seven, Mario regained his scoring touch, compiling 92 points in sixty-seven games, but his team missed the playoffs. Mario's second comeback was short-lived because the NHL owners' lockout canceled the 2004-2005 season. The following year, the Penguins won the draft lottery and chose Sidney Crosby. Mario opened his home to the young rookie and mentored him in hockey and in life. The two played together only briefly because Mario had an atrial fibrillation.

On January 24, 2006, Mario announced his retirement; however, he remained the owner of the Penguins. The ownership group announced it intended to relocate the Penguins if a new arena were not built. In 2007, the Penguins' ownership group and the city of Pittsburgh struck a deal to build the long-promised arena, and the Penguins stayed in Pittsburgh. In retirement, Mario resided in Sewickley, Pennsylvania, a suburb of Pittsburgh, and maintained his star status around the area and the sports world.

Summary

Mario Lemieux rose to hockey stardom with breathtaking speed. He dominated his sport as an amateur and as a young professional before coming to the NHL. Once in the NHL, he led his team to two Stanley Cup Championships. For a time, he rivaled Wayne Gretzky for recognition as hockey's greatest player, a feat that may have been his most impressive of all.

Jan Giel, updated by Timothy C. Hemmis

Additional Sources

Bynum, Mike, Ron Cook, Chuck Finder, and Dave Molinari, eds. *Mario Lemieux: Best There Ever Was.* Toronto: Macmillan Canada, 1997.

Christopher, Matt. *On the Ice with Mario Lemieux.* Boston: Little, Brown, 2002.

Goyens, Chrys, and Frank Orr. *Mario Lemieux: Over Time, Sixty-six.* New York: Universe, 2001.

Hughes, Morgan. *Mario Lemieux: Beating the Odds.* Minneapolis: Lerner, 1996.

McKinley, Michael. *The Magnificent One: The Story of Mario Lemieux.* New York: Grosset & Dunlap, 2002.

Rossiter, Sean. *Mario Lemieux.* Vancouver, B.C.: Greystone Books, 2001.

Willes, Ed. *Gretzky to Lemieux: The Story of the 1987 Canada Cup.* Toronto: McClelland & Stewart, 2007.

Carl Lewis

Born: July 1, 1961
      Birmingham, Alabama
Also known as: Frederick Carlton Lewis (full
name)

Early Life
Frederick Carlton Lewis, the third son of William
and Evelyn Lawlor Lewis, was born on July 1, 1961,
in Birmingham, Alabama. Two years later, Carl's

Carl Lewis jumping during the 1992 Olympic Games in Barcelona.
(Mike Powell/Getty Images)

sister, Carol, was born and his family moved to
Willingboro, New Jersey, a suburb of Philadelphia,
where both parents became high school track
coaches.

Carl had a typical American middle-class childhood. His life revolved around family, church, and
school. He spent summers with relatives in Alabama. Carl had a newspaper route, took cello and
drum lessons, and played Little League baseball.
Unlike his athletic brothers and sister,
however, he did not excel in sports and
was considered the family "runt."

The Road to Excellence
By the age of eight, Carl was running with
his parents' track club. In 1971, when
he was ten, Carl attended his first Jesse
Owens track meet and met Owens himself. Two years later, Carl placed first in
the long jump at an Jesse Owens long
jump event in Philadelphia.

Carl's parents were his first coaches,
and Carl worked constantly with them to
improve his athletic skills. In his sophomore year of high school, Carl finally began to grow physically and his abilities
improved rapidly. By the end of his junior
year, his long jump distance improved
from less than 23 feet to 25 feet 9 inches.
By the time he graduated from Willingboro High School in 1979, he was the
New Jersey long jumper of the year and
the top-ranked high school track athlete
in the United States.

Carl was heavily recruited by several
colleges, including Fairleigh Dickinson
University, Villanova University, and the
University of Houston. In the end, he decided to work with coach Tom Tellez at
Houston. Tellez used the laws of physics
to help Carl develop an unusual jumping
technique called the double-hitch kick.
Tellez also became Carl's lifelong athletic counselor and friend.

At the National Collegiate Athletic As-

Major Sprint and Jumping Championships

Year	Competition	Event	Place	Time/Distance
1979	Pan-American Games	Long jump	3d	26′ 8″
	U.S. Nationals	Long jump	2d	26′ 6½″
1980	NCAA Outdoor Championships	Long jump	1st	27′ 4¾″
	NCAA Indoor Championships	Long jump	1st	26′ 4½″
1981	World Cup	Long jump	1st	—
	NCAA Outdoor Championships	100 meters	1st	—
		Long jump	1st	—
	NCAA Indoor Championships	55 meters	1st	6.16
		Long jump	1st	27′ 10″
	U.S. Nationals	100 meters	1st	10.13
		Long jump	1st	28′ 3½″
1982	USA/Mobil Indoor Championships	Long jump	1st	28′ ¾″
	U.S. Nationals	100 meters	1st	10.11
		Long jump	1st	27′ 10″
1983	World Championships	100 meters	1st	10.07
		4×100-meter relay	1st	37.86
		Long jump	1st	28′ ¾″
	U.S. Nationals	100 meters	1st	10.27
		200 meters	1st	
		Long jump	Gold	28′ 10¼″
	USA/Mobil Indoor Championships	55 meters	1st	6.04 AR
		Long jump	1st	27′ 4¾″
1984	Olympic Games	100 meters	Gold	9.99
		200 meters	Gold	19.80 OR
		4×100-meter relay	Gold	37.83 WR, OR
		Long jump	Gold	28′ ¼″
	USA/Mobil Indoor Championships	Long jump	1st	27′ 10¾″
1986	Goodwill Games	100 meters	3d	10.06
		4×100-meter relay	1st	37.98
	U.S. Nationals	100 meters	1st	9.91
		Long jump	1st	28′ 5½″
1987	World Championships	100 meters	2d	9.93 AR
		4×100-meter relay	1st	37.90
		Long jump	1st	28′ 5½″
	Pan-American Games	4×100-meter relay	1st	38.41
		Long jump	1st	28′ 8½″
	U.S. Nationals	100 meters	2d	10.05
		200 meters	1st	20.12
		Long jump	1st	28′ 4½″
1988	Olympic Games	100 meters	Gold	9.92 OR
		200 meters	Silver	19.79
		Long jump	Gold	28′ 7½″
1990	Goodwill Games	100 meters	2d	10.08
		Long jump	1st	27′ 6″
1991	World Championships	100 meters	1st	9.86 WR
		4×100-meter relay	1st	37.50 WR
		Long jump	2d	29′
	U.S. Nationals	100-meters	2d	
		Long jump	1st	
1992	Olympic Games	Long jump	Gold	28′ 5½″
		4×100-meter relay	Gold	37.50 WR
1995	U.S. Nationals	Long jump	2d	
1996	Olympic Games	Long jump	Gold	27′ 10¾″

Notes: OR = Olympic Record; WR = World Record; AR = American Record

sociation (NCAA) Outdoor Track and Field Championships in 1980, Carl won the long jump with a distance of 27 feet 4¾ inches. Although both Carl and his sister Carol made the 1980 U.S. Olympic track team, they did not compete, because the United States boycotted the Games in Moscow as a protest against the Soviet Union's invasion of Afghanistan.

The Emerging Champion

In 1981 and 1982, Carl dominated national collegiate track and field events. He won indoor and outdoor titles in long jump and sprints, a feat last performed by Jesse Owens in 1936. He also set records for indoor and outdoor long jumps and the 100-meter dash at sea level. He received the Amateur Athletic Union's (AAU's) Sullivan Award, for the year's outstanding U.S. amateur athlete, in 1981, and the Jesse Owens Award, for outstanding track and field performance, in 1982.

Disqualified as an amateur collegiate athlete in 1982 because of low grades, Carl started competing for the Santa Monica Track Club under the guidance of Coach Joe Douglas. In 1983, Carl set several new records, including the indoor 60-yard dash and the 100-meter dash at sea level. He also won gold medals in the 100 meters, the long jump, and the 4×100-meter relay at the first World Track and Field Championships in Helsinki, Finland.

Carl majored in communications in college and continued to train after graduation for a career in show business. He took acting lessons and, just before the 1984 Olympics, cut a record called "Going for the Gold," which met with some success in Europe.

Carl's career reached a high

Honors and Awards

1979	Dieges Award
1981	James E. Sullivan Award
1982	Jesse Owens Award
1982, 1984	*Track and Field News* World Athlete of the Year
1983-84	Associated Press Male Athlete of the Year
1985	Inducted into U.S. Olympic Hall of Fame
1999	World Sports Awards of the Century
	Selected as the International Olympic Committee's "Sportsman of the Century"
	Selected as the International Association of Athletics Federations "World Athlete of the Century"
	Selected as *Sports Illustrated*'s "Olympian of the Century"
2000	Received Library of Congress' Living Legends Award

---

point with the 1984 Olympics in Los Angeles, where he matched Jesse Owens's record of four gold medals in the long jump, 100 meters, 200 meters, and 4×100-meter relay. He also set Olympic records in the 200 meters and the 4×100-meter relay. At the Olympics, Carl was criticized for waving a large American flag during the victory lap following the 100-meter race and for passing up several opportunities to break Bob Beamon's long jump record of 29 feet 2½ inches.

Continuing the Story

Carl's career as a track and field athlete was memorable. In the 1988 Olympics in Seoul, South Korea, Ben Johnson, a Canadian runner, beat Carl in the 100-meter race but was disqualified when he tested positive for drug use. At Seoul, Carl won gold medals in the 100 meters and long jump and set a new Olympic record of 9.92 seconds in the 100-meter race. At the 1991 World Track and Field Championships in Tokyo, Japan, he set a new world record and won the gold medal in the 100 meters with a time of 9.86. Many consider this race to be the greatest 100-meter dash of all time: The top two finishers broke the world record; six of the finalists ran the race in under 10 seconds; and the fourth, fifth, and sixth place finishers all set national records for their home countries. Furthermore, with an astonishing leap of 29 feet, Carl took the silver medal in the long jump competition.

Carl had publicity problems during most of his career. He was often labeled a showoff and even accused of using drugs. Carl denied all these accusations and was an outspoken opponent of the use of performance-enhancing drugs in athletics. He was quietly self-confident rather than arrogant. He was religious. He was a member of Lay Witnesses for Christ and had a close friendship with an Indian guru named Sri Chinmoy.

Carl also had problems with promotional contracts. Shortly before the 1988 Olympics, Carl reached an out-of-court settlement with his longtime sponsor Nike and accepted a new shoe contract with Mizuno. Although technically an amateur, Carl earned a large trust fund from promotional contracts and appearance fees, and he lived comfortably in Houston. Not surprisingly, Carl advocated a redefinition of amateur status to allow athletes like himself to earn money directly from their talents.

Carl continued to excel in the 1992 Olympic Games, winning the gold in the long jump and the men's 4×100-meter relay, in which the U.S. team set a world record mark of 37.40. In 1996, Carl won his fourth consecutive Olympic gold medal in the long jump in Atlanta, bringing his medal total in Olympic competition to ten: nine gold and one silver. Following the 1997 season, he announced his retirement from competition. The International Olympic Committee (IOC) named him the athlete of the twentieth century.

Summary

Carl Lewis finished his career with nine Olympic gold medals, eight world championships, and ten world records. Although he did not achieve his goal of breaking Bob Beamon's long-jump record, Carl will be remembered as one of the most dominant track and field athletes in history.

Thomas J. Sienkewicz

Additional Sources

Lewis, Carl, and Jeffrey Marx. *Inside Track: My Professional Life in Amateur Track and Field.* New York: Simon & Schuster, 1990.

Swift, E. M. "Carl Lewis." *Sports Illustrated* 105, no. 24 (December 15, 2006): 37.

Wallechinsky, David, and Jaime Loucky. *The Complete Book of the Olympics: 2008 Edition.* London: Aurum Press, 2008.

Jason Lezak

Born: November 12, 1975
      Irvine, California
Also known as: Jason Edward Lezak (full name)

Early Life

Jason Edward Lezak, of Polish and Slovak descent on his father's side, was raised in Irvine, California. As a young man, Jason excelled at several sports, including basketball, water polo, baseball, soccer, and swimming. At the age of five, he began to compete in the latter sport with the Irvine Novaquatics. In 2008, at the age of thirty-two, Jason continued to train with the same team.

At ten years old, Jason was faced with a tough decision. He had two important events scheduled on the same day: a baseball run, hit, and throw competition at Anaheim Stadium and the swimming Junior Olympics. He chose swimming and quickly became nationally prominent in his age group. He continued to play basketball until his sophomore year in high school. By his senior year in high school, he was 6 feet 4 inches and 205 pounds and an all-American swimmer. He received a swimming scholarship at the University of California at Santa Barbara. As a freshman and sophomore, he was not an outstanding swimmer, but by his junior year he placed fifth and sixth for the 50- and 100-yard freestyle events, respectively, in the National Collegiate Athletic Association (NCAA) ratings. In 1998, he finished his college swimming career and turned professional. The following year, he graduated with a degree in business and economics.

The Road to Excellence

Jason was unusual among swimmers in that he did not become a world-class sprinter until after he was twenty-five years old. Furthermore, he did not train with a coach, although he drew inspiration from several who taught him along the way. He said that Dave Salo at Irvine Novaquatics taught him to coach himself.

Jason developed a history of responding

to other swimmers' braggadocio with record sprints in the pool. At the 2004 Olympic trials, eight-time Olympic medalist Gary Hall, Jr., called Jason a "professional relay swimmer" before they were matched in the 100-meter freestyle. Jason responded with a time of 48.17 seconds, the third-fastest in the world at that time and an American record. He won in the finals of that race in 48.41 seconds, as Hall, who botched his start, finished third. After the race, Jason and Hall shook hands in the pool. Hall then edged out Jason in the 50-meter freestyle and went on to win that event at Athens at the 2004 Olympics.

The Emerging Champion

In 2000, Jason competed in his first Olympic Games, winning a silver medal in the 4×100-meter freestyle relay and a gold medal in the 4×100 medley relay. During the 2004 Olympic trials in Long Beach, Cal-

---

Major Swimming Championships

Year	Competition	Event	Place
1999	Pan-Pacific Championships	4×100-meter freestyle	2d
2000	Olympic Games	4×100-meter medley	Gold
		4×100-meter freestyle	Silver
2002	World Short Course Championships	4×100-meter freestyle	1st
		4×100-meter medley	1st
	Pan-Pacific Championships	50-meter freestyle	1st
		4×100-meter medley	1st
2004	World Short Course Championships	100-meter freestyle	1st
		4×100-meter freestyle	1st
		4×100-meter medley	1st
	Olympic Games	4×100-meter medley	Gold
		4×100-meter freestyle	Bronze
2005	World Long Course Championships	4×100-meter freestyle	1st
		4×100-meter medley	1st
2006	World Short Course Championships	4×100-meter medley	2d
		4×100-meter freestyle	3d
	Pan-Pacific Championships	4×100-meter freestyle	1st
		4×100-meter medley	1st
		100-meter freestyle	2d
2007	World Long Course Championships	4×100-meter freestyle	1st
2008	Olympic Games	4×100-meter freestyle	Gold
		4×100-meter medley	Gold
		100-meter freestyle	Bronze

---

ifornia, he broke the U.S. national record in the 100-meter freestyle, qualifying in that event and the 50-meter freestyle sprint.

At the 2004 Olympics, Jason was a member of the medley relay team that won a gold medal and broke the world record. He also won a bronze medal in the 4×100-meter freestyle relay. He failed to qualify in the individual 100 meters, however, because he did not take the preliminaries seriously. He finished fifth in the 50-meter freestyle at the 2004 Olympics.

At the 2008 Olympic trials in Omaha, Nebraska, Jason twice broke the U.S. national record in the 100-meter freestyle and qualified for his third consecutive Olympic team. At the Beijing Olympics, Jason won gold medals in the 4×100-meter medley relay and 4×100-meter freestyle relay. He won a bronze in the 100-meter freestyle, in which he tied Brazilian swimmer César Cielo with a time of 47.67 seconds.

Continuing the Story

In Beijing, Jason took part in his third Olympic Games as the oldest man on the American team. As a member of the U.S. 4×100-meter freestyle relay team, Jason swam the fastest split in the history of the 100-meter freestyle relay, making up a body length and beating French team anchor Alain Bernard, who was the holder of the world record in the 100-meter freestyle at the time. Jason's effort secured the gold medal for the U.S. team.

Some observers believed that Jason's astounding final leg on the 4×100-meter freestyle relay was the single most memorable performance of the Games, even eclipsing Michael Phelps's eight gold medals. The relay team set a world record of 3:08:24, 3.99 seconds better than the previous standard. Jason, who admitted that he could not sleep the night before, wondered from where his strength had come. A consummate competitor, he was spurred by Bernard's bragging prior to the race that the French would "smash" the American team.

Jason said the relay was the second-best day of his life, after his wedding. In April, 2004, Jason had married Danielle DeAlva, whom he had met in high school. She represented Mexico at the Athens Olympics. DeAlva was working as an emergency-room nurse in Anaheim when Jason's historic race took place.

Summary

By the summer of 2008, Jason Lezak held or shared three world records and five American records. During the 2008 Olympic Games at Beijing, his 46.06 seconds anchor leg on the winning U.S. 4×100-meter freestyle relay team made him internationally famous. Though he competed in three Olympic Games, he will be remembered for his improbable swim in Beijing, in which he came from behind to catch Alain Bernard and give his team the gold medal.

Bruce E. Johansen

Additional Sources

Dillman, Lisa. "Anchor Jason Lezak's Stunning 400-meter Relay Performance Proves He's a Team Player." *Los Angeles Times*, August 12, 2008.

"Jason Lezak Storms Rose Bowl Aquatics Invite." *Swimming World Magazine*, June 20, 2008.

Phelps, Michael. *Beneath the Surface.* Champaign, Ill.: Sports, 2005.

Siegman, Joseph M. *Jewish Sports Legends: The International Jewish Sports Hall of Fame.* 4th ed. Dulles, Va.: Potomac Books, 2005.

Eric Liddell

Born: January 16, 1902
 Tianjin, China
Died: February 21, 1945
 Weihsien internment camp, China
Also known as: Eric Henry Liddell (full name);
 Flying Scotsman
Other major sport: Rugby

Eric Liddell winning the 400-meter race during the 1924 Olympic Games in Paris. (Getty Images)

Early Life

Eric Henry Liddell's spectacular 400-meter victory in the 1924 Paris Olympics was highlighted in the celebrated film *Chariots of Fire* (1981). The "Flying Scotsman," as he came to be known, was born on January 16, 1902, in Tianjin, China. His parents were Scottish, and his father was a Christian missionary. Missionary work inevitably became important in Eric's life. From the time he was five years old, Eric lived in Scotland. Although small, he was athletic and grew up enjoying rugby.

The Road to Excellence

Eric excelled as a rugby player and competed in seven international matches for Scotland. He could have pursued rugby as a career. Eventually, he devoted himself more to running. The Scots were the first to revive the kind of athletic competition lost since the days of the Greco-Roman world, and the Scottish Highland Games, already prominent in the nineteenth century, constituted the forerunner of modern track and field competition. Scottish heritage and pride were inherent in these and other local games.

Eric quickly became a local sports hero and attracted sizable crowds wherever he competed. He answered critics who found his enjoyment of sport too frivolous by using his athleticism and the attention it received to help spread a Christian message.

The Emerging Champion

Eric first gained national attention when he won both sprints at the Amateur Athletic Association (AAA) championships in 1923. In a meet with England and Ireland the next week, he was tripped and fell while running the 440-yard race. Undaunted, he got up and re-sumed the race. Although twenty yards behind, he caught his competition, passed them, and won. Word about the inspired Christian sprinter spread quickly. Eric simply explained that he did not like to be beaten.

By the time of the 1924 Paris Olympics, Eric was a divinity student at the University of Edinburgh and Scotland's greatest athlete. He was also British champion and record holder in the 100-yard dash. Eric was sent to Paris as a member of the British Olympic squad. No European had ever won a gold medal in the 100 meters, and the best that anyone from Great Britain had done was third place in the Antwerp Games. Eric's chances to win the first gold—or at least a medal—must have appeared a strong possibility to his Scottish and British fans.

As fate would have it, Eric never had the opportunity to compete in the 100 meters. Eric had always had difficulties balancing his athletic career with his religion, and when he learned six months in advance that he would have to compete on a Sunday, his religious convictions forced him to withdraw. His respect for the Sabbath was more important than a chance for an Olympic medal in the 100 meters. Eric's teammate Harold Abrahams ultimately won the event. For the same religious reason, Eric did not compete in the relays. His decision drew a great deal of criticism, and he was accused of a lack of patriotism, selfishness, and religious fanaticism. He would still compete in the 200- and 400-meter races at Paris.

Continuing the Story

Once in Paris, Eric emphasized his convictions by delivering the sermon in a Scottish church on the Sunday of the 100-meter heats. On July 9, he competed in the 200 meters and came in third. He was the third successive third-place finisher for Great Britain in the event, but his time of 21.9 seconds was best of the three.

In the 400 meters, however, Eric achieved Olympic immortality. On July 10, he qualified for the semifinals, but his time attracted little attention. The next day, he qualified for the finals by running 48.2 seconds, by far the fastest he had ever run, but still not impressive—earlier heats had been won in 48.0. The finals were run later the same day, and Liddell literally ran the race of his life. Running in

Major Sprint Championships

Year	Competition	Event	Place	Time
1923	AAA Championships	200 meters	1st	—
		400 meters	1st	—
	British/Irish meet	440 yards	1st	—
1924	Olympic Games	200 meters	Bronze	21.9
		400 meters	Gold	47.6 WR, OR

Notes: OR = Olympic Record; WR = World Record

the outside lane, he defied all conventional track wisdom by racing flat out. He led from start to finish and covered the 400 meters as if it were a sprint. No one could keep up with him or even get near him. By the time he finished, he was more than five meters ahead of his closest opponent and had established an Olympic record time of 47.6 seconds. Few athletic performances were ever as electrifying—or as inspired.

Eric returned to Scotland a national hero and was paraded through the streets of Edinburgh. A month later, his fellow students carried him from the university to St. Giles Cathedral, where he received his divinity degree. No athlete could have had a more spectacular end to his career, as Eric then turned his attention fully to his religious duties. A year later, he returned to China, where his family continued its missionary work.

In China, Eric taught science and athletics at the Anglo-Chinese college in Tianjin. In 1934, he married a fellow missionary's daughter, a nurse named Florence, and engaged in evangelical work in rural China. When the Japanese invaded China in 1937, Eric's pregnant wife and two daughters left for Canada while he continued his work. In 1941, he was taken prisoner by the Japanese. On February 21, 1945, he died of a brain tumor in a prisoner-of-war camp at the age of forty-three.

Summary

Eric Liddell combined a life of athletic prowess and Christian faith to become Scotland's greatest athlete and to win one of the most spectacular single victories in Olympic history. In the 400-meter race at the 1924 Paris Olympics, he inspired and amazed the athletic world by setting an Olympic record and outdistancing his opponents by more than five meters in a race that no one expected him to win. He overcame criticism and hostility for his religious convictions and, ultimately, won the praise of his compatriots and the world. In particular, he gave the Scots a national hero. The so-called "muscular Christian" died doing what was most important to him in occupied China during World War II.

Robert B. Kebric

Additional Sources

Benge, Janet, and Geoff Benge. *Eric Liddell: Something Greater than Gold.* Seattle, Wash.: Youth with a Mission, 1998.

Caughey, Ellen W. *Eric Liddell: Gold Medal Missionary.* Uhrichsville, Ohio: Barbour, 2006.

McCasland, Dave. *Eric Liddell: Pure Gold—A New Biography of the Olympic Champion Who Inspired Chariots of Fire.* Grand Rapids, Mich.: Discovery House, 2001.

Eddie Liddie

Born: July 24, 1959
 Delones, France
Also known as: Edward J. Liddie (full name)

Early Life

Edward J. "Eddie" Liddie was born on July 24, 1959, on a United States Army base in Delones, France. Arriving in the United States at the age of five, he settled with his family in New York City, where his father, Edward, opened a *dojo*, a judo school that he called Judoka Ltd. Having learned judo in France while in the Army, Eddie's father decided to spread his love for the sport to his students, many of whom included police officers of the New York City Police Department. He trained these police officers in the art of self-defense and how to handcuff and subdue. Also among his pupils was his wife, Arlene, who developed into a fine competitor and was the New York City judo champion at 114 pounds for four years. Eddie's younger brother, Jean Claude, also grew up with judo, but it was Eddie who emerged as his father's star pupil.

The Road to Excellence

Under his father's tutelage, Eddie developed great skill and quickness. He entered his first competition at the age of seven and soon dominated his weight class in competitions throughout New York and New Jersey. Around age eleven, his family realized that Eddie had great potential and a desire to continue serious competition and made a commitment to assist in making Eddie's Olympic dreams become a reality. For the next several years, the Liddies ventured to judo nationals, hosted in a different city each year. Eddie earned his first black belt at the age of seventeen; each year, he showed marked improvement. He began to attract the attention of a number of college judo coaches looking to recruit athletes to their programs. Eddie decided to attend Cumberland College in Williamsburg, Kentucky, after he was approached with a scholarship offer by Dr. Omer "O. J." Helvey, the school's head judo coach. Cumberland was the alma mater of Doug Nelson and Leo White, Jr., both members of the U.S. Olympic judo team.

Eddie enrolled in the fall of 1979 after winning a silver medal in the 1979 Pan-American Games. At Cumberland, Eddie dominated his 60-kilogram (132-pound) weight class and earned all-American honors from the National Collegiate Judo Association three times. In 1981, he was named team most valuable player when his squad dethroned San Jose State University and won the national title. In 1983, he graduated with a teaching degree in physical education, health, and psychology, and made his second appearance in the Pan-American Games, placing fourth.

The Emerging Champion

In May of 1983, having secured national attention with the success that his aggressive style produced, Eddie traveled to Colorado Springs, Colorado, and took up residence at the U.S. Olympic Training Center as a member of the U.S. Judo national team. For his first two years there, he trained under John Saylor, and he earned a spot on the team that represented the United States in the 1984 Summer Olympics hosted in Los Angeles, California. He earned a bronze medal, becoming the first American ever to win an Olympic judo medal in his extra-lightweight weight class (132 pounds). He placed in every Olympic Sports Festival for the first ten years of the program.

Continuing the Story

Returning to Colorado with the confidence and respect that an Olympic bronze medal produced,

Major Judo Championships

Year	Competition	Weight Class	Place
1979	Pan-American Games	60 kilograms	2d
1982, 1986	U.S. Nationals	60 kilograms	1st
1983	U.S. Nationals	60 kilograms	1st
	World Championships	60 kilograms	5th
	Pan-American Games	60 kilograms	4th
1984	Olympic Games	60 kilograms	Bronze
1986	U.S. Open	60 kilograms	2d
	Cuban Open	60 kilograms	2d
1989	World Championships	60 kilograms	4th
1991	U.S. Nationals	60 kilograms	1st

Eddie set his sights on another Olympic appearance and began training in 1985, under Phil Porter. Continuing with running, weightlifting, *randori* (fighting sessions), and other exercises designed to improve his cardiovascular and overall fitness level, Eddie traveled to competitions throughout the world, including Japan, France, South Africa, and the Netherlands. Employment with the Olympic Job Opportunities Program, which places elite athletes in part-time jobs to assist with rigorous training schedules, allowed Eddie to devote the attention to his judo that his international schedule required. He worked for several years in the Olympics Drug Education program, coordinating the drug-testing efforts for amateur sports throughout the country.

Eddie made great strides in three years of training and remained relatively healthy in a sport that has a tremendous risk of injury. He suffered only separations of the shoulder and elbow but never sustained an injury that jeopardized his future in judo. Eddie suffered the biggest setback of his career, however, at the Olympic trials in 1988. In a decisive match, Eddie threw his opponent and the official made a judgment call, ruling that Eddie was out of bounds when the incident occurred. The controversial call made Eddie an alternate on the 1988 U.S. Olympic team and essentially kept him out of that year's Olympics.

After achieving a fifth-degree black belt, Eddie continued to train in Colorado Springs, Colorado, hoping to represent the United States at the 1992 Olympic Games in Barcelona, Spain. He finished fourth at the 1989 World Judo Championships in Yugoslavia. He trained at the National Judo Institute, a veteran among a group of world-class athletes competing for a coveted spot on the next Olympic team.

Eddie won a gold medal at the Olympic Festival in 1990 and a bronze medal the following year, becoming the only person to win at least one medal in each of the eleven Olympic Festivals. Eddie also won the U.S. National Championships in 1991. Competing in the U.S. Olympic trials in 1992, Eddie missed a berth on the U.S. Olympic team by one point in his loss to Tony Okada, but he was named an alternate.

Eddie turned his attention to coaching, earning recognition as a finalist for the 1996 U.S. Olympic Committee development coach of the year award and winning the U.S. Judo, Inc., developmental coach of the year award in 1996 and 1998. He coached at the National Judo Institute, was an assistant coach for the 1996 women's Olympic judo team, and served as head coach for the U.S. world judo team in 1997. In 1998, Eddie became the resident judo coach at the Olympic Training Center (OTC) in Colorado Springs. In 2000, he was selected as the judo coach for the 2000 U.S. Olympic team. His OTC Judo club sent five athletes to the 2004 Athens Olympics. In 2005, he became the director of coaching and athletic development for USA Judo.

Summary

Eddie Liddie was the first American to win an Olympic medal in the 132-pound extra lightweight class. He won eleven medals in eleven consecutive Olympic Festivals, the most of any athlete in any sport. As a coach, Eddie has drawn on his success as a two-time national judo champion to train the next generation of Olympic athletes at the Olympic Training Center. Married and the father of three, Eddie also directs the training of his family, all of whom participate in judo.

Jan Giel

Additional Sources

Brousse, Michel, and David Ricky Matsumoto. *Judo in the U.S.: A Century of Dedication.* Berkeley, Calif.: North Atlantic Books, 2005.

Soames, Nicolas, Roy Inman, David Finch. *Olympic Judo: History and Techniques.* Swindon, England: Ippon/Crowood, 1990.

Lin Dan

Born: October 14, 1983
　　　　Longyan, Fujian Province, China
Also known as: Super Dan

Early Life

Lin Dan was born on October 14, 1983, in Long-yan, a metropolitan center in the mountainous interior of Fujian Province on China's southeastern coast. He grew up during the height of China's political tensions with the West, and little is known of his childhood. He demonstrated promising skills in Longyan's junior badminton leagues, distinguishing himself by the age of five with his ability to master the subtle dynamics of the game and its combinations of long smashes and delicate drop-shots. Given that Dan was naturally left-handed, relatively rare in the game but a characteristic of some of the sport's finest champions, government coaches quickly recognized his potential in a sport that had become the country's premier sport beginning in the 1970's.

Lin Dan competing in the badminton singles final during the 2008 Olympic Games in Beijing. (Cameron Spencer/Getty Images)

The Road to Excellence

By the age of eighteen, Dan was already a member of the prestigious national badminton squad. Although the sport had rarely captured the attention of audiences outside of Asia, the Western media immediately took notice of the spiky-haired nineteen-year-old phenom when Dan battled to a third-place finish in the 2002 All-England Open, one of the oldest and most widely covered international badminton competitions. With his less than 5-foot 10-inch, 150-pound wiry frame, he commanded the court, maintaining pressure on opponents by displaying a fierce intensity that expressed itself in a range of shots executed with pinpoint accuracy. On court, he maintained an explosive speed—critical because the shuttlecock does not travel at a consistent rate—and, with his remarkable leg strength, exhibited a gift for leaping that helped him control matches.

However, as with many athletic prodigies whose gifts bring them reputation and success early, Dan also demonstrated a penchant for boorish behavior. He disputed calls, glared at line judges and opposing coaches, and dismissed his obligation to speak with the press. Far more remarkable for a Chinese athlete, however, was how he played to the crowd, pumping his fists and strutting about the court with theatrical intensity. Within the next year, given his court presence and his high-voltage game, Dan began to dominate play on the international circuit, winning his first singles title at the Korea Open in 2002.

The Emerging Champion

Beginning with his singles title at the Denmark Open in 2003, Dan commenced the kind of domination that drew comparisons to Pete Sampras's tennis mastery a decade earlier, winning thirteen major singles titles in a little more than two

625

years. With his visual acuity, court savvy, and quick reaction time, Dan mowed his opponents. He celebrated each victory with a four-cornered military salute; like all of China's premier athletes, he maintained an officer's position in the Chinese army. His brash style of play and his rock-star charisma created an international buzz, something unprecedented for the sport. With the help of the Internet, he became an international celebrity, nicknamed "Super Dan."

In addition to his athleticism and mastery of the subtle dynamics of the game, Dan was a personality. He recalled the tennis prima donnas of the 1970's and 1980's, regularly interrupting matches with his hot-tempered reactions to calls and complaining publicly about other players and even his own coaches. Fans loved it. Lin became the sport's hottest commodity; his presence guaranteed to sell seats. When he began a public relationship with China's reigning female badminton champion, Xie Xingfang, the two athletes quickly became China's most famous sports couple.

Nonetheless, Dan was more than a show. Incredibly, between 2004 and 2008, he maintained a nearly unbroken streak as the sport's top-ranked player. In 2007, he became only the second male player in the history of the sport to win consecutive world championships. Still in his early twenties, he was his country's dominant athlete.

Continuing the Story

However, in badminton, a legacy is defined in Olympic competition. This is particularly true for China, which, since the sport was introduced into play at the 1992 Barcelona Olympic Games, garnered twenty-two medals in the sport's five events, including eight golds. Entering competition at the 2004 Athens Olympic Games ranked number one in the world, Dan was eliminated in the first round. His defenders quickly pointed out that the 15-point Olympic scoring system—versus the 21-point arrangement in international competition—tended to favor underdogs. In fact, no top-seeded player had ever won the gold medal.

Dan then set his sights on the 2008 Olympic Games in Beijing. There, before a home crowd, at twenty-five years old and at the height of his ath-

Major Badminton Championships

Year	Competition	Event	Place
2002	Asian Games	Team	3d
	All-England Open	Singles	3d
2002, 2007	Korea Open Super Series	Singles	1st
2003	German Open	Singles	2d
2003-04	China Open	Singles	1st
2003-04, 2007	Denmark Open Super Series	Singles	1st
2003, 2005-06	Hong Kong Open	Singles	1st
2004	Indonesia Open	Singles	3d
	Japan Open	Singles	3d
	Swiss Open	Singles	1st
2004-05, 2007	German Open	Singles	1st
2004, 2006-07	All-England Open	Singles	1st
2004, 2006, 2008	Thomas and Uber Cup	Team	1st
2005	Singapore Open	Singles	3d
	World Championships	Singles	2d
2005-06	Japan Open	Singles	1st
	Malaysia Open	Singles	2d
2005, 2007	China Masters Super Series	Singles	1st
2005, 2008	All-England Open	Singles	2d
2006	World Championships	Singles	1st
	Asian Games	Team	1st
		Singles	2d
	Macau Open	Singles	1st
	Chinese Taipei Open	Singles	1st
	China Open	Singles	3d
	German Open	Singles	3d
	China Masters	Singles	3d
2007	World Championships	Singles	1st
	Hong Kong Super Series	Singles	1st
2008	Olympic Games	Singles	Gold
	Swiss Super Series	Singles	1st
	Korea Super Series	Singles	2d

letic prowess, he was to be the heavy favorite. However, in the months leading up to the Games, he was embroiled in two public run-ins, one with an opposing coach over a disputed line call at the Korea Open, the other, far more serious, included unsubstantiated charges that he had punched his own coach. Many speculated that Dan was struggling to handle the enormous pressure of claiming the gold medal. Nonetheless, in Beijing, Dan dominated play, beating his opponents often by double-digit margins, to claim the gold medal, all the while playing to the fanatic cheers of the Beijing crowds.

Summary

With his tenacious attacking style, balletic grace, remarkable arsenal of shots, vertical leap, and mercurial temperament, Lin Dan has represented a new kind of sports phenomena for China. He has been a striking contrast to the often faceless athlete produced by the Chinese system of an earlier era.

He brought a distinctly Western sense of arrogance and celebrity that compelled China to reassess the privileged position its superior athletes had long held. Many in the Chinese media objected vociferously to Dan's status as a role model for contemporary Chinese athletes. In that regard, he represented a pivotal challenge to China's developing relationship with the West.

Joseph Dewey

Additional Sources

Bloss, Margaret Varner. *Badminton.* New York: McGraw-Hill, 2000.

Guoqi Xu. *Olympic Dreams: China and Sports 1895-2008.* Cambridge, Mass.: Harvard University Press, 2008.

Price, Monroe, and Daniel Dayard, eds. *Owning the Olympics: Narratives of the New China.* Ann Arbor, Mich.: Digital Culture, 2008.

Gerry Lindgren

Born: March 6, 1946
Spokane, Washington
Also known as: Gerald Paul Lindgren (full name)

Early Life

Gerald "Gerry" Paul Lindgren was born March 6, 1946, in Spokane, Washington. Gerry's parents, Eleanor and Myrl, had two older sons, Lyle and Mickey. Gerry grew up in Spokane. He was a small, fragile boy who was rejected by his father and favored by his mother. He became a class clown in school to gain acceptance from his peers because he did not get much positive feedback at home.

In junior high school, Gerry began to run long distances while he delivered newspapers. He tried out for the track team, but the longest race was 660 yards. He had only moderate early running success but found that he enjoyed running and that it was about the only sport in which he could physically participate.

The Road to Excellence

Gerry attended Rogers High School in Spokane and was coached by Tracey Walters. Walters became a father figure to Gerry, encouraging him to work hard and to develop discipline in his training.

Gerry did not believe he had much talent for distance running, but under the guidance of Coach Walters, he felt that if he worked hard, he would succeed. Gerry trained twice a day, often running hard intervals in the morning and racing long distances in the afternoon. He remained fairly injury-free even though he probably overtrained during his teenage years. He did, however, suffer from stomach ulcers throughout his career.

As a high school sophomore, Gerry finished second at the state cross-country meet. Walters recognized that Gerry had tremendous potential. Gerry, however, did not accept the idea that he might be talented. He felt that he was unworthy of winning races and unable to beat more talented runners. Walters berated Gerry for not pushing himself harder, particularly when he held back in a practice meet and let an upperclassman beat him. Gerry responded by winning the state mile run as a junior.

By the time Gerry graduated from Rogers High School, he had set national high school records for the mile, two-mile, and three-mile runs, as well as the 5,000-meter distance. In 1964, he qualified for the U.S. track and field team. He was chosen to

Gerry Lindgren (127) leading in a 5,000-meter race in Los Angeles in 1967. (AP/Wide World Photos)

Major Running Championships

Year	Competition	Event	Place	Time
1960	NCAA Outdoor Championships	3 miles	1st	13:47.2
1964	Olympic Games	10,000 meters	9th	29:20.6
	U.S. v. U.S.S.R. meet	10,000 meters	1st	—
1965	National AAU Championships	3 miles	1st	13:10.6
	National AAU Outdoor Championships	6 miles	1st	27:11.6 WR
1966	NCAA Indoor Championships	3,000 meters	1st	8:41.3
	NCAA Outdoor Championships	3 miles	1st	13:33.7
		6 miles	1st	28:07.0
1967	NCAA Indoor Championships	3,000 meters	1st	8:34.7
	NCAA Outdoor Championships	3 miles	1st	13:33.7
		6 miles	1st	28:44.0
	National AAU Outdoor Championships	3 miles	1st	13:10.6
1968	NCAA Outdoor Championships	6 miles	1st	—

Note: WR = World Record

race 10,000 meters in the annual United States versus Soviet Union dual meet, a competition that had come to exemplify the Cold War tensions between the two major political powers.

The Emerging Champion

No American had ever won the 10,000-meter race against the Soviets. Gerry was only 5 feet 6 inches tall and was dwarfed by the taller Soviets in the race. However, Gerry burst away at about four miles into the race and won handily. The more than fifty thousand fans at the meet cheered him throughout the final mile.

Gerry's victory against the Soviets made him a national hero. He became known as the small high school boy who beat the older, more mature Soviets. The media noted that Gerry's victory also epitomized the political system of the United States and its citizens' strong sense of nationalism.

Later in 1964, Gerry qualified for the 10,000-meter run in the Tokyo Olympic Games. However, he injured an ankle in practice and finished in ninth place, while his teammate, Billy Mills, won in an upset.

Gerry went to Washington State University (WSU) and was coached by Jack Mooberry. While at WSU, Gerry won an unprecedented eleven national championships in cross country and indoor and outdoor track.

Continuing the Story

In 1965, Gerry was caught in the middle of a power struggle between the National Collegiate Athletic Association (NCAA) and the Amateur Athletic Union (AAU), the two major governing bodies for track and field. The NCAA threatened to terminate the athletic scholarship of any athlete who competed in AAU-sanctioned races. In the summer, Gerry ignored the NCAA boycott and set a shared world record with Billy Mills in the six-mile run at the National AAU meet. He was not penalized, and he actually became a hero to those in the track and field community who disapproved of the feud between the two governing bodies.

Gerry trained for the 1968 Mexico City Olympics, but an injured Achilles tendon ruined his opportunity. Following his graduation from WSU with a major in political science, Gerry had difficulty finding a job that allowed him to make a decent living while continuing to train. He became a motivational speaker in the early 1970's and gave seminars on how to fulfill one's potential.

In 1971, Gerry resumed heavy training in preparation for the 1972 Munich Olympics. Once again he suffered an injury prior to the Olympic trials and did not qualify. He signed a professional track contract with the International Track Association later in the year, but the group had folded by 1976. Gerry never made it back to world-class running levels after 1972. He had married in 1970, and he and his wife, Betty, had two sons, Steven and Jeremy.

Records

Held world 6-mile record (27:11.6)

Held American collegiate records in distance events

Best mark for 1 mile (4:01.5), 2 miles (8:35.4), 3 miles (12:53.0), 5,000 meters (13:33.8), 10,000 meters (28:40.2)

Honors and Awards

1964 *Track and Field News* High School Runner of the Year

Strangely, Gerry disappeared in 1980; he left his family and dropped out of society. His close friend and rival, Kenny Moore, later contacted Gerry and attributed Gerry's sudden departure to his inability to cope with his early phenomenal running success and later performance failures. Gerry relocated to Hawaii; in 2005, he became the woman's track and field coach at the University of Hawaii.

Summary

For many track and field fans, Gerry Lindgren will be remembered as the small, fragile high school boy who beat the mighty Soviet runners in the 1964 10,000-meter race. To others, he will be remembered as an outstanding track athlete who was not afraid to stand up to authority.

Tinker D. Murray

Additional Sources

Dunne, Jim, and Joe Henderson. *The Gerry Lindgren Story.* Mountain View, Calif.: Runner's World Magazine, 1971.

Friedman, Steve. *The Agony of Victory: When Winning Isn't Enough.* New York: Arcade, 2007.

_____. "Lost and Found." *Runner's World* 39, no. 7 (July, 2004): 62.

Lindgren, Gerry. *Gerry Lindgren's Book on Running.* Honolulu, Hawaii: Author, 2005.

Eric Lindros

Born: February 28, 1973
    London, Ontario, Canada
Also known as: Eric Bryan Lindros (full name);
    the Big E; Captain Crunch, E-Train

Early Life

Eric Bryan Lindros was born to Carl and Bonnie Lindros on February 28, 1973, in London, Ontario, Canada. Both parents achieved some success as amateur athletes and conveyed their love of sport and their competitive spirits to Eric, his younger brother, Brett, and his sister, Robin. Eric and his father practiced for hours throughout the Canadian winters on backyard ice rinks. When Eric was six, his mother enrolled him in a noncontact hockey league, hoping to drain some of his excess energy. He quickly developed an appreciation for the complexity of the sport.

The Road to Excellence

Blessed with skill, determination, and size, Eric often played in leagues with boys two years older than him. When he was fourteen, a year in which he grew 7 inches, he decided to become a professional hockey player. By 1989, he qualified to play in the Ontario Hockey League, a stepping-stone to the NHL. However, when the Sault Sainte Marie Greyhounds drafted him, Eric refused to report to a team so far from his home. In the fall of 1989, he finished high school and played in a league that was less competitive.

In early 1990, Eric joined the Canadian national junior team, which competed for the junior world championship in Finland. He was the youngest player in the tournament, but he scored 4 goals in seven games to help Canada win the competition. He returned to discover that the Ontario Hockey League had changed its rules to let Eric join the Oshawa Generals, closer to home. That spring Oshawa captured the Memorial Cup, the championship of the Canadian Hockey League.

During the 1990-1991 season, Eric dominated the Ontario Hockey League and won

the prestigious Canadian Hockey League player of the year award. He was the obvious top choice for the NHL draft in June, 1991. Eric and his parents warned the Quebec Nordiques, who had the first pick, that Eric would not sign with them. He did not speak French, nor would he receive sufficient salary and recognition in Quebec. The Lindroses emphasized that the Nordiques' owner was not committed to winning. Nevertheless, the Nordiques drafted Eric, and he refused to sign.

The Emerging Champion

While waiting for the Nordiques to capitulate to his demands and trade him, Eric completed a remarkable amateur hockey career. In the 1991 world ju-

Eric Lindros celebrating a goal during an NHL game in late 2005. (Dave Sandford/Getty Images)

NHL Statistics

Season	GP	G	Ast.	Pts.	PIM
1992-93	61	41	34	75	147
1993-94	65	44	53	97	103
1994-95	46	29	41	70	60
1995-96	73	47	68	115	163
1996-97	52	32	47	79	136
1997-98	63	30	41	71	134
1998-99	71	40	53	93	120
1999-00	55	27	32	59	83
2001-02	72	37	36	73	138
2002-03	81	19	34	53	141
2003-04	39	10	22	32	60
2005-06	33	11	11	22	43
2006-07	49	5	21	26	70
Totals	711	367	472	839	1,328

Notes: GP = games played; G = goals; Ast. = assists; Pts. = points; PIM = penalties in minutes. 2004-05 NHL season canceled because of lockout.

nior championships, he dominated the competition, scoring 6 goals and adding 11 assists in only seven games. The victory represented the first time Canada won back-to-back gold medals in that tournament. Later that year, Eric made Team Canada as an eighteen-year-old amateur, the youngest Canadian ever to compete against other nations for the Canada Cup. Playing against NHL stars, Eric scored 3 goals, had 2 assists, and delivered dozens of devastating body checks. Team Canada was victorious. In the 1992 Olympics, Eric tallied 5 goals and 6 assists in eight games for the all-amateur squad, but the Unified Team, of the former Soviet Union, captured the gold.

Continuing the Story

On June 30, 1992, the Quebec Nordiques traded Eric to two different teams. An arbitrator decided that the Philadelphia Flyers had obtained Eric. Philadelphia gave Quebec its starting goaltender, five other players, two first-round draft picks, and $15 million. The Flyers' management knew that Eric was the star around whom it could build a championship team.

Eric missed two months of his first season with knee injuries, costing him the Calder Memorial Trophy as the top rookie. He still scored 41 goals and had 34 assists, remarkable for a center on a next-to-last-place team.

The strike-shortened 1994-1995 season did

not stop Eric's rise. Only twenty-one, Eric became team captain and led the Flyers to the team's first playoff appearance in five years. Eric won the Hart Memorial Trophy as the most valuable player. The following year Eric scored 115 points and finished second to Mario Lemieux for the Hart Trophy.

In 1996-1997 the forward line of Eric, John LeClair, and Mikael Renberg, nicknamed the "Legion of Doom," led the Flyers to the Stanley Cup Finals. The three players supplied a physical presence and scoring punch that few teams could match. Eric led all scorers in the playoffs. In the finals, however, the talented Detroit Red Wings stopped the Legion, and the Flyers lost in four straight games. Late in the next season, Eric scored his 500th point; only four players had achieved that goal in fewer games. Eric was only twenty-five years old, but he was named captain of the Canadian team for the 1998 Winter Olympics in Nagano, Japan.

On March 7, 1998, Darius Kasparaitis of the Pittsburgh Penguins checked Eric so hard that the latter suffered a serious concussion. A year later, a freak injury during a game in Nashville sent him to the hospital with a collapsed and bleeding lung. The life-threatening condition kept him out of the playoffs and prevented him from achieving another 100-point season.

Physical problems continued to plague Eric's career. In the last half of the 1999-2000 season, he suf-

Honors and Awards

1990	Memorial Cup All-Star Team
1991	Canadian Hockey League Player of the Year
	Canadian Hockey League Plus/Minus Award
	Canadian Hockey League Top Draft Prospect Award
	Youngest-ever member of Team Canada
	Red Tilson Trophy
	Eddie Powers Memorial Trophy
	Ontario Hockey League All-Star First Team
1992	Silver medal with Team Canada at the Olympic Games
1993	NHL All-Rookie Team
1994-96, 1999	Bobby Clarke Trophy
1994, 1996-2000	NHL All-Star Game
1995	*Sporting News* NHL Player of the Year
	Hart Memorial Trophy
	Sporting News All-Star First Team
	Lester B. Pearson Award
1996	Team Canada
1998	Team Canada captain
2002	Gold medal with Team Canada Olympic Games

fered three more concussions. He rejoined the Flyers during the third round of the playoffs, but on May 26, 2000, a vicious hit by an opponent knocked Eric unconscious. Many feel that Eric's career as an elite player ended with that concussion. Although healthy enough to play by November, 2000, Eric was determined to change teams because of strained relations with Flyers' management. After Eric sat out the entire 2000-2001 season, the Flyers traded him to the New York Rangers in August, 2001.

In 2001-2002, Eric enjoyed a productive season with 73 points. Eric's production decreased dramatically the following two seasons with the Rangers and one with the Toronto Maple Leafs, and he suffered his eighth concussion. In his final season, 2006-2007, Eric played for the Dallas Stars, but he scored only 5 goals. On November 8, 2007, Eric announced his retirement.

The preceding summer Eric had begun working with the NHL Player's Association. He was instrumental in choosing a new executive director to address the incompetence and corruption that hampered the union's leadership. On November 11, 2007, Eric was appointed the NHL Players' Association ombudsman. Players praised his efforts to make the union's activities transparent and to help the NHL overcome the lingering negative feelings from the 2004-2005 lockout season. Eric also spoke out against violent aspects of hockey, such as checks to the head.

Summary

Bobby Clarke, a Hockey Hall of Famer, concluded that at the age of sixteen Eric Lindros was ready for the NHL. Eric had a quick and hard wrist shot, and he was a graceful yet powerful skater. At 6 feet 4 inches and 235 pounds, he was difficult for opponents to control. Known as the "Big E," "Captain Crunch," and the "E-Train," Eric delivered checks that left opponents dazed and intimidated. His skillful passing made the "Legion of Doom" a scoring machine. Despite his final seasons, Eric averaged a remarkable 1.14 points per game during his career.

Eric's refusal to play for Sault Sainte Marie and Quebec led to accusations of arrogance. He contradicted those claims through his willingness to represent his country in numerous international events, by gaining his teammates' respect, and through his work for the Children's Miracle Network. Eric gave $5 million to the Health Science Center in London, Ontario, which is believed to be the largest contribution by an athlete in Canada. Only injuries limited Eric's achievements in the NHL.

M. Philip Lucas

Additional Sources

Greenberg, Jay. *Full Spectrum: The Complete History of the Philadelphia Flyers.* Chicago: Triumph Books, 1997.

Kennedy, Kostya. "Eric Lindros: Worthy of the Hall?" *Sports Illustrated* 107, no. 20 (November 19, 2007).

Lindros, Eric. *Pursue Your Goals.* Dallas, Tex.: Taylor, 1999.

Lindros, Eric, and Randy Starkman. *Fire on Ice.* Toronto: HarperCollins, 1991.

Poulin, Daniel. *Lindros: Doing What's Right for Eric.* Markham, Ont.: Panda, 1992.

Savage, Jeff. *Eric Lindros: High Flying Center.* Minneapolis: Lerner, 1998.

Ted Lindsay

Born: July 29, 1925
  Renfrew, Ontario, Canada
Also known as: Robert Blake Theodore Lindsay
  (full name)

Early Life

Robert Blake Theodore "Ted" Lindsay was born on July 29, 1925, in Renfrew, Ontario, Canada. His father, Bert Lindsay, had played goaltender for the Renfrew Millionaires, a hockey team that was famous before the National Hockey League (NHL) existed. Later in his career, the elder Lindsay played part of a season with the NHL Toronto Arenas, later known as the Toronto Maple Leafs. Young Ted was determined to follow in his father's footsteps and become a professional hockey player. He got his first set of skates from a neighbor at the age of nine. These did not last long as Ted wore them out by practicing long hours.

The Road to Excellence

Although small of stature for a hockey player at 5 feet 8 inches tall and 155 pounds, Ted had the fierce determination to succeed. Throughout his career, he made a point of never backing down from another player. His ability and competitiveness earned him the respect of all his teammates and opposing players. While playing for a junior hockey team in Ontario, Ted attracted the attention of several major-league scouts. In 1944, he helped the Oshawa Generals win the Memorial Cup, which was Canada's junior hockey title. That same year, at the age of nineteen, Ted was signed to a professional contract with the Detroit Red Wings. His first year in professional hockey was a good one; he scored 17 goals in forty-five games.

The Emerging Champion

Ted was always known as a tough hockey player and usually was at, or near, the top of the penalties list each year. Along with

that, he was a fine playmaker and always a team player. His talents were best displayed when he was teamed with center Sid Abel and left winger Gordie Howe. That trio, known as the "Production Line," helped the Red Wings to win eight league titles and four Stanley Cup championships in the late 1940's and early 1950's. Ted was the heart of that line. He was not the biggest player, but he played tough every game. He was a hard worker along the boards, where few players liked to be.

Ted made the NHL all-star team nine times and once led the league in scoring, which would be an incredible accomplishment during any era. The National Hockey League had only six teams, and each squad was loaded with talent. To be a tough

Ted Lindsay in 1955. (Bruce Bennett/Getty Images)

player who could skate, pass, and score was difficult, but Ted possessed the talent to do just that.

Continuing the Story

Prior to the 1957-1958 season, Ted was traded to the Chicago Blackhawks. In his three seasons there, he was able to help the Blackhawks get out of last place and into the playoffs twice. However, he never thought highly of Chicago, and finally, after sixteen years in the big leagues with Detroit and Chicago, Ted retired.

Four years later, however, at the age of thirty-nine, Ted returned to the game. His return was not inspired by money; his business ventures had been successful and he was well off. Rather, the thrill of the game and the desire to end his career in a Detroit uniform brought him back. The Detroit management wanted him back because they knew their team played better when he was around. Nobody slacked off when Ted was in uniform.

From hockey's earliest days, good teams had a variety of players. There were the flashy skaters, the goal scorers, the playmakers, and the policemen. During every era of the sport, the policemen helped control the mood and tempo of each game so as to give the scorers an opportunity to perform their magic on the ice. Ted filled this role of "ice cop" throughout his career. In Ted's case, however, he brought considerably more to the game. Not only did his rugged style set the tone of the contest, but his natural ability also made him into a scorer and playmaker. This was a rare combination and one that was recognized by fans, teammates, and management. Finally, in the summer of 1965, at the age of forty, Ted decided it was time to quit for good.

In 1966, Ted was elected to the Hockey Hall of Fame. While honored by the selection, he declined to attend the ceremonies when he learned that members' wives and families would be excluded from some of the events. True to form, Ted scowled, "If my wife and kids can't see the old man honored,

NHL Statistics

Season	GP	G	Ast.	Pts.	PIM
1944-45	45	17	6	23	43
1945-46	47	7	10	17	14
1946-47	59	27	15	42	57
1947-48	60	33	19	52	95
1948-49	50	26	28	54	97
1949-50	69	23	55	78	141
1950-51	67	24	35	59	110
1951-52	70	30	39	69	123
1952-53	70	32	39	71	111
1953-54	70	26	36	62	110
1954-55	49	19	19	38	85
1955-56	67	27	23	50	161
1956-57	70	30	55	85	103
1957-58	68	15	24	39	110
1958-59	70	22	36	58	184
1959-60	68	7	19	26	91
1964-65	69	14	14	28	173
Totals	1,068	379	472	851	1,808

Notes: GP = games played; G = goals; Ast. = assists; Pts. = points; PIM = penalties in minutes

what's the point?" Rather than leave the family out, Ted stayed home.

Summary

No man on skates was ever too big or too tough for Ted Lindsay to challenge. His fierce determination, his ability, and his team-first attitude gave him the edge as a hockey player. At the start of his comeback with Detroit, league president Clarence Campbell scoffed at the idea, believing it to be a publicity stunt by both the team and the player. After the season was over, he called it one of the most amazing comebacks in professional sports. To Ted, it was just a matter of playing a game he loved. His induction into the hall of fame proved that Ted was one of the greatest left wingers ever to play the game.

Carmi Brandis

Additional Sources

Dryden, Steve, and Michael Ulmer, eds. *The Top One Hundred NHL Hockey Players of All Time.* Toronto: McClelland & Stewart, 1999.

McDonell, Chris. *For the Love of Hockey: Hockey Stars' Personal Stories.* Richmond Hill, Ont.: Firefly Books, 2004.

_____. *Hockey's Greatest Stars: Legends and Young Lions.* Richmond Hill, Ont.: Firefly Books, 2005.

Podnieks, Andrew. *Lord Stanley's Cup.* Bolton, Ont.: Fenn, 2004.

Honors and Awards

1948, 1950-54, 1956-57	NHL First Team All-Star
1949	NHL Second Team All-Star
1950	Art Ross Trophy
1966	Inducted into Hockey Hall of Fame

Elizabeth Lipă

Born: October 26, 1964
    Siret, Romania
Also known as: Elisabeta Oleniuc (birth name)

Early Life

Elizabeth Lipă was born Elisabeta Oleniuc on October 26, 1964, in the northeastern Romanian town of Siret, near the Ukrainian border. Her family moved to Botosani on the Moldavian border, where Elisabeth grew up. As a child, Elizabeth excelled in sports, distinguishing herself as a multi-sport prodigy who relished the thrill of competition. In her second year of high school, she was recruited by communist government coaches who routinely scouted secondary schools for promising talent.

Assessing her muscular frame, her powerful legs, and her tremendous endurance, coaches directed Elizabeth to take up rowing, a sport she had never attempted. Romania had a long and proud history of rowing, and in the years after World War II, it had become one of Romania's national sports. To be asked to train in rowing was a high honor. Elizabeth had to move to Bucharest; only sixteen, she had no relatives in the capital city, but with the support of her family, she made the difficult move.

The Road to Excellence

Between training in Romania's national Olympic rowing center and completing her high school degree, Elizabeth had little time for homesickness. She loved rowing—she trained in both single-oar sweeping and double-oar sculling—because it necessitated a combination of aerobic endurance and upper-body strength. Raised in an area of Romania with many rivers, Elizabeth greatly enjoyed her time on the water. Her commitment to the sport was absolute—she suspended attending classes and came to school only for exams.

By nineteen years old, she was a formidable rower. She participated in European competitions in both 1982 and 1983 without distinction but used the experience to prepare for the Olympic Games. She made the Romanian Olympic team sent to the Los Angeles Games in 1984. She had an immediate impact, capturing a gold medal in double scull. In the last years of the Cold War, Elizabeth embodied the communist-athlete ideal: She seldom smiled or played to the cameras. Rather, she went about the business of rowing with machine-like efficiency, an intimidating demeanor, and total focus. What media attention she garnered amid the hoopla of the Olympics focused on her government career as a police chief commissioner in the Romanian equivalent of the Central Intelligence Agency.

The Emerging Champion

In the 1988 Olympic Games in Seoul, South Korea, Elizabeth won a silver medal in the double scull and a bronze in the quadruple scull. However, the media largely ignored the achievement, assuming that, given the toll row-

Major Rowing Championships

Year	Competition	Event	Place
1982	Rowing World Championships	Quadruple scull	3d
1983	Rowing World Championships	Double scull	3d
1984	Olympic Games	Double scull	Gold
1985	Rowing World Championships	Double scull	2d
1986	Rowing World Championships	Double scull	2d
1987	Rowing World Championships	Double scull	2d
1988	Olympic Games	Double scull	Silver
		Quadruple scull	Bronze
1989	Rowing World Championships	Double scull	2d
		Single scull	1st
1991	Rowing World Championships	Single scull	2d
		Double scull	2d
1992	Olympic Games	Double scull	Silver
		Single scull	Gold
1994	Rowing World Championships	Eight with coxswain	3d
		Double scull	2d
1996	Olympic Games	Eight with coxswain	Gold
2000	Olympic Games	Eight with coxswain	Gold
2003	Rowing World Championships	Eight with coxswain	2d
2004	Olympic Games	Eight with coxswain	Gold

ing routinely takes, Elizabeth's career was coming to an end.

However, Elizabeth maintained her rigorous training. She returned to the Bucharest training facility and reworked her pull-and-lunge techniques; she practiced tirelessly along the channels of the Snagov River. Despite Romania's long tradition of Olympic championships in rowing, the country's facilities were not the caliber of other national powerhouses. Given unfolding political uncertainties as Romania became a sovereign nation in the wake of the collapse of the Soviet Union in the early 1990's, the maintenance of such sports facilities lagged even further behind the Greek, Dutch, and Russian teams. Furthermore, the river channels lacked signposts and timers and their bottoms were choked with weeds.

At the next Summer Games, the 1992 Olympics in Barcelona, Spain, the Romanians and Elizabeth—in her third Olympiad and approaching thirty years old—finally captured international attention. Elizabeth claimed a silver medal in the double scull and a gold in the prestigious single-scull event, considered by many to be the defining competition in the sport. In this event, a lone rower must physically control the progress of the skiff and remain mentally strong.

Continuing the Story

Many assumed that Elizabeth would retire following the 1992 Games because she had established her legacy. She hinted she was ready to concentrate on her government career and her family: A devoted mother, she regularly brought her son and daughter to the training facility and relied on a family caregiver during the Olympic season. However, she found retirement difficult and returned to training with new resolve. She focused on team events, particularly the eight-oared team runs. At the 1996 centennial Olympic Games in Atlanta, Georgia, Elizabeth made Olympic medal history, claiming a gold medal, her sixth career medal, which was unprecedented in her sport.

In 2000, determined not to concede to the inevitability of time and committed to a team and to a sport that she regarded as part of her national identity, Elizabeth returned to the Olympic Games. At the millennium Games in Sydney, Australia, she scored her second gold in the eight-with-coxswain event. Most remarkably, she repeated that performance at the 2004 Games in Athens, Greece. At forty years old, she competed against athletes half her age. Her career medal total—five golds, two silvers, and one bronze—and her legacy of competitive excellence in both sculling and sweeping and in both individual and team formats made her the most decorated female athlete the sport had ever produced.

Summary

Elizabeth Lipă's rowing achievements were unprecedented in a sport in which high-performance athletes are fortunate to last a decade. To have dominated a sport across six Olympiads placed Elizabeth in historic company—only four athletes have ever done that. Furthermore, Elizabeth's career illustrates how former Soviet athletes helped define identities for their emerging nations.

Joseph Dewey

Additional Sources

Dodd, Christopher. "Rowing: Expect a Fiesta of Fancy Dress and Fast Women at Henley." The Guardian, June 30, 1993.

Guttmann, Allen. *The Olympics: A History of the Modern Games.* Champaign: University of Illinois Press, 2002.

Tara Lipinski

Born: June 10, 1982
　　　Philadelphia, Pennsylvania
Also known as: Tara Kristen Lipinski (full name)

Early Life
Born on June 10, 1982, Tara Kristen Lipinski is the only child of Jack Lipinski, an oil refinery executive, and Pat Lipinski, a former Wall Street secretary. Although Tara was born in Philadelphia, the Lipinskis soon moved to Sewell, New Jersey, where they lived until Tara was nine.

Tara was an active toddler, and her mother was alert to anything that might help channel the little girl's energy. When Tara was three, her mother signed her up for roller-skating lessons. Tara showed a natural talent for roller skating and loved skating in front of an audience. Soon she was entering and winning roller-skating competitions, including a regional and a national championship.

The Road to Excellence
When Tara was six, her parents took her ice skating at the urging of a family friend. By watching the other skaters she quickly learned to keep her balance on the ice and soon was performing jumps from her roller-skating repertoire. She fell in love with ice skating and immediately started taking lessons.

In 1991, the Lipinskis moved to Sugar Land, Texas, near Houston. Tara tried to continue figure skating in Texas, but she and her mother had to get up at four every morning and drive to the nearest rink so Tara could practice. In 1993, Tara and her mother moved to Delaware so she could pursue her skating on a less taxing schedule, while her father remained in Texas. A year later, Tara and her mother moved once again, this time to Bloomfield, Michigan, where Tara began training with coach Richard Callaghan.

The Emerging Champion
In 1994, twelve-year-old Tara gained national attention as the youngest athlete ever to win a gold medal at the Olympic Festival. Two years later at the World Figure Skating Championships she placed fifteenth, a respectable accomplishment for a newcomer, and third at the U.S. Championships. She also set a record, becoming the first woman to land a triple loop, triple loop combination jump in competition.

In 1997, Tara unexpectedly swept the World Figure Skating Championships, the U.S. Championships, and Champions Series, placing first in each competition. At

Tara Lipinski skating during the 1998 Winter Olympic Games in Nagano. (Clive Brunskill/Allsport/Getty Images)

Major Figure-Skating Championships

Year	Competition	Place
1994	Midwestern Novice	1st
	Southwestern Novice	1st
	National Novice	2d
	U.S. Olympic Festival	1st
	Blue Swords	1st
1995	Nebelhorn Trophy	4th
	National Juniors	2d
	World Junior Championships	4th
1996	World Junior Selections	2d
	Skate Canada	2d
	South Atlantic Juniors	1st
	Nations Cup	2d
	Trophée Lalique	3d
	World Championships	15th
	National Championships	3d
	World Juniors	5th
1997	Trophée Lalique	2d
	World Championships	1st
	Hershey's Challenge (team)	1st
	National Championships	1st
	Skate America	2d
1997-98	Champions Series Final	1st
1998	Jefferson Pilot Financial Championships	1st
	National Championships	2d
	Olympic Games	Gold
	Skate TV Championships	1st
	Ice Wars	1st Team USA
		1st Ladies
	Team Ice Wars	2d Team USA
1998-99	Team Ice Wars	1st Ladies
1999	World Pros	1st
	Team Ice Wars	1st Team USA
	Pro Superteam Challenge	1st

Tara entered the Olympic Village determined to experience everything possible about the event, so that she would have wonderful memories even if she did not win a medal. Her approach contrasted with that of figure skater Michelle Kwan, who eschewed much of the camaraderie with other athletes and possibilities for entertainment in the Olympic Village. Kwan was expected to win the gold medal, but Tara's wins at the national and World Figure Skating Championships proved that she was also a serious contender for the gold.

The media focused on a rivalry between the two young women, although Tara and Kwan had been casually friendly. Increasingly distraught by the pressure of competing and the public perception that she was skating to defeat Kwan, Tara briefly considered dropping out of the competition after her short program.

After deciding to go forward, Tara skated a perfect long program. Her seven triple jumps included her trademark triple-loop combination, a harder element than Kwan's combination jump. Tara won the gold medal. At fifteen she was the youngest woman to place first in ladies' figure skating at the Olympics.

Continuing the Story

After her gold-medal win in Nagano, Tara immediately wanted to start training for the 2002 Winter Olympics. However, after years of sacrifice and complete dedication to her daughter's skating career, Tara's mother wanted to move home to Texas. Tara understood and made the decision to leave amateur competition. She officially became a professional figure skater in April, 1998.

In the years immediately following her Olympic victory, Tara skated professionally with Scott Hamilton's Stars on Ice tour and made several television specials. She began an acting career as a guest star in prime-time television programs and in a brief role as a college student on the daytime soap opera *The Young and the Restless*. Tara also signed contracts to endorse many products, from Capezio dancewear to Snapple fruit drinks.

Tara taught at skating clinics for young hopeful skaters around the country, visited children in hospitals, and gave lessons to sick children for the

fourteen, she set a record as the youngest world champion in the history of the sport. At the 1998 U.S. Championships Tara landed seven triple jumps in her long program and placed second, qualifying for the U.S. Olympic team.

Despite her successes, Tara was criticized as a robotic jumper, impressive in her athleticism but unable to interpret music with emotional maturity on the ice. To correct this, she worked with a ballet instructor—while polishing her Olympic programs—and began to create a more sophisticated image. She used practice sessions to improve her artistic presentation in the days before the Olympic competition. She watched daily videotapes of practice sessions and discussed the balletic elements of her program with her choreographer, Sandra Bezic. Small changes in her movements improved the overall look of her program.

Make-A-Wish Foundation. She was also a national spokesperson for Tobacco-Free Kids and for the Boys and Girls Clubs of America. Although she was able to move back to Texas with her parents, her schedule still required many hours of practice and constant travel to make personal appearances.

Summary

Tara Lipinski's Olympic win, her dedication to her sport, and her naturally bubbly personality made her a heroine to many young women and opened up countless opportunities for other young athletes. Her determination was rewarded as she set new records in figure skating and achieved her ultimate dream at the Olympics.

Maureen J. Puffer-Rothenberg

Additional Sources

Hines, James R. *Figure Skating: A History.* Urbana: University of Illinois Press, 2006.

Lipinski, Tara, and Emily Costello. *Tara Lipinski: Triumph on Ice—an Autobiography.* New York: Bantam Books, 1998.

Ryan, Joan. *Little Girls in Pretty Boxes: The Making and Breaking of Elite Gymnasts and Figure Skaters.* New York: Warner Books, 2000.

Natalya Lisovskaya

Born: July 16, 1962
     Alegazy, Soviet Union (now in Russia)

Early Life

Natalya Lisovskaya was born on July 16, 1962, in Alegazy, Soviet Union (now in Russia). At the age of eleven, she began sports school in Tashkent, Uzbekistan, where her sister, Ludmila, was a student. Coach Robert Naumovich Zisman trained Natalya in the shot put and the discus. In 1980, Natalya enrolled at Moscow's central sports college and trained for three years with former Olympian Paina Melnik. Practicing at the famous Spartak Sports Club in Moscow, Natalya made rapid progress.

The Road to Excellence

With her physical attributes and dedication, Natalya's potential was recognized by several Soviet coaches. The shot put is a demanding sport that requires great strength and superb technique. Shot-putters developed various methods to gain the greatest momentum in hurling the 8-pound 14-ounce metal shot used in women's competition. The most prevalent techniques in modern shot

Natalya Lisovskaya. (Bob Thomas/Getty Images)

put are the glide and the spin. The putter must release the shot while staying in the 7-foot throwing circle. In most competitions, including the Olympics, competitors have three throws in a round. Reflecting the technique and mental concentration required to excel in the sport, leading shot-putters are usually in their late twenties. At 220 pounds and 6 feet 1 inch and possessing excellent technique, Natalya emerged as a dominant force in women's shot put. She was also a talented discus thrower with a personal record of 62.28 meters (204 feet 4 inches).

In September, 1981, at a meet in Moscow, Natalya shot the put 18.66 meters (61 feet 2 inches), becoming the Soviet champion. In 1982, she improved to 19.64 meters (64 feet 5 inches). One year later, Natalya surpassed the 20-meter (65-foot 7-inch) barrier for the first time and threw 20.02 meters (65 feet 8 inches) at the first International Association of Athletics Federations (IAAF) World Track and Field Championships. In May, 1984, after intensive training to perfect her technique, Natalya broke the Soviet women's record of 21.45 meters (70 feet 4 inches), set by Nadeshda Tchizova in 1973, with a throw of 21.75 meters (71 feet 4 inches). Seven days later, in the Soviet resort city of Sochi, she broke the world record throw of 22.45 meters (73 feet 8 inches), set by Ilona Slupianek in 1980, with a throw of 22.53 meters (73 feet 11 inches).

The Emerging Champion

Already the world-record holder, Natalya continued winning titles and extending her world record. In 1985, she came in first at the IAAF World Indoor Games in Paris, France, with a throw of 20.07 meters (65 feet 10 inches). In 1987, she won the outdoor world championship for the third time and bested her own world record with a throw of 22.60 meters (74 feet 2 inches). She won gold medals at both the World Indoor Track and Field Championships in Indianapolis, Indiana, with a throw of 20.52 meters (67 feet 4 inches), and the World Track and Field Championships, with a throw of 21.24 meters (69 feet 8 inches). Natalya set her per-

Major Shot Put Championships

Year	Competition	Place
1985	IAAF World Indoor Games	1st
1987	World Championships	1st
	World Indoor Track and Field Championships	1st
1988	Olympic Games	Gold
1990	European Championships	2d
1991	World Championships	2d
	World Indoor Track and Field Championships	3d
1992	Olympic Games	9th

sonal best indoor record of 22.14 meters (72 feet 8 inches) in Penza, Russia, on July 2, 1987.

At an outdoor meet in Moscow, in July, 1987, Natalya improved her world record with a shot put of 22.63 meters (74 feet 3 inches). Her domination continued in the Summer Olympics held in Seoul, South Korea, the following year. On September 30, 1988, twenty-six competitors vied for the twelve spots in the final round of the shot-put competition, an outdoor event. Natalya easily qualified with a throw of 19.78 meters (64 feet 11 inches). On October 1, 1988, the final round in the shot put event was held. All the competitors had six throws. Natalya won the Olympic gold medal with her final throw of 22.24 meters (73 feet). Incredibly, any of her five previous throws would have been enough to win the gold medal; the silver medalist threw 21.07 meters (69 feet 2 inches).

Continuing the Story

At the 1988 Soviet championship, Natalya came close to her world record with a shot put of 22.55 meters (74 feet). With this shot put, Natalya had made the four longest shot puts by a female athlete. However, allegations arose claiming the record-breaking shot puts of the 1980's and 1990's had been accomplished by athletes under the influence of performance-enhancing drugs. At the 1990 European Championships in athletics, Natalya won a silver medal with a throw of 20.06 meters (65 feet 10 inches). In the 1991 World Track and Field Championships, in Tokyo, Japan, she again won silver, with a throw of 20.29 meters (66 feet 7 inches). She also won a bronze medal that year in the World Indoor Track and Field Championships in Seville, Spain.

Although Natalya was no longer the dominating shot-putter that she had been in the late

1980's, she continued to compete. She made the finals in the 1992 Summer Olympics in Barcelona, Spain, although her shot put of 18.60 meters (61 feet) was good for only ninth place. She competed in occasional French meets in the late 1990's and early 2000's. Her last meet was in Dreux, France, in June, 2002.

Natalya married Yuri Sedykh, a Soviet hammer-throw champion. Their daughter, Alexia, was born in 1992. They settled in Paris. Natalya and Yuri hosted joint hammer-throw and shot-put clinics for top athletes at various locales around the world. They offered helpful critiques and video reviews of throws by budding athletes.

Summary

Natalya Lisovskaya is considered one of the greatest female shot-putters of all time. In the late 1980's, she was a triple champion, winning Olympic gold and several outdoor and indoor world championships. She won a gold medal at the 1988 Olympics, with one of the most dominating performances in Olympic history. She set the world record for shot put in 1987. This record stood for more than two decades. In addition, she set the record for the four longest shot puts by a female in history.

Howard Bromberg

Additional Sources

Berenyi, I. "Natalya Lisovskaya: A Profile of the Olympic Champion in the Shot." *Athletics* (July, 1989): 14-15.

Conner, Floyd. *The Olympics Most Wanted: The Top Ten Book of Gold Medal Gaffes, Impossible Triumphs and Other Oddities.* Washington, D.C.: Brassey's, 2001.

Gifford, Clive. *Summer Olympics: The Definitive Guide to the World's Greatest Sports Celebration.* Boston: Houghton Mifflin, 2004.

Silvester, Jay, ed. *Complete Book of Throws.* Champaign, Ill.: Human Kinetics, 2003.

Records

In 1984, set Soviet women's record of 21.75 meters (71 feet 4 inches)

In 1984, set the world record of 22.53 meters (73 feet 11 inches)

In 1987, improved world record at 22.63 meters (74 feet 3 inches)

Set the record for the four longest shot puts by a woman in history

Sergei Litvinov

Born: January 23, 1958
      Tsukarov, Krasnodar district, Soviet Union
      (now in Russia)
Also known as: Sergei Nikolayevich Litvinov (full name)

Early Life

Sergei Nikolayevich Litvinov was born on January 23, 1958, in Tsukarov, Krasnodar district, near the Black Sea, in what was then part of the Soviet Union. Born during the Cold War, Sergei was drawn into a life in the Soviet Army. He was also interested in athletics. His military career was a factor in his choice of individual athletic competition as opposed to team competition.

Sergei grew to a height of almost 5 feet 11 inches and a weight of nearly 240 pounds. His muscular build led to a natural interest in events of strength such as the hammer throw. In 1972, at the age of fourteen, he entered his first official competition. In 1974, at the age of sixteen, he threw the hammer 60.68 meters (199 feet).

The Road to Excellence

In 1976, Sergei gained international recognition when he set a world junior record with a throw of 72.38 meters (237 feet six inches). In 1977, he raised that record and also became a member of the Soviet national track and field team.

Sergei's athletic development was paralleled by his training as a Soviet Army officer. His physical training in the military helped him to develop the arm, shoulder, and back muscles vital to hammer-throw success. Because the hammer is thrown with both hands, tremendous upper-body strength and excellent coordination are required for a championship performance. The hammer is actually a sixteen-pound metal sphere attached to a grip by a steel spring wire, which is almost four feet long. The event—which is believed to have its origin in sledgehammer throwing in England and Scotland during the fifteenth and sixteenth centuries—first appeared in the Olympics in 1900.

I. Timashkov coached Sergei in the hammer throw. In 1978, Sergei improved his best to 76.32 meters (250 feet 5 inches), a mark he raised to 79.82 meters (261 feet 11 inches)in 1979. This performance enabled Sergei to join Yuri Sedykh and Yuri Tamm in a Soviet trio that dominated the hammer throw through the next decade.

The Emerging Champion

By 1980, the members of the trio were repeatedly setting and breaking world records. In May, the world record, which was then held by the German Karl-Hans Reihm, was first broken by Sedykh. Tamm followed with a new record, which was erased immediately by Sedykh. Eight days later, Sergei beat both of his countrymen and set his first world record with a mighty throw of 81.66 meters (267 feet 11 inches).

Sergei Litvinov throwing the hammer during the German national championships in 2008. (AP/Wide World Photos)

In the 1980 Summer Olympics in Moscow, the Soviet trio had the field to themselves. Because the United States and many Western European nations boycotted the Games in response to the Soviet invasion of Afghanistan, Karl-Hans Reihm, the only threat to the Soviets, could not compete.

Sedykh had won his first gold medal in the 1976 Olympics in Montreal, and he repeated as champion in 1980, with a throw of 81.80 meters (268 feet 5 inches). Sergei's first toss in Moscow was 80.64 meters (264 feet 7 inches), enough for the silver medal. Tamm won the bronze.

Following the 1980 Olympics, the competition between Sergei and Sedykh intensified, inspiring both men to previously unthinkable performances. Because Sedykh was three years older and had more experience than Sergei, his advantage held through the next three years; however, Sergei was rapidly narrowing the gap. In 1982, he set his second world record with a throw of 83.98 meters (275 feet 6 inches). Sergei placed third in the European Championships that year.

The year of 1983 marked a major summit in Sergei's career. Not only did he win the World Track and Field Championships in Helsinki, Finland, with a throw of 82.68 meters (271 feet 4 inches), but he also defeated Sedykh for the first time in a major competition—Sedykh's first such defeat since 1976. In 1983, Sergei's best effort was a tremendous 84.14 meters (276 feet) for his third world record.

In 1984, the personal duel again turned in favor of Sedykh. Although Sergei threw more than 85 meters for the first time at a meet in Cork, Ireland, he placed second to Sedykh, who set a new world record at 86.34 meters (283 feet 4 inches). The So-

Major Hammer Throw Championships

Year	Competition	Place	Distance
1980	Olympic Games	Silver	80.6 meters/264 feet 7 inches
1982	European Championships	3d	78.6 meters/257.9 feet
1983	World Championships	Gold	82.7 meters/271 feet 4 inches
1986	European Championships	2d	85.7 meters/281.2 feet
1987	World Championships	Gold	83.0 meters/272.3 feet
1988	Olympic Games	Gold	84.8 meters/278.2 feet

viet trio missed the 1984 Olympics in Los Angeles as a result of a Soviet boycott.

In 1986, Sergei reached his personal high point when he threw the hammer 86.04 meters (282 feet 4 inches). Sedykh, however, again surpassed him with a new world record of 86.74 meters (284 feet 7 inches). In 1987, Sedykh did not enter any official competition as he trained for the 1988 Olympics. This gave Sergei an easy road to win the European Cup in Prague in June and to defend his world championship successfully in Rome in September.

The climax of Sergei's career came in the 1988 Summer Olympics in Seoul, South Korea. As in 1980, the Soviet trio won all three medals, but this time, the top two positions were reversed. Sergei won the gold medal with a throw of 84.80 meters (278 feet 2 inches). Sedykh followed with 83.76 meters (274 feet 10 inches) for the silver, and Tamm again received the bronze.

Continuing the Story

The friendly rivalry between Sergei and Sedykh left a lasting impact on athletic events with individual competition. With the added incentive of both to stay a throw in front of Tamm, the impact was even greater. Sergei and Sedykh are the only men ever to throw the hammer more than 85 meters (279 feet).

The Soviet Union had many honors for its outstanding athletes. Many were awarded the title of Master of Sport; only the elite, however, were honored as Merited Masters of Sport. Along with Sedykh and Tamm, Sergei was awarded this highest title.

Sergei and his closest rival, Sedykh, retired from active competition after the 1988 Olympics. After the breakup of the Soviet Union in 1991, Tamm competed in the 1992 Barcelona Olympics for his native republic of Estonia.

Sergei retired as a Soviet Army officer about

Records and Milestones

Set world record in the hammer throw in 1980 (81.66 meters/267 feet 11 inches), 1982 (83.98 meters/275 feet 6 inches), and 1983 (84.14 meters/276 feet 2 inches)

Set world junior records in the hammer throw in 1976 (72.38 meters/237 feet 6 inches) and 1977 (78.22 meters/256 feet 7 inches)

Honors and Awards

USSR Merited Master of Sport

the same time as his retirement from track and field. At the time, he was living in Rostov-on-Don, not far from his place of birth. For several years, Sergei had been a student working on a diploma in physical education and after his retirement from the army, he began a new career as a physical-education teacher.

Summary

Throughout his many years of training, Sergei Litvinov exhibited tremendous determination to become a champion. His fierce competitive spirit, his consistent improvements, and his many awards all serve as examples of what an athlete can accomplish with hard work and dedication.

Glenn L. Swygart

Additional Sources

Greenberg, Stan. *Whitaker's Olympic Almanack: An Encyclopaedia of the Olympic Games.* Chicago: Fitzroy Dearborn, 2000.

Wallechinsky, David, and Jaime Loucky. *The Complete Book of the Olympics: 2008 Edition.* London: Aurum Press, 2008.

Liu Xiang

Born: July 13, 1983
    Shanghai, China
Also known as: Flying Man

Early Life

Liu Xiang was born July 13, 1983, in Shanghai, China, the only son of truck driver Liu Xuegen. His mother worked at a food factory. A good athlete as a child, Xiang underwent bone scans and X-rays that determined his best sport would be high jumping.

Xiang grew fast, eventually becoming 6 feet 2 inches, and by his teens developed a wiry, long-legged build. At the age of fifteen, while he attended Yichuan High School, he was tested again. This time, experts and athletic coaches concluded that with his particular musculature and bone density, Xiang would never be able to compete at a world-class level as a high jumper, and he was asked to give up the event.

The Road to Excellence

Undaunted by the prognosis, Xiang switched to hurdles, aiming to compete in 60-meter and 110-meter events. He trained hard under the guidance of Coach Sun Haiping. Though his technique was flawed, by 2000, Xiang was ready to test himself against an international field. He debuted that year at the World Junior Track and Field Championships, finishing in fourth place in the 110-meter hurdles.

After graduating from high school, Xiang enrolled at East China Normal University. By 2001, with his technique improving, he began to attract attention on the track. In May that year, he finished first in the 110-meter hurdles, in a time of 13.42 seconds, at the East Asian Games in Osaka, Japan. In August, he captured the same event at the World University Games in Beijing, winning in 13.33 seconds.

Though occasionally bothered by hamstring and tendon problems, Xiang continued to improve. In 2002, he won the gold medal in the 110-meter hurdles at the Asian Games in Pusan, Korea. At the Super Grand Prix in Switzerland he also broke world junior and Asian records for the event with a time of 13.12 seconds. The following year, he took bronze in the 60-meter hurdles at the World Indoor Track and Field Championships in Birmingham, England. He also captured third place in the 110-meter hurdles at the 2003 World Track and Field Championships in Paris, France. This performance marked him as a contender for a hurdling medal at the 2004 Summer Olympics. However, he was not considered a favorite because of his typically slow reaction off the starting blocks.

The Emerging Champion

In 2004, Xiang tuned up for the Summer Olympics by taking the silver medal in the 60-meter hurdles at the World Indoor Track and Field Championships in Budapest, Hungary. In late spring that year, at an International Association of Athletics Federations (IAAF) race in Osaka, Xiang recorded a personal best in the 110-meter hurdles: 13.06 seconds.

At the 2004 Olympics in Athens, Greece, Xiang outdid himself. With nearly flawless technique, he cleanly cleared each hurdle over 110 meters and won by almost 10 feet, tying the world record of 12.91 seconds. His victory sent the Chinese nation into a frenzy of adoration for the modest, personable athlete. Xiang had claimed the first gold medal ever won by China in a men's track and field event and dashed the widely held, and obviously er-

Major 110-Meter Hurdles Championships

Year	Competition	Place
2001	East Asian Games	1st
	World University Games	1st
2002	Asian Championships	1st
	Asian Games	1st
2003	World Championships	3d
2004	Olympic Games	Gold
2005	World Championships	2d
	East Asian Games	1st
2006	World Athletics Final	1st
	East Asian Games	1st
2007	World Championships	1st

roneous, cultural and racial stereotype that Asians were incapable of winning sprints. Xiang, who proudly accepted the Olympic gold medal while draped in a Chinese flag, was an instant hero in his home country. In the wake of his victory, he was showered with accolades and commercial sponsorship honors. Almost overnight, his image was seen on billboards and in print and television advertisements across China. With lucrative deals from Nike, McDonald's, Coca-Cola, Cadillac, and a host of other products, Xiang became a multimillionaire—he donated a quarter of the total to state and provincial athletic facilities—and a celebrity. Xiang was suddenly a more popular sports star in China than Yao Ming, the center for the Houston Rockets of the National Basketball Association.

Continuing the Story

After the Olympics, Xiang returned to competition, eyeing the 2008 Olympics in Beijing, where his athletic talents would be showcased for the whole world as he defended his hurdling title. He took silver in the 110-meter hurdles at the 2005 World Track and Field Championships in Helsinki, Finland. He won gold at the East Asian Games in Macau.

In 2006, at the Super Grand Prix in Lausanne, Switzerland, Xiang set a new world record of 12.88 seconds. He also won at the 2006 World Athletics Final in Germany. The following year, he captured a gold medal in the 110-meter hurdles at the World Track and Field Championships in Osaka, becoming the first Chinese athlete to accomplish a coveted "triple crown" as world champion, world-record holder, and Olympic champion.

Though Xiang won the gold medal in the 60-meter hurdles at the 2008 World Indoor Track and Field Championships in Valencia, Spain, trouble soon came. A bad hamstring forced him to withdraw from the Reebok Grand Prix. He false-started at the Prefontaine Classic. He declined to participate on the European circuit in order to train in China.

Finally, the 2008 Beijing Olympics arrived, and Chinese fans anticipated that Xiang would repeat as Olympic gold medalist. However, in pain from a chronic Achilles-tendon inflammation, he was forced to withdraw from the 110-meter hurdles. Faced with possible surgery, he hoped to return to competition in 2009 in preparation for the 2012 Olympics.

Summary

The most popular athlete in China, Liu Xiang was the first Asian male to win an Olympic gold medal in a short-distance track-and-field event. Winner of many international competitions in the 110- and 60-meter hurdles, and a former world-record holder, Xiang disappointed his nation when he was unable to repeat as champion at the 2008 Olympics because of injury. However, he remained a revered athlete in China.

Jack Ewing

Additional Sources

Brownell, Susan. *Beijing's Games: What the Olympics Mean to China.* Lanham, Md.: Rowman & Littlefield, 2008.

Li, Lillian M., Alison Dray-Novey, and Haili Kong. *Beijing: From Imperial Capital to Olympic City.* Basingstoke, Hampshire, England: Palgrave Macmillan, 2008.

Price, Monroe, and Daniel Dayan, eds. *Owning the Olympics: Narratives of the New China.* Ann Arbor, Mich.: Digital Culture Books, 2008.

Xu, Guogi. *Olympic Dreams: China and Sports, 1895-2008.* Cambridge, Mass.: Harvard University Press, 2008.

Nastia Liukin

Born: October 30, 1989
      Moscow, Soviet Union (now in Russia)
Also known as: Anastasia Valeryevna Liukin (full name); Anastasia; Nast

Early Life

Anastasia "Nastia" Valeryevna Liukin was born to a family of star Soviet gymnasts. Her mother, Anna Kotchneva, was the 1987 world champion in rhythmic gymnastics, and she won bronze medals in rope and hoop. Valeri, Nastia's father, won four gymnastics medals, two of them gold, at the 1988 Olympics in Seoul, South Korea. When Nastia was two years old, her family moved to New Orleans, Louisiana, where her parents obtained jobs teaching gymnastics. They brought Nastia to the gym, and she was mesmerized by the gymnastics moves. When Nastia was four, her family moved to Plano, Texas, where they opened their own gymnastics studio. Nastia began training with her father, and,

by age six, she was ready for competition. She made rapid progress, becoming a member of the junior U.S. women's artistic-gymnastics team at twelve years old.

The Road to Excellence

Nastia's first big success was her third-place finish in the all-around at the 2002 Women's U.S. Classic. In 2003, she followed that with numerous top scores in junior-division events: She earned first place in the all-around, uneven bars, balance beam, and floor exercise in the Podium Meet; she finished first in the all-around and floor exercise in the American Classic; and she was the winner in the all-around, vault, uneven bars, balance beam, and floor exercise in the Women's U.S. Classic. Most impressively, Nastia scored first in the all-around, uneven bars, balance beam, and floor exercise at the 2003 National Gymnastics Championships. Although, at fourteen, Nastia was too young to com-

Nastia Liukin performing on the uneven bars during the 2008 Olympic Games in Beijing. (Kazuhiro Nogi/AFP/Getty Images)

Major Gymnastics Championships

Year	Competition	Event	Place
2003	Pan-American Games	Team	1st
		Balance beam	1st
		All-around	2d
		Uneven bars	3d
		Floor exercise	3d
2005	World Championships	All-around	2d
		Floor	2d
		Uneven bars	1st
		Balance beam	1st
	American Cup	Balance beam	1st
2006	World Championships	Team	2d
		Uneven bars	2d
	Pacific Alliance Championships	All-around	1st
		Team	1st
		Uneven bars	1st
	American Cup	All-around	1st
2007	World Championships	Uneven bars	2d
		Team	1st
		Balance beam	1st
	Pan-American Games	Uneven bars	2d
		Team	1st
		Balance beam	2d
	Pacific Rim Championships	All-around	1st
		Team	1st
		Balance beam	1st
		Uneven bars	2d
2008	American Cup	All-around	1st
	Olympic Games	All-around	Gold
		Team	Silver
		Uneven bars	Silver
		Balance beam	Silver
		Floor	Bronze

pete in the 2004 Olympics, her Olympic dreams became more tangible after she watched her good friend and training partner Carly Patterson become the 2004 all-around Olympic champion. While preparing for the 2008 Olympics, Nastia continued her march to the top of her sport. Coached by her father, she practiced for seven hours a day, six days a week.

At 5 feet 3 inches, Nastia was tall for a gymnast. Height can be a disadvantage for gymnasts because, as Mary Lou Retton, the 1984 Olympic gold medalist in the all-around, explained, a taller body rotates more slowly. Despite her height, Nastia mastered difficult skills. She developed superb technique and featured such impressive moves as an Ono-half on uneven bars, a double front in floor exercises, and a front ariel to arabesque on the beam. In addition, she utilized her longer than usual build to add elegance, beauty, and balletic moves to her routines. Her clean, elongated lines and extreme attention to details, such as pointing her toes and fully extending her arms and legs, evoked the moves of a dancer.

Nastia won the all-around title at the 2004, 2005, and 2006 U.S. National Gymnastics Championships. At the 2005 World Gymnastics Championships, she won the uneven bars and balance beam and finished second in the all-around by only .001 point. However, in October, 2006, Nastia injured her ankle practicing a jump and was sidelined for a year because of surgery, rehabilitation, and recuperation. In July, 2007, she returned to competition but not to her previous dominating self. Questions remained about how she would do in the 2008 Olympics, although she qualified easily at the U.S. Olympic trials. Although Nastia had been hampered by inconsistent landings, she won the balance beam at the 2007 World Gymnastics Championships with a fine two and one-half twist dismount. Her first place in the 2008 American Cup boded well for her Olympic dreams.

The Emerging Champion

The women's 2008 U.S. Olympic team consisted of Nastia, Shawn Johnson, captain Alicia Sacramone, Chelsea Memmel, Samantha Peszek, and Bridget Sloan. Nastia and Johnson, who was the U.S. and world all-around champion in 2007 and the U.S. all-around champion in 2008, were favored to win. The U.S. team counted on Nastia's uneven bar routine, which was one of the most difficult in the world, to help it achieve a high team score.

At the Olympics, the U.S. team finished second in the qualifying round, despite the fact that two of the stronger members, Memmel and Peszek, had become injured after arriving in Beijing and were unable to compete. This increased the pressure on Nastia and Johnson. The performances in the qualifying round determined who would compete in the individual events, and Nastia's scores enabled her to advance to the all-around competition and the individual-event finals in bars, beam, and floor exercise.

Honors and Awards

2005	International Gymnast Hall of Fame Gymnast of the Year
	United States of America Gymnastics Athlete of the Year
2006	United States of America Gymnastics Athlete of the Year (award shared)
2008	United States of America Gymnastics Sportswoman of the Year

---

As the reigning world champion, the U.S. team had originally been favored to win. In the team finals competition, Nastia came in first in the uneven bars and third in the balance beam, helping the U.S. team to a second-place finish behind the young, up-and-coming Chinese team. Two days later, Nastia won the gold medal in the women's all-around competition. Over the next few days, she added a bronze medal in the floor exercise, a silver medal on the uneven bars, and a silver medal on beam. Although Nastia tied for the highest score on the uneven bars, the gold medal was awarded to He Kexin of China in a tiebreaker. Nastia performed her difficult routines with great precision and showed the world her graceful, artistic style. Overall, Nastia earned medals in five of the six Olympic gymnastics events, taking home a medal in every event for which she had qualified. By winning five gymnastics medals, Nastia tied the record set by Retton and Shannon Miller for the most medals won by an American female gymnast in a single Olympics.

Continuing the Story

Nastia came home from the Beijing Olympics a celebrity. She was chosen as a role model by B*tween Productions, performed in the Tour of Gymnastics Superstars, and appeared on numerous television talk shows. Following in the footsteps of Retton and Patterson, Nastia appeared on the cover of the Wheaties cereal box. After graduating from Texas Spring Creek Academy, she entered Southern Methodist University and majored in international business. She appeared in the movie *Stick It* (2006) and was interested in additional acting opportunities. She planned to compete at the 2012 London Olympics.

Summary

With her performance at the 2008 Olympics, Nastia Liukin joined the ranks of the greatest American gymnasts. Her elegant, balletic lines added artistry to an American gymnastics tradition that had been criticized for overemphasizing technical proficiency. Nastia won the world championship four times and, with nine world medals in all, tied Shannon Miller's U.S. record for most world championship medals. Furthermore, she was a four-time U.S. champion and was named gymnast of the year and a world top athlete.

Howard Bromberg

Additional Sources

Marcovitz, Hal. *Russian Americans.* Philadelphia: Mason Crest, 2008.

Olsen, Leigh. *Going for Gold: 2008 U.S. Women's Olympic Gymnastics.* New York: Price Stern Sloan, 2008.

Reinstein, Mara. "USA Women Gymnasts: Tears, Joy, and Scandal." *Us Weekly,* September 1, 2008, 46-51.

Van Deusen, Amy. "Dynamic Duel." *International Gymnast* 50, no. 6 (July/August, 2008): 30-33.

Ryan Lochte

Born: August 3, 1984
    Rochester, New York
Also known as: Ryan Steven Lochte (full name);
    the Lochtenator

Early Life
Ryan Steven Lochte was born in 1984 in upstate New York. As a young swimmer, he was coached by his mother, Ike, and father, Steve. He started swimming competitively at the age of nine. Both of his parents coached swimming, therefore competing in the sport seemed natural to Ryan. However, he often fooled around during practice and near the pool. Nonetheless, though Ryan impersonated a slacker, he swam with determination.

When Ryan was eleven, he moved with his family from New York to Daytona Beach, Florida, where his father became aquatics director at a local YMCA. By the year he graduated from Spruce Creek High School in Port Orange, Florida, Ryan had swum three top-ten race times at the U.S. National Championships. His best finish was fourth place in the 800-meter freestyle. His mother was stunned; she had promised to buy him a video game system if he did well. Ryan, a keen competitor, was spurred on by stiff swimming competition in Florida.

The Road to Excellence
At the age of eight, Ryan watched Pablo Morales win a gold medal in the 100-meter butterfly at the 1992 Olympics. Ryan thought he could represent his country and win a gold medal. It took him twelve years to make a reality of his dream, working with his parents and University of Florida head swim coach Gregg Troy. Beginning in 2002, Troy focused Ryan's attention on the 2004 Olympics. During his first year at the University of Florida, Ryan was named Southeastern Conference (SEC) male swimmer of the year, SEC freshman of the year, and SEC male high-point-award winner.

An outstanding high school swimmer, Ryan earned a scholarship at the University of Florida, one of the best college swim teams in the country. He also majored in sports management. As a sophomore, he was undefeated during the regular season in nine separate events. One of the best all-around swimmers in the history of college competition, Ryan broke U.S. Open and National Collegiate Athletic Association (NCAA) short-course records in the 400-yard individual medley.

At 6 feet 2 inches and 190 pounds, Ryan earned a reputation as a spontaneous and laid-back guy who was always ready to play a joke. However, once the starter's signal sounded when he was in the blocks, he was a serious competitor. Between his sophomore and junior years at Florida, Ryan qualified for the 2004 U.S. Olympic team in the 200-meter individual medley and the 4×200-meter freestyle relay. In Athens, he advanced to the 200-meter individual medley final and swam the second-fastest time in Olympic history, taking the silver medal behind Michael Phelps. The two swimmers were part of the gold-medal-winning 4×200-meter freestyle relay team. The team, which also included Klete Keller and Peter Vanderkaay, upset the favored Australian squad.

Ryan Lochte competing in the 400-meter individual medley during the 2008 Olympic Games in Beijing. (Ezra Shaw/Getty Images)

651

The Emerging Champion

After the 2004 Olympics, Ryan continued to improve. At the 2006 NCAA men's swimming and diving national championships, held at the Georgia Tech Aquatic Center in Atlanta, Georgia, he won three individual events, setting U.S. national short-course records in the 200-yard individual medley and the 200-yard backstroke.

At the 2006 World Short Course Swimming Championships, Ryan won the 200-meter individual medley and the 200-meter backstroke in world-record time. He set an American record at the same meet, swimming the backstroke leg in the 4×100-meter medley relay. In the race, he became the first person to swim the 100-meter backstroke in less than 50 seconds. The International Swimming Federation (FINA) named him the male swimmer of the meet.

Continuing the Story

In 2006, after graduating from college, Ryan signed a ten-year, seven-figure endorsement contract with Speedo. At the 2007 World Swimming Championships in Melbourne, Australia, he won his first individual gold medal in a long-course (50 meters) world-championship meet, beating American Aaron Peirsol in the 200-meter backstroke. Thus, he broke Peirsol's world record in the event as well as his seven-year winning streak.

Ryan has been known for his flamboyance during award ceremonies, occasionally sporting a silver, diamond-studded tooth grill, an accessory often used by rap musicians. He wore the grill at a medal ceremony during the 2007 World Swimming Championships and nearly laughed it out of his mouth when Phelps broke up giggling at the sight.

At the 2008 Olympics in Beijing, China, Ryan won a gold medal in the 200-meter backstroke, setting a long-course world record at 1:53.94. Peirsol took silver in 1:54.33. Peirsol had narrowly beaten Ryan at the Olympic trials weeks earlier. This was Ryan's first individual Olympic gold medal. He also shared a gold medal in the 4×200-meter freestyle relay and won bronze medals in the 200- and 400-meter individual medleys.

Major Swimming Championships

Year	Competition	Event	Place
2003	Pan-American Games	4×200-meter freestyle	1st
2004	Olympic Games	4×200-meter freestyle	Gold
		200-meter medley	Silver
	World Short Course Championships	4×200-meter freestyle	1st
		200-meter medley	2d
		200-meter freestyle	3d
2005	World Long Course Championships	4×200 meter freestyle	1st
		200-meter backstroke	3d
		200-meter medley	3d
2006	Pan-Pacific Championships	4×200-meter freestyle	1st
		100-meter backstroke	2d
		200-meter medley	2d
	World Short Course Championships	400-meter medley	1st
		200-meter backstroke	1st
		200-meter medley	1st
		4×100-meter medley	2d
		4×100-meter freestyle	3d
		4×200-meter freestyle	3d
	NCAA Championships	200-yard individual medley	1st
		200-yard backstroke	1st
		4×100-yard medley relay	1st
2007	World Long Course Championships	4×200-meter freestyle	1st
		200-meter backstroke	1st
		100-meter backstroke	2d
		200-meter medley	2d
		400-meter medley	2d
2008	Olympic Games	200-meter backstroke	Gold
		4×200-meter freestyle	Gold
		200-meter individual medley	Bronze
		400-meter individual medley	Bronze
	World Short Course Championships	100-meter medley	1st
		200-meter medley	1st
		400-meter medley	1st
		4×100-meter freestyle	1st
		200-meter backstroke	2d
		4×100-meter medley	2d

Records

2004	Set the U.S. short-course record in the 200-yard individual medley
	Set the U.S. short-course record in the 200-yard backstroke
2006	Set the U.S. record in the 200-yard individual medley
	Set the U.S. record in the 200-yard backstroke
2007	Set the world record in the 200-meter backstroke
2008	Set the world long-course record in the 200-meter backstroke

Summary

By 2008, Ryan Lochte had become a world-class swimmer in the individual-medley, backstroke, and freestyle events. Well-known for the length he was able to kick underwater, Ryan was a rival of Phelps in the individual medley and Peirsol in the back-stroke. However, the three swimmers remained friends. After the 2008 Olympics, Ryan continued to train in Daytona Beach.

Bruce E. Johansen

Additional Sources

Crouse, Karen. "With an Eye on Olympics, Lochte Is a Fish, in and out of Water." *The New York Times*, November 28, 2007.

Phelps, Michael. *Beneath the Surface*. Champaign, Ill.: Sports, 2005.

Wallechinsky, David, and Jaime Loucky. *The Complete Book of the Olympics: 2008 Edition*. London: Aurum Press, 2008.

Jonah Lomu

Born: May 12, 1975
       Auckland, New Zealand
Also known as: Jonah Tali Lomu (full name)

Early Life

Born of Tongan parentage and raised in Mangere, a poor section of Auckland, New Zealand, Jonah Tali Lomu rose from rough and humble origins to gain international fame. He began playing rugby at a young age, and his talent blossomed under the tutelage of Coach Chris Grinter at Wesley College. Jonah began by playing for Auckland primary schools but joined the Counties Manukau at the age of fourteen. Jonah represented New Zealand in the Under-17 (U-17) side in 1991-1992, the New Zealand Secondary Schools in 1992-1993, and the national U-19 side in 1993.

Jonah transferred to New Zealand's national rugby team, the All Blacks, leaving Weymouth, his former rugby club. His All Blacks debut was on June 26, 1994, when New Zealand played France in Christchurch. Jonah was nineteen years and forty-five days old, becoming the youngest All Black test player. The All Blacks lost 22-8, but Jonah played well enough to play in the second match, against France, which New Zealand also lost.

The Road to Excellence

Jonah first gained international attention during the 1995 Rugby World Cup. While competing in South Africa, he managed to score seven tries in the five matches in which the All Blacks participated. In the first match of the tournament and Jonah's first-ever Rugby World Cup match, he scored twice against Ireland; New Zealand won the match. In the second round, he did not play, but the All Blacks were again victorious. New Zealand also won the third round against Japan and the quarter-final against Scotland. In the semifinal against England, Jonah scored four tries and helped the All Blacks win 45-29. The final game of the 1995 Rugby World Cup was played in Ellis Park against the South Africa Springboks. Jonah was unable to score, and the whole team struggled, eventually losing 15-12.

In 1996, the first Tri Nations Series was held, and Jonah helped the All Blacks beat both South Africa and the Australian Wallabies to capture the inaugural championship of the tournament. That same year, Jonah was diagnosed with nephrotic syndrome, an unusual but serious kidney disorder. He was unable to play in the 1997 Tri Nations Series but did compete in the All Blacks tour of the Northern Hemisphere. He played in three matches, two against England and one against Wales, but did not score in any of the games. In the 1998 Commonwealth Games held in Kuala Lumpur, Malaysia, Jonah won a gold medal while representing New Zealand in the "sevens rugby" event, a game similar to traditional rugby but with only seven players on

Jonah Lomu playing rugby in 2000. (Will Burgess/ Reuters/Landov)

each side. That same year, Jonah played in two matches against England, scoring in the first. In the 1998 Tri Nations Series, the All Blacks lost all four games in one of its worst series competitions ever.

The Emerging Champion

In the 1999 Tri Nations Series Jonah appeared unstoppable, as the All Blacks defeated the Springboks 28-0. He also played in the test against Australia and the second test against South Africa, both of which New Zealand won. The All Blacks lost in the final game against Australia but were still crowned the champions for the year. In the 1999 Rugby World Cup Jonah scored twice against Tonga, once against England, twice against Italy, once against Scotland in the quarterfinals, and twice against France in the semifinals.

In the 2001 Tri Nations Series the All Blacks narrowly defeated Australia when Jonah scored at the last second. The second match Australia won against South Africa; New Zealand won the third game and, eventually, the entire series. That year, Jonah played on the winning side against France. Jonah represented New Zealand in the 2001 Sevens World Cup, which the team won. During the 2001 Tri Nations Series Jonah played in his fiftieth series for the All Blacks.

Jonah started off the 2002 season scoring against Italy and Ireland. He played against South Africa in the first game of the 2002 Tri Nations Series but did not play again in the tournament. Later that year he scored against England and then played against France. On November 23, 2002, against the Welsh team in Cardiff, Wales, he played in his final game.

Continuing the Story

Jonah's career achievements are made more impressive because he was suffering from a severe

Honors, Awards, and Milestones
Youngest All Black test player (1994)
Rugby World Cup all-time scorer (15)
Gold medal, Commonwealth Games (1998)
International Rugby Players Association special merit award (2003)
Inducted into International Rugby Hall of Fame (2007)

health problem. Jonah was a sensational athlete and helped bring international attention to the sport of rugby. He played in fifty-nine Super-12 games—twenty-two for the Auckland Blues, eight for the Waikato Chiefs, and twenty-nine for the Wellington Hurricanes. In 1995 and 1999, Jonah was sensational, with an incomparable physical presence. In 2003, he was presented the special merit award at the International Rugby Players Association ceremony. He was also featured in Adidas's "Impossible is Nothing" campaign. In 2007, he was inducted into the International Rugby Hall of Fame.

Summary

Through his drive and determination, Jonah Lomu, 6 feet 7 inches and 262 pounds, became the most recognizable player in international rugby. He competed in seventy-three matches for the New Zealand All Blacks, scoring a total of 185 points. His prowess on the field was unmatched, and he set the record for fifteen scoring tries in the Rugby World Cup.

Kathryn A. Cochran

Additional Sources

Lomu, Jonah. *Jonah Lomu Autobiography.* Auckland, New Zealand: Hodder Moa Beckett, 2004.

Shirley, Phil. *Blood and Thunder: The Unofficial Biography of Jonah Lomu.* Auckland, New Zealand: Harper Collins, 1999.

Steven Lopez

Born: November 9, 1978
New York, New York

Early Life

Steven Lopez was born in New York, New York, in 1978. His family moved to Sugar Land, Texas, when he was a boy. At the age of five, he began training in Tae Kwon Do with his older brother Jean. Their father, who was a huge fan of Kung Fu movies, located a Tae Kwon Do school in suburban Houston, Texas, where the Lopez boys started their journey to sports fame. Eventually, the Lopezes had two more children, Mark and Diana, both of whom also became Tae Kwon Do Olympians for the United States in the 2008 Beijing Games.

Steven Lopez (left) competing during the 2004 Olympic Games in Athens. (Nick Laham/Getty Images)

The Road to Excellence

Early in his life, Steven excelled in various sports; however, Tae Kwon Do became his passion. He enjoyed this Korean martial art because it allowed him to compete on an individual level. Furthermore, many children his age focused on more traditional sports like baseball and basketball; Steven was able to express his individuality through Tae Kwon Do.

The Lopez children practiced religiously: They woke up early in the morning to train before school; after completing their homework, they trained again in the evening. They turned the oil-stained, cold, dark family garage into their dojo. During the winter months, Steven's mother, Ondina, started the clothes dryer 15 minutes before the children trained so they had some warmth while practicing. Despite his grueling training schedule, Steven maintained good grades and was an honor student at Kempner High School in Sugar Land. However, his schedule caused some sacrifices. He was unable to attend either his homecoming dance or his prom because of upcoming national competitions.

The Emerging Champion

For Steven, the sacrifices he had to make were worth the rewards; he started winning more and more of his matches. In 1994 and 1996, both Steven and his older brother Jean were a part of the U.S. national team. Jean later left competition in order to become Steven's coach. In 1997, Steven expanded his dominance when he won the World Gold Cup in Cairo, Egypt. From 1996 to 2000, he placed first in international Tae Kwon Do competitions as a featherweight.

In 1998, Sugar Land celebrated its first Olympic star when Tara Lipinski won the gold medal in women's figure skating. Steven hoped that she would not be Sugar Land's only Olympic champion. Before he was ready for the Olympics, however, he had several more years of rigorous training and brutal competition. In 1999, he finished second in the Pan-American regional qualification tournament in his weight class.

The outcome of this match helped propel him to the Olympic trials in May, 2000. Tae Kwon Do was a debut Olympic sport in Sydney, Australia, and Steven hoped to represent the United States. He was just one of three Lopezes competing in those trials. His brother Mark finished third in the men's flyweight division, and his sister, Diana, finished third in the women's welterweight division. Steven made the U.S. team by defeating Glenn Lainfiesta at the trials. He had the possibility of becoming Sugar Land's second Olympic champion.

Continuing the Story

During his first three preliminary matches at the 2000 Olympics, Steven won all three matches easily. In fact, opponents scored only 1 point against him. In his semifinal round he earned an easy victory over Germany's Aziz Arhrki, to whom he had lost in an Olympic qualifying tournament in Croatia. During the bout, Steven dislocated his little finger. However, the pain was no distraction, and he went on to defeat South Korean champion Sin Jun-sik. Although the match ended in a 1-1 tie, Steven won the gold medal because of Sin's penalties. Steven became the first Latino and the first American to win a gold medal in the new Olympic sport of Tae Kwon Do.

Major Tae Kwon Do Championships

Year	Competition	Division	Place
1992	U.S. Open Championships	Junior Finweight	1st
1993	U.S. Open Championships	Junior Finweight	1st
	U.S. Junior Olympic Championships	Flyweight	Silver
1994	U.S. Open Championships	Junior Flyweight	1st
	U.S. National Championships	Finweight	2d
	U.S. National Team Trials	Finweight	1st
	World Cup Championships	Finweight	3d
	Pan American Championships	Finweight	2d
1995	Pan American Games Team Member	Finweight	
	U.S. National Championships	Flyweight	2d
	U.S. National Team Trials	Flyweight	3d
	U.S. Junior Olympic Championships	Featherweight	1st
	U.S. Olympic Festival	Flyweight	1st
1996	U.S. Open Championships	Featherweight	3d
	U.S. National Junior Team Trials	Lightweight	1st
	U.S. National Championships	Featherweight	1st
	U.S. National Team Trials	Featherweight	1st
	World Junior Championships	Lightweight	1st
	Pan American Championships	Featherweight	1st
1997	U.S. Open Championships	Featherweight	1st
	World Cup Championships	Featherweight	1st
	U.S. National Team Trials	Featherweight	1st
1998	U.S. Open Championships	Lightweight	1st
	Spain Open Championships	Lightweight	1st
	World Cup Championships	Featherweight	3d
	U.S. National Team Trials	Featherweight	1st
	U.S. Olympic Weight Division Tournament	Featherweight	Gold
	National Collegiate Championships	Featherweight	1st
	Choson International Cup	Featherweight	1st
	Pan American Championships	Featherweight	1st
1999	U.S. Olympic Weight/Pan Am Games Team Trials	Featherweight	1st
	U.S. National Team Trials	Lightweight	1st
	Pan American Games	Featherweight	1st
	Pan Am Olympic Qualification Tournament	Featherweight	2d
2000	U.S. Olympic Team Trials	Featherweight	1st
	U.S. National Team Trials	Lightweight	1st
	Olympic Games	Featherweight	Gold
2001	World Championships	Lightweight	1st
2002	World Cup Championships	Lightweight	3d
	Pan American Games	Lightweight	1st
2003	World Championships	Lightweight	1st
	World Qualification Tournament	Lightweight	3d
	Pan American Games	Welterweight	1st
2004	Olympic Games	Welterweight	Gold
	U.S. Olympic Team Trials	Welterweight	1st
2005	World Championships	Welterweight	1st
2006	Sr. National Team Trials	Welterweight	1st
2007	World Championships	Welterweight	1st
	Olympic Trials	Lightweight/Welterweight	1st
	Sr. National Team Trials	Welterweight	1st
2008	Olympic Games	Welterweight	Bronze

Four years later in Athens, Greece, Steven regained his title of Olympic gold-medal champion in the 80-kilogram (welterweight) weight class, becoming the first repeat champion in Tae Kwon Do. After the Games, he continued his dominance, fighting in competitions in both the United States and abroad. In fact, in 2007, in Beijing, China, he won an unprecedented fourth consecutive World Tae Kwon Do Championship, securing a bid to represent the United States in another Olympics.

A favorite to win a third gold medal in 2008, Steven, at twenty-nine years old, won all of his preliminary fights, leading him to the quarterfinal match against Italy's 80kg champion, Mauro Sarmiento. At the end of the second of three rounds, Steven was winning 2 to 0. With 1 minute 35 seconds left in the third round, Sarmiento scored. Then with 49 seconds left in the match, Steven was penalized for an illegal kick, causing the match to go to overtime. During the first minute of the overtime round, Sarmiento scored with a kick to Steven's back, giving Steven his first loss since 2002. Jean, Steven's brother and coach, immediately filed a complaint with the World Tae Kwon Do Federation regarding the questionable penalty point against his brother. The federation rejected the protest. Steven, although disappointed with the federation's decision, won the bronze medal match the following day.

Summary

Steven Lopez's bronze medal finish in the 2008 Beijing Games put him into an elite category in Tae Kwon Do. With two gold medals and one bronze medal in the Olympics and his four world titles, Steven became one of the most accomplished Tae Kwon Do competitors in American history.

Furthermore, the Lopez trio was the second set of three siblings ever to compete in the Summer Games in the same sport; the first were three American brothers who competed in gymnastics in the 1904 Games. In the 2008 Beijing Games, sister Diana won a bronze, while brother Mark finished with a silver medal, allowing the three Lopezes to become the first family trio to medal in an Olympics.

Deborah Service, updated by Paul M. Klenowski

Additional Sources

Baranger, Walter R. "Lopez Takes Gold." *The New York Times*, September 29, 2000, p. 5.

"Lopez, U.S. Win Inaugural Gold." *The Washington Post*, September 29, 2000, p. D12.

Mihoces, Gary. "USA's Steven Lopez Adds Bronze to Family's Medal Haul." *USA Today*, August 22, 2008.

"One Hundred Olympic Athletes to Watch." *Time* 172, no. 5 (August 4, 2008): 44-61.

Tegla Loroupe

Born: May 9, 1973
Kapsait, Kapenguria District, Kenya

Early Life

Tegla Loroupe was born in the rural village of Kapsait, Kapenguria District, Kenya near the Ugandan border on May 9, 1973. As a child, Tegla ran six miles each way to school and back home every day. Until she was seven years old, she made this daily run barefoot. She also honed her running skills weekly while helping her parents herd cattle on the family farm. By the time Tegla was nine years old, she, her family, and her teachers realized that she had a natural talent for distance running. That year, her school district sponsored a track meet with competitions in various long-distance events. Tegla competed in and won all of the races that day except for the 800-meter event.

The Road to Excellence

Tegla fell in love with running and expressed an interest in becoming a professional runner. Her parents, in support of her dream, sent her to a private boarding school where she could practice her running and receive professional training. In 1989, at the age of sixteen, Tegla finally received her first pair of running shoes. While at the boarding school, Tegla followed a strict training program that incorporated rigid running, nutrition, and sleep schedules. She also spent four months a year in Detmold, Germany, where she worked exclusively with her coach, Volker Werner.

The Emerging Champion

In 1993, at the World Track and Field Championships, Tegla competed in her first major 10-kilometer race and finished in fourth place. In November, 1994, at the age of twenty-one, she competed in the New York City Marathon. She won the race in 2 hours 27 minutes 37 seconds (2:27:37). By finishing first, she became the first African woman to ever win an international marathon. She also became the first black woman and the youngest competitor to ever win the New York City Marathon. The president of Kenya at the time, Daniel Arap Moi, was so proud of Tegla's accomplishment that he honored her by giving her parents a gift of livestock. The value of the livestock made her family wealthy by Kenyan standards.

Tegla's success also inspired other Kenyan women to pursue running. In order to support their dreams, Tegla began providing running shoes to these female athletes. In 1995, she ran the Boston Marathon and finished in ninth place among the female runners. That same year, in Göteborg, Sweden, she again competed in the World Track and Field Championships. She earned a bronze medal for finishing the 10-kilometer run in 31:17.

Tegla Loroupe winning the 1994 New York City Marathon. (Darrell Ingham/Allsport/Getty Images)

In November, 1995, she again competed in and won the New York City Marathon, a victory which qualified her for the 1996 Olympic Summer Games in Atlanta, Georgia. During the Olympics, she competed in the 10,000-meter race and came in sixth, with a time of 31:23.

Also, in 1996, Tegla ran the Boston Marathon again and finished in second place among women. She attempted a third win at the New York City Marathon but finished in seventh place, with a time of 2:32:07. Shortly after the race, she was diagnosed with stress fractures of the spine and had to take time off to heal. In 1997, she won the Rotterdam Marathon in the Netherlands. In 1998, she not only won the Rotterdam Marathon again but also set a new women's world record with a time of 2:20:47. In 1999, at the Berlin Marathon, she broke her own world record by four seconds. At the 2000 Olympic Summer Games in Sydney, Australia, Tegla competed in the Olympic Marathon but finished in thirteenth place. However, that same year, she won marathons in Rome, Italy, and London, England. Her other accomplishments that year included finishing first in the women's category at the Kenyan National Track and Field Competitions and receiving the Golden Shoe Award from the Association of International Marathons and Road Races. By the end of 2000, she was forced to reduce her training schedule because of back pain.

Continuing the Story

In 2003, Tegla established the Tegla Loroupe Peace Foundation in Kenya. The organization funds conflict resolution programs and also sponsors "Peace through Sports" marathons, in which teams of government officials and ordinary citizens participate in relay races. The courses are designed to run through violence-plagued areas in Kenya, Uganda, and Sudan. Tegla also financed a school and an orphanage in her hometown. In 2006, she became a United Nations Ambassador of Sport.

Summary

As a professional long-distance runner, Tegla Loroupe achieved an enormous amount of success. Her original reasons for pursuing a professional career in running involved

Major Marathon Competitions

Year	Event	Place
1993	10-kilometer, World Track and Field Championships	4th
1994	New York City Marathon	1st
1995	New York City Marathon	1st
	10-kilometer, World Track and Field Championships	3d
1996	10,000-meters, Olympic Games	6th
	Boston Marathon	2d
1997	Rotterdam (Netherlands) Marathon	1st
1998	Rotterdam (Netherlands) Marathon	1st
1999	10-kilometer, World Track and Field Championships	3d
2000	Olympic Marathon	13th
	London Marathon	1st
	Rome Marathon	1st
2003	Cologne (Germany) Women's Marathon	1st
2004	Leipzig (Germany) Women's Marathon	1st
2006	Hong Kong Half-Marathon	1st

not only her love of the sport but also her desire to avoid the typical life of a Kenyan woman. Through diligence and hard work, she became internationally famous and financially independent. Equally important, she became a role model for women athletes from all over the world.

Bernadette Zbicki Heiney

Additional Sources

O'Reilly, Jean, and Susan K. Cahn, eds. *Women and Sports in the United States: A Documentary Reader.* Boston, Mass.: Northwestern University Press, 2007.

Pendergast, Sara, and Tom Pendergast. *Contemporary Black Biography: Profiles from the International Black Community,* vol. 59. Detroit: Thomson Gale, 2007.

Slomanson, Joan Kanel. *A Short History: Thumbnail Sketches of Fifty Little Giants.* New York: Abbeville Press, 1998.

Switzer, Kathrine, and Roger Roberson. *26.2: Marathon Stories.* Emmaus, Pa.: Runner's World, 2006.

Honors, Awards, and Milestones

Year	
1994	First African woman to win international marathon
1997-99	Winner, AAF World Half-Marathon Championships
1998	Set women's marathon world record at Rotterdam Marathon (2:20:47)
1998-2001	Held the world record for marathon
1999	Improved her marathon record at Berlin Marathon (2:20:43)
2000	Association of International Marathons and Road Races Golden Shoe Award
2006	United Nations Ambassador of Sport
2007	Kenyan sports personality of the year, community hero category

Greg Louganis

Born: January 29, 1960
  El Cajon, California
Also known as: Gregory Efthimios Louganis (full
  name)

Early Life

Gregory Efthimios Louganis is of Samoan and northern European background. He was adopted by Frances and Peter Louganis nine months after his birth on January 29, 1960. Greg has an older sister, Despina, who is also adopted. They grew up in El Cajon, a working-class suburb of San Diego, California. Both children began taking dancing lessons when they were young.

Greg's early school experiences were difficult. Other children ridiculed him because of his dancing. They called him stupid because he stammered and had a severe reading problem. He was even a physical misfit, with dark hair and skin in a school of mostly blond, blue-eyed children. Greg also had problems with his father, a hard-living tuna fisherman who could not understand his more sensitive son.

The Road to Excellence

Greg learned gymnastics as a child. When he began tumbling off the diving board in the family's backyard pool, Peter Louganis decided to enroll his son in local diving classes. To make up for his difficulties at school, Greg concentrated on his only success: diving. At the age of eleven, just two years after starting lessons, Greg scored a perfect ten in diving at the 1971 Amateur Athletic Union (AAU) Junior Olympics in Colorado Springs, Colorado.

At this competition, Greg impressed the spectators, including Dr. Sammy Lee, the gold medalist in diving in both the 1948 and 1952 Olympics. Four years later, when Peter Louganis asked Dr. Lee to coach Greg for the 1976 Olympics, Lee quickly agreed.

Meanwhile, life at home was growing increasingly difficult for Greg, so he moved in with his coach's family. Lee was a strict disciplinarian. He set up a rigorous training schedule and helped Greg to build self-confidence. Under Lee's coaching, Greg qualified for both the springboard and platform events for the 1976 Olympics. He finished sixth in springboard diving. He did even better in platform diving, finishing second behind the favorite, two-time gold medalist Klaus Dibiasi. Nevertheless, Greg returned home feeling that he had failed.

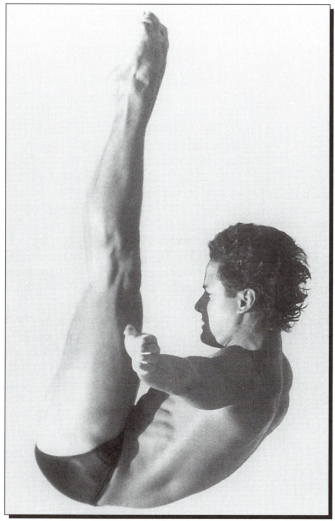

Greg Louganis. (LAOOC Collection, Department of Special Collections, University Research Library, UCLA)

661

Major Diving Championships

Year	Competition	Event	Place	Points
1976	Olympic Games	3-meter springboard	6th	528.96
		10-meter platform	Silver	576.99
1978	World Championships	10-meter platform	1st	844.11
1979	World Cup	10-meter platform	1st	588.90
	Pan-American Games	3-meter springboard	1st	627.84
		10-meter platform	1st	592.71
1981	World Cup	3-meter springboard	1st	643.20
1982	World Championships	3-meter springboard	1st	752.67
		10-meter platform	1st	643.26
1983	World Cup	3-meter springboard	1st	717.03
		10-meter platform	1st	687.90
	Pan-American Games	3-meter springboard	1st	724.02 PAR
		10-meter platform	1st	677.58 PAR
	World University Games	3-meter springboard	1st	—
		10-meter platform	1st	—
1984	Olympic Games	3-meter springboard	Gold	754.41
		10-meter platform	Gold	710.91
1986	World Championships	3-meter springboard	1st	750.06
		10-meter platform	1st	668.58
1987	World Cup	3-meter springboard	1st	707.46
	Pan-American Games	3-meter springboard	1st	754.14
		10-meter platform	1st	694.68
1988	Olympic Games	3-meter springboard	Gold	730.80
		10-meter platform	Gold	638.61

Note: PAR = Pan-American Record

Back in his high school, he had become a hero, but he was still withdrawn and without real friends. Greg experienced a long period of illness and injuries. As he became more and more unhappy, he started to smoke and drink.

For a while, Greg did not train much or compete. By spring, 1978, however, he was again winning titles at competitions such as the National AAU Indoor and Outdoor Diving Championships, the Hall of Fame International Diving Meet, and the World Aquatic Championship.

The Emerging Champion

In the fall of 1978, Greg accepted a scholarship at the University of Miami, mostly because it was far away from his life in California. He learned for the first time that his reading problem was caused by a learning disorder—dyslexia. He finally believed that he was not really intellectually limited.

Greg continued to dive fearlessly. Experts expected him to win two gold medals at the 1980 Olympics. However, the United States boycotted the 1980 games to protest the Soviet Union's invasion of Afghanistan, and Greg was unable to compete. In January, 1981, he transferred to the University of California at Irvine so he could train with Ron O'Brien, the head coach at the famous Mission Viejo Swim Club. In 1983, Greg received his B.A., with a theater major and dance minor.

During these years, Greg was virtually unchallenged in diving competitions. In the 1982 World Aquatic Championship, he became the first diver ever to earn a perfect score from all seven judges in international competition. In 1982, he won the 1-meter and 3-meter springboard and the 10-meter platform diving events at the national indoor and outdoor diving championships. His winning streak was not broken until 1987.

Greg developed difficult new dives and introduced them into his sport. He was classically proportioned for a diver. He had great flexibility and balance because of early dance and gymnastic training. Because his legs were strong, he was able to jump high off the board and have more time for twists and turns in his dives. By raising his own standards of excellence, Greg also raised the standards of world diving competition.

Despite his diving success, Greg still had personal problems. In 1983, an incident gave Greg the strength to change his life. During a break in a swim meet, he saw a young diver smoking. When questioned, the boy said he wanted to be just like Greg Louganis, and Greg Louganis smoked. Greg took a long, hard look at himself. He stopped smoking and drinking and started to accept himself for what he was. He began to take himself less seriously and decided that it was acceptable to be shy.

When the time came for the 1984 Olympic competition, Greg was prepared both physically and

Honors and Awards

1984	James E. Sullivan Award
1985	Inducted into U.S. Olympic Hall of Fame
1986	Jesse Owens International Trophy
1988	Olympic Spirit Award
1993	Inducted into International Swimming Hall of Fame

mentally. He won gold medals in both the spring-board and platform diving competitions, becoming the first man in fifty-six years to do so. He also became the first diver ever to earn more than 700 points in a single Olympic event.

Continuing the Story

After facing his own fears, Greg felt that he had something to offer others. He began telling his story to thousands of teenagers at school assemblies. He did television commercials and public-service spots, moving toward his long-time goal of an acting career. In 1984, Greg won the prestigious James E. Sullivan Memorial Award as the outstanding amateur athlete of the year. In 1985, he was inducted into the U.S. Olympic Hall of Fame. In 1986, he was awarded the Jesse Owens International Trophy for excellence in athletics and international relations.

In the 1988 Olympics, Greg again won both the springboard and platform competitions, as he had done in 1984. This time, though, he did so after hitting his head on the springboard in a preliminary dive. With stitches in his scalp and his confidence shaken, Greg immediately went back to dive again and did so almost perfectly. The coach of the Chinese team later said: "We must all learn from Louganis's grit and determination. In adversity, he was able to rise up and win the championship."

Unlike many world-class athletes, Greg was motivated by an inner search for artistic perfection rather than an outer desire to excel. In this, he had been encouraged by his mother, who told him to do his best and that she would love him no matter what.

In 1988, Greg retired from competitive diving. He spent time speaking to dyslexia organizations, youth clubs, drug and alcohol rehabilitation groups, and diving clinics about the challenges in his life. He made his professional dance debut with the Indiana Repertory Theatre and continued to pursue a serious acting career.

In 1995, Greg published his autobiography, *Breaking the Surface*, in which he discussed openly for the first time his struggle for acceptance as a gay man and the turmoil of living with HIV. In the years following his historic diving career, he became an inspiration to athletes and fans alike.

In addition to a growing list of film and theater credits, Greg also received recognition as an advocate for those living with AIDS. He was inducted into the International Swimming Hall of Fame in 1993. In 1999, he published his second book: *For the Life of Your Dog: A Complete Guide to Having a Dog in Your Life, from Adoption and Birth Through Sickness and Health.*

Summary

Greg Louganis is considered to be one of the greatest divers of all time. An equally important achievement may be his personal victory over self-doubt. By recognizing his fears and rising above them, Greg grew from an introverted, troubled child into a relaxed, confident adult who is comfortable with himself and others.

Greg was a diver of unequaled grace and power. His goal was not only to win but also to raise his own level of performance and the standards of his sport. Greg said, "I don't want to be remembered as the greatest diver who ever lived. I want to be able to see the greatest diver. I hope I live to see the day when my records are broken."

Jean C. Fulton

Additional Sources

Edelson, Paula. *Superstars of Men's Swimming and Diving.* Philadelphia: Chelsea House, 1999.

Knapp, Ron. *Top Ten American Men's Olympic Gold Medalists.* Springfield, N.J.: Enslow, 2000.

Louganis, Greg, and Eric Marcus. *Breaking the Surface.* Naperville, Ill.: Sourcebooks, 2006.

Louganis, Greg, and Betsy Sikora Siino. *For the Life of Your Dog: A Complete Guide to Having a Dog in Your Life, from Adoption and Birth Through Sickness and Health.* New York: Pocket Books, 1999.

Wallechinsky, David, and Jaime Loucky. *The Complete Book of the Olympics: 2008 Edition.* London: Aurum Press, 2008.

Lu Li

Born: August 30, 1976
Changsha, Hunan Province, China

Early Life

Lu Li was born August 30, 1976, in Changsha, Hunan Province in southern China. Because of her government's one-child-per-family policy, Li was an only child. Chinese parents have a custom of naming a child for a quality they hope he or she will grow to embody. Li's name means "earth flower." Lu is her family name, Li her given name.

Li began gymnastics when her mother, thinking the slim five-year-old should do something to build her physique, took her to the gym. Sports training is provided free by the Chinese government with an eye toward Olympic success.

Li's short, strong, yet flexible body proved to be well suited for the sport. So was her mentality: quick, tough, and obedient. She would need these qualities for the hard work ahead. Young gymnasts in China follow a strict regimen of stretching and strengthening exercises that allow them to perform the spectacular moves modern gymnastics requires. China, with its long acrobatic tradition, is also known for the innovative and artistic gymnastics made possible by this disciplined foundation.

Li rose through the ranks of youth competitions and eventually was selected to train at the national training center in Beijing. There, gymnasts live together and train with the national coaches—at the time Gao Jian and Luo Xe Lian—who keep close watch on their prodigies. Meals, schooling, and housing are furnished by the state. National team members see their parents just once or twice a year, but families know that their children enjoy a better standard of living than they could have at home. In addition, top athletes are able to travel abroad, an opportunity denied the average Chinese citizen.

The Road to Excellence

In the spring of 1991, fourteen-year-old Li attended Moscow's prestigious Stars of the World competition. The meet often functions as a coming-out

Lu Li performing on the balance beam during the 1992 Olympic Games in Barcelona. (David Cannon/Getty Images)

Major Gymnastics Championships

Year	Competition	Event	Place
1992	Olympic Games	Balance beam	Silver
		Uneven bars	Gold
	Pacific Alliance Championships	All-around	1st
		Floor exercise	1st
		Uneven bars	2d
	World Championships	Uneven bars	4th
1993	Chunichi Cup	All-around	7th
		Balance beam	3d
		Uneven bars	1st
	Tokyo Cup	Balance beam	1st
		Uneven bars	1st

party for young gymnasts of the former Eastern Bloc countries, but Li failed to make a big impression. The winner that year, Tatiana Gutsu of the then-Soviet Union, later became the 1992 Olympic all-around champion.

Li's world debut came at the World Gymnastics Championships in Paris a year later. The competition boasted a new, individual-events-only format, which should have worked to the advantage of the Chinese gymnasts. Though they are often weak on vaulting and floor exercise, the Chinese women are acknowledged as the best in the world on the bars and beam. Finally, they would be able to focus on their strong points and with luck, bring home medals.

In Paris, Li dazzled the knowledgeable crowd with her unique bars work, swinging with superb technique and amplitude. The 4-foot 6-inch, 66-pounder set a new standard for the event, using complicated elements her coaches had adapted from the men's horizontal bar. Her routine included inverted giant swings—swinging around the bar with the shoulders literally inside out—which require a high degree of both flexibility and strength. If the shoulders are too tight, inverted giants are impossible, but without sufficient strength, injury results. Thanks to her early training, Li was able to walk that fine line with consummate ease.

Li had the lead after preliminary competition, and it looked as if she would become the first Chinese woman to win a world title in three years. After cruising through a perfect set in the finals, however, Li made a classic mistake. She jumped forward on her difficult double layout dismount, and the resulting deduction kept her out of the medals.

She—and her many new fans—would have to wait for the Olympic Games.

The Emerging Champion

Her disappointing finish in Paris motivated Li, and she arrived in Barcelona for the 1992 Summer Olympics well prepared. She worked well through the early stages of competition, qualifying for the finals of the all-around, the balance beam, and her specialty, the uneven bars.

During the all-around finals, though, Li fell twice from the beam. Her resulting drop to thirty-fourth out of thirty-six competitors was less devastating than the psychological impact of such a disaster in the Olympic Games. Fortunately for her, she had two days to collect herself for the finals.

The uneven bars final was one of the toughest of the Games. Two world champions and several medalists packed the field. Li, with her novel combinations, precision, and technical superiority, was the favorite, but she would have to "stick" her dismount to win.

As she had in Paris, Li performed a superb set. This time, she erased her memories of Paris with a perfect landing. The judges were unanimous, giving Li her first 10.0, one of just two perfect scores in the 1992 Games. Li was the Olympic champion. Immediately after receiving her gold medal, Li almost won another on the very apparatus that had foiled her two days before, the beam. The delighted sixteen-year-old happily claimed a silver medal, but some observers felt she deserved gold.

In October, Li took her act to a previous Olympic city, Seoul, South Korea, where she won the all-around and floor exercise at the Pacific Alliance Championships, featuring the best from Asia, Australia, and the Americas. However, the Olympic champion was just second on the bars. Afterward, she dropped out of sight. Some future Chinese stars graced the World Gymnastics Championships in April, 1993, but Li was missing.

Continuing the Story

Finally, in late fall, a familiar name appeared at Japan's prestigious internationals, the Chunichi and Tokyo Cups. Li was back, taller, leggier, and better than ever. Her Olympic bars set was already well ahead of its time, but she added even more difficulty, winning easily in both meets. Additionally, Li pranced through a new beam routine as if she had never been away.

Instead of pursuing coaching or exhibitions at the end of her competitive career, like most gymnasts, Li went on to college. There she studied English and international cultures. In 2000, she moved to the United States and began coaching gymnastics in Northern California. She eventually opened her own gym in Fremont, California.

Summary

The Chinese gymnasts have never failed to impress gymnastics fans, but they often fail to rise to the occasion with world and Olympic medals at stake. However, Lu Li earned a perfect score and aced two of the best routines of the 1992 Olympics while the world watched.

Nancy Raymond

Additional Sources

Greenberg, Stan. *Whitaker's Olympic Almanack: An Encyclopaedia of the Olympic Games.* Chicago: Fitzroy Dearborn, 2000.

Wallechinsky, David, and Jaime Loucky. *The Complete Book of the Olympics: 2008 Edition.* London: Aurum Press, 2008.

Pierre Lueders

Born: September 26, 1970
        Edmonton, Alberta, Canada
Also known as: Pierre Fritz Lueders (full name)

Early Life

Pierre Fritz Lueders was born September 26, 1970, in Edmonton, Alberta, Canada. Bobsledding was not Pierre's first sport of choice. As a youth, he had hoped to become an Olympic decathlete for Canada, for which he trained vigorously until August, 1989. At that time, Pierre visited relatives in the former East Germany. A cousin, sportswriter Gunnar Meinhart, suggested that the 6 foot 1 inch, 218-pound Pierre was better built for bobsledding than the decathlon. Based on this recommendation, Pierre began training as a bobsledder.

The Road to Excellence

In 1989, after abandoning his quest to become an Olympic decathlete, Pierre began serving as a brakeman for the Canadian two-man bobsled team. He remained in this position until 1991 when he was promoted to the front of the sled as driver. Partly because of his youthful naivete, he thought bobsledding was going to be easy and that he would be successful without much work. Quick success reinforced this attitude when in 1992, just a year after becoming driver, he won the first World Cup race he entered, defeating the 1992 Olympic champion in Calgary, Alberta, Canada. Although Pierre experienced success quickly, he was soon reminded of the difficulty of mastering a sport; he finished seventh in the two-man event at the 1994 Olympics in Lillehammer, Norway. He realized that bobsled competition was not as easy as he had thought.

The Emerging Champion

The 1994-1995 season was memorable for Pierre. At the end of the season, he had made history by winning the overall bobsledding World Cup title in both the two-man and the four-man events. Never before had anyone accomplished such an achievement in World Cup competition.

Three years later, in what many consider one of the greatest achievements in Olympic bobsled history, Pierre and brakeman Dave MacEachern won Olympic gold at the 1998 Winter Olympics in Nagano, Japan. This amazing event took place at the "Spiral" in Asakawa. Incredibly, at the conclusion of four heats over two days, Pierre and MacEachern, in their bobsled *Canada One*, had tied the Italian team of Guenther Huber and Antonio Tartaglia in the two-man competition, with identical times of 3:37.24. In each heat, both teams drove their sleds down the run in a little more than 54 seconds. However, the final run shocked everyone. Trailing the Italians by three hundredths of a second, Pierre and MacEachern drove *Canada One* into history. Against massive odds Pierre piloted the sled into the first-ever tie in Olympic bobsled history. In 1968, there had been a tie, but Olympic rules at the time required a tiebreaker to determine the gold and silver medalist. This time, Olympic rules provided for both teams to receive gold medals. After the race, Pierre told reporters that, considering the conditions in which they had competed over the two days, he would have been disappointed if the race had not ended as it did. Both the Canadian team and the Italian team felt they had made history together.

Continuing the Story

The two-man competition in Nagano was only the second time a Canadian team had won an Olympic medal in bobsledding. The only other Canadian team medal in bobsledding was won by Vic Emery, John Emery, Doug Anakin, and Peter Kirby, who

---

Major Bobsled Championships

Year	Competition	Event	Place
1995	World Championships	Two-man	2d
1996	World Championships	Two-man	2d
1998	Olympic Games	Two-man	Gold
1999	World Championships	Four-man	3d
2003	World Championships	Two-man	2d
2004	World Championships	Two-man	1st
2005	World Championships	Four-man	3d
		Two-man	1st
2006	Olympic Games	Two-man	Silver
2007	World Championships	Four-man	2d

won gold in the four-man event at Innsbruck, Austria, in 1964.

Although Pierre was best known for his success piloting the two-man sled, he also piloted a Canadian four-man sled. After a less than inspiring performance at the 2002 Winter Olympic Games in Salt Lake City, Utah, in which Pierre finished fifth in the two-man and ninth in the four-man competitions, he set out on a three-year plan to improve his world rankings in both sleds. As part of the plan, he did not compete in the four-man event during the 2002-2003 season. The next year he piloted his team and brought home the silver medal at the World Cup in Corina, Italy. His plan was taking form. In 2005, Pierre completed the season with nine medals and was ranked second in the two-man sled and third in the four-man sled.

Pierre, with brakeman Lascelles Brown, added another medal to the Canadian collection, winning the silver medal in 2006 at the Winter Games in Turin, Italy. He collected numerous World Cup medals and seven World Cup Championships to accompany his two medals from the Winter Olympic Games.

Pierre committed himself to the Canadian team through the 2010 Olympic Games in Vancouver, British Columbia, Canada. There, he planned to make his last run on the ice, in his home country. Vancouver provided him with his last chance to win the Olympic four-man bobsledding medal that had eluded him throughout his career.

Summary

Pierre Fritz Lueders competed in the Olympic bobsled four times, in 1994, 1998, 2002, and 2006. He was the first man to win the overall World Cup title six times in the two-man bobsled event, doing so in 1994, 1995, 1997, 1998, 2003, and 2006. He was the most decorated bobsledder in Canadian history. In 1999, he was inducted into the Alberta Sports Hall of Fame and Museum.

Michael D. Cummings, Jr.

Additional Sources

Farber, Michael. "Pierre Lueders." *Sports Illustrated* 88, no. 5 (February 9, 1998): 124.

Starkman, Randy. "On the Road to 2010: Canadian Olympians Will Have a Lot More than Home-Field Advantage Going For Them at Games." *Toronto Star*, February 10, 2008, p. S1.

Wallechinsky, David, and Jaime Loucky. *The Complete Book of the Winter Olympics.* Wilmington, Del.: Sport Media, 2005.

Jon Lugbill

Born: May 27, 1961
Wauseon, Ohio

Early Life

Jon Lugbill was born on May 27, 1961, in the northwestern Ohio farming community of Wauseon, some thirty miles west of Toledo. Jon was one of four children of Ralph and Viva Lugbill. When he was three, his family moved to Fairfax, Virginia, a suburb of Washington, D.C. Life in the middle-class neighborhood was good. In his younger years, Jon had a strong interest in sports, particularly football and basketball.

At the age of ten, Jon went on a whitewater raft trip in West Virginia, with his father and older brother. This trip changed Jon's life. He saw his first canoe and kayak race. Upon the family's return home, they purchased a canoe and launched a career. A year later, Jon was back in West Virginia to enter the Petersburg downriver race.

The Road to Excellence

Jon and his older brother, Ron, began paddling in slalom races. In slalom, a series of "gates" are hung over a whitewater course. Racers are scored on the

basis of elapsed time with penalty points added for hitting or missing gates. Slalom was more challenging than downriver racing.

Early in his high school career, Jon made a major decision. Naturally athletic, he was also short. At 5 feet 9 inches, his height was a major disadvantage in basketball and football. In canoeing, his height was an advantage, giving him a lower center of gravity and greater boat stability. He decided to concentrate his efforts on canoeing.

Jon took full advantage of both the number of competitions and the quality of the athletes found in the Washington, D.C., area and along the Eastern seaboard. Quick to learn and with a natural love of whitewater, he progressed quickly and rose through the ranks. In 1975, the year he graduated from Oakton High School, he made the U.S. national canoe team.

The Emerging Champion

A month after graduation, Jon went to Yugoslavia to compete in his first World Slalom Championships. That first taste of championship competition led to a commitment: Jon wanted to train hard and push himself to the limits. He promised himself to become as good as he possibly could. In 1977, Jon found a mentor in Bill Endicott, a former world-class paddler who had moved to Bethesda, Maryland. Endicott assumed coaching duties for the U.S. team.

Under the watchful eye of his coach and with a practice schedule that demanded twenty hours a week on the water and additional time for endurance and weight training, Jon began a program that molded him into a world-class athlete. "I liked the day-to-day training, being fine-tuned," says Jon. "I also liked competition and doing well, and I really enjoyed paddling on whitewater." With that combination of desire and dedication, Jon was able to advance his canoeing skills steadily and, at the same time, continue his education: He eventually received a B.A. in environmental science from the University of Virginia.

Jon's first World Championships wins came

Major Canoeing Championships

Year	Competition	Event	Place
1978	Pan-American Championships	One-person canoe	1st
1979	World Championships	One-person canoe	1st
		Team canoe	1st
1981	World Championships	One-person canoe	1st
		Team canoe	1st
1983	World Championships	One-person canoe	1st
		Team canoe	1st
1984	Europa Cup	One-person canoe	1st
	Pan-American Championships	One-person canoe	1st
1985	World Championships	Team canoe	1st
		One-person canoe	2d
1987	World Championships	One-person canoe	1st
		Team canoe	1st
1988	Europa Cup	One-person canoe	1st
1988-90	World Cup	One-person canoe	1st
1989	World Championships	One-person canoe	1st
		Team canoe	1st
1991	World Championships	Team canoe	1st

in 1979, at Jonquière, Quebec, Canada. He took both the individual gold medal and the team gold (three boats race together) in C-1 (one-person canoe), signifying the beginning of a remarkable string.

Continuing the Story

Between 1979 and 1990, Jon won a total of eleven gold medals in the biennial World Championships competitions. Five golds were in individual events, six in team. Only in 1985, when he placed second, a fraction of a second behind teammate Davy Hearn in the one-person event, did he fall short in a World Championship effort. In that same time span, Jon won the World Cup Championship each of the three years it was held, the Pan-American Games Championship once, and the Europa Cup twice.

Perhaps Jon's greatest accomplishment, the one that gave him the most satisfaction, came at the 1989 World Championships on Western Maryland's Savage River. Jon's second run of two was ranked by many as the best effort in the history of whitewater slalom.

In a sport in which world championships are usually decided by tenths or even hundredths of a second, Jon blazed through the twenty-five gates hung along 600 meters of thrashing Savage whitewater in 205 seconds. He beat the second-place boat by an unheard of margin of nearly 12 seconds.

"In spite of winning, one seldom paddles to his full potential," says Jon. "This is one time I could say 'I did the best I could,' and that is really rare." To do it under the pressure of the World Championships and the difficult course made it all the more spectacular. The fact that it was in the United States simply added to the thrill.

Jon continued his reign as one of the world's best in whitewater slalom by winning the gold medal at the 1991 World Championships and was the heavy favorite to win the gold in Barcelona in 1992. In fact, he did win the race by a narrow margin of .007 seconds. However, the judges determined that his life-vest had brushed one of the gates, incurring a five-second penalty that removed him from medal contention altogether.

After retiring from competition, Jon became a commentator for NBC-TV. He later became the executive director of Richmond Sports Backers, which was chosen as the 2006 National Association of Sports Commissions' (NASC's) member of the year.

Summary

Many things contributed to Jon Lugbill's outstanding career, including his natural athletic ability and his ability to manage priorities. He completed an education and raised a family while performing at the highest level in his sport. Also, he had a quiet inner strength that is best illustrated by an incident at the World Championships on the Savage River. Between runs, Jon retired to the privacy of his car. There, away from the crowds and his fellow competitors, he spent time by himself. He looked within and found the strength and determination to return to the course for that remarkable second run to the gold.

Chuck Weis

Additional Sources

Levinson, David, and Karen Christensen. *Encyclopedia of World Sport: From Ancient Times to the Present.* Santa Barbara, Calif.: ABC-Clio, 1996.

Wallechinsky, David, and Jaime Loucky. *The Complete Book of the Olympics: 2008 Edition.* London: Aurum Press, 2008.